IFIP Advances in Information and Communication Technology 350

IFIP – The International Federation for Information Processing

IFIP was founded in 1960 under the auspices of UNESCO, following the First World Computer Congress held in Paris the previous year. An umbrella organization for societies working in information processing, IFIP's aim is two-fold: to support information processing within ist member countries and to encourage technology transfer to developing nations. As ist mission statement clearly states,

> *IFIP's mission is to be the leading, truly international, apolitical organization which encourages and assists in the development, exploitation and application of information technology for the bene t of all people.*

IFIP is a non-profitmaking organization, run almost solely by 2500 volunteers. It operates through a number of technical committees, which organize events and publications. IFIP's events range from an international congress to local seminars, but the most important are:

- The IFIP World Computer Congress, held every second year;
- Open conferences;
- Working conferences.

The flagship event is the IFIP World Computer Congress, at which both invited and contributed papers are presented. Contributed papers are rigorously refereed and the rejection rate is high.

As with the Congress, participation in the open conferences is open to all and papers may be invited or submitted. Again, submitted papers are stringently refereed.

The working conferences are structured differently. They are usually run by a working group and attendance is small and by invitation only. Their purpose is to create an atmosphere conducive to innovation and development. Refereeing is less rigorous and papers are subjected to extensive group discussion.

Publications arising from IFIP events vary. The papers presented at the IFIP World Computer Congress and at open conferences are published as conference proceedings, while the results of the working conferences are often published as collections of selected and edited papers.

Any national society whose primary activity is in information may apply to become a full member of IFIP, although full membership is restricted to one society per country. Full members are entitled to vote at the annual General Assembly, National societies preferring a less committed involvement may apply for associate or corresponding membership. Associate members enjoy the same benefits as full members, but without voting rights. Corresponding members are not represented in IFIP bodies. Affiliated membership is open to non-national societies, and individual and honorary membership schemes are also offered.

John Impagliazzo   Per Lundin
Benkt Wangler (Eds.)

History of
Nordic Computing 3

Third IFIP WG 9.7 Conference, HiNC 3
Stockholm, Sweden, October 18-20, 2010
Revised Selected Papers

 Springer

Volume Editors

John Impagliazzo
Hofstra University
Department of Computer Science
Hempstead, NY 11549-1030, USA
E-mail: john.impagliazzo@hofstra.edu

Per Lundin
KTH Royal Institute of Technology
Division of History of Science and Technology
100 44 Stockholm, Sweden
E-mail: per.lundin@abe.kth.se

Benkt Wangler
Stockholm University
Department of Computer and Systems Sciences
164 40 Kista, Sweden
E-mail: benktw@gmail.com

ISSN 1868-4238   e-ISSN 1868-422X
ISBN 978-3-642-27019-2   ISBN 978-3-642-23315-9 (eBook)
DOI 10.1007/978-3-642-23315-9
Springer Heidelberg Dordrecht London New York

CR Subject Classification (1998): K.2, K.1, K.3, K.7

Typesetting: Camera-ready by author, data conversion by Scientific Publishing Services, Chennai, India

Printed on acid-free paper

Springer is part of Springer Science+Business Media (www.springer.com)

Dedication

We dedicate this book

to professor emeritus **Hans Andersin** *of Aalto University, who was deeply involved in the preparations for HiNC3 as well as HiNC1 and HiNC2. He was unable to participate in the HiNC3 conference due to a brief period of illness that ended his life just a few days after the conference.*

Professor Andersin was a Finnish pioneer within the applied computing field. He was a respected friend and colleague of many IT professionals and academicians throughout the Nordic countries. He played an important role in building the first Finnish computer and later he worked with computer support for newspaper production and industrial automation, areas that also became important research fields for him and the profession. In 1969, Andersin became a professor of information processing at Helsinki University of Technology, now part of Aalto University.

Hans Andersin's work bestowed upon him international recognition. Organizations often consulted with him as an expert in various scientific contexts. After his retirement in 1993, he continued to give lectures and in later years, he devoted much time to various initiatives for preserving the history of Nordic computing. Many friends at Nordic universities and throughout the world will miss his gentle wit and creative fantasy.

Preface

These proceedings derive from the Third IFIP Conference on the History of Nordic Computing, described simply as the "History of Nordic Computing 3" (HiNC3). This conference was the third of a series of conferences that has taken place under the auspices of the International Federation for Information Processing (IFIP). This volume consists of a collection of articles presented at the HiNC3 conference held during October 18–20, 2010 in Stockholm, Sweden. The papers presented cover a wide variety of historical and computing perspectives. The HiNC3 conference represents a joint effort between the Department of Computer and Systems Sciences at Stockholm University and the IFIP Working Group 9.7 on the History of Computing. The Department of Computer and Systems Sciences, Riksbankens Jubileumsfond, the Swedish Research Council, and the Swedish Computer Society sponsored the conference.

The HiNC3 conference has brought to light a broad spectrum of issues. It illustrates topics in computing as they occurred mostly in the "early days" of computing; those ramifications and overtones remain with us today. Indeed, many of the early challenges are still part of a historical tapestry woven by pioneers from the Nordic countries. Therefore, these proceedings provide additional value to the reader as they reflect the past and in so doing they provide fodder for the future Nordic development of computing.

The First Conference on the History of Nordic Computing (HiNC1) took place in Trondheim in June 2003. HiNC1 focused on the early years of computing, mostly the years from the 1940s through the 1960s. While developing hardware was a necessity for the first professionals, computer scientists as well as others became increasingly interested in programming and application software. Progress in these areas from the 1960s through the 1980s became the focus of the HiNC2 conference held in Turku, Finland, in August 2007. During the closing discussion of the HiNC2 conference, participants were already looking forward to the next HiNC event. Iceland and Sweden were possible locations; due to the successful completion of a large project on Swedish ICT history, "From Computing Machines to IT," Sweden became the obvious choice. The first HiNC3 planning session occurred in Stockholm in February of 2009. Thereafter, members of various committees worked diligently throughout the days of the conference and beyond.

HiNC3 took place at the Department of Computer and Systems Sciences at Stockholm University. There was a great deal of interest around the conference, revealed through the large number of papers submitted. Hence, more than 50 contributions authored by more than 70 historians of science and technology, senior researchers in computing sciences and senior practitioners from the industry, are included in the conference proceedings. The conference reflected a positive atmosphere and continued with comradely enthusiasm. Sixty-five people attended the conference.

The theme of the conference was twofold, namely:

1. The application and use of ICT
2. Ways in which technical progress affected the conditions for the development and use of ICT systems

Furthermore, the historical period at the center of attention at the conference covers the years from around 1970 until around 1995. This leads up to the beginning of the era of the Internet and global networks.

We did indeed receive many papers on applications – from computer use for music composition and for digital dating to real-time systems for control of train movements and the flow of electricity. Changes in conditions of use were reflected, for instance, in papers that dealt with networking and the Internet. Papers on software engineering and systems development mirror how the conditions for developers have changed over time. When it comes to time, one paper reflected history from 100 years ago; we chose to include this paper since it provided a very nice background to the Nordic development of digital computing that started around 1950. However, the conference in general focused on the 1970s, 1980s, and beginning of the 1990s.

The publication of the conference proceedings has given authors the opportunity to modify and improve their papers based on comments received in the conference and by reviewers. Although this effort has made the work of the editors more tedious, they believe the effort has captured Nordic computing history more accurately.

The HiNC3 Program Committee expresses it gratitude to the organizers and sponsors of the HiNC3 conference for their support. Again, participants anticipate a follow-up event. The plan is to organize the next conference on the History of Nordic Computing 4 (HiNC4) in Denmark in 2014.

September 2011   John Impagliazzo
                                                                        Per Lundin
                                                                    Benkt Wangler

HiNC3 Conference Organization

General Conference Co-chairs

Janis Bubenko, Jr.	Stockholm Unversity and KTH, Sweden
Per Olof Persson	Athena Konsult, Sweden

IFIP Representative

John Impagliazzo	Former IFIP WG 9.7 Chair, Hofstra University, USA

Steering Committee

Janis Bubenko, Jr. (Co-chair)	Stockholm University and KTH, Sweden
Anita Kollerbaur (Co-chair)	Stockholm University, Sweden
Benkt Wangler	Stockholm University, Sweden
Gunnar Hesse	Formerly of Unisys Nordics, Sweden
Harold (Bud) Lawson	Lawson Konsult AB, Sweden
Per Lundin	KTH, Sweden
Tomas Ohlin	Formerly of Linköping University and Stockholm University, Sweden
Per Olof Persson	Athena Konsult, Sweden
Björn Thodenius	Stockholm School of Economics, Sweden

Advisory Committee

Hans Andersin	Aalto University, Finland
Christian Gram	Technical University of Denmark
Jóhann Gunnarsson	Formerly of Ministry of Finance, Iceland
Páll Jensson	University of Iceland
Harold (Bud) Lawson	Lawson Konsult AB, Sweden
Eva Lindencrona	Vinnova, Sweden
Bjørn Nagell	Devoteam daVinci, Norway
Søren Duus Østergaard	Duus.Communications ApS, Denmark
Arne Sølvberg	Norwegian University of Science and Technology
Jussi Tuori	Formerly of the Finnish Computer Society and Kanallis-Osake-Pankki, Finland

Organizing Committee

Gunnar Hesse (Co-chair)	Formerly of Unisys Nordics, Sweden
Anita Kollerbaur (Co-chair)	Stockholm University, Sweden
Paula Berglund	Stockholm University, Sweden
Karl Kajbjer	Stockholm University, Sweden
Britt-Marie Nordström	Stockholm University, Sweden
Per Olofsson	Stockholm University, Sweden
Ann-Marie Philipsson	Stockholm University, Sweden
Angela Westin	Stockholm University, Sweden

Program Committee

Benkt Wangler (Co-chair)	Stockholm University, Sweden
Per Lundin (Co-chair)	KTH, Sweden
Hans Andersin	Aalto University, Finland
Kjell Bratbergsengen	Norwegian University of Science and Technology
Janis Bubenko Jr.	Stockholm University and KTH
Hasse Clausen	University of Copenhagen, Denmark
Hilde Corneliussen	University of Bergen, Norway
Christian Gram	Technical University of Denmark
Jóhann Gunnarsson	Formerly of Ministry of Finance, Iceland
Lars Heide	Copenhagen Business School, Denmark
Magnus Johansson	Linköping University, Sweden
Harold (Bud) Lawson	Lawson Konsult AB, Sweden
Arne Maus	University of Oslo, Norway
Panu Nykänen	Aalto University, Finland
Tomas Ohlin	Formerly of Linköping University and Stockholm University, Sweden
Anna Orrghen	Uppsala University, Sweden
Petri Paju	University of Turku, Finland
Stefán Pálsson	Orkuveita Reykjavíkur, Iceland
Petri Saarikoski	University Consortium of Pori, Finland
Airi Salminen	University of Jyväskylä, Finland
Gustav Sjöblom	Chalmers University of Technology, Sweden
Arne Sølvberg	Norwegian University of Science and Technology
Björn Thodenius	Stockholm School of Economics, Sweden
Louise Yngström	Stockholm University, Sweden

Acknowledgments

The conference was organized as an activity within IFIP's Working Group 9.7 (History of Computing) of its Technical Committee 9 (Relationship Between Computers and Society). It was sponsored and organized jointly by the Department of Computer and Systems Sciences at Stockholm University and the Swedish Computer Society.

The Organizing Committee of the Third Conference on the History of Nordic Computing wishes to extend its particular appreciation to the following organizations, without whose support the conference would not have occurred:

- Department of Computer and Systems Sciences at Stockholm University for hosting the conference and for monetary support
- Riksbankens Jubileumsfond for monetary support
- Swedish Research Council for monetary support
- The Swedish Computer Society

We also thank the following groups for support:

- Silicon Vikings
- Datasaabs vänner

Table of Contents

Keynote Address

A World Full of Computers: How Did That Happen? 1
   James W. Cortada

Computerizing Public Sector Industries

Computerization of the Norwegian Land Register: An Early Example
of Outsourcing and Still a Model for Good Practice 13
   Bjørn Nagell

Controlling the Battlefield: Computing and Operational Command in
the Swedish Armed Forces, 1966–1989 22
   Johan Gribbe

The Use of Computers for Controlling Electricity Flows in Sweden,
1950–1980 28
   Arne Kaijser

Operations Analysis Computing at FFI, 1970–1995 35
   Norodd Hagenson

Re-engineering Norwegian Research Libraries, 1970–1980 43
   Ingeborg Torvik Sølvberg

Instruments of Surveillance Welfare: Computerizing Unemployment
and Health in 1960s and 1970s Sweden 56
   Isabelle Dussauge and Julia Peralta

History of Electronic Prescriptions in Sweden: From Time-Sharing
Systems via Smartcards to EDI 65
   Gunnar O. Klein

Electronic Health Records in Sweden: From Administrative
Management to Clinical Decision Support 74
   Karin Kajbjer, Ragnar Nordberg, and Gunnar O. Klein

Computerizing Management and Financial Industries

The Totally Integrated Management Information System in 1960s
Sweden 83
   Gustav Sjöblom

The History of the Swedish ATM: Sparfrämjandet and Metior   92
  Björn Thodenius, Bernardo Bátiz-Lazo, and Tobias Karlsson

Electronic Securities: The Introduction of an Electronic Registration
and Settlement System for the Norwegian Securities Market   101
  Jan Hellstrøm

How New Computing Technology Reformed the Audit Profession   108
  Bjørn Barth Jacobsen

Computerizing Art, Media, and Schools

History of Digital Dating: "Computer-Balls" and Digital Pairing in
Finland from the 1960s to the Present   117
  Jaakko Suominen

Collaborations between Engineers and Artists in the Making of
Computer Art in Sweden, 1967–1986   127
  Anna Orrghen

IBM's Norwegian Grammar Project, 1988–1991   137
  Jan Engh

Computer Courses in Finnish Schools, 1980–1995   150
  Petri Saarikoski

Teacher Pioneers in the Introduction of Computing Technology in the
Swedish Upper Secondary School   159
  Lennart Rolandsson

Users and Systems Development

Computing on the Desktop: From Batch to Online in Two Large
Danish Service Bureaus   168
  Anker Helms Jørgensen

UTOPIA: Participatory Design from Scandinavia to the World   176
  Yngve Sundblad

Designing Democracy: The UTOPIA-Project and the Role of the
Nordic Labor Movement in Technological Change during the 1970s and
1980s   187
  Per Lundin

The Making of a Nordic Computing Industry

Early History of Computing in Denmark   196
  Søren Duus Østergaard

Making Business of a Revolutionary New Technology:
The Eckert-Mauchly Company, 1945–1951   207
  Lars Heide

IBM Manufacturing in the Nordic Countries   215
  Petri Paju

The Presence of the IBM Branch Office in Iceland, 1967–1992   228
  Sverrir Ólafsson

Personal Computers: A Gateway to Personal Computing   234
  Kari Kotiranta

Norwegian Computer Technology: Founding a New Industry   240
  Yngvar Lundh

The Founding, Fantastic Growth, and Fast Decline of Norsk Data AS . . .   249
  Tor Olav Steine

The Norwegian National IT Plan, 1987–1990: Whence It Came, What
It Was, and How It Ended   258
  Arne Sølvberg

Nordic Networking

Before the Internet: Early Experiences of Computer Mediated
Communication   271
  Jacob Palme

The Baby Networks: Nordic Positions Before the Internet   278
  Tomas Ohlin

Development of Internet Technology and Norwegian Participation   287
  Yngvar Lundh

The Internet Development Process: Observations and Reflections   297
  Pål Spilling

Nordic Software Development

The Use of Interpretation for Data Acquisition and Control: Its Impact
on Software Development and Project Management   305
  Otto Vinter

Computer Systems Performance Engineering in Trondheim: Origins
and Development, 1970–1995   315
  Peter H. Hughes

Provisioning of Highly Reliable Real-Time Systems   323
  Harold (Bud) Lawson and Kurt-Lennart Lundbäck

Information Modeling: Forty Years of Friendship   331
  Stig Berild and Eva Lindencrona

Scandinavian Contributions to Object-Oriented Modeling Languages . . .   339
  Birger Møller-Pedersen

Nordic Research in Software and Systems Development

Dansk Datamatik Center   350
  Dines Bjørner, Christian Gram, Ole N. Oest, and Leif Rystrøm

SISU: The Swedish Institute for Systems Development   360
  Janis A. Bubenko, Jr.

Cloud Computing in the 1970s: The Discovery of Hash Based Relational
Algebra   368
  Kjell Bratbergsengen

The TEMPORA Approach: Information Systems Development Based
on Explicit Business Rules with Time   375
  Benkt Wangler

RAMATIC: A Case Shell Platform   383
  Lars-Åke Johansson and Mats Gustafsson

Teaching at Nordic Universities

Computer Science Education at Helsinki University of Technology: The
First Ten Years (1968–1978)   390
  Hans Andersin, Reijo Sulonen, and Markku Syrjänen

Provincial Designer Design: A Creative Mix of Hard Restrictions and
Soft Visions of an Information Systems Educational Program   399
  *Darek Haftor, Stig C. Holmberg, Ulrica Löfstedt,
  Christina Amcoff Nyström, and Lena-Maria Öberg*

Teaching Image Analysis at DIKU   409
  Peter Johansen

Simula: Mother Tongue for a Generation of Nordic Programmers   416
  Yngve Sundblad

New Historiographical Approaches and Methodological Reflections

Precursors of the IT Nation: Computer Use and Control in Swedish
Society, 1955–1985 425
  Isabelle Dussauge, Johan Gribbe, Arne Kaijser, Per Lundin,
  Julia Peralta, Gustav Sjöblom, and Björn Thodenius

Text Mining and Qualitative Analysis of an IT History Interview
Collection 433
  Petri Paju, Eric Malmi, and Timo Honkela

A Classification of Methods and Contributions in the Historiography of
Nordic Computing 444
  Henry Oinas-Kukkonen, Harri Oinas-Kukkonen, and
  Veronika Sušová

Research Directions Profile in the Computing Museum of the Institute
of Mathematics and Computer Science, University of Latvia (IMCS) ... 453
  Rihards Balodis, Juris Borzovs, Inara Opmane, Andrejs Skuja, and
  Evija Ziemele

Panel Discussion

What Can We Learn from the History of Nordic Computing? 462
  Tomas Ohlin, Harold (Bud) Lawson, Søren Duus Østergaard,
  Ingeborg Torvik Sølvberg, and Nina Wormbs

Author Index 465

A World Full of Computers: How Did That Happen?

James W. Cortada

IBM Institute for Business Value
2917 Irvington Way, Madison, Wisconsin 53713 USA
jwcorta@us.ibm.com

Abstract. This paper argues in favor of more national and global histories of computing, describes the author's current research, and presents preliminary findings about the global diffusion of IT with particular emphasis on developments in the pan-Atlantic community of North America and Europe from to 1940s to 2000. The author introduces a new model for dating events in the diffusion of computing.

Keywords: European ICT, global diffusion, historical trends, history of computing, Wave One.

1 Introduction

At the end of World War II there were probably up to a dozen devices one might call computers. By the early 1950s, almost every country in Western Europe had at least one computer project underway; many had several. By 1960, there were over six thousand systems around the world, and after the diffusion of personal computers in the 1980s, observers counted the number of newly acquired systems in the millions of units per year. By the end of the 1980s, many other machines had computers in them such as automobiles, microwave ovens, early mobile phones, and in the following decade, cameras. Today, there are so many computers in so many places and things that we no longer know actually how many there are. Rather, we measure IT differently. Instead of asking how many computers exist, we want to know how much traffic is flowing through the international fiber-optic cables that carry all the internet traffic—its volume doubles every eighteen months and just over half of all this internet traffic is made up of videos, while Facebook messages now surpass all the e-mail combined worldwide [1]. To complicate matters, the number of machines—not computers—that have computational components in them attaching to the internet is now increasing so fast that it will not be long before they outnumber the quantity of people using the internet through mobile phones and other human-used computers.

How did all these things happen? How is it there exists so much computing in extensive use throughout the world that we have difficulty tracking the volume involved? Indeed, how did that infusion of technology into human societies happen so quickly? These are not easy questions to answer. The story of computing is highly fragmented; the quantity of sources historians can study too few; and the number of experts available to do the work insufficient to the task. That is why the efforts of computer professionals, computer scientists, historians, economists, librarians and

J. Impagliazzo, P. Lundin, and B. Wangler (Eds.): HiNC3, IFIP AICT 350, pp. 1–12, 2011.

archivists in the Nordic countries collaborating in the study of computing's history is so important.

As this conference—and the two previous ones—make very clear, there are collaborative ways to study the subject, thereby expanding the pool of researchers, increasing the availability of information, and enriching discussions about the history of computing. What your activities have indicated so far, along with the research of others in dozens of countries, is that the history of ICT is bigger, more complex, and central to the history of the twentieth century than historians might have thought even as recently as two decades ago. For example, your work to preserve and study the history of Nordic computing and telecommunications established that all countries in this part of Europe played an enormous role in the lives of the region and in the history of modern Europe. We did not know that even as recently as ten years ago. Other countries can learn from what you are doing today.

First, the importance of the subject warrants discussion. It is not enough to say that there are billions of computers around the world. It is more important to look at their use. To be brief, we know that global diffusion of computers is so great that almost the majority of all data now available are in digital forms and will increase in quantity over time. Today, the majority of digital data consists of images, such as video and still photography, and the greatest amount of text is in English with Chinese increasing rapidly its presence. Libraries and publishers are transforming texts of all languages into digital formats, what French historian, Lucien X. Polastron considers a challenge to even such traditional modes of presenting information as the book and the nature—even the existence—of libraries. To him, digitization is placing libraries and all of us "at a historical turning point" [2, p.161]. I think he is correct. IBM's lens—often forecasting how much computer storage customers will buy—confirms the same, with the volume of exabytes of data going from an estimated 500 just two years ago (2008) to over double that amount by the end of 2012.[1]

Second, the software and hardware emerging in support of the use of digital information continues to appear quickly, as it has for the past fifty years with no evidence that the process of new product introductions is slowing down even in difficult economic times. One has only to observe what has happened at any company, such as all the products that have come from Apple just in the past five years, or by type of device, such as the functions available in mobile phones, cameras, and e-book readers. Kindle and iPad are only two of over two dozen such devices. Over twenty vendors have committed publicly in 2010 to introduce newer versions over the next several years.

However, even more important is the fact that consumers and institutional customers of ICT over time have acquired these technologies faster than prior versions. There are many measures of such adoptions; we all have seen charts that show percents of penetration with electricity taking seventy-five years for modern societies to have 100 percent adoption; that 75 percent of the pan-Atlantic community acquired VCRs in thirty years; that nearly 100 percent had television sets in twenty-five years. It took the pan-Atlantic community less than fifteen years to have nearly

---

[1] One exabyte is equal to one quintillion bytes of data, or 1,000,000,000,000,000,000. In early 2010 the internet's total volume of material amounted to about 22 exabytes. Keep in mind that not all data passes through the internet so there is more than 22 exabytes of digitized information in the world.

half its homes and businesses using PCs, barely a decade for 75 percent of Western Europeans to have mobile phones and over half the population access to the internet. Consumers bought digital television sets sooner than they did PCs, because they had learned how to buy digital devices; they did not hesitate to rid themselves of film for digital photography and are now replacing first generation flat screen TVs. Hence, people and institutions are acquiring digital devices even faster than in the past and in the process are embracing a digital social *zeitgeist*. The wealthiest economies are doing it the fastest and most extensively, of course. Nevertheless, as the costs of digital technologies shrink as they also come in smaller, hence less expensive, products their affordability spreads. That is one important reason why Africa and China are now the fastest growing markets for mobile phones, which we all know are small computational devices, with smart phones rapidly becoming platforms for "apps," potentially the most important evolution in IT hardware that we might see in this decade.

2   The Historian's Challenge

For historians of ICT the challenge is more than just describing the use of computers in earlier decades, when mostly large organizations acquired them. We now need to explain the diffusion of the technology into consumer and industrial goods as well. It is not an exaggeration to say that almost everyone in a developed or developing economy is a user of ICT. Currently over an additional billion people are moving into the middle class for the first time as well. They too are expected to become users of various ICTs, but, also in different ways than others in early-adopter societies. Given that we know enough about the history of computing to realize that we understand too little in a time of great churn, what are the questions historians must now ask of ICT at this time? There are basic questions among many such as:

- What diffused into the world? When? To whom? Where?
- How did that happen? Was the experience the same in each country? If not, what was it? How did they vary? Moreover, the historian's favorite question—Why?
- What were the specific causes of such a diffusion and why so quickly?
- What roles did various factors play such as technological evolutions, cultural, political and historical realities, economics, and government policies and programs?
- Are there common patterns of diffusion? If so, what were they and how did that happen?

Students of the history of ICT need to deal with these fundamental questions for several reasons. First, the diffusion of massive quantities of computing happened and indeed, they were widespread. Second, current business and government leaders need—and want—to understand how "high tech" uses spread and affect societies, economies and their own organizations. Third, as Spanish sociologist Manuel Castells has been reminding us for over three decades, we may all be entering some post-industrial networked information age that potentially could be quite different in form and style from what the world lived in since the start of the First Industrial

Revolution. Fourth, we need to study ICT because technological diffusion is a subject of great interest to economists, historians, political scientists, public administrators, businesses, technologists, sociologists, philosophers, computer scientists, and engineers with too many of them not understanding what the others are saying, yet each creating a large body of literature on the role, and sometimes the parallel histories of ICT.

After seventy years of using computers, are we not due for some consensus about humankind's experience with ICT? So a fifth reason: historians in many fields of history are now writing world histories to make sense of how humankind has evolved. Since ICT is such a global phenomenon, it too will become part of the global story. So far, no serious attempts have been made by historians to look at the history of ICT globally; at best their work remains narrowly focused on specific applications, industries, devices, types of technology, and user groups. The most broadly conceived take a national perspective, as we saw recently by French historian Pierre Mounier-Kuhn with his book on France [3]. Trans-national comparative studies are few, although recently one of Europe's leading historians of ICT, Denmark's own Lars Heide, published an excellent example [4].

Several problems must be overcome, however. There are, for example, too few historians of ICT, but probably enough experts on telecommunications. Scholars in other fields and archivists are helping these students of technology; as the Swedes are demonstrating, computer pioneers and ICT professionals are also helping. The work being done in Sweden, that of the IT History Society, the Internet Archives, and the Computer Museum in California are examples of projects and initiatives appearing in many countries that help. Another problem mentioned above is that much research is fragmented, but there is progress. Collaborative or multi-national research projects are appearing more frequently by:

- examining classes of technologies such as European software, Asian printing, and American hardware,
- class of user such as those accessing the internet in various countries, and others about programmers, women in IT, and ICT professionals,
- type of application such as supply chains, banking ATMs, mobile phones, and computing in government,
- industry and country such as banking, government, military, France, Finland, Great Britain, and Sweden, and
- time periods such as the 1930s through the 1950s, the 1970s–1980s, and now beginning, the study of the 1990s.

The problem of fragmentation has many causes and manifestations. Among the causes we can list include too little or too much material to examine with too little done so far. There still is insufficient consensus and inadequate clarity about what issues to study since the subject is so new. Archival collections are too few and what exists are scattered about—European historians too frequently have to go to the middle of the United States—Minneapolis, Minnesota—to study Europe's history of ICT! This situation borders on the ridiculous yet is a remediable problem, as Tom Misa showed at the last Nordic history conference with his discussion on the Charles Babbage Institute (CBI) experience [5]. An important problem for trans-national historiography is that one must deal with too many languages to conduct research, not to mention the accommodation of cultural considerations. The few historians expert in this subject are also just now beginning to collaborate on projects, with Europeans leading the way now, in part because of EU funding of pan-European initiatives. Yet most historical research still remains too narrowly focused, with an insufficient number of the sort of what one might call "big history" projects that we see in other sub-fields of history. Moreover, as historians are quick to point out, there is insufficient funding and other resources to support their work, although that is beginning to change with the EU helping in Europe and the National Science Foundation in the United States.

3   A Way Forward

Each must do what we can to address these problems and seize upon the opportunities. I am currently examining the way ICT spread around the world between 1940 and the end of the century. While I am only just over halfway through the project, there are a number of observations that can be made about the patterns of deployment. I offer these as a small contribution to the field of ICT history. There are four questions to answer in the project.

- In what countries did ICT emerge?
- How did that happen in each country? And in general?
- What were the factors that made diffusion happen?
- What made possible their speed of diffusion? Was it great technology, other influences, or some combination of factors?

These questions are discussed on a country-by-country basis, selecting some but not all nations that extant evidence suggests might provide answers to these queries and that also allows one to generalize about global patterns. These nations include the United States and the largest in Europe, from Great Britain, France, Germany, and Italy to Russia, but also East Germany and some of its immediate Comecon neighbors, and smaller states such as the Netherlands and Sweden to understand better the pan-European and pan-Atlantic experiences. In Asia there is Japan, where computing first began in the region, but also South Korea, Singapore, Taiwan, and, of course, most recently India and China. There are nations in Latin America to examine such as Mexico and Brazil, but also in Africa too, a continent with over fifty countries.

The story is told in roughly chronological order of diffusion, beginning with the United States, next with Western Europe, followed by Eastern Europe, across East Asia, through Latin America, and finally Africa. Many countries are examined that will not be written up in my study, however, such as smaller states or others that reflected patterns of diffusion of neighboring countries that I do describe in detail. Some are left out because of insufficient space in my project, others because of lack of data. I plan to donate all my research notes, records, and books from this project to CBI as a way of helping future historians continue this sort of historical inquiry. My focus is on technological, economic, political and managerial issues relying on contemporary reports, secondary literature, and archival materials where available and relevant.

The story line is becoming clear. First, countries with the most extensive and quick starts did it through national investments in information technologies. World War II and the Cold War led to early starts in the United States, United Kingdom and its Commonwealth nations, Sweden, and the Soviet Union with military, then scientific computing, and ultimately civilian applications. Second, the pan-Atlantic community was able to transfer quickly findings and technologies that originated from military applications and projects to civilian products and uses originating in the United States and in other European nations. Communist states generally blocked movement of military ICT into civilian uses. Asian countries began adopting ICT after initial civilian successes in Europe. Third, almost every country in developed and developing economies simultaneously began small experiments in building computers between the late 1940s and early 1950s; the academic literature has not documented many of these, while those in the pan-Atlantic community always received publication. Speed of diffusion was generally a function of the speed of acquisition and the funding amount. The quickest technology transfers occurred in pan-Atlantic nations in the 1950s and 1960s, and in East Asia beginning with the 1970s. American computer vendors, most notably IBM, were the fastest to scale up their work, investments, sales, and infrastructures to support customers. Almost all national ICT champion programs failed to meet their original objectives with the exception of Japan and South Korea.

Several factors were in evidence in nations that adopted computing most extensively the quickest, while a number of environmental issues conversely slowed diffusion. In support of diffusion, one has to begin with the military investments in Cold War ICT, which many scholars have already studied. In the pan-Atlantic community, however, we must also recognize the legal protections provided for contracts and patents, because these protections for vendors facilitated development and sale of ICTs. All over the world, those nations that allowed the free flow of information did well. Having a capitalist economy helped enormously by providing economic incentives for innovation and risk taking, and for making available investment capital. Another economic factor was the availability of stable currencies and private sector venture capitalists, the first for cash liquidity and the second for competent investment and managerial "know-how." The existence of technical universities, institutes and academies populated with engineers, scientists, mathematicians, and individuals interested in practical construction of ICT and their use was and continues to be essential to diffusion. Finally, and very importantly, having public policies that promoted the diffusion of computing proved to be as crucial as the military investments.

We now also know there existed practices and circumstances that slowed the rate and extent of diffusion of ICT in the twentieth century, with many of the lessons coming from behind the Iron Curtain. These included secrecy in public administration and related to that lack of accurate information or inadequate free flow of knowledge, particularly among potential users, but, also to some extent, for computer builders and programmers. Centralized communist economic planning and control created havoc in the supply chains of whole industries and nations, particularly if these led to incentives that discouraged innovation or reduced the hunt for economic productivity—a major problem across all of communist dominated Central and Eastern Europe from the 1950s through the 1980s, and still a lingering heritage in contemporary Russia. Lack of contract and patent protection slowed innovation and adoptions. Just as educated people were needed to develop ICTs and then to use them, so too weak educational programs and inadequate technical human resources proved harmful. Regarding infrastructures, good telephone networks and adequate supplies of electricity were needed for the "I" and the "C" of ICT as well. In short, ICTs needed a broad, complex and supportive eco-system to flourish comprised of technological, scientific, economic, political, social and educational infrastructures.

A few surprises also emerged from the country-level research that one would do well to take into account in future studies of ICT, three in particular because they have global implications. First, technological and economic effects of Moore's Law were only marginally important in promoting diffusion and innovation, surprising because economists have maintained for decades that it was paramount in diffusion. The Law was—and continues to be—most important to North Americans and South Koreans in their highly competitive economies and ICT industries and *de rigueur* in the semiconductor industry. It proved of no consequence in the USSR where it was routine to use ten to fifteen year-old technologies regardless of their cost of operation or lost opportunities for improved operational productivity. Many West European, American, and Japanese users knew ICT was very costly in the 1950s through the 1970s; however, they incurred most of their expenses for software and in programming and staff needs.

Second, national initiatives to upgrade and improve telecommunications taught policy makers how they thought they should manage national champions and ICT diffusion as well. For example, their generally positive experience with telecommunications profoundly influenced French regulators and political leaders. On the other hand, Central Europeans and the Russians had poor telecommunications networks, which they never fixed properly by replacing older ones with more modern systems that could handle voice and data at greater volumes and quality or by diffusing sufficiently ICT throughout an economy during the entire period of communist rule. These necessary changes only began in earnest during the early 1990s. Poor telecommunications constrained adoption of online computing and later use of the internet and other networks. Most developing economies in the 1990s and 2000s turned first to modernizing their telecommunications infrastructures before launching campaigns to increase the diffusion of computing.

Third, smaller countries often proved more agile in adopting ICT. These included all the Nordics, Netherlands, Belgium, Canada, Singapore, Latvia, and Costa Rica as examples. Not all small countries were so effective; for example, Trinidad & Tobago, Venezuela, and Greece reinforce my major finding that multiple factors in combination influenced diffusion of ICT when they played either positive or negative roles.

Historians of all kinds of technologies are enamored with the special roles played by parties with a direct material interest in a technology such as programmers and hardware vendors in IT. So, what influence did they have on the spread of computing? It turns out that in every country, they played a very important role and we should study them in considerable detail. Advocates included all manner of IT professionals, vendors, sociologists, and other social commentators discussing telematic societies and end users with interest in ICT or in need of such technologies.

American, Dutch, Danish and Swedish experiences demonstrated that internal IT advocates, local culture, and organization of specific institutions influenced profoundly the kinds of ICTs and rates of adoption they achieved. Centralized institutions were attracted to large computers, while decentralized organizations favored mini- and distributed systems. International firms exported ICT to their offices and factories in other countries, regardless of local practices, stimulating regional diffusions of ICT knowledge and uses. ICT vendors and their collaborators played important roles in shaping governmental initiatives and public opinion about the value of the technology, both often collaborating with business partners and the press in discussing computing's role and value, usually in very positive terms. Commentators about the future of society originally came from academies and universities in the 1950s and 1960s; then the media and business commentators joined them in the 1970s and 1980s, but only in the most advanced economies.

The top third of all OECD countries were early and extensive adopters, as measured by per capita GDP, beginning in the early 1950s. The second tier were seven to ten years behind in rates of adoption (began in the early 1960s) while the bottom one third were the late adopters, most beginning in the 1980s. Economies with large companies and agencies were early and continuing adopters surpassing those nations that had smaller institutions, regardless of land mass and population size such as the very large and extensively populated Western Russia, Eastern China and all regions of Italy, which were technological laggards.

All various data points lead to several fundamental conclusions that could alter our perception of the broad issue of computing's diffusion. First, technology alone seemed to play a less influential role in diffusion than did other factors such as political issues and availability of information, skills and funding. Second, historians need to de-emphasize—but not ignore—features and costs of a particular device or software in general and instead increase their focus on how a technology was used in different industries, organizations, and cultures; so, the history of applications must be studied in considerable detail, as is already beginning to happen.

Third, the world went through one major wave of diffusion so far but also a second wave also seems to have started in many countries, typically in all top tier OECD nations and many smaller states in second tier countries. We will come back to the definition of the waves later. The notion that the world has just finished its first round of diffusion of IT suggests that we should de-emphasize old notions of hardware generations in describing ICT eras if for no other reason than multiple generations of equipment were in simultaneous use in all countries. We should become cautious about generalized rules of ICT and economic behavior in characterizing patterns of behavior, such as an over reliance on Moore's Law, but not discard them, and in particular, emerging rules and insights about the behavior of users and networks. We must pay more attention to economic literature on diffusion of ICT to understand fundamental motivations and practices concerning adoption of technologies. Yet, looking at technologies themselves can conveniently help differentiate between first and second waves of computing. Hence, we should not be absolute in our conclusions.

Fourth, as we look at the role of ICT in any society, we should realize that the subject cannot be discussed outside the context of the national events and culture of the day. The days of just writing about specific ICTs, or of their industries, with minimal attention to political, social, cultural, economic, and business issues must end. I found ICTs a central feature of modern societies, and that was not an observation of just the period involving the internet. A number of years ago Paul Edwards made that obvious in his book dealing with the role of computing and the Cold War, dating it as far back as the 1950s [6]. In an extreme case, one can conclude after examining the role of ICT and IT politics in East Germany that one of the reasons this country's government failed was due to its poor management of IT. Additionally, today we also know that IT's importance to East Germany was one of the reasons why the Berlin wall went up in the first place, namely, to keep computer experts from leaving the country along with other technically skilled workers and scientists [7].

4   The Role of Historic Waves in Information Technologies

If we discard the old IT paradigm of defining computer eras by the generations of hardware and software introduced by IT vendors and, instead, define periods by a more comprehensive results-centered approach as historians do for other technologies, then we are given the opportunity to organize information about computing in new ways. For example, I have concluded that between roughly 1940 and 1990 or 1995, the most economically endowed nations have gone through one era, not four or five in their use of computers. It is too early to give this one era a good descriptive name, so I propose an uncomfortable, unpolished temporary placeholder: Wave One. Eventually, someone will come up with a more elegant name such as was done for the Spanish Golden Age, the Napoleonic Era, or the Victorian Era. We need the placeholder because it appears that a Wave Two is underway that must be differentiated from the first as events will not wait for the historians to catch up.

So, what is Wave One all about? Wave One has several features. First, it relied very much on mainframe computers and their associated technologies with a particular emphasis on centralized computing as the dominant form of IT in those nations that used ICT. IT was embedded the most in the largest organizations in society and increasingly during Wave One in smaller organizations as more modular digital IT became more available such as in the forms of minicomputers, later personal computers, and then early telecommunications networks. During this wave, institutions were the dominant users of communication infrastructures linked to IT, and this happened during the second half of Wave One that evolved into ICT. ICT remained very expensive relative to other ways of processing options, but individuals began using computing at home and online such as with PCs. Because we are so close in time to Wave One—a wave still alive and emerging in dozens of countries—the boundaries between it and Wave Two are not always evident—yet.

I am noticing the emergence of early features of Wave Two—again a placeholder of a name until someone can later define the era better. Wave Two already has some visible elements. First, it continues to do all the things users, vendors and societies did in Wave One, as those activities remain. Swedish government agencies still do the same data processing today as they did a few years ago, yet Sweden, for example, is clearly moving into Wave Two. However, new activities are integrated into those of Wave One, or are in addition to the earlier one such as a citizen accessing government services through mobile phones and websites that in prior years they did by filling out forms, making telephone calls, or by visiting a government office. A bigger difference is that individuals in Wave Two play a role almost equal economically to that of Wave One participants, who in the first wave were mostly managers that acquired and used IT on behalf of their enterprises and public agencies. In Wave Two economies, consumers spend almost as much as enterprises on such digital technologies as consumer electronics, and mobile communications, and own vast quantities of digital data they store in their phones, laptops, digital cameras, CDs, and DVDs. The percent of GDP spent by people on ICT approaches Wave One rates—it is no accident that Apple is prosperous—it evolved into a Wave Two enterprise, while Amazon.com and eBay were born into that new era.

In Wave Two whole societies begin to think and act as if they were telematic, networked cultures. Four behaviors seem to be in evidence. There is more discourse about the information age as present society or one soon to be. Manuel Castells publishes another book about telematic societies in Great Britain through Oxford University Press and knows that the largest number of readers of his book will be in those countries that are already extensive users of ICT, not in Central Africa or in Western China, where publications about telematic societies are virtually non-existent. Another characteristic of Wave Two is more training of technical and knowledge workers, and labor that use brains more than brawn, resulting in extended economic activity coming from high-tech endowed products and services, and more knowledge work than before. IT is everywhere and digital, embedded in ever smaller forms and products, even in the air—wireless—and physically in almost all buildings, spaces inhabited by people, and on one's person in our pockets and sticking out of their ears. Wave Two is a time when bandwidth is something everyone "must have." In some countries it is seen as a citizen's entitlement as part of their legal and moral civil right to have access to information, for example Finland which recently passed a law making access to the internet a human right. The Finns were not alone in their views. A recent BBC poll reported that 87 percent of people in twenty-seven countries agreed with this idea [1]. Leaders of the eighteenth century French Enlightenment would be quite at home in Wave Two societies. Finally, one should note that Wave Two is coming in spurts and pieces, just as Wave One did and to such an extent that no clear global pattern is yet fully evident except mobile telephony, which is the most studied technological feature of Wave Two that we have today. Spurts and pieces of similarly repeated events and patterns explain why I use the word Wave. Finally, let us recognize that the study of mobile telephony will inform greatly the first generation of ICT historians who someday will describe Wave Two.

5 How Should Students of ICT's History Proceed?

This question can be answered with a list of questions—issues—that future historians can address. Waves One and Two are simply literary scaffolds to help get scholars to various parts and issues of IT's global history. I believe there are a few questions that we can start addressing to both waves. My list includes the following.

- How did culture and politics of one nation affect use of computing in a broad region?
- To what extent is the country format I am using the best one for understanding the global history of ICT, or should we discard it in favor of some other model or models? What are these other models?
- How do we overcome the reluctance of scholars in one country to comment on the history of another? Lars Heide is willing to do that but will a Southern European be prepared to critique the digital history of Northern European nations, or Chinese digital history by a Japanese scholar?
- Since it appears that the Iron Curtain of the Cold War era was more like a chain link fence rather than some solid impenetrable barrier, what does ICT's history teach us about the economies, societies, and flow of information in communist Europe—an area as big and as populated as Western Europe. What does Cold War Eastern Europe teach us about the general movement of ICT knowledge globally to other communist regions, "Third World," "Unaligned Nations" of the twentieth century, and today's totalitarian societies?
- How do we overcome problems of so many languages to work with to build global histories of ICT themes? We all cannot be like the great twentieth century French historian, Fernand Braudel, who seemed comfortable working with so many languages.
- Finally, what can we do to build trans-national repositories of primary materials?

There are various actions we can take, however, that my limited study of global history of computing suggests are possible and useful. The collective experiences of the Nordics are additionally demonstrating how trans-national history collaboration is possible, engaging pioneers, users, scholars, and institutions. Let us use them as a laboratory in which to learn how to do well in other regions of the world. That means the Nordics are going to have to share more in English and in other languages how they are doing their histories of ICT, in particular the Swedes who currently seem to be the most advanced in the world in such collaborative work.

I ask Nordic scholars to write more in English because so few people in the world can read Swedish, Danish, Norwegian, or Finnish. Many speak and often write well in English or German. So for the Nordics and scholars in other countries, either write your histories in widely used languages or arrange for translations, not just translated summaries of your work. Otherwise your history will not be taken into account when writing global histories and your nation's accomplishments will remain marginalized as they normally have been in the past, denying scholars all over the world a fuller knowledge of the history of computing. Publishing in English proceedings of the Nordic computer history conferences is a wonderful example of what is possible. Without the first two volumes, many historians in other parts of the world would know almost nothing about the history of IT in northern Europe.

Just as Nordics were smart in how they used so many forms of ICTs, let us encourage them to help find solutions for reconstructing ICT's history of Central Europe. For a half century or more the archives of the communist countries were sealed from scholarly study, but now are open. We need historians to examine these, to reconstruct the history of 350 million people across all aspects of society, not just about computing. I believe this is one of the biggest research requirements for historians of all kinds for the next half century and certainly the biggest one for European history for at least several generations.

Write more national ICT histories in any language otherwise we Americans will continue to dominate the narrative. We need country histories of IT for almost all of Continental Europe, for each country in Latin America, for three-quarters of Asia, for a handful of nations in Africa, and for the entire Middle East. National histories are the bricks we need with which to build really good global histories of specific ICTs, uses, and themes.

Finally, continue encouraging the European Union and various national institutions to support pan-European ICT history and the development of pan-European ICT archival and history centers. As much as I love the Charles Babbage Institute in the middle of North America, if I were a European, I would have to say, "CBI is too far away from Stockholm, Paris or Helsinki."

Some final thoughts about global ICT trends are in order. ICT history is going global, because ICT is now used in every country, in almost all its current technological formats, by almost four billion people, soon by over five billion (largely cell phones). It is diffusing faster than the population of the world is growing. ICT is as important to understand within the histories of the late twentieth century, as are the political, business, economic and military events of the era. In short, ICT history is now mainstream. Yet, ICT is still emerging and changing, as it has not stabilized into some mature set of technologies, uses, or results and consequences. That continuing churn makes the work of historians very difficult. Finally, more than historians are interested in learning from the history of ICT—and the audience at this conference represents some of the best qualified people to assist in creating and using the insights of history to help them.

References

1. Economist Intelligence Unit: Digital Economy Rankings 2010: Beyond e-Readiness. EIU, London (2010)
2. Polastron, L.X.: The Great Digitalization and the Quest to Know Everything. Inner Traditions, Rochester, Vermont (2006)
3. Mounier-Kuhn, P.: L'informatique en France. PUPS, Paris (2010)
4. Heide, L.: Punched-Card Systems and the Early Information Explosion, 1880–1945. Johns Hopkins University Press, Baltimore (2009)
5. Misa, T.: Organizing the History of Computing: "Lessons Learned" at the Charles Babbage Institute. In: Impagliazzo, J., Järvi, T., Paju, P. (eds.) History of Nordic Computing, vol. 2. Springer, Berlin (2009)
6. Edwards, P.N.: The Closed World. MIT Press, Cambridge (1996)
7. Stokes, R.G.: Constructing Socialism: Technology and Change in East Germany, 1945–1990. Johns Hopkins University Press, Baltimore (2000)

Computerization of the Norwegian Land Register: An Early Example of Outsourcing and Still a Model for Good Practice

Bjørn Nagell

Devoteam daVinci
bjorn.nagell@devoteam.com

Abstract. Computerization of the Ground Book and the property rights registration, led to a major improvement of the service quality. The computerizing, which started in the late 1980s, resulted in considerable cost savings for the government, citizens, banks, real estate agents, and other private enterprises using the register. At the time, the government made a bold decision to outsource the total effort to private consortium. The author reflects on some experiences from this successful implementation of new computer-based services for the registration and publication of property rights.

Keywords: Digitalization, e-government, outsourcing, public administration.

1 Historical Background

The disposal of real estate property is one of the most basic rights in all countries. Scandinavia, including Norway, Denmark, Sweden and, to some extent, Finland, have very similar traditions developed through trade and cultural exchange across borders for more than a thousand years.

During the Viking period, the old courts were called, "Tinget," and Tinget announced a declaration of rights related to land. Since that time, the announcement of property rights was part of the court system. A law regulation in 1633 required the registration of such announcements. This led to the establishment of the first land register in 1665, which contained most real estate properties in Norway, including information about the user of the land and his tax liability.

Two hundred years later, a new law established the existing land register, the Ground Book (GB). In this register, both a block and a parcel number defined the properties, an identification that is still in use today. The old Ground Book had one page per property defined by block and parcel number, and it contained information on the title and other rights related to it.

2 The Purpose of Registration

Individuals, companies, the government, or joint ownership could hold title to the land. In addition, a separate law regulates leasehold. The rights to real estate

J. Impagliazzo, P. Lundin, and B. Wangler (Eds.): HiNC3, IFIP AICT 350, pp. 13–21, 2011.

properties can serve as security for loans. Consequently, a mortgage deed would be registered as a financial encumbrance on the property, which could limit the owner's right of use of the land such as the right of first refusal if the property is sold, right of way, and the right to hunt, among others.

Before someone buys an asset or takes an asset as security for a loan, it is important to be able to check

- o that the one who sells the object or gives it as security has the right to do so
- o whether the object has already been used as collateral for loans from other sources, and
- o that there is no other encumbrance or restriction that might limit the rights to dispose of the object or reduce its value.

It is important that such information is available to the public so that potential buyers and lenders can easily search for such information prior to purchase.

3 The Need for Computerization

During 1985, approximately 1.1 million transactions were entered into the manual land register. Of this total, 120 to 140 thousand transactions were transfers of title. The annual growth that year was 11 percent compared with an average of 3 percent growth over the last ten years. The number of requests for information from the register in 1986 was estimated at 2.6 million per year:

- o Certified extracts from the books: 30,000 per year
- o Uncertified extracts from the books: 600,000 per year
- o Questions by phone or from visitors to the office: 2,000,000 per year

While the courts experienced a heavy workload, the public experienced problems with long processing times for the transactions – more than thirty days on average. The government considered additional personnel; but at the same time a need to bring the Ground Book up-to-date, including reorganizing and restructuring the information in the books had been identified. Therefore, they decided to introduce modern information technology to improve the efficiency and quality of the registration. The idea of computerizing the books was expected to improve the current situation and lead to major cost savings.

Making information available online meant a value-added service for which the external users should be willing to pay. In this way, the distribution of digital information from the land register represented a business opportunity that could provide financing for the implementation of computer technology in the local courts.

4 Implementation Strategy

The planning of a computerized land register started in 1984. During this stage, the Ministry of Justice (MOJ) identified three critical factors for which it had to make provisions; these include:

o The implementation required a large project and the government did not have the staff, skills, and experience to carry out such a major enterprise,
o The introduction of information technology should be carried out for the land register and include the computerization of all the courts at the same time.
o Sources of financing should be sought outside the government budgets. External users (banks, insurance companies, real estate agents) would benefit from increasing the speed and reliability of the transfer of title and financing.

Initially, through their National Commercial Bank Association, the MOJ proposed, that the Norwegian banks could take on the register project as a joint venture, since they would be major users of a mortgage register. After some discussions, the Bank Association refused the offer.

5 The Contract – Terms and Conditions

The MOJ decided to issue an invitation to major information technology companies for open tenders for a national land register system. The tenders should include systems development, equipment and communication, conversion of manual books, training, operation, as well as maintenance and support. In return, the contractor would receive a part of the fees for registration and requests for information from the register.

Thus, the contractor had the right to commercialize the information within certain market segments. The contract period defined a timeframe that would give the bidders a reasonable return on their investments. However, the MOJ had the possibility to terminate it at any time; in doing so, however, they would then have to repay the other party their investments including interest. The MOJ also had an option to take certain corrective actions if the profitability proved to be far above expectations. The MOJ kept the ownership of the register database.

The terms of reference specified the following tasks related to the land register (GB):

o Introduction of a system with the necessary registration and report functions to produce the Ground Book (GR), the journal of transactions, certified printout of encumbrances, and other information on registered documents according to the Norwegian Law for Legal Registration,
o Establishment of an accounting system for the collection of fees for registration and use of information from the database,
o Conversion of the paper files.

In addition, one important task was the implementation of general office automation systems for the local courts. Through separate agreements with the MOJ, the contractor would supervise the installation of computer equipment and provide user, maintenance, and operational support.

6 Organization

Because of the procurement process, the contract was awarded to a joint venture between Statens datasentral (SDS) and Kommunedata (KD) through Tinglysningsdata

AS (TD), founded in 1987. In 1994, the organization changed its name to Norsk Eiendomsinformasjon AS (NE). Tinglysningedata had the following business idea:

o   Assure that the court system in Norway utilized IT in the most efficient way
o   Produce a reliable and easily accessible Ground Book, which could be used for the purpose of economical assessment of individuals and companies, available to the public

The TD was supposed to stay small and to concentrate on project management and other key functions. Most of the project was subcontracted, mainly to the owners. The mother companies carried the necessary guarantees for the fulfillment of the contract.

KD owned 60 percent of TD and SDS owned 40 percent, with a share capital of six million NOK. Both of these companies were major providers of data processing services, including the operation of nationwide computer networks. KD was a joint venture of seven regional computer centers owned by municipalities. Later, the regional centers merged and privatized into two separate companies—NIT and Allianse. SDS was a government owned share holding company, originally established to provide data processing services for the central government.

The MOJ retained a strong controlling and monitoring position, but it avoided taking part in the day-to-day management. Representatives for the MOJ held two positions on the board of directors. In addition, a steering committee had a co-coordinating role.

7   The Implementation Project

The technical solution consisted of the following main elements:

o   Each local court received a UNIX server with workstations in a local area network used for registration. Each local system kept a complete copy of the register for the actual court district. There was 100 percent terminal coverage in the court system.
o   A centralized database on a mainframe computer comprised the legal place of record. The daily transaction data transferred to the central database, which was updated each day.
o   The local court using the local system to download printouts from the central system issued all authorized extracts from the GB. All phone or counter inquiries were answered by accessing the local database.
o   The central database had gateways to the distributors' value added networks giving external users access to information.

When the implementation project was finished, 120 servers and 1,500 workstations were installed in 102 local courts, providing a 100 percent terminal coverage.

Providing information and training to all court personnel was regarded a key factor for success. A total of twelve thousand days of training was given through the project to government employees, distributors, and customers. A first class support service was also essential for the success of the project. A technical group of seven people provided hotline telephone support; they answered eleven thousand inquiries in 1993.

8 Conversion of Manual Books

The conversion ensured that the required information from the manual books was transferred into the new system with the right structure and quality, but the court system did not have the capacity to take on any additional workload. They were already behind with current tasks.

Then, the conversion was organized as a project. Four conversion centers were established in different rural areas of Norway with high unemployment rates. Each center comprised approximately twenty-five people. The local court offices thus had a temporary increase in their workload, taking on training and dedicating some key people to support the project. They also had a peak work period when the results of the conversion were under approval. However, at this stage they were using computers for all new registrations, thus taking advantage of the improved efficiency.

Initial estimates showed that conversion of full text from the manual book would require 4 kbyte of storage per property. The use of codes and secondary files for the corresponding textual description reduced the registration volume to half. During the project, the daily production was 2,700 properties per day, which was somewhat more than they estimated.

The conversion started in 1988 and it included 2.4 million properties in 97 local courts. It required an average of four months to complete one local court. The conversion centers accomplished their tasks in 1993; the centers closed down as the workload reduced.

9 Marketing and Distribution

From the beginning, the strategy had been to work solely through distributors. TD put much effort into marketing and external information, because they needed it to educate the market and develop the demand for the services provided.

Active marketing started in 1989. Advertising material was produced aiming at professional users in the financial industry, the public in general, and the government. Newspaper advertisements had little effect; better results were obtained from using courts to inform and encourage customers to go online, and advertisements in professional magazines.

Market surveys were conducted to identify needs and test various pricing policies and institutions with large potential customers, such as commercial banks and local tax collection offices. A market poll of users in October 1990 showed that 90 percent were very satisfied. At that point, there were 800 customers, of whom 70 percent were bank and finance and 30 percent were insurance and government.

A number of PR activities were carried out including participation in meetings, conferences for customers and contact with associations for various customer groups. As many as 30 seminars with 400–500 participants were arranged for customers and salesmen from the distributors. In addition, TD established an incentive program for the salesmen.

By the end of 1993, TD's market coverage was 60 percent of all requests for information from the land register; the rest was inquiries directly to the courts. The financial market (banks, insurance, financing and credit information providers) represented 80 percent of this traffic.

10 Financing

Actual revenues followed the projected pattern over the first three years, but were delayed by one year. The reasons were a combination of three factors:

(a) The downturn of the real estate market in 1989–1992 led to a decrease of volume by 27 percent over the three years. Then the market started to rise again.
(b) It took longer than anticipated to get the financial market to start using the services. This was partly due to necessary changes of systems and working procedures, and partly related to the rate of conversion. The volume of transactions increased significantly after the completion of about two thirds of the conversions.
(c) The development after five years of operation far exceeded expectations. However, the increase in volume might have been even higher with lower transaction charges, although the market did not seem to be very price sensitive with regard to the level of fees imposed.

11 Refinancing Government Buyout

In 1992, Tinglysningsdata A/S was on the edge of bankruptcy and the government had taken it over. The project had progressed according to the plans and the costs were close to budget. However, revenues did not develop as anticipated, mainly due to market conditions, which led to a situation where the company had to obtain additional funding. The owners asked the government to increase TD's share of the legal fees and made this a condition for providing additional funding. Instead, the government decided to buy the company and to compensate existing owners. TD was the owner of all the local computer equipment and the workstations in the courts. The MOJ transferred title of equipment to the government and paid all debts.

However, the current organization of the project was running so well that no one would take the risk of disturbing its ongoing activities. Therefore, the MOJ decided not to change TD until the project was completed.

Because the government was criticized for involving the ordinary administrative tasks of running the court system with those of providing services to the public on a commercial basis, it was decided to divide the further financing into two separate activities.

A. *Distribution of online information*: TD retained the exclusive right to sell information from the register and had to bear all costs involved with the marketing and distribution of online services and the computer operation related to these activities.
B. *Computerization of government activities*: The MOJ paid separately all services related to the computerization of the court system according to a management contract.

The MOJ also received criticism for having officers on the board of directors, because it meant combining responsibilities for the administrative and controlling role with the tasks of operational issues. Because of this criticism, a general policy was introduced restricting ministry representatives from sitting on the board of directors of a company. The ministry should execute its control solely through the owners' meetings and its power to appoint the board of directors.

On the other hand, we should note that the success of the project was largely due to such mixed roles by which the few people involved from the MOJ were able to control efficiently the implementation and secure coordinating activities. In this role, representatives of the MOJ could simultaneously design the concept, propose the required legal adjustments, instruct the court system, and control the project management.

12   After Refinancing

By 1993, after completion of the implementation project, the organization was left with the tasks of normal operations and support. At this point, the MOJ started to discuss alternative ways of organizing the activities in the future.

From 1987 to 1994, TD had twenty-six employees of which sixteen were part-time or contracted. On 1 January 1995, they transferred all support for the local courts, and the personnel involved in this, was transferred to a new agency (RIFT) established to provide training and support to all organization units under the MOJ's jurisdiction. RIFT was also responsible for acquisition, development, implementation, maintenance, and support for systems used in the legal sector of the government, including the local land register systems.

Thereafter, TD was purely dedicated to the task of operating, maintaining and supporting the central register, including the distribution of information from the register on a commercial basis. The company was also given the operation of the GAB register[1] on behalf of the Ministry of Environment, which was the start of diversification into new and related services.

They kept the organization small and transparent. Most activities ware outsourced to subcontractors for a limited term, which keeps costs low due to market competition. By 1 January 1995, TD's staff comprised eleven people. The MOJ was the sole owner and the only participant at the owner's meeting.

13   Costs and Benefits

The cost of local equipment was around 70 million NOK and included 1,600 terminals and the necessary site computers for the whole court system, of which only 350 terminals were used for registration.

The cost of software development is difficult to estimate, but probably amounts to 15–20 million NOK including systems for local registration, central database register, and conversions. In addition, it included software for case handling, office automation, and a general accounting system.

The total costs of conversion were approximately 160 million NOK. These costs were mainly expenses paid to subcontractors who were responsible for the establishment, operation, and dismantling of the four temporary conversion centers.

If the operation had continued according to its original form in private hands, the profit would have stabilized around 22 million NOK from 1993, with a turnover of about 65–70 million NOK (more than 30 percent), which means a repayment period of fifteen years for the project, excluding financial costs.

The time to register a transaction was reduced from 30 to 1.2 (1.4) days. Already in 1990, it was found that phone calls to the registry office at the local court had been reduced by 75 percent when the information became available online.

In 1987, 350 people were working with land registration in the local courts. Based on experience obtained in a trial project at a local court, the introduction of a computerized system would make it possible to handle the expected growth of transaction volume with the same number of employees.

The MOJ conducted a study in 1993 to measure benefits of the computerization, when the conversion was completed and the system was fully operating. The result of this analysis showed an improvement in efficiency of 30 percent for the land register activities.

One has to remember that the project also included financing the computerization of the whole court system. The income from registration fees, from which the project received a small part during implementation, covered more than twice the cost of registration and brought in another 250 million NOK per year for the government.

The savings within registration in the local courts was 30 percent, which meant a further 40 million NOK per year in addition to the annual profit from online sales. With such a total amount from profit and productivity gains, the repayment time was four years from completion of the implementation project.

14 Learning Experience

We must regard the entire project for the computerization of the Ground Book and the courts a success story. Outsourcing of the whole process was a bold decision initiated by some leading civil servants in the Ministry of Justice. The contractual model that was developed proved to work well for the government and made it possible to deal with the experienced problems in an adequate way. It is most likely that the project would also have been successful, even if it had survived in private hands.

Time and cost estimates turned out to be in the right range, the projected income was delayed for a year due to several factors. Nevertheless, the business case proved to be sound. One factor that was underestimated was the time it takes to introduce new services that radically change current working procedures for the users.

Since 2010, all registrations in the Ground Book are centralized, which could have taken place from the very beginning and would have increased the overall reduction of operating costs. However, if the registration activities had been removed from the court, the remaining tasks in many of the courts would have been below critical mass for these local institutions and would have initiated an even more comprehensive reform. Due to the political situation at that time, this would have been extremely difficult to accomplish.

After the recent centralization of the Ground Book with the Norwegian Mapping Agency, the original mission of Norsk Eiendomsinformasjon is less important. However, Norsk Eiendomsinformasjon is still a vital institution under the jurisdiction of the Ministry of Trade and Industry, having diversified with other services related to the former ones.

References

1. Nagell, B.: Establishment of Property Right Registries in IDA Countries: A Framework for Development Based on Concepts and Experiences from Norway (1997)
2. Forespørsel om tilbud på et landsomfattende system for tinglysning, Justisdepartementet 19/6-1986
3. Årsberetninger i Tinglysningsdata A/S
4. En eiendomssaga 1987–1997. Et jubileumsskrift utgitt av Norsk Eiendomsinformasjon
5. Ejendomsregistrering i de nordiske lande: Et samarbeid mellom faginstitusjoner og universiteter i Norden; ISBN: 87-7866-412-8

Controlling the Battlefield: Computing and Operational Command in the Swedish Armed Forces, 1966–1989

Johan Gribbe

Div. of History of Science and Technology, KTH
100 44 Stockholm, Sweden
johan.gribbe@abe.kth.se

Abstract. In the late 1960s, the Swedish Defence Staff initiated the development of a computerized command and control system that was later to be known as the LEO-system. From the mid-1970s to 1989, more than two hundred million SEK were spent on the project, which involved private computer consultants and with military staff officers acting as project leaders and customers. In the end, however, only the intelligence application was introduced and put into operational use in the Swedish intelligence service during the 1990s. This paper will tell the story of the LEO-system and outline some of the reasons behind its failure. It is based on a witness seminar held at the Swedish Armed Forces Headquarters in Stockholm on January 15, 2008.

Keywords: Cold war, main frame computer, military technology, security.

1 Introduction

In the late 1960s, the Swedish Defence Staff initiated the development of a computerized command and control system that was later to be known as the LEO-system. The decision followed a reorganization of the national command structure and the system was intended to help central and regional military headquarters conduct wartime operations. Each headquarter was to have one LEO terminal system, with a number of workstations, containing information about all aspects of the battlefield. Information about friendly and enemy forces, fuel and ammunition supplies, were to be stored in a central database and a secure messaging system was to provide fast and reliable communications. Additional applications were developed to handle computations and simulations of transports and mobilization times. From the mid-1970s to 1989, more than two hundred million SEK were spent on the project, which involved private computer consultants and with military staff officers acting as project leaders and customers. In the end, however, only the intelligence application was introduced and put into operational use in the Swedish intelligence service during the 1990s.

This paper will tell the story of the LEO-system and outline some of the reasons behind its failure. One problem, that many insiders point out, was the considerable passive resistance which the system encountered from both end users and senior commanders when new computer technology was to be introduced in old organizational

J. Impagliazzo, P. Lundin, and B. Wangler (Eds.): HiNC3, IFIP AICT 350, pp. 22–27, 2011.

structures. The critical problem in this case was security. To develop an integrated and computerized command system meant that highly classified information about war plans, communications and intelligence was concentrated in a single computer system, which run counter to the fundamental military principle that an officer should know no more than absolutely necessary to execute the task assigned to him. Measures developed to control access, and to guarantee electronic security, provided little assurance to critics within the officers corps.

Other problems concerned the core technology involved. During more than twenty years of development, the LEO-system survived several different generations of computers, from the mainframes of the early 1970s to the personal computers of the late 1980s, with the basic system architecture intact. How did these technology shifts affect system development? Or put differently: How come the project was not cancelled but rather re-equipped with new computer hardware despite the apparent problems? Finally, it could be argued that the reason behind its failure was cultural and related to the grand ambitions of the system. In fact, there are many similarities between the LEO command system and the management information systems (MIS) developed in the private sector during the second half of the 1960s. The similarities concern both the basic technology and the overall function of the system, and the reasons behind the failures of LEO and other MIS-systems are probably similar [1].

Some parts of the LEO command system are still in use within the Swedish military intelligence (MUST) and all written documentation about the system and its development is classified. Instead, this paper is based on oral accounts given at a witness seminar held at the Swedish Armed Forces Headquarters in Stockholm on 15 January 2008 [2].

2   Project Initiation and Early Tests

In 1966, the command structure of the Swedish Armed Forces was reorganized. Sweden was organized in so called military areas. The general in command of a military area commanded the army divisions stationed in the region, the regional naval command and the regional air defence sector. The commander answered directly to the Supreme Commander. Each area was named according to the geographical area it covered. After the 1966 command reform, there were eight military areas, from the Upper Norrland Military Area (Övre Norrlands militärområde) in the north to the Eastern Military Area (Östra militärområdet), covering Stockholm and most parts of Södermanland and Uppland to the Southern Military Area [3]. In connection to this reorganization of regional command, the Supreme Commander ordered an investigation of a possible computerization of the military command structure. In terms of ideas, the project had close connections to the Management Information Systems (MIS) that were introduced at this time in many large private corporations. For a discussion on Management Information Systems in private industry, see Gustav Sjöblom's contribution to this volume [4].

Work on the new project was formally initiated in 1969–70. As the new system was intended as an integrated operational command, control and communications system for all three service branches, overall systems responsibility was given to the head of the Operations section within the Defence Staff (Försvarsstabens Sektion III).

This department was responsible for warplanning. Military officers from deparments within the Operations section acted as "buyers", specifying the functionality of the system, working in team with the computer specialists in charge of applications development. Meanwhile, personnel from the Data processing department of the Defence Staff (Försvarsstabens ADB-avdelning) and computer consultants from private companies were to handle systems development. A military officer, colonel Torbjörn Ottosson, was put in charge of applications development. In 1970, the project was formally named LEO after a headquarters command excercise with the same name. This division of labour between military officers, acting as customers of the applications and subsystems developed for their particular area of responsibility, and the computer specialists in charge of software development – with no project manager in charge of the project – was later to be a subject of much debate and criticism.

Technologically, the LEO systems architecture was closely linked to the large mainframe computers that appeared in the mid and late 1960s. Each headquarter was to have one terminal system, with a number of workstations connected to it, containing information about all aspects of the battlefield. Information about friendly and enemy forces, fuel and ammunition supplies, was to be stored in a central database and a secure communications system, the LEO Message Control System (LEO:MCS) was to provide fast and reliable communications. Information about military forces, their level of preparedness, their fighting values and losses was handled in an application called LEO:SK. Another important area in which computer power could support decision making was transport planning, handled in an application called LEO Transport Planning (LEO:TP) that contained maps and information about roads and railroads and their capacity. Using the transport planning application, military commanders could calculate alternate routes or the consequenses of the enemy knocking out a bridge or a railroad junction. The intelligence application, called LEO:UND, was essentially a mirror image twin of these applications, intended to store the same information about the enemy, his supplies and his fighting capacity.

3 Computer Procurement

A major user of mainframe computers in the military organization was the the National Service Administration in need of computing and storage capacity to process information about the tens of thousands of young men who did their compulsary military service each year. The computing division of the service administration in Kristianstad had aquired a Burroughs B2500 mainframe computer that was used to test an early version of LEO. A particular advantage of the Burroughs mainframe system was that it already contained a powerful data base handler colled FORTE. After an initial period of testing, formal technical and operational specifications of the LEO computers were issued in 1977–78. While most of the software development hade been handled by personnel of the computer department (ADB-avdelningen), or external consultants tied to it, the procurement of systems hardware was handled by the Swedish Agency for Public Management (Statskontoret) in cooperation with the Swedish Defence Material Administration (Försvarets materielverk, FMV). In the end, four competing companies/systems remained: Norsk Data/Nord-series, Datasaab/Censor 932, DEC/VAX-11 and minicomputer from Burroughs. In November 1979, Norsk Data was chosen as the supplier and three of its Nord 100 computers were ordered to be used with Alfaskop data terminals.

At the same time the first problems started to appear. By the late 1970s, the LEO-project had already dragged on for almost a decade without an operational system even being close to completion. Several technical problems had come to light. A major problem was still limitations in computer graphics and presentation technology and in addition, the security of information stored in the system started to be a concern. It was clear that the LEO-system, while functioning at exercises, could not live up to previous expectations. Gert Schyborger, then project manager at the Defence Staff, recalls two opposing sides at this time. On the one hand, those who considered the problems to be causes of delay, not reasons to discontinue the entire project. According to them, the project should be allowed to continue with the hopes of a technological fix along the way. On the other hand, those who considered the whole idea of a central computerized system for operational command to be premature and who thought that it should be abandoned right away. The dispute ended in what could be labelled an organizational compromise. The position as project leader was separated from the position as chief of the operations section within the Defence Staff, and a special project manager was appointed. The task of implementing the LEO-system on a smaller scale, while awaiting new technological developments, was assigned to colonel Orvar Lundberg in 1981. The fundamental issues, however, were not resolved and the project was to become a source of conflict throughout the 1980s.

This internal debate on the future of the system coincided with shifts on several important positions within the military high command. Throughout the project supreme commander general Stig Synnergren had been a keen supporter, but he was replaced in 1978 by the more sceptical army general Lennart Ljung. The most important shift, however, took place at the position as head of the Defence Staff where vice admiral Bror Stefenson succeeded Bengt Schuback in 1981. Stefenson, like a number of other high-ranking officers, believed LEO to be a waste of both time and money and openly declared to the new project manager Orvar Lundberg that "he did not believe in automated computer processing and that there should be no new system". By this time, however, the decision to build the system was firmly anchored in decisions within both the military high command and the government. Stefenson did not have the authority to discontinue the project, but he did control the funds and during the course of the 1980s, Lundberg saw his project increasingly stripped of economic resources and manpower. Behind the resistance from Stefenson and other senior officers, however, lay deeper concerns than just the short term financial aspects of the project. Which would be the wider consequences of introducing computer technology in the military command structure?

4 Security Problems and the End of the Project

On the one hand, the idea of commanding the armed forces through an integrated and centralized computer system – with the supreme commander and his staff in the center – seemed almost congenial with the hierarchic nature of the military command structure. If properly used, computer technology could be a means of strengthening and consolidating the traditional military chain of command. On the other hand, however, the system architecture violated other equally important military principles in a way that was not obvious when the system was first conceived. To develop a computerized command system meant that highly classified information about war plans, mobilization schemes, communications and intelligence was gathered in a single computer system, something which ran counter to the fundamental rule of military security that an officer should know no more than absolutely necessary to execute the task assigned to him. What would, for example, prevent a military officer from tapping the system and handing over classified information to the enemy? And how could orders issued within the system be authenticated? Wouldn't it be possible for lower level commanders in wartime to issue orders that were either outside their area of responsibility or, in worst case, deliberately false and misleading?

These weaknesses could not easily be corrected without changing the overall systems architecture. Measures developed to control access, and to guarantee the security of classified information stored in the system, provided little assurance to the critics within the organization and these problems were probably an important reason behind the considerably passive reaction the project encountered among influential senior commanders. Another problem subject to much debate at this time was that of electronic security. In the late 1970s, it was discovered that computers, and monitors in particular, emitted relatively strong electronic signals that could be picked up and used to tap the system of secret information. The resulting measures to secure the system caused the cost of systems hardware to increase threefold, while the cost of communications and installation increased almost by a factor of ten, causing a severe strain on the already limited project budget and resulted in further delays. This increase in the cost of communications resulted in large part from the addition of a fiber optic communications network, a new and unproven technology at that time.

Despite the security problems, the dramatic cost increases and the lacking support from senior military commanders, the project dragged on during the first half of the 1980s under the leadership of Orvar Lundberg. Development work was allowed to continue, the many internal computer programmers and external consultants tied to the project were paid, and several new applications were added to the system. A limited test version of the system called LEO-80 was installed at the military headquarters in Stockholm, beginning in 1981. However, despite a formal decision in 1984 to implement the system, no additional funds were made available to buy new hardware and more computers that could meet the new security standards.

This situation continued until 1987 when the most outspoken critic of the project, vice admiral Bror Stefenson, finally retired and was replaced by general Torsten Engberg as head of the Defence Staff. Engberg had a more sympathetic attitude towards the project in general and decided that the by now largely dormant LEO-system should be refurbished with new hardware and put into operational use. The annual budget assigned to LEO was doubled to thirty million SEK and to mark the shift the new name LEO-85 was decided. At the same time, the project management was renewed when commander Lars-Erik Hoff, who had served under Engberg at the navy staff, replaced Orvar Lundberg as project manager. Hoff faced a fundamentally different situation than his predecessor both in terms of funding and support, and a period of rapid expansion ensued. After less than two years, in 1989, all regional headquarters had been equipped and the system was declared operational.

In the end, however, this proved to be only a temporary success. In 1994, work on a replacement system called ORION was initiated. Originally, ORION like LEO was intended to be a secure wartime communication system for military operational command, capable of handling both open, secret and top secret information, but this goal was never achieved. During the 1990s, the system, as used by central and regional headquarters, had gradually evolved into a system for the handling of intelligence. In 1999, development work on all ORION applications but the intelligence subsystem was discontinued, almost thirty years after the LEO project was initiated. This latter part of the system is still in use within the Swedish military intelligence organization.

Acknowledgments. I am grateful to Handelsbankens forskningsstiftelser for supporting the research for this paper. I am also grateful to my colleagues within the project, "Precursors of the IT Nation: Computer Use and Control in Swedish Society, 1955–1985" for comments on earlier versions of the paper.

References

1. Haig, T.: Inventing Information Systems: The Systems Men and the Computer. Business History Review 75(1), 15–60 (2001)
2. Gribbe, J.: LEO: Databehandling och operativ ledning inom försvaret, 1972–89: Transkript av ett vittnesseminarium vid Högkvarteret i Stockholm den 15 januari 2008. Avdelningen för teknik- och vetenskapshistoria, KTH, Stockholm (2008)
3. Cars, H. C., Skoglund, C., Zetterberg, K.: Svensk försvarspolitik under efterkrigstiden. Probus förlag, Stockholm (1986)
4. Sjöblom, G.: The Totally Integrated Management Information System in 1960s Sweden. In: Wangler, B. (ed.) HiNC3. IFIP AICT, vol. 350, pp. 83–91. Springer, Heidelberg (2011)

The Use of Computers for Controlling Electricity Flows in Sweden, 1950–1980

Arne Kaijser

Div. of History of Science and Technology, KTH
100 44 Stockholm, Sweden
arne.kaijser@abe.kth.se

Abstract. An important application of computers from the 1950s and onwards has been for designing and operating complex infrastructural systems like air traffic, telephony, railways, and electricity. This paper tells the story about how computers from the 1950s and onwards became an important tool for designing and operating the Swedish power grid. It describes two phases of this development. In the 1950s and 1960s, computers were used for making complicated *calculations* for designing power grids in a reliable way and optimizing the use of the different power plants. In a second phase starting in the late 1960s, computer systems were developed for *real time monitoring* supporting human control of the power grid. The paper analyzes by whom and for what purposes computers became tools for controlling electricity flows. In the conclusion, it also discusses the wider implications of computers for the development of the Swedish power system.

Keywords: Control, computers, efficiency, power systems, stability, Sweden TIDAS.

1 The Challenge of Stability

In Sweden, many of the large rivers and hydropower resources are located in the northern part of the country, while most of the population and industries are located in the south. Starting in the 1930s, long power lines were built to enable transmission of power from the north to the south and these lines became the backbone in a national power grid. However, the power grid also entailed a new kind of vulnerability due to the increasing complexity and the tight coupling between all the components. This meant that a disturbance in one part of the country could spread quickly to other parts of the system [1].

Power engineers were particularly concerned about so-called power oscillations: a sudden accident in a power plant or transformer station could cause major oscillations in the transmission lines. Such oscillations could affect transformers and power plants far away. In the mid 1920s, a young engineer at ASEA, Ivar Herlitz, studied this problem and developed a mathematical method for designing stable and robust transmission lines. His method was a forerunner of what became the new discipline of control theory in the 1950s. It was used when the first Swedish 220 kV power lines from the north of Sweden were designed in the early 1930s [2, 3].

J. Impagliazzo, P. Lundin, and B. Wangler (Eds.): HiNC3, IFIP AICT 350, pp. 28–34, 2011.

As the number of power lines increased, so did the complexity of the power system and Herlitz' method led to ever-larger calculations. In the early 1950s, the State Power Board, or Vattenfall as it is usually called, built a special laboratory where a physical model of the Swedish power system was constructed. (Vattenfall was responsible for operating the national grid.) It was a so-called network analyzer similar to the one built by Vannevar Bush at MIT in the 1930s [4]. This network analyzer made it possible for engineers at Vattenfall's Planning Division to simulate different kinds of disturbances in the grid. It was also possible to test different configurations of future power lines, but the preparation of these configurations was very time consuming.

When the computer BESK became available in the mid-1950s, Åke Ölwegård at Vattenfall's Planning Division developed a model for simulating the Swedish power system on BESK. Because of the limited capacity of BESK, the model was simplified – for example, it had only six power stations – yet, it behaved similar to the more "correct" model of the network analyzer. Moreover, the big advantage was that the parameters could change notably faster between subsequent simulations. A simulation that would take two days to prepare on the network analyzer could take only fifteen minutes to prepare with BESK [5].

When more powerful computers became available in the early 1960s, Ölwegård and his colleagues at Vattenfall's Planning Division developed a more comprehensive computer model of the Swedish power system called Dynamic Stability (DYN STAB). Vattenfall was able to make simulations at night on a big IBM 7090 computer, owned by the Swedish Defense Research Institute, FOA, until Vattenfall bought a computer of its own in the mid-1960s [5].

In the 1960s and 1970s, the complexity of the Swedish power system grew substantially, first because many power lines were built to neighboring countries and a Nordic grid emerged, secondly because huge nuclear power plants were built and taken into operation. These changes altered the system properties of the power system in a fundamental way [6]. The computer models described above were very important tools for planning and designing this expanding system in such a way that it would be robust and stable. These computer models were also used to make instructions for the personnel operating the grid. In particular, safety margins were calculated so the grid would be able to withstand a major disturbance, for example, the loss of a transformer or a high-tension line, without affecting consumers.

2 The Challenge of Efficiency

In all large-scale power systems, an important challenge is to use the various power plants in an efficient way. In the 1960s, twelve large power producers dominated the Swedish power industry. The largest one of these was Vattenfall, which owned almost 50 percent of all generating capacity. Each of the twelve power companies had a regional monopoly in some part of Sweden where it sold power to local utilities and industries [7].

Until the 1960s, Swedish electricity supply was predominantly based on hydropower, and yearly variations in precipitation and winter temperature influenced the availability of power in different parts of the country. The risk of shortage could be diminished by building storage dams and thermal power plants for backup, but such facilities were expensive and managers of the power companies realized that they had much to gain from mutual cooperation. If companies with a surplus of water in their dams could sell power to those with a shortage and if many companies could use thermal backup plants jointly, it could substantially lower the overall cost for reserve capacity.

Nonetheless, the selling and buying of power called for common rules for calculating the marginal cost for power. For thermal power, the marginal cost was rather easy to calculate. The dominant cost element was the cost of fuel. However, the marginal cost of hydropower was much more complicated to estimate. It had to take into account not only the operation costs, which were minimal, but also the risks for having to use thermal power later on or to ration electricity. These risks were dependent on the water level in the up-stream water reservoirs and the expected precipitation. In the 1950s, two engineers at the Sydkraft power company, Sven Stage and Yngve Larsson, developed a rather sophisticated mathematical theory for such calculations. The latter developed a computer program for these calculations that ran on BESK [8]. Ölwegård recalls that he and Larsson met each other sometimes while running their respective programs at night on BESK [5]!

Vattenfall developed a similar method for calculating marginal costs and there was a certain tug of war between the two methods. Nonetheless, a power pool agreement was reached in 1965 between the twelve largest power companies. This power exchange made possible a coordinated and very efficient use of almost all Swedish power plants and storage dams. In parallel, with negotiations about a power pool in Sweden, there were also efforts to establish power exchange among the Nordic countries. In 1963, a new Nordic organization for power cooperation, Nordel, was established. A few years later, the same principles for power exchange as in Sweden were adopted for the entire Nordic region.

3 Monitoring the Grid with Telephones

In the 1930s, Vattenfall established a central control room for the daily operation of their power plants and transmission lines. In 1947, the Swedish parliament made Vattenfall responsible for the management and operation of the entire Swedish power grid and Vattenfall's central control room became the national control center. The physical location of the control room was in Vattenfall's office in central Stockholm until 1962, when it moved to Vattenfall's new huge office building in Råcksta, a suburb of Stockholm.

The most important measuring instrument in the control room was a frequency gauge. The frequency should be as close to 50 Hz as possible and if it started deviating from 50 Hz this was a sign that *something* un-normal and unwanted was happening, but not what it was. Therefore, the key technical tool in the control center was the telephone. If an incident happened somewhere in the power system the engineers in the national control center were informed of what had happened through a telephone call from colleagues out in the country. When the control room engineers had made an analysis of the situation and what actions were needed, they phoned back and gave orders. Thus, when major disturbances occurred there was a very intensive calling [9]!

Normally two people worked in the central control room. One of them was responsible for the safe *operations* of the national power system. He gave orders to control centers around the country to start or stop power plants so that the total generation closely followed the total consumption. This was a prerequisite for keeping the frequency close to 50 Hz. He also checked that safety margins remained at all critical nodes in the grid. The other engineer was responsible for the economic *optimization* of the power system. His task was to make assessments and forecasts of which power plants in the country were most economical to use at each point in time and in the coming day and week, and to make offers to other companies to buy or sell certain quantities of power. He also registered all sale and buy deals so that they could settle them afterwards. Similar deals were also made with power producers in Denmark, Finland, and Norway. Both engineers used simple rule of thumb calculations for most of their decisions and these rules were based on the computer models mentioned above [9].

Daily control of the power system in Sweden was thus remarkably "low-tech" until the mid-1970s. This was possible because the power system – designed with the help of computer programs – was as stable and robust as possible. In addition, strict safety margins were established with these programs. Furthermore, many small disturbances were handled automatically without any human interference at all. For example, if the frequency dropped below a certain level, some designated hydro power plants or gas turbines would start automatically within seconds.

The engineers in the national control center had a large responsibility and mistakes could – literally – have far-reaching consequences. For example, Gunnar Ålfors, who worked many years in the control room, had a nightmare experience in the early 1970s when he was new on this job in the control center. To compensate for a burnt electronic component in a transformer station near Östersund, he ordered the closing down of a transmission line to Karlstad, but by mistake he said the wrong name and another power line between Karlstad and Gothenburg was closed down. This led to a power loss and oscillations in the southern part of Norway and within a few seconds a power line to Oslo broke down and the whole city became black [9]!

4   Monitoring the Grid with Computers

Another much larger blackout had occurred some years earlier abroad. On 9 November 1965, a fault occurred at the Niagara power station and within ten minutes, overloads had cascaded through the interconnected power grid in the northeastern states of the US and the whole of Ontario in Canada. Approximately twenty-five million people were left without electricity for up to twelve hours. That an electric blackout could have this magnitude was a shock to the public, politicians, and engineers alike.

The shock waves went far beyond the North American continent, and alarmed the engineers responsible for the operation of the Swedish power grid. In the mid-1960s, Sweden was connected with transmission links to the neighboring Nordic countries. This meant that up to fifteen million people in the four Nordic countries could be affected if a major blackout would occur in Sweden. Moreover, in the coming decade new big nuclear power plants would come into operation, which would make the Nordic power system even more complex.

Shortly after the big American blackout, Lars Gustafsson, the head of the Operations Division at Vattenfall, initiated an investigation concerning measures to avoid similar events in the Swedish grid. The investigators recommended the procurement of a computer system for monitoring the grid. The system could *collect* current data from power plants and transformer stations from all over the country approximately every ten seconds, *process* these data and present them in a lucid and usable way, and make *calculations* to determine the optimal mode of operation of the power system a week ahead. The system was called *T*otally *I*ntegrated *D*ata *A*cquisition *S*ystem (TIDAS), a name that tells something of the ambitions [10].

In the spring of 1971, a call for tenders was sent out to about twenty potential bidders, and the incoming tenders were carefully assessed half a year later. In 1972, the Swedish firm ASEA, which had been a major supplier of equipment to Vattenfall for half a century, was chosen as the main supplier for the new computer system. To be more precise, a new subsidiary called ASEA-LME Automation was responsible for the project. They established this subsidiary the previous year and recruited engineers from both ASEA and the telephone manufacturer LM Ericsson. ASEA engaged TRW Control, as a subcontractor for the computer part of the project. TRW was a company with headquarters in Houston, Texas and specialized in control engineering for the space and automobile industry, but also with some experience from the power industry. It was absolutely crucial for Vattenfall that the computer system would be reliable; therefore, Vattenfall participated actively in the development of TIDAS. Vattenfall engineers went both to Houston and to Västerås and Ludvika in order to follow the development work and to make sure that the computer system would be well adapted to the Swedish grid.

ASEA-LME Automation was responsible for the transmission part of the system. At an early stage some of the engineers read an article in an IEEE publication on "Adaptive Routing Techniques for Computer Communication Networks" describing the new ARPA network, [11]. The ASEA engineers found this promising and decided to embark on this road. However, the communication network for TIDAS was more complex than the ARPA network and contained more nodes. According to Torsten Cegrell, one of the ASEA engineers, they redesigned the ARPA network to achieve a robust and stable system, and according to him, this new design was important for the further development of the internet [12].

In parallel, TRW Control worked on the data processing part of the project, called TIDAS-D. TRW in turn worked closely with Xerox Data Systems. Two Sigma 9 computers from Xerox were chosen as the hardware for the system. A whole series of very extensive tests had taken place before Vattenfall would accept the new system. When the Houston team had completed its work, the computers and all the peripherals were flown to Stockholm in a chartered Boeing 747 Jumbo Jet [12].

In Stockholm, the computer part was merged with the communication networks from ASEA. The combined TIDAS system was very carefully tested and personnel from the central control room as well as the regional control centers were thoroughly trained before Vattenfall dared make the decision to take it into operation. The TIDAS system went into service at 7 AM on 7 February 1977 and it worked [13].

The cost to develop and install the entire TIDAS system amounted to about a hundred million SEK. It was unique in several respects. In particular, the data transmission part was very advanced at the time. Data accumulated at 150 power plants and transformer stations and about a thousand measurements went to the national control center via sixteen nodes with eight-second intervals using packet switching technology. ASEA managed to develop a robust and stable routing mechanism with very high reliability. The data processing part was also advanced. It consisted of two identical Sigma 9 computers, one of which was in continual operation while the other was on stand-by and used for the training of personnel. The computer linked a number of workstations and key boards. The operators could look at no less than eight-hundred different graphs of the current situation in the power system. In addition, the computer automatically made statistical compilations of all incoming data to serve as a basis for planning the operations for the coming week [10].

TIDAS was not an automatic control system, but a monitoring system that assisted control room engineers. Through TIDAS, they had a much better overview of the entire power system and they did not have to rely on rule of thumb calculations any more. This led to a more efficient use of the generating (and storage) capacity in the power system. The estimated gain equaled a medium sized hydropower station. Moreover, the national power grid could operate with more precise safety margins than before. This meant that the system operated at a higher capacity, as the earlier rules of thumb had been more conservative in compensating for the insufficient overview. One could compare this with a driver in a new car with better breaks and controls who is tempted to drive faster than in his or her old car. We should note, however, that TIDAS did not prevent some major blackouts; for example, a major blackout occurred 27 December 1983 when all of southern Sweden lost power.

5 Conclusion

Let me finally briefly discuss the wider implications of computers for the development of the Swedish power system at large. This paper has described how computers from the 1950s and onwards became an important tool for designing and operating the Swedish power grid. It has outlined two phases of this development. In the 1950s and 1960s, computers were used for making complicated *calculations* for designing power grids in a robust and reliable way, and for optimizing the use of the different power plants. In a second phase starting in the late 1960s, computer systems were developed for *real time monitoring* supporting human control of the power grid. We should note that Vattenfall did not dare introduce the kind of automatic process control systems that for example IBM had developed for industrial purposes [14]. Instead, they developed a system "with a man in the loop"; that is, one in which a human operator made the crucial decisions but continuously received data about all components in the system. The responsibility for controlling electricity flows thus remained in human hands and minds.

The introduction of TIDAS meant rather big changes in the daily operation of the Swedish power grid, and this spurred certain resistance. One kind of resistance came from inside Vattenfall, because TIDAS altered the tasks and responsibilities for different divisions and groups as well as for individual people. Another resistance came from other power companies as TIDAS gave Vattenfall a much better overview of the entire Swedish power system than any other entity. However, the advocates of TIDAS overcame these different kinds of resistance.

TIDAS was only one part of the computerization of the Swedish power industry. In parallel, also other parts of the industry were computerized, including the local distribution and the billing of customers. This meant that the ability to monitor and control electricity flows from the power plants all the way to the final consumers increased rather dramatically, and this in turn was a technical prerequisite for the deregulation of the power industry that occurred in Sweden during the 1990s. This is arguably the most profound effect of TIDAS and other computer systems in the industry. However, no one anticipated this effect when computerization was initiated in the late 1960s.

Acknowledgments. I am grateful to Handelsbankens forskningsstiftelser for supporting the research for this paper. I am also grateful to my colleagues within the project, "Precursors of the IT Nation: Computer Use and Control in Swedish Society, 1955–1985" for comments on earlier versions of the paper.

References

1. Perrow, C.: Normal Accidents. Princeton University Press, Princeton (1984)
2. Herlitz, I.: The Dynamic Stability of Long Transmission Lines. Royal Institute of Technology, Stockholm (1928)
3. Fridlund, M.: Den gemensamma utvecklingen. Symposion, Eslöv (1999)
4. Mindell, D.: Between Human and Machine. Johns Hopkins University Press, Baltimore (2002)
5. Interview with Åke Ölwegård by the author
6. The Swedish State Power Board, The Swedish 380 kV System. Stockholm (1960)
7. Högselius, P., Kaijser, A.: När folkhemselen blev internationell: Avregleringen i historiskt perspektiv. SNS förlag, Stockholm (2007)
8. Larsson, Y.: Autobiography, http://www.tekniskamuseet.se/
9. Interview with Gunnar Ålfors by the author, who worked in the control room ca 1970–2000
10. The Vattenfall archive in Arninge has a special file on the TIDAS project
11. Fultz, G., Kleinrock, L.: Adaptive Routing Techniques for Store-and-Forward Computer-Communication Networks. In: Proceedings of the IEEE International Conference on Communications on Conference Record, Montreal, Canada, pp. 39-1–39-8 (June 1971)
12. Cegrell, T.: A Routing Procedure for the TIDAS Message-Switching Network. IEEE Transaction on Communications 23(6) (1975)
13. Vedin, B.-A.: Technology, Tumbling Walls of. Institute for Management of Innovation and Technology, Göteborg (1990)
14. Åström, K.J.: Oral history interview by Per Lundin October 3, 2007 National Museum of Science and Technology, Stockholm, Från matematikmaskin till IT, interview 3

Operations Analysis Computing at FFI, 1970–1995

Norodd Hagenson

Forsvarets forskningsinstitutt, P.O. Box 25, N-2027 Kjeller, Norway
norodd.hagenson@ffi.no

Abstract. By initially presenting FFI and its operations analysis (OA) activity, this paper illustrates the use of OA computing at FFI in three ways, in defense analysis, Simula, and various analyses of air defense. The paper focuses on methods, particularly the use of discrete event simulation. Most examples are from 1978–1995, and Simula's role is highlighted.

Keywords: Defense, ground-based air defense, history, long-term planning, operations analysis, Simula, simulation.

1 FFI and Operations Analysis

The Defense Research Institute (Forsvarets forskningsinstitutt, FFI) was established 1946 and is Norway's major defense research and development organization [1] with a staff of 716 and an annual turnover of 754 MNOK (2009) [2]. FFI not only provides scientific and technological advice to the Norwegian Ministry of Defense and the armed forces, but also carries out research, development, and analysis in support of the structures of the armed forces. In addition, it undertakes weapons and equipment development as a basis for a competitive national defense industry.

FFI established its Systems Analysis Group in 1959 [1]. The main idea was to use operations analysis (OA) for defense planning purposes, but a further notion was that emerging computer power could play a role in our OA activity. The group later became the Division for Systems Analysis and eventually the Analysis Division. It has focused on long-term defense planning, using operations analysis that includes simulation, which is used to experiment with new systems in a future environment.

Various kinds of computing power were employed for OA since the group was establishment in 1959. Analyses have ranged from weapons testing through weapon system evaluation and tactical employment to analyses of defense service structures and the full defense structure. Service and defense wide analyses were performed for the first time in the 1970s. Such high-level analyses have had a major impact on defense planning and defense structuring in Norway. Delivering relevant advice on time was of paramount importance; analyzing the wrong problem or providing a good answer too late was of little use. User involvement was another key to success.

J. Impagliazzo, P. Lundin, and B. Wangler (Eds.): HiNC3, IFIP AICT 350, pp. 35–42, 2011.
© IFIP International Federation for Information Processing 2011

2 Defense Analyses

Having successfully used OA for specific problems such as weapon system development in the 1960s, FFI's Systems Analysis Group saw an opportunity to influence major and important decisions. The Royal Norwegian Air Force was going to acquire new combat aircraft. FFI's first air force analysis was carried out 1970–1974 [1, 3, 4] and addressed not only the question of aircraft selection posed by the Air Force, but also important issues which the customer did not ask, for example, what support was needed in terms of airbases and aircraft service capacity. A discrete event Simula-model, the Base Model [5], was used in this analysis, simulating combat aircraft sortie production.

The navy and army were also analyzed, as were the entire Norwegian armed forces from 1974 onwards [1, 3]. System dynamics (SD), the main tool in the latter project, models dynamic effects in systems with feedback and is often applied to, but not restricted to economic and social systems. SD really describes a system by coupled linear differential equations. In the armed forces' study, SD modeled their flow and attrition, and was later used at FFI in other contexts. Our experience of SD has been good. High-level studies of defense structures were repeated in the 1980s and 1990s, and they are now a continuous activity.

The cost of defense structure is an important example of continuous computing activity. While the first version of the main model, BUDSJ [3, 6], was FORTRAN based, today's version, KOSTMOD [3, 7], is a database. Involving the customer is one of the first commandments in OA. A couple of attempts to transfer data collection and cost analysis to defense headquarters were made during the 1980s. However, the coming and going of officers in key positions made the task difficult and it was never completely successful. These attempts clearly demonstrated the necessity of dealing with a community that has sufficient continuity to maintain knowledge, methods, and data. Thus, the estimation and analysis of defense costs have become permanent activities at FFI.

3 The Use of Simula at FFI

Simula is considered to be the world's first object-oriented programming language. It was developed by Kristen Nygaard and Ole-Johan Dahl at the Norwegian Computing Center in the 1960s [8]. Both had recognized the need for more powerful programming languages when they worked at FFI in the 1950s. Simula, based on Algol, had added important concepts such as classes and objects, subclasses, inheritance, and virtual procedures. System classes are used to implement connected lists and events, enabling discrete event simulation by quasi-parallel processes. The clean concepts in Simula will easily leave a lasting impression on programmers' way of thinking.

Simula was an important programming language at FFI. RBK (Regneanlegget Blindern-Kjeller) was established and obtained its Cyber-74 computer in 1972 [9]. A Simula complier was included, but its quality was not satisfactory. FFI therefore developed a new Simula complier for Cyber-74, starting in 1973 [10]. This compiler was marketed and sold by CDC (Control Data Corporation, the maker of Cyber-74), but it was owned and maintained by FFI. The quality of this compiler was good and it was able to handle large programs, even featuring the separate compilation of program modules. The only major drawback was its inability to nest SIMSET- and SIMULATION-blocks while maintaining correct qualification for variables belonging to the outer SIMSET-block, when seen from the inner SIMULATION-block. However, this flaw was easy to circumvent with a few auxiliary functions. Nevertheless, the defect appeared to be common in other Simula implementations as well.

Simulation with Simula represented a radically new and different approach to computing. Formerly, a program was a sequence of statements often described by a flow chart, but by using Class Simulation, a program could now consist of several separate co-routines that would execute in some order that was not always directly predictable, allowing for complex interaction between processes.

During the 1980s, in-house minicomputers from Norsk Data, with Tandberg terminals, partially took over programming and computing. Simula became available on ND computers in the 1980s. Lund Simula was used on UNIX workstations at FFI until 2001.

The use of Simula at FFI gradually dwindled. In the 1980s and 1990s, other languages, such as Simscript and Modsim II, were also employed for simulation model development. Simula was still used for models that had initially been developed in Simula and were being reused and further developed. Simscript was employed for a US model. Modsim II replaced Simula for the new development of discrete event simulation models. Simula's role at FFI is further illustrated through the following examples.

4 Application of Simula for Analyses of Air Defense Systems

Several projects have analyzed ground-based air defense, of which some serve as examples here. A number of important studies using Simula were omitted, however, such as air defense of maritime patrol boats.

A model is a catalyst that stimulates thinking. Modeling problems usually provide better understanding than modeling systems. A model is an abstraction that should include the key factors, but not more details than necessary.

4.1 The Air Defense Model

The Air Defense Model (AD-model) [11], simulating ground-based air defense, was the longest-lasting Simula model at FFI; it was used between 1978 and 2001. During this period, it was reused, expanded, and adapted to new problems and new weapon systems several times. Initially, the model ran on Cyber-74 with the FFI Simula compiler, but the compiler needed an update as the AD-model grew in size.

The AD-model is a closed, discrete event Monte Carlo model that simulates several ground-based fire units engaging several airborne targets in a digital terrain. It would typically execute hundred replications in a run. The model simulates fire units sitting in fixed positions engaging targets moving in 3D over a digital terrain. The airborne targets fly along predetermined tracks, while the ground-based air defense is modeled with considerably more detail. Some important features are reaction times, weapon ranges, and velocities. Officers were involved in establishing scenarios and input.

The Air Defense Model utilized almost every feature in Simula. Cancelling processes was the only feature that was used for a short time and then abandoned. An experience with a bug that caused a process to cancel itself taught us a lesson. It led to a strange situation where processes were in disarray and difficult to debug with the available tools. When cancelling a process, it may be necessary to keep close track of each procedure, including its state. A more elegant and manageable approach to the programming of process interaction was to reactivate a process when there was an event which might influence it, let the process analyze the situation as it was being perceived, and then allow the process itself decide what to do. A useful way of thinking is to assume that it is not necessary to know very much about how a program reached a certain state, and to just handle the present state regardless of its history.

Simula facilitated a structure where new weapon systems could easily be added, using the powerful concept of virtual procedures to model weapon system specific features. From the start, it used digital terrain initially based on in-house manually digitized iso height curves. It was soon apparent that a grid-based terrain database was preferable, and the change was implemented, initially using terrain from the Defense Mapping Agency and later from Norges Geografiske Oppmåling, now the Norwegian Mapping Authority (Statens Kartverk).

Virtual procedures were particularly useful and included generic classes for a fire unit, a missile, and a gun. Every class related to weapons was derived from such generic classes and used virtual procedures for specific properties, for example, 3D weapon range or the random drawing of a reaction time. The concept was flexible enough to allow the easy addition of new weapon systems, once their properties were specified. Even new concepts could be accommodated. Without the adaptability and growth potential of virtual procedures, the AD-model might have been short-lived, perhaps only surviving through its first project.

To a computer, a program is blind calculation. A human must always interpret the results and the meaningfulness of results must be checked. On one occasion, the digital terrain played us a trick. Through an error, a flight track had the incorrect height and passed through a mountain. The AD-model did not check for terrain collision, but faithfully represented the aircraft as obscured by terrain where its flight track passed through the mountain. The mistake was easily spotted and corrected, and gave us a good laugh.

The AD-model was born when Hollerith cards were still being used. Despite the jokes and comments about old-fashioned technology, it was actually faster, easier and more practical to edit and arrange cards than it was to use the primitive line-oriented editors, which were available at the time. Cyber-74 had a very useful program called Update, which could delete and add lines of code in a file, thus, only incremental changes needed to be accumulated. When we acquired the first page-oriented editors from Norsk Data, conditions changed, and Hollerith cards soon disappeared.

An attempt was made to compile the AD-model on an ND machine using an early version of their Simula compiler. The attempt failed due to the program's size and complexity, but it was eventually possible to compile and run the AD-model on an ND-500 machine by splitting it into modules.

About 1990, the AD-model was transferred to a UNIX environment, initially to an Apollo workstation and later to an HP workstation. The compiler was the Lund Simula compiler, which was of good quality.

4.2 Command and Control of the Air Stations' Low-Level Ground-Based Air Defense

This project gave rise to the Air Defense Model (AD-model) [11]. At the time, Norway was planning to buy the Roland II. An important issue was how to coordinate several fire units with high firepower avoiding other fire units engaging the same target at the same time. The AD-model was used to simulate the effectiveness of various ground-based air defense systems in a given scenario, which contributed the principles of deployment. This project established a basic understanding of ground-based air defense and the effects involved [3].

Additionally, coordination between fire units was simulated by passing messages that might be delayed or backlogged. Thus, decisions were made based on a perceived situation rather than on absolutely correct information. This led to the concept of decentralized coordination, which was analyzed with the AD-model. Cost-effectiveness was also calculated, using the simple idea that the maximum value of coordination was confined to the cost of the missiles that could be saved. When this concept was presented to Hughes, they stated that this was the first time they had met a customer who knew what he wanted, why he wanted it, and how much he was willing to pay.

4.3 The Hawk Study

Roland II turned out to be expensive. Some people wanted Hawk instead. No analysis had compared the two. In late 1982, FFI was asked to provide a study in about three months [11], and something unique and drastic happened. Other tasks were put aside and most of the Systems Analysis Group worked on the study. Developing two new systems in the AD-model was considered to be too risky in such a short time. In addition, there was the terrain issue, since our in-house digitized terrain did not cover all the air stations in question. It was, therefore, initially decided to carry out hand simulations using maps, templates, and calculators. Tactical situations involving six airbases were to be analyzed. A program being developed to aid the construction of flight tracks got to a flying start, and was put to use before it was fully developed.

However, three of us were allowed to make an attempt to modify the AD-model, by introducing new weapons and changing the digital terrain interface to a grid-based one. The programming was completed two weeks ahead of schedule. In the meantime, the hand simulations had taken more time than anticipated and had only covered about one third of the planned work. In just one week, the AD-model completed the rest.

Based on FFI's analysis and the priorities made by the Chief of Defense, a modified Hawk system was chosen. Named NOAH, Norwegian Adapted Hawk, the system had new surveillance radar and, most significantly, a new fire control system from Kongsberg. This fire control system has subsequently been updated and adapted, becoming the backbone of Norway's ground-based air defense.

During the Hawk study, we obtained a small plotter that used colored pens on paper and plastic foils, for which a creative soul found a very good use. He visualized simulation outcomes such as bomb patterns, which aided our own understanding and analysis. The plots were also a useful means of communication. By the end of the study, the plotter had more or less been written-off, but remained usable, nevertheless, for several more years. It was a very useful investment.

4.4   Triangulation of Jamming Strobes

In the Hawk study, it was noted that jamming could degrade the ground-based air defense radars. The jamming signal (noise) from a jamming pod would show up as a strobe on the radarscope, denying range information, but still providing some directional information. By combining information from two or more radars, it seemed possible to locate the jammers by triangulation [11], which a new project examined. The main problem was the large number of ghosts, which occur when strobes cross in positions with no jammers. A few simple tests could eliminate some of the ghosts, but most of the eliminations came by tracking the PJLs (Probable Jammer Location), using advanced statistical methods. By observing each PJL over a period, some PJLs would increase their likelihood of being a target, while others would decrease and be eliminated. A dedicated FORTRAN model was used for the triangulation study. The developed triangulation method was implemented in NOAH's fire control system. Norway was actually first to automatically triangulate jamming strobes.

4.5   NASAMS

Leasing the Hawk missiles was expensive and the Nike system needed replacement. An idea surfaced at the Air Materiel Command in the mid-1980s: Could they use an air-to-air missile like AMRAAM placed in a simple container on a truck? After FFI analyzed some critical issues, employing a specially modified AD-model [11], NASAMS (Norwegian Advanced Surface to Air Missile System) was born. NOAH had been transformed into a very different air defense system while retaining Kongsberg's fire control system as its backbone.

A few years later, there was a question about a more thorough evaluation of NASAMS' effectiveness. Thus, in 1993 and 1994, the AD-model was modified and put to use again.

5   Vulnerability of Air Stations

After the 1967 war between Israel, Egypt, Jordan, and Syria, the low-level threat to air stations remained in focus for twenty years. Ground-based air defense was only one element; the runway was vulnerable and hard to protect. This project focused on runway bombing and repair in an operational context [11], using a couple of dedicated simulation models, of which one was RunBom (for Runway Bombing), a Pascal model. Its main purpose was to find the optimal MOS (Minimum Operating Strip – a sufficiently large stretch of runway on which a combat aircraft could operate), by calculating the least possible number of craters that need to be repaired after a bomb attack on a runway. This problem had been addressed in a model (BABO) from STC (SHAPE Technical Centre), but the model was quite slow. RunBom utilized the fact that fighter-bombers could cut across the runway with series of bombs instead of the heavy bomber method of carpet bombing. It was thus sufficient to place a MOS through one of the cuts, a calculation that RunBom could do quite fast. Therefore, it was expanded to include runway repair as well, simulating repeated attacks in order to study the operational effect of runway bombing and repair over time, deriving requirements for runway repair capacity.

6   A Computer with Personality

Some computers behave in such ways that make one feel they have personalities of their own. A ND500 machine from Norsk Data was our strangest computer. We named it Sisyfos (Norwegian spelling), for the Greek King Sisyphus who was condemned for eternity to roll a rock up a mountain, lose his grip almost at the top, watch the rock roll back down the mountain, then have to start all over again. This computer, Sisyfos, would sometimes unexpectedly stop executing a program at some random point. When we tried the program again, it would often run flawlessly, but we never knew for sure whether it would execute completely. Later I learnt that the ND 500 was supposed to have hardware faults that could, on occasion, be encountered during heavy computing, and thus could cause non-repeatable execution errors.

7   Final Discussion

Simula pioneered powerful qualities and has had a major impact on all other object-oriented languages that followed. However, Simula lacked graphics, and it had no modern debugging tools. Simula's initial high price was undoubtedly a major obstacle for the distribution of the language at the beginning. The subsequent lack of development and support resulted in an unavoidable slow death.

Simulation combines a number of effects in such a way as to reveal complex interactions and relationships that would not be readily derived with less powerful tools. When starting an analysis, one often has some expectations about what the results will be. A model helps to quantify effects and adds them in a way that is hard for a human to keep track of simultaneously and completely. A model often demonstrates its power by showing some results that initially seem strange and unexpected, but are logical on closer examination. At the end of an analysis, the results often seem obvious. The model may no longer be needed, but without its quality of being a catalyst that stimulates thinking, those obvious results would not have become apparent. A good model may thus render itself superfluous.

A key success factor for operations analysis is to maintain a community of skilled experts where knowledge is maintained and further developed. An organization's collective memory is very important and people are often more important than tools. Regarding both simulation and cost estimation, the tools and individuals involved may have changed, but the community lives on. Another key factor is to analyze the right problems; analyzing the wrong ones leads to irrelevance, no matter how good the tools are.

The use of hardware and associated software tools at FFI has been both strategic and pragmatic. Strategic choices, such as a shared mainframe and FFIs own Simula compiler, were particularly important in the early years. In addition, although FFI's own version of digital terrain from the late 1970s was short lived, it provided a needed tool at an initial stage. As more IT products appeared, market forces have played an increasingly important role in product survivability and the kinds of tools that users are steered towards.

Many studies and computing tools have not been mentioned in this paper, which can only provide some examples and a sense of the computing history of operations analysis at FFI.

References

1. Njølstad, O., Wicken, O.: Kunnskap som våpen, Forsvarets forskningsinstitutt 1946–1975. Tano Aschehoug, Oslo (1997)
2. FFI Årsrapport 2009, Forsvarets forskningsinstitutt, Kjeller (2010)
3. Solstrand, R.H.: Langsiktig planlegging i Forsvaret – vitenskap i skjæringspunktet mellom politikk, byråkrati og kommandostyring, FFI-Rapport 2010/01924, Forsvarets forskningsinstitutt, Kjeller (2010)
4. Sandnes, H.O.: The 1970–1974 Combat Aircraft Analysis: Priority to Defensive Counter Air and Anti-Shipping Operations: How Optimizing Defense Resources Altered the Use of RNoAF Fighters. Tapir Academic Press, Trondheim (2010)
5. Vebjør, K.T.: Basemodellen – en modell av sortieproduksjon fra et basesystem under en begrenset konflikt. FFI Notat 74/TN-S-362, Forsvarets forskningsinstitutt, Kjeller (1974)
6. Nielsen, S.A., Magnus, E.: Kortfattet beskrivelse av budsjettmodellen "BUDSJ", FFI Notat 77/TN-S-477, Forsvarets forskningsinstitutt, Kjeller (1977)
7. Gullichsen, S.: Long term cost analysis and KOSTMOD 4.0, FFI Notat 2007/01169, Forsvarets forskningsinstitutt, Kjeller (2007)
8. Nygaard, K., Dahl, O.J.: The development of the Simula languages. In: Wexelblat, R.L. (ed.) History of Programming Languages, pp. 439–493. Academic Press, New York (1981)
9. IT-historien @ UiO,
   http://www.usit.uio.no/om/it-historien/ forskning/rbk.html
10. Heistad, E.: Telephone interview by Norodd Hagenson (June 1, 2010)
11. Hagenson, N.: Luftvern og sårbarhet av egne flystasjoner. In: Skogen, E. (ed.) Fra Forsvarets Forskningsinstitutts Historie, vol. 8, pp. 4–12. Forsvarets forskningsinstitutt, Kjeller (2004)

Re-engineering Norwegian Research Libraries, 1970–1980

Ingeborg Torvik Sølvberg

Department of Computer and Information Science,
Norwegian University of Science and Technology,
7491 Trondheim, Norway
ingeborg.solvberg@idi.ntnu.no

Abstract. The Norwegian shared library system BIBSYS is in 2010 used by more than hundred university-, college-, and research libraries, including the Norwegian National Library. The BIBSYS project was initiated in 1970 and it led to a complete re-engineering of the Norwegian research libraries. The paper describes the project, how the system was initiated and discusses important decisions made during project development. The two most important factors for the success of BIBSYS are discussed. One is that the project started with a detailed information analysis prior to coding and data base design, using a good software tool. The other factor is that the potential users of the system, the librarians, were included in the project loop from the beginning.

Keywords: BIBSYS, information systems, library automation, re-engineering, systems design.

1 Introduction

In 1970, a process started that resulted in a reorganization of the Norwegian research libraries. The advances in computer technology drove the change process. It was decided to start a "library automation" project at the Norwegian Institute of Technology, NTH, Norges Tekniske Høgskole. The project very quickly was expanded to the two other research libraries in Trondheim, and gradually to other research libraries to become a nationwide project.

The first operational data processing system, for acquisition of library documents, was operational from 1976. Other systems to cover all library work processes followed over the next few years. The system was called BIBSYS, and its successor is still operational in 2010, forty years after its conception [1]. The original information system design of BIBSYS has survived thirty-five years of computer technology development. The design process was based on the information systems development approach, which was pioneered by Langefors in the late 1960s [2]. Key elements were

- o participatory design
- o separating information aspects (infology) and data aspects (datalogy)
- o developing detailed requirements prior to coding and data base design

J. Impagliazzo, P. Lundin, and B. Wangler (Eds.): HiNC3, IFIP AICT 350, pp. 43–55, 2011.
© IFIP International Federation for Information Processing 2011

BIBSYS embarked on a "business process re-engineering" project many years before the phrase was coined and became fashionable. After the initial design and implementation phases, the system became the basis for a nationwide re-organization of the Norwegian research libraries. BIBSYS took over the operational responsibilities for the computerized parts of the libraries' operations as well as the responsibility for keeping up with advances in information technology.

The following paper gives an account of the first years of the BIBSYS project, as well as a short analysis of its impact.

1.1   The BIBSYS Project – Initiated in 1970

Today's libraries use information technology for their internal routines as well as in order to give the public access to their collections. The Norwegian shared library system BIBSYS is used by all Norwegian university libraries, the National Library, a number of college libraries, and other research libraries, altogether more than hundred libraries. Currently the shared bibliographic database contains information about more than 5,000,000 unique titles and more than 15,000,000 physical objects, when copies are included. In 2009, the bibliographic search system handled 20,700,000 searches from all over the world [1].

It all started in 1970. The Director of SINTEF, Karl Stenstadvold, took an initiative to investigate how computers could be used in the daily routines of the Library at the Norwegian Institute of Technology (NTH). He was willing to use Sintef resources to get a project off the ground.

I was a young researcher at Regnesenteret NTH (later called RUNIT) interested in exploring how we could use computers in new and exciting applications. The Head of the NTH Library, Knut Thalberg, was interested in such a project; the same was my superior, Director Karl G. Schjetne. This was a good match!

The first question that surfaced was: What is the status world wide of how libraries use computers? The next question was: What should and could we do at our university?

2   The Traditional Library in 1970s

The information objects in the traditional library were the physical objects such as books, journals, reports, maps, patent-descriptions and others. The library objects were mainly paper based, even if in the 1970s many libraries included music recordings and movies on physical media in their collections. The objects were catalogued and the catalogue records were printed, mainly on small catalogue cards, which were filed in catalogue card cabinets according to specific rules. Hence, information about objects could be found in many card catalogues serving different purposes, and they were geographically distributed. Only one catalogue at the NTH Library contained information about *all* the objects owned by the library; this was the Main Catalogue located in the reading room of the Main Library. The Main Catalogue was used by the library staff as well as by the public. The NTH library had several branches on campus; each branch maintained a card catalogue of their own holdings.

The NTH Library, like most other large university libraries, used international cataloguing standards, with local adjustments. Cataloguing and classification were costly processes. A rule of thumb was that it was just as expensive to catalogue an object as to purchase the object. All libraries catalogued all the objects in their own collections.

During the late 1960s and early 1970s, a few projects involving computers were initiated in Europe and USA. Many of the first library automation projects produced local catalogues in the form of sorted lists or in book-form. The lists could easily be produced in many copies and they were distributed throughout the library and could even be sent to cooperating libraries. A drawback with the lists and books was that they were produced periodically, such as monthly or even annually, with smaller weekly or monthly additions for the new acquisitions. Hence, there were many lists to look through in order to find a specific object. In Europe, the university libraries in Bochum and in Bielefeld were well known for their computerized book catalogues. They were the European leaders in the emerging field of library automation. Soon microfilm was used instead of paper when distributing the catalogues. The microfilms were used by other libraries as a support to cataloguing and for locating specific documents. Other universities as the University of Southampton, UK, developed circulation systems based on punched cards. In the late 1960s and early 1970s, the Library of Congress (LC) developed the MARC standard (MARC: Machine Readable Cataloguing). The MARC format contains information describing the intellectual content of an object as well as administrative data. The MARC standards have been of great importance to the library community worldwide [3, 4]. The MARC format is described later in the paper.

3   The Library Automation Project

At NTH we agreed that the library could benefit by using computers, but there were no clear ideas of where to start. In 1970, I did some minor projects; I learned about the different library departments and their working routines, I produced various types of sorted lists, I looked into the possibility to reuse cataloguing records coming from MARC magnetic tapes from Library of Congress, USA (LC). In a report of November 1970, I gave a brief description of the workings of the library and presented some project ideas [5]. The number one recommendation was to conduct a user study in order to clarify the requirements of the library users: NTH's scientific personnel and students. If the project mainly should be aimed to have the librarians work more efficient there were interesting starting points in all of the library departments. I also proposed that the Library of Congress' MARC format should be used for the cataloguing work. It could be beneficial for the NTH Library to use MARC magnetic tapes from Library of Congress. Initially this proposal was deemed silly. However, not too long time afterwards did the library subscribe to MARC tapes.

RUNIT's library volunteered to be a pilot, if the NTH Library found a project to be too risky to self- serve as a pilot. At that point, the Library was not interested in a user study; they wanted to aim the project at supporting the internal processes in the library.

The organization of the university sector in Trondheim was restructured at this time. NTH was loosely coupled with two other scientific organizations in Trondheim under the UNIT "umbrella" (UNIT: Universitetet i Trondheim). UNIT had two university libraries, in addition to NTH Library there was the DKNVS Library (DKNVSB: Det Kongelige Norske Videnskabers Selskabs Bibliotek) which just had merged with the library at the other university college in Trondheim, the College of Arts and Letters (AVH). Early in 1971 DKNVSB's Head librarian, Sten Vedi, made contact and wanted his library to join the library automation project together with the NTH Library and RUNIT. This speeded up the process; the NTH Library suddenly had a competitor!

RUNIT was asked, "Is it possible to support the work processes in the two libraries with the same IT-system?" This was an interesting challenge. The NTH Head Librarian Knut Thalberg proposed the starting point for such a project to be the work process where information about the documents was registered in the library for the first time: the ordering department.

I made a proposal for a common project for the two university libraries: "A proposal for mechanization of the accession processes in two scientific libraries" [6]. In February 1972, the proposal was presented for the leaders of the two university libraries, Runit's director and a few other key persons, and it was decided to initiate a common project with an ambitious goal:

> The project's goal is to develop a system to automate ALL of the
> internal routines in the libraries; acquisition, cataloguing, circulation,
> search and serials control. The first departments to be automated are
> the two Acquisition departments.

BIBSYS was born, both as a project and an organization, even if the name BIBSYS was not invented at this point; this was still the "Library Automation Project."

The project needed persons with a variety of competences, in librarianship as well as information technology, in order to embark on a participative development where IT persons and Domain experts could work together following the so-called "Scandinavian approach" to Information System development.

The libraries approached the project with the opinion that the work could be done by data experts alone with minimal involvement from the libraries. RUNIT had to insist that librarians should be included in the project team; "no librarians – no project." Eventually we got a great team together with me as Project Leader and the main IT-person together with two part time librarians from each of the two libraries. They learned how to program and they got insight in what computers could do and not do. They participated in the development of the systems- and user requirements and were important intermediaries between the IT department and the libraries. After a while, RUNIT allocated one more IT person to the project.

Shortly after, in 1974, a formal Steering Committee was established, The University of Trondheim (UNIT) appointed Associate Professor Jørgen Løvset from the Physics department as the Steering Committee Leader. Jørgen Løvset did a great job. He realized the complexity of the project as well as the shortcoming of the available technology. From time to time, he had to stand up and defend the technical proposals from the project team. The user community did not always understand that there was not a straight way forward to develop such a complex system and that we were breaking new ground. Jørgen Løvset was of crucially importance for making the library automation project a success.

3.1 A Master Plan

It soon became obvious that all departments of the libraries would be influenced by the library automation project. We needed a Master Plan for establishing the information system for the whole library, which could also serve several autonomous libraries.

We defined the Universe of Discourse to have three main components; the Library, the Vendors, and the Users. The Library had three subsystems: Acquisition, Circulation, and Administration.

The central questions were: Which kinds of data are produced, used, changed, deleted – where and by whom? Who makes the decisions, e.g., about new acquisitions? What kind of information and messages are exchanged inside a library department, between the departments, and communicated with the outside world? These questions and many more needed to be answered.

In the Information Systems Group at RUNIT, the CASCADE research project was based on Börje Langefors' theories of Information Systems development. CASCADE offered computer-assistance for information analysis and information systems design. The tool produced graphical presentations of the information flow on all levels of the system description, systematic storage and presentation of information objects and information processing tasks, automatic testing of the system descriptions, and gave warnings about inconsistencies and broken links [7–9]. This was deemed an excellent tool for the analysis phase.

In 1972, we made a detailed system analysis of the Acquisition department and in 1973 of the Circulation department using CASCADE.

3.2 An Example from the Acquisition Subsystem

The Acquisition subsystem had two component systems: the Ordering Department and the Cataloguing Department [10]. Fig. 1 shows an original CASCADE diagram of the Ordering Department process. Because of low print quality, we have added additional identifiers to the original in order to make the figure readable.

In 1972, the Ordering department was responsible for the production and maintenance of three bibliographic card catalogues:

- o The Ordering Catalogue contained everything that was ordered but not received, and in addition, claims and other information regarded to be of importance. ("Bestillings katalog")
- o One catalogue contained information about the objects that had been received in the library and had been forwarded to the cataloguing department in order to be catalogued ("Akse Katalog")
- o The library did often consult professors and university departments before buying an object. This information was kept in a special catalogue, "Gjennomsynskatalog"

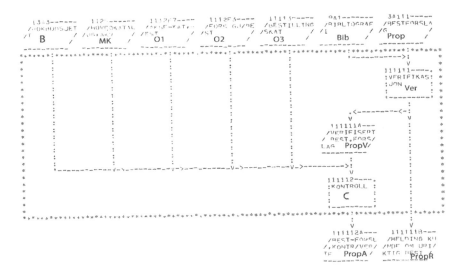

Fig. 1. The Ordering department, *Receiving a Proposal for buying an object*

Legend:
Ver: Verification process; **C:** Control process , **Prop**: Proposal;
PropA: Accepted Proposal, **PropR**: Rejected proposal

Bibliographic Catalogues: **MK**: Main Catalogue; **O1**: AkseCat;
O2: GjennomsysnKat; **O3**: OrderingCat; **Bib**: bibliographies **B**: Budgets

The Ordering subsystem had two processes: Verification and Control. A process in the Ordering department was initiated when the department received a proposal for acquiring an object. The proposal came either from someone inside the library world, e.g., a professor, a student, a librarian, or it came from the outside, e.g., a publisher.

Fig. 1 shows what happened when the library received a proposal for buying an object. The incoming Proposal triggered the Verification process. The librarian consulted external bibliographic sources, bibliographies, to verify whether the proposed object existed, e.g. whether the proposed book was published or not. If 'yes' the verified proposal was sent to the Control Subsystem. The Main Card catalogue was accessed in order to check if the object already was in the library's collection. If it was not, the three bibliographic card catalogues in the Ordering Department were searched. Finally, the budget files in the Administration Department had to be consulted in order to check whether there was money available for the scientific area of the proposed object.

When an ordered object arrived in the library, this is not shown in the figure, the order record (of the library of 1972) was physically transferred from the Ordering Catalogue ("Bestillings katalog") to the "Akse Katalog" and new relevant information was added to the card. The order form resided in "Akse Katalog" in the Ordering

Department until the Cataloguing Department sent a message, on paper, that the object has been catalogued and classified. Information about the object could now be found on catalogue cards in the Main Catalogue in the Main Reading Room.

In the analysis of the Ordering department, we described around three hundred objects. This description was used in the design phase when proposing processes, forms, and for describing the proposals for data and file structures.

4 Systems Design and Development

4.1 Systems Design

The information analysis described in detail the relations between work processes and the logical files (catalogues) and whether a process reads, modifies, generates or deletes a record or another data item. Based upon the analysis results we defined the logical file structure. Many of the existing catalogues were merged. The information analysis gave guidance when defining the search terms for the index files: author, title, ISBN, DOKID, vendor-identifier, vendor-name, a.o.

The systems analysis described processes in the information system. Some of these processes could be automated immediately, and we could develop computer programs right away, while other processes might be automated later when more mature technology would become available (such as decision support systems), some processes were completely dependent on human decision-making and could never be automated [11–14].

In designing the new system, much emphasis was put on that there should not be introduced limitations through unnecessary borders between the different processes. In the design of the computerized system, the border between ordering and cataloguing of an object became blurred. An object is pre-catalogued when the order is registered; the cataloguing process is a continuation of the ordering process using the already recorded order information. In the manual system, bibliographic information was distributed over many bibliographic card catalogues. We proposed these catalogues to be merged so all descriptions about bibliographic objects should be stored in one catalogue/file only. A Status variable was added to the bibliographic record, the value of the Status could be *ordered, received, on the shelf, cataloguing-in-process, in circulation,* et cetera.

The bibliographic record should be updated when new information became available. Pre-cataloguing gave new responsibility to the persons in the Ordering Departments, as they had to register bibliographic data as correctly as possible. At this processing stage, however, only limited bibliographic data were usually available. A quality test was conducted to find if the proposed solution was viable. The bibliographic entries of approximately two hundred orders were compared to the final catalogue records of the same documents. Only 5 percent of the order records had needed to be modified. It was subsequently decided to merge the bibliographic catalogues in the Ordering Department with the Main Catalogue.

The Project team had been instructed by the libraries not to look into organizational or administrative matters. In spite of this, the libraries were restructured when the consequences of the computerization became apparent. The decision to pre-catalogue a document in the Ordering Department is just one example on how the automated system influenced the internal library organization.

A summary of the overall design objectives include the following.

- To create an online system with shared catalogues, for participating libraries; vertical integration within a library; horizontal integration between libraries. This required that routines and standards needed to be harmonized.
- The system must be accessible online and searchable for anyone; public as well as library personnel.
- Bibliographic data shall be written once; starting in the ordering department(s). The record shall be updated in later processes; verified, changed, expanded, or deleted.
- When there are more than one copy of a document, local information shall be added for each specific copy (e.g. physical location, classification)
- Each physical object shall have a unique identifier, a DOKID, to be used also in the circulation sub-system.

4.2 Representation and Communication of Bibliographic and Related Information

The central part of the system is the database containing the bibliographical records; the digital descriptions about the documents related to the libraries.

In the late 1960s and early 1970s, the Library of Congress (LC) developed the MARC standard (MARC: Machine Readable Cataloging). *"The MARC standards consist of the MARC formats which are standards for the representation and communication of bibliographic and related information in machine-readable form, and related documentation. It defines a bibliographic data format … It provides the protocol by which computers exchange, use, and interprets bibliographic information"* [3].

The MARC standard was originally developed as a format for interchange of Library of Congress cataloguing information using magnetic tapes – MARC-tapes. The tapes were originally intended to produce catalogue cards, but they were soon used for book catalogue production and a variety of listings, such as acquisitions lists. In April 1969, the Library of Congress began to distribute to other libraries its cataloging services on machine-readable magnetic tape [4].

Most MARC fields contain several related pieces of data. Each type of data within the field is called a subfield, and each subfield is preceded by a subfield code. The field, or tag, "100" is used for a person as author, subfield "$a" is used for the author's name, "$d" is used for the author's birth and death year. The field (or tag) "245" title statement, for example, contains the title and the statement of responsibility area of a bibliographic record, where "$a" denotes the title proper, "$b" the reminder of the title ("sub-title"), and "$c" other title information such as statement(s) of responsibility. Tag "240" is used for the document's original title.

The libraries have different kinds of materials in their collections: monographs, serials, maps, movies, photos, and others. Already from the beginning did the MARC format identify data common to different types of material with the same content designators (fields or tag), while unique fields (tags) are assigned for data elements peculiar to any one format of material. As an example, the four kinds of information objects Monographs, Serials, Maps, and Movies all use tag "245" for title statement while tag "255" is used only when describing Maps such as "255 $a Scale 1:12.500".

BIBSYS developed its own variant of the MARC format, there taking into account the Norwegian cataloguing rules and local practice. From the basic MARC format, different presentation formats can be generated.

As an example a search for "A doll's house" and author "Henrik Ibsen" in BIBSYS of 2010 gives seventy-four matches, one of them is:

```
Title:    A doll's house / by Henrik Ibsen; translated by
          William Archer; with an introduction by M.Yassin
          El-Ayouty
Author:   Ibsen, Henrik 1828-1906
Year:     [1957]
Printed:  Cairo: Anglo-Egyptian Bookshop
Pages:    122 s.
```

This is generated from a record in the BIBSYS MARC-format:

```
100 $a Ibsen, Henrik $d 1828-1906
240 $a Et dukkehjem
245 $a A doll's house $c by Henrik Ibsen ; translated by
        William Archer ; with an introduction by M. Yassin
        El-Ayouty
260 $a Cairo $b Anglo-Egyptian Bookshop $c [1957]
300 $a 122 s.
```

The University Library at Oslo University started around 1971 to develop a Norwegian version of the MARC format, NORMARC, and the BIBSYS Cataloguing User Group defined UNITMARC (later called BIBSYS-MARC), taking into account the need for future cooperation [15]. The University Library at Oslo University did not originally participate in the BIBSYS project. A special branch of the University of Oslo's Library acted as National Library until 1989, when the National Library of Norway was established.

4.3 Database Structure

It was decided to use the MARC format in the bibliographic descriptions. This MARC structure was a perfect match for a database system, which was under development at RUNIT: the randomized file system RA1. This was a win-win situation both for the library automation project and for the Database group. We were able to use RA1 and gave feedback and new requirement for the Database group's next database system, RA2, which the BIBSYS project also used for some years [16].

4.4 Expert User Groups

The participative development approach included the users of the system, the librarians. Several Expert User Groups were established as early as possible, starting with the Expert User Group on Cataloguing and the Expert User Group on Acquisition. The participants in the Groups were experts in their fields and represented their libraries.

The groups' main objectives were to develop the user requirements for the subsystems, harmonizing rules and work procedures inside as well as between the libraries, and later in the process, to test the system prototypes and prepare instructions for their use within the libraries.

In the early years, 1970–75, when talking with representatives from the libraries we were met with phrases like "of course we want to cooperate with other departments and libraries, but *my* department is very special." However, when the representatives from the different libraries had met a few times they realized that they had similar problems and challenges and that working with colleagues from other organizations was fun!

The sizes of the user groups increased as the number of participating libraries increased, because all participating libraries should be represented in every group. The User Groups' influence on the planning, development, testing, operation, and, not least, the acceptance – of BIBSYS cannot be over-estimated.

Including the librarians in the project team and in the User Groups eased the introduction of computers in the libraries. There were many small as well as a number of large problems when introducing such dramatic changes in the working environments. The librarians had ownership to the system and they were eager to find solutions.

As more and more libraries became users of BIBSYS, User Groups developed de-facto standards for the Norwegian university- and research libraries. They became major actors in the reorganization of the Norwegian library community.

4.5   Immature Technology, Possible Stumbling Blocks

During the system design phase we made some bold, someone would say naïve, decisions on proposing solutions that were ahead of the technological state-of-the-art:

- Only upper case letters were available in the 1970s on our equipment, e.g. on the printers and the input terminals. This was insufficient for our libraries, and we developed an interim solution for upper- and lowercase letters. Multikey strokes had to be widely used.
- In the very early days, BIBSYS was a one-user system. The operating systems were not designed for multi-using. An ad-hoc solution was developed and used until multiuser facilities were included in the standard software of time-shared computers. The ad-hoc solution permitted five to ten simultaneous users.
- Due to limitations of the data nets, only one library at a time could use the system during the first year (1976). The two participating libraries in Trondheim each used the system two days a week, and half day Friday! The multiuser solution permitted the librarians to use the system in parallel.
- We wanted full screen terminals to be used when ordering and cataloguing objects. Only tele-type terminals were available the first years. We bought a few screen terminals, UNISCOPE-100, in 1974. According to the vendor, they were the first of their kind in Norway. UNISCOPE-100 was expensive, NOK 50,000 apiece, comparable to an average annual wage.

4.6 Operational System Modules

As the first acquisition and search modules became operational, the NTH Library registered the first real document using the acquisition module in March of 1976. More modules were added to the system; cataloguing pre-testing began in 1978 and became operational in 1980 with circulation control and Online Public Access (OPAC) in 1983. The last module was serials control, which was added in 1994.

During the first years, we used RUNIT's main computer, UNIVAC 1108, the programming language FORTRAN and tele-type terminals. Today BIBSYS has its own IBM computer.

5 Discussion

5.1 Going from a Dynamic Developing Environment to an Operational and Service Environment

The project became well known in the Norwegian library community and abroad. The number of research libraries participating in the project increased quickly and the size of the project team and the expert user groups became larger. So did the steering committee and the project budget.

When the steering committee obtained new members, the first question usually was, "Why don't we just buy a library automation system? There must be hundreds of suitable systems on the market." Several surveys, investigations, and visits were made, but the result was always negative; commercial systems that covered certain functions like circulation or catalogue productions existed, but no system was found that could give all the functionality and flexibility that our libraries demanded.

Large resources are required for developing and operating a system of BIBSYS kind so there is a substantial shift in the use and distribution of the organizations' budgets. During the first ten years, the BIBSYS staff grew from a handful to twenty persons.

It can be hard to accept that new technology requires continuously technological development – which consequently results in continuous change and budget redistribution. The administrative leadership of the participating organizations wanted of course to increase their influence on the further development of BIBSYS. Administrative leaders became members of the steering committees. In many ways, this was beneficial to the project, but it did also hamper development both because "change" can be scary, but also because change initially costs money.

The resistance to change was always felt and had to be continuously combated. There were some tense situations over the years. My first report [5] became so controversial and radical that key persons in the library declared that this report had better disappear from the surface of the earth. This may be due to "cultural" differences. I am educated as a physicist and may have used a different vocabulary and described procedures in the library differently than the librarians were used to. Another example: In the very early years there was a formal meeting at the university where we discussed some proposals I had made without having received any feedback. A leading person in the university administration mentioned these proposals and said that more time was needed before a conclusion could be made. I was enthusiastic and proud because I could tell *the good news*: "We have already completed that part!" The administrative leader became furious and shouted back: "You are a galloping elephant!" For me, this comment was a compliment I appreciated – and I do so more and more. Over the years, I have stumbled into bureaucracy several times; in a bureaucratic world, maybe more "galloping elephants" are needed?

BIBSYS was in a good shape in the early 1980s. The computerized system was in front worldwide. We had a great project team with competent, enthusiastic and dedicated persons. We were part of an excellent IT community at RUNIT and the university. The necessary developments for the nearest years were planned.

The steering committee focused increasingly on minor additions required by the users, and day-to-day operation filled the days. I proposed a couple of times that we should look into new challenges and technological opportunities for the library community, for example, to use some resources for including full-text documents in the library information system, or to make it possible to have information exchange with other online information systems. Some of the prominent leaders of the organizations said that they did not want to be in front of the technological development and use; "let the others do research, develop, use, and think, and we may follow later" was one phrase. The libraries were pleased with the situation and wanted to consolidate.

In many ways, this is easy to understand. The libraries had been through dramatic re-engineering over a relatively short time. They had been very courageous during the changing times, they had been eager to change, learn and to include new technology into their daily work. Now they had an operational system: No more changes for a while! Further change would cost more money. To propose inclusion of full text electronic documents was perhaps overdoing the level of ambition when remembering that a few years before we could only handle capital letters!

5.2   What Did We Learn?

BIBSYS has been in operation for many decades. The design principles from the 1970s are still valid. The computer programs have been re-written, adjusted and expanded several times over the years to fit with the continuously changing technology.

Looking back I find that one important factor to the success is that we started with a pioneer approach. We were able to work without a large bureaucracy during the first years. We were not bothered with people who wanted to lead without understanding what they were leading. This gave us flexibility, and flexibility is important for a pioneer project.

In addition, there were two other crucial success factors:

1. The project started with a detailed information analysis, analyzing the whole library information structure, developing detailed requirements prior to coding and data base design. The master plan and detailed systems analysis occurred before programming (the "think first – program later" approach). We had a good tool at hand assisting in the information analysis and design

2. Participatory design people, potential users of the system, and librarians were included in the project loop from the beginning, in the project group and in the expert

user groups. However, we must realize that the participants come from different "cultures." The terminology is different, so is the problem solving approach, sometimes even the human values. The different cultures must respect the differences and trust each other if the project shall succeed. In the BIBSYS project, we were lucky enough to have this mutual respect for each other.

References

1. BIBSYS, http://www.bibsys.no/english/pages/index.php
2. Langefors, B.: Theoretical Analysis of Information Systems. Studentlitteratur, Lund (1966)
3. MARC Standards, http://en.wikipedia.org/wiki/MARC_standards
4. Kilgour, F.: OCLC. Summary of Marc. (1970), http://www.ideals.illinois.edu/bitstream/handle/2142/858/Kilgour.pdf?sequence=2
5. Sølvberg, I.: En grov beskrivelse av Hovedbiblioteket NTNU. Biblioteksautomatisering. Arbeidsnotat 1. SINTEF, Trondheim (1970)
6. Sølvberg, I.: Forslag til mekanisering av aksesjon ved to vitenskapelige bibliotek. Biblioteksautomatisering, Arbeidsnotat 2. SINTEF, Trondheim (1972)
7. Sølvberg, A.: Experimenter med Nyere Metoder i Systemarbeidet. In: Bubenko Jr., J.A., Källhammar, O., Langefors, B., Lundeberg, M., Sølvberg, A. (eds.) Systemering 70, Studentlitteratur, Lund (1970)
8. Aanstad, P., Skylstad, G., Solvberg, A.: CASCADE – A Computer-based Documentation System. In: Bubenko Jr., J.A., Langefors, B., Sølvberg, A. (eds.) Computer-aided Information Analysis and Design, pp. 93–118. Studentlitteratur, Lund (1971)
9. CASCADE: SINTEF Årsmelding (1972), http://www.idi.ntnu.no/datamuseum/dokumentasjonssenter/aarsmeldinger/sintef-aarsmelding-1972.pdf
10. Sølvberg, I.: Informasjonsanalyse av tilvekstsystemet. Biblioteksautomatisering. Arbeidsnotat 3. SINTEF, Trondheim (1972)
11. Sølvberg, I.: Systemforslag for tilveksten ved bibliotekene tilknyttet Universitetet i Trondheim. Biblioteksautomatisering. Arbeidsnotat 4. Trondheim, Sintef (1972)
12. Sølvberg, I.: Oversiktsrapport om biblioteksautomatisering ved UNIT. Biblioteksautomatisering, Arbeidsnotat 7. RUNIT, Trondheim (1973)
13. Bibliotekautomatisering (BIBSYS): RUNIT Årsmelding, p. 14 (1974), http://www.idi.ntnu.no/datamuseum/dokumentasjonssenter/aarsmeldinger/runit-aarsberetning-1974.pdf
14. Bibliotekautomatisering (BIBSYS): RUNIT Årsmelding, pp. 23–24 (1978), http://www.idi.ntnu.no/datamuseum/dokumentasjonssenter/aarsmeldinger/runit-aarsberetning-1978.pdf
15. Sølvberg, I., Aas, G., Vikan, M.: Katalogavdelingene ved bibliotekene tilknyttet Universitetet i Trondheim, Bibliotekautomatisering, Arbeidsnotat 8. RUNIT, Trondheim (1973)
16. RA1: RUNIT Årsmelding, p. 16 (1974), http://www.idi.ntnu.no/datamuseum/dokumentasjonssenter/aarsmeldinger/runit-aarsberetning-1974.pdf

Instruments of Surveillance Welfare: Computerizing Unemployment and Health in 1960s and 1970s Sweden

Isabelle Dussauge[1] and Julia Peralta[2]

[1] Dept. of Thematic Studies – Technology and Social Change
Linköping University, 581 83 Linköping, Sweden
isabelle.dussauge@liu.se
[2] Swedish Institute for Disability Research
Örebro University, 701 82 Örebro, Sweden, and
Div. of History of Science and Technology, KTH
100 44 Stockholm, Sweden
julia.peralta@oru.se

Abstract. The object of this paper is the role of computerization in the establishment of a specific form of "surveillance welfare" after World War II. Was computerization used as a technology of mass-welfaring to produce a governable population in the frame of an expanding welfare state? Large-scale welfare practices such as health screenings and databasing of the unemployed seem to have a common purpose: making the population into a governable, partially self-regulating, collective body–a welfare body. The paper analyzes the use of computers in the implementation of regional health screenings in the 1960s and the 1970s and in the transformation of (un)employment procedures in the 1970s as two sites for the exercise of state control in post-WWII Sweden.

Keywords: Control, health screenings, history, unemployment policy, welfare.

1 Introduction

In line with many other sectors, the Swedish public administration introduced computerized applications in the 1960s. The post-WWII industrial growth had led to a tremendous expansion of the public sector and services. Computers made possible a breakthrough in data processing and they became an important tool in the rationalization of administrative tasks. For the public administration, they became instruments for the control of welfare procedures. Decision-makers (politicians and civil servants) saw computerization as a way to eliminate loopholes in the tax and social insurance systems and to enhance welfare services. One major aspect of these developments was the establishment of computed systems for the production and classification of data covering the population [1–3].

From *Discipline and Punish* through *History of Sexuality* (1977–1984), the French philosopher Michel Foucault inquired into the emergence and installation of modern and postmodern means of societal control, which he refers to as *surveillance*. These

J. Impagliazzo, P. Lundin, and B. Wangler (Eds.): HiNC3, IFIP AICT 350, pp. 56–64, 2011.
© IFIP International Federation for Information Processing 2011

forms of control did not always explicitly derive from concrete policies or political measures; instead, they were indirect and exerted by means of disciplining technologies through which individual and collective bodies/subjects were rendered manageable and compliant to societal orderings. Here, health care system and labor market policies are considered as two such instances of surveillant control of the population.

This paper will explore two cases in the use of computerization in the expansion and/or strengthening of two welfare institutions: health screenings as an instance of public health and employment agencies as an instance of labor market policies. In our conclusions, we will come back to the following two questions: Which were the goals of computerization in these two instances of the Swedish welfare system? How did the computerization of these welfare practices possibly affect the definition of the social problems (unemployment, health), which they were used to manage?

2 Automating the Collective Body: The Värmland Screening

In Sweden, health care policy and services as well as the National Board of Health (*Medicinalstyrelsen*) have had a central place in the establishment and post-WWII expansion of the Swedish welfare system. The Värmland Mass Screening Pilot Program[1] was initiated by the National Board of Health and started in 1962. This was the first time in Sweden a health control was conducted that was conceived as a total screening, encompassing a whole geographical population and seeking to identify a large battery of possible diseases with the help of automated and computerized technologies.

In 1948, a governmental committee led by the Director-General of the Swedish Medical Board, Axel Höjer, released a major government report on outpatient care, which had been described as Höjer's political legacy. In this document, Höjer argued that the focus of public health care services should be to maintain the population's health and prevent diseases, rather than focusing on the treatment of known diseases, thus continuing a trend that in Sweden had emerged in the 1930s [4]. The 1948 report also recommended that public authorities conduct a series of pilot screenings [5]. It was not until in 1961 that the Board of Health received its first governmental funding for a pilot program [*försöksverksamhet*] of general health control "on a larger scale" [6].

The Board referred later to the lack of doctors in Sweden in the 1950s as the reason why the large-scale health screenings had to wait [6]. In hindsight, the Board also wrote that "the classification of the healthy [and sick] among the people examined" had to be done "without concrete participation of a doctor. We considered that this condition was fulfilled by the development achieved in clinical-chemical laboratory technology" [7].

2.1 Technologies of Mass-Screening

The Board of Health decided that the main screening instrument in the Värmland screening would be automated blood chemical analysis, i.e. the use of an automated

---

[1] *Allmän hälsokontroll i Värmlands län, försöksversamhet* – here referred to in short as the Värmland Screening.

apparatus conducting a pre-defined range of chemical analyses of blood samples. More precisely, the Board recruited the services of clinical chemist Gunnar Jungner's and doctor Ingmar Jungner's new automated laboratory, MEKALAB [7]. The Jungners were largely inspired by growing visions of mass screening at the US American National Institute of Health in the late 1950s where Gunnar Jungner had spent a sabbatical in 1959–1960. By 1961, the Jungners had designed automated machinery for chemical analysis of large amounts of blood samples [8].

Whereas Höjer's 1948 report argued for a yearly health control of everyone aiming at a healthy and well-informed population, the goals of the Värmland Screening were, in comparison, more modest. By the 1960s, the agenda was reduced to test the value of the specific screening method as a way to identify sick and diseased patients [5, 9]. In a nutshell, the argument for this was that common diseases could be identified in patients before they themselves felt the symptoms [5, 10]. Early detection of diseases was argued to be an instrument for the health authorities to better fight diseases and make health care services, as a whole, more effective by referring patients to a larger extent to primary health care [5].

Forty years later, Ingmar Jungner explained that "[t]he Värmland Screening could be considered an extreme attempt to conduct a mass screening in an effective manner" [8]. The Värmland Screening was "planned as a methodological study in order to determine if chemical blood analysis can be used as a method for mass screening … in a general health control in the same way as x-ray examination [tuberculosis screenings]." Ivar Friman, a doctor centrally involved in the Board of Health's coordination of the Värmland Screening, also indicated that the criteria of assessment of the method would be not only the medical results of the screening but also the costs of blood-chemical testing as a method for screening. Further, Friman described the Jungners' "automated laboratory" as "precondition in order to conduct a health control of the [Värmland Screening] kind for an acceptable cost" [9]. Balancing health results and costs was an organizational equation that was not specific to the Värmland Screening, as witnessed by documents on other health controls in planning during the first half of the 1960s (which awaited the conclusions from the Värmland Screening) [11].

Thus, although improving the population health was a general long-term rationale for the large-scale health controls, such screenings were not only aimed at controlling health but also at controlling the costs of the publically funded health services and their use of personnel resources. The Värmland Screening was an assessment of a certain kind of infrastructure and automatized laboratory for this job.

2.2 Computers in a Socio-Technical System of Control

The Värmland screening started on 1 October 1962 in the area of Arvika with the official goal to examine about 100,000 inhabitants in a three-year period [9]. "Among the 88,959 who were screened, 7,620 (8.6 percent) were singled out and sent to follow-up control with examination by a doctor. Among those, previously unknown disease was identified in 3,014 individuals," Ingmar Jungner writes [8].

The Värmland Screening marked the Board of Health's implementation of a mass-scale infrastructure designed to mobilize, examine, screen and potentially treat a whole population, a collective body. Huge amounts of work were required to make the infrastructure work, along three dimensions:

Firstly, it mobilized the collective body of the population. The Värmland Screening created and relied on a large-scale organization reaching all the way down to the population with the creation of "local committees" in each municipality, whose role was to attempt to achieve 100 percent participation of the population. In some organizational aspects (e.g. producing lists of people to call in to the screening), the Värmland Screening was drawing on an existing structure of x-ray screening for tuberculosis. The administration of calling in the population was computerized, and the participants were registered with their "national identification number" (date of birth).

Secondly, at the core of the screening procedure were the production and analysis of health data on the participants. A Central Committee and the municipalities shared the responsibility to arrange rooms, personnel, instruments and standardized procedures for physical examination and the taking of samples for laboratory examinations. Blood samples were sent to MEKALAB, where the Jungners' automated apparatus was made to perform a huge number of analyses of bodily fluids.

Thirdly, the data produced on the health of the participants had to be analyzed for each participant in order to decide who should be contacted for a more thorough medical examination. In the first year of the Värmland Screening, doctors and subsequently automated through computerized processing conducted centrally this preliminary screening decision. Concretely, a program that identified abnormal values interpreted the health data of each participant. Data cards with abnormal values were sent to the central medical assessment group of the Värmland Screening that "made a judgment" and categorized patients for further referral [12]. The purpose of this computerization was to minimize the involvement of doctors, for two reasons: to minimize the amount of errors (in the identification of samples and data; in the originally manual transposition of data values; and in the identification of abnormal data for further medical interpretation); and to use personnel efficiently.[2]

2.3   Interpretation: Controlling the Cost of Health Screenings

The Värmland Screening was part of a historical shift in medical regimes in the Western world: from managing the sick to monitoring the healthy [13]. In that sense, computerization and automation were part of the historical installation of surveillance medicine and its qualitatively new object: health and healthy populations.

Although the Värmland Screening in many ways was a technical and organizational success (it worked, people participated to a large extent, diseases were diagnosed in patients), it was finally evaluated as evidence against mass-scale general screenings. Such general screenings were dismissed as a general tool for health monitoring of the population because they were too demanding on health care resources: costs and personnel; and their clinical value was therefore questioned [5]. This illustrates that the function of the ideal screening was not so much to control population health but rather to control the costs and organization of producing population health.

However, new pilot screenings were generated in the dawn of the Värmland Screening. According to a later governmental report, the debates that arose around the

---

[2] Additionally, the computerized processing was supposed to enable sorting the newly archived screening data by birth date (*folkbokföringsnummer*) – thus opening up for easier retrieval of data.

Värmland Screening triggered many counties and municipalities to plan and conduct their own screening programs.[3]

3 Matching Labor Supply and Demand: Computerization of Employment Agencies

The computerization of the Swedish public employment services began in the late 1960s, divided into three phases. A first phase involved the development of all administrative systems. The second phase came to focus on the application of computer resources to the placement process, i.e. the service in which the unemployed were offered work positions that suited their competence profile. The third and final phase consisted in the construction of a totally integrated information management system. In the present text we inquire on the second phase and, more specifically, on the computerization of the placement work of the Swedish employment agencies in the period 1968–1984. The application of computer technology in the employment agencies became an important instrument in their efforts to achieve social policy goals, which in turn were closely related to the government's key socio-economic objectives [14].

On 6 November 1972, the National Labor Market Board (*Arbetsmarknads-styrelsen*, AMS) appointed a working group named *AMS-ADB-utredning* [15], who identified a few main problems in the functioning of the labor market. The average length of periods of unemployment and the vacancy times (the time when an available position is unoccupied) had become longer in comparison with earlier periods with similar conditions of overall demand for labor. Moreover, by the early 1970s, there were large regional, sectorial and social disparities in unemployment and labor supply. The participation of women in the labor force had increased, whereas the overall employment rate had decreased; young as well as older people experienced more difficulties in employment. Regional disparities in unemployment rates and shortages of high-skilled workforce were evident [14].

The employment services envisaged computerization as a means to implement two main strategies: the production and analysis of better information on the labor market, and the improved placement of the unemployed based on this information. With these two strategies, they aimed to solve the problems connected with periods of unemployment, vacancy times, and disparities in labor supply and demand [14]. By exploring these strategic *improvements* in information and placement, we aim to shed light on the rationale of the computerization of employment services.

3.1 ADB in the Employment Service

In the 1970s and until 1984, three interdependent projects dominated the computerization of the employment services: Creation of job listings (*platslistor*); development of a search engine (*terminalsökning*) and a matching engine (*bevakningsmatchningen*); and finally a pilot employment agency (*modellkontor*). The last two projects had an experimental character and they were followed up regularly during the period studied.

---

[3] About fifteen health screening projects were conducted in Sweden on different scales between 1963 and 1978, to be compared to five projects until 1962, see [16].

3.2 Job Listings

In December 1971, a pilot project of computerized production of daily job listings was launched in Stockholm. The job listings were easily produced, and they were introduced in Gothenburg in 1974–75 and later in Malmö. *AMS-ADB-utredning* suggested a rapid expansion of computerized job lists all over the country. The *AMS-ADB-utredning* settled in its first report, published in 1974, that the simple job listings would be replaced by computerized regional job listings in tabloid format, which would be produced using computer graphic techniques [15]. The information on each job became more extensive and more clearly structured which was an improvement in relation to the previous system [17].

3.3 Search Engine and Matching Engine

In its first report, the *AMS-ADB-utredning* suggested the introduction of terminals for searching and matching to achieve greater effectiveness in the placement process.[4] A comprehensive and well-structured job database was developed in connection with the computerized production of job listings, which at that time were produced in nineteen counties. The job database stored and made available computerized information on vacant jobs, which was a central prerequisite for testing the search engines and matching engines [17].

During the study period, the scope of the search and matching engine projects gradually expanded to include 158 terminals, located at some 90 employment offices, each terminal shared between several employment agency officers [14]. These computer-based tools were adequate and they brought an improvement in the quality of job placement. The opinion of the employment office staff was that terminals "gave a better overview of the labor market and helped them activate the unemployed" [14].

3.4 Pilot Agency

The third operation consisted in developing two instances of a "pilot employment agency," carried out in two employment services districts in Södermanland. It started in 1980. The pilot projects aimed to test the implementation of organizationally and technologically more advanced terminal-assisted job placement. In these pilot projects, all employment agency staff accessed their own individual terminal. They used the terminals to search and monitor vacancies, to register job descriptions, and to produce follow-up lists of unemployed and jobs. Parallel with this development, the issuing of printed job listings was reduced [18]. The pilot agencies soon became the basis for the system of job placement that AMS would come to propose.

A computer system was constructed, an inventory of facilities and work environment was conducted, and new equipment was installed. The pilot agency staff went through comprehensive training in "methods of placement with terminal"

---

[4] Search through the terminal in the form that the investigation proposed had not previously been used in other countries. The benefits of search were assessed to be primarily on the qualitative side, while the match was expected to save time.

(*förmedlingsmetodik med terminal*). Changes in the organizational and operational procedures were implemented in the pilot agencies.

In the new pilot organization, the employment officer had to follow a work schedule that included times for the new visits of unemployed as well as their return visits, appointments with companies, monitoring of placement opportunities and following-up of the arrangements made for unemployed individuals. A system of fixed-length appointments for the unemployed was introduced. Furthermore, the need for services of each unemployed person would be assessed at each contact with the employment agency. On the one hand, this assessment formed the basis for decisions about the situation of the unemployed individual, and on the other hand, such assessments were used in the agency's overall planning of labor market programs such as education, internship positions, and introductory programs.

On the companies' side, the bigger firms engaged their own contact person at the employment agencies, who was in charge of receiving new vacant job notifications from these companies and following up their previously notified jobs [19].

The computerization of the employment agencies was a concrete step towards better conditions for the crucial process of matching jobs with the unemployed. Computerization of the employment agencies came to provide the employment services with two enhanced forms of control: First, a more accurate and updated overview of the labor market; and second, saving time in the task of matching supply and demand of labor.

The matching of work and labor is strongly associated with the emergence of a modern labor market and more specifically with industrialization, which resulted in both wage work expansion and the separation of workers and employers. In a welfare state like Sweden, the link between matching and unemployment is of central importance: it concerns issues of economic stability and social security [20]. In this context, the employment services are a national institution with the central aim to influence directly the process of "matching" in the labor market. This political commitment was manifested in defining the role of the employment agency staff in the computerized agencies, whose main task was to contribute to creating a marketplace of labor where workforce (supply) and jobs (demand) could meet.

4 Discussion

With the present investigation, we have aimed to clarify general political aspects of the computerization process in the Swedish welfare state in the 1960s and 1970s.

The Board of Health strived to enhance the management of a population and to upscale the scope of that management to encompass a broader range of (un)health. Automation and computerization seem to have filled two different functions in building up the new screening infrastructure. On the one hand, the automation of laboratory procedures functioned as a means to upscale the analysis capacity. Here we could argue that these technologies created and managed a historically new collective body: a healthy population. On the other hand, we could argue that these new health technologies were conservative of the orders they were part of. That is, the new screenings were based in part on older organizations of screening for disease (tuberculosis), and the main goal with the new screening and their technologies was to maintain and produce population health at an acceptable cost.

The National Labor Market Board strived to display a control of unemployment consisting in a shorter unemployment period for the unemployed, shorter job vacancy times, and a more geographically flexible workforce: the attributes of a well functioning market machinery of supply and demand of labor. For the involved authorities, the necessary oil in this market machinery was the computerized, effective overview of, and matching between, supply and demand of work/workforce. With the computerization of the employment agencies as a tool, the authorities could intensify the shaping of the labor market as a market.

We have observed that surveillance was exerted and enhanced by computerization at three levels. It included the mobilization of a population (the improvement of which was not a goal in the computerization of employment agencies), the production and analysis of information about that population, and the actions taken by the authorities based on that information.

Our interpretation is thus that computerization afforded the Board of Health and the Labor Market Board through the employment agencies, the possibility to re-shape, technologically and organizationally, the objects of their control – (un)health and (un)employment. *The same* tasks could be conducted at a higher pace, and therefore possibly on a larger scale. However, we want to emphasize that these Swedish welfare institutions used computer technology primarily to improve the efficacy of their welfare procedures, and therefore as an *intensification* of their control of the very objects of welfare. Thus, computerization was historically a part of the re-definition of social issues in the welfare state, as those became more manageable.

Acknowledgments. We thank Handelsbankens forskningsstiftelser for supporting the research for this paper. We are also grateful to our colleagues within the project, "Precursors of the IT Nation: Computer Use and Control in Swedish Society, 1955–1985" for comments on earlier versions of the paper.

References

1. Agar, J.: The Government Machine: A Revolutionary History of the Computer. MIT Press, Cambridge (2003)
2. Annerstedt, J.: Datorer och politik: Studier i en ny tekniks politiska effekter på det svenska samhället. Cavefors, Staffanstorp (1970)
3. Waara, L.: Offentliga sektorns tillväxt. LiberLäromedel, Malmö (1981)
4. Berg, A.: Den gränslösa hälsan: Signe och Axel Höjer, folkhälsan och expertisen. Uppsala Universitet, Uppsala (2009)
5. Hälsoundersökningen i Värmland 1962-1965. Socialstyrelsen, Stockholm (1968)
6. National Archives of Sweden (Riksarkivet), Hv FLIV:1: Nilsson, G. and T. Johanson (Letter March 15, 1962)
7. National Archives of Sweden (Riksarkivet), Hv FLIV:4: Engel, A., H. Dunér, et al., (Draft of the final report) (1968)
8. Jungner, I.: Berättelsen om AutoChemist (2007), http://www.tekniskamuseet.se/1/262.html (accessed on May 17, 2010)
9. National Archives of Sweden (Riksarkivet), Hv FLIV:1: Friman, I.: P.M. angående pågående försöksverksamhet med utökad hälsokontroll i Värmlands län (Memo March 25, 1963)

10. National Archives of Sweden (Riksarkivet), Hv FLIV:4: WHO Regional Committee for Europe, The pre-symptomatic diagnosis of diseases by organized screening procedures (Summary Report September 25, 1964)
11. Ett förslag till allmän hälsokontroll av 4-åringar. Socialstyrelsen, Stockholm (1968)
12. National Archives of Sweden (Riksarkivet), Hv FLIV:1: Friman, I.: P.M. angående uppläggning av databehandling och statistik för Värmlandsundersökningen (Memo April 14, 1964)
13. Armstrong, D.: The rise of surveillance medicine. Sociology of Health & Illness 17(3), 393–404 (1995)
14. Arbetsförmedling med ADB-resurser. Rapport 8, Förslag till ADB-system för platsförmedling. Arbetsmarknadsstyrelsen, Stockholm (1983)
15. Arbetsförmedling med ADB-resurser. Rapport 1, En utvecklingsplan. Arbetsmarknadsstyrelsen, Stockholm (1974)
16. Hälsoundersökningar och annan förebyggande hälsovård – utvecklingstendenser [Hälsokontrollutredningen]. Socialstyrelsen / Liber, Stockholm (1978)
17. Arbetsförmedling med ADB-resurser. Rapport 2, Målstudie, verksamhet 1976/1977. Arbetsmarknadsstyrelsen, Stockholm (1976)
18. Arbetsförmedling med ADB-resurser. Rapport 7, Försöksverksamhet 1980/1981 och planering för 1981/82 m m. Arbetsmarknadsstyrelsen, Stockholm (1981)
19. Arbetsförmedling med ADB-resurser. Rapport 6, Försöksverksamhet 1979/1980 och planering under 1980/1981 m m. Arbetsmarknadsstyrelsen, Stockholm (1980)
20. Walter, L.: Som hand i handske: En studie av matchning i ett personaluthyrnings-företag. BAS, Göteborg (2005)

History of Electronic Prescriptions in Sweden: From Time-Sharing Systems via Smartcards to EDI

Gunnar O. Klein

Department of Microbiology, Tumor and Cell Biology
Karolinska Institutet, Stockholm, Sweden
gunnar.klein@ki.se

Abstract. Managing prescriptions for medication, using ICT support, started in the 1970s with the computerization of the pharmacy branch offices where local systems registered handwritten prescriptions and to print labels. In 1984, the first online prescribing started with physicians connected to their local pharmacy system in a pilot test. Then in 1987, the first pilot test started with an off-line system in which PC-based prescriber support systems transferred data to patient-held smart cards that were taken to the pharmacy. In the 1990s, we had the first use of messaging using EDIFACT syntax for prescriptions. These had a relatively small volume until 2000, when an XML version of a European standard based on object-oriented modeling became popular and made electronic prescribing the normal practice, which meant important quality gains.

Keywords: Decision support, electronic prescriptions, Infocard, messaging, standards.

1 Introduction

Computer support for the process of managing medication prescriptions is an interesting example of the developments of what we now call eHealth[1]. There were a number of relatively early developments in this sector using computers, but the large-scale adoption of the new techniques has been slower than in many other sectors. However, the history of ICT use for prescriptions in Sweden offers several interesting aspects that touch upon technology as well as informatics and societal issues. Today, these techniques affect almost every citizen, since most people use prescription medication at one time or another.

Some of the medication issues addressed by ICT are:

- Decision support for the prescribing physicians improves the quality of medication selections, optimizes the possibility of efficacy, and minimizes the risk of adverse reactions. In Sweden alone, an estimated three thousand deaths occur yearly due to errors in medication.

---

[1] http://www.ehealthweek2010.org/ this year's EU ministerial and scientific conference.

J. Impagliazzo, P. Lundin, and B. Wangler (Eds.): HiNC3, IFIP AICT 350, pp. 65–73, 2011.
© IFIP International Federation for Information Processing 2011

- Improved cost-efficiency for the pharmacies has occurred by changing almost illegible paper scripts to computerized support for retail, billing, and safety checks.
- Improved services provided to customers/patients.

2 Background

This paper is based on a literature study and the experience of the author who, in leadership positions, has had the privilege of not only observing, but also actively participating in the developments described herein.

During the period 1972–73, the author worked for Philips Bank Terminal Systems where an interesting and not very well-known computer was constructed based on developments from the Arenco Company bought by Philips. This was a mini-computer, with a set of special printers, displays and keyboards, also manufactured by the same company, to manage five working terminals at a bank branch office. The author designed the testing software for the factory and service personnel, including the design of a simple time-sharing operating system (OS). The computer had no general OS available at first. It had a core memory and sixteen instructions pro-grammed, using punched cards at the beginning, with an assembly code that trans-ferred to a machine code 20 kilometers away, once daily. Much of the debugging took place using a special hardwired unit with bit switches and lights, which allowed patching in the core memory. Apoteksbolaget (the National Corporation of Swedish Pharmacies) bought these printers for all the pharmacies in Sweden in the 1970s.

In 1987, the author had become a medical doctor with some limited experience of writing prescriptions, and a PhD in cancer research with many data management projects at Karolinska Institutet. He then founded the company, Infocard Nordiska AB, in which a staff of ten worked to pioneer the development of applications for the new memory card technologies in Sweden. Firstly, laser optical cards from Canon were used that could hold some 500 kB of data. The aim was to compile an entire medical record that the patient could hold. This technique had several problems, such as poor reliability and the expense of the equipment needed for reading/writing. Focus then switched to smartcards. Besides Bull, Infocard was the only significant company in Sweden with such expertise, and for some five years worked closely with Telever-ket (the National Telecommunications Administration) in several projects crowned by the system for GSM. The cards and the personalization systems for all the Nordic countries came from Infocard. Nevertheless, the heart of the author was with the med-ical applications and he led the development of the prescribing system described in this article.

During 1993–2000, the author worked for both the Swedish Institute for Health Services Development (Spri) and Karolinska Institutet where he started the Centre for Health Telematics in 1996. He was working both with European R&D projects and standardization for health IT, first with health care cards, later information security, and object oriented information models and semantic interoperability. In addition, the author was the coordinator of the EU project, Trusted Health Information Systems, which developed the principles for the use of cryptographic services in health care using PKI and smart cards as electronic identity cards for use by the health professionals. In 1997, he became chair of all European standardization for health informatics, operating with EU mandates and financing. Then in 1998, he co-founded the corresponding ISO committee. During this period, Europe developed both a formal standard for electronic prescriptions and various important security standards. The patient card standardization became global and now it has an eight-part ISO standard that includes a part for electronic prescriptions.

Since 2000, the author has continued to work for health care standards and other issues in medical informatics. He was instrumental in the development of the Swedish e-prescription specification, which is a profile of the European standard expressed in XML. In 2007, his long-term work for electronic prescriptions was published as an ISO Technical report [1]. Since 2008, the author's main job is as primary care physician who makes daily use of the electronic prescription and various decision support systems.

3   Pharmacy Computerization in Sweden – The Early Phase

Between 1970 and 2009, the National Corporation of Swedish Pharmacies (Apoteksbolaget AB) was the sole pharmacy retailer in Sweden. This unusual situation enabled it to invest in ICT developments much earlier than in the other Nordic countries and in Europe as a whole. During the 1970s, all the nine hundred branch offices received a minicomputer with custom-built software from the Swedish branch of Data General. Special dot matrix printers were custom-built to meet the size requirements of the labels for the patient's name and dosing instructions for the medication package. This computerization, first made to simplify the retail and safety checks, also led to the development of a national database for all prescriptions, at a very early stage, compared internationally. This has been very useful for many studies of medication use as well as finding side effects. The National Corporation of Swedish Pharmacies compiled it and then it transferred to the National Board of Health and Welfare for analysis.

There have been a number of generations of this system for the pharmacies. Different methods that also included the prescribing physicians were considered and tested. The first trial was in Bankeryd in the Småland region where the pharmacy and the primary care center were located in the same building. A module was slightly adapted from the one that the pharmacists use to enter paper prescription data. Some of the physicians who received terminals (the 80x25 line text ones used by minicomputers at the time) to the pharmacy computer, on which they could enter their prescriptions, used this. The physicians had access to a list of all the products with names and packages, but not much decision support.

4   The Communication and Security Problems

During the 1980s, the networks did not reach all the primary care centers in the country; dial-up connections using standard telephone lines were all that was available.

The speed, 9,600 baud, could be enough to send an occasional prescription, but it was not enough to browse through databases for pharmaceutical information for the prescriber, for example. There were also serious security concerns regarding the need to protect the confidentiality of patients' health information and the authenticity of legally regulated documents such as prescriptions. These concerns meant that new solutions had to be found for the prescription communication.

This was one reason for our idea of using the new microprocessor cards (named Smartcards by Roy Bright) for prescriptions. Our new concept was not only a means of protecting the confidentiality during a one-time transfer from the prescriber to the pharmacy, it also included allowing the patient to carry a complete history of all current medication, often prescribed by different providers, to hospitals as well as outpatient clinics. A national database, which could have been an alternative solution, was, at the time, not considered feasible, due to data protection regulations.

The first commercially available smartcards were the BULL CP8 cards with 8 kbit=1 kbyte of storage. This was insufficient for the application, which would allow patients to take a complete medication history and other data, such as allergies, to medical facilities. However, Infocard became a distributor for Matsushita/Panasonic that introduced 2- and 8-kbyte smartcards in 1986. Most of the pilot tests used the 2-kbyte smartcards, whose capacity, with our compact storage, was enough for fifteen current prescriptions and fifty old ones, as well as some other information.

5   The Prescriber Support System

The prescriber support system developed by Infocard in 1986–88 was innovative in several ways. It received considerable attention from the smartcard community and it enjoyed presentations at various conferences [2].

This rather advanced decision support system could be presented, with all the previously prescribed medicines, possible allergies and renal function, to the prescribing physician. In addition, it also included information on the products and their use, data that was derived from three sources:

- The Product database used by the pharmacies, updated each month on a diskette, contained the name of the product, its ingredients, strength, packages, and prices.
- The Pharmaceutical information, "Läkemedelsregistret," included about two pages of information on each product with Indications, Contraindications, Recommended Dose, Side effects, and several more items.
- The Problem-Oriented Drug Book, "Läkemedelsboken," a five hundred page volume with some twenty chapters for each major disease or problem category (i.e., Pain is not a disease but an important reason for medication). Named experts wrote this book that build on scientific references and various consensus guidelines, and they still publish it regularly. It not only provides advice on the major classes of drugs for illness such as depression, but it also provides guidance for diagnoses and alternative therapies that do not involve medicines. Previously only available in print, it is now also accessible as a PDF version on the web. Our team acquired the magnetic tape used for the

typesetting machine at the printers and, because it was systematically organized with various control codes for chapter, subchapters, and so on, they
were able to automatically create a very adequate database from this book for
use in the local system,

The above-mentioned last part about guidance, based on the intended problem to be
treated, was one of the unique features of the support system. Interestingly, now over
twenty years later, none of the prescriber support systems has such a feature, partly
because the source book does not appear to be a database [3]. Fig. 1 depicts the
workflow using these three sources.

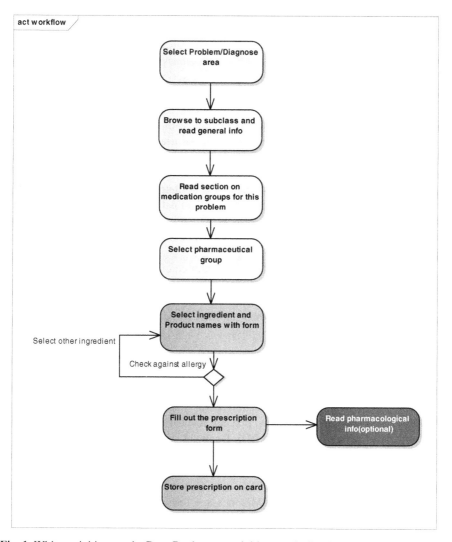

Fig. 1. White activities use the Drug Book, gray activities use the Product database and the dark
gray activity uses the Pharmacology database

The system also used some other important features, which are common today, to complete the prescription form, thus it was possible to calculate the total dosage from the number of portions and intended period of medication. A specific detail of this system was the search for the optimal package (amount of medication and appropriate sizes), to obtain the lowest possible total price.

The control of access to the data on the patient card was based on the interaction between the keys on this card and those on the doctor's card (now generally called Health Professional Cards). The doctor's card used here was a forerunner of the electronic ID card concept and at the time, in 1987, rather unique. Since 1998, the use of smartcards by professionals has been generally accepted and recommended, but despite small trials very few systems still use them, although, for example, fifty thousand cards have been issued in Stockholm [4–6].

The site of the trial for the Patient prescription card was on the island of Tjörn in west Sweden. The County Council and the Pharmacy Corporation participated, of which the latter developed software to read the prescriptions from the cards and integrate them with the software used to process paper prescriptions, the ATS system. Infocard developed all the software for the doctor's office. An approximate three hundred patients and four physicians were included in the pilot study. Although the participants were generally quite positive about the trial, for most of the physicians, this was their first encounter with a PC, and some of the initial problems encountered were related to inexperience in handling a computer with a mouse.

However, the Federation of County Councils hesitated, due to the costs associated with supplying all physicians with computers and all patients with cards, the latter at a cost of approximately 100 SEK per card at the time. Consequently, this initiative, which had the keen support of the Pharmacy Corporation for several years, was never implemented on a large scale.

The focus of the investments in ICT for health care became instead the electronic health records, as reported in another contribution to this conference [7]. These included, in many cases but not all, a module for prescriptions, but for years, these modules were much less advanced than this first Swedish Prescriber Support system and are, in some ways, still not as progressive.

6   Messaging and Standard Formats

During the 1990s, when electronic health record systems at the desktop of outpatient clinics increased from 5 percent to 90 percent, there was renewed interest in the electronic transfer of prescriptions using EDI. Denmark was a pioneering country for this method and an Electronic Data Interchange For Administration, Commerce and Transport (EDIFACT) message format was developed on a European scale to represent an electronic prescription. This was adapted to Sweden and used until about 2001 when it was replaced by an XML message format based on the European pre-standard ENV 13607. A Danish GP led this development, which had an object-oriented model of the prescription message and some related ones that dealt with an intermediate relaying agent. Initially, they sent all prescriptions directly to one named pharmacy; however, it is now possible to send them to a national prescription store from which they are retrieved when patients want them filled.

7   Public Web Based Knowledge Bases

The product database has only been available for software producers, but the pharmacological information most widely used in Sweden today is Fass[2]. Fass was available since the mid-1990s without restrictions; it includes a version that uses less technical language and less detail, especially for patients/citizens. Software companies that allow their users to open a window to read from while they are prescribing also use this database. However, there is no link to the different elements of this to allow more informed prescribing. Other national developments offer software companies the opportunity of linking to a database with prescriber information in a different way.

8   Patient/Citizen Inclusion

One important aim behind our development of the Prescription system in 1986–88 was to include patients and make them more aware of their complete current medication as prescribed by, unfortunately, often several different care facilities with no connectivity or common database. Therefore, the concept of the patient held data card was important. Our intention was to make this card interoperable internationally as well, at least in Europe. Patient cards based on smartcards were in use much more in certain other countries like France, Germany, and Spain, but prescriptions have only been part of such systems on a relatively small scale.

The patient held data was a practical way of moving the information to all the facilities that patients would need to visit (health care and pharmacies). Very importantly, the system also provided a means of putting the patient in control of the access to the information because only those who received the card could read it. Presuming no one stole it, if such was the case it would probably not have been possible for the thief to read it, the patient decided who to trust to read the medical information the card contained. The data could be quite sensitive, also indirectly informing the reader which diseases were present.

The early system of the 1980s also encouraged doctors to print a table adapted to patient use that listed all the current medication with dosage, to facilitate the correct use. This feature is available in many systems today, but it is, unfortunately, often not adapted well enough to the patients' needs and not used as much as it should be.

Today, despite the advanced general technology with electronic IDs widely used by citizens, only a few places offer patients the service of being able to log onto their record of medication data. A promising approach is the National Patient Overview, which started in 2010 in Örebro County.

---

[2] FASS.SE is published by LINFO, the organization for the pharmaceutical industry, and is not controlled by any authority.

However, the Pharmacy Corporation has offered citizens online access to their new prescriptions in the national prescription store, which any pharmacy could fill, and a printout of all prescription medication they have bought since 2009. While this is all very well, it does not replace the need for access to current ordination, since dosages do change and some medicines found unsuitable and suspended, despite doctors prescribing them.

9   Discussion

The evolution of the use of ICT for improving the use of prescription medication has been far from straightforward. It has included various alternative developments including what now appears to be a parenthesis, the use of patient held smartcards with all prescription information. This is partly due to the rather advanced level of other network-based services including PKI-based security infrastructures. Sweden and Denmark are clearly world leaders with regard to the use of messaging for prescriptions. Nevertheless, even in these two countries, they still use several million paper forms, although most of the sixty million prescriptions in Sweden are now transmitted electronically. This has resulted in a reduction of problems associated with poor handwriting. It is usually a quick and convenient service to patients, since after a phone call to the doctor, a prescription could go directly to any pharmacy and there is no need for the patient to collect a paper form printed by the computer, which is still the main method in most European countries.

However, the most important benefits of ICT support do not relate to the Electronic Transfer, but the associated development of decision support for the prescriber. This support should include a number of different issues, which are only partly available even today.

- A current record of all ordinated medication wherever the patient goes, preferably also internationally
- Access to several types of integrated decision support processes, in addition to books in a web browser
- Integration of the information in the general health record with the pharmaceutical information source to allow, for example, links to diagnosis and the appropriate medications for the illness. In addition, a linkage that automatically creates an alert if a diagnosis or any laboratory tested value creates a reason to avoid prescribing a certain medication or to alter the standard dose
- Support for patients that enables them to manage their medication, including non-prescription items and natural remedies, herbal medicinal products, and traditional herbal medicinal products.

The development of electronic prescribing support in Sweden is an interesting example of different technologies that include the computer on the card. The microprocessor card has become a very important security tool for personnel in Swedish health care, and patient data cards are now in use in many countries, but not in the Nordic ones. The initial standards developed in Europe were adopted as global ISO standards, including a part for prescriptions on cards.

References

1. Klein, G.O.: ISO/TR 22790 Health informatics – Functional characteristics of prescriber support systems (2007)
2. Klein, G.O.: Infocard in Pharmacy. In: Proceedings of the North American Conference on Patient Cards, New Orleans, pp. 1–3 (March 1992)
3. Klein, G.O.: The Swedish Prescription Card Trial: A Technical Report. Published by Apoteksbolaget in the co-operation between Sweden and the French Ministry of Health, p. 29 (1992)
4. Klein, G.O.: Final report of the project Trustworthy Health Telematics 1 (Trusthealth). Deliverable D1.4, p. 16 (1998)
5. Klein, G.O.: Security principles for patient card systems. In: Köhler, C.O., Waegeman (eds.) Proceedings of the Fourth Global Congress on Patient Cards and Computerization of Health Records, pp. 77–87. Medical Records Institute, Newton (1992)
6. Klein, G.O.: Smart Cards: A tool for carrying medical information by patients and creating digital signatures by professionals. In: Information Security – The Next Decade Conference of the International Federation of Information processing/TC 11 Security, Annex Information Security on the Electronic highways of Sweden, Cape Town, pp. 1–20. Chapman & Hall, Boca Raton (1995)
7. Kajbjer, K., Nordberg, R., Klein, G.O.: Electronic Health Records in Sweden: From Administrative Support to Clinical Decision Support. In: Lundin, P., Impagliazzo, J., Wangler, B. (eds.) HiNC3. IFIP AICT, vol. 350, pp. 65–73. Springer, Heidelberg (2011)

Electronic Health Records in Sweden: From Administrative Management to Clinical Decision Support

Karin Kajbjer[1], Ragnar Nordberg[2], and Gunnar O. Klein[3]

[1] Department of Computer and Information Science, Linköping University
Linköping, Sweden
karin.kajbjer@telia.com
[2] JMP Research & Development AB, Mölndal, Sweden
ragnar.nordberg@jmprd.se
[3] Department of Microbiology, Tumour and Cell Biology
Karolinska Institutet, Stockholm, Sweden
gunnar.klein@ki.se

Abstract. Computer support for health care started in Sweden in the mid-1960s, with a series of pilot tests using clinical records at the Karolinska Hospital. This had very little impact in health care due to its limited volume and scope. In addition, the first automation of chemistry laboratories that created many benefits in the form of increased efficiency from the early 1970s, rapid results delivery and the possibilities of quality control also occurred in the mid-1960s. The 1970s and first part of the 1980s saw the independent development of several patient administration systems, based on central mainframes in the counties, as well as a large number of dumb terminals in the hospitals and later also in the outpatient clinics. From the early 1990s, we saw an explosion of primary care electronic health records with twenty-seven different products in 1995.

Keywords: Electronic health records, Melior, patient administrative system, PAX, Swedestar.

1   Introduction

Health care is a large part of modern societies, accounting for nearly 9 percent of the GDP and a similar proportion of the labor. Although it is also a person-centric manual service, it is a business that is very information rich and in which knowledge is rapidly developing. It has been stated that owing to the large and growing amount of information that needs to be managed, a situation where the capacity of the unaided human brain no longer meets the requirements is approaching. There have also been many interesting attempts, using computers for a very long time, to provide decision support for medicine, but few of the advanced AI techniques often first developed for medical problems have actually had a broad impact.

The very first account of automatic decision support for medicine dates back to the thirteenth century with Ramon Llul, who was a scholar in Mallorca. Llul was knowledgeable in the mathematics of Arabia, as well as in European Medicine, and a

J. Impagliazzo, P. Lundin, and B. Wangler (Eds.): HiNC3, IFIP AICT 350, pp. 74–82, 2011.

practicing physician that influenced Leibniz in the early theory of computation. Llul invented a machine, now called the Lullian Circle, which consisted of three paper discs inscribed with alphabetical letters or symbols that referred to lists of attributes. The discs rotated individually to generate a large number of combinations of ideas. For medical decision support, one of the circles described possible symptoms, the next indicated possible causes/diagnoses, and the third included a set of remedies or treatments indicated by turning the circles.

Computers in health care, as studied in the scientific field of medical informatics, were used in a large number of areas and are today essential in many fields such as digital imaging and bioinformatics analysis of DNA and proteins.

However, we dedicate this paper to the history of computer support for routine tasks in health care where information, often in the form of a simple line of text or a single numeric value, manages both the medical understanding of a patient as well as to improve the management of the processes of investigation and treatment. Estimates show that nurses and physicians spend about 40 to 50 percent of their working time on information management in a broad sense.

Despite many internationally advanced and pioneering projects, it has taken quite a long time for the health sector to use the advantages of computer technology. This paper describes the early developments in Sweden, until 1995, and discusses some of the reasons for the somewhat slow, large-scale introduction.

2   Materials and Methods

This paper is based on a literature study and on interviews with Gert Ljungkvist, project manager at SPRI, the Swedish National Institute for Health Services Development owned by the Department of Health and Welfare (Socialdepartmentet) and the Federation of County Councils (Landstingsförbundet). In Sweden, this institute played a very important role in the development of good practices for documentation, first in the paper world, and computerized records from the early 1980s. We have also used the documented personal accounts of early Swedish IT history, particularly those of Hans Peterson, Paul Hall, and Torsten Seeman [1–3].

3   Results

Computer support for health care started in Sweden in the mid-1960s, which at an international level was very early. This was a series of pilot tests with clinical records at the Karolinska Hospital in the Stockholm region, which was using batch processing. Although these tests achieved some international fame, they had very little impact in health care due to their limited volume and scope.

The automation of chemistry laboratories and various administrative systems soon followed. It was not until the mid-1980s that computer support for medical records really started to emerge with an explosive development in primary *care* and with hospitals generally following fifteen years later.

3.1   Laboratory Systems

From the early 1970s onwards, the next step of automating the chemistry laboratories created many benefits in the form of increased efficiency, rapid delivery of results and possibilities of quality control.

At that time, all laboratory instruments delivered readings in analogue form, which was unsuitable for data processing and therefore required digitization. The first computerization step was therefore to develop or introduce commercial analogue for digital converters and equipment, which triggered a precise reading rate. Thereafter, automated data processing grew rapidly within the laboratories and with automated analysis instruments; the Swedish AutoChemist, the English Vickers, and the Swiss Greiner analyzers all had interfaces that made them compatible with most computers. The automated processing of the laboratory data increased productivity and made it possible to achieve a much higher level of quality. This also meant that one could send laboratory results to the wards and primary care units electronically, where they arrived at the same moment, as the results were ready at the laboratory.

The laboratory data was also stored in databases at the laboratory, which made it possible to obtain a cumulative laboratory test report per patient, even before they installed computer systems in the clinics. As hospitals had installed PAS and electronic health record (EHR) systems, they interfaced with the laboratory systems and both requests and transmitted the results automatically.

3.2   Patient Administrative System – PAS

The 1970s and first part of the 1980s also saw the independent development of several patient administration systems, based on central mainframes in the counties, as well as a large number of dumb terminals in the hospitals and later also in the outpatient clinics. These managed invoicing as well as the allocation of hospital beds and certain related tasks.

One of the systems developed was PAX, in Gothenburg. This was created in-house, after a number of other incompatible systems had been installed, tested and disqualified. There were many discussions and arguments about which system was the best and should be used, before it was decided to develop a totally new system based on the experiences from the others and peace was established, thereof the name PAX.

They developed the basic version of this new system in two years and installations started in 1988. It took several years to install the system due to financial problems with supplying all the wards with the necessary equipment and the training of the staff. They continuously improved the system during the years and it is still in use in the region of Västra Götaland and the county of Dalarna. Another system was called PAS in SLL, the county of Stockholm; the third largest region around Malmö in Skåne developed yet another system that included diagnosis codes, codes for admission, and referrals among others.

3.3   Primary Care Record Systems

Due to the difficulties of creating computer support for the clinical staff, physicians, and nurses, it took almost twenty years after the first trials before electronic health records made their successful entry into primary care rather than in the more demanding general hospital sector.

One of the most interesting systems in Swedish primary care was called Swedestar, introduced in Lerum [4] and Sundbyberg in 1984, which is still, with minor modifications, in use in several places. Swedestar was a modification of Costar, developed in Boston, closely associated with the MUMPS operating system that included an integrated database function. A similar development in Finland was the Finnstar system. An important and novel idea at the time was to record all clinical information according to certain keywords from a defined local terminology. This allowed both a fast selection of the relevant parts of individual case histories for presentation and, perhaps more importantly, the easy and efficient compiling of data from groups of patients. The latter can be used both for scientific studies on various clinical issues and for quality management of the core clinical work. The system was based on a local minicomputer server for a primary care centre with asynchronous terminals, later PC workstations. This relatively innovative system came from the high-tech advanced, academic environment of Harvard.

The next step was the proliferation of a large number of small PC-based systems that in many cases were more like word processing systems rather than for the advanced management of structured data. They were often developed by a physician in co-operation with one or several, more or less, self-made software engineers. Data from a SPRI report [4] illustrated in Fig. 1 shows the rapid deployment of record systems.

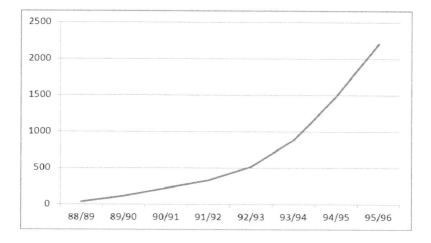

Fig. 1. Number of installed EHR systems in Sweden 1988–96

In 1994, EHR systems operated in 85 percent of the primary care centers. As shown in Table 1, there were twenty-seven different products available on the Swedish market [5]. Note that the Melior and Bedside systems were intended only for hospital care.

Table 1. Systems for electronic health records in Sweden 1994

System name	Supplier
AMA	Mediflex Data AB
APEX	DDE Sverige AB
Axept (formerly called Aesculap)	INEQ AB
Bedside	Celsius Information System
BIOSIS	Health Allocation System AB
BMS journal	Bonjour Medical System AB
Dialog Journal	Celsius Information System
Dr Grans Datorsystem	Gran Data AB
Infodoc	Sysdeco Profdoc AB
Journal II and Journal III	Sysdeco Profdoc AB
Journalia	Journalia AB
Mac Adapt	Frontec Care System AB
MacDoc II	Esmeralda AB
Medex	Medex Sverige AB
Medicus	Data 16 AB
Medidoc	Medidoc AB
Medilite	PCD Applitron AB
Melior	Siemens AB
Mia vård	Infoservice Sweden AB
Patientjournalen	Patientjournalen AB
PC-Praxis	Lap Power
PMS	Bergsjö Data- och Systemutveckling AB
Promed	PRO International AB
Swede Star 2.0	Celsius Information System
VANIA	CAP Programator
VAS	CAP Programator Stockholm AB
WordPics	DAFA Syd AB

We believe that an important reason for the popularity of these small-scale developments was the sense of participation that the clinical staff felt in being able to influence many details of the systems. This was in contrast to the later production of in some ways more advanced systems introduced through the central IT management of the various counties and often developed by large, or at least somewhat larger, software companies. Only a few clinicians were able to influence the design and many felt alienated from these systems.

Also contributing to the popularity of the small-scale systems were the improved user interfaces, employing windows techniques especially designed for the record systems and later based on Microsoft Windows with a mouse and with color.

Unfortunately, they had already forgotten some of the important design principles of earlier systems from the 1960s such as using defined terminologies and structuring data based on headings and subheadings useful for keyword-based searches and for the compilation of statistics.

The developments of electronic health record systems during the 1990s and into the new millennium included a large number of integration projects that had aspects such as laboratory referrals and results, electronic prescriptions and, with the patient administration systems, national and regional population registers and reporting for invoicing.

There has also been a successive return to the goals of recording clinical data in structures based on both process analysis and medical ontologies as well as using more internationally based health terminologies that are very large compared to those used in other sectors. The current and very promising clinical terminology SNOMED CT, translated into Danish and Swedish, contains some 308,000 concepts with 900,000 terms and 1.5 million relations.

3.4   Hospital Record Systems

The large-scale use of electronic health records in hospitals came considerably later than in primary care. However, already by the 1980s, a number of specialized record systems were developed particularly for various university hospital departments. Nevertheless, these mainly complemented the paper-based record systems rather than replaced them. However, we will describe two early hospital implementations. One is the adoption of what was really a primary care system in Ystad; the other is the comprehensive development in Gothenburg, first installed in 1994.

The Ystad Case

The first Swedish hospital to use comprehensively an electronic health record system was Ystad, a small hospital in the southern Swedish region of Skåne. This 190-bed hospital also had 74,000 outpatient visits a year, including 21,000 for acute illness, which installed the Swedestar system.

In 1989, HC Lennér, chief physician at the department of internal medicine, initiated the project [6]. The hospital management was enthusiastic, and although they received some external grants, the hospital financed some 80 to 90 percent of the investment costs from their normal budget, believing it would pay off. They divided the goals into two sets – short- and long-term goals.

The short-term goals include:

- Less manual work for notes, referrals, and lab results,
- More efficient care through better access to information,
- Support for nurses and the evaluation of the nursing care,
- Possibilities for change and trials of new processes in outpatient clinics and clinical wards,

- Improved privacy protection,
- Improved work situation for the assistant nurses by providing more direct patient care and reducing the time spent on paper work.

The long-term goals include:

- Improved assessment of the production and costs,
- Improved quality management,
- Improved competence of staff.

They first used the system in 1991 in the clinical wards for internal medicine and certain outpatient clinics. There were many initial difficulties with frequent stops of the system and much integration was required for referrals and lab-test results that were not ready. Interestingly, the ways of working with records and rounds changed. Doctors and nurses now first sat down in front of a computer and discussed all the patients and then the doctors made their rounds alone, with very little documentation and no computer support. Not everyone applauded this approach. In 1994, they computerized almost the entire set of hospital's records. In the overall assessment, they at least partially met the goals in all aspects, but 25 percent of the staff felt that the computer records functioned worse or much worse than anticipated.

Melior – The Sahlgrenska Development

Sahlgrenska University Hospital is a large teaching facility in Gothenburg. They started to develop their own EHR system in 1988, using a then rather modern Microsoft technology and allowing different departments to choose their own key words and specific graphical user interfaces to create an efficient and user-friendly display for the presentation and collection of data. Although this was very popular, it caused problems for the doctors and nurses when they moved between the wards, because they did not recognize the screen-layouts. Therefore, they decided to develop one common user interface, which was very similar in appearance to an ordinary paper-based health record. This version was ready in 1993 and the installation began the following year. Unfortunately, it had taken a long time to install the system in the whole hospital for the same reasons as with the PAX system.

3.5   Attempts to Standardize Systems for Interoperability

From the early 1990s, there have also been several attempts to develop standards for record structures. In Sweden, the government organization, Swedish Institute for Health Services Development, SPRI [7], had an important influence in setting standards for certain elements of records, actually starting with the paper-based ones of the 1980s, but also used many in the 1990s EHRs. European standardization started in CEN/TC 251 from 1992 onwards and the first elements of the Electronic Health Record Architecture appeared in 1995 under the leadership of doctor Petter Hurlen from Norway. An object-oriented information model followed these design principles in the pre-standard 13606 in 1999. This in turn was further developed into what is now state of the art in electronic health record architecture. Based on the two-level modeling, it uses so-called archetypes for specific clinical purposes that represent constraint models of the relatively small reference model. Since 2008–09 this has been both a European CEN and an ISO standard and thus a national standard in all the Nordic countries.

4   Discussion

The paper presents how computer support in primary care was rapidly developed and implemented on a large scale in Sweden during the early 1990s. At an international level, this is quite early, although our neighboring countries had similar developments but somewhat later. One reason has been the public financing of health care in Sweden through the now twenty independent county councils. These had enough financial strength to support the introduction of record systems in all the primary care centers of their respective areas. The general size of a rather large group practice of four-to-ten doctors and perhaps ten-to-thirty other staff members also meant that there was a power of scale that facilitated the investment, installation, and management of the small server-based systems on a local area network with relatively advanced software. In many countries, even in European ones such as France, a single doctor's office largely manages primary care and there is little capacity to manage a computer system let alone its development.

It is interesting to note that during the rather few years of the early 1990s, when this market took off, there was a huge proliferation of at least twenty-seven different products, developed with a quite similar range, although some of them were imports from Norway, Denmark, or Iceland. This was clearly too many and ten years later only four remained as commercial products, although in some locations many of the early systems are still running. Three of the systems used in 1994 are now among the leaders in terms of number of users, Journal III, Melior, and VAS. Relatively little has happened to them in fifteen years, even if no new installations occur.

It is noteworthy that Electronic Health Record systems rarely succeed in other countries than in their country of development; many also have problems reaching beyond the region in which the company is located. In some respects, a hospital EHR system is much more demanding. Use was still very low in 1995 and it was not until 2009 that as many as 85 percent of hospital wards were using computerized records.

The goals of the early pioneers not only targeted improving the efficiency of routine activities in health care, but also the prospects of easy and comprehensive follow ups of medical results, as quality management and research into the future were often mentioned. Unfortunately, the systems of the 1990s that still dominate the scene do not provide such features, partly because medical facilities did not fully appreciate the difficulties of standardizing EHR structures and their associated medical terminologies.

Acknowledgments. The authors are indebted to Mr Gert Ljungkvist, retired from SPRI – the Swedish Institute for Health Services Development – for sharing his private archive and answering many questions.

References

1. Seeman,T.: Oral history interview by Isabelle Dussuage, Urban Rosenquist, and Hans Peterson, National Museum of Science and Technology, Stockholm, Från matematikmaskin till IT, interview 61 (November 20, 2007)
2. Dávila, M. (ed.): Datorisering av medicinsk laboratorieverksamhet 1: En översikt: Transkript av ett vittnesseminarium vid Svenska Läkaresällskapet i Stockholm den (February 17, 2006) Avdelningen för teknik- och vetenskapshistoria, Kungliga Tekniska högskolan, Stockholm (2008)
3. Den svenska it-historien, http://ithistoria.se/
4. Dahlin, B.: Datagrundjournal: datorisering av informationssystem vid Gråbo vårdcentral. Spri rapport 282, Stockholm (1990)
5. Lundberg, B., Ljungkvist, G.: Patientjournaler med datorstöd – Spridning, marknadsläge och systemöversikt. Spri tryck 270, Stockholm (1995)
6. Nordestedt, B.: Datoriserad journalhantering vid Ystad lasarett – en uppföljning hösten (1994) Spri rapport 402, Stockholm (1995)
7. Spri:Styrelsen för teknisk utveckling: DASIS – datorstött informationssytem i sjukvården: datorisering i vården – ett måste. Spri tryck 67, Stockholm (1985)

The Totally Integrated Management Information System in 1960s Sweden

Gustav Sjöblom

Department of Technology Management and Economics,
Chalmers University of Technology, 412 96 Gothenburg, Sweden
gustav.sjoblom@chalmers.se

Abstract. The availability from the mid-1960s of powerful mainframe computer systems such as IBM's System 360 allowed computer specialists and rationalization experts to pursue what appeared to be the logical next step in the evolution of office rationalization: from the automation of clerical routines to the automation of decision-making. This paper argues that despite the rapid diffusion of the idea of the totally integrated, firm-wide, centralized management information system (MIS) – which, besides data processing, allowed business executives real-time information on a desktop terminal – there are few real examples of MIS implementations. A survey of the MIS projects at Volvo, Saab, Asea and SAS shows that in practice these projects had limited ambitions to provide executive information, were scaled down owing to early problems and resulted in limited systems for material requirements planning.

Keywords: 1960s, Asea, big business, EDP, management information systems, MIS, Saab, SAS, Volvo.

1 From Office Automation to Information Systems

The first digital computers for office purposes were used for the mechanization of clerical routines and had little impact on decision-making. Nevertheless, from the very beginning the new technology accompanied a dream of one-day extending office automation to include strategic decision-making by top management. With the arrival in the mid-1960s of third-generation computers with operating systems and improved storage devices, this prospect developed into a widespread idea of totally integrated management information systems (MIS). The purpose of this paper is to review and analyze the implementation of MIS in Sweden during the height of its popularity in the late 1960s, and to evaluate the phenomenon in the light of Tom Haigh's work on MIS in the United States [1]. The paper deals only with the particular vision of the total system that dominated the MIS concept in the 1960s. While MIS later came to represent an academic and professional field as well as more limited executive information systems (EIS), we will not address these here. The paper is based on contemporary business and computer press, complemented by oral history evidence and deals with, in turn, the context in which MIS emerged; which Swedish firms embarked on efforts to develop total information systems; the outcome of the implementations; the question of who promoted MIS; and its historiographical legacy.

J. Impagliazzo, P. Lundin, and B. Wangler (Eds.): HiNC3, IFIP AICT 350, pp. 83–91, 2011.

According to Haigh, many systems developers and management scientists in the 1960s had a common vision of "a comprehensive computerized system designed to span all administrative and managerial activities. While the lower level of this gargantuan information system would process the payroll and bill customers, its upper levels would provide executives with constantly updated forecasts and models of their company's position." With that, the "computer's role had been transformed, rhetorically at least, from a simple clerk-replacing processor of *data* into a mighty *information* system sitting at the very heart of management, serving executives with vital intelligence about every aspect of their firm's past, present, and future" [1].

Technologically, the MIS concept linked closely linked to the appearance of more powerful mainframe computer platforms in the mid-1960s, notably IBM's System 360. The majority of larger and medium-sized corporations were likely to have first encountered computer technology in the form of second-generation digital computers like IBM 1401, a transistorized computer with substantially higher performance compared to its predecessors. However, second generation computers had a number of limitations which mostly limited their application to batch data processing tasks: input was based on punch cards, output consisted mostly in printed reports, and magnetic tape with long access times was the usual means of secondary data storage. Third generation computer systems allowed direct-access storage devices and multiprogramming, and they set the stage for new visions of integrated information systems, spanning the entire organizations and extending the application from the operative to the strategic level [2].

In terms of ideas, MIS represented the continuation of a longstanding desire to improve productivity through rationalization and in particular automation. Whereas rationalization had previously been mainly concerned with the shop floor, from the 1950s, attention increasingly turned towards the office. In the 1950s, a popular keyword was integrated data processing (IDP), implying that data entered into a system of electromechanical or electronic data processing machines and transferred on punch cards or paper tape between machines, and even between offices using telex. As Haigh has pointed out, "MIS was IDP writ large, emphasizing better decision making rather than operational efficiency and applying techniques from operations research to transform mere data into managerially relevant information" [1]. Unlike the visions of 1950s, scholars such as Herbert Simon, Thomas Leavitt and Harold Whisler, MIS did not imply the automation of management decision- making, but the provision of information to management.

The course of events in Sweden had a lot in common with those in the United States. Electronic data processing (EDP) was introduced in the mid-1950s, beginning from 1956 with the installation of digital computers in a number of insurance companies, insurance being a very information- and transaction-intensive industry [3]. The first digital computer for office applications in Sweden, the IBM 650 machine at Folksam, was used for calculations related to life insurance, for motorcar and life insurance statistics, and for some of the office work involved in motorcar insurance previously carried out by means of conventional punch card machines [4]. The introduction of EDP in Sweden coincided with hype for the keyword automation, which promised something far more advanced than mere mechanization [5]. According to a leading expert on office technology in 1960, with EDP, one could not only "process large quantities of paperwork at a fantastic speed". More significantly, one could "provide management with concise, absolutely fresh information about the market situation and the firm's position from the point of view of accounting" – thus returning some of the managerial control which had been lost during the growth of complex organization in the twentieth century [6]. EDP advertising for computer suppliers and service bureaus around 1960 displayed images of business managers accompanied by slogans like "if one only had the facts," or "I get the statistics while they are still relevant." Thus, by the late 1950s, the vision of the fully automated office had begun to spread in Sweden. The idea was usually not automating decision-making per se, but rather automating the provision of information for managers (just as described by Haigh). For a commentator in 1958, the internal functions of the firm would remain "to mechanical brains and mass producing machines" [7]. Machines would gradually replace clerical office personnel, whereas managers remained with access to superior data for control and management of the firm. This would result in the rise of a new professional class, namely that "brain trust" which was to be in charge of the programming and development of automation [7]. The hope for automated information provision was inspired by the recent success – or at least publicity – of the new discipline of operations research, loosely defined as "a "scientific method for the provision of the basis of decision for top management" [8, 9]. Rather than a coherent set of methods or techniques, operations research was a generic term for a set of rather disparate techniques, including Monte Carlo experiments, queue theory, linear programming and game theory.

2 Third Generation Computer Systems and MIS

By the mid-1960s, the arrival of third generation computer systems, operations research, and the vision of taking automation to the strategic level had merged into a particular vision of the management information system. The term management information system has later taken on several different meanings. In the mid-1960s, it was strongly associated with a rather particular vision of a totally integrated, firm-wide information system that allowed the managing director (and sometimes his vice presidents) to access current information about the firm, preferably from a terminal on his desktop and in real-time. Using the terminal, the manager could access up-to-date information from the firm's data bank and run simulations that allowed him to improve decision-making.

Turning from the realm of ideas and to business practices, a salient aspect of MIS is the rarity of attempts to implement such systems – at least if we keep with the narrow definition of a totally integrated system. In practice, only a small number of the biggest and technologically most advanced firms in engineering and financial services endorsed MIS. At Volvo, the transport equipment manufacturer based in Gothenburg, an explicit attempt to develop a MIS entitled "Volvo Information System" (VIS). Volvo initiated it in 1964, formalized it in 1967, and ultimately discontinued in it 1972. VIS was to integrate twenty major application areas such as construction data, materials and production control, and payroll. The initial budget was SEK 30 million and 300 person-years. At the electrical engineering giant Asea in Västerås, an effort to develop an Asea Management Information System (AMIS) was undertaken marginally later than the project at Volvo, but it did not really take off. At the aerospace, motor car, and electronics firm Saab in Linköping, TIPS (initially shorthand for "Totalt Informationssystem På Saab," later for "Totalt Informations system för Produktions-Styrning") was initiated as a preliminary study in June 1967 and led to a four-year development plan by 1969 [10]. In the financial services sectors, there were also some attempts at totally integrated systems such as TOBA (TOtalt BAnksystem) at the savings banks service bureau Spadab, conceived as "a total bank system with complete integration." TOBA was one of the first online systems in Sweden driven by visions of the local savings bank manager retrieving information and running simulations on a terminal [11]. The airline company SAS did not endorse the MIS discourse, but it probably came closer to building an integrated total information system than any other Swedish firm. In 1963, on the recommendation of a department dealing with efficiency and rationalization, the SAS management decided to join all computing into a single department with offices in Copenhagen and Stockholm. SAS Data then produced an EDP Long Range Plan (ELOP), which had no explicit ambition to provide management information but in practice went further than attempts elsewhere in integrating subsystems and databases. Raine Dahlberg, at the time responsible for long-range planning at SAS Data, recalls an early decision not to aim at a "well-developed and integrated MIS system," but rather to present a set of ten different monthly Management Information Reports, MIR. [12, 13]

It is evident that the firms in question were the largest and technologically leading enterprises in Sweden. In 1964, ASEA and Volvo were the biggest groups in Sweden in terms of number of employees and Saab ranked ninth [14]. Just like SAS they moreover belonged to the top in terms of being technologically advanced. MIS was essentially a big business concept and it is debatable whether many more Swedish firms were big enough to qualify. Certainly, many other firms initiated large information systems around the same time, but few met the typical description of MIS in the trade journals – the total integration of data processing into a system providing information for top management.[1]

3   MIS at Volvo, Asea, and Saab

Since there is not enough space here to describe the individual projects in detail, instead I will present three main themes that characterize the Swedish MIS endeavors. First, although the provision of management information was often mentioned in presentations of the various MIS systems, in practice the implementation of MIS was guided by other organizational objectives. VIS was primarily "a large scale effort to integrate the many diverse applications of data processing within the Volvo company" [15]. Around 1964, Volvo ran the risk of ending up with four different incompatible computer systems within the group. In addition to the IBM machines in Gothenburg and the Saab D21 at Trollhättan, there were plans to purchase a Bull Gamma 10 at the Köping plant and a Univac system at Skövde. The head of systems development, Karl-Henrik Hübinette, and the head of operations, Anders Svedberg, notified vice

---

[1] These firms include the steel company Fagersta and the forest and paper company SCA.

president Per Ekström who in turn referred the issue to Stanford Research Institute (SRI). SRI strongly recommended a centralized data processing system for Volvo and in response to the SRI Report, Volvo set up Volvo Data as a separate subsidiary responsible for all data processing in the group (except Trollhättan) [16]. The TIPS project was motivated by the intention of Saab's top management to decrease the dependence on the Swedish Air Force and expand the firm's activities in the market for civilian products, which required a makeover of administration. Moreover, there was a desire to substitute Saab's own D22 mainframe computer for the existing IBM 7070/1401 and Saab D21. Cost savings remained a very important rationale for TIPS, through savings on the materials flow, operational control, and administrative personnel [17].

Second, the MIS projects ran into problems and they scaled down soon after initiation. VIS was off to a slow start in 1964 since the formation of Volvo Data and systems development for the new Torslanda plant in Göteborg took up most of the available resources. Around 1967, they formalized with a steering group and a project group (which met on neutral ground in Laxå, roughly equal distance from the various Volvo sites). It soon became apparent that the centralization effort underlying VIS ran counter to a wider trend in the Volvo group towards a more decentralized structure, with Passenger cars, Lorries, and Buses becoming separate subsidiaries within the group in 1969. VIS was scrapped in 1972, although many of the subprojects lived on as separate systems and VIS may have led to more systematic procedures for data processing and analyses and investigations useful in later stages [18]. As for AMIS, after about a year the project reduced to a three-person mapping of the operative functions at Asea. The resulting table showed that most of the relevant functions were difficult to integrate into a centralized system [19].

Third, what in the end came out of the MIS systems development consisted largely of systems for materials and inventory control, and to some extent production planning. These systems led to a certain degree of automation of decision-making and improved statistical data, but not at the strategic level implied by the MIS vision. At Volvo, systems for spare parts and inventory control were at the heart of data processing in general as well as the MIS modules. TIPS resulted in the projects MOPS (Material- och Produktionsstyrning) and IOL (Inmatning on line av ekonomitransaktioner) [18]. AMIS was downscaled to address specific problems of materials control, where the problem of lacking centralized control was most obvious, and they relabeled it CM (Centralt Materialstyrsystem), Central Materials Control System [19]. At SAS, MOPS (Maintenance and Overhaul Planning System) alone required some four hundred person-years of systems development and programming work; MATS (Material Supply and Inventory Control) was another major effort in the 1960s [12, 13]. The focus on materials and inventory was not coincidental. It matches the findings of contemporary investigations of computer use in Sweden [20]. Indeed, these areas correspond to those where operations research had first found its main applications in the 1950s [21]. Moreover, the eventual emergence of enterprise resource planning (ERP) systems in the 1980s owed a lot to the preceding developments in materials and production planning.

4 Explaining the MIS Legacy

Technical systems never materialize unless powerful groups of actors conceive, endorse, and promote them. In the case of MIS, Thomas Haigh has claimed that a particular professional group spread the idea: the "systems men" of the Systems and Procedures Association (SPA). Although systems men were often systems developers or other computer specialists, they were also "an alliance of staff specialists in administrative methods, management consultants, and business professors, who were all seeking to legitimate themselves as technical experts in management" [1]. For Haigh, the prominence of MIS in 1960s management discourse and (to a somewhat lower degree) practice was the outcome of the endeavors of this professional group. They tried to establish their jurisdiction "over the burgeoning world of corporate computing," to improve their status from clerical specialists to a key function in corporate management, and to extend their control into new domains, such as management reports, organizational restructuring, and strategic planning [1].

In the Swedish context, it is difficult to identify an equivalent of Haigh's systems men. In Sweden, systems men as a professional category emerged only with the onset of data processing. Specialists in administrative methods were like a subcategory of general rationalization expertise – implying a very strong focus on time and motion studies – and organized in the Swedish Rationalization Association. As a rule, the time study men did not find a place in the increasingly computer-oriented offices of the 1960s. Computer specialists instead emerged as a new group organized in the organizations *Svenska Dataföreningen* and *SSI*, which do not appear as major promoters of MIS. Neither do leading management science scholars with an interest in computing. Börje Langefors at the Royal Institute of Technology, the first professor in information processing in Sweden and a doyen of Swedish computing, was critical because of the difficulty of defining a total-optimal objective for such a system [22, 23]. The idea that management control was too elusive to be part of a system seems to have been widespread. In 1969, Sam Sjöberg at the Gothenburg School of Economics, one of the most frequent commentators on MIS, talked about "the propaganda for 'On Line Real Time Management Information Systems' promoted by machine vendors and other should be met with a no mean measure of skepticism" [24]. Olle Dopping, another leading information scholar, mentioned MIS in 1972 as "the pompous piling of one prestigious word after another" [25].[2]

In all likelihood, the MIS vision derived largely from the United States and it transferred to Sweden through the written work of management scientists and the activities in Sweden of computer supplier and management consultants. The Swedish MIS firms studied above have in common a substantial reliance on IBM as supplier of computer equipment and on Stanford Research Institute in helping to organize the firm's reorganization, long range planning, and centralization of systems development and data processing facilities. While MIS partly represented a continuation of ideas of

---

[2] There were certainly more enthusiastic voices, such as Hans B. Thorelli, Walter Goldberg at the Gothenburg School of Economics.

earlier domestic origin, these American influences were decisive in bringing about the MIS projects. SRI gained a very influential position in Sweden through the intermediation of the industrialist Marcus Wallenberg, who was chair of the board of SAS and ASEA at the time.

MIS as a term did not disappear in the early 1970s, but it received new life by the formation of the Society for Management Information Systems and its journal *Management Information Systems Quarterly*. However, the term now carried a different and more fragmented meaning, as an academic discipline or as a general framework for information systems development. Only in the 1980s, other terms replaced it like "decision support systems" or "executive information systems." However, in its late 1960s totally integrated version, MIS never achieved realization. According to Haigh, "there is no record of any major company managing to produce a fully integrated, firm wide MIS during the 1960s, or even the 1970s – still less one that included elaborate economic forecasts or linked suppliers and producers" [1]. The Swedish record tells a similar story, with even fewer attempts at building MIS systems.

Yet, the "MIS period" had left behind a negative legacy often mentioned in historical overviews of systems development in Sweden. According to a 1978 handbook in industrial production, "some of the biggest Swedish enterprises invested a couple of millions in management information systems (MIS) and discontinued the projects as they were approaching implementation. The computer fell into disrepute and there was a computer backlash in the line departments" [26]. An overview of accounting systems in Sweden, also from 1978, claimed, "the failed management information systems in large corporations in the 1960s has led to a more cautious coordination of different modules into coordinated accounting systems in the 1970s" [27]. Similar passing statements about the existence and legacy of MIS in Sweden are not hard to find in the literature [28]. It is quite possible that MIS in these statements has become a symbol of a wider tendency in the 1960s towards centralization in corporate computing – or in planning more generally for that matter – and in particular the centralization of computer facilities and control of information systems to the computer departments.

This overview of MIS implementations in Sweden has shown that the totally integrated management information system in practice was a rare phenomenon. Based on the few implementations, it hardly deserves the attention it has attracted and it may seem surprising that the MIS era in Sweden received stature by latter-day commentators. Nevertheless, MIS was always more of an idea than a practice, and the Swedish discourse of the late 1960s and early 1970s closely interlinked with the discussions of leading computer specialists and management scientists in the United States.

Acknowledgments. I am grateful to Handelsbankens forskningsstiftelser for supporting the research for this paper. I would also like to thank Thomas Haigh, my colleagues within the project, "Precursors of the IT Nation: Computer Use and Control in Swedish Society, 1955–1985," and the participants of HiNC3 for comments on earlier versions of this paper.

References

1. Haigh, T.: Inventing Information Systems: The Systems Men and the Computer, 1950–1968. Business History Review 75, 15–60 (2001)
2. Dickson, G.W.: Management Information Systems: Evolution and Status. In: Rubinoff, M., Yovits, M.C. (eds.) Advances in Computers, vol. 20, pp. 1–39. Academic Press, New York (1981)
3. Yates, J.: Structuring the Information Age: Life Insurance and Technology in the Twentieth Century. Johns Hopkins University Press, Baltimore (2005)
4. Folksams elektronmaskin först i Skandinavien, Affärsekonomi 25, 939 (1956)
5. Carlsson, A.: Elektroniska hjärnor: Debatten om datorer, automation och ingenjörer, 1955-1958. In: Widmalm, S., Fors, H. (eds.) Artefakter: Industrin, vetenskapen och de tekniska nätverken, Gidlund, Hedemora, pp. 245–285 (2004)
6. Cervin, K.: Automatisk databehandling – behövs det? Affärsekonomi 29, 1272 (1960)
7. Palmskog, F.: Individuell contra automatisk kontorsteknik. Affärsekonomi 27, 1040 (1958)
8. Dannerstedt, G.: Operationsanalys – ett praktiskt hjälpmedel i företagens tjänst. Affärsekonomi 25, 919 (1956)
9. Andrén, B.: USA-intryck av EDP-teknik. Affärsekonomi 27, 1202 (1958)
10. Murhed, C.: Kundernas syn på saken 1: Internkunden Saab. In: Yngvell, S. (ed.) Tema D22-D23: Tunga linjens uppgång och fall, Datasaabs vänner, Linköping, pp. 90–95 (1997)
11. Flyger ni för högt herr Wetterholm. Modern Datateknik 4, 33–35 (1968)
12. Sjöblom, G. (ed.): Systemutveckling och långtidsplanering vid SAS Data i Stockholm, 1964-1982: Transkript av ett vittnesseminarium vid Tekniska museet i Stockholm den (December 5, 2007) Avdelningen för teknik- och vetenskapshistoria, Kungliga Tekniska högskolan, Stockholm (2008)
13. Bergner, T.: Oral history interview by Gustav Sjöblom. National Museum of Science and Technology, Stockholm, Från matematikmaskin till IT, interview 17 (October 8, 2007)
14. Ägande och inflytande inom det privata näringslivet. SOU 1968:7. Stockholm (1968)
15. IBM: Volvo Study Report. (n.d. [probably c. 1970])
16. Dana Jr., A., Jack, W.: A Study of Centralized vs Decentralized EDP at Volvo. Stanford Research Institute Memorandum Report (November 1964)
17. Administration för 70-talet. Modern Datateknik 4, 13–15 (1968)
18. af Geijerstam, Jan (ed.): VIS/MIS – visionen om den kompletta informationen: Transkript av ett vittnesseminarium vid Chalmers tekniska högskola i Göteborg den (May 8, 2008) Avdelningen för teknik- och vetenskapshistoria, Kungliga Tekniska högskolan, Stockholm (2008)
19. Eriksson, G.: Oral history interview by Jan af Geijerstam. National Museum of Science and Technology, Stockholm, Från matematikmaskin till IT, interview 85 (October 1, 2007)
20. ADB i Sverige: Tillämpningar. Modern Datateknik 5, 21 (1969)
21. Debatt om operationsanalysen i företagens tjänst. Affärsekonomi 25, 1341 (1956)
22. Langefors, B.: System för företagsstyrning. Studentlitteratur, Lund (1968)
23. Lundin, P. (ed.): Administrativ systemutveckling i teori och praktik, 1960-1980: Transkript av ett vittnesseminarium vid Tekniska museet i Stockholm den (November 26, 2007) Avdelningen för teknik- och vetenskapshistoria, Kungliga Tekniska högskolan, Stockholm (2008)

24. Sjöberg, S.: Vilka skall ha terminaler? Modern Datateknik 5, 49–50 (1969)
25. Dopping, O.: Data via tråd. Ekonomen 49, 11 (1972)
26. Giertz, E., Andersson, J.: Industriell Produktion. Norstedt i samarbete med Sv. Civilekonomfören, Stockholm (1978)
27. Frenckner, P.: Ekonomisystem i Sverige – lite historia. In: Samuelson, L.A. (ed.) Ekonomi, pp. 9–19. Norstedt i samarbete med Sv. Civilekonomfören, Stockholm (1978)
28. Sandell, K.: Frigoscandias datachef kritisk: Misstror datasystem. Dagens Industri (February 24,1981)

The History of the Swedish ATM:
Sparfrämjandet and Metior

Björn Thodenius[1], Bernardo Bátiz-Lazo[2], and Tobias Karlsson[3]

[1] Dept. of Management and Organization, Stockholm School of Economics, Sweden
bjorn.thodenius@hhs.se
[2] University of Leicester and Bangor University, UK
b.batiz-lazo@le.ac.uk
[3] Department of Economic History, Lund University, Sweden
tobias.karlsson@ekh.lu.se

Abstract. In this paper, we describe the first decades of the history of the Swedish Automated Teller Machine (ATM). Sweden was one of the pioneers in using ATMs, starting with cash dispensers or cash machines in 1967. The first machine was made operational and shown to the press on 6 July 1967 in Uppsala at Upsala Sparbank, only one week after the first cash machine in the world was made operational in the UK. The Malmö-based company Metior manufactured the Swedish machine. This paper seeks to document the origins and the early development of cash machines by Swedish savings banks, employing oral as well as archival sources. Interestingly, we find that the key actor behind the ATM technology was not Spadab, the computer company of the saving banks, but Sparfrämjandet, a company most well known for its campaigns to encourage thrift among children.

Keywords: Automated teller machines (ATM), cash dispensers, savings banks, Sweden, technological change.

1 Introduction

Automated teller machines (ATMs) have been around for some forty years and today we can use the same card to withdraw cash all over the world. In this paper we describe the first decades of the history of the Swedish ATM. Sweden was one of the pioneers in using ATMs, starting with cash dispensers or cash machines in 1967 [1]. The first machine was made operational and shown to the press on 6 July 1967 in Uppsala at Upsala Sparbank, only one week after the first cash machine in the world was made operational in the UK [2]. The Malmö based company Metior manufactured the Swedish machine. This paper seeks to document the origins and the early development of cash machines in Sweden, employing oral as well as archival sources. Interestingly, we find that the key actor behind the ATM technology was not Spadab the computer company of the saving banks, but Sparfrämjandet, a company most well known for its campaigns to encourage thrift among children. This finding is, however, not as surprising as it may seem, since Sparfrämjandet also had the task to rationalize administrative functions among the savings banks. The ATM

J. Impagliazzo, P. Lundin, and B. Wangler (Eds.): HiNC3, IFIP AICT 350, pp. 92–100, 2011.
© IFIP International Federation for Information Processing 2011

technology was not a coincidental innovation made by technicians. Rather, we should view it as part of a modernization process within the savings banks movement that took place in the light of intensified competition and rising transaction costs.

The reminder of this paper proceeds as follows. The next section provides some background regarding the origins and the growth of savings banks in Sweden. The third section documents the adoption of cash machines by Swedish savings banks and the way this development intertwined with the history of the engineering firm Metior (later to be Asea-Metior). The fourth and final section encompasses our conclusions.

2 The Swedish Savings Banks – A Brief Overview

During the first half of the twentieth century, competition between savings banks and commercial banks in Sweden was rather weak. Each bank had different customers and offered different services. In some instances they even came together to collaborate in joint projects. Whereas the commercial banks had experienced serious problems during the inter-war period, savings banks flourished while operating mainly in local and regional markets. Although their number had already started a downtrend (approaching 450 in 1945 and as few as 60 in 2008), their joint share of total deposits increased from 26 to 43 percent between 1920 and 1950 and profits were high [3].

The decades that followed the end of World War II were characterized by overall economic growth, increased affluence and expansion of the welfare state in Sweden. This era also saw increased competition in the banking sector as the commercial banks began to widen their customer base (while aiming to attract all sorts of new customers, from companies to wage earners). Handelsbanken, for example, launched itself as the "people's bank" in 1950. Shortly afterwards, Handelsbanken and other commercial banks used the contacts developed while financing the working capital of manufacturing companies to offer these companies direct payroll deposit services.

The savings banks were initially hesitating to this new service. However, a group of younger managers pushed for a more aggressive corporate strategy [1, 3]. Throughout the 1950s, these young managers were under the leadership of Sven G. Svensson, director of Sparfrämjandet, who also organized annual conferences in Saltsjöbaden to facilitate the meeting of like-minded young managers [3]. They united with the idea that the savings banks had to adjust to ongoing social change. Furthermore, their conviction was that the savings banks should meet the challenge of Handelsbanken and other commercial banks, not by demanding protection from the state but by introducing better services. Many ideas that emerged from the conferences at Saltsjöbaden were implemented during the 1960s as the attendants reached influential positions within the savings banks. As a result, the Swedish savings banks evolved from small-scale savings institutions to "modern" business-oriented banks. During this process, the emphasis on thrift was downplayed while savings banks began to view depositors more like customers than savers.

Rocketing administrative costs provided a strong incentive for the savings banks to seek greater labor efficiency through the application of new technologies. As suggested by Table 1, the increase in the nominal value of deposits accompanied an increase in the value of administrative costs (measured as a percent of total deposits). It is with this background that they intensified efforts to introduce mainframe computers for various tasks during the 1960s.

Table 1. Administration costs in the 80 biggest Swedish savings banks, 1962–67 [1]

Year	Million SEK	% of deposits
1962	114	0.847
1963	128	0.895
1964	150	0.963
1965	176	1.063
1966	213	1.124
1967	257	1.194

As mentioned, the savings banks were late to respond to the direct payment of payroll service offered by commercial banks. This attitude was to change in 1960 when most of the bigger savings bank introduced that service. However, unfortunately, the number of individual accounts they managed to attract proved to be much lower than expected. This became evident two years later in 1962 when the commercial banks had more than twice as many accounts as the savings banks (387,000 and 143,000, respectively). However, close links with trade unions helped the savings banks to transform their position and eventually dominate the direct payroll payment service. By the end of 1970, the savings banks had no less than 870,000 accounts [1, 3]. Table 2 below illustrates the way growth in business volume accompanied an increase in staff in Sweden.

Table 2. Estimated number of employees and deposits in Swedish savings banks, 1962–67 [1]

Year	Number of employees	Increase in %	Deposits million SEK	Increase in %
1962	3,500		17,699	
1963	4,100	17	18,957	7
1964	4,700	15	20,531	8
1965	5,200	11	22,263	8
1966	5,800	12	24,511	10
1967	6,400	10	27,259	11

While increased involvement in direct deposit of payroll reduced the number of checks passing through the banking system, the savings banks found that this involvement was not without costs. To keep up with the commercial banks, the savings banks had to expand their workforce. This resulted in payroll and related costs growing faster than the pace at which the value of total deposits increased. Consequently, administration costs bolted. Administration costs (expressed as a share of deposits) increased by 40 percent between 1962 and 1967. Table 3 below summarizes a closer study of the four largest savings banks. It revealed that the number of transactions (withdrawals and deposits) increased by 125 percent, whereas their total funds increased by 64 percent [1].

Table 3. Transaction volume and deposits in the four biggest Swedish savings banks, 1962–67 [1]

Year	Number of deposits and withdrawals	Value of deposits in million SEK
1962	2,011,600	989
1963	3,077,600	1,062
1964	3,528,900	1,147
1965	3,843,300	1,246
1966	4,473,000	1,425
1967	4,526,700	1,626

Another aspect of the modernization of the Swedish savings banks that took place in the 1960s was concentration. In the beginning of the 1960s, there were still over 400 individual savings banks in Sweden. Because of amalgamation between small units operating in the countryside and city-based entities, only 273 savings banks remained in 1970. The concentration process went on during the following decades with merges between the biggest banks. By 1989, there were 109 savings banks left, but this population consisted of 20 big banks with regional coverage holding 80 percent of total deposits, and 95 local banks [3].

Rising administrative costs and an increasing number of accounts in the late 1950s and the 1960s required Swedish savings banks to take urgent action. A major step towards computerization occurred in 1958 when a Technical Committee formed within the Swedish savings banks association. Per Olov Rimvall, a committee member was a driving force behind research to solve the "bookkeeping problem" in the savings banks. Eventually he initiated the formation of a commonly owned computer and data processing company in 1961, later called Spadab. However, to all appearances, Spadab did not play a central role in the development of cash machines. Within the saving banks movement, the agent of change occurred in another organization, namely Sparfrämjandet.

3   Sparfrämjandet and Metior

3.1   Sparfrämjandet

Originally, Sparfrämjandet was the propaganda department of the Swedish savings banks association. According to Hessling [4], this department had three main aims. First, the department encouraged thrift, both internally within the savings banks and externally among the public. Second, it served as a publishing house. Third, the department became a central purchasing unit to coordinate purchases of material that the savings banks needed in their retail branches. The department regularly published printed material and was responsible for launching national campaigns. In 1941, the propaganda department was renamed Sparfrämjandet and in 1943, it became an independent company. One reason to change the name was the negative connotation of the term "propaganda." The new Sparfrämjandet had three departments, namely publishing, external relations, and central purchasing.

Sparfrämjandet was the initial driving force for savings banks to adopt cash dispensers because the central purchasing department of Sparfrämjandet had a parallel development within automation. In 1960, Hans Rausing and the Rausing company started to develop and sell coin sorting machines to the savings banks. This later became the firm Restello, a company within the Tetra Pak group.

For some years, the saving banks and Sparfrämjandet had been discussing the possibilities of automating cash dispensing to rationalize the bank tellers' handling of cash in the bank offices. One other need was to make it possible to distribute cash when the bank offices were closed, especially as had been the case in Britain, after the banks closed retail branches on Saturdays in 1969.

3.2 The Metior Cash Dispenser

Sparfrämjandet wanted some type of machine or automat that was able to dispense bank notes and discussed the issue with Metior, a company in the Tetra-Pak group that manufactured automatic petrol pumps and had taken over production of the Restello coin sorting machines. The discussions went on for some time but the co-operation was not fully successful. Metior then contacted the commercial bank Svenska Handelsbanken who became the new partner in the development of a cash dispenser [1, 5]. According to Körberg [1], Bengt Wetterholm, the CEO of Spadab at that time, reinitiated the contacts with Metior when learning about the interest of Svenska Handelsbanken [1, 6].

Here it is worth noting that there are very few references to Spadab in Metior's archives. It seems like the company mainly had contacts with Sparfrämjandet and that this organization influenced the design of the first generations of cash dispensers in Sweden. For example, when Metior was about to demonstrate its first machine in December 1966, it invited a representative from Sparfrämjandet but no one from Spadab.

The initial demonstration was planned for 11 January 1967 in Malmö. There were also plans to start testing the machines in Uppsala in January or February that same year. It is unclear whether the demonstration and subsequent tests actually took place according to plans, but we can establish that the first Swedish cash machine became operational and shown to the press on 6 July 1967 in Uppsala. This was only nine days after the first British cash machine was operational by Barclays Bank and De La Rue, and a couple of days before Svenska Handelsbanken showed its first Metior machine.

After some months of testing, the public started to use the cash dispenser in Uppsala twenty-four hours a day in September of 1967. The first machine had some problems and it took some time to get them sorted and make the machine operational most of the time.

In early 1968, Metior had manufactured five machines. Metior still called them prototypes and of these five machines, the savings banks had two and the commercial banks three. In the spring of 1968, mass production began because Sparfrämjandet ordering twenty machines. This order included a number of specific requirements, indicating that the savings banks actively contributed to shape the new technology.

They delivered about twenty machines to Switzerland and one to the Netherlands. Each machine sold at 58,000 to 59,000 SEK. About a year later, in April 1969, the

Swedish savings banks ordered Metior cash dispensers for 1.8 million SEK, Metior's biggest order so far. By February 1970, Metior had delivered 37 cash dispensers for the Swedish market, of which savings banks bought 24. At the same time, Metior had exported 141 cash dispensers. For instance, Metior had achieved a dominating position in Switzerland, where De La Rue had left the market, and was about to enter the French market in collaboration with Transac, a division of Compagnie Industrielle des Télécommunications (CIT).

The first cash dispenser went under the name "utbetalningsautomat" and later "Bankomat." However, Svenska Handelsbanken and the commercial banks soon acquired this name as the brand name for their dispensers. During its initial years, Metior developed four generations of cash dispensers. The first generation was not sold commercially. They developed the second and third generations for savings banks and the fourth for commercial banks and the French market.

Bankomat Mark 2 and 3 were made of steel and had punched holes for identification, while in the UK Chubb's plastic card had punched holes, Barclay-De La Rue used a cheque-sized voucher with a magnetic stripe and Speytec-Burroughs' plastic card had a magnetic stripe on the back [7]. Bankomat Mark 4 used a card with information embedded in a magnetic stripe that had been developed by the French Société Générale de Automation. To withdraw money from the Metior machines, a one used a PIN-code together with the card.

Whereas UK banks had been adamant not to deploy machines until their security had been tested [7], some years after the first Swedish machines were being used the security of the system became an issue. Withdrawals using fake cards started to appear. Someone had discovered the algorithm used to associate card numbers with the PIN-code. One Easter holiday someone travelled around Sweden, withdrawing money from each machine visited. This led Metior to contact Bofors in order to help with the security issues. The cooperation led to Bofors buying 80 percent of Metior's shares on 31 August 31 1969. However, Bofors' interest and competence on these security issues regarding cash dispenser were insufficient. New problems emerged in October of 1971 and of such magnitude that the savings banks considered closing down its whole fleet of Metior machines. As a result, Bofors sold the control of Metior to ASEA in 1973.

It is interesting to note that the Easter holiday incident lead to a change in the internal regulations of the savings banks. Before the incident, the retail branch that had the dispensers was solely responsible for losses that might arise. This changed after the incident so that all savings banks collectively shared any losses resulting from the malfunction of cash machines.

Already at an early stage, in May 1968, Metior delivered the first machine connected online to the Malmö computer center. The second to fourth generations of Bankomats were all able to connect online via modem and Mark 4 connected to a call system. However, most cash machines at the savings banks operated as stand-alone, off-line machines.

A turning point came in 1971 because of two developments. First, commercial banks within the Swedish Bankers Association, the post office, and the Federation of Swedish Rural Credit Societies set up the Automatic Cash Dispenser Center. The aim of this independent company was to install and run cash dispensing equipment for the consortia, determine where the machines would be located, market its services (under the Bankomat brand) and administer card registration, data processing, clearing and statistical information. In November 1972, fifteen Asea-Metior cash machines became operational for the consortia in Stockholm. In 1973, thirteen machines became operational in Gothenburg and one more in Stockholm. The following year, ten more dispensers became operational in Stockholm. By 1974, the savings banks remained outside of the consortia that, at the same time, aimed to deploy one hundred machines throughout Sweden to service 1.8 million direct payroll deposit accounts. Between November 1972 and January 1974, banks in the Automatic Cash Dispenser Center consortia issued 29,443 cash machine cards and dispensed some SEK 66 million (USD 14.54 million), with an average withdrawal equal to SEK 268 (USD 59).

A second important development took place when the new director of Spadab, Jan Rydh, attended the Automated Teller Machine Conference in Chicago in 1971. Rydh reminisced that during discussions dwelling on investments in off-line dispensers on the fringes of the conference, out of impulse he made the sudden decision to regard investments in off-line machines a sunk (i.e. irrecoverable) cost [8]. Colleagues attending the conference received the decision; upon their return to Sweden, engineers at Spadab were free to start what became the Minuten project. The aim of this project was the adoption of online cash dispensers by the savings banks. In search of potential suppliers, they made contacts with a number of manufacturers of cash dispensers and in the end, three companies competed for the project. These were the Swedish company Asea-Metior, the British company Chubb, and the US-based Docutel. Resulting deliberations caused savings banks to abandon Metior in 1975 by choosing Docutel as their supplier of ATM devices (online cash machines).

There are several competing explanations behind the move by the savings banks to abandon Metior. One major factor, however, was the weak US dollar at that time which made the Asea-Metior dispenser more costly than the Docutel machine [8]. Datasaab handled the installation and service in Sweden. This engineering company was at the start of its collaboration with Leif Lundblad and his Stockholm-based Inter Innovation company. Lundblad had developed its own cash dispensing mechanism to accommodate the differences between dollar notes and European currencies. The experience which Datasaab had acquired of the Docutel machines combined with Lundblad's dispensing mechanism, led to the decision to develop a Datasaab ATM. However, before presenting a working machine, Datasaab became part of Ericsson Information Systems. It produced and installed a few machines in a number of countries.

The savings banks were the first to use this new generation of ATMs. These ATMs were initially known as mini-banks and 'Minuten' and the first machine was installed on 24 May 1977 in the city of Falun. In total, Docutel installed 600 machines [5]. From the beginning, all Minuten machines were connected online. In 1982, Spadab searched the market for a new generation of ATMs. Spadab wanted to buy 1,000 new ATMs. The machine that Datasaab had started to develop did not fulfill the demands of Spadab. Instead, Ericsson contacted Omron; in 1984, they signed a contract and started deploying new ATMs. In total, they delivered to the savings banks 900 ATMs of this type.

The Minuten network competed with the network built around the commercial banks (called "Bankomat"). In later years, clearing agreements between the two networks allowed bank customers to use each other's network.

4 Conclusion

In this paper, we have explored the first steps in the emergence of self-service technology in banking. The focus has been on the savings banks, since they played an especially important part in the early development. It would also be interesting to investigate closer the early development in Svenska Handelsbanken before 1966–67.

Our purpose has been to research technology and corporate strategy in their social and historical context, that is, the dynamics of the design, construction, development, implementation and use of specialized technology [9, 10].

What we find among the most interesting aspects in the early development is the key role of Sparfrämjandet and that the interest of the saving banks' computer company Spadab seems to have been low in the beginning. This finding is, however, and as stated before, not as surprising as it may seem, since Sparfrämjandet also had the task to rationalize administrative functions among the savings banks.

We also note that the ATM technology was not a coincidental innovation made by technicians. Rather, we should see it as a part of a modernization process in the savings banks movement that took place in the light of intensified competition and rising transaction costs.

The role of the company Metior is also crucial for the early development and it would be interesting to make deeper studies of the company and its roots. The exact story of the first online machines also requires further investigation.

References

1. Körberg, I.: Förnyelsen: Sparbankernas historia 1945–1980. Ekerlids förlag, Stockholm (2006)
2. Bátiz-Lazo, B.: Emergence and Evolution of ATM Networks in the UK, 1967–2000. Business History 51(1), 1–27 (2009)
3. Forsell, A.: Moderna tider i Sparbanken: Om organisatorisk omvandling i ett institutionellt perspektiv. Nerenius & Santérus förlag, Stockholm (2002)
4. Hessling, T.: Att spara eller inte spara – vilken fråga! Den sparfrämjande verksamheten 1920–1970. Sparfrämjandet, Stockholm (1990)
5. Wentzel, V.: Pengar på Minuten. In: Hallberg, T.J. (ed.) Tema bank: Datasaab och bankerna (1996)
6. Elanders, A.B.: Västerås, The Archive of Metior AB (MAB), Huvud- och dagböcker (HD) 1966–1971, (series 1), vol. 8–14
7. Bátiz-Lazo, B., Reid, R.: Evidence from the Patent Record on the Development of Cash Dispensers and ATM Technology. In: IEEE History of Telecommunications Conference, Paris (2008)
8. Thodenius, B.: Teknisk utveckling i bankerna fram till 1985: Transkript av ett vittnesseminarium vid Tekniska museet. Trita-HST 2008:26. KTH, Philosophy and History of Technology, Stockholm (2008)
9. Orlikowski, W., Barley, S.: Technology and Institutions: What can Research on Information Technology and Research on Organizations Learn from Each Other? MIS Quarterly 25, 145–165 (2001)
10. Bridgman, T., Willmott, H.: Institutions and Technology: Frameworks for Understanding Organizational Change – the Case of a Major ICT Outsourcing Contract. Journal of Applied Behavioural Science 42(1), 110–126 (2006)

Appendix: Secondary Sources

Bátiz-Lazo, B., Del Angel, G.: Competitive Collaboration and Market Contestability: Cases in Mexican and UK banking (1945–1975). Accounting, Business and Financial History 13(3), 1–30 (2003)

Bátiz-Lazo, B., Maixé-Altés, J.C.: Managing Technological Change by Committee: The Computerization of Savings Banks in Spain and the UK (circa 1960-1988). In: BHC/EBHA Joint Conference, Milan (2009)

Bátiz-Lazo, B., Maixé-Altés, J. C.: Organisational Change and the Computerisation of British and Spanish Savings Banks, circa 1950-1985. XVth World Economic History Congress Utrecht (2009)

Bátiz-Lazo, B., Wardley, P.: Banking on Change: Information Systems and Technologies in UK High Street Banking, 1919-1969. Financial History Review 14(2), 177–205 (2007)

Bridgman, T., Willmott, H.: Institutions and Technology: Frameworks for Understanding Organizational Change – the Case of a Major ICT Outsourcing Contract. Journal of Applied Behavioural Science 42(1), 110–126 (2006)

Ekebrink, I.: Cash Dispensing: A Joint Venture in Sweden. Magazine of Bank Administration: 10–12 and 63 (1974)

Elanders A.B.: Västerås: Metior AB (MAB), Huvud- och dagböcker (HD) 1966–1971, (series 1), volumes 8–14

Frame, W. S., White, L.J.: Technological Change, Financial Innovation, and Diffusion in Banking. Federal Reserve Bank of Atlanta, Atlanta (2009)

Guerriero Wilson, R.: 'The Machine Should Fit the Work': Organisation and Method and British Approaches to New Technology in Business. History and Technology 24(4), 321–333 (2008)

Spadab: Från fjäderpenna till microchip: Den tekniska utvecklingen i sparbankerna. Stockholm, Sparfrämjandet (1987)

Swedbank Central Archive, Stockholm: Spadab files, several. Anonymous, 'Diverse' (May 6, 1965)

Electronic Securities:
The Introduction of an Electronic Registration and Settlement System for the Norwegian Securities Market

Jan Hellstrøm

Novanta, Rasmus Winderens vei 36, 0373 Oslo
janhell@me.com

Abstract. The development of computerized systems in the financial industry facilitated the growth of the stock exchange market for institutional and private investors. Paperless settlement systems for stocks and bonds were first introduced in the Nordic region. The successful introduction of the new infrastructure for the securities markets was the result of solid cooperation between market participants and authorities, which made it possible to implement major changes in the incumbent manual systems in record time.

Keywords: Central Securities Depository (CSD), electronic registration, financial industry, stock exchange market.

1 Introduction

Back in the first half of the 1980s, the Norwegian securities market experienced a tremendous growth. The stock exchange market started to develop from a rather closed community to an open marketplace with a large number of both institutional and small private investors. The number of transactions challenged the incumbent manual systems. Equity turnover increased from NOK 1.7 billion in 1982 to 31.8 billion in 1985, and bond turnover increased from 5.8 billion in 1983 to 75.9 billion in 1985. At its worst, it had taken over three months before a transaction at the stock exchange was settled and new share certificates were issued to the buyer.

The market was close to a systemic crisis and among its participants there was broad consensus for a major change. The idea of a dematerialized Central Securities Register developed rapidly. In 1982, the Minister of Finance, Rolf Presthus, announced the need for a modern securities infrastructure, and urged the banks and the other market participants to find a solution. He said that a central securities depository would make it possible to introduce tax deduction for individual savings in shares as well as generally improve control regarding taxation of securities, which at that time was an important political issue. There was strong potential for an efficient operation to replace the physical securities of book-entries with an electronic register. The rights to shares and bonds would be linked to a registration rather than to a document.

J. Impagliazzo, P. Lundin, and B. Wangler (Eds.): HiNC3, IFIP AICT 350, pp. 101–107, 2011.

Against this background, Norway's three main banks (Den norske Creditbank, Christiania Bank og Kreditkasse and Bergen Bank) established a committee in 1982 to study the introduction of a Central Securities Depository (CSD) in Norway. The conclusion from the committee was generally accepted, but there was a need for broader support from all participants in the market. An all-embracing project group was launched in May of 1983 to study technical and legal implications of an electronic system. Denmark had introduced the paperless registration of listed bonds in 1983 and the project group was much inspired by the Danish CSD organization VP. The project group delivered its recommendation in June 1984 and at the same time an interim company (Verdipapirsentralen under establishment) was set up. This organization immediately began to hire people to plan for the implementation of the ICT system and to prepare for market readiness.

2 The Stakeholders

It was a challenging task establishing a new entity, like a CSD, in the network of players in the financial market. Some of them had an interest in retaining their existing business, or at least as much of it as possible. It was a reality that the new paperless system would result in substantial cost reductions due to the major decrease of manual operations and consequent cuts in manpower. This was broadly accepted, even by the employees' organizations. The financial industry was experiencing tremendous growth and it was possible to move people to other positions. This situation lasted at least until Norway's bank crisis in the early 1990s, when thousands of people were laid off, partly as a result of the use of computerized systems and the reduction of manual tasks in the industry.

The stakeholders were more concerned that the new system would change the balance between the players. Until then, the largest players had invested in ICT systems and staff training to provide specialized securities handling. In addition, the companies had outsourced the operation of the share-register and corporate action handling to the banks. The largest players had economy of scale compared to the smaller ones and there was a major concern that the new system would change the balance of competition in the market. There was also a worry that the new entity would be too powerful and initiate a disintermediation of function from users and expand the scope of business.

3 The Business Model and the Legal Foundation

The challenge was finding the right combination of a technical system and a legal platform. Traditionally, the legal rights to a share had been linked to a physical document, the share or bond certificate. In order to exploit the efficiency of a fully computerized system, it was imperative to remove such paper handling and to change the regulation to allow electronic registration of securities.

In the record time of just one year, a new law for a Central Securities Register was enacted, including changes to the law governing companies, and other related regulations. Some legal specialists later criticized some detailed parts of this law, for example, what amount of time in the computer systems should be used for priorities between concurrent claims and pledges. It subsequently took a period of three years to solve these detailed issues.

The legal and organizational design was based on some important cornerstones: the electronic register would be based on the concept of accounts for the owners' securities and on sub-registers for information about the issued securities.

The CSD was regulated in a special law, which determined its status and organization. The law also regulated the legal conditions and implications of electronic registrations. VPS was given exclusive rights to carry out registrations according to the law. The new entity's scope of business was strictly prescribed to running the securities register and some connected tasks, like operating the securities' settlement system.

The company would be organized as a self-owned and self-financed institution led by a broad-based council and a smaller board of directors.

To utilize the current network of customer services, account operators such as banks and brokers were to carry out all registrations. The concept of central and de-central registration was not only an efficient way of utilizing the current infrastructure, but also an important division of work. The banks and brokers network would maintain their customer relations, and the CSD would provide the technical infrastructure and operate the register.

There were, however, discussions about direct access for large investors and companies. Some of these were worried that intermediaries would add costs to the use of the system. The banks, for their part, were concerned that the CSD would bypass their business and offer services directly to their clients. After many years of operation, the experience is that the bank/broker network still has the customer relation, but most of the services connected to the register information are delivered by the CSD as an application service provider. The added cost of the banks/brokers for the basic services has been reduced over the years and more or less covers "cost plus" today.

Political problems emerged in the government during the processes. The right wing government supported the introduction of the proposed new securities system, with the exception of the mandatory registration of all Norwegian bonds and securities listed at the Oslo Stock Exchange. The Ministry of Finance stated that VPS would be a rational and efficient central securities register and that mandatory registration was regarded as unnecessary. The regulation was, however, changed a couple of years later, imposing compulsory registration of the main financial instruments in the Norwegian market. This amendment was primarily explained as a consideration for efficient tax control.

4 The IT Design

The planning and analysis of the business architecture started in parallel. Since the business model was based on central registration and decentralized customer service, it was rational to use the current banking network for data entry, inquiries, and reports. Most of the brokers had in-house ICT systems for client ledgers and accounting, but trading at the Stock Exchange was still floor-based, which required that personnel from the brokerage firms were present at the stock exchange. The ICT architecture had to combine the current network with the new application requirement for reliability, safety, and privacy. Leased direct lines were regarded as providing acceptable security against fraud and misuse of information. While decryption of the lines was an option for the customers, it was never made a requirement for access to the system and, not surprising, was never used. There was, however, much effort spent in setting up an extensive end-to-end control to identify the connected terminals and users. The weak point regarding control was the existing connected bank/broker network. The central system had limited control over the reliability and protection of the local networks at the customer premises, which had to be regulated through agreements to reduce a potential loss for the CSD, due to security breaks at the locations of the connected users. After years of operation, no unauthorized access to the system has ever been discovered.

The design of the central system was a major issue. Time and costs were essential. Since it was too time-consuming to analyze and implement a new architecture from scratch, a quick decision was made to reuse the main architecture, platform, and application of the Danish system. The Danes had spent much effort designing and developing a state-of-the-art ICT system, applying the slogan "make it simple," both for functionality and technical implementation. The Danish platform was based on Yourdon's structured analysis and had a robust architecture with separate communication and application layers. The implementation was carried out on an IBM mainframe system, utilizing software components such as the S2000 database system, Rovsing spooling facilities, PL/I programming language, CICS transaction server, and other popular facilities from the 1980s. The book "Up and Running" by Dines Hansen from 1984 describes the design and implementation of the Danish securities system.

In retrospect, not all of these choices were the best ones. The S2000 database system was replaced with DB2 after some years. In addition, the industry's use of PL/I decreased over the years and it was difficult to hire people with PL/I knowledge. This made the company vulnerable with respect to critical know-how. The architecture was robust for many years, until the Internet applications required more flexible functionality for the end-users. On the other hand, the system was up and running in a very short time and the operation cost proved to be competitive. The cooperation with the Danes was very helpful and the system was in use by mid-1986, after less than two years developing and implementing it.

The support agreement with the Danish VP for systems and implementation had a price tag of DKK 25 million, which mainly covered the basic system for the bond market. VPS had to develop the functionality for equity and other requirements for the Norwegian market. After eighteen months developing and testing the system, the first production started in May 1986. The total investment in systems, hardware, and software was approximately NOK 100 million, of which about one half was for system development, including the fee to VP in Denmark.

5 Up and Running

The practical preparations for the establishment of the company VPS were started at the same time as the working committee delivered their recommendations. In June

1984 the main players took the chance to finance and establish an interim company. This organization began to hire people, rent office space, acquire hardware and software, and make agreements with the Danish CSD organization VP. The cooperation with VP was crucial. The use of the Danish architecture and platform saved a lot of time for the approximately sixty people who were recruited during a six-month period. There was no time to discuss basic architectural ICT issues.

The planning of the project was a crucial task. This complex project had many stakeholders who all needed strong coordination. In spite of this, simple milestone planning with a minimum of paper and reporting was implemented. The master plan for the project was written on one A4 paper, and was the only report that the project leader used for the board of directors.

All employees were sent to Denmark for introduction training of the main framework of the system. In that way people were able to start with systems development for the Norwegian functionality directly. It was, however, a challenge that most of the people who were recruited had little knowledge about the highly specialized securities market. There was well-pronounced skepticism from the specialists in the banks and the brokerage firms about the new IT people. Nevertheless, bridges were built, user groups engaged, decisions taken and, after some time, respect was generated.

The first transfer to electronic securities in VPS started in May of 1986 with the commercial banks qua public limited companies. The rest of the companies were converted in September/October and all the bonds in November of 1986. Later, services have been expanded to other financial instruments like derivatives and mutual funds.

6 Who Should Pay?

After implementation, one major question remained. Who should pay? Everyone was in agreement that the total cost was lower than before. However, should the new prices be related to the savings compared to the old system, to the use of the resources in the electronic system, or to a kind of market price? The annual cost of running the new system was approximately NOK 100 million for the first years and covered amortizations and operations' costs. In the plans and the analysis done prior to the start-up, it was stated that the fees for the users of the system should be cost-based. The challenge was to devise a model of how to distribute costs in a system with a 90 percent fixed cost-base. Another main problem was which elements should be charged for and who should pay for them. In the old document-based system, the costs were to a large degree connected to the manual handling and even to the value of the transaction. A political barrier was that the authorities had clearly stated that the small investors should not pay more for their ownership of shares and bonds than they had in the old system. For the broad majority this was close to zero, because most people had their share or bond certificates in a drawer or under the mattress at home. Some people may have had their documents together with other valuables in a safe deposit box in a bank, but only the larger investors had their securities under safe-keeping in a bank, for which they paid an annual fee.

A purely cost-based model was in contradiction to main pricing models in the financial sector. It was not natural that a company or a bond with a capital of one billion should pay the same as one with ten million, which raised a new debate between the bond issuing firms and the public limited companies. The bonds usually had substantially higher value than equity, especially when we include the government bonds. The problem with prices based on a purely cost-based model was that all units tended to cost the same, for example, the fee for an investor account for Goldman Sachs would be the same as one for Aunt Olga. It became obvious that we had to combine a cost-based model with one that was broadly accepted in the industry, taking the political limitations into account. A long debate started among the board members and in the trade organizations for the different user groups, going so far that the board and management were threatened with legal action. At one point, the employees' representative in the board asked the members; "If you really think the costs are so high, why did you start this project?" He was assured that everyone was better off than before and that it was purely a debate on how to divide the cost between the different user groups.

In Denmark, a quite different approach to dividing the cost had been taken. There, a small group of the users had been gathered and the main distribution of costs between them had been determined. At the end of the year, any discrepancies in the budget were cleared and settled. We sometimes regretted that we had not chosen the Danish approach.

After some hard work, the company managed to produce a cost and price model which was broadly accepted by all user groups. The concept was based on an analysis of all cost generators of the main services. For example, the distribution of costs from the computer system was calculated according to the use of computer resources such as use of CPU minutes, disk access, use of storage, network utilization, back-up capabilities, and operating hours, among others. An internationally recognized consultancy firm controlled the model and the figures. This gave the company a cost base, which was used to calculate fees according to a set of business principles, the main ones of which included the following:

- The user who generates a transaction has to pay for the service
- Some services should have fees based on capital value rather than costs
- Small investors are exempted from paying for the use of a securities account
- A special fee for large investors should cover the costs of the small non-paying clients
- The banks should receive compensation from the issuers for customer service to the small investors
- Some charges should have volume discounts

The distribution between user groups after the new cost/price model was that the investor group should pay approximately 25 percent, the brokers 25 percent, the bond issuers 15 percent, and the issuers of equity 35 percent. Over the years, this distribution has changed with the development of the market and the introduction of new services.

After years with a high degree of tension, the pricing system ended up in a hybrid resource/market pricing schedule which still uses the main principles, but with some adjustments. The cost model has been developed to reflect the fact that today's cost generators are manpower and not computer resources. The fees have been gradually reduced, because the volumes have increased substantially more than the costs.

7 Lessons Learned

The establishment of VPS and the transition to a dematerialized securities system has, without doubt, been a great success. One of the reasons was that new regimes were continuously implemented. The old workflows were not copied, the banks, brokers, and issuers had to decommission their old systems and implement new business rules for the processing of settlement, custody, and corporate action. In fact, the changes were so substantial that they would probably not have been possible to implement, if the market had not been in crisis. Of course, it helped that the authorities could introduce better tax control of securities capital and transactions. The years after have proven that all participants in the market have benefited from better control of the securities market facilitated by increased transparency and consistent procedures.

Later analysis has shown substantial cost savings, better control, and faster market operations for both intermediaries and end-customers. A major player in the London market put it this way, "In Norway you have created a national securities infrastructure with integrated custody, registrars and settlement agents for less than 25 mill € pr year, no one can beat that."

References

1. Odelstingsproposisjon nr. 83 (1984-1985)
2. Innstilling fra arbeidsgruppe nedsatt for å utrede de juridiske og tekniske sider ved etablering av en Verdipapirsentral i Norge. Oslo (June 22, 1984)
3. Annual Reports, Verdipapirsentralen
4. Dines Hansen, H.: Up & Running: A Case Study of Successful Systems Development. Yourdon Press, N.Y (1984)

How New Computing Technology Reformed the Audit Profession

Bjørn Barth Jacobsen

University of Nordland
bjorn.barth.jacobsen@stud.hibo.no

Abstract. This paper describes how the audit profession went through a paradigm restructuring itself, by taking advantage of ICT, which led to a wave of mergers from 1987 to 1998. The paper also presents two cases of fraud; the Kreuger and the Enron affairs. The latter led to the conviction of Arthur Andersen for obstruction of justice, which resulted in the termination of the company's activities, due to lack of confidence.

Keywords: Accounting, Andersen Consulting, audit, computing technology, Enron, fraud, ICT, Ivar Kreuger.

1 Prologue

When Ivar Kreuger committed suicide in March 1932, the Swedish government called upon the U.S. audit firm Price Waterhouse (PW), which revealed that a quarter of a billion dollars in assets did not exist. The largest case of fraud in history initiated the reformation process that created the U.S. Securities and Exchange Commission (SEC) in 1934. It was given authority to determine the improved accounting practices which became known as Generally Accepted Accounting Principles (GAAP) that provided auditors with the tools and authority to create order in the financial markets. These markets had been governed by *animal spirits;* irrational financial acts resembling casino behaviour.

In this historically-based text, I focus on the auditor, his roles and tools before and after World War II. One of the roles was to detect fraud. Pre-war auditors used mechanical bookkeeping machines such as Facit, Underwood, Olivetti, and IBM. How could these machines be trusted? In an old audit magazine I found the following statement from a Danish auditor, "the auditor cannot accept all mechanical calculations. All machines may fail in their automatic functions, and an operator may purposely manipulate the machines" [1]. He also advised that two independent accounts should be drawn up to improve controls, particularly when auditing banks and insurance companies.

The war brought new challenges to the audit profession, which contributed to the U.S. military efforts and spurred new approaches for achieving economic objectives and raising money. Increasingly complex wartime Treasury and IRS regulations in the U.S. resulted in specialized tax practices that diverged from GAAP. The logistics of war strained the *mechanized* pre-war clerical routines. Audit testing and internal

J. Impagliazzo, P. Lundin, and B. Wangler (Eds.): HiNC3, IFIP AICT 350, pp. 108–116, 2011.

control procedures were introduced in defence-related systems driven by tight deadlines and expanded the scope of work. New technology that could manage large amounts of information was required, which contributed to the development of the first *electronic computers* ENIAC & EDVAC during 1943–47.

The wartime experience with computers provided a foundation for post-war accountants, transforming audit reporting systems into useful management tools. After the war, Price Waterhouse separated these activities into a *Systems Department*, the first consulting function of which, later named Management Advisory Services (MAS), staffed by specialists without an accounting background, contributed to a significant strategic change of the profession's direction.   These professional consultants, attached to audit companies, were working for the government, large industries, banks, and insurance companies which required experts in hard- and software and applied system engineering.

The first commercial computer, UNIVAC I, was developed by Remington Rand (RR) and installed at the U.S. Bureau of Census in 1951, followed by forty-five units to governmental and business institutions.   In 1953, General Electric hired MAS-consultants from Arthur Andersen (AA), PW's main competitor, to program their first payrolls on the UNIVAC I.

The diversion into MAS changed the focus of AA's business, gradually reforming the firm's strategic concept. Specializing into computing consulting applications created a new profitable line of business. They aggressively used colour films in advertising to attract big clients and adopted a distinctive strategy into computing consulting. Their assertive approach transformed the audit profession. PW were concerned about the impact of MAS on the firm's relationship with audit clients and kept a lower profile than AA.

Remington Rand's UNIVAC became the leading mainframe for technical purposes, while IBM tailored their 700/7000 computers for business applications. The consulting wing of the auditing professions developed rapidly during the 1950s and 1960s. By the 1970s, it had become an important line of business, growing faster than the established auditing practice. AA took the lead among the Big Eight – also in Scandinavia.

Who was Arthur Andersen and why is he important in this historical context? His parents migrated to the U.S. from Denmark and Norway and died in 1901 when the ambitious youngster was sixteen. After graduating in 1908 as a Chartered Public Accountant (CPA), he worked for PW prior to starting on his own firm in Chicago in 1913. He left his mark on the profession long after his death in 1947. I have interviewed former auditors of AA who still refer to the firm as "Arthur." Let us therefore look at AA's audit and computing venture in Norway from the 1970s to illustrate how they developed new audit standards, computer applications, and institutional structures, as well as how they contended with fraud, attracted big clients, and promised ICT-improvements and better audit effectiveness.

2   How AA Developed Computing into Scandinavian Audit in the 1970s

AA was the largest auditing firm in Norway in 1970. Finn Berg Jacobsen, with a Harvard background, took the firm into computing at an early stage and recruited a core of talented engineers, economists, and auditors. He also engaged in fighting fraud, writing an article in 1977, "EDB-svindel" (Computing Fraud) [2]. The text illustrates AA's strategy in designing computer systems tailor-made to customers' needs. The extracts also show AA's marketing skills in making the clients dependent on their auditor's advice:

> Computing fraud is a growing problem typically ten times larger than old-fashioned embezzlement, but so far they are quite rare in Norway. The problem with computing frauds is difficult to detect. There are three types:
>
> o Financial crime, embezzling money or securities
> o Information crime, including copying data or information
> o Property crime, stealing assets or equipment.
>
> Financial crime is a growing field for fraud. It is difficult for auditors to detect, due to lack of competence. In the U.S., three cases of computer fraud have recently been discovered that have cost the audit companies $39 million in indemnity charges, paid from the auditors' insurance. This trend will obviously result in economic consequences for the profession. Information and property crime is also an expanding business where we need better computer competence and controls.
>
> How do we protect ourselves against computer fraud? Computer Controls have to be part of the system design phase. Some claim that auditors ought to contribute to the system design. According to our standards, the auditor should not participate fully, but as a consultant. The auditor should limit activities to developing a control philosophy, advising when auditors should be actively engaged, and developing check-points where they should be consulted.
>
> The role of auditors is important, but limited. Unnecessary discussions on computing technology is outside the scope of work for auditors, but consulting ought to be charged on separate accounts and fees. Auditors should, however, be key specialists with regards to efforts to expose fraud, according to the four phases of diagnosis illustrated below.

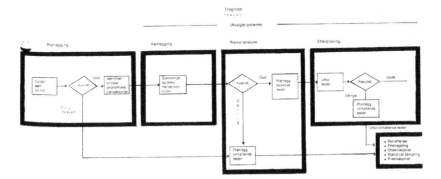

Fig. 1. Diagram illustrating how to prevent computing fraud. Extracts from article in Revisjon og Regnskap 3/77.

Berg Jacobsen's advice provides historical evidence about the status of computing, accounting, system consulting, and distinguishing the auditor's clean financial reports from their commercial activities. It introduces statistical sampling and risk-analyses, and identifies threats and weaknesses in critical transactions. The article introduces the term *system revision,* which audits the process more than the end product, the balance sheet.

He concludes that new professional demands require computer and audit technology as well as knowledge of the client's strengths and weaknesses. The auditor must also be able to motivate the client's employees into participating in risk-analyses and assessment. Due to the wide range of tasks, the auditor's advice is a teamwork approach, although this subject raises the question of the auditor's independence. He states that the risk of computer fraud is increasing. I interpret that remark as an important sales argument. Neither auditors nor their clients were normally covered by insurance.

He also remarks that computer software was designed for maximizing efficiency, *not* security. There was little fraud protection built into software. His punch line is that auditors who do not master risk-analyses could end up in prison, while the smart computer expert with fraudulent behaviour goes free. Control systems should be shifted from software to hardware and suppliers should design audit systems in a way that protects them from being manipulated by unauthorized personnel. The hidden message was clear; to avoid prison, engage AA as MAS-consultant *and* auditor. Those of us who worked with computers in the 1970s recognize the message. Tailor your own software and stay in control of your business using the minicomputer's competitive flexibility.

3 1980s: ICT Shapes a New Paradigm for the Audit Profession

MAS became a very profitable segment of growth for AA. The international audit firms emulated their strategies by using the audit function as an entrance ticket to lucrative ICT-contracts. PW, which had been represented in Norway and Sweden since 1933 in alliance with local firms, and in Denmark since 1948, was a hesitant follower, while Cooper & Lybrand, which had established footholds in the Scandinavian market, was a professional contender for second place. The advent of minicomputers created a new segment when medium-size audit clients bought their own equipment, but lacked the expertise to run it. They all needed help.

In 1982–83, AA's chief ICT consultant in Norway, Arve Sogn Andersen, published several articles in the auditor's community magazine about the information revolution, micro-computers' application and experience, auditing with mini-computers, and how to choose systems. All the articles were illustrated with the AA-trademark and used tantalizing cartoons [3–7]. Mr Andersen had a professional technical background from Norsk Data and SI, a Norwegian research institute.

Throughout the 1980s, many computer engineers found interesting employment with the Scandinavian branches of the Big Eight. By 1983, the National Norwegian Audit Society had organized a computing committee, headed by Lasse Birkeland, a CPA and computing specialist partner in a small Oslo firm. He published three articles about auditing and minicomputers, focusing on statistics, the random selection of transactions, mathematical calculations, and so on [6, 7].

Fig. 2. AA cartoon promoting ICT-solutions for minicomputers

Lasse Birkeland also recommended using fantasy in the construction of software to take the drudgery out of the tedious work of the auditor. His articles won him fame and so much respect at AA that he was headhunted and sent to the U.S. to improve his computer competence. Returning to Norway, he presented a paper at the Nordic Auditor Congress in Gothenburg in August 1986, suggesting new methods to *automate auditors work effectively.* As a historian, the Gothenburg event seems to be a major *shift of paradigm for ICT- systems for Scandinavian auditing.* Birkeland coined his lecture as follows:

> I hope I have given some ideas on how to use ICT as a tool for improving effectiveness in auditing. Furthermore, I hope we here in Gothenburg together can develop new Nordic solutions to common challenges. In this field, we will not be judged better than the weakest of us, by society and politicians. We must adapt to the new environments we shall be working in [8].

In hindsight, these words may sound prophetic. AA may have adapted too well to new times. ICT became a mixed blessing. From now on, computer transactions reduced the volume of manual control. This meant that the audit methods of using ledgers, checking cash transactions against paper files disappeared. The old auditor partners competed with young consultants dealing with clients; focus was on HW-terminals, ICT-systems, and new technology.

The new paradigm also created new opportunities for fraud, required improved monitoring systems, passwords, and so on, accelerating the importance of computer knowledge over audit judgement. Consulting practices within the major firms expanded dramatically. The complexity and applications of information and communication technology were no longer restricted to automating back office functions. New manufacturing methodologies required a new breed of non-CPA partners who advised clients about how to participate in global business development. Clients also asked the Big Eight to assist them in making use of electronic financial information. Computing technology was now essential for professional survival. It was also a rich source of profit.

The flip side was darker. It contained a hidden element of self-destruction. How? Consulting fees among Norwegian auditors had, by 1987, increased to 37 percent of revenues. Together with tax work, consulting fees were sometimes *larger* than audit fees. On a global scale, AA earned $2 billion for *designing and operating computing systems.* MAS-consulting became a battlefield where the Big Eight competed with banks, lawyers, and financial planners on a global basis. The campaigns were fought by well-trained experts and specialists, the weapons were sophisticated software systems and the ability to interface with the client through the Trojan gate of audits.

The struggle between the auditor's independence and MAS-role created an internal conflict within each of the Big Eight audit firms. They were forced to grow with their clients' frantic hunt for global dominance, which led to a wave of mergers and acquisitions. It was a question of grow or die. The audit profession followed suit. This is the traditional historical explanation for the structural changes within the global auditing firms.

Another explanation is that the ICT-paradigm changed the audit processes. The routine manual work of checking transactional files against cash controls, which had earlier contributed to most of the income, vanished. Poorly paid manual work was replaced by computers, and the successful partners were the ones who gained status through highly paid consulting and advisory work. The big clients were conversant with high fees in the class of McKinsey, and Boston, among others, where they rarely complained about costs. The large audit firms now made their mark and money from MAS, and the Big Eight also emulated the consulting companies' organisational models. Young ambitious people climbed the steep career ladders, becoming partners before the age of thirty years. The old ones were stuck in a detour.

The merger processes commenced in 1984 with talks between PW and *Deloitte, Haskins & Sells*. They were met with public resistance. PW then merged with *Computech Corporation* and with *Consumer Finance Institute*, combining computer systems with the analysis of financial planning programs. The results came quickly. By 1988, only 25 percent of PW's U.S. consultants were Chartered Accountants. The traditional audit was no longer their main focus, but used as an entryway for MAS-work.

In 1986–87, *Peat Marwick* joined hands with European *KMG* to become the world's largest accounting organisation, *KPMG*. In Norway, they introduced themselves to customers in 1987, while KPMG became operative in Sweden by 1989, when it became affiliated with the highly respected audit firm *Bohlins Revisionsbyrå*, which had forebears as far back as 1923. *Arthur Young* and *Ernst & Whiney* merged into *Ernst & Young* and *Deloitte* formed a global firm with *Touche* in 1990.

The two largest companies, AA and PW, started to talk about a merger, but failed. Their company cultures were too different. There was also a growing conflict within AA about the distribution of profits from ICT-consulting, which led to a deep split among partners. A separate daughter company, *Andersen Consulting*, was created in 1989 and became an immediate success, which escalated the internal conflicts with AA, the parent company. Andersen Consulting integrated Management with ICT, in a very professional way. AA tried to combine the remains with audit independency. The two different lines of business were not compatible under a common umbrella, and the conflict was settled through arbitration in August 2000, when Andersen Consulting changed its name to *Accenture*.

AA continued on its own after the split, competing with its former daughter company. Driven by animal-like spirits, they now expanded into new consulting activities. Profits hovered between $3–5 million and nearly doubled during 1996–2001. The *dot.com*-wave triggered opportunities for expansion where energy companies such as Enron was one of AA's most loyal clients.

How could AA grow so fast? One historic explanation can be that the audit branch had become accustomed to the high income business, and the partners became greedy for greater profits. Without deeper reflection, they continued the consulting business to compete with the other major auditors. In order to stay in the competitive battle you had to be big. When the two remaining major audit firms, PW and Coopers & Lybrand, merged in 1998 to become PwC, they created the world's largest integrated audit and service company with 150,000 employees, many of them ICT-experts.

AA's audit partners were continually encouraged to seek out opportunities for consulting fees from existing audit clients. By the late 1990s, AA had succeeded in tripling the per-share revenues of its partners. Predictably, AA struggled to balance the need to maintain its faithfulness to accounting standards with its clients' desire to maximize profits, particularly in the area of quarterly earnings reports. AA was alleged to be involved in the *fraudulent* auditing of several large international companies. Even other audit firms had problems during the dot.com-wave.

Computing technology had, in my opinion, transformed the audit firms by enabling them to control companies from the inside. By the end of the 1990s, the Finance Service Authorities in Norway reported that at some of the major audit firms consulting fees contributed as much as 70 percent of total revenues, most of it from MAS, ICT, and Tax Advisory work. The fees from *clean* audit reports were put under competitive pressure and such work was often provided free of charge to secure the bigger clients.

Another source of potential fraud was to assist in the valuation of airy assets. There were two types of valuation principles; historic value and *fair value,* the latter based on the estimation of future income. During the dot.com years, this was a risky activity governed by the hopes and animal-like spirits of the financial markets. The bubble economy was, by 2000, no more solid than the optimistic times of 1929 which led to the Kreuger crash in 1932. Thus concludes my official story about computing.

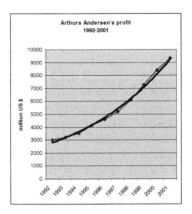

Fig. 3. AA's exponential growth before the Enron collapse

4 Epilogue: The End of Enron, AA, and Confidence in the Audit Profession

This story about the manual and mechanical to electronic computing paradigm in the audit profession 1932–2001 has an epilogue. As a former electrical engineer who has actively worked with computers in the 1960s and 1970s at NTH, Shell, and Kongsberg, I have found pleasure preparing this paper and discovering that the field of computing contributed to the reformation of the audit profession.

Through the research, I discovered a story about fraud that was driven by what Keynes coined *animal spirits,* which ended in the collapse of the firm AA, for the same reasons. AA was, by 2001, in an enviable global position, having regained leadership after the split from its daughter company, Anderson Consulting. Its reputation as the one of the leading Big Five auditors of the world created a streak of arrogance that distinguished their corporate culture from the less assertive firms.

One of the biggest clients of their Houston office was Enron, which handsomely paid AA more than $50 million annually to maintain the impression that their books were in order. They were not.

By concealing enormous loans and providing proof that the increasing profits were real, AA also helped Enron in persuading the stock market to believe that Enron's broadband plans were valued at $35 billion, which supported the stock price of $90 by the year 2000. One year later the company was broke. Loans fraudulently hidden and capitalizing on future profits were the popular songs that attracted investors. The similarity to the Kreuger case is striking. People could not believe it was true. By the end of October 2001, The New York Times wrote:

> At the beginning of 2001, The Enron Corporation, the world's dominant energy trader, appeared unstoppable. The company's decade-long effort to persuade lawmakers to deregulate electricity markets had succeeded from California to New York. Its ties to the Bush administration assured that its views would be heard in Washington. Its sales, profits and stock were soaring.

Enron was bankrupt. AA was dismissed as Enron's auditor, citing the firm's accounting advice and the destruction of documents. AA countered that they had already severed ties with the company when Enron entered bankruptcy. But public confidence in AA vanished when the firm was charged with *obstruction of justice* and found guilty in June 2002 for shredding thousands of documents and deleting e-mails and company files that tied the firm to its audit of Enron. The conviction barred them from auditing public companies. The loss of the public's confidence frightened the remaining global auditors into withdrawing from MAS-consulting. PwC in Norway sold their consultancy group of 350 ICT experts to IBM.

Although only a small number of Arthur Andersen's employees were involved with the scandal, the firm was finished, and 85,000 employees lost their jobs. Most of the Nordic AA-people found new jobs with the remaining Big Four firms. Almost ten years later, the loss of public confidence and reputation is still a touchy subject among auditors. To restore confidence in the audit profession, the Sarbanes–Oxley Act was established by Congress in 2002, to protect investors against future accounting scandals. New regulations were also introduced in Europe.

The audit profession is still struggling to re-establish its reputation. To this day, many people still have no faith in banking, insurance, as well as in their auditors, after the financial crisis of 2007. The global economy is as unstable as in the 1930s, driven by animal spirits and weak public regulation.

The trust in auditors and their tools – the computers – must be re-established. If we cannot trust our auditors and our banks, our money is not safe. My research thus far has, however, made me reasonably confident that we can restore faith in the audit profession and their ICT-solutions, if there is public pressure for transparency. So far, the profession seems to have a way to go.

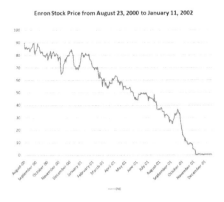

Fig. 4. Enron's share price 2000–2001

References

1. Revisjon og Regnskap. No. 2 (1980)
2. Revisjon og Regnskap. No. 3 (1977)
3. Revisjon og Regnskap. No. 6 (1982)
4. Revisjon og Regnskap. No. 8 (1982)
5. Revisjon og Regnskap. No. 2 (1983)
6. Revisjon og Regnskap. No. 4 (1983)
7. Revisjon og Regnskap. No. 6 (1983)
8. Revisjon og Regnskap. No. 7 (1986)

History of Digital Dating: "Computer-Balls" and Digital Pairing in Finland from the 1960s to the Present

Jaakko Suominen

Degree Program in Cultural Production and Landscape Studies
University of Turku, P.O. Box 124
28101 Pori, Finland
jaakko.suominen@utu.fi

Abstract. This paper focuses on the cultural history of digital matchmaking from a Finnish point of view. By using examples from the mainframe computer era, personal computer applications, as well as from the age of the Internet, the paper argues that three reasons, popularization of technology, modernization of conventional partner seeking practices and the scientification of intimate relationships, are constantly adapted and appropriated to the language of the newest media and computing technology.

Keywords: Computer-aided matchmaking, cultural history of computing, Finland, love, online dating, popular culture.

1   Introduction

Matti Kosola, who advertised "The Computer Ball" at the Student Art Exhibition in Finland in 1968, used the following words.

> A computer is a necessary tool in conquering space. It helps us in many other ways too: why not also in business, which could be far more interesting than the dark side of the Moon? A standard ball normally consists of a homogenized group, where we are most likely to find a suitable companion. During the event, we only have time to get to know ten to twenty people quite superficially and the selection criteria we apply are ridiculous compared to the scientific methods. In a dim light we – us men – carry out our selection on the basis of female appearance, or of the faces of those who are not on the dance floor at the time. And then, women have to choose between those ten to twenty male candidates who ask them to dance [1].

At the ball, the perfect dance partners were supposed to be selected with the help of a computer. Participants only had to fill in a form containing dozens of questions about their own personal features and qualities, state what their expectations of an ideal partner were – and then hope for the best from this "scientific method" [1].

"The Computer Ball," organized by the Student Union of the University of Technology in Espoo, Finland, was one example of the small boom in computer balls

J. Impagliazzo, P. Lundin, and B. Wangler (Eds.): HiNC3, IFIP AICT 350, pp. 117–126, 2011.

that, in all probability, followed American models. From today's perspective, those events appear as the pre-history of Internet dating services, and they certainly share some similarities. Computer-aided partner seeking has at least three different motives or themes: the popularization of technology, modernization of conventional partner seeking practices, and scientification of intimate relationships.

Love, emotions, and sensations are matters regularly used to introduce new computing technology [2–4]. This paper focuses on the cultural history of digital partner seeking from a Finnish perspective. By using examples from the mainframe computer era, personal computer applications, as well as from the age of the Internet, the paper argues that the three above-mentioned motives have been constantly adapted and appropriated to the language of the newest media and computing technology.

The paper is empirically based on interviews, archival material, cartoons, press clippings as well as films and TV-programs on digital dating. It is also related to the author's other studies on the cultural history of computing and popular media.

2 Entertainment of Classification

The American pioneer of punch card technology, Herman Hollerith used to travel on the railways at the end of the nineteenth century. Hollerith became acquainted with the system, which ensured conductors that a passenger's ticket was really the travel document of that particular passenger. He had seen how railway officers punched a "punch photograph" onto the ticket. This was a code, which, among other things, revealed the color of the eyes and hair – as well as the size of the passenger's nose.

At the same time, the population of the United States was increasing and the government was struggling with the Census, which it conducted every ten years. However, when the population grew rapidly, there was a risk that the task of calculating, listing, and tabulating would last more than ten years each time.

Hollerith won a contest, which sought a system that would speed up the computation. He had devised a method that was a kind of adaptation of the conductors' punch photographs, thereby generating punch card technology, which was successfully used since the 1890 Census [5].

Punch card machines – and computers thereafter – brought about the prospect of the statistical analysis of human characteristics. These developments led to different experimentations and applications, which were marketed commercially and popularized in different media. One particularly interesting topic was related to computer-aided matchmaking.

Rolf Strehl wrote in his book *Die Roboter Sind Unter Uns,* which was translated into Finnish in 1954, about "Machine Amor," a global business innovation and technology that American Clara Lane used for partner selection, by applying the "newest scientific principles of medicine, psychology and graphology." Candidates, seeking a spouse, also had to answer the most intimate questions, submit a handwriting sample, and do a drawing test. Strehl stated that the machine had brought about twenty thousand marriages, for judges, revue girls, teachers, opera singers, as well as for millionaires. Everything worked firmly and efficiently: "Robots provide quickly as lightning 'the absolute' partner for the customer, the partner who is the most suitable with his/her view of life, education, character, temperament, hobbies, orientations and cultivation" [6]. The computer accelerated the matchmaking as well as reduced the possibilities of "human errors" in choosing a suitable partner.

Although Strehl depicted the rationalization of matchmaking, the novel machinery was not only associated with the reasoning or scientification and technologization of aspects of human life. Popular media also eagerly introduced the new technology with humor and mysticism. The public seemed to become excited about the particular technological innovations and entertaining experiments that touched their emotional lives and mirrored the collective grand hopes, expectations, and threats of technologies.

From the 1950s onwards, the general public encountered computing technology, for the most part, through science fiction and popular media, which typically played with characteristics of machines, although developers wanted to emphasize the speed, rationality, and calculation abilities of computers and "electronic brains" [7, 4, 2]. Emotions and humor intermingled with work and efficiency in the Age of Automation. Computer-aided matchmaking, in this sense, titillated the public as well as the producers of new technology.

On 13 July 1957, a popular Finnish family magazine *Apu* ("Help") wrote about an American TV-show where couples find each other with the aid of a computer. The article popularized two essential technological innovations of that time, television and the computer. The journalist Lionel Crane described an episode of the People Are Funny TV-show where "The Love Robot" selected a man and a woman who suited each other perfectly, from over 2,500 candidates. The couple, Barbara Smith and John Caran, became quickly engaged: "It feels absolutely amazing that some sort of machine would have been able to define the tastes of both of us so infallibly like the robot did. After the first TV appearance I asked Barbara to have dinner with me – and then I proposed to her to marry me" [8]. In the story, the emotionless computer "knows" people; it is able to analyze details and can answer the specific questions posed.

3   Computer at the Dance Halls

Similar experiments and stories functioned as models for Finns when they conceived ideas about computer-aided dating during the 1960s. Moreover, Finnish cartoon makers and humorists had brainwaves on such occasions, devising comedy sketches about potential computer errors and the odds of too efficient computerized matchmaking. [9–16]

The first practical application took place within the Finnish dancehall culture, in the midst of the musical and economic changes of the 1960s. After the repeal of dance prohibition (which occurred during World War II), many new dance halls emerged and tried to compete by offering a choice of artists, as well as initiating all kinds of marketing campaigns [17]. Due to better roads and transport, the dancehall audience was more mobile than before, and sport clubs and other associations sought funding by organizing events during the short Finnish summer. Although huge events posed bigger risks, they could generate more funds. Dancehalls attracted people, and cultural geographer Pentti Yli-Jokipii notes, "dancehalls have been the essential stage for the matchmaking play in the Finnish summer" [18]. Soon they bought a computer to direct the arena of passion.

During the summers of 1966 and 1967, Mr. Kauko Lehtonen worked as "half a manager" of a dance pavilion that had been erected in Vehmassalmi, South West Finland, in 1963. As Lehtonen was strolling past the IBM computing centre in Turku, he remembered reading about American computerized matchmaking experiments at some exhibition. Lehtonen also decided to test the system with the help of the IBM centre [19], which was situated in a central place in Turku and had large display windows. People could therefore get together regularly to see the computer work [7].

"The Computer Ball" was also a way of promoting other balls organized in Vehmassalmi. Lehtonen portrays the process the following way:

> The particular time was chosen to be at the beginning of June, the prime Midsummer period [when there would be a big festival with major artists]. The previous Saturday, every participant received a ticket on which they marked five characteristics of a desired partner. During the following week, the data was transferred to a computer. The machine analyzed the data and chose each participant's most suitable partner. The following Saturday everyone received a number on their chest and then found the partner with the same number in the audience [19].

4   I Make Love with Pleasure – Students in Computer Dance

After the Vehmassalmi experience, computer balls were also organized in the Helsinki area. Now the "scientific method" was portrayed as more advanced, and this scientification discourse legitimized the use of expensive computer technology for play and entertainment applications. One had to look for business in pleasure. This took place, when a computer ball was organized during the student art happening at Helsinki University of Technology (HUT) at the Espoo Dipoli in 1968.

The organizing team was not fully aware of the previous trial in Vehmassalmi and in a preliminary memo, the HUT organizers claimed that the computer ball was the first in Finland, which was quite typical rhetoric when introducing and popularizing new computing technology [1, 2, 7]. However, the *Helsingin Sanomat* newspaper returned the honour to Vehmassalmi and declared that the Vehmassalmi computer ball was the first in the whole of Europe. The newspaper did however state that the matchmaking by "the mechanical thinker" at the Dipoli was to be based on more substantial background research and material than before [20]. In addition, student psychologists, M.Soc.Sci Pekka Kansi and M.Soc.Sci Leif Sonkin, who had helped with the questionnaire, planned to write several academic papers based on the survey answers as well [21–24].

Students of technology, Ralf Saxén, Pieter Sigmudt, and Arno Wirzenius, were the fathers of the computer ball idea. As Lehtonen in Vehmassalmi, the trio got the idea from the American press. The students were responsible for mathematical planning as well as practical arrangements. In an interview, Saxén revealed that the software development was his and Sigmundt's practical work for technical physics and it was the most amusing laboratory work he had ever done in his studies. They also wanted maximum publicity for the recently completed Dipoli, a large and economically demanding building project for the Student Union of Helsinki University of Technology [25].

The organizers had managed to attract some sponsors for the event as well. IBM and the Computer Centre of the Finnish State helped to sort out the computer services and the major Nordic travel agency Spies provided a trip to Mallorca in Spain, as the lottery prize for the participants. Tillander promised to provide rings to the first couple to become engaged after the event. In addition, the couple most suited to each other, according to the computer, received a bottle of Italian sparkling wine. Therefore, the sale of the party tickets was marketed with the contemporary glamour ideals in mind, to which new technology added its own flavor. All these elements together created the promise of an experience that was exotic and imaginary, which hopefully was possible to achieve. The analysis of this popular cultural and technological utopian media field provides an opportunity to interpret a mixture of cultural values and ideologies attached to the phenomenon.

A total of seven hundred tickets were released for the festivity. In order to achieve an equal number of male and female participants, organizers not only marketed tickets to students of technology, but also to those at the Helsinki Schools (both Finnish and Swedish) of Economy, the University of Helsinki, the Nursing Academy as well as the Handicraft School [26].

Archival material does not reveal whether the event was a great success or not. However, according to Saxén, the occasion attracted wide media attention and was well received by the participants. At the start of the ball, participants searched for their partner, selected by the mainframe. This was followed by a dinner including wine to create a pleasant and relaxed atmosphere. The after party with dance was organized at the student union house and, according to Saxén, the ambience was eager and exciting. He estimates that two hundred of the seven hundred participants joined the after party, which was "one of the funniest" he had ever participated in. It transpired that the most suitable couple matched by the computer had actually dated before, but broken up. However, for a little while, their passions flared again due to the computer. The couple that won the trip to Mallorca pointed out later that the holiday was nice, but they did not continue dating. The morning after the party, two couples attempted to be the first ones to become engaged and obtain rings from Tillander [25].

The couple that happened to be the first was followed afterwards by the afternoon newspaper *Ilta-Sanomat*, which reported about their relationship a couple of times. However, they later broke their engagement. The organizers of the party were interviewed for several newspapers, magazines, radio, as well as television. A popular cartoonist Kari Suomalainen even drew a cartoon about the event: "What do you become when you are an adult? A computer pimp." Two firms contacted the organizers to obtain permission to use the application for their own parties (only one of them used it). Another student party was also organized, but it was not as popular as the first one. The organizers did not continue the computer dating experiments and one of the participant psychologists was even slightly worried about any erroneous impression of psychological work caused by the large media coverage of the event [25]. However, the popular and emotionally charged introduction of the computer matchmaking application did seem to be mostly successful.

It is also fascinating to focus more carefully on the computer ball questionnaires, because they reveal the context of the partner seeking, the survey method, and student life of the 1960s. The survey forms (different ones for the male and female participants) comprised dozens of questions. The organizers explained the aim of the event as follows: "[P]artners will together enjoy a night, not necessarily for rest of their lives. Therefore, the main focus is on hobbies, outlook, and relation to sex life. Socio-economical background, which is one of the most important factors in a successful marriage, is mostly avoided" [1].

Respondents were asked to provide information about their attitudes to religion, alcohol, sex, gambling, fishing, animals, colors, comics, handcrafts, technical student humor, theatre, tobacco, politics, *Ylioppilaslehti* (a student newspaper), jazz, classical music, tennis, slalom or sailing (last three together), travelling, and dancing. They also had to comment on the following statements: "I make love with pleasure," "I am of the opinion that the woman should pay [food and drinks, etc.] herself," "I could accept living together without marriage." The questions appeared to relate to common values and sought answers about how students regarded other academic fields. As mentioned, the survey was based on an enjoyable evening, the primary aim of which was not necessarily marriage, as was the case with many other heterosexual matchmaking services [27].

The survey questions were understandable in the context of the 1960s and student life. At the time, according to historian Laura Kolbe, various student cultural activities were bound to tradition, just when the public discussion about relations between culture and society were increasing rapidly. Such discussions included debates on the value of modern art, popular culture, and so on. At the end of the decade, a rupture occurred and 1968 is known as "the mad year" of student radicalism. In Finland, students occupied the Old Student House in Helsinki [28].

5 A Spouse for a Farmer?

During the following decades, rationalization and popularization were repeatedly intermixed within computer-aided partner seeking. The Finnish TV program Napakymppi ("Bull's eye," 1985–2002) popularized the phenomenon, even though the role of the computer in deciding the most suited couple was not that explicit.

There was one other application that also received wide media attention without weekly television coverage: Leo Vimpari created the Choice of Man/Lady of the House (IEVA) application, which had its premiere at the Oulu agricultural exhibition in August 1982 and mainly targeted farm owners who were single. Just as in the previous cases, one had to fill in a form with the details of one's requirements. Vimpari explains the conditions of the service:

IEVA was created to cater for the needs of bachelor farmers. In many cases, low birth rates and risks that bachelor farmers posed for the continuity of life in the countryside had been noted. There were stories about villages where over half of the farms were occupied by bachelors ... So everything was about ... a farmer hoping to have some woman to share the life at the farm ... How to fix the situation? Modern technology in agriculture as well – a computer – that was it [29].

Again, it was a question of the rationalization of matchmaking with the help of modern technology. In this case, the matchmaking form comprised questions about wealth, hobbies, education, sociability, sobriety, and agricultural experience/competence. The user could put more emphasis on certain aspects by using some important factors (as in online matchmaking services and in digital election machines later on).

IEVA was used at Farmers Exhibitions between 1982 and the 1990s. For example, by the end of 1986 almost 27,000 persons had participated. Vimpari argues that about 15 percent of participants filled in the form as a joke, but 85 percent were more or less serious about finding a partner. He also cites a study that claims that 8 percent of the participants had managed to find a partner—but not necessarily with the direct help of computers [29].

Fairs and exhibitions are good opportunities for the introduction and presentation of new technology, especially in cases where the fairs did not focus on technology itself. Fairs attract large crowds of people who want to see novelties and have fun together. IEVA received much exposure and interest on such occasions, people became accustomed to it, and they expected to see it at agricultural exhibitions.

IEVA was also featured in many newspaper and magazine articles, TV-programs, cartoons, and even in a fictional movie. The publicity was, according to Vimpari, very positive in general; he also received an award from the Society of Agricultural Journalists of Finland [29]. Likewise, in some 1960s cartoons, the publicity played with a combination of new technology, emotions, and rural culture. Behind this, there was concern about rural depression and the hope of creating a new life – literally, for the countryside, with the help of information technology. As an application, it consisted of many symbolic meanings connected to physical and mental reproduction.

6   Online Matchmaking

Matchmaking on the Internet partially differs from the previous examples.

> Googling for love is not the last resort for a desperate single anymore. The Internet acts as a meeting forum for just ordinary people [30].

In this case, the computer not only calculates and suggests the best partners, but it also provides a possibility for the participants to communicate with each other. Net dating services started to flourish just after the popularization of the Internet in the mid-1990s. Finnish Deitti.net ("Dates") started in 1995 and Sinkut.net ("Singles") in 1996. One reason for the popularization of these services, as well as the Internet in general, was the constant media attention in newspapers, magazines, TV-programs and the cinema. The first major net dating boom was connected internationally to the movie *You've got m@il* (1998), which starred Meg Ryan and Tom Hanks. The movie, which also promoted the American Online Corporation, also encouraged discussion in Finland about the dangers and possibilities of net dating [31].

One can cautiously argue that in the last ten years online dating services have become simpler and more focused on serving the needs of different users and age groups. Currently, some of the services are free (obtaining income from advertising, etc.), but others are based on user fees. Moreover, nowadays, users must publish a recognizable photo on their profile page. In addition, a kind of online flirting and dating flourishes in different net environments such as Facebook and SecondLife, and not just on particular online dating services like match.com.

Today, the utilization of these services is no longer publicly presented as something odd, as in the past, but there is still a certain shamefulness linked to the use of the online dating application:

> [Finnish Prime Minister Matti] Vanhanen and [Susan] Kuronen's love affair started to burn in early 2006. The relationship was revealed to the public in March. At first, the couple said that they met at Ikea, but they actually got together on the net, when Matti Vanhanen answered the dating advert of Susan Kuronen on Suomi24.fi-netportal. According to Kuronen, Matti Vanhanen wanted to keep the online dating secret; therefore she [or he] made up the Ikea-story … After the break up, Susan revealed that the couple first met through the online dating services. In the interview for the Me Naiset magazine [Us Women] Susan said that Matti left her by announcing the fact in an SMS-message [32].

7   A Computer: The Emotional Problem Solver

The previous examples illustrate that people have regularly harnessed technology to serve love and emotions. Typically, new information technology has acted as a solution for the difficulty of finding a partner—and sometimes for the trouble of breaking up with a partner. Often, the rationalization of the pair selection process is not the only goal. The application and services were also used to answer the needs of education, regional or national politics—or hegemonic scientific discourse. Even the resolutions were used to obtain wide public attention for new technology or certain values of the producers.

When popularizing science and technology, these aspects have been adjusted to the needs of everyday life and experiences. In addition, science and technology have been adapted to dominant economic and political objectives. They have been tuned to slowly altering ideas about emotions, love, human relations, sex and marriage, and finding Mr. or Mrs. Right.

References

1. Taidetapahtuma järjestää tietokonetanssit. Etukäteismuistio tai lehdistötiedoteluonnos [Art Happening organizes Computer Ball. A Preliminary Memo]. Polyteekkarimuseon arkisto, Otaniemi
2. Suominen, J.: Koneen kokemus. Tietoteknistyvä kulttuuri modernisoituvassa Suomessa 1920-luvulta 1970-luvulle [Experiences with machines. Computerised culture in the process of Finnish Modernisation from the 1920s to the 1970s]. Vastapaino, Tampere (2003)

3. Suominen, J.: Computer as a Tool for Love – A Cultural History of Technology. In: Proceedings of 8th Annual IAS-STS Conference Critical Issues in Science and Technology Studies, CD-ROM. IAS-STS, Graz, May 4-5 (2009), http://www.ifz.tugraz.at/index_en.php/filemanager/download/1558/Jaakko%20Suominen.pdf

4. Suominen, J., Parikka, J.: Sublimated Attractions – The Introduction of Early Computers in Finland in the late 1950s as a Mediated Experience. Media History 16(3), 319–340 (2010)

5. Campbell-Kelly, M., Aspray, W.: Computer. A History of the Information Machine, pp. 20–26. BasicBooks, New York (1996)

6. Strehl, R.: Aikamme robotit. German origin Die Roboter Sind Unter Uns. Finnish translation O. E. Huhtamo. WSOY, Helsinki, pp. 195–196 (1954)

7. Suominen, J.: Sähköaivo sinuiksi, tietokone tutuksi. Tietotekniikan kulttuurihistoriaa [Getting familiar with the electric brain, getting to know the computer. A cultural history of information technology]. Jyväskylän yliopiston nykykulttuurin tutkimuskeskuksen julkaisuja 67. Jyväskylän yliopisto, Jyväskylä (2000)

8. Crane, L.: Uusin avioliiton välittäjä – koneaivot [The newest marriage arranger – machine brains] Apu (July 13,1957)

9. Alenius, S.: Reikäkorttien avioliitto" [Marriage of punch cards.] Apu 36 pp. 38–39 (1963)

10. Hurmerinta, O.: Tietokoneen tahdissa [In the pace of computer, a cartoon]. Apu 46, p. 18 (1963)

11. Hurmerinta, O.: Treffiautomaatti [A date automat]. Apu 37 p. 22 (1964)

12. Bygrave, H.: Kuinka hyvän vaimon tietokone valitsee [How good wife does a computer select]. Pirkka 3 pp. 26–27 (1967)

13. Introduction of the TV-programme Eddien isä (Eddie's father). Apu 5/, p. 13 1970 (in which episode aired on the A computer arranges a girlfriend for Eddie's father, but they don't really trust the possibilities of the machine (February 6, 1970)

14. I.S.: Vaarallista huvittelua: tietokoneella avioon [dangerous entertainment: to marriage with the help of computer]. Kymppi 8, 36–37 (1973)

15. Valitut Palat 12/, p.163 (1972) (an advertisement: "Oletko ylittänyt 40:n ja edelleen "yksinäinen susi". Tie ulos yksinäisyydestä on ehkä lyhyempi kuin luuletkaan. Jos etsit itsellesi elämäntoveria, Markus voi olla avuksi. Tietokonetekniikkaan ja arvostelukykyynsä nojaten Markuksen erikoistuntijat etsivät esille ihmisiä, joilla on hyvät edellytykset sopia yhteen kanssasi." [Are you over 40 and still a "lonely wolf". The road out of loneliness is shorter than you expect. If you seek a life partner, Markus can be of help for you. Experts of Markus based their knowledge on computing technology, and their own judgement and look for people who had good opportunities to get together with you]

16. Viki: Tietokoneiltamat [computer evening party]. Tekniikan Maailma 9, 98 (1968)

17. Pesola, S.: Kun suomalaiset äänestivät jaloillaan. Toisen maailmansodan tanssikiellosta tanssilavojen kukoistukseen. In. Terho, H. (ed.): Hetkiä historiassa. Cultural history – kulttuurihistoria 2. Turun yliopisto, Turku (2002)

18. Yli-Jokipii, P.: Paikallisyhteisöjen muutos Suomessa kesäisten tanssilavojen kuvastamana. In: Löytönen, M. & Kolbe, L.: Suomi. Maa, kansa, kulttuurit. SKS, Helsinki (1999)

19. Lehtonen, K.: Vehmassalmi muistoissani [Vehmassalmi in my memories]. Uudenkaupungin Sanomat (July 3, 2003)

20. Tietokonerakkautta taidetapahtumassa [Computer love in art happening] Helsingin Sanomat (March 8,1968)

21. Taidetapahtuma järjestää tietokonetanssit [The art happening organizes computer ball]. Contactor, 3 (March 8,1968)
22. Otahuuto 7/1968
23. Ylioppilaslehti (March 8, 1968)
24. Ylioppilaslehti (March 15,1968)
25. Saxen, R.: A phone interview by Jaakko Suominen (July 17, 2009)
26. Tietokonetanssilippujen jakelu. Muistio [Deliverance of Computer Ball Tickets. A Memo] Polyteekkarimuseon arkisto, Otaniemi
27. Tietokonetanssien kyselykaavakkeiden luonnokset [Outlines for survey forms of Computer Ball]. Polyteekkarimuseon arkisto, Otaniemi.
28. Kolbe, L.: Eliitti, traditio, murros. Helsingin yliopiston ylioppilaskunta 1960–1990. Otava, Helsinki (1996)
29. Vimpari, L.: Ieva ja muut puhemiehet. Oulu (1986)
30. Elomaa, J.: Nettideittailun @bc [@BC for Netdating] Ilta-Sanomat (December 9, 2006)
31. Turtiainen, R.: Tunne netissä. In: Saarikoski, P., Suominen, J., Turtiainen, R., Östman, S.: Funetista Facebookiin. Internetin Kulttuurihistoria [From Funet to Facebook. A Cultural History of the Internet]. Gaudeamus, Helsinki (2009)
32. Näin rakkaustarina eteni [So went the love story]. Ilta-Sanomat (February 20, 2007)

Collaborations between Engineers and Artists in the Making of Computer Art in Sweden, 1967–1986

Anna Orrghen

Dept. of Art History, Uppsala University, Box 630, 751 26 Uppsala, Sweden
anna.orrghen@konstvet.uu.se

Abstract. The aim of this paper is to describe and analyze collaborations between artists and engineers working together in the making of computer art in Sweden 1967–1986. The paper is based on interviews with artists and engineers who collaborated during this time. By using the theoretical concept "co-construction," I map the phenomenon and discuss the driving forces behind the social, as well as the economical and institutional conditions of the collaborations.

Keywords: Art and technology, art and science, computer art, computer pioneers, human computer interaction.

1 Introduction

During the mid-1960s, when artists started to gain access to computer departments at universities and research departments in large industrial companies, a new kind of collaborations between artists and engineers developed [1]. Next to the US, Germany and Great Britain, Sweden is put to the fore as one of the countries where artists and engineers at an early stage explored the possibilities of using computers for creating art [2, 3]. For instance, the programmer Göran Sundqvist at Saab in Linköping, and later at AB Skandinaviska Elverk, used the Saab manufactured computer D21 at Skandinaviska Elverk to help the composer and artist Jan W Morthenson. He also used the ABC 80 computer with a XY-plotter for collaboration with the composer and artist Lars-Gunnar Bodin. Another example is the long-term collaboration between IBM employed programmer Sten Kallin and the artist Sture Johannesson, which began in 1969 and resulted in the projects *Intra* and *Exploring Picture Space (EPICS)*. Johannesson and Kallin worked with *Intra* at IBM in Stockholm where they used an IBM 1130 computer to elaborate on different kind of patterns. A third example is Mikael Jern who developed the program Color for the Color Ink Jet Plotter at the computer department at Lund University in 1970s. The artists Beck & Jung, among others, used Color on a UNIVAC 1108 for making computer art.

We can regard contemporary art in general and computer art in particular as complex negotiation processes between artists and other actors. The foundation of the American organization Experiments in Art and Technology (E.A.T.) in 1966 and their famous event 9 Evenings: Theatre and Engineering in October that same year must be considered as crucial events regarding the changing possibilities for these kinds of

J. Impagliazzo, P. Lundin, and B. Wangler (Eds.): HiNC3, IFIP AICT 350, pp. 127–136, 2011.

collaborations [4]. Art today increasingly seems to turn into interdisciplinary projects involving a number of different actors.

How can we understand these collaborations? In this paper, I use the insights made within the interdisciplinary field of Science and Technology Studies (STS). A basic assumption in the STS approach is that we should describe scientific and technological activities as the result of relations between different actors rather than the result of singular individuals, disciplines or groups. By adopting such a perspective, we regard scientific knowledge and its use as a conscious cooperation between different actors who produce and use this knowledge [5].

An STS concept particularly apt to study collaborations between different actors is "co-construction." Nelly Oudshoorn and Trevor Pinch introduced the concept in their book How Users Matter from 2003. Their main argument is that researchers interested in users and technology had a narrowly focused view on users as separate objects of study. By using the term co-construction as a point of departure, they aim at changing the perspective and instead, they underscore the development of new products as a co-operation effort between "producers" and "consumers" and that the use of the products is the result of a negotiating process between these two groups. Hence, the term emphasizes the importance of studying production and consumption of knowledge together rather than as separate phenomena. Oudshoorn and Pinch pay attention to the role of the user in technological development in general and they are interested in how users consume, modify and resist technologies. Although their primary focus includes "what users do with technology," they are also interested in "what technology does with users" [6].

The aim of this paper is to describe and analyze collaborations between artists and engineers working together in the making of computer art in Sweden 1967–1986. Earlier, the Swedish art historian Gary Svensson has studied the introduction of computer art in Sweden. Although he also mentions that the collaborations took place, he focuses mainly on mapping the actors and the art works, as well as placing the Swedish development in an art historical context [7]. In my approach, on the other hand, attention is paid to the collaborations only. I am particularly interested in questions on three different levels. The first one deals with mapping the phenomenon, i.e. which artists and engineers participated in collaborations and which art works did they create during those collaborations? The second one concerns the driving forces behind the collaborations: Why did they collaborate? What did they expect to gain and what did they gain from the collaborations? How do they consider their role in the collaboration? What impact did the collaboration have on their work as artists as well as engineers?

The third question includes the social, economic, and institutional conditions of the collaborations. How did the artists and engineers get into contact? How did they carry through the collaboration? Where did it take place? Which computers did they use? How did they finance the collaborations? By taking Oudshoorn and Pinch's concept co-construction as a theoretical point of departure, I shed light upon these questions from the point of view of the artists as well as the engineers. I argue that early Swedish computer art illustrates a kind of co-constructed contemporary art.

The sources for this paper are mainly interviews with Swedish artists and engineers who collaborated to create computer art. I conducted these interviews within the documentation project "From Computing Machines to IT." The project aimed at documenting the Swedish IT history; it was collaboration between the Div. of History of Technology at KTH in Stockholm, the National Museum of Science, and Technology in Stockholm and the Swedish Computer Society [8].

Although these oral sources are necessary to be able to study these collaborations, there are, however, a number of difficulties concerning source criticism related to interviews as a methodology. One such difficulty concerns how the researcher is to relate to an interview conducted several years after the case in question. This underlines the importance of being aware of memory and time in relation to oral history as a method [9]. However, one way of dealing with this question is to supplement the oral sources with written sources.

2 Three Case Studies

This paper contains three case studies followed by a concluding discussion.

2.1 Case 1: Göran Sundqvist, Jan W Morthenson and Lars-Gunnar Bodin

One of the earliest collaborations took place between the programmer Göran Sundqvist (b. 1937) and the composer and artist Jan W Morthenson (b. 1940). Sundqvist, at Saab in Linköping, and later at AB Skandinaviska Elverk, used the Saab manufactured computer D21 at Skandinaviska Elverk to create a digital sound for Morthenson's musical piece *Neutron Star* in 1967. In 1969, Sundqvist made the computer animations for *Supersonics*, a TV-film Morthenson made for Westdeutscher Rundfunk [7, 10, 11]. Morthenson met Sundqvist at Fylkingen, a society committed to experimental and unestablished forms of contemporary art, where the latter's musical experiments with the computer D21 had gained him a reputation for being interested in the field of art, music and computers [11]. At Fylkingen, Sundqvist also made acquaintance with the composer and artist Lars-Gunnar Bodin (b. 1935). In 1968, he used the Saab manufactured computer D21 at Skandinaviska Elverk to realize Bodin's work on stochastic compositions and in 1979, the collaboration continued, although this time Sundqvist used the ABC 80 computer with a XY-plotter to continue the elaboration on the same theme.

Morthenson and Bodin nursed an interest in new aesthetic expressions, which led them to the computer. Although they lacked access to computers, they were both well acquainted with the international development within the field and they had ideas of how to use this new technology for artistic purposes. Sundqvist, who earlier had elaborated with SARA at Saab and later with D21 at AB Skandinaviska Elverk, also shared this interest to create sound and images. Hence, the main reason for Morthenson and Bodin to approach Sundqvist was twofold: he could offer access to a computer, and he knew how to use it. Alternatively, as Morthenson puts it: "He was important since he was the first one who could offer access to a computer, a so called D21" [11]. Even though Sundqvist, Morthenson and Bodin shared a mutual interest in the artistic possibilities of computer technology, it is nonetheless clear that they had different roles. Describing their roles during the work with *Supersonics,* Morthenson says, "I drew pictures and courses [of events], pretty much the same thing as when one makes an animated movie. I made him a storyboard and then he tried to realize it as well as he could by using the oscilloscope" [11]. Moreover, when Sundqvist describes their collaboration on *Neutron Star*, he says, "He wanted short sound beats with a number of different frequencies, and I made that" [12]. Afterwards, Morthenson himself put the piece together. The collaboration with Bodin follows a similar pattern which Bodin expresses, "I gave a number of rules for how these should be" [13], and Sundqvist explains, "I was curious and he had ideas" [12].

The quotations illustrate their different roles where they asked Sundqvist to perform a specific task that made it possible for the artists to realize their ideas. Sundqvist's description of his role in the collaborations is similar to his description of the working tasks that he received and carried through at Saab and AB Skandinaviska Elverk. There he occasionally was asked to elaborate on the computer, preferably by creating sound and images to demonstrate its possibilities for presumable clients. In 1960, he received a similar task to impress on a group from the military air force interested in the computer D2:

> ... [Bernt Magnusson] gave me the equation of a trajectory, and I managed to draw it by the help of sub programs for sinus and cosinus that they used on SARA, the large copy of BESK at SAAB. [...] I kept on experimenting with it for many years after that, in order to make different pictures [12].

Today, the program described is probably considered the first computer game created in Sweden [14]. I would like to dwell upon the later part of Sundqvist's answer, which I find particularly interesting. On one hand, he received instructions and followed them, but on the other hand, he also used these instructions as a springboard to continue to elaborate on and develop his knowledge of how to create sound and images with the computer for his own sake of interest. Of course, it is not possible to say whether those collaborations really contributed to Sundqvist's development as a programmer. However, considering that he carried out these tasks in a similar way as he did at AB Skandinaviska Elverk and Saab, and that he wrote his own programs to realize Morthenson's and Bodin's artistic ideas, one might assume that this was the case.

Financially, AB Skandinaviska Elverk sponsored the collaborations since Sundqvist could use their computers. Although Sundqvist often used the D21 in his spare time, occasionally he also used it during working hours while waiting for the result of his programming to appear [12].

2.2 Case 2: Sten Kallin and Sture Johannesson

In 1969, the artist Sture Johannesson (b. 1935) approached IBM in Sweden. Inspired by the development in the U.S., where the computers were reported to be able to "draw pictures," Johannesson was anxious to find out more about this new technology and its possibilities. The request ended up at Sten Kallin's (b. 1928) desk and became the starting point of a long time collaboration that resulted in the projects *Intra* (1969–1974) and *EPICS* (1986–present) [15]. Kallin was an instructor in programming languages and program design and development, a "systems engineer," and in the 1980s "senior consultant." Similar to Sundqvist, Kallin was well known among his colleagues at IBM because of his interest in elaborating with the computer for his own sake, and thus he had gained a reputation to have "some strange ideas and projects going on" [16].

Before Johannesson contacted IBM, he had elaborated with a number of different artistic techniques such as painting, drawing, screen print and clay. The subjects of the pictures were often taken from an "alphabet" he had developed containing different symbols, e.g. a key, a heart and a combination of both. With *Intra* he continued to elaborate on these symbols in yet another technique: computer technology. Johannesson and Kallin worked with *Intra* at IBM in Stockholm where they used an IBM 1130 computer to elaborate on graphical pictures constructed by mathematical curves.

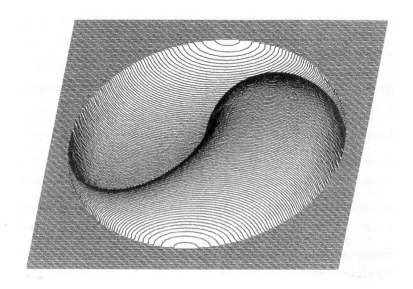

Fig. 1. Spirals 106, from *Intra* 1969/70–1974. Courtesy of Sture Johannesson

In 1986, Kallin's and Johannesson's second project started, *EPICS* [7, 16]. *EPICS* was carried out with a PC-AT and a graphic screen. However, this time, Kallin approached Johannesson by saying:

> I think we should make a project together, I have an idea. And I think we should continue our exploring of a picture space. But not a picture space with the keyhole, the heart and stuff like that, because it's difficult to figure out how we could develop it. My idea is that we let simple graphic elements on a picture space be surrounded by some kind of aesthetical power field, a power field similar to gravitation or an electrostatic field that reduces by distance. [...] And I would like to elaborate on this aesthetical power field and be able to visualize it graphically in one way or another. [---] And he jumped at it and we gave it a thought and made a number of suggestions and I probably made a simple prototype of something. After that we went to IBM and said that we would like to do this. I will only do it during my spare time but Sture needs equipment. IBM Malmö lends him a pretty good PC-AT, the third generation of IBM PC's and a graphic screen [16].

Kallin's thorough description of how *EPICS* started and how it was realized puts to the fore a number of interesting things. For instance, it illustrates the interaction that was taking place between Kallin's involvement in artistic projects and his regular working tasks at IBM. Kallin's driving forces behind the collaboration were twofold. On one hand, he was interested in "the huge possibilities of visualizing with the help of computer technology" [17]. On the other, he had always been interested in solving problems. By collaborating with Johannesson he gained new experiences of how to visualize with the computer. Some might interpret the fact that he wanted to continue the collaboration to develop his newly achieved skills as a sign of the impact of the collaboration on his work as an engineer. Kallin confirms the interpretation by claiming, "Yes indeed. Everything I have done has taught me a lot one can use later on" [16].

An interest in visualizing by using new technology was also the main driving force for Johannesson. Before Johannesson started to work with Kallin he had tried different printing techniques. Hence, turning to the computer should be a natural step in his artistic development. However, another important factor needs mentioning. Before contacting IBM, Johannesson had gained a reputation of being a troublemaker, which, according to himself, froze him out within the art world. Contacting IBM was for him a way of finding a new arena "free of prejudices" where he could continue to elaborate with his art [18].

Given that Johannesson initiated *Intra* and Kallin initiated *EPICS*, makes the question of their different roles particularly apt to study. On one hand, one can easily assign them different roles where Kallin possessed the technical knowledge and access to computer technology and Johannesson had a broader experience of visualizing in different techniques. There is, however, another question brought to the fore by Kallin who touches upon a highly interesting, yet difficult, question of creativity while describing the collaboration:

> I completed the program but gave him as many parameters as I could, so he could do that on his own, so he would feel that at least he was participating. That is of course a sensitive question concerning creativity, where the creativity is… And I do think that the main creativity comes from the one who designs the program since that is the one who completely decides the frames [16].

Thus, on the other hand it is much harder to claim one of the roles as the more creative one. Kallin's description of his interest and involvement in what became *EPICS* makes their collaboration an interesting illustration of Oudshoorn's and Pinch's co-construction. Although Kallin initiated *EPICS* and had a clear idea of what he wanted to do, he needed Johannesson's artistic experience to realize his ideas, just as Johannesson needed Kallin's knowledge of and access to computers.

However, Kallin's description also tells something about the economical conditions of the collaboration. Economically, IBM financed the collaboration in terms of allowing Kallin to use their computers. IBM also sponsored Johannesson's participation in a couple of international conferences in Denmark, Germany and Switzerland where he and Kallin demonstrated *EPICS* as well as lent him the technical equipment he needed. One might also talk about an important institutional support from IBM since according to Kallin the collaboration was "heavily supported" [16] by the information department at IBM that also initiated the contact between Kallin and Johannesson. This institutional support also reflects when Johannesson describes IBM as a space free of prejudices against him where he – contrary to the art world – was trusted and given an artistic freedom: "I borrowed a key to IBM's laboratory in Solna and went there by myself and unlocked and locked when I left" [18].

Fig. 2. Sten Kallin (left) and Sture Johannesson (right) during their work with *Intra* at IBM Stockholm in the early 1970s. Courtesy of Sture Johannesson.

2.3 Case 3: Mikael Jern and Beck and Jung

In 1965, the artist Holger Bäckström (1939–1997) and the mathematician Bo Ljungberg (1939–2007) started out on a lifelong collaboration. They called themselves Beck & Jung and were early users of computer technology. The computer technology was specifically apt for combining their mathematical and artistic skills and their early experimentations with computer graphics have gained them an international reputation [7, 19, 20].

Initially, they started to develop a new kind of alphabet called *Bildalfabetet* (the Picture Alphabet) based on a module system consisting of eleven basic forms. In 1966, Beck & Jung began to collaborate with Leif Svensson at IBM in Malmö where they used the IBM manufactured computer IBM/1401 to examine the possibilities of *Bildalfabetet*. The collaboration lasted until 1967 and *Felixsnurran* (the Felix Pivot) (1967–1968) is one of their most famous works during this time [21].

From 1970 to 1976, the programmer Mikael Jern (b. 1946) worked together with Professor Hellmuth Hertz (b. 1920) on a project where they developed the first color plotter in the world, the Color Ink Jet Plotter [22]. The Color Ink Jet Plotter was developed because of collaboration between the department of Building Function Analysis, the Department of Electrical Measurement, and the University Computing Center at Lund University. As such, it was an important step in the development of computer graphics [7]. Jern developed the program Color that made it possible to draw color pictures and he continued to develop the idea during the years to come [23]. Jern was an early and ardent advocate of raster graphics, instead of vector graphics, and he argues that one way of interpreting his work with Color might be considered as a way of visualizing the advantages and possibilities of raster graphics [24]. Color was used on a UNIVAC 1108, mainly for environmental research such as visualizing community planning [7]. However, although they formed a relatively almost invisible group, a few artists used the Color Ink Jet Plotter such as Beck & Jung. In 1972, they made their first color pictures by using the Color Ink Jet Plotter [21].

In 1979, Jern used Color to create the Color Cube (consisting of 17x17x17 small cubes). The Color Cube was a way of demonstrating the 3D graphics as well as visualizing the color system itself. Although the principle for the color cube had been described before, this was the first time it was possible to visualize the technique by a computer. Beck & Jung became interested in the color cube and approached Jern to ask whether they could use it and Jern agreed [24]. The result became their project *The Chromo Cube* that started in 1980. Between 1982 and 1986, Beck & Jung continued to elaborate with different forms. However, this time they worked together with Bob Wissler, a technician at Lund University, who helped them to use the program developed by Jern [21].

When Jern describes the collaboration with Beck & Jung it becomes quite obvious that they had different roles:

> Beck & Jung came to me and asked if they were allowed to use my programs that made these cubes. And I made the first one for them, but after that I didn't have time for it, instead there was a guy called Bob Wissler in Lund, who was a programmer, who became their programmer and helped them to use my programs [24].

This collaboration is different from the two other cases discussed in this paper, since in this case Jern had already made the program as well as the color cube for another purpose. Hence, the color cube "was *used* but not invented by Beck & Jung" [7]. There is also a difference in the economical conditions surrounding the collaboration between Jern and Beck & Jung. At the computer department, one was able to rent time at the computer according to a specific rate. There were also additional costs in relation to color prints [25].

3 Conclusion

In this paper, I show that the number of computers used for making art during this time was rather limited. The computers were mainly at the computer department at Lund University and large companies such as Saab and IBM. Another important place was Fylkingen. Given the conditions that the knowledge of using computers during this time was limited to a few persons, mainly engineers, we can assume that the artistic projects carried out during this time more or less required collaborations between artists and engineers. In this manner, the artists needed access to the computers as well as the knowledge of how to use them to create their artworks. However, I also demonstrate that the engineers, by participating in these collaborations, might have further developed in their role as programmers since the artist´s ideas on how to use the technology often stimulated the development of their programming skills. This interpretation finds support in the international development during this time, as it happened that large international companies and universities supported these kinds of collaborations with the aim to foster interactions between artists and the industry; early examples are IBM, AT&T Bell Labs, and Lincoln Laboratory at MIT [2, 26]. A later example is PAIR, the PARC Artist-in-Residence program at Xerox Parc in Paolo Alto that started in the early 1990s [27].

Initially, I claimed that early computer art was a co-construction. I would like to end this paper by suggesting that it is not only the art made by those collaborations – but also the computer technology being used in the collaborations – that might be considered as co-constructed.

Acknowledgments. The author wishes to thank Stiftelsen Längmanska kulturfonden, Helge Ax:son Johnsons stiftelse and Anna Ahlströms och Ellen Terserus Stiftelse for valuable financial support. Per Lundin has given valuable comments on earlier versions of this manuscript.

References

1. Shanken, E.A.: Artist in Industry and the Academy: Collaborative Research, Interdisciplinary Scholarship and the Creation and Interpretation of Hybrid Forms. Leonardo 38, 415–418 (2005)
2. Davis, D.: Art and the Future: A History/Prophecy of the Collaboration Between Science, Technology and Art. Thames & Hudson, London (1973)
3. Bijvoet, M.: Art as Inquiry: Toward New Collaborations Between Art, Science, and Technology. Peter Lang, New York (1997)
4. Loewen, N.: Experiments in Art and Technology: A Descriptive History of the Organization. PhD Dissertation New York University, New York (1975)
5. Hackett, E.J., et al. (eds.): The Handbook of Science and Technology Studies. MIT Press, Cambridge (2008)
6. Oudshoorn, N., Pinch, T.: How Users Matter. MIT Press, Cambridge (2003)
7. Svensson, G.: Digitala pionjärer: Datakonstens introduktion i Sverige. Carlssons, Stockholm (2000)
8. Lundin, P.: Documenting the Use of Computers in Swedish Society between 1950 and 1980. KTH, Avdelningen för teknik- och vetenskapshistoria, Stockholm (2009)
9. Portelli, A.: The Death of Luigi Trastulli: Memory and the Event. In: The Death of Luigi Trastulli and Other Stories: Form and Meaning in Oral History, State University of New York Press, Albany (1991)
10. Broman, P.O.: Kort historik över Framtidens musik: Elektronmusiken och framtidstanken i svenskt 1950- och 60-tal. Gidlunds, Hedemora (2007)
11. Morthenson, J.W.: Interview from 2007 by Anna Orrghen, medie- ochkommuni kationsvetenskap, Institutionen för kultur och kommunikation, Södertörns högskola, Stockholm
12. Sundqvist, G.: Interview from 2007 by Anna Orrghen, medie- och kommunikations vetenskap, Institutionen för kultur och kommunikation, Södertörns högskola, Stockholm
13. Bodin, L.-G.: Interview from 2007 by Anna Orrghen, medie- och kommunikations vetenskap, Institutionen för kultur och kommunikation, Södertörns högskola, Stockholm

14. Ernkvist, M. (ed.): Svensk dataspelsutveckling, 1960–1995. Transkript av ett vittnessemi narium vid Tekniska musset i Stockholm den 12 december 2007. KTH, Avdelningen för teknik- och vetenskapshistoria, Stockholm (2008)

15. Bang Larsen, L., Johannesson, S.: Sture Johannesson. Lukas & Sternberg, New York (2002)

16. Kallin, S.: Interview from 2007 by Anna Orrghen, medie- och kommunikationsvetenskap, Institutionen för kultur och kommunikation, Södertörns högskola, Stockholm

17. Åkerman, C.: Dekorerad IBMare gör vad han vill. Datateknik 1 (1989)

18. Johannesson, S., Johannesson, A.C.: Interview from 2007 by Anna Orrghen, medie- och kommunikationsvetenskap, Institutionen för kultur och kommunikation, Södertörns högskola, Stockholm

19. Popper, F.: Art of the Electronic Age. Thames & Hudson, London (1993)

20. Nilsson, B., Bruhn, P.-O., Ljungberg, S.: Beck & Jung med glada hälsningar! Torekovs Kulturstiftelse, Torekov (2009)

21. Eriksson, L., Beck & Jung: Chromo Cube. Wedgepress & Cheese, Bjärred (1981–1982)

22. Hertz, H., Jern, M.: Hard Copy Color Display System Using Ink Jets. Computer Graphics in Planning (1972)

23. Jern, M.: Color Jet Plotter. In: International Conference, Computer Graphics, SIGRAPH-ACM, vol. II(1), pp. 18–31 (Spring 1977)

24. Jern, M.: Interview from 2007 by Anna Orrghen, medie- och kommunikationsvetenskap, Institutionen för kultur och kommunikation, Södertörns högskola, Stockholm

25. Information given by phone by Ingemar Dahlstrand (August 2007)

26. Century, M.: Encoding Motion in the Early Computer: Knowledge Transfers between Studio and Laboratory. In: Broeckmann, A., Nadarajan, G. (eds.) Place Studies in Art, Media, Science and Technology: Historical Investigations on the Sites and the Migration of Knowledge, pp. 29–45. VDG, Weimar (2008)

27. Harris, C. (ed.): Art and Innovation: The Xerox Parc Artist-in-Residence Program. MIT Press, Cambridge (1999)

IBM's Norwegian Grammar Project, 1988–1991

Jan Engh

Oslo University Library, Norway
jan.engh@ub.uio.no

Abstract. During the years 1988–1991, IBM Norway developed a broad-coverage grammar for Norwegian Bokmål as part of an international corporate effort to create writing tools for all platforms and for all major language communities where IBM had business at that time. The grammar was based on IBM's own lexicon and morphology modules and a key factor of the technology was the programming language PLNLP. The main project halted in 1990 because of the world's economic crisis. However, local development continued with a view to a different application: Machine translation between Norwegian Bokmål and Nynorsk. Unfortunately, even this project did not reach a natural conclusion for economic reasons. In addition to producing linguistic results, the project showed how difficult it is to rely on one unique source of corporate funding for a comprehensive long-term project. It also showed how a national subsidiary of an international corporation could not count on local public support.

Keywords: Broad coverage grammar, syntax, natural languages, Norwegian, machine translation, public funding.

1 Introduction

During the period 1988–91, IBM Norway developed its own grammar for Norwegian Bokmål as a natural follow-up project after the company's lexicographical projects of the mid-1980s [1]. The project was funded by IBM's Advanced Systems' Development (ASD)[1] as part of a plan to create writing tools for all IBM platforms – for all major language communities of Western Europe, the Middle East, and East Asia.[2]

Initially, two main components were implied: A broad-coverage analysis grammar including a component for post syntax processing and a style module. Various other applications were planned. Since an unannounced product was involved, the project was confidential. Later, when international funding failed, IBM Norway decided to carry on with the project as an open research program at a reduced pace and with a different application as its primary objective [2, 3].

The basic idea behind the project was to link modules of syntax, semantics, and discourse analysis to form a unified whole on a firm morphological basis, using a unified formalism called "Programming Language for Natural Language Processing" or PLNLP.

---

[1] Based in Bethesda, Maryland.
[2] With the notable exception of Finnish and Icelandic.

J. Impagliazzo, P. Lundin, and B. Wangler (Eds.): HiNC3, IFIP AICT 350, pp. 137–149, 2011.

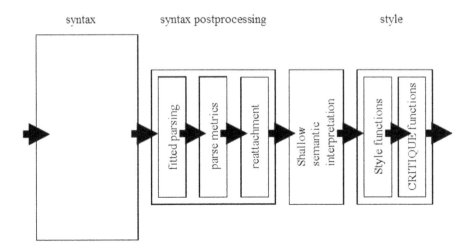

Unfortunately, the project was cancelled because of a lack of funding. At the time of its termination, though, the principal component of the grammar, the analytic syntax, had reached a comparatively high functioning level. However, only partial experimental implementations of the remaining components had been made.

In this article, I shall focus on the part of the grammar that was actually implemented, the syntax, and the national continuation project, a system for machine translation between Norwegian Bokmål and Nynorsk.[3] I shall only give a brief sketch of the general technology, which has been thoroughly represented elsewhere [5–9]. The implementation, including aspects of the linguistic development, will be given and I will account for the general experience gained from the project.

2 The Project

2.1 Goals and Means

The main goal of the project was to create a grammar with the capacity of processing every possible input string of Norwegian words: To analyse fully any sequence generally recognised as correct, and to analyse as much as possible any other sequence. This was motivated, of course, by the simple fact that a grammar without a broad coverage is useless for commercial purposes. Developing such a grammar was quite a challenge, however, since one had to face the often unexpected variety and complexity of natural language. On the other hand, with a full-scale design, one would not run the risk of ending up in an "it doesn't scale up" situation. In the 1980s, most grammars developed in a scientific environment only worked on a very small subset of a given language.[4]

---

[3] For those unfamiliar with the language situation of Norway, see [4], pp. 53–57 and pp. 98–104.

[4] E.g. the only predecessor of IBM's Norwegian grammar [10].

The task of the Norwegian development group was twofold. It consisted in the adaptation of the general technology provided by ASD, so that it could handle the peculiarities of Norwegian and, above all, in implementing the grammar rules based on thorough linguistic insight.

2.2 Technology

The key factor of the grammar technology was "Programming Language for Natural Language Processing" (PLNLP), a rule-based language specially designed for the purpose. All software was written in PLNLP and an entire development environment was available for grammar writing, including tools for debugging and regression testing. The PLNLP environment provided a shell into which the user loaded a grammar definition as a set of PLNLP rules. Subsequently, the program could decode a language sequence according to the rules of the grammar. Details of the decoding process were displayed by selecting from a variety of tracing options.

2.3 Linguistics

From a linguistics point of view, a grammar written in PLNLP was an augmented phrase structure grammar: It consisted of phrase structure rewriting rules "augmented" by specifications and conditions for the application of the rules. Independently of the linguistic meaning that the grammarian would like to assign to them, basic descriptive entities such as 'head', 'premodifier', and 'postmodifier' already had a rather concrete meaning in the PLNLP system. Apart from this, PLNLP could be considered neutral to linguistic theory. In principle, any theoretical approach or linguistic model could be implemented by means of PLNLP. Neither was PLNLP characterized by any latent bias as far as the structure of the language under analysis was concerned. In fact, PLNLP proved itself a valuable tool for the representation of languages as different as English, Arabic, and Japanese.

One important characteristic of actual use of the formalism in the grammar was the "relaxed" approach:[5] to parse as extensively as possible every sequence found in actual texts submitted for analysis and in an "extrinsic" way. No claim was made of creating any "intrinsic" representation of "how the language really is." The grammar was constructed based on actual language use and the surface text provided the clues for parsing. Thus, in order to identify any sentence level constituents, the parsing rules had to contain information about what (form of a) word could be followed by (what form of) another word.

2.3 The Lexicon

A prerequisite for high coverage as well as for correct parsing was an extensive lexicon and a corresponding morphology. Such data were provided by the current updated version of the Norwegian Bokmål base dictionary and morphology module [1]. The former contained more than 64,777 entry words and the latter was, in

---

[5] Adopted from the English PLNLP grammar, cf. [7].

principle, complete.[6] Together, they covered close to 99 percent of the word forms of most running text.

Additional properties of words were stored in auxiliary files. They included traditional grammatical information such as valency, types of complement, and control characteristics for verbs, as well as collocation data and information that is more specific; these attributes are not usually found in linguistic literature. For instance, information about a given adverb's ability to appear in front of, in the middle of, or at the very end of a sentence, whether a given adjective could appear in an attributive position or not or whether an adverb could modify an adjective phrase as premodifier. As such, information for Norwegian was not accessible or simply inexistent at that time, quite a few person-months were invested in this type of basic descriptive linguistic research.

3 The Syntax

3.1 Architecture

The syntax had a sequential architecture: each step in the analysis added to the final structural description of the input string, thus producing a more precise and "deeper" analysis. When parsing began, the grammar received, from the lexicon, information about each word, in the form of collections of attribute-value pairs called records. During the processing, grammar rules combined the word records into constituent records, and then put these records together to form even larger record structures. Whether a particular rule would be applicable to a certain set of constituents was governed by the presence or absence of certain attributes, and their values, in the record structures. Some attributes were provided by the dictionary and some added by the rules themselves. Hence, the syntax produced a description of a sentence by incrementally building a record structure. Every possible combination of the records according to the syntax rules was tried until one (or more) successful parse(s) of the input string had been found. This meant that a high number of records that had not been used for the current successful parse(s) were created as well.

3.2 Records

Record structures could have as many attributes as necessary. Fig. 1 illustrates one example. On the left-hand side, are attribute names; to the right of each attribute name is its value.[7] Values could be either simple or complex. Many of the values are themselves other records. Five attributes were essential: PRMODS 'premodifiers', HEAD, PSMODS 'postmodifiers', SEGTYPE 'segment type', and STR '(input) string'. Of the remaining attributes, some were provided by the system, the others chosen by the grammarian. The RULES attribute gave the derivational history of the

---

[6] Generating more than 485,000 unique (i.e. non-duplicate) wordforms. This particular dictionary module could easily be exchanged for a new, updated and still more extensive one. The last Bokmål module actually produced by IBM, contained approximately 160,000 lexemes (including some 30,000 proper nouns) generating 1,133,633 unique wordforms.

[7] "NP" and "VP" are abbreviations for 'noun phrase' and 'verb phrase' respectively.

```
Skriv en setning på norsk eller en kommando:

(prtrec 1)
              SEGTYPE    'FHSETN'
              STR        " Den ikke altfor flinke snekkeren sendte Kari en vakker faktura ."
              RULES      2040 2500 2500 2400 2900
              RULE       2900 SNTBEG1 VP1 PUNC1
              COPYOF     VP1 "Den ikke altfor flinke snekkeren sendte Kari en vakker faktura" ' SENDE'
              BASE       'SENDE'
              DICT       'sendte'
              INDIC      PRET V3
              PRMODS     NP1 "Den ikke altfor flinke snekkeren" 'SNEKKER'
              HEAD       VERB1 "sendte" 'SENDE'
              PSMODS     NP2 "Kari" 'KARI'
              PSMODS     NP3 "en vakker faktura" 'FAKTURA'
              PSMODS     PUNC1 "." '.'
              INDOBJ     NP2 "Kari" 'KARI
              FREMSTEV   VERB1 "sendte" 'SENDE'
              OBJEKT     NP3 "en vakker faktura" 'FAKTURA'
              TOOBJ      1
              NOKOBJ     1
              SUBJEKT    NP1 "Den ikke altfor flinke snekkeren" 'SNEKKER'
              HOVEDV     VERB1 "sendte" 'SENDE'
              PARSENO    1
              PRED       'SENDE'
              DSUB       NP1 "Den ikke altfor flinke snekkeren" 'SNEKKER'
              DIND       NP2 "Kari" 'KARI'
              DOBJ       NP3 "en vakker faktura" 'FAKTURA'
              XVPMODS    1
              NODENAME   'FHSETN1'
Value = NIL
```

Fig. 1. Record structure

parse by displaying an ordered list of rules, which had been applied at that level of constituent analysis. Feature markings on words and phrases were shown by the INDIC attribute. BASE showed the lemmatised form of the head word for any constituent. A POS attribute would have told what possible parts of speech that were returned from the lexicon for any given word. Functional information was also added to the record whenever possible. In the case above, both the subject, the direct and the indirect object of the sentence have been identified as the values of the SUBJEKT, OBJEKT, and INDOBJ attributes, respectively.

3.3 Rules

With very few exceptions, all the rules of the grammar were binary. As opposed to configurational rules, they have the advantage of predicting correctly the flexible order and the theoretically unlimited branching capacity of natural language constituent structures. Another characteristic of the rules was recursion. In general, PLNLP rules could apply several times. Further, attributions made at the first application could be changed at a later one. For instance, the verb complement pick-up rule was not only intended to handle direct object attachment, but also attachment of indirect object as well as subject and object predicatives. Each time the rule applied, the (preliminary) role attributed to each of the NPs of the VP was reconsidered in the light of information provided by the newly attached NP: An NP would be given the role of direct object in case there was not one there already, i.e., in the first pass of the rule. In a possible second pass, an NP already attributed the role of direct object, would be re-evaluated and given the role of indirect object, and the NP

```
(2500)      VP((---)
                    /// for å få til at 2500 virker to ganger /////////
                    /// etter verb som tar objektspredikativ //////////
                <OBJPRED1^METT>,
                    (---)
                    /// for å hindre "(gi den ut)VP nåNP"      /////////
                ^NOKOBJ,
                    (---))

            NP(---)

        --> VP(
                    (---)
                    /// får til indirekte og direkte objekt  //////////
                <^OBJPRED,INDOBJ=OBJEKT,OBJEKT=NP,+TOOBJ>,
                    /// får til direkte objekt og objektspred. /////////
                <OBJPRED,
                <OBJEKT,OBJPREDIK=NP>,
                <^OBJEKT,OBJEKT=NP>>,
                    (---))
```

Fig. 2. Extract of the verb complement pickup rule

attached in the current pass would be marked as a direct object instead – unless the main verb required an object predicative. In the latter case, the NP attributed the function of direct object in the first pass, would continue to be the direct object, and the new NP attached in the second pass, would be marked as object predicative. Cf. the extract from the rule in Fig. 2.

4 Development

Writing the syntactic rules constituted the central activity of the project. This is why I shall elaborate on rule writing, while just mentioning the post syntax components in passing.

4.1 Staff

The project leader[8] acted as the "grammarian," i.e. the person actually implementing the rules and testing them. He also coordinated the maintenance of the lexicon and the morphology as well as the development of the auxiliary material (syntactic information, corpora etc.). Research assistants were instructed to find and document combinability properties of words as well as information that might be of value for the future style component.

4.2 Rule Writing

To limit the scope of the phrase structure rules, thus preventing incorrect and otherwise unwanted parses, syntactic markers and conditions were used. In practice, the grammar writing was carried out as a process of rule writing and subsequent

---

[8] Jan Engh.

testing, involving both individual utterances and corpora.[9] Debugging functions allowed the user to pinpoint the exact place in a rule where a parse failed, or the exact differences between two ambiguous parses.

First, a rule was set to apply to a certain linguistic structure. Then the grammarian's task was to make that rule as precise as possible and to put limits to its scope so that it actually parsed the type of linguistic structure that the grammarian had in mind and nothing else. One simple example is direct object selection. For instance, the verb KJØPE 'buy' cannot take an infinitive as its direct object, while ØNSKE 'wish' can. In order to block object infinitives, a simple condition had to be written in the verb complement pick-up rule.

The first task was carried out partly based on the grammarian's own linguistic competence as a native language user and partly based on documented linguistic knowledge. Now, it is common knowledge that the description of all natural languages is far from complete. Based on what is actually stated in syntax literature, rules will never cover nor provide adequate structural descriptions of the sentences produced. This even holds for rules based on introspection. Hence, the use of corpora was essential.

Inevitably, rules may also produce unforeseen results, not least given the rapid complication of the rule structure itself. A consequence of the extrinsic and relaxed approach of rule writing was, thus, a proliferation of unintended parses. So, in a second phase, the grammarian had to set conditions – often in other rules – that would block these partly unpredictable and in any case unwanted parses. Some incorrect, others, in fact, correct, however inconvenient. In fact, a few central rules carried a heavy burden containing numerous filtering conditions, simply because they were to be applied after most other rules, offering the possibility to "control" the well-formedness of the input graphs generated by previous rules. These conditions were of a general nature, as already illustrated by the complement selection. However, there were exceptions. One was the case of "man."

Although there are sentences whose subject is an indefinite singular, such as (1),

(1)   Regn faller fra himmelen.
        'Rain falls from the sky'[10]

"man", the indefinite singular a form of MAN 'mane' – a homonym of the indefinite pronoun MAN 'one' – had, in fact, to be blocked in subject position, i.e. an ad hoc blocking. This was done to prevent a highly improbable alternative parse of the sentence (2).

---

[9] Two types of corpora were created for the purpose. One constructed with systematically fully expanded Norwegian sentences selected to contain well identified structures – each sentence with variants containing all possible word orders (both grammatical and ungrammatical). One "authentic" with ordinary Norwegian texts drawn from various areas of language use, partly typed in, as no Norwegian common language corpus was available to the project (examples from linguistics literature, samples of literary texts etc.), partly harvested from corporate business correspondence. Finally, a corpus consisting of grammar school pupils' essays – uncorrected and containing authentic errors and weaknesses – was purchased.

[10] Here and later, the expression in single quotes represents a rough, word-by-word English gloss of the content of the Norwegian example – regardless of the possible ungrammaticality of the English rendering.

(2)   Man hørte rop i det fjerne.
         'One heard shouts in the far', i.e. 'One heard distant shouts'

The last example illustrates yet another characteristic of PLNLP-based syntax: information usually attributed little importance – or ignored – by grammarians is quite useful. One more example: There are lexemes (word types) that never appear as the subject of a sentence, for instance, the one marked for 'reciprocity'. Why bother? The syntax will never be given an absurd sentence such as (3) as input. However, the feature 'reciprocity' will provide a clue for producing only the correct parse of sentences such as (4). Without this clue, a second – and incorrect – parse would also be possible (5). [11]

(3)   *Hverandre kjøpte mat.
         'Each other bought food'

(4)   De så på hverandre tenkte sitt og gikk hvert til sitt.
         [De så på hverandre] [tenkte sitt] [og gikk hvert til sitt].
         '[They looked at each other], [made up their own minds], [and went away]'

(5)   *[De så på] [hverandre tenkte sitt] [og gikk hvert til sitt].
         '[They looked at] [each other made up their own minds] [and went away]'

As already mentioned, an amazingly high number of unexpected parses turned out to be – just correct parses. For instance, (6) has, surprisingly, two correct interpretations, (7) and (8), as shown by the analysis trees in Fig. 3.

(6)   De kjøpte huset.

(7)   DeNP/SUBJECT kjøpteVP husetNP/DIRECT OBJECT.
         'They bought the house'

(8)   [De kjøpte]NP/SUBJECT husetVP.
         '[The bought ones] gave shelter'

```
Skriv en setning på norsk eller en kommando:

De kjøpte huset.

------------------------------------------------------------
FHSETN1NP1            ADJ1       "De"
                                 VERB1*      "kjøpte"
                     VERB2*     "huset"
                     PUNC1      "."
------------------------------------------------------------
FHSETN2NP2           PRON1*     "De"
                     VERB1*     "kjøpte"
                     NP3        NOUN1*      "huset"
                     PUNC1      "."
------------------------------------------------------------
```

Fig. 3. Analysis trees

---

[11] Theoretically, one might have avoided the problem in this particular case by means of a comma rule. However, that would have made it more difficult to process sentences with a comma error, which, among other things, would have made the syntax unsuited as the base of a text critiquing system.

It would be wrong to block the unexpected parse since, theoretically, it will always be possible to use (8), for instance as the response to a question (9), which, in turn, cannot be discarded on syntactic grounds. Cf. its structural resemblance with sentences such as (10).

(9)   Hvem var det som huset [dem]?
        'Who was it that let them stay in their house?'

(10)   [Hva var det de oppsagte arbeiderne gjorde?] De oppsagte streiket.
        '[What was it that the dismissed workers did?] The dismissed (ones) started a strike'

However, not all unexpected correct parses were that awkward. One perfectly normal sentence was (11), where the preposition phrase may be interpreted in two distinct ways, cf. (12) and (13), according to the context.

(11)   Han spiste det brødet han bakte i går.
        'He ate the bread that he baked yesterday'

(12)   Han spiste [det brødet [han bakte [i går]ADVP]RELATIVECLAUSE]NP/DIRECT OBJECT.

(13)   Han spiste [det brødet [han bakte]RELATIVECLAUSE]NP/DIRECT OBJECT. [i går]ADVP.

In fact, the most common type of real ambiguity concerns attachment of this kind, which was marked in the parse tree to be solved later.

5 Post Syntax Processing

In a number of cases, one may find sentence internal clues for adjunct attachment. Cf. (14) and the two possible attachments for the preposition phrase, (15) and the somewhat awkward (16).

(14)   Hun renset fisken med en kniv.

(15)   Hun renset fisken [med en kniv]PP.
        'She cleaned the fish by means of a knife'

(16)   Hun renset [fisken med en kniv]NP.
        'She cleaned the fish which had a knife'

Such cases were supposed to be taken care of by the reattachment component, which would use the information from a conventional lexicon to decide which one of the parses was the more probable. In its most primitive manner, simply by looking for the possible co-occurrence of "clean (a fish)" and "knife" within the same dictionary definition. However, this subcomponent was not fully developed. Neither were the ones for fitted parsing (assigning some reasonable structure to non-parsed input by the use of a "fitting" procedure, see [11]) and parse-metrics (evaluation of multiple correct parses for applications requiring unique parses, see [12, 13]). In addition, the component for surface structure interpretation, operating on the output of the reassignment components and intended to serve as the basis for further semantic processing, did not exceed the stage of prototype.

6 Style Component

The style component had two subcomponents, the style procedures and the features pertaining to the style critiquing application system, CRITIQUE. The former would detect stylistic errors. The latter would produce a set of explanations, ranging from the simple identification of the style error via advice for action to the relevant paragraph in an on-line textbook on correct style. Whenever required, a syntactic change such as moving a constituent was prepared – for later execution on request from the application user. For instance, one could identify "heavy" adjuncts between the finite and the infinite verb of (17), proposing a move to the front of the sentence (18).

(17)   (?) Jeg ble i dag morges påkjørt av en sykkel.
        'I was this morning run into by a bicycle.'
(18)   I dag morges ble jeg påkjørt av en sykkel.

This example also illustrates the unclear border between style and syntax. On the other hand, it also shows how the style procedures could be used for borderline cases.

7 Project History

The project started in the late autumn of 1988, and was carried out in close cooperation with its sister projects abroad. In addition to the project leader/grammarian, five part-time assistants participated in the development, which was carried out on an IBM 370 mainframe under VM/CMS at IBM Norway premises. The development work went on until ASD cut the funding prematurely as of 3 August 1990. Still, significant results had been made. Most important: the first broad coverage analytic syntax for Norwegian.

8 The Continuation Project – Machine Translation

After the corporate funding cut, IBM Norway decided to continue the grammar project on its own. As a continuation of the writing tool development was out of question, grammar development was continued in order to produce a commercial system for automatic translation from Norwegian Bokmål to Nynorsk.

The machine translation technology adopted was a transfer based system developed at IBM Portugal [14–16]. A rough sketch of its architecture and the dataflow appears in Fig. 4. The width of the lines indicates the degree of completion at the time of the conclusion of this project. The Bokmål and Nynorsk lexica and morphologies were ready, the analytic syntax was extensive but not yet ready for commercial purposes, the transfer rules were also more or less ready, and the production syntax development was under way. The bilingual dictionary, however, was small.

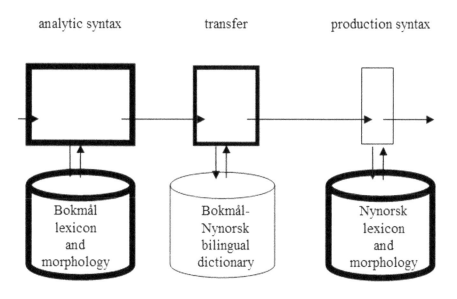

Fig. 4. Architecture and dataflow

The Bokmål-Nynorsk machine translation engine was a possible product with good market perspectives (in public sector administration and, above all, in the production of schoolbooks). Unfortunately, even this project turned out to be too expensive, and IBM Norway invited The Ministry of Administration as a partner in the application for a grant from Statens industrifond,[12] NOK 1,300,000, intended to finance Portuguese education and support and, above all, the compilation of an extensive bilingual Bokmål-Nynorsk dictionary. After half a year's reflection, the invitation was turned down (1991) on the grounds that IBM had not proved that it was possible to realise the project – strangely enough, since the prototype with fully developed system modules had been demonstrated to top officials and their technical aids.

9   Experience Gained

As for linguistics, unknown aspects of Norwegian syntax were discovered, relating to valency, preposition selection, and subject predicative agreement etc. One general observation: Actual Norwegian sentences are far more open to interpretation than usually acknowledged, as long as a strict separation of syntax and semantics is observed. From a methodological point of view, it became clear that a working broad coverage grammar could, in fact, be made without drawing heavily on modern linguistic syntactic and semantic theory. What turned out to be essential was extensive

---

[12] The Norwegian State's Fund for Industrial Development.

descriptive knowledge of Norwegian, for instance based on traditional and structuralist (positional) syntax.

As far as economy was concerned, the final, "national" phase of the project showed that relying on public grants for this type of development was a daring venture. The project obviously stumbled owing to higher public management's attitudes and personal antipathies, irrational factors that it will always be difficult to control. On the rational side, however, the main experience was probably that a huge and expensive enterprise such as the entire broad-coverage grammar project ought to be financed in several stages: Funding needs to be generated from successive implementation of modules in products and services already from an early phase of the project. The IBM grammar project depended on one unique corporate source of long term funding. There were no plans to generate funding before the very end of the project and this became critical when the world's economic crisis hit the corporation.

Acknowledgments. I would like to thank Diana Santos for having read the manuscript and confirmed my recollections.

References

1. Engh, J.: Lexicography for IBM. Developing Norwegian Linguistic Resources in the 1980s. In: Impagliazzo, J., Järvi, T., Paju, P. (eds.) HiNC2. IFIP AICT, vol. 303, pp. 258–270. Springer, Heidelberg (2009)
2. Engh, J.: Språkforskning i IBM Norge [Paper read at Møte om norsk språk (MONS) IV, Oslo 15.-17.11.1991] Printed in NORSKRIFT 72, pp. 16–36 (1992)
3. Engh, J.: Developing Grammar at IBM Norway 1988–1991. Unpublished report, Oslo (1994)
4. Vikør, L.: The Nordic languages. Their Status and Interrelations. 3rd edn. (Nordic Language Secretariat. Publication 14) Novus, Oslo (2001)
5. Heidorn, G.: Natural language inputs to a simulation programming system. Ph.D. dissertation. Technical report, NPS-55HD72101A. Naval Postgraduate School, Monterey. Monterey, Cal. (1972)
6. Heidorn, G.: Augmented Phrase Structure Grammars. In: Nash Webber, B.L., Schank, R. (eds.) Theoretical Issues in Natural Language Processing, pp. 1–7. ACL (1975)
7. Jensen, K.: PEG 1986: a Broad-coverage Computational Syntax of English. IBM research report. T.J. Watson research center, Yorktown Heights, N.Y. (1986)
8. Jensen, K., Heidorn, G., Richardson, S., Haas, N.: PLNLP, PEG, and CRITIQUE: Three Contributions to Computing in the Humanities. In: Proceedings of the 8th International Conference on Computers and the Humanities, Toronto, Canada (1986)
9. Jensen, K., Heidorn, G., Richardson, S. (eds.): Natural Language Processing: The PLNLP Approach. Natural Language Processing and Machine Translation. The Kluwer International Series in Engineering and Computer Science, vol. 196. Kluwer, Hingham (1993)
10. Lie, S.: Automatisk syntaktisk analyse. 1, Grammatikken (Rapportserie 17) NAVFs EDB-senter for humanistisk forskning, Oslo (1980)
11. Jensen, K., Heidorn, G., Miller, L., Ravin, Y.: Parse Fitting and Prose Fixing: Getting a Hold on Ill-formedness. American Journal of Computational Linguistics 9, 3–4 (1983)

12. Heidorn, G.: An Easily Computed Metric for Ranking Alternative Parses. Paper Presented at the 14th Annual Meeting of the ACL (1976)
13. Heidorn, G.: Experience with an Easily Computed Metric for Ranking Alternative Parses. In: Proceedings of the 20th Annual Meeting of the ACL (1982)
14. Santos, D.: An MT Prototype from English to Portuguese. In: Proceedings of the IBM Conference on Natural Language Processing, Thornwood, USA, October 24-26 (1988)
15. Santos, D.: Broad-coverage Machine Translation. In: Jensen, K., Heidorn, G., Richardson, S. (eds.) Natural Language Processing: The PLNLP Approach, pp. 101–115, (118). Kluwer, Hingham (1993)
16. Engh, J., Santos, D.: Use of PORTUGA for the two Norwegian Written Standards. In: Jensen, K., Heidorn, G., Richardson, S. (eds.) Natural Language Processing: The PLNLP Approach, pp. 115–118. Kluwer, Hingham (1993)

Computer Courses in Finnish Schools, 1980–1995

Petri Saarikoski

Digital Culture, Degree Program in Cultural Production and Landscape Studies
PL 124, 28101 University Consortium of Pori, Finland
petsaari@utu.fi

Abstract. The early history of computers in Finnish schools occurred during the period 1978–1995. In high schools, courses were officially included in the curricula in 1982, while at the upper level of comprehensive school, computer courses started in 1987. This paper describes and analyzes the challenges and results of the first wave of computer education in the Finnish school system.

Keywords: Comprehensive schools, computer clubs, computer courses, computer literacy, Finland, high schools, history of computer education.

1 Introduction

"Discussion about the computerization of our school system has mainly been dominated by computer consultants and the computer industry. This has been affected by the myth of the information society. It is regrettable that, in this way, parents and teachers have suddenly and sadly lost their self-respect."

The above sentences were included at the start of a research publication [1] written by Jarkko Alajääski, Senior Lecturer of Didactics of Mathematics. The work, which was published in the spring of 1987, strongly criticized the way in which computers and information technology had so far been introduced into schools. In the late 1980s, there were relatively few academic studies available about the use of computers in Finnish schools. Some researchers had collected data and material from high schools where computer teaching (more commonly known in the early 1980s as "teaching of Automatic Data Processing" or more simply "ADP-teaching") had started in the 1980s. The results had mainly been embarrassing; high school students and teachers had declared that "ADP-teaching" did not work as the National Board of Education had planned it [2].

In media publicity, the computerization of schools was more commonly associated with "the computer literacy project." I have studied the computerization of schools in a couple of publications and partly in my doctoral thesis [3, 4, 2]. In this article, I examine how the adoption of computers started in schools during 1980–1995. What were the politics of this computerization project? In what ways were the interaction between schools and computer clubs established? It is also important to study the collaboration of teachers and pupils. What was the role of the ordinary pupil, seen as an integral part of the computer culture, which was already taking shape?

J. Impagliazzo, P. Lundin, and B. Wangler (Eds.): HiNC3, IFIP AICT 350, pp. 150–158, 2011.

2 Background of the Early Computer Courses

The teaching of data processing and information technology began in the Finnish universities during the 1960s, and some basic courses were available in some schools and institutes in the late 1960s and early 1970s. In Finland, this was combined with the educational and do-it-yourself aspects of IT-learning. Early courses were usually joint ventures between local schools, universities, and computer companies. This kind of activity started in major cities, especially in the metropolitan area. Sources have indicated that Tapiola co-educational school in Espoo offered ADP-courses already in 1965. This particular school was well known for its reformist curriculum and open-mindedness towards the use of new technology. During these first experimental courses, pupils had the opportunity to learn the basics of programming. After their graduation, some of the more talented pupils started to study ADP at university [5, 6].

Computers and information technology, more generally, still had no official status in the Finnish school system during the 1970s. ADP-teaching was only available in some special courses and in unofficial computer clubs founded by some far-sighted teachers. In fact, during the 1970s and early 1980s, ADP-teaching and the hobby of microcomputers were socially and culturally very close to each other. However, things had begun to change from the mid-1970s onwards. Finland was in a deep economic depression during the late 1970s. Traditional heavy industry was in crisis and companies were rapidly seeking solutions for production problems from computerization, the use of electronics, and industrial automation. Economic life and society was clearly changing. The policy of the information society was established by the state and the usage of information technology was seen as part of everyday life. This also meant fundamental challenges for the Finnish school system [7, 4].

The consultative committee for the development of ADP in Finnish society – funded by Sitra, the Finnish Innovation Fund – started a major research project in the spring of 1977, in which the challenges and opportunities of IT in schools were studied. The ulterior motive of this project was the formalization of ADP for the Finnish school system. The research report published in 1978 indicated that there were indeed many challenges; very few schools had computers or any other ADP-infrastructure available. When the situation was compared to other Nordic countries, the results showed that Finland's readiness for ADP-education in schools was weak. As a conclusion, the report proposed that drastic measures were necessary before the first ADP-courses could be started. Primarily, this meant that schools were obligated to purchase computers and other hardware. Computer training should also be arranged for the teachers. According to the report, this reform was to be first started in high schools and then in comprehensive schools. The proposal argued that from the economic point of view, the fast computerization of high schools was realistic, because in doing so learning results would be quickly utilized [8, 9].

The early 1980s was a crucial turning point for the Finnish school system. The reform of the comprehensive school system, started in the 1970s, was already completed, and the computerization of schools, initiated by the government, was a major addition to the whole school system. This project was, in fact, a combination of separate IT-projects that took place during the 1980s. The basic goal of each of these projects was the foundation and maintenance of IT-infrastructure for the Finnish educational sector. These projects had a clear and understandable connection to other similar projects that had started in the 1970s and 1980s in Europe (for example, in Britain, France, and the Nordic countries). The concept of "computer literacy" was very popular during the 1980s and it was mostly linked to the domestication of the home computer. It had strong connections to the use of home computers during leisure time, but also to the computerization of schools. A typical early adopter of computer literacy was the computer hobbyist. The concept became common during the late 1970s, but it gained more popularity in the media during the early 1980s. The whole concept, and especially its media exposure, was the counterpart of a similar kind of public discussion that was going on in Europe at the same time. The best-known example was Britain's "The Computer Literacy Project," started by the Ministry of Education in the late 1970s and early 1980s [10, 11].

In Finland, the concept of "literacy" has a very strong connection to the emergence of the welfare state after World War II. Free education provided by the state became the very cornerstone of Finnish society. Therefore, in Finland, "literacy" was both a privilege and an obligation at the same time. This evocative concept was also analyzed in the media by a series of experts, who underlined that in coming decades the knowledge and mastery of computers was to become a strong part of general education. This marks the point at which computers came to be seen as a tool in the education of youth and children, making it possible for them to acquire the basics of computer literacy that were to be so valued in the future. This is, of course, only a generalization. Families typically bought their first home computers as a leisure tool for technically-oriented boys. On the other hand, the early 1980s was a period characterized by a strengthening of the optimistic, symbolic meanings associated with home computers [12, 2]. The concept of computer literacy has similarities to the concept of digital literacy, which became popular during the first decade of the twenty-first century [13].

In addition, the concept of computer literacy linked closely to the emergence of the microcomputer hobby and the opening of home computer markets during the early 1980s. Unofficial computer clubs in schools were also part of this development. These clubs operated like earlier technically oriented clubs founded by radio amateurs and electronics enthusiasts [3]. The importance of these clubs was also noticed in reports published by the Ministry of Education. Such clubs became important staging posts in some schools before the official introduction of ADP-courses.

The official start of computerization in schools offered new markets for the computer industry. Computer systems, designed for educational purposes and home computing, were also manufactured and designed in the Nordic countries. Perhaps the best-known example was the ABC80 microcomputer engineered by the Swedish corporation Dataindustrier AB (DIAB) and manufactured by Luxor. The growth of the educational computer market was also noticed in Finland, and sources indicate that the Finnish IT-industry was also interested in starting its own serial production of home computers. Nokia became the most successful manufacturer of microcomputers in Finland during the 1980s and early 1990s. The Nokia MikroMikko series was sold to industry, schools, and households [14, 3].

In Finland, the number of computer systems ordered by schools increased slowly, but in 1980 and 1981, computerization began to escalate, when more state aid was available. In 1979, one high school out of ten had purchased computers and associated peripherals, but in 1981, almost 33 percent of high schools had some sort of

ADP-infrastructure. Furthermore, in high schools, ADP-courses were officially included in the curricula in 1982 and, during the autumn term of the same year, ADP-courses were arranged in 320 high schools, which comprised almost 70 percent of all upper secondary schools. During the following spring term, almost 87 percent of all high schools could arrange ADP-courses. In the autumn term of 1983, ADP-teaching was offered in practically every Finnish high school. The National Board of Education calculated that about one third of upper secondary students took a computer course as a free elective [2, 9].

The most popular computers used in high schools during these years were ABC80, Apple II, Nokia MikroMikko, and AMC-100, which the National Board of Education recommended. The machines usually operated with 32–128 kB memory and the most common operating system was CP/M, provided by Digital Research. Furthermore, the most typical computer system was AMC-100, manufactured by Finnish Auditek. One AMC-100 classroom system consisted of one minicomputer for the teacher, six terminals for pupils, educational software, and associated peripherals, which constituted extremely expensive investments for high schools [12, 9].

3 Finnish Model for Computer Education

The ADP-education of institute members had many problems right from the start. The main problem was that in the 1980s, educational software support was very weak. There was also a lack of decent course material and difficulties with teacher training. In most of the cases, teachers had no other alternative than to start courses with the programming exercises. BASIC programming language was widely criticized for dominating the computer curriculum. Many IT-experts criticized these courses for having no real value in working life, where the need for skilled ADP-workers was growing all the time. These problems were also noticed by the Ministry of Education, but the lack of extra resources and relatively bureaucratic policymaking, led to the situation in which most of the problems remained unsolved [15]. ADP-courses were mostly successful if teachers were motivated and had taken part in the education provided in computer clubs. Most of these teachers were also computer hobbyists who also quickly learned that it was more effective and affordable to buy home computers for classrooms. For example, Commodore Vic-20 and especially Commodore 64, both very successful home computers in computer clubs, were purchased for some schools. In this way, computer clubs were also established in some comprehensive schools [16–19].

During the 1980s, a characteristic of the Finnish "computer education model" was that computers did not belong to the lower level of the comprehensive school. In reports and memoranda produced by the Ministry of Education, there are still references to experts who recommended that some sort of ADP-education should be available at the lower level of the comprehensive school. However, these recommendations were mostly ignored when plans for the computerization of the upper level of comprehensive schools began in 1984 [20, 6].

On 12 October 1984, ADP was officially accepted as a free elective in the new reform order for the Finnish comprehensive school (which was roughly translated in the late 1980s simply as "Computer course"). The curriculum for these new computer courses was mainly planned by the "Tietokone opetuksessa" (Computing at School) working committee. The first draft was presented in the spring of 1985. It had several interesting features, for example, the working committee insisted that the mistakes made in high schools should be avoided. This meant the reduction of the importance of programming languages. The draft included several modules: the basics of computer use, information networks, programming, and computer-aided education. The latter module included the idea that teachers could use computer software in drawing and language courses. BASIC was still considered a good option for the programming module, but the committee recommended that simpler LOGO programming language should be included as an alternative. The most ambitious idea of these first drafts was that in future years all school courses could be computer-aided, the long-term elaboration of which was left open [2, 6].

During 1985–1987, the state gave special funding to ten schools where computers had been partly used in unofficial computer clubs. The best-known examples include the computer club of Herttoniemi Primary School (started in 1984) from Helsinki and the computer club of Uomarinne Primary School (started in 1985) from Vantaa (Fig.1). Computer courses officially began at the upper level of comprehensive school during the autumn term of 1987 (eighth grade) and the autumn term of 1988 (ninth grade). 20 percent of municipalities postponed the start for one year and, according to some statistics, about 60 percent of pupils did choose the computer course during 1988–1989. The computerization of Finnish society had clearly put some demands on the Finnish school system. The first waves of the home computer boom were already starting to diminish in 1985–1987, but PC-microcomputers, more common in business use, had clearly gained some foothold in consumer markets. In this way, PC, an industry standard, was slowly but steadily becoming the most common computer platform in households and schools. The National Board of Education decided that schools should primarily purchase MS-DOS -compatible PCs, and by the spring of 1988, some eight thousand microcomputers were available in schools, although only half were PCs. These new instructions were criticized because PC-compatible microcomputers were usually very expensive. Schools had already saved money when they had purchased affordable home computers. It is interesting that this politically and technically motivated decision also helped Nokia to increase the sale of MikroMikko computers to schools [21–25, 6].

The time schedule for the launch of computer teaching in comprehensive schools was extremely tight and criticism of the politics of computerization was growing in 1987, as Jarkko Alajääski's study had shown. Some of the teachers and researchers were very skeptical about the successful embrace of the new computer education program [1]. Insufficient teacher training was a major problem; most of the teachers started their first computer course after only one week of training. Pekka Lehtiö, who was involved with the Computing at School working committee, had later stated in an interview that the National Board of Education had a clear tendency to statistically show that there were more and more computers in schools and the Finnish school system was therefore being updated to meet the demands of the information society. On the other hand, little attention was being paid to the implementation of the curriculum itself [22]. This once again created problems at the grass root level of computer education.

Fig. 1. Sixth grade pupils, from Uomarinne primary school in Vantaa, using Commodore 64 at their school's computer club (spring 1987). Courtesy of A-lehdet.

During the late 1980s, the lack of decent educational software and course material was a continuous problem. Once again, programming exercises played an important part in most of the computer courses. Some of the problems can be explained by teaching politics; computer courses were mostly given to the teachers of mathematics and physics. The Trade Union mostly backed this policy for Teachers of Mathematics and Physics ("Matemaattisten Aineiden Opettajien Liito," MAOL) [22]. This might have given a boost to the mathematically oriented "teaching philosophy;" if computer literacy was the essential ability of the information society, then programming was its official language.

The expensive license fees can partly explain the lack of decent software. Programming languages remained in the curriculum most of the 1990s, but were slowly substituted for the computer-aided teaching methods. This was also a time of growth for educational software systems, primarily due to the advent of more affordable computers and the Internet. For example, pupils could try out Visual Basic programming environments later, in connection with their education. Pascal programming language has also been used in the illustration of programming principles. This education has undoubtedly been particularly useful for the technical and mathematical oriented high school students. The technical simplicity of LOGO programming language has also extended its life cycle. In Finland, LOGO is still occasionally used in teacher education [2].

Although computer courses were less technically oriented in the late 1980s and early 1990s than in the early 1980s, sources indicate that learning results were controversial. While some of the pupils had difficulties in following the teaching because they had absolutely no foreknowledge of computer use, some of the computer hobbyists, typically boys, could feel that course exercises were too easy. In questionnaires and interviews collected some fifteen years later, informants criticized these computer courses. Some of them thought that the teachers had not enough experience and that the pupils knew more about the subject than their instructors [26]. These levels of difference between user generations and groups had already been common in the 1960s and 1970s, when the first computer courses became available. There are also examples where informants criticized the authority of teachers; pupils were instructed to strictly follow the course exercises and not to try anything independently. On the other hand, there are also a number of neutral examples where computer courses in schools were classified as the first steps towards more advanced computer education. When teachers were motivated and pupils had the ability to co-operate, learning results were even better. The usability of computer courses improved when word processing, spreadsheets, computer graphics, music, and even games became more common in the curriculum during the 1990s. During these years, computers were also more widely introduced into the lower level of comprehensive school [27, 2]. Despite advances in computer education, the challenges and problems continued in the 1990s. The economic depression in Finland had a severe negative effect on the Finnish school system. During 1991–1995, schools had less money for the purchase of new computers, associated peripherals, and software. A major turning point occurred in 1995 when the government started to intensify information society programs [28].

During these years, the emergence of information networks began to increase. Already in the late 1980s, some pupils and students were also active users of information networks, such as BBS (Bulletin Board System) and several other systems. BBS networks were especially important in Finland before the country was connected to the Internet in the late 1980s. This tradition also continued in the 1990s, when the culture of information networks began to spread. In universities and other institutions, local networks were important points of connection for hobbyists, students, and professionals of information technology. These socially constructed networks led to more benefits and more use. The short cultural history of this development includes the communal spirit and mutual support of USENET, BBS, and the early Internet, in general, and leads into the Open Source movement as its contemporary successor [4].

4 Conclusion

In the late 1980s, the prominence of information technology was contradictory in the Finnish society. The domestication of microcomputers was more clearly regarded as an integral part of the Finnish society, but there was still a wide discussion about the purpose and usability of information technology. The early years of computer literacy and information technology in Finnish schools were challenging in many ways. Computerization started hastily and led to several problems. For policymakers, it was easy to show that the computerization project was advancing, because computer hardware was being steadily purchased for schools. Nevertheless, there were indications that too little attention was being paid to the implementation of the curriculum itself. Insufficient teacher training was one of the main problems, and for some pupils, parts of the curriculum modules also had an orientation that was too technical. In addition, the programming language was widely criticized for dominating the curriculum. Still, for many pupils, these initial computer courses were the first opportunity to learn the basics of computing, when the domestication of computers was in its early stages.

On the other hand, computer hobbyists could feel that courses were too simple or they had other motivation problems regarding the authoritarian teacher. In recent studies [4], I have noticed that some of the "success stories of computer education" have links to the unofficial computer clubs. During the 1980s, these clubs also had links to the culture of computer hobbyists, who created a range of subcultures, where different kinds of communities began to emerge. Networks of these communities formed a very strong social base for the emergence of the computer culture of the 1990s.

References

1. Alajääski, J.: Tietokoneopetus peruskoulun ala-asteella: Johdanto ja käsitteitä. Jatko-opiskeluun liittyvä tutkielma. Turun yliopiston kasvatustieteellinen tiedekunta, Turku (1987)
2. Saarikoski P.: Koneen ja koulun ensikohtaaminen Suomalaisen atk-koulutuksen varhaisvaiheet peruskoulussa ja lukiossa. Tekniikan Waiheita, (3) (2006)
3. Saarikoski, P.: Koneen lumo. Mikrotietokoneharrastus Suomessa 1970-luvulta 1990-luvun puoliväliin. (The Lure of the Machine. The Personal Computer Interest in Finland from the 1970s to the mid-1990s) Väitöskirja, yleinen historia, Turun yliopisto (Doctoral thesis, Department of History, general history, University of Turku, October 2004). Jyväskylän nykykulttuurin tutkimuskeskuksen julkaisuja 83 (publisher: The Research Centre for Contemporary Culture). Jyväskylä (2004)
4. Saarikoski, P., Suominen, J., Turtiainen, R., Östman, S.: FUNETIsta Facebookiin. Internetin kulttuurihistoria. (From FUNET to Facebook: Cultural History of Internet in Finland), Gaudeamus, Helsinki (2009)
5. Saarikoski P.: Koneen lumo, pp. 44–45 (2004)
6. Tietokone opetuksessa -projektin (TOP) mietintö. Tietotekniikan integroiminen kouluopetukseen. Tulosten arviointi ja jatkotoimet. Opetusministeriö. Helsinki Liite 1, 2 (1989)
7. Saarikoski P.: Koneen lumo, pp. 58–59 (2004)
8. Parkkinen, M., Rantanen, J., Valli, T.: Tietokone opetuksessa. Suomen itsenäisyyden Juhlarahasto Sarja A 56, 63–64 (1978)
9. Lukion atk-laitteita ja ohjelmistoja selvittäneen työryhmän (ATLAS) muistio. Kouluhallitus, Helsinki, 5–8 (1982)
10. Haddon, L.: The Roots And Early History of the British Home Computer Market: Origins of the Masculine Micro. Management School Imperial College. University of London, London (1988)
11. Saarikoski P.: Koneen lumo, p. 145 (2004)
12. Tietokone 3/ 9 1983
13. Digitaalinen sisältötuotanto - strategiset tavoitteet ja toimintaehdotukset. Opetusministeriö, Sisältötuotantotyöryhmän raportti Helsinki (2002)
14. Radiokauppias, October 28-29 (1981)
15. Saarikoski P.: Koneen lumo, pp. 45–46 (2004)

16. Kivinen, A.: Taulukkolaskentaohjelma mikrotietokoneen opetuskäytössä. Suomen kasvatustieteellinen aikakauskirja Kasvatus 16(5), 347–352 (1985)
17. Raivola, R.: Uusi informaatioteknologia edellyttää koulun muuttumista. Suomen kasvatustieteellinen aikakauskirja Kasvatus 16(5), 359–366 (1985)
18. Tietokone, February 66-67 (1983)
19. Printti 12, 4 (1986); Printti 14, 9, 26 (1986)
20. Aikuisväestön tietotekniikan peruskoulutus. Tietotekniikan aikuiskoulutuksen suunnitteluryhmän muistio. Opetusministeriön työryhmien muistioita 5, 1–15 (1986)
21. Saarikoski, P.: Koneen lumo, p. 118 (2004)
22. Lehtiö P.: Interview (January 21, 2005)
23. Printti 1,3 (1985) Printti 1,16 (1986) Printti 5, 3 (1986) Printti 4, 16-18 (1987) Printti 19, 16–17 (1987)
24. Opettaja 9, 22–24 (1986) Opettaja 5, 4–5 (1987)
25. Tietokone opetuksessa -projektin (TOP) mietintö, 42–43
26. TIESU-kysely (2003), http://kultmais.utu.fi/tiesu (June 12, 2010)
27. Kajosvaara, J.: Tietotekniikka ala-asteen koulutyössä. Loppuraportti. Opetushallitus, TAKO-projekti 1.1.1990-30.6.1991, Rauma, pp. i-ii (1991)
28. Valtioneuvosto, Suomi tietoyhteiskunnaksi. Kansalliset linjaukset. Edita: Helsinki (1995)

Teacher Pioneers in the Introduction of Computing Technology in the Swedish Upper Secondary School

Lennart Rolandsson

Department of Education in Arts and Professions
Stockholm University, SE-106 91 Stockholm, Sweden
lennart.rolandsson@utep.su.se

Abstract. The paper elaborates on programming and computing 1970 to 1983 in the Swedish upper secondary school. Articles from contemporary journals and firsthand text sources are used. During that period, programming never qualified as a separate subject; it was a tool for problem solving in engineering, economics, and mathematics, and did become a literacy subject in its own right. Early adopters of computers in education became important pioneers in the production of discourses about "how-to" and "what-to" teach. The diffusion of computer technology was substantiated in a curriculum for computing in natural sciences, which embraced programming.

Keywords: Curriculum development, education in computing, programming, system architecture, teacher, upper secondary school.

1 Introduction

The paper describes the period from 1970 to 1983 when computing was under considerable elaboration in experimental works at schools. Computer technology had been in universities and Swedish industry since the 1940s, but the 1970s was the decade of important reforms when the gymnasium (upper secondary school) merged with vocational education into one school system. Three perspectives describe this historical movement: 1) the pedagogy offered by hardware and software, 2) the experimental works initiated by the National Board of Education, NBE (Skolöverstyrelsen) in some of the major projects concerning the adoption of computing into education, and 3) the voices of teacher pioneers concerning programming.

This paper is part of my thesis project that explores programming as a subject topic experienced by teachers in upper secondary school. The perspective of computing history is important to appreciate better the constraints that technology offers.

2 Hardware and Software Constraints in Education

The learning processes of students when constructing software have always been dependent on features in peripheral and internal hardware. Students could consider

J. Impagliazzo, P. Lundin, and B. Wangler (Eds.): HiNC3, IFIP AICT 350, pp. 159–167, 2011.
© IFIP International Federation for Information Processing 2011

themselves lucky if they did not have to load the computers, by hand for half an hour, with necessary software before beginning the work of programming.

In the fall of 1979, NBE made an inventory of different computer technologies used in schools [1]. Fig. 1 displays the computer hardware shifts in upper secondary school during the 1970s. The figure reveals a huge investment from 1977 to 1979 when many schools purchased single unit computers.[1]

According to the DIS-report, the investment for five working places with a connection to a mainframe computer or minicomputer would be approximately 25–35 million SEK [1]. The prices of single unit computers were much more affordable at the time. However, technological development was rapid, which possibly led to some caution with regard to investments. According to NBE's enquiry in 1979, more than 50 percent of the schools had only one or two single unit computers and 88 percent of the schools had at most five single unit computers. In other words, schools were cautious.

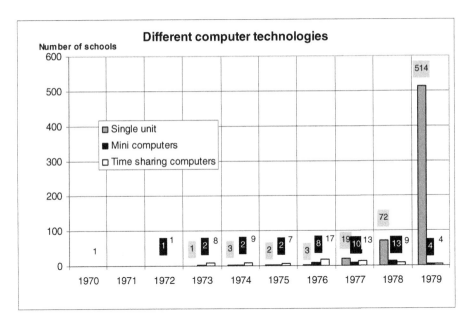

Fig. 1. How computer hardware changed in upper secondary school during the 1970s [1]

2.1 Mainframe Computer

In the spring of 1970, a programming project called "Zimmermanska skolan," together with ASEA Education AB, began at an upper secondary school in Västerås, Sweden [2]. The working group consisted of three part-time teachers plus a full-time teacher assistant who worked together with students from the technical upper secondary school. Together they developed courses in Automatic Data Processing

---

[1] Commodore PET came on the market 1977, Apple II in June 1977, TRS 80 in December 1977, ABC 80 in August 1978, and Compis in 1984.

(ADP) combined with the regular mathematical education for natural science students. At their disposal, they had a mainframe computer, DEC PDP-8 8k/word, which was equipped with disk memory 32 k/word, seven terminals, and eleven monitors. The educational method fell into one of the following two categories:

1. Classroom teaching where the teacher used a monitor to demonstrate, for example, the parabola of moving objects in physics;
2. Students working in groups of four at typing machine terminals and monitors connected to a common computer in the classroom.

The documentation reveals that it took about ten hours of students' work before they could construct their own programs in some applied subject.

2.2 Desktop Calculator

In Sunnerboskolan, teachers had their first experience of computing in 1970 when they used terminals connected via modems to companies such as IBM, Honeywell Bull, and Datema [3]. The educational setting was expensive and constrained to special times during the day and year. Due to the complex connecting procedures, the education consisted primarily of teacher led demonstrations. At first, teaching focused on programming in FORTRAN, and later in BASIC. The shift was based on the higher threshold for learning FORTRAN.

Due to economic constraints, teachers decided to use the desktop calculator, Compucorp 122E, which offered a higher threshold because of the lack of any advanced level language. The calculator, however, enabled more flexible classroom activities, since students could work more interactively with their algorithms. The students prepared the executable programs in assembly language, which were translated to code on card(s) that were loaded into the calculator later. They then had to wait in a line before they could see the results of their work. If students discovered errors in the code, they had to check their algorithms and repeat the process.

2.3 Minicomputer

Sunnerboskolan was also one of the very first schools that purchased a minicomputer in 1973, the PDP 8, with three teletype devices [3]. The computer's construction meant that you had to load the machine for twenty minutes with a BASIC compiler before one could use it in class. The connection between the teletypes and the minicomputer was slow; the teletypes printed ten characters per second. Therefore, in 1975, the school decided to buy a minicomputer, the Alpha LSI, with a magnetic secondary memory, which resolved many of the tedious preparations. According to documentation, they purchased their third minicomputer in 1978, the Nord 10, which had a much bigger primary memory and a faster response rate with its terminals. The monitors responded one hundred times faster than the teletypes could ever print. In conclusion, the educational setting for computing transformed considerably in a period of five years.

3 The Introduction of Programming in Upper Secondary School

The first secondary schools to offer computing courses in the 1960s were located in one of the following areas: Stockholm (Fridhemsplan), Västerås, Gothenburg, and Malmö. Computing was offered as advanced special courses at upper secondary school; as a student, you could choose between one-year specializations in administrative ADP or technical ADP [4]. Due to its success and to meet industry standards at the time, these first schools were soon followed by eleven others [5] located in Solna, Växjö, Västervik, Norrköping, Linköping, Örebro, Karlstad, Uppsala, Gävle, Umeå, and Sundsvall [2]. The courses reached a peak or "programming boom" at the end of the 1960s with thirty-five to forty classes [5] all over Sweden. The programming languages offered were Assembler, FORTRAN, PL/I, Simula, Basic, Simscript, Cobol, and script languages [6, 7].

In 1977, reorganization from NBE to National Board of Universities and Colleges (Universitets- och högskoleämbetet, UHÄ) meant that many schools were organized under higher education and municipality colleges. However, three schools included a local upper secondary school in the following cities: Umeå, Uppsala, and Linköping [5].

In 1980, collaboration occurred between one college and Berzeliusskolan in Linköping where they carried out the education for the natural sciences computer alignment (from now on named CANS) and evening courses for the municipal adult education [5]. In Malmö, a municipal college offered courses for teachers at upper secondary level and a college in Växjö offered courses for the municipal adult education.

3.1 Early Adopters of Programming in Technical Upper Secondary Schools

The result of an enquiry in 1970 initiated by NBE identified fourteen different technical upper secondary schools as users of computers for scrutinizing laboratory data [2]. A report from 1973 reveals the existence of local experimental work carried out at nine different upper secondary schools [8]. The educational content differed in some aspects between the schools, but the main intention was to enhance calculation and problem solving in mathematics and applied subjects. According to the report, education allocated to programming varied between the schools from a few to fifty-one hours, in languages like BASIC, FORTRAN and COBOL. Furthermore, the DIS-report reveals that some schools had received special support from NBE for investments in computer technology since 1973: Erik Dahlbergsskolan in Jönköping, Berzeliusskolan in Linköping[2], Sunnerboskolan in Ljungby, and Zimmermanska skolan in Västerås [1, 8].

Another report from NBE [9] reveals that students of electrical engineering were taught how to program simpler tasks (mainly in BASIC), by the mathematics teacher. Students would acquire procedural knowledge about computing and programming to the extent that:

---

[2] During that time the head master of Berzeliusskolan was also one of those responsible for the report "Computers in the school municipality," DISK report (translated from "Datorn I SkolKommunen").

... [students] themselves sometimes have to code and sometimes they have to use established programs. It is important that the computer interaction is not time consuming and that students do not perceive computer interaction as an unusually complex way of solving problems [9].

The report from 1976, DIS Bygg, explicitly indicates how teachers of the building/construction course perceived the necessity of programming in education [10]. Some excerpts from these teachers' opinions reveal that there was a tendency to work more with established programs:

... only one of three building/construction teachers had spent much energy in creating programs ... If the school had a computer park with BASIC-compilers and enough terminals, students with interest could probably create their own programs, and in that way also learn a diversity of calculating methods [10].

The role of computers was a calculation tool used for statistics, printing graphs, or sorting data, which would infer programming work. According to a report, the time allocated to the objectives of learning computing, with a major focus on programming, was a suggested two hundred hours distributed over four years at upper secondary school [11].

3.2 A Broad Initiative with Many Projects

During the 1970s, the NBE expressed a sincere ambition to draw up a curriculum for developing computing literacy among students in secondary school. They realized early in the process that computer technology would become a pervasive technology with a huge impact on the whole of society. NBE therefore had to reach a common understanding of how to organize and standardize computing education in secondary school. Some countries considered the importance of a new subject [1] with advanced technical content, while Sweden and NBE, based on recommendations from the DISK report [8], decided to adopt their own implementation strategy, as quickly as possible, in different subjects while experimental work would determine best practices. Subsequently, they would introduce a new subject called "Datalära."

NBE formed a working group in 1974, "Computers in school," a DIS[3] group that based its work on the assumption that computing is better taught as non-specialized knowledge with the potential to facilitate and enhance conceptual understanding in other subjects like mathematics, natural, and social sciences.

3.3 The Computing Alignment in Natural Science Program

Meanwhile, in 1976 [12], experimental work for eight to nine hours per week started in the Natural Science Program with a computer alignment (CANS). The intention was to "increase the number of students in natural science for the purpose of making the Natural Science Program more practical with regard to connections to society as a whole" [13]. The intention described in 1981 was:

---

[3] Acronym for "Datorn I Skolan."

...not intended as a difficult alternative... Hopefully students will experience learning about computing in harmony, partly by doing their own programs, mainly in BASIC, and partly by using developed programs in different subject domains. In addition, it will lead to a better understanding of computers in society. The overall objective of the work is to expose the natural scientist to the use of computers, instead of it being regarded as an education for computer specialists [14].

This was one of four different alignments in the Natural Science Program. The other three were in energy, healthcare, and environment, of which computing was considered the most popular. One of the persons in charge of the implementation of CANS describes the process in the following way:

The experiences so far are good, with a positive attitude from students and teachers. Because of the Natural Science Program and the [computing] alignment's future, it will be very important that education in the subject does not put too much pressure on students. One of the major concerns with the alignment is to give students more time for natural science... [15].

At a conference in 1981 [16], teachers involved with computing alignment shared their experiences while emphasizing special concern about the importance of structure and sound habits when students use system architecture in programming. The language COMAL (a dialect of BASIC) was considered suitable for fostering sound habits because of its implicit structure.

Based on work in the DIS-project [1], NBE devised a new curriculum, in 1983 [17], for Computer Science or "Datakunskap," which became the course subject and guideline for the computing alignment in the Natural Science Program. It was explicitly drawn up with 190 to 240 hours [18] of computing. The curriculum was extraordinary because of its descriptive texts to facilitate the teaching of computer science. Teachers in favor were mainly from the mathematics domain [19]:

Software development in a methodological sense is a relatively new knowledge domain undergoing huge change. The subject is not part of any teacher education [for upper secondary school]. Due to this, extensive commentaries about the module [concerning program development and programming] have been included to clarify and describe a strict educational design and overview of the subject for inexperienced teachers [17].

The commentaries, divided into three levels, are worth reading. They consist of features of the language, elaboration about the programming concepts, and a major work project; a pattern still found today in programming courses A, B and C in upper secondary school. The curriculum description contained twenty-five pages, divided into five different modules:

1. Computer system
2. Program development and programming
3. Use of computers in natural sciences
4. Use of computers in social sciences
5. System technology

A clear statement about the purpose of studying "Datakunskap" is made at the beginning of the document [17]:

> ... the education should be designed to enhance the development of students' ability to work with computers as users ... The intention is not to educate people for the programming industry," meanwhile one of the objectives for the course is to "develop students knowledge in problem analysis and programming."

One of the first schools carrying out experimental work with CANS was Berzeliusskolan in Linköping. Bandhagen upper secondary in Stockholm started in autumn 1977 [19] and was followed in autumn 1978 by eleven other schools.

Table 1. Number of schools carrying out experimental work within the Natural Science Program (CANS) [14, 15, 19]

	Number of schools within CANS	Number of students
1978	11	
1980	20	
1981	35	500 students in year two
1983	47	1,956 students in year two, 1,029 students in year three
1985		2,345 students

3.4 Step-Wise Integration of Programming into Mathematics

Some teachers perceived computing as different from the rest of mathematics and sometimes too advanced for the ordinary mathematics curriculum. They state:

> The change of curriculum [with numerical methods] could drastically influence mathematics education, mainly because of the implicit demands of the new way of thinking, which above all shall be integrated with the other chapters [in the literature] ...teachers with not enough confidence dare not experiment with technical facilities and therefore [numerical methods] become another example of a theorized module, practiced according to the student literature mainly before central assignments [20].

In 1976–77, twenty classes were doing experimental work within mathematics [21] where step-wise iterations were introduced for solving differential equations which were later enlarged with numerical equations, numerical integration, simulation, and applications in physics, all under the name of the NUMA[4] project [12]. The material originated from a group of teachers at Sunnerboskolan in Ljungby. The overall

---

[4] NUMA is an acronym for "Numerisk matematik."

intention of the NUMA project was to study how practical mathematics could be established in a school context with computers [22]. The following excerpt describes some of the ideas that surrounded their pedagogy:

> The 1980s is the decade for problem solving in mathematics … In school we are trying different strategies for problem solving. Computers and calculators foremost affect the trial and error methods and the simulation methods. With a computer as a tool, students could experience how mathematics could be used experimentally to solve different problems. Computers in the proper hands open up possibilities for the enhancement of creative thinking [12].

Teachers in general considered programming as synonymous with tedious work that took time away from the original subject, mathematics [13]. The dilemma between time-consuming technicalities in programming and increased conceptual understanding in mathematics is obvious. The author of the previous excerpt states:

> If you intend to really do programming you should do it with a broader perspective; formulate your problem, pick one of many solution methods, code it in a language, try the algorithm and document your solution [12].

Another excerpt reveals the importance of a sound and social connection when implementing programming in the school context:

> We have to aim for a broader perspective of computer technology that goes beyond the common dialectic view of either the public fear of hostile technical database registries or the computer technician's light blue optimism. It is also important that a general broader perspective even includes hackers (compulsion programming) among our students and teachers [12].

4   Analysis and Discussion

In the development of the computing curriculum, two intersecting objectives have emerged [8]: 1) the implementation of computing as a non-specialist subject offering literacy, and 2) computing as a tool to facilitate the education in applied subjects. The paper has exposed the existence of programming, during the time span, in different experimental works; in advanced mathematical courses (numerical methods and algorithm construction), in applied subjects for engineering in upper secondary school, and as a module in computing alignment for the Natural Science Program.

The paper also reveals the tension between the features inherent in computing devices and the intent to teach programming in an educational setting. Furthermore, the paper presents the existence of teacher pioneers who succeeded in merging technology and pedagogy to such an extent that their work became exemplary for NBE in the development of the computing curricula. Programming, however, does not appear as a subject itself, during this period, which could be understood from the contextualized view and the programming perspective as a natural tool in problem solving [24]. Nevertheless, one of the teacher pioneers explains the beauty of the conceptual understanding of loops[5], when he writes:

---

[5] A learning object in programming.

The class have conquered the computer with a simple BASIC program and forced it to deliver the true answer with few loops! Is not that a miracle in itself? [12]

Finally, I would like to pose the question concerning advanced special courses in upper secondary school within ADP. Why did the legacy from these courses not have a greater influence in the development of computing education? They obviously used the same resources for several years.

References

1. Skolöverstyrelsen: Datorn i skolan. SÖ:s handlingsprogram och slutrapport SÖ-projekt 628, Stockholm, pp. 8–9, 13, 51–56 (1980)
2. Andersson, Å.: Datorn i skolan (DIS): förstudie 1. Kungl. Skolöverstyrelsen, p. 4, 14. Stockholm (1970)
3. Emanuelsson, G., Nilsson, R.: En gymnasieskola med lång erfarenhet. In: Att köpa datorer, pp. 89–91. Liber Utbildningsförlag, Stockholm (1984)
4. Skolöverstyrelsen: Aktuellt från Skolöverstyrelsen, vol. 68, p. 3 (1972/1973)
5. ADB-lärarföreningen: Alfanumeriska meddelanden, 6(1), 3–11 (1980) In private collection
6. Skolöverstyrelsen: Aktuellt från Skolöverstyrelsen, vol. (42), pp. 24–25 (1976/1977)
7. Skolöverstyrelsen: Aktuellt från Skolöverstyrelsen, vol. (5), p. 3 (1975/1976)
8. Fagerström, P.: Datorn i skolkommunen (DISK): Kartläggning, beskrivning: Förslag till åtgärd, p. iv, Appendix 3. Linköping (1973)
9. Skolöverstyrelsen: Datoranvändning i eltekniska ämnen (DISEL). In: National Archives, Arninge, Sweden. Dnr L 77:809, p. 7 (September 1, 1977)
10. Skolöverstyrelsen: Datorns användning i byggtekniska ämnen: Delrapport (DIS Bygg). In: National Archives, Arninge, Sweden. Dnr L 76:1897 (August 13, 1976)
11. PRODIS report. In: National Archives, Arninge Dnr L 81:530 (June 16, 1981
12. Björk, L.-E.: Datorns intåg i svenska skolan. J. Nämnaren 1, 32–33 (1983)
13. Wendelöv, L.: Fortbildning i datalära Mer tid för matematik. Remissvar på kursplaneförslag för NT-linjerna. J. Nämnaren 3, 7–11 (1980)
14. Borg, K.: N-linjens datatekniska variant. J. Nämnaren 2, 55 (1981)
15. Wendelöv, L.: Gymnasielinjernas matematik. J. Nämnaren 1, 7 (1981)
16. Wendelöv, L.: Gymnasielinjernas matematik. J. Nämnaren 4, 7 (1981)
17. Skolöverstyrelsen: Läroplan för gymnasieskolan, Supplement, 95, Datakunskap. Liber Utbildningsförlag, Stockholm (1983)
18. Wettstam, L.: Datakunskap. J. Nämnaren 2, 12 (1984)
19. Borg, K.: Varierande undervisning på datateknisk variant. J. Nämnaren 4, 60 (1981)
20. Schreiber, B., Schreiber, A.: Vad blev det av NUMA? J. Nämnaren 2, 41–42 (1984)
21. Vejde, O.: Några fakta om NUMA försöket. J. Nämnaren 2, 40 (1984)
22. Borg, K.: Några terminer vid en minidator. J. Nämnaren T, 122–124 (1976)
23. Björk, L.-E.: ADM-projektet. Några synpunkter på gymnasieskolans datakunskap. Rapport 27, 13–15 (1987)

Computing on the Desktop: From Batch to Online in Two Large Danish Service Bureaus

Anker Helms Jørgensen

IT University of Copenhagen
Rued Langaardsvej 7, DK-2300 Copenhagen S, Denmark
anker@itu.dk

Abstract. This paper addresses the change from batch mode to online mode in offices and workplaces in the 1970s and 1980s. Particular focus is on the role of IBM and the 3270 display terminal. The change had profound implications for users and system developers. The paper is based on oral history interviews with former employees of the two large Danish service bureaus, Datacentralen and Kommunedata, and addresses a number of themes: driving forces, technology, education and training, skills and knowledge, and systems development practice.

Keywords: Batch, display terminal, IBM 3270, online.

1 Introduction

The term "computing on the desktop" is today associated with the personal computer. Indeed, the personal computer resides on many desktops and has been doing so for many years. However, the desktop was invaded by computing facilities in the decades before the personal computer. The display terminal made its way to offices and workshops in the 1970s and 1980s, facilitated by emerging timesharing capabilities, increasingly powerful computers, the growing need for fast access to information, and more user-friendly types of dialog.

This introduction implied a considerable change for users and system developers. The former batch processing mode involved cumbersome and slow punch card technology, huge piles of print, and turn-around times counted in hours, while in online mode users could access information quickly. This development took place over several decades. Although online technology matured in the 1960s, the change from batch to online did not take place in most organizations until the 1970s and 1980s. As an example, online access only became available in the Danish Civil Registration System (CPR-register) in 1981, although the system had already been established in 1968 [1].

In these decades the state-of-art in commercial computing has been called "IBM and the seven small dwarfs" [2, p. 129], referring to the dominant role IBM had with its market share of 60 to 70 percent. The foundation was laid when IBM released the groundbreaking, general purpose IBM 360 computer in 1964. It was designed to

J. Impagliazzo, P. Lundin, and B. Wangler (Eds.): HiNC3, IFIP AICT 350, pp. 168–175, 2011.
© IFIP International Federation for Information Processing 2011

handle batch and online alike, but performed poorly in the latter [3, p. 155], which later versions of the 360 and in particular the 370 remedied. IBM also played a significant role in the proliferation of online computing, with the 3270 display terminal family, released in 1971 [4].

As to significance of the display terminal at large, I will make a comparison with other significant technologies. Mike Mahoney [5] compared IBM to the canonical Ford T: "Much as Henry Ford taught the nation to use an automobile (by way of Ford T), IBM and its competitors taught the nation's businesses (and government) how to use the computer." Accordingly, the basic thesis in this paper is that IBM and its competitors taught employees in the nation's businesses to use the computer in online mode, largely with the IBM 3270 and compatible display terminals, backed by the dominance of the IBM 360 and 370 computers. The paper is an initial attempt to create grounds for substantiating this basic thesis. A twofold approach is used: literature study and oral history – later to be supplemented by archive studies.

2 Batch Mode and Online Mode

Batch is a mode of operation with a computer, where programs or systems ("jobs") are executed without human intervention. This mode is well suited to high-volume, repetitive processing. Originally, mainframe computers only employed this mode. The typical input media were magnetic tape and punch cards, prepared by punch card operators, while the typical output medium was punch cards and print, often in massive amounts. The turn-around time was counted in hours. Batch designated processing of a large amount of data usually occurred at regular intervals: daily, weekly, or monthly. Working with the information involved huge piles of printed material, so-called Leporello lists. As batch jobs were run infrequently, the administrative routines supported were not necessarily based on up-to-date data. Although the online mode is prevalent today, batch is still alive and well. It is employed for background processing such as database updating, report generation, and high volume printing.

Online is a mode of operation where the human user interacts directly with the system, using either a screen or a paper terminal.[1] Processing took place one-at-a-time in real time – as opposed to batches – with data stored on disks or diskettes with (almost) instant access time. Working online implied that information was up-to-date and answers to queries were provided immediately. Response time was counted in seconds.

As to the novelty of the online mode, William D. Orr stated "conversational interaction with computers is a major new phenomenon in its own right, not simply another 'application' of computers" [6]. A way of characterizing the differences is suggested by Long and colleagues [7, p. 39]: "In batch systems, the end-user's relationship with the computer is indirect. Specialists write the programs, enter the data and operate the machine ... the role of the user is restricted to specifying the task

---

[1] Although the Teletype (TTY) played a significant role as terminal in the 1970s and 1980s, I have decided to focus solely on the display terminal as the visual appearance has survived into today's interactive systems.

in sufficient detail for the computer specialists to do their work." This statement points to the heart of the distinction between batch and online, namely the directness and connectedness in the dialogue.

While the turn-around time in batch mode was several hours, the interaction in online mode took place "instantly." But "instantly" was not necessarily instantly. Response time was often unbearably slow and highly variable, hence response time became crucial and the subject of research [8]. This variability made Nobel Laureate Herbert Simon suggest that the system should deliberately delay the response to ten minutes, if the system could not respond within a short timeframe [9].

Throughout the 1960s, the interest in batch mode and online mode was significant. Harold Sackman conducted a series of studies on programmer productivity in the two modes, finding that online programming was in general quicker. However, the most important finding was the large differences between individual programmers: up to a factor of ten [10].

The advent of online mode incurred a flurry of papers and reports addressing user-system dialog design. A landmark book appeared in 1973: James Martin's *Design of Man-Computer Dialogues* [11]. The book listed numerous dialog techniques and included a section on psychological considerations. Papers and reports focusing on dialog design guidelines appeared, such as the one by Engel and Granda [12]. These guidelines were aggregated in huge reports in the 1980s, culminating in 1986 with *Guidelines for Designing User Interface Software* by Smith and Mosier [13]. This report contained no less than 944 guidelines.

The Sackman studies and the guideline endeavors were examples of forerunners of a new academic field: Human-Computer Interaction (HCI). The focus of HCI is the interaction between a human user and the computer system, connected through a display terminal. The seeds emerged in the 1970s, but the field gained momentum in the 1980s. Oddly enough, in batch mode there was also significant interaction between the user and the computer, albeit much more indirect and asynchronous. Nevertheless, apart from a very limited number of studies, this interaction was not given much attention by researchers.

3   The 3270 Display Terminal and Protocol

The 3270 terminal family was manufactured from 1971 to 1977, ending with the 3278 and 3279 high resolution display terminals with colors and graphics [4]. As the first 3270 display terminals were monochrome (green), they were called "green screens" and referred to as "dumb" terminals. The latter is true from today's perspective, but the 3270 terminal was by then not "dumb," since it came with an efficient protocol based on data streams – not unlike today's HTTP-protocol used in World Wide Web – and an innovative small memory facilitating local operations, such as syntax checking. This solution served to off-load the central computer and the communication lines. The 3270 protocol continued to live – a witness to technological momentum. Even today, many applications rooted in the 1970s and 1980s are using the 3270 protocol emulated on PCs. As part of their approach towards online computer use, IBM presented Systems Network Architecture (SNA) in 1974, which significantly advanced the state of the art in teleprocessing software systems.

As IBM's blueprint for future teleprocessing products, SNA provided a unified design for IBM's data communications products [14, p. 399]. It is noteworthy that the 3270 display terminal family, the 3270 protocol, and SNA all adhered to the principle behind the successful IBM 360 computer: uniformity and generality.

4 Two Large Danish Service Bureaus

Datacentralen (now CSC) and Kommunedata were cutting edge service Bureaus in the Danish data processing business, established in 1959 and 1972 respectively. Together they covered a considerable share of the data processing needs of public authorities, Datacentralen aiming primarily at Government institutions and Kommunedata at regional and local authorities [15–17]. The term "service bureau" calls for a comment as Kommunedata and Datacentralen both undertook substantial software development in addition to operations and service.

5 An Exploratory Pilot Study

In order to probe the general attitude to the 3270 era, I conducted an informal survey among five experienced IT-colleagues, eliciting their free association responses to the question: "When I say 3270, what do you say?" The following comprises the essence of their answers:

○ It was a dumb terminal and at the same time the first intelligent terminal
○ It set the standard for a long time and had a fantastic lifetime as protocol
○ It employed full screen mode, but validation of fields was difficult
○ The navigation was difficult and a nuisance for users for many years

These answers supported the planning of the interviews presented in the next section.

6 Oral History Interviews

Three staff members or former employees at Kommunedata were interviewed on June 1, 2010. Employed in 1957, 1967, and 1974 respectively, they had occupied various positions: punch card operator, plug-board programming, programming, management, project management, servicing clients, and SAP customization. The interview, which took 1.5 hours, was recorded and shortly after transcribed.

One ex-staff member of Dacatentralen was interviewed on June 16, 2010. He had been employed at Datacentralen since 1980 and had worked with programming, testing, standards development, teaching, and technical writing. This interview also took 1.5 hours. The main interview themes were: driving forces, technology, education/training, skills and knowledge, and systems development practice. The interview focused on batch and online, but a lot of other aspects were covered, some of which are included below, in the interest of context.

Both companies primarily employed IBM and IBM-compatible hardware, soft-ware, and display terminals (Stansaab Alfaskop, fully 3270-compatible).

Kommune-data used assembly language at an early stage. PL/I, along with COBOL, entered the scene with the online operations and SAP later became the overall development framework.

The transition from batch to online came in many disguises. One of the first steps in Kommunedata was installing a display terminal in a municipality and providing the option of requesting the "instant execution" of jobs. Therefore, instead of turn-around times of a day or so and waiting for the mail to deliver the paper output, the users in the municipality could see the result of the job execution via their terminal, immediately after the "instant execution." This mode resembled a hybrid of batch and online operations – of which many existed [18]. Similarly, at Datacentralen, a hybrid form of queuing online requests and processing them in small, fast batch jobs was employed. In addition, at Datacentralen, a fast punch card terminal was installed, which reduced turn-around time considerably. On a good day, one could submit one's stack of cards, walk to the print desk and watch the print appear.

Interestingly, a major influence on online operations was bills passed in the Danish parliament. In the 1960s, two major reforms were implemented: the Danish Civil Registration System (CPR-register) in 1968, upon which the Pay-as-You-Earn Taxation scheme of 1970 was based. These batch systems and the accompanying opportunities helped in bolstering the need for local municipalities to access centrally stored data online, as every citizen in Denmark was given a unique identification number.

Other incentives included the internal competition among departments in Kommunedata to provide the municipalities with the most advanced systems, and the inspiration resulting from the regular trips to IBM sites in the US, where Kommunedata staff, at the invitation of their primary supplier IBM, was presented with the newest developments. In addition, IBM handled almost all the education of Kommunedata personnel such as project management courses at Lidingö in Sweden.

In spite of the interest and pressure from many municipalities, there was also resistance, not least in small municipalities. During a presentation of the features of online access for the board of a municipality in Southern Jutland, a member of the board insisted: "Three second response time ... it can't be done ... it is a lie!" He was heading the IT Department of a local enterprise that had not yet discovered the virtues of online access. At the same event, the mayor questioned the need for such rapid access in the social sector. A bright member of the Kommunedata team replied that everybody could become a social case, fast handling time was in the interest of the person in question – hinting at the mayor himself.

With regard to the system developers and programmers, one of the first consequences of the introduction of display terminals in Kommunedata was that they had to punch their programs themselves instead of punch card operators carrying out the task. However, even after the introduction of the terminals, they asked the best punch card operators to punch their programs, as these operators were very skilled in detecting syntactic errors in the code. The most significant change for the programmers was turn-around time. With batch development, they had one – or sometimes two or even three – shots per day. This meant that a lot of time was spent on hand-testing the programs, but with online access this discipline soon vanished. Nevertheless, the conditions in the early days were far from those of today, since there could be as many as twenty-five developers sharing one display terminal.

Regarding user interface design, the Kommunedata employees admitted that some of the 3270 applications were not that self-evident and user friendly. The user interface design skill and experience gradually evolved during the transition to online operations, without any external sources such as literature, conferences, and consultants seemingly having played a role. The attitude was that a system should be a natural part of the users' workday, requiring user involvement. As an example, the sequence of the fields on the screen, which is of great importance to users' everyday activities, was mentioned. No particular activities, such as courses, standards, handbooks or the accumulation of systematic experience, seem to have been established early on, but user interface standards did emerge later. When the focus on user interfaces was peaking in the 1990s, special dialog designers were used in Kommunedata. In user interface design, one of the most fundamental principles is consistency, which is manifested in organizations as standards. In Datacentralen, agreement on a user interface standard was a bumpy process that lasted three years. Regarding the organizational push for user friendliness, the creation of the Usability Test Center in the 1990s, at Kommunedata in Copenhagen, resulted in the publishing of guidelines. This was accompanied by fairly strict requirements regarding usability testing, which were later eased. With the current SAP foundation, this has changed; in the words of a SAP customizer: "We can fiddle a bit here and there, do things a bit smarter, but the options are really limited."

In the early days at Kommunedata, there was close contact between the developers and the customers and users in the municipalities. These would even call the Kommunedata staff and abuse them, if they had made errors. The developers took pride in what they did – later, a certain degree of alienation crept in. Gradually, the collaboration became more organized and formalized, not least when the Association of Danish Municipalities (KL) was established in 1970. Steering committees were established that worked out the specs between users and developers jointly, primarily focusing on functionality. The developers wrote the specs and the users were not really involved in the design of the user interface.

As mentioned before, the 3270 display family and protocol were introduced in 1972. The "green screens" are long gone, but the protocol is not. A good number of 3270-based applications are still operational at Kommunedata, simulated on PCs. In many of these older applications, the central components are from the 1970s or 1980s. Some PL/I -based applications also still exist, as well as some applications where the kernel is written in assembler. Therefore, as history evolves, software persists, but hardware disappears. This also happens to people; assembly programmers are becoming rare – as are PL/I programmers.

At times, the introduction of display terminals evoked odd situations. In planning a new building, some employees strongly argued that space for one display terminal for every three developers had to be allocated, a hard to win argument, but they succeeded.

At Datacentralen, two local software systems that support online operations were developed in 1973 (DDBS and TDSS), to facilitate telecommunication-based access to databases. The reason was the lack of suitable software from IBM. In a later heroic effort, the developers of these systems "shoehorned" these systems into the general IBM online Information Management System (IMS).

With regard to the interview mentioned previously, a question was also included concerning the significance of the transition from batch to online in the broader perspective of important innovations over the last sixty years, such as miniaturization, client/server architecture, the personal computer, the graphical interface, and the Internet. The Kommunedata employees agreed that the significant change was the personal computer, not the display terminal. However, being in the middle of it in the 1970s and 1980s, the display terminal was a big thing. The Datacentralen interviewee responded to this question in terms of database access (DB2) – an accompanying and necessary feature of online mode. However, when I repeated the question the interviewee stated that the display terminal was a revelation and thereby significant.

7 Discussion and Conclusions

Due to the limited number of interviewees, the paper does not warrant strong conclusions, but a few points are worth mentioning. First, the transition involved a number of batch/online hybrid forms – of which this study has undoubtedly only shed light on a few; see [18] for another survey. This calls for a comment on the classical question of evolution or revolution in technology and computer history. I think is safe to say that the batch/online transition took place in a number of different stages and that the display terminal has paved the evolutionary path for the personal computer with its much more elaborated capabilities. Perhaps it may even be more meaningful to think of the "batch to online" issue as "batch and online"? It seems that the new craft of online user interface design was not generally informed by existing knowledge sources such as literature, courses, and consultants. User interface design was approached locally, perhaps another manifestation of the "not invented here" syndrome not unknown in the IT realm. Throughout the interviews, it was often difficult to maintain focus on the core issue from batch to online, such as user interface design in online mode and the accumulation of experience from this novel aspect of development. It seems that this central theme has not played an important role in the interviewees' professional lives. Nevertheless, it seems that the introduction of the display terminal and online operations has had a significant impact on users and developers alike and that IBM played a significant role in this transition.

Acknowledgments. I thank Søren Lauesen, Rolf Molich, Peter Carstensen, and Jan Clausen for comments on an earlier version of this paper.

References

1. Nielsen, H.: CPR – Danmarks Folkeregister. CPR-Kontoret (April 1991), http://www.cpr.dk/cpr_artikler/Files/Fil1/4392.pdf (accessed on June 10, 2010)
2. Campbell-Kelly, M., Aspray, W.: Computer: A History of the Information Machine. Westview Press, Boulder (1996)
3. Ceruzzi, P.E.: A History of Modern Computing. MIT Press, Cambridge (1998)

4. IBM 3270 Information Display System Component Description. Report IBM GA 27-2749-1, 1972. IBM Systems Development Division, Product Publications, Kingston, NY 12401
5. Mahoney, M.S.: The History of Computing in the History of Technology. Annals of the History of Computing 10, 113–125 (1988)
6. Orr, W.D. (ed.): Conversational computers. Wiley, Chichester (1968)
7. Long, J., Hammond, N.V., Barnard, P., Morton, J., Clark, I.A.: Introducing the interactive computer at work: The users' views. Behaviour and Information Technology 2, 39–106 (1983)
8. Miller, R.B.: Response time in man-computer coversational transactions. In: AFIPS Fall Joint Computer Conference, vol. 33, part 1, pp. 267–277 (1968)
9. Simon, H.A.: Reflections on time sharing from a user's point of view. Computer Science Research Review, 43–51 (1966)
10. Sackman, H.: Man-computer problem solving. Auerbach, New York (1970)
11. Martin, J.: Design of Man-Computer Dialogues. Prentice-Hall, Englewood Cliffs (1973)
12. Engel, S.E., Granda, R.E.: Guidelines for Man/Display Interfaces. Report TR 00.2720. Poughkeepsie, NY, IBM (1975)
13. Smith, S.L., Mosier, J.N.: Guidelines for designing user interface software. The MITRE Corporation, Bedford Mass, USA, rapport ESD-TR-86-278 (August 1986)
14. Jarema, D.R., Sussenguth, E.H.: IBM data communications: A quarter of evolution and progress. IBM Journal of Research and Development 25(5), 391–404 (1981)
15. I/S Datacentralen af 1959 igennem 25 år. Datacentralen, Copenhagen (1984)
16. Falk, R.: Fra hulkort til EDB: Jyske Kommuners Hulkortcentral. Aalborg Stadsarkiv and KMD (2006)
17. Laursen, A.: Historien om en central. Kommunedata, Aalborg (1991)
18. Jørgensen, A.H.: Exploring the Transition From Batch to Online: Datamation as Source of Evidence. In: Hertzum, M., Hansen, M. (eds.) Proc. DHRS 2010: 10th Danish Human-Computer Interaction Research Symposium, Roskilde, pp. 27–30. (November 2010), http://magenta.ruc.dk/dat_en/research/reports/132/ (accessed November 21, 2010)

UTOPIA: Participatory Design
from Scandinavia to the World

Yngve Sundblad

Human-Computer Interaction, Computer Science and Communication
KTH, 10044, Stockholm, Sweden
y@kth.se

Abstract. Studies and design of information technology support for workplaces, especially workshop floors, office floors and hospital floors, have a strong tradition in Scandinavia, involving workplace users and their trade unions and other stakeholders. The projects emphasize the active cooperation between researchers and workers in the organizations to help improve their work situation. This tradition is analyzed in its historic perspective, starting with the roots in Norway in the early 1970s while highlighting the seminal UTOPIA project from the early 1980s. Today computer use and interaction possibilities are changing quickly with use contexts and application types radically broadening. Technology no longer consists of static tools belonging only to the workplace; it permeates work activity, homes, and everyday lives. The Scandinavian tradition of user involvement in development is facing up with the challenges of new contexts. The influence on past and current practices for international ICT system design is described and analyzed.

Keywords: Cooperative design, human computer interaction, participatory design, Scandinavian model of ICT systems development, user involvement, working life applications.

1 Introduction

The study and design of information technology support for workplaces, especially workshop floors, office floors and hospital floors, have a strong tradition in Scandinavia involving workplace users, their trade unions, and other stakeholders.

The projects emphasize the active cooperation between researchers and workers of the organization to help improve their work situation.

Since the early days, the obvious idea to involve as early as possible users in systems and interface design with low and high tech prototypes, has become a standard to which most developers at least pay lip service. That the practice is not necessarily followed is usually because of time constraints and lack of insight rather than reluctance. However, there are also inherent difficulties.

In the early 1970s, computer technology and use in Scandinavia was dominated by mainframes in "computer centers," guarded by technicians in white frocks, with text

J. Impagliazzo, P. Lundin, and B. Wangler (Eds.): HiNC3, IFIP AICT 350, pp. 176–186, 2011.
© IFIP International Federation for Information Processing 2011

input and output, and rudimentary communication between installations. Few were aware of the future that promised broad and powerful use of computers that were developing in laboratories, especially in California.

1.1 Historical Roots – Kristen Nygaard

We all owe great gratitude to Kristen Nygaard as the father of worker involvement in workplace for computer development and use. His project with the Norwegian Iron and Metal Workers Union (NJMF) in 1972 made an initial move from traditional research and development of computer systems to working *with* people, directly changing and making more active the role of the local unions [1, 2]. This project has had great influence on all succeeding research and development of user participation in systems development leading into cooperative (or participatory) design. In general, the tradition has developed strategies and techniques for workers to influence the design and use of computer applications at the workplace. Not only did Kristen give a generation of academic computer scientists in Scandinavia their mother tongue for computer programming, SIMULA, inventing all main object-oriented concepts [3, 4], he also gave us the tradition of workplace user involvement.

Kristen Nygaard (1978)

Fig. 1. Kristen Nygaard (1926–2002)

1.2 Inspiration to Other Scandinavians

Kristen soon inspired Danish, Norwegian, and Swedish young computer and information science researchers and students. One of these was Pelle Ehn, who in 1975 initiated the DEMOS (DEMOkratisk planering och Styrning i arbetslivet = Democratic Planning and Control in Working Life) project [5, 6]. A similar project was DUE (Demokratisk Utveckling og EDB = Democratic Development and Computer Processing) with researchers from Aarhus such as Morten Kyng [7].

These projects emphasized the active cooperation between researchers and workers of the organization to help improve their work situation. One strong goal was to 'give the end users a voice' in design and development of computer support in work places, thus enhancing the quality of the resulting system. The projects were part of the start of the "Scandinavian tradition" in system design.

2 UTOPIA

Based on the DEMOS and DUE experience and the shortcomings when using and adapting the technical systems at hand, Pelle Ehn and Morten Kyng decided to try a more offensive ("utopist") strategy for worker involvement – direct participation in all design and development phases of computerized tools and systems in the workplace.

They found a good partner through their contacts with newspaper graphic workers, the Nordic Graphic Union (NGU), which became so interested that it financed half-time participation of six graphic workers from Stockholm and Aarhus, and formed a reference group led by the Norwegian NGU board member Gunnar Kokaas.

The natural choice for the project leader was Pelle Ehn, then researcher at ALC, the Center for Working Life in Stockholm, from which an interdisciplinary group with social and information sciences background became involved.

NADA's (the KTH Computer Science department) involvement came when Pelle, whom I knew from other contexts, asked me about our interest to contribute with "technical imagination." As head of department, I could get us, including about five other young researchers, involved in this for NADA somewhat unorthodox project. The other university partner was DAIMI (Computer Science) at Aarhus University.

UTOPIA is a somewhat far-fetched, acronym: Utbildning, Teknik Och Produkt I Arbetskvalitetsperspektiv (workable in all Scandinavian languages); that is, Training, Technology and Product in Work Quality Perspective, inspired by the name of classical book on an ideal society.

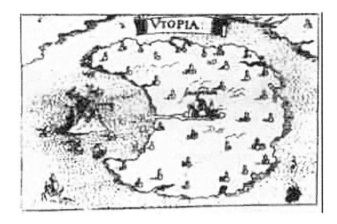

Fig. 2. From an edition of Thomas More's UTOPIA from

Fig. 3. UTOPIA participants 1981–1986, from ALC, DAIMI, NADA, NGU

2.1 Objective

The overall research objective of UTOPIA was to contribute to the development of methods for involving end users in all phases of design and development of IT support for their activities. This objective was based on experience from a concrete case, the development of powerful skill enhancing tools for graphic workers in the light of the emerging graphic workstation technology. Quality of work and product was crucial. Both technical and social prerequisites, as well as obstacles and limitations were examined. The labor processes of page make-up and image processing in integrated computer-based newspaper production were in focus.

2.2 UTOPIA Activities

Main activities during UTOPIA were as follows.

- o *Mutual learning* between the active participants: graphic workers, computer and social researchers
- o *Common study tours* to graphic industry exhibitions and to important laboratories in the US, including Xerox PARC and Stanford University, where Terry Winograd was an important contact and supporter
- o *Requirement specification* for a system for newspaper text and image pre-press production, under development by a Swedish manufacturer
- o *Studying a pilot installation* of the image system in real production at the Swedish newspaper Aftonbladet
- o *Dissemination*, especially to the graphic workers and to the scientific community, see below under "International recognition."

They produced twenty "UTOPIA reports" in Swedish or Danish on different aspects of technology, work organization, and work environment. All (about 50,000) members of NGU received the final, 48-page edition no.7 of the project newsletter, Graffiti, translated into Danish, Finnish, Norwegian, Swedish, English, and Italian.

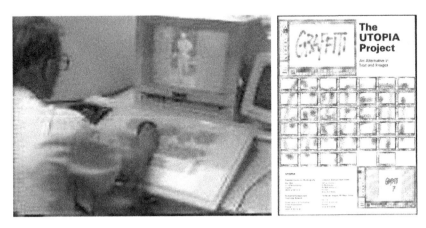

Fig. 4 & 5. Pilot installation at Aftonbladet & the newsletter GRAFFITI

2.3 UTOPIA Tools

The tools and methods in the laboratory were innovations in the early 1980s. These include:

- o Color slide mock-ups with picture sequences that were also pasted on the walls, for simulation of work processes
- o Low-tech mock-ups of equipment (wooden mouse, cardboard laser writer etc.), material and menus (paper and plastic)
- o A graphic workstation for illustrating prototypes of computer based tools
- o A tool kit (box with waxed cards) for modeling and experimenting with work organization

Fig. 6 & 7. Mock-up situation & work process simulation

Fig. 8 & 9. Graphic work station with A4 screen (Perq, 1983, first commercially available in Scandinavia) & page make-up simulation

2.4 UTOPIA Results

UTOPIA became a seminal project on methods for involving end users in all phases of design and development of IT support for their activities.

The main results were not so much the pilot computer tool built and used at Aftonbladet as compared to the experience and methods:

- o *for the Nordic Graphic Union members*, who from UTOPIA knew, at least as well as their employers, the pros and cons of the emerging technology and what to require from it, for functionally and socially acceptable tools and systems in their work

- o *for the researchers,* the challenging insight that the human interface is very important for how useful a computer based tool will be, inspiration for establishing IPLab (Interaction and Presentation Lab) 1985 at NADA and similar efforts in Aarhus
- o *for the researchers and the design community* in general a methodology, Cooperative Design / Participatory Design, for involvement of end users together with interface designers and program developers on equal footing in computer application projects

3 UTOPIA Long-Term Experience

In retrospect, we can see the following four main features of quality and experience from UTOPIA.

3.1 Where Workers Craft Technology

This characterization comes from the MIT Technical Review [8], with the observation that UTOPIA showed that it is possible to design information technology based on use requirements such as work organization, work environment, forms of cooperation, and working skills. At that time, this idea was almost blasphemy in some management circles and more mainstream today.

3.2 Setting the Stage for Design in Action

UTOPIA was precursor to current practices in interaction design in staging active design exercises such as the organizational toolbox and use of mock-ups and prototypes as a way to involve end users in design. Crucial are the means to create meaningful design objects for all participants (different groups of users and designers).

3.3 Playing the Language Game of Design and Use

UTOPIA gave a lasting contribution to the theoretical understanding of design with users through contributions such as Pelle Ehn's [9] and Susanne Bødker's [10] dissertations and several other papers. Today, a "Communities of Practice" perspective is the mainstream for understanding design and learning.

3.4 Bringing Design to Software

The title of this section, borrowed from Terry Winograd [11], underscores the fact that we could view UTOPIA as a "paradigmatic example" of how design thinking and practice can be brought into software development.

4 International Recognition – Cooperative / Participatory Design

The UTOPIA and "Scandinavian model" experience formed a main theme of the 1985 Computers and Democracy conference in Aarhus as shown by the seminal paper [12].

At the 1988 CSCW (Computer Supported Cooperative Work) conference in Portland, Oregon, UTOPIA results appeared in an invited paper [13]. There were several more contributions by UTOPIA members and others from Scandinavia on cooperative design and collaboration. Many scientists from the US and Europe were involved and they greatly contributed to the further development and spread of these ideas.

The term "Scandinavian model of ICT design" is frequently used today in many contexts all over the world to characterize the approaches and practices emanating from these experiences. The "secondary result" of UTOPIA, the methodology, with ingredients such as low-tech prototyping, early design sessions with users, and iterations has had a great impact on ICT design in general.

We still maintain the term "cooperative design" but we recognize that the term "participatory design" has gained greater international use. In addition, biennial international Participatory Design Conferences (PDC) have taken place since 1992, arranged the first five times in the US, and then also in Sweden, Canada, Italy and Australia.

5   Impact on ICT Design in Practice Since the 1980s

The UTOPIA approach, with ingredients such as low-tech prototyping and early design sessions with users, has had a great impact on ICT design in general. This is the case not only where the methods were a main ingredient as in cooperative design / participatory design, but also as part of current common practices in HCI and in CSCW in general, and in later methodologies such as consensus participation, contextual design [14], and cooperative inquiry [15].

Since then, the methodology has developed (e.g. extended to involvement of all stakeholders in system design projects, see [16]) and been complemented with a battery of other methods into strategies for involving users for better-suited IT support. Some examples, many from Scandinavia, are use scenarios [17], technical probes [18], video prototyping [19], vision games [20], close cooperation with joint user experience between ethnographer, industrial designer and programmer [21], and overall process design. For example, the Cooperative Experimental Systems Development [22], and MUST [23] have provided an industrial method for the early phases of design.

The methodology has in my practice been used successfully for design, study and evaluation of ICT support for people such as graphic workers, office workers, programmers, teachers, school childs, family members for intergenerational communication, call center workers, and artists [24]. A current project based on the UTOPIA experience is user assessment of IT quality in workplaces, the Users Award [25]. Other researchers and developers in the cooperative design tradition could extend the list of projects considerably.

6   Conclusions – Still as Relevant Today

It is clear from the aforementioned experiences that the "Scandinavian model" for ICT system development and use, as it was conceived in the 1970s and 1980s notably through the UTOPIA project, has been of utmost importance for forming design practice of today. It is often argued that the conditions in Scandinavia in the 1980s were uniquely favorable for a worker driven IT project, both politically and academically. There were resources available both for participation (in UTOPIA from trade union funding) and for research and development (from academic and research institute funding, including Arbetslivscentrum, for working life studies). This does not mean that the funding was without obstacles. The funding of the participation of a traditional computer science department NADA at KTH depended on its own priorities. The funding authority, STU, first denied it; later, it obtained a technology procurement grant to the newspaper Aftonbladet.

Though projects with such extensive work place user participation are rare, we should consider UTOPIA as a movement showing what is achievable and it should serve as an example for ambitions even under less favorable conditions.

The previous section showed many examples of methods developed in the 1990s that were improvements and modifications of the original methods and practices of the cooperative design approach for different conditions and situations; they illustrate the sound basis of the approach. The approach gives users a voice, an understanding, and knowledge as well as the cooperative design methodology. Even at early stages where they did not know the purpose of the design, it is important to focus on multiple users and uses and on the experience of use. Post-design evaluation was not enough. For exploring the many innovative new forms of interaction today and their use in mixing old and new technologies, multiplicity and ad-hoc configuration everywhere and anytime, for tailorability, adaptation and awareness in networks and communities, the "Scandinavian" cooperative design with users is needed at least as much as before.

Often the problems of user participation are discussed from the point of view of researchers getting access to the users. Yet, we should see user participation from the point of view of the conditions of the participation process, that is, how the conditions are set for users to participate together with designers (and managers). Experiences from cooperative design projects show problems that cooperative design research still needs to deal with.

There are indeed a number of difficulties to overcome. It is important to find the right set of participants, the right tools and techniques as well as the right location and physical space for cooperative design. Furthermore, it is important to create a setting where all involved groups can make active contributions that are meaningful to themselves as well as to other groups of participants. In our experience, this usually requires a serious change in attitude from some of the groups involved.

It is often seen that influence in non-work use of technology goes through consumerism and "voting with the users'/buyers' feet", which could also be a lever for workplace democracy when it comes to ICT support. The ideal that everyone could have full participation and control, and make use of head, hand and heart in their whole life, including work, can move closer as a result of cooperative ICT design and use.

"Common" workplaces can be as challenging and inspiring, e.g. in UsersAward [25], as the more "fancy" new mobile workplaces for media design etc. We need to work with all, old and new, workplaces in the spirit of "Digital Bauhaus" [26].

Acknowledgments. The cooperative design tradition owes its development to a large number of practitioners and researchers. I recognize the importance of discussions with many of them for our understanding of possibilities and limitations.

Specifically I want to thank the researchers and users in the projects here described. The UTOPIA group should be mentioned for a great experience of fruitful cooperation of lifelong importance:

o Gunnar Kokaas, chairman of Nordic Graphic Union reference group;
o Gunnar Rasmussen, graphic worker in Aarhus;
o Björn Burell, Bernt Eriksson, Bo Eric Ericsson, Malte Eriksson, Martin Eriksson and Björn Sporsén, graphic workers in Stockholm;
o Pelle Ehn, Angelika Dilschmann, Ewa Gunnarsson, Åke Sandberg and Dan Sjögren, Centre for Working Life Research, Stockholm;
o Merete Bartholdy, Susanne Bødker, Kurt Jensen, John Kammersgaard and Morten Kyng, DAIMI, Aarhus University;
o Björn Eiderbäck, Kerstin Frenckner, Caroline Nordquist, Staffan Romberger and Kerstin Severinson Eklundh, NADA, KTH.

References

1. Nygaard, K., Bergo, O.T.: Planning, Control, and Computing. Basic Book for the Trade Unions (Planlegging, Styring og databehandling. Grunnbok for Fagbevegelsen) Tiden Norsk Forlag, Oslo (1974)
2. Nygaard, K.: The Iron and Metal Project: Trade Union Participation. In: Sandberg, Å. (ed.) Computers Dividing Man and Work, Utbildningsproduktion, Malmö, pp. 94–107 (1979)
3. Dahl, O.J., Myhrhaug, B., Nygaard, K.: SIMULA Common Base Language, Norwegian Computing Centre (1968, 1970)
4. Holmevik, J.R.: Compiling SIMULA: A historical study of technological genesis. IEEE Annals of the History of Computing 16(4), 25–37 (1994)
5. Carlsson, J., Ehn, P., Erlander, B., Perby, M.-L., Sandberg, Å.: Planning and control from the perspective of labour - A short presentation of the Demos project. Accounting, Organizations and Society 3, 249–260 (1978)
6. DEMOS Project Group: The Demos Project: A Presentation. In: Sandberg, Å. (ed.) Computers Dividing Man and Work, Utbildningsproduktion, Malmö, pp. 122–130 (1979)
7. DUE Project Group (1979): Project DUE: Democracy, Development, and EDP. In: Sandberg, Å. (ed.) Computers Dividing Man and Work, Utbildningsproduktion, Malmö, pp. 122–130 (1979)
8. Howard, R.: Utopia – Where Workers Craft New Technology. Technological Review 88(3), 43–49 (1985)
9. Ehn, P.: Work-oriented design of computer artifacts. Doctoral disseratation. Almqvist & Wiksell International / Lawrence Erlbaum, Hillsdalae, N.J (1988)
10. Bødker, S.: Computer applications as mediators of design and use – a developmental perspective. Doctoral dissertation, Department of Computer Science, University of Aarhus (1999)
11. Winograd, T., Bennett, J., De Young, L., Hartfield, B.: Bringing design to software. Addison-Wesley, Reading (1996)

12. Bødker, S., Ehn, P., Kammersgaard, J., Kyng, M., Sundblad, Y.: A Utopian experience. In: Bjerknes, G., Ehn, P., Kyng, M. (eds.) Computers and Democracy: A Scandinavian Challenge, pp. 251–278. Avebury, Aldershot (1987)

13. Bødker, S., Ehn, P., Lindskov Knudsen, J., Kyng, M., Halskov Madsen, K.: Computer Support for Cooperative Design. In: Proceedings of the conference on Computer Supported Cooperative Work, Portland, Oregon, pp. 377–394. ACM, New York (1988)

14. Beyer, H., Holtzblatt, K.: Contextual Design: Defining Customer-Centred Systems. Morgan Kaufmann Publishers, San Francisco (1998)

15. Druin, A.: Co-operative Inquiry – Developing New Technology for Children with Children. In: Proceedings of CHI 1999, Pittsburgh, pp. 223–230 (1999)

16. Bødker, S., Ehn, P., Sjögren, D., Sundblad, Y.: Co-operative Design - perspectives on 20 years with 'the Scandinavian IT Design Model. Invited paper in Proceedings of the NordiCHI 2000 Conference, pp. 1–11. KTH, Stockholm (2000)

17. Kyng, M.: Creating Contexts for Design. In: Carroll, J.M. (ed.) Scenario-based Design: Envisioning Work and Technology in System Development, pp. 85–108. Wiley, New York (1995)

18. Hutchinson, H., Mackay, W., Westerlund, B., Bederson, B., Druin, A., Plaisant, C., Beaudouin-Lafon, M., Conversy, S., Evans, H., Hansen, H., Roussel, M., Eiderbäck, B., Lindquist, K., Sundblad, Y.: Technology Probes: Inspiring Design for and with Families. In: Proc. CHI 2003, Fort Lauderdale, pp. 17–24 (2003)

19. Mackay, W.E., Ratzer, A.V., Janecek, P.: Video artefact for design: Bridging the gap between abstraction and detail. In: Proc. of ACM DIS 2000, pp. 72–82. ACM Press, New York (2000)

20. Hornecker, E., Buur, J.: Getting a grip on tangible interaction: A framework on physical space and social interaction. In: Proceedings of the CHI 2006 Conference on Human Factors in Computing Systems, pp. 437–446. ACM Press, New York (2006)

21. Westerlund, B., Lindqvist, K., Mackay, W., Sundblad, Y.: Co-designing methods for designing with and for families. In: Proc. 5th European Academy of Design Conference, Barcelona (2003)

22. Grønbæk, K., Kyng, M., Mogensen, P.: Toward a Cooperative Experimental System Development Approach. In: Kyng, M., Mathiassen, L. (eds.) Computers and Design in Context, pp. 201–238. MIT press, Cambridge (1997)

23. Kensing, F., Simonsen, J., Bødker, K.: MUST: A Method for Participatory Design. Human-Computer Interaction 13(2), 167–198 (1998)

24. Bødker, S., Sundblad, Y.: Usability and Interaction Design – new challenges for the Scandinavian tradition. Behaviour and Information Technology 27(4), 293–300 (2008)

25. Walldius, Å., Sundblad, Y., Sandblad, B., Bengtsson, L., Gulliksen, J.: User certification of Workplace Software – Assessing both Artefact and Usage. BIT (Behaviour & Information Technology) 28(2), 101–120 (2009)

26. Sundblad, Y.: From Utopia 1981 to Utopia 2008. In: Binder, T., Löwgren, J., Malmborg, L. (eds.) (Re)searching the Digital Bauhaus, pp. 13–41. Springer, Heidelberg (2008)

Designing Democracy: The UTOPIA-Project and the Role of the Nordic Labor Movement in Technological Change during the 1970s and 1980s

Per Lundin

Div. of History of Science and Technology, KTH
100 44 Stockholm, Sweden
per.lundin@abe.kth.se

Abstract. By using the UTOPIA-project as an example, this paper highlights the role of the Nordic labor movement in technological change and underlines that there are different incentives for technological change. While corporations developing technology usually pursued increased efficiency in production, the UTOPIA-project aimed at other, alternative goals such as translating social values regarding job skills, quality of work, and quality of products into new computer hardware and software for the graphic industries. In the larger context, the UTOPIA-project can be seen as an attempt by the labor movement to revitalize and realize the old dream of industrial democracy by designing computing technology.

Keywords: Graphic industries, history of computing, industrial democracy, IT-history, labor movement, Sweden, trade unions, users.

1 Introduction

When the computer-based wave of rationalization hit industry, trade, business, and the public sector during the 1970s and the 1980s, many occupational groups feared they would lose control of their work and eventually their jobs. The "microelectronics revolution" during the mid-1970s transformed the job made by graphic workers [1, 2]. Many of them lost their jobs, and especially in the United States and Great Britain, extinction threatened the very existence of the occupation. In the Anglo-Saxon countries, the counter-strategies developed by organized labor were in general Ludditian, i.e. characterized by a resistance towards technological change [3–5].

This paper demonstrates that the responses articulated by the labor movement in the Nordic countries developed along a different path. The Nordic trade unions argued that if new technology could be developed on the premises of workers, it would be possible for them to keep their occupations. By investigating the conscious counter-strategies elaborated by Nordic trade unions and politically radical computer scientists during the 1970s and 1980s, this paper shows that they aimed to organize themselves *with the help of* technology rather than *against* technology. Particular attention will be paid to the UTOPIA-project and its attempts to develop computer hardware and software for the graphic industries. The important contextual elements discussed are

J. Impagliazzo, P. Lundin, and B. Wangler (Eds.): HiNC3, IFIP AICT 350, pp. 187–195, 2011.

the altering notions of technological change during the post-war period, the question and old dream of industrial democracy, the strong welfare states and long-lasting social democratic rule in the Nordic countries, and the belief in allegedly Nordic/Scandinavian values such as consensus, participation and democracy.

2 The UTOPIA-Project

The UTOPIA-project was a Nordic research project on trade union based development of, and training in, computer technology and work organization, especially text and image processing in the graphic industries.[1] It occurred between 1981 and 1986. UTOPIA was an acronym in Swedish for training, technology, and products from a skilled worker's perspective, "Utbildning, teknik och produkt i arbetskvalitetsperspektiv." UTOPIA was conducted, in close cooperation with the Nordic Graphic Workers' Union (Nordisk Grafisk Union, NGU), at the Swedish Center for Working Life (Arbetslivscentrum, ALC), the Royal Institute of Technology in Stockholm, Sweden, and Aarhus University in Denmark. The project received the majority of its funding from the Swedish Center for Working Life and the National Board for Technical Development (Styrelsen för teknisk utveckling, STU) [6].

Two different social groups were brought together in the project: on the one hand, system designers, computer scientists, and work-efficiency experts; and on the other, activists and officials from unions representing some 120,000 printers, typographers, lithographers, and other skilled workers in the newspaper and printing industries of the five Nordic countries. The combination of politically radical scientists (which were influenced by the social movements of the late 1960s as well as the radicalization of the universities the following decade) and graphic workers' unions (which, in comparison with other unions, were unusually intellectual, radical and technology-minded) was probably decisive for the outcome of the project. About fifteen people participated in the project. The Nordic Graphic Workers' Union appointed a group consisting of representatives from Denmark, Finland, Norway and Sweden who followed the project. At various stages the project cooperated with the Swedish state-owned publishing company and computer supplier Liber and its development project Text and Image Processing System (TIPS), the Swedish Social Democratic newspaper *Aftonbladet*, and the Danish independent center-leftist newspaper *Information* that was owned by its co-workers between 1970 and 1986 [6].

Obviously, UTOPIA developed in a very particular setting. State- or union-owned companies and cooperatively owned newspapers agreed either to support the project financially and ideologically or to participate as customers. Without this complex of government agencies, the realization of the project would probably not have occurred.

3 Technology as Ideology

The Norwegian mathematician and computer scientist Kristen Nygaard, who worked at the Norwegian Defense Research Agency (Forsvarets forskningsinstitutt) and later

---

[1] Yngve Sundblad presents the UTOPIA-project from an insider's perspective in the paper "UTOPIA: Participatory Design from Scandinavia to the World" (in this volume).

at Norsk Regnesentral, inspired the researchers in the UTOPIA-project. Originally liberal in his views, he was influenced by the social movements of the 1960s and engaged himself politically to the left. His interests moved toward the social consequences of computerization. Together with Olav Terje Bergo, he cooperated in the early 1970s with the Norwegian Iron and Metal Workers' Union (Norsk Jern- og Metallarbeiderforbund, NJMF) on a project that dealt with planning, control, and data processing in enterprises from the perspectives of the employees [7]. Another important source of inspiration was Harry Braverman's seminal book from 1974 on the degradation of work, *Labor and Monopoly Capital*, which was translated into Swedish in 1977 [8, 9].

The NJMF-project received a couple of Nordic successors in the 1970s: the Danish DUE-project and the Swedish DEMOS-project. DEMOS, an acronym for Demokratisk styrning och planering (Democratic Control and Planning in Working Life) took place between 1975 and 1980, as a form of cooperation between the Swedish Center for Working Life and a number of trade unions. It dealt with planning, control and the use of computers from a wage-earner perspective, aiming to accumulate knowledge for the union movement [10].

Like its precursors, UTOPIA was an explicitly ideological project from the outset. The research program for the project from 1980 stated:

> The experience gained by organized labor and the research conducted by trade unions during the 1970s into the ability to influence new technology and the organization of work at local level highlighted a number of problems. One fundamental experience gained is that the "degrees of freedom" available to design the content and organization of work utilizes existing technology is often considerably less than that required to meet trade unions demands. Or expressed another way: Existing production technology more and more often constitutes an insurmountable barrier preventing the realization of trade union demands for the quality of work and a meaningful job [11, p. 255].

According to its participants, technology was an expression of the sort of society in which we live. It was value-laden – and the participants argued that existing technology and new technology largely reflected corporate interests instead of the interests of workers. Hence, it constrained the demands of workers and trade unions. In contrast to the trade unions' earlier "defensive strategies" for coping with technological change (e.g., reducing the negative effects of technology on employees by demanding reforms in legislation and concluding agreements), the participants in the UTOPIA-project worked with a "yet untried offensive strategy." The trade unions themselves were supposed to develop alternative technologies that mirrored the interests of trade unions rather than the ones of corporations:

> The trade union movement itself draws up the technological and training alternatives and takes the sole responsibility for their implementation and development at local level [11, p. 256].

Thus, the aim with the UTOPIA-project was to help unions translate their social values regarding the job skills, quality of work, and quality of products into new computer hardware and software for the printing industry. Its participants held a strong belief that technology largely shaped working conditions. The underlying notion of technology being deterministic led them to argue that it was crucial for workers to develop and control alternative technologies.

4 Altering Notions of Technological Change

The concept of technological determinism ruled during the post-war period. However, as pointed out by David Edgerton, we should distinguish it from the notion of technology as autonomous – as out-of-control – an important theme in Western thought during the 1950s and the 1960s [12, 13]. Thus, the trade unions and the UTOPIA-project questioned the inevitability of technological change, not the technological determinism in social change *per se*. On the contrary, UTOPIA presupposed a 'soft' technological determinism [14, p. 2]. The point of departure for the project was that technology largely shapes the workers' conditions.

In the following, the paper will examine the governing Social Democrats' and the labor movement's approach to technology and technological change during the post-war period. Already in the *Arbetarrörelsens efterkrigsprogram* from 1944, a joint labor movement program set up by the Social Democrats and the Swedish Trade Union Confederation (Landsorganisationen i Sverige, LO), a growing technological optimism could be sensed. It was through technological progress that material and social welfare should be reached. The so-called Rigoletto conference organized by the Social Democrats in 1955, with participating scientists, technicians and politicians as well as representatives for trade and industry, received public attention. It resulted in the publication *Tekniken och morgondagens samhälle* (Technology and the Society of Tomorrow) and manifested an optimistic belief in technology and science [15]. This belief was established as a "supreme ideology," an ideology above all other ideologies, an ideology that unified all the existing political ideologies. It was also reflected in the discourse on the "death of ideologies" that took place in the Western world during the mid-1950s [16]. The notion of technological change as autonomous was strong. Thinking in the inevitability of technological progress, there was no need for considering alternative directions. There was only one way to go. The overall strategy was "total adaptation" to the demands of the assaulting technology. People understood that technology determined social change. Thus, both the belief that technology is autonomous and the belief that technology is largely deterministic in its character, existed side by side. Trade unions largely shared this approach. For example, the Trade Union Confederation adopted a "rationalization friendly approach," i.e., a strategy of adaptation towards technological change [17, p. 355].

In the aftermath of the "Boom Years" of the 1950s and the 1960s came the crisis of the 1970s. Technology changed from a promise to a threat. The rationalization that followed technological change did not produce prosperity to the same extent as before; instead, it increasingly made workers redundant and ultimately led to unemployment. A broad spectrum of political organizations and interest groups began to question the inevitability of technological change. It was almost as a discovery: technology is political! Instead of adapting ourselves to the inevitable technological progress, they argued, we should choose technology, thus choose our future; we should take control over technology in order to take control over work; etc. [18].

A very strong labor movement expanded its ambitions from wage negotiations into changing work organization and eventually technology [19]. For instance, the Trade Union Confederation established a Committee for Computing (LO:s dataråd) in 1976, the Workers' Educational Association (Arbetarnas Bildningsförbund, ABF); it conducted courses on the role of computers in social change; the Social Democratic Party presented an action program on computers and politics [20–25]. They moved – in their own words – from a "defensive" to an "offensive" strategy. Instead of being the passive object of automation, they argued that the worker should be an active subject in shaping technological change.

Tage Erlander's Computer Symposium became an important political manifestation of this new posture. The symposium took place in 1980 at the Social Democratic residence Bommersvik and resulted in, among other things, the publication *Datorerna och samhällsutvecklingen* (Computers and the Development of Society). This labor movement summit conference consisted of participants such as the Social Democratic party secretary Sten Andersson (later Minister for Health and Social Affairs, and Foreign Minister), the president of the Swedish Confederation of Professional Employees (Tjänstemännens centralorganisation, TCO) Lennart Bodström (later Foreign Minister, and Minister for Education and Science), the member of the Social Democratic party executive Kjell-Olof Feldt (later Minister for Finance), the secretary for the Swedish Trade Union Confederation Rune Molin (later Minister for Industry), Hans Gustafsson (later Minister for Housing), Anders Ferm (managing director for the leading Social Democratic publishing house Tidens förlag) as well as the social democratic icons such as former Prime Minister Tage Erlander and former Minister for Finance Gunnar Sträng [26].

The well-known Finnish philosopher Georg Henrik von Wright opened the symposium with a reflection over Man, Technology, and the Future. He drew the attention to the profound social consequences of modern technology and thus addressed the overall themes of the conference: What social consequences does technological change have? Of special concern at the conference were the effects of technological change on employment. Given the profound consequences of technology: Who influenced and controlled technological change? Was it possible to control the progress of technology or was humanity forced to adapt itself to this development? Different visions and strategies for confronting technological change were suggested. The participants from trade unions, such as Rune Molin, emphasized that trade unions had to take command over technological change; another participant demanded "offensive decisions." In short: the employees needed to create their own alternatives [26].

Thus, during the 1970s it is possible to discern a shift in the notion of technological change from a belief that it was autonomous and out-of-control, towards a belief that it is controllable. However, the notion that technological change determined social change was as strong as before; it also was a very important incentive for the trade unions to take control over technological change. It is in this vein that we should understand the attempts of the Scandinavian labor movement to take control over work organization and technology and, consequently, projects such as NJMF, DEMOS, DUE, and above all, UTOPIA.

5   Industrial Democracy Reborn

Henry Ford's assertion that "democracy stops at the factory gates" strikingly illustrates a problem that gained attention during the 1920s in connection with the wave of democratization that swept through Europe after World War I. It dealt with the employees' influence in companies. After the seminal Saltsjöbaden agreement in 1938 between the Swedish Trade Union Confederation and the Swedish Employers' Confederation (Svenska arbetsgivareföreningen, SAF) the question gained renewed attention. The so-called Swedish Model was established during the 1930s and the 1940s and it became a role model manifesting technological optimism during the Boom Years of the 1950s and the 1960s [27, 28]. The social conflicts that arose at the end of the 1960s politized the industrial rationalization and the Swedish Model was questioned by the trade unions who protested against the "over-profits" made by corporations which they claimed did not sufficiently reach the employees. As a response, the powerful Social Democratic Party carried through a number of legislations during the 1970s that considerably strengthened the position of the employees in private companies. For instance, a law concerning the right of participation in decision-making, the Codetermination Act (Medbestämmandelagen, MBL) was legislated in 1976, and in the wake of these many reforms the question of industrial democracy called for attention once again [20]. Pelle Ehn, UTOPIA's project leader, rephrased Ford's assertion as, "democracy stops at the office door and the factory gate" [29].

The attempts to re-vitalize the question of industrial democracy had important parallels in other Scandinavian countries. Norway was pioneering with its program for industrial democracy during the 1960s and a number of experiments in work organization were completed. Similar attempts took place in Denmark, where several experiments in industrial democracy were conducted between 1969 and 1973. It should be noted that this trend is also discernible outside Scandinavia, and particularly in West Germany, which, among other things, carried through a similar Codetermination Act in 1976 [30, 31].

In conjunction with passing the Codetermination Act, the Swedish Parliament decided in June 1976 to establish a research institute with the purpose of bringing the research community and trade unions together. The Work Environment Fund (Arbetsmiljöfonden)[2], based on a wage tax paid by all employers, financed the Swedish Center for Working Life [32]. One of the aims of the center was to "promote democracy in working life," and the concept of industrial democracy so to speak, was built in its regulations [33 p. 9, p. 13]. Furthermore, it edited (and financed) the international quarterly journal *Economic and Industrial Democracy* published by Sage Publications starting in 1980. The Center for Working Life carried out three big research projects dealing with trade unions and development of technology and organization: DEMOS (1975–1980), UTOPIA (1981–1986), and FRONT [34]. In the statutes of the Center for Working Life, it legislated that the research conducted should not consist of traditional reflective, analytic social science. Instead, it should take the form of "action research" where the "researcher's contribution as well as the reporting" should be "highly dependent on the actions of local parties" [33, p. 12].

---

[2] Former Occupational Safety Foundation (Arbetarskyddsfonden).

The argument supported by the Center for Working Life was that trade unions needed to develop independently knowledge in order to shape technology and work organization actively. The center took a seminal role in the DEMOS and UTOPIA projects [33].

To conclude this section, the 1970s and the first half of the 1980s was a period when powerful trade unions made several attempts to realize the old dream of economic or industrial democracy. Through a number of governmental decisions, several new institutions with affinities to the labor movement such as the Work Environment Fund and the Center for Working Life took place on stage and quickly gained in strength. A state-supported complex giving voice to the demands of the labor movement was established and it became an important prerequisite for projects such as DEMOS and UTOPIA.

6 Democracy by Design

A "technology laboratory" where researchers and workers worked closely together was established at the Swedish Center for Working Life. The American Robert Howard reviewed UTOPIA for the MIT-based journal *Technology Review*, and was amazed at what he saw when visiting the laboratory. He reported that it could be a research department at any high-tech manufacturer; instead, the lab belonged to the government-funded Swedish Center for Working Life in Stockholm and he described the scene where graphic workers and computer scientists sat side by side as "an intriguing experiment in technology development" [11, 35].

One of the more important results was the publication of requirement specifications (kravspecifikationer) in 1983. The requirement specifications acted as guidelines for what workers should require of new technologies or organizations when introduced, and they were used in collective bargaining and local negotiations [36].

The UTOPIA-project presented its results at a conference in May 1984 at the Social Democratic Youth League's (Sveriges Socialdemokratiska Ungdomsförbund, SSU) residential study center Bommersvik [11, p. 259]. The choice of place symbolized and manifested the strong connections with the labor movement; during the latter half of the twentieth century, the Bommersvik residence was a political and cultural center for the Swedish labor movement.

Should the UTOPIA-project be evaluated as a success or as a failure? According to the researchers, the project led to "a successful conclusion" as a "single demonstration example." It demonstrated that alternative technological and organizational solutions for newspapers could be developed, which gave possibilities for graphic workers to improve their skills and keep their jobs. The participating researchers nurtured a dream that the project would contribute to a "new Scandinavian model" for technological development. However, as they later pointed out, the lack of trade union cooperation put an end to this dream [6, 11, p. 260]. Nevertheless, as a project on participatory design it must be considered seminal. It gave rise to the so-called Scandinavian School of System Development (Den skandinaviska skolan), where the users' participation in system development has become a key element [37]. Moreover, quite interestingly, an observer noted in 1990 that graphic workers in Sweden had managed to keep their occupations to a considerably higher extent than in the

Anglo-Saxon countries [28]. To sum up, the counter-strategies against a computer-based wave of rationalization developed by the Nordic trade unions differed fundamentally from those articulated by trade unions in the Anglo-Saxon countries.

Acknowledgments. Handelsbankens forskningsstiftelser and Ridderstads stiftelse för historisk grafisk forskning have provided financial support for the research carried out in connection with this paper. Isabelle Dussauge, Johan Gribbe, Arne Kaijser, Anna Orrghen, Julia Peralta, Gustav Sjöblom, and Björn Thodenius have given valuable comments on earlier versions of this manuscript.

References

1. Magnusson, L.: Den tredje revolutionen – och den svenska arbetsmarknaden. Prisma, Stockholm (2000)
2. Wennersten, B.G.: Mikrodatoriseringen: Den tysta revolutionen: En guide för beslutsfattare. Affärsförlaget, Stockholm (1980)
3. Noble, D.F.: Progress without People: New Technology, Unemployment, and the Message of Resistance. Between the Lines, Toronto (1995)
4. Bix, A.S.: Inventing Ourselves Out of Jobs? America's Debate over Technological Unemployment, 1929-1981. Johns Hopkins University Press, Baltimore (2000)
5. Moore, R., Levie, H.: New Technology and the Trade Unions. Workers' Control (2), 13–21 (1982)
6. UTOPIA-projektet: Alternativ i text och bild. Graffiti (7) (1984)
7. Nygaard, K., Bergo, O.T.: Databehandling, planlegging og styring: Grunnbok for fagbevegelsen. Norsk regnesentral, Oslo (1972)
8. Braverman, H.: Labor and Monopoly Capital: The Degradation of Work in the Twentieth Century. Monthly Review Press, New York (1974)
9. Braverman, H.: Arbete och monopolkapital: Arbetets degradering i det tjugonde århundradet. Rabén & Sjögren, Stockholm (1977)
10. Ehn, P., Perby, M.-L., Sandberg, Å.: Brytningstid: Teknik, arbete och facklig kamp i grafiska branschen: Rapport från samarbetet mellan Svenska Dagbladets Kamratklubb och Demos-projektet. Arbetslivscentrum, Stockholm (1983)
11. Bødker, S., et al.: A UTOPIAN Experience: On Design of Powerful Computer-Based Tools for Skilled Graphic Workers. In: Bjerknes, G., Ehn, P., Kyng, M. (eds.) Computers and Democracy: A Scandinavian Challenge, Avebury, Aldershot (1987)
12. Winner, L.: Autonomous Technology: Technics-Out-of-Control as a Theme in Political Thought. MIT Press, Cambridge (1977)
13. Edgerton, D.: Tilting at Paper Tigers. The British Journal for the History of Science 26(1), 67–75 (1993)
14. Smith, M.R.: Technological Determinism in American Culture. In: Smith, M.R., Marx, L. (eds.) Does Technology Drive History? The Dilemma of Technological Determinism. MIT Press, Cambridge (1994)
15. Tekniken och morgondagens samhälle. Tiden, Stockholm (1956)
16. Skovdahl, B.: Tingsten, totalitarismen och ideologierna. Symposion, Stockholm (1992)
17. Weinberger, H.: Nätverksentreprenören: En historia om teknisk forskning och industriellt utvecklingsarbete från den Malmska utredningen till Styrelsen för teknisk utveckling. KTH, Avd. för teknik- och vetenskapshistoria, Stockholm (1997)

18. Att välja framtid: Ett underlag för diskussion och överväganden om framtidsstudier i Sverige: Betänkande. Statens offentliga utredningar (SOU), 1972:59, Stockholm (1972)
19. Isacson, M.: Arbetets organisation och ledning. In: Berggren, L., et al.: Det lyser en framtid: Svenska Metallindustriarbetareförbundet 1957-1981. IF Metall, Stockholm (2008)
20. Företagsdemokrati och data: Sammanfattning av LOs handlingsprogram. LO, Stockholm (1976)
21. Solidariskt medbestämmande: Rapport till LO-kongressen 1976: Med kongressens beslut. Prisma i samarbete med Landsorganisationen i Sverige, Stockholm (1976)
22. Birgitta Frejhagen, interview by Per Lundin (November 29, 2007)
23. Datoranvändning: Från samråd till medbestämmande. LO och Brevskolan, Stockholm (1978)
24. Datorer på människans villkor. ABF, Stockholm (1979)
25. Datorer på människans villkor: Program för datapolitiken. Socialdemokraterna, Stockholm (1979)
26. Datorerna och samhällsutvecklingen: Debattinlägg vid Tage Erlanders datasymposium 1980. Tiden, Stockholm (1980)
27. Johansson, A.: Taylorismen och arbetarrörelsen: En problemdiskussion. In: Schiller, B., Svensson, T. (eds.) Arbete och arbetsmarknad i Norden: Nya linjer inom den nordiska arbetslivsforskningen, Arkiv, Lund (1988)
28. Johansson, A.L.: Teknikoptimismen i den svenska modellen. In: Beckman, S. (ed.) Teknokrati, arbete, makt. Carlsson, Stockholm (1990)
29. Bjerknes, G., Ehn, P., Kyng, M. (eds.): Computers and Democracy: A Scandinavian Challenge. Avebury, Aldershot (1987)
30. Pedersen, U.S.: Fagbevægelsen og spørsmålet om industrielt demokrati i Skandinavien: Nogle problemstillinger og resultater fra et komparativt skandinavisk project. In: Schiller, B., Svensson, T. (eds.) Arbete och arbetsmarknad i Norden: Nya linjer inom den nordiska arbetslivsforskningen, Arkiv, Lund (1988)
31. Judt, T.: Postwar: A History of Europe since 1945. Heinemann, London (2005)
32. Johansson, J.: Arbetsmiljöfonden: Lagen om avsättning till arbetsmiljöfond. Tholin/Larsson-gruppen, Göteborg (1974)
33. The Swedish Center for Working Life, 1976-1987: ALC Review Committee. Arbetslivscentrum, Stockholm (1987)
34. Sandberg, Å. (ed.): Arbete, ledning och teknik: Resultat från ett forskningsprogram om omvandling i företag och fack vid Arbetslivscentrum 1975-1991. Arbetslivscentrum, Stockholm (1991)
35. Howard, R.: UTOPIA: Where Workers Craft New Technology. Technology Review 88(3), 43–49 (1985)
36. Kravspecifikation – teknik, arbete och utbildning. Graffiti (7), 24–25 (1984)
37. Asp, M., James, S.: Trender inom skandinavisk systemutveckling. Unpublished report, MSI, Växjö universitet (June 2003)

Early History of Computing in Denmark

Søren Duus Østergaard

Duus.Communications ApS
soren@duus.com

Abstract. This paper describes how the predecessors to modern computers, the family of equipment we describe as The Punch Card Machines, entered the Danish and Nordic Markets. It also describes how it paved the way for the relatively rapid take-off in the Nordic market of the 'real' computers. The paper also sheds light on the competitive situation, the key applications, and the heavy influence of public regulations on market development. Written in conjunction with the studies on the roots of IBM Denmark, founded as a limited company as late as 1950, the paper makes use of archives and material hitherto not published.

Keywords: Bull, CTM, Hollerith, IBM, Max Bodenhoff, Powers, punched cards, Remington.

1 Introduction

Although the focus of the HINC3-conference is the development and take-up of IT in the Nordic countries, this did not just happen "out of the blue," but was the logical consequence of hard work and scientific breakthrough abroad and within the Nordic regions. It was also definitely useful because the market situation was well prepared for this type of practical application created to increase the human capacity for calculating, storing, and analyzing vast amounts of data.

Even more interesting to social and organizational researchers is the way punched-card based companies and customers were organized, how the competitive landscape, patterns of competition, the constant pressure on innovation, and the need for skilled employees actually mirrors what we have witnessed from 1960 onwards. It was during that time when 'real computing' was a matter of making companies more efficient and competitive as well as increasing the speed, accuracy, and accountability of the public sector.

As this paper is based on research into the roots and origins of IBM Denmark, the focus is on the Danish market. However, it is evident that much Nordic cooperation was actually unfolding before and even during World War II.

2 The First Automatic Calculation Machines in Denmark

As early as 1911, the Danish Central Bureau of Statistics ordered the first set of so-called Hollerith machines from the German agent, Mr. W. Williams, in Berlin to

J. Impagliazzo, P. Lundin, and B. Wangler (Eds.): HiNC3, IFIP AICT 350, pp. 196–206, 2011.
© IFIP International Federation for Information Processing 2011

assist in finalizing the census of 1910 [1]. The Hollerith equipment, first used in connection with the U.S. Census in 1890, was based on patents owned by Herman Hollerith who developed the equipment specifically with large statistical applications in mind. These machines were rented (as all Hollerith equipment and indeed for many years IBM computers and equipment also) and no service specialists accompanied the machines that comprised two vertical sorters, one tabulator, six hand punches, and one hand gang punch. These machines – except the hand punches – were returned in 1912 and, according to employees, they were difficult to use and had been out of order for most of the time.

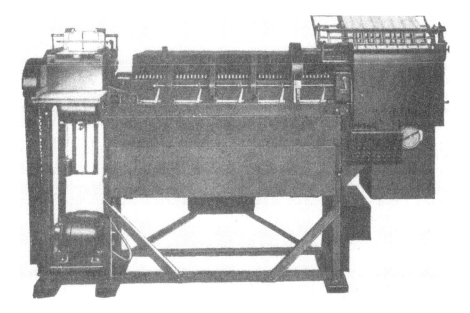

Fig. 1. A Hollerith Tabulator unit with an automatic writing unit [1]

In 1915, the Danish insurance company Hafnia entered into an agreement with the Hollerith agent in Berlin to deliver equipment and punched cards, in order to celebrate Hafnia's fifty-year anniversary in 1922. The machines were delivered in 1920 – a vertical sorter (15,000 cards/hour), and a small tabulator which was replaced after a period by a tabulator that arrived directly from the U.S.. The technician that received this parcel was astonished that he was able to put it together and have it operational in a short time. His name was Henrik Hartzner, later to become CEO of Machines Bull in Denmark [1].

3 The Danish Hollerith Agency

Max Bodenhoff, a dynamic young Danish businessman, was an agent for the Royal Typewriter Company when he received a letter in 1920 from a former Royal salesman, Mr. Jennings, who now represented IBM in Europe. In Max B's own words:

> In 1920 I got a letter from Paris inviting me to participate in an international training course in Berlin so I could learn about the so-called Hollerith System.
> ... This was the first international course created as a pilot and run by Mr. Jennings and an extremely nice teacher, Mr. Hide, from the U.S. These two persons were supposed to train us in this extremely odd system [2].

The course consisted of one week of technical training that obviously mostly went over Max Bodenhoff's head, and a one-week sales course that he took to his heart.

The "canvassing technique," as Max Bodenhoff learned, brought him some success relatively soon. He first targeted the Central Bureau of Statistics – and was almost thrown out, as they recalled their experiences from 1911–12. He was asked not to return, but Max Bodenhoff went instead to the manager of the Bureau, Mr. Cohn, and complained that he, who represented one of the world's largest companies, was being treated as a mere seller of shoe strings; he asked for information and numbers so he could make a detailed and realistic offer. Surprisingly, Mr. Einar Cohn agreed and gave him the requested information. Armed with this, he went to Hafnia, the only other company with experience in Hollerith equipment, and asked Mr. Hartzner to help him calculate that the Bureau of Statistics could have saved 36,000 DKK had they used Hollerith equipment for the 1920 census. This helped, and after a month he had his first order.

Max Bodenhoff's second customer became the Danish National Railways. He focused the attack on its statistics department, but the manager did not want any changes; fortunately, a younger manager, Mr. Herschend, replaced him. In Max Bodenhoff's own words:

> I arrived packed with papers and descriptions, and told Mr. Herschend that he was probably very able to extract the lesson from these papers. I also informed him that Swedish Railways had recently sent a committee of three specialists to New York to study the system [2].

Mr. Herschend did indeed take the opportunity and used the Hollerith system to keep track of goods and railway wagons in a way never done before. In Max Bodenhoff's own words:

> This department – until now just looked upon as dull and unimportant – was suddenly able to produce information and data at a detail and speed that no Ministry for Public Works had been able to obtain before [2].

Herschend thus became a star in the Railways – and Max Bodenhoff could point to an important reference. Success materialized when he negotiated a contract for Hollerith equipment with the Danish Employers' organization in 1924.

4 Competition in the Early Days

4.1 Hollerith and Powers

Max Bodenhoff and Hollerith were not the only players in the field of punched cards. A creative engineer, James Powers, had already developed an improved keypunch in the U.S. in 1910 and incorporated his own company in 1911, just when some of Hollerith's original patents were running out. In addition, the U.S. Census for 1910 was now deploying Powers' equipment [1].

The previous occurrences were some of the reasons Herman Hollerith sold his company to the Computing-Tabulating-Recording Company that later developed into IBM. In addition, the rental business approach required large investments that Hollerith and his investors were not ready to fund. Apart from some technical improvements of the original Hollerith equipment, Powers also had another business strategy, where customers were also able to buy his equipment, while CTR ruthlessly maintained Hollerith's original lease/rental strategy. The other major difference between the two original systems was that while Hollerith was a sworn fanatic of electro-mechanical solutions, Powers invented a low-cost yet still effective mechanical solution.

There is no doubt, however, that the presence of two vendors gave rise to fierce competition that required constant innovation and improvements in both companies, and soon Powers, as Hollerith, looked to Europe as a potential growth market. The first orders for Powers' equipment in Europe seemed to have come from the Swedish Bureau of Statistics as early as 1913, but soon Powers entered some of the major markets where Hollerith Equipment had until then been the only vendor. In the UK, the Powers Company fiercely competed with British Tabulating Machines, an independent vendor selling Hollerith equipment, and on the continent, the main battle was between Powers Germany and DeHoMag – Deutsche Hollerith Machinen AG [1]. All of these local companies invented new devices and improvements and took out patents to protect themselves. This later became the artillery for intense legal battles that would be fought during the 1930s – a trend we also saw in the 1970s (Peripherals, mainframes) and in the 1980s (PCs) – as well as in SW Patent disputes since the 1990s.

4.2 Frederik Rosing Bull Enters the Danish Market

In Norway, Frederik Rosing Bull was a consultant for the Storebrand Insurance Company, who in 1918 began to construct an improved accounting machine – or as he called it – an automatic registration machine for statistical or similar purposes [1]. The patent was issued in 1919, the first machine was sold to Storebrand, of course, but the second was sold to Hafnia in Denmark. Henrik Hartzner tells us:

> As his managing director in a Nordic insurance magazine had read about 'Storebrand's new machine, I was sent to look at it, and as result we bought one 'registration machine' that was installed on September 30 1922. It was a combined sorting and accounting machine with 3 x 9-digits counters [2].

After some correspondence with Frederik Bull, additional orders were placed and Hafnia returned all Hollerith equipment on July 18 of 1923, at which time the new Bull accounting machines arrived. They were produced at Kr. Ormestad's machine shop and arrived together with Frederik R. Bull, who supervised the installation. Hafnia kept these machines until 1930, when they were replaced by newer Bull equipment.

Henrik Hartzner became general agent for Bull in Denmark in 1925, and already the same year sold a Bull machine to the Central Bureau of Statistics and later the same year to the Tryg Insurance Company. Hafnia updated the Bull equipment during the 1930s and became the reference customer in Denmark. This early success explains part of the relative strength of Danish Machines Bull in the 1950s and 1960s [3].

However, Frederik Bull died young, already in 1925, and willed his patents to the Norwegian Cancer Foundation, from where they were eventually bought to become the foundation of the Compagnie Machines Bull.

5 Service Bureau Business – Challenges and Disappointments

5.1 Early Attempts to Create an IBM/Hollerith Service Business

Already in 1921, Max Bodenhoff recognized the need to create a Service Bureau business, as he was approached by (RFI) Revisions- og Forvaltningsinstitutet (Later Deloitte DK), an institution with 150+ traveling auditors who controlled banking companies [4]. However, RFI demanded an exclusive contract with the Service Bureau business for ten years, and since the general manager of IBM in Europe, Mr. Jennings, would only agree to five years and a cap of fifty thousand punched cards to be used annually, this effectively ended the negotiations and RFI went to Powers for help.

However, Max Bodenhoff did not give in so easily. In 1930, he managed to get together a large group of medium-small insurance companies for the purpose of creating a fully developed service bureau, even hiring the best person from the Central Bureau of Statistics as the operating manager. Nevertheless, when the general manager of IBM Europe arrived, now a Mr. Jones, Max Bodenhoff was disappointed again:

> However, it was against the policy of the company that the agents ran a service bureau and I had to give up the plans and pay the man I had hired six months' salary for doing nothing!

Moreover, to make matters worse, all the insurance companies went to Powers. Still, he kept focus on what we today would have called the SMB-segment, recognizing that a service bureau sales channel was the only way to create a long lasting customer relationship with smaller clients and to keep them growing until they were convinced of the value of renting equipment themselves [2].

One might wonder why Max Bodenhoff did not dissolve the relationship with IBM. He said himself that he maintained the relationship because he was simply so impressed by the IBM global management, in particular the general manager, Thomas Watson, who returned the friendship and in many presentations referred to Max Bodenhoff as one of the most well run IBM agencies. Max Bodenhoff and his wife not only enjoyed the friendship of Thomas Watson, but also of his wife and four children, who used to travel with "Daddy" when he was abroad inspecting business partners in Europe. From Max Bodenhoff's notes, we also learn that Thomas Watson also personally worked to maintain the relationship between the agents and the Nordic general managers of the IBM companies, which showed their value during World

War II and beyond. The charisma of T. Watson was legendary, and he was a sort of icon for multinational companies during his lifetime.

5.2 Depression and Foreign Exchange Control

In 1931, the Danish Government created the Exchange Center (Valutacentralen), in order to meet the worldwide crisis and its impact on Danish foreign exchange reserves. Consequently, in order to spend foreign exchange, importers had to seek permission. Since the policy of this organization was extremely tough, in practice, only government import allowances for punched card equipment were granted – including permission to import equipment for the exchange center itself. This was an important order as the need for calculations rose dramatically during the 1930s. The only other important order in 1932 was a contract with Unilever Denmark, delivered in 1933 [5].

Max Bodenhoff's reason for pushing for a service bureau approach did not diminish as the 1930 crisis advanced; in addition to this, Denmark was primarily an agricultural nation that at the time only had ten companies and institutions with more than one thousand employees.

Finally, IBM company policy changed and Mr. Jones, the new general manager of IBM Europe, informed Max Bodenhoff that he would receive the green light to create a service bureau. This proved not to be at all too early and the creation of the service bureau actually helped the business of Hollerith Equipment to survive during the Second World War. However, the take-up was slow, as almost all insurance companies were now using Powers (now UK-based Powers-Samas). The turnover for the service business in 1932 was $645, rising to $2,527 in 1933, causing stagnation again [2].

The portfolio of customers grew with AU (the Employer Organization's insurance company) in 1934 and another minor insurance company two years later. In 1938, Max Bodenhoff decided to increase the sales force. He employed eight people, and had a turnover of $6,000 at the service bureau plus $5,000 per month from rental equipment.

6 A Short Overview of the Competitive Situation in the 1930s

Much happened technically during the late 1920s to strengthen the competitiveness of the machinery developed by the two, soon to become three, major players in the punch card arena. The battle for applications was mirrored in the explosion of new devices able to print, carry over intermediary results, cross-tabulate, perform simpler accounting applications and, not least, increase the speed capacity. An 80-column card replaced the original 45-column punched card that Hollerith introduced in a very clever way that meant existing machinery only needed small changes to adapt to the new standard. This was the first major "systems migration."

Nevertheless, considering the market and the machinery, there was little doubt that the Powers-Samas products were better than the Hollerith equipment, which was, however, more than offset by the IBM's sales force – they simply had more customers.

Powers-Samas in the UK became Remington Rand in the U.S. and Europe, as the Rand Corporation acquired the Powers' patents. There had been minor disputes between IBM and Powers Germany up to then, but with Remington-Rand's greater muscle, a serious struggle over patents developed between DeHoMag and Remington [6, 7].

In addition, the battle for Frederik Bull's patents also started in the early 1930s [1]. An exhibition in Paris in 1930 displayed Bull machines produced by the Swiss Egli Company that had acquired the Bull patents from Norway. The Egli Company was not ready for production and it was looking for partners. Both IBM and Remington Rand flirted with the idea of taking over Cie des Machines Bull, as the incorporated French production company and Egli affiliate was called. The vice president of Bull actually invited IBM management to inspect the quality of the equipment in 1932, and the proposal was presented to Tom Watson. He hesitated, and eventually turned down the proposal, in spite of the technical evaluation that the machines definitely had growth potential. It was obvious that the threat of the inspection of IBM's monopolistic behavior that the U.S. Ministry of Justice had announced it would start kept Tom Watson away from a direct confrontation.

However, although French IBM had bought 85 percent of the shares in Egli, the Swiss Bull Company, all production and growth took place in the French Bull Compagnie. Due to this, IBM and Cie des Machines Bull also continued the legal battle over who owned which patents until the war broke out [1, 8]

This is therefore the brief account of why an excellent Norwegian invention ended up in France, why the antitrust legislation of the U.S. (as much later in EU/Europe), just by its presence, would influence business decisions, in order to strengthen competition – and why international companies and their behavior had considerable impact on the Nordic customers' daily operations.

7   War – Emergency Operations and Innovative Actions

When the German Wehrmacht occupied Denmark and attacked Norway on April 9 1940, Max Bodenhoff received a visit from two high-ranking German officers that wanted to inspect the service bureau. However, since the U.S., at that point in time, was not yet in the war, they left without further notice. Even after the attack on Pearl Harbor, they did not interfere with the Hollerith Service Bureau and it was the general opinion that its work was of importance for the Danish administration and production upon which the Germans were depending. This may be easier to understand after seeing the proposal prepared by Max Bodenhoff for the National Bank of Denmark on how to administer the so-called Clearing Account, which the German Wehrmacht used to have Denmark finance all the costs of keeping the Wehrmacht operational in Denmark [2].

During the first few years, business was very slow, but after the German defeat at Stalingrad in the winter of 1941–42 trading and industrial companies became interested in starting accounting at the Service Bureau, and soon it was necessary to have a two-shift operation.

Getting punched cards had already become a major problem in 1941; but, thanks to his connections with Swedish IBM, Max Bodenhoff managed to get hold of a worn-out printing machine from the Swedish postal service and negotiated an agreement with Munksjö paper mill for the export of cardboard material, so that card manufacturing could begin in Denmark from early 1942. All import of equipment was cancelled, and the Service Bureau plus the skilled customer engineers kept the machinery going for the duration of the war. Similar arrangements were made between IBM Sweden and IBM Finland [2].

On January 27 1943, the Royal Air Force attacked Burmeister & Wain, the large Danish industrial company located at Christianshavn. This raid was supposed to demonstrate what the Allied forces would do unless the Danish Resistance started its sabotage. Included in the collateral damage were the deaths of several civilians and the destruction of dwelling houses. As Max Bodenhoff's office was, at the time, located in the center of Copenhagen, he felt obliged to move to the suburbs and finally to the House of Danish Industry at a considerable increase in rent.

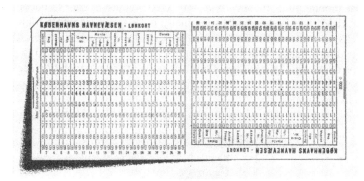

Fig. 2. An 80-column Punched Card used for calculation of salaries and wages, Copenhagen Harbor 1943–46

Nevertheless, when peace finally came on the eve of May 4, 1945, Max Bodenhoff could tally up, with satisfaction, an intact business operation, twenty-five employees, a rental base that was still around $5,500 per month, but a turnover at the Service Bureau amounting to $28,000 per year. The situation indicated that new customers had been acquired and the outlook on this evening was as bright as ever. In addition to this, his staff had used the war years to develop a variety of applications and demonstrations for different industries ranging from shipyards to retail to manufacturing and government, based on the strategy that applications were, after all, more important than machinery. In a way, this attitude preceded the much later change in IBM from a hardware company to a services company during the 1990s [2].

8 The Postwar Years

The plans were already drawn – Max Bodenhoff never lacked initiative [4]. His ambition was to establish affiliates and service bureaus in the three large provincial cities – but optimism soon disappeared as it became clear that the import restrictions were not going to eased in the near future; no new machinery was allowed entry into

Denmark until 1948. In addition, the many sales pitches, presentations, as well as application descriptions that had been developed and offered to customers and prospects during and immediately after the war could even turn against the Hollerith department. This was because the National Bank of Denmark categorically denied the use of U.S. dollars to buy new equipment, and it would grant only a very restricted quota on extensions of installed equipment. Similar restrictions were *not* imposed on Powers-Samas (UK based) or on Cie Machines Bull (French), as the European currencies were not being managed as restrictively. Thus, all the effort of creating interest and understanding might have resulted in victories for the competition.

Furthermore, the installed rental based equipment was worn out as was the machinery in the Service Bureau. Fortunately, in 1946, the authorities gave permission to import a complete set of IBM machinery that the U.S. Army used during the campaign in Northern Germany, 1944–45. Permission had also been granted by IBM's European headquarter in Geneva, but there was a problem finding the so-called mobile unit. In May 1946, Mr. Lykke Hansen, later to become general manager of IBM, was dispatched to Germany on a troop transport train and after several weeks he located two rather enormous trucks with what he described as "a service bureau on wheels," which had been placed at an airfield close to Bremen, and drove the lorries home. As a matter of curiosity, the installed tabulating/accumulating unit at Max Bodenhoff's Service Bureau stopped working the moment its replacement was placed in the room.

Fig. 3. One of the two lorries containing the so-called army machines brought back to Copenhagen from the U.S. Army in Germany. Parts of the machines were later installed in the City of Copenhagen's Bureau of Statistics, while the remaining parts were used at the Service Bureau [4].

Some prospective customers were lost during the first years after the war, while many others patiently waited for things to clear up. Consequently, when news of the Marshall Plan spread, customers first contracted with the Service Bureau and eventually, when restrictions were lifted, rented their own equipment.

Some very strategic sales to the City of Copenhagen and the City of Frederiksberg marked the beginning of the large number of municipal applications that later became the foundation of first the regional Punched Card centers, later the EDP-centers that finally emerged as Kommunedata, while the central government applications led to the foundation of Datacentralen I/S in 1959. An additional user group was founded – Dansk Hulkortforening – that much later in 1958, developed into Data-behandlingsforeningen, now Dansk IT [9].

It is not a coincidence that the first manager of the Jutland EDP-center JKEC, Mr. Renner Andresen, was a salesman with Max Bodenhoff's Hollerith Department during the 1940s, as was Willy Olsen, Datacentralen's (Center for Danish Government Data Processing) first CEO. When IT history is told, it is important to remember the pioneers and where they were first trained and employed. This pattern of recruiting trained former IBM employees was to continue and took-off with the later introduction of the computer era; but the trend actually started in the 1940s [5].

In 1949 Max Bodenhoff's "Hollerith Department" consisted of forty-nine persons, the turnover at the Service Bureau amounted to $112,000/year and the rental base, thanks to the lifting of the import restrictions, now represented a turnover of $20,000 per month [5].

9   Creation of IBM Denmark in 1950

In 1947, Viggo Troels-Smith, the future first CEO of IBM DK [4], joined the Max Bodenhoff Hollerith organization; he had studied in the U.S. before the war and was hired as a salesman by IBM U.S. in 1937. During the War, he had enlisted in the Navy and participated in a punched card logistics unit. He returned back to Europe to assist in re-establishing the Nordic IBM companies and to Denmark to ensure the creation of a fully developed affiliate company. Max Bodenhoff very soon declared that he wanted to remain an independent merchant, and so the job naturally went to Troels-Smith, while T.J. Watson, who awarded a pension to Max Bodenhoff, was described by him as "more impressive than any Department Manager of a Danish Ministry" [2]. The entire Hollerith staff joined the new IBM A/S that opened its doors on 1 January 1950 in Vestre Boulevard 38 (later H.C. Andersens Boulevard).

10   Summary – What Can We Learn from History?

From the beginning of the automatic "punch card era," it seems that the patterns of development, operations, marketing, and competition have followed the trends repeatedly witnessed in every phase of the 'real' computer era. The driving force behind the market place was and is the intelligent combination of creative engineers and the key applications needed by advanced companies and institutions. While the characteristics for this first generation of (semi) intelligent computing were the sheer volume of the computations needed, it soon became clear that information management, cross-tabulating, and new ways of reusing large bulks of data have given rise to new business opportunities as well as cost savings. Originally focused on statistical departments in government and insurance, the toolbox of applications soon spread to other parts of society. In the case of Denmark, the specific challenges imposed by the German Occupation led to a pressure on creativity, particularly in the applications area, which was inherited by the newly formed IBM Denmark organization and which ensured a firm position in the market when the age of electronic computing really took off. In 1950, the tradition of efficient marketing, already introduced by Max Bodenhoff in 1920, the close partnership with customers, and the importance of employee education and training as well as educational facilities for customers were already a matter of fact.

References

1. Conolly, J.: A History of Computing in Europe. IBM, New York (1967)
2. Private correspondence of Mr. Max Bodenhoff, IBM Denmark Archives
3. Bashe, C.J., Johnson, L.R., Palmer, J.H., Pugh, E.W.: IBM's Early Computers. MIT Press, Cambridge (1986)
4. Private archives of Mrs. Elin Hansen, secretary of first CEO of IBM Denmark
5. IBM Denmark Archives
6. Powers Magazine (April 1938)
7. Before the Computers Came (Powers- Samas and more references), http://www.westwoodworks.net/HowItWas/BeforeComputers/index.htm
8. Science et Vie Micro Magazine. History of Bull (74) (July-August 1990), http://www.riemarfamily.com/BullHistory/history.html
9. Heide, L.: Hulkort og EDB i Danmark 1911-1970. Systime, e-book (2005)

Making Business of a Revolutionary New Technology: The Eckert-Mauchly Company, 1945–1951

Lars Heide

Copenhagen Business School, Porcelænshaven 18B
2000 Frederiksberg, Denmark
heide@cbs.dk

Abstract. The paper analyzes John Presper Eckert and John William Mauchly's endeavours to design, sell, and build the revolutionary new technology of the first large, commercial computers. It discusses how Eckert and Mauchly's conceptualization of the computer grew out of their ENIAC and EDVAC projects at University of Pennsylvania. They incorporated their own business to gain profit from production and attain the freedom needed to develop their revolutionary new computer technology through a series of small, separate computer projects with private and government customers. It approaches innovation as a chaotic process and uses uncertainty to conceptualize the basic relations between actors and organizations.

Keywords: Eckert-Mauchly Company, EDVAC, ENIAC, John Presper Eckert, John William Mauchly, UNIVAC, University of Pennsylvania.

1   Introduction[1]

> *"… did you ever think it was going to turn out like this? … my colleague Mr. Eckert and I, independently I think, have developed about the same answer: that, yes, we felt it was going to turn out to be a big thing. It was just to our disappointment that it took so long. But then it always takes a long time to change people's minds, and it takes even longer for us to change an institution."* [2]

This was how John W. Mauchly, in 1973, recalled the development of the first UNIVAC computer, completed in 1951. He acknowledged that he and John Presper

---

[1] The paper is based upon extensive material in the archives of Hagley Museum and Library, Wilmington, Delaware, USA (Sperry Corporation Records (acc. 1825), Sperry-Rand Corporation Administrative Records (acc. 1910)) and at the Charles Babbage Institute at University of Minnesota, Minneapolis, Minnesota, USA (Margaret R. Fox Papers (CBI 45), C. E. Berkeley Papers (CBI 50), Mauchly talk 1973 (OH 44)) and extensive literature. Research for this paper was accomplished based upon a grant from Hagley Museum and Library, Wilmington, Delaware, and an Arthur L. Norberg Travel Grant from the Charles Babbage Institute at University of Minnesota.

[2] John Mauchly, talk to UNIVAC meeting in Rome in 1973, p.1, interview OH 44, Charles Babbage Institute.

J. Impagliazzo, P. Lundin, and B. Wangler (Eds.): HiNC3, IFIP AICT 350, pp. 207–214, 2011.
© IFIP International Federation for Information Processing 2011

Eckert did not know where the development would end, when it started in the mid-1940s. In contrasts, the histories of the computer industry subscribed to a linear narrative from the ENIAC project during World War II to the IBM System/360 mainframe computer closure in the mid-1960s, and to personal computers and beyond. They discuss either engineering (hardware and software) or business aspects of the development and they, therefore, miss the shaping interaction between markets and engineering, and the crucial role of government in both funding projects and acquiring computers.

An integrated analysis of business, technology, private market, and government market is essential in order to understand how mainframe computers emerged. Further, the linear narrative ignores the size of the endeavor that Eckert and Mauchly faced in the mid-1940s of designing and building a revolutionary new technology, and it ignores the complexity of subsequent development, until IBM established the mainframe computer closure by introducing its System 360 in 1964. The development of revolutionary new technology and establishing its production was never a simple rational simple process. In the mid-1940s, designing and producing mainframe computers required revolutionary new design and basic elements, like adders, memory, storage, and input and output media.

The paper analyzes Eckert and Mauchly's endeavours between 1945 and 1951 to design, build, and sell the revolutionary new technology of the first large, commercial computers in interaction with private and government customers. It approaches innovation as being chaotic and uses uncertainty to conceptualize the basic relations between actors and organizations.

2   ENIAC and EDVAC: Technical Feasibility and Design of an Operational Computer

In late 1945, John William Mauchly and John Presper Eckert started exploring what a computer should be and its commercial potential. This was based upon the ENIAC project, which had proved the feasibility of building a large electronic computer, and the EDVAC project, which had produced a feasible rapid-access memory, the stored program design and opened for more complex use than calculating the third root of 2,589 raised to the sixteenth power.

In August 1942, John Mauchly wrote a memorandum on a large high-speed vacuum-tube calculator for the Army Ordnance Department. The proposal outlined the main features of a digital vacuum-tube calculator and focused on its technical feasibility. This became the basis for a contract on a large electronic computer, which the Army awarded to the Moore School. Eckert and Mauchly's project team designed new electronic circuits and built a reasonably reliable machine. By June 1944, the formal design of the computer was completed and it was dedicated in February 1946 as the Electronic Numerical Integrator and Computer (ENIAC).

ENIAC proved the feasibility of building a large electronic computer, but it did not have reliability, size, moderate energy consumption, and user friendliness needed in order to make it attractive for a wider range of public and private organizations.

Based on discussions between Moore School and Army Ballistics Research Laboratory, in October 1944, the Army granted a supplement to the ENIAC contract to develop a computer, EDVAC, which was easier to use for calculations. During 1945, this project ran in parallel with the completion of ENIAC, which had priority.

3   Shaping a Computer

In the summer of 1945, the building of large computers became technically feasible. ENIAC was being completed and had proven the feasibility of large electronic computers.

In December 1945 – while completing the ENIAC – Eckert and Mauchly started envisioning commercial possibilities. They approached the Bureau of the Census in order to sell the idea of a large-scale electronic digital computer as an efficient tool for census work. For this end Mauchly and Eckert studied census data processing, and probably magnetic tape was a significant sales argument. In the summer of 1945, the EDVAC design applied magnetic tape or wire for input and output.

However, it was not simple to accommodate commercial production at a non-profit university, such as University of Pennsylvania. In the spring of 1946, Eckert and Mauchly resigned from Moore School because they wanted to exploit the commercial opportunities of building computers.

The ENIAC and EDVAC projects had been classified because of World War II. The end of hostilities facilitated declassification, which enabled Eckert and Mauchly to use their expertise for business. In addition, war-funding disappeared and public funding would again have to be based upon Congressional appropriations. The new funding structure was probably a major reason that Eckert and Mauchly since December 1945 worked to attain a contract to build a computer for the Bureau of the Census. By the spring of 1946, the Census Bureau was definitely interested in Mauchly's proposal.

At their resignation from University of Pennsylvania in March 1946, the possible census contact was the only contract, which they found was at hand. They started to work for establishing a company to develop a multi-purpose rapid computing machine. Though they only were negotiating a contract with the Bureau of the Census, they optimistically envisioned many business opportunities in scientific computations, bookkeeping, and record management. They cited scientific calculations at universities, government agencies, and industries, bookkeeping in large companies, particularly insurance and railroad, and record management in insurance companies and libraries. This was a revolutionary new way to see computers compared to ENIAC and EDVAC.

However, the end of World War II caused a fundamental change in public funding of projects. During the war, funds were amble for war-related projects like ENIAC and the EDVAC pre-project and the trust needed for funding was accomplished quite informally, when the project was located at a well-estimated institution like the Moore School. Now, peacetime appropriation made it essential for a public organization to establish the trust needed to award a project to an organization. Was the project feasible? Was the price reasonable? Did the organization have the technological and financial capabilities needed to complete the contract in due time? It was not simple answering these questions for funding a project with Eckert and Mauchly of building a computer for the Census Bureau. They had substantial technological expertise;

however, did it suffice to build a revolutionary new device? Moreover, Eckert and Mauchly's business was not yet incorporated and had little assets. It was essential to find a way to establish the needed trust, which required assessment by experts, public or private, acting as intermediaries between the Census Bureau and Eckert and Mauchly. The National Bureau of Standards rose to become the intermediary for civilian and military government computer projects.

By June of 1946, the National Bureau of Standards had decided to award a study contract to Eckert and Mauchly. The two inventors then formed a partnership, but the study contract only became effective in October 1946. Originally, they anticipated that the research and study phase would last six months. They expected to complete the design phase within the next six months. This schedule proved to be overly optimistic. The research and study phase itself lasted a full year. Moreover, it was not until June 1948, that they signed the actual design contract.

The Census Bureau was prepared to spend $300,000 on the Eckert-Mauchly computer, of which $55,400 went to the National Bureau of Standards for services as the intermediary. In June 1946, Eckert and Mauchly's had estimated the development cost at $400,000. Anyhow, despite their limited assets, the two men were willing to absorb the anticipated loss, because they believed that if they were successful, additional machines could be sold to both government and industry at substantial profits.

The Census Bureau needed a different computer than the sophisticated calculator, which was the objective of building ENIAC and EDVAC. Census processing required facilities for producing double entry tables and it took advantage of the plan to use magnetic tape in the EDVAC project. It needed fast and reliable sorting, which Eckert and Mauchly suggested could be achieved through transmission of data between two magnet tapes operating at separate stations. This made construction of tape stations and fast exchange of data between tape and the computer a key element of the Census Bureau contract. The computer was changing from a fast calculator into a smart punched card machine. This transformation was more complicated and time consuming than Eckert and Mauchly anticipated.

The situation of late assignment of government contracts, which were smaller than expected, and more work in designing and building the computer than anticipated made Eckert and Mauchly open for approaches for additional contracts from A. C. Nielsen Company, and Prudential Insurance Company.

The A. C. Nielsen Company was founded in 1923 in Chicago, Illinois, by Arthur C. Nielsen, Sr., in order to give marketers reliable statistics on impact of marketing and sales programs. In the mid-1940s, A. C. Nielsen Company used large punched card installations to process the data for their market statistics. Nielsen was interested in investing in new development, even in a small company, despite the obvious risk and started negotiations with Eckert and Mauchly in December 1946.

In January 1947, Eckert and Mauchly offered to sell A. C. Nielsen Company a computer system equipped with a key-to-tape recorder and a printer, all units to be completed within a year. This implied changing the basis for Nielsen's data processing from punched cards to magnetic tape, which they accepted. But A. C. Nielsen Company was reluctant to sign a purchase agreement with Eckert and Mauchly's company because of its precarious financial position. Nielsen wanted Eckert and Mauchly to develop their equipment and gain more business in order to establish the trust, which it needed for awarding a contract for a computer system.

Over the next year, Eckert and Mauchly reshaped their computer system and particularly its peripherals based upon their discussions with Prudential Insurance Company. The A. C. Nielsen Company only needed a computer similar to that already promised to the Bureau of the Census. In April 1948, Nielsen signed a contract for a computer system with several peripherals. The system included one computer, six tape units, six key-to-tape units, and one printer.

Simultaneously with the negotiations with A. C. Nielsen Company, Eckert and Mauchly negotiated with Prudential Insurance Company of Newark, New Jersey. The negotiations with Prudential made Eckert and Mauchly extend the scope of their computer project to encompass alphanumeric data processing, because the Eckert Mauchly Company realized that Prudential demanded equipment for premium billing, mortality studies, and group insurance. Premium billing presupposed letters and numbers.

Prudential's data processing was based on IBM equipment since the 1920s. Therefore, it viewed the Eckert and Mauchly's use of magnetic tape for input and output with concern. Although the concept seemed attractive, there yet was no working model to prove its feasibility, and the use of tapes in place of cards would mean that Prudential's entire data processing operation would need conversion to tape. Eckert and Mauchly convinced Prudential that their computer system was feasible and a superior alternative to its current IBM punch-card systems, which caused two concerns at Prudential. Eckert and Mauchly's uncertain financial position was a serious obstacle. Prudential was unwilling to sign a large contract with a small company that had serious financial problems, particularly when sizable investment was required to complete the contract. This was the case, because Eckert and Mauchly had not yet accomplished designing the statistics computer for the contracts with the Bureau of the Census and A. C. Nielsen Company, and Prudential's alphanumeric requirements would imply additional research and development as well as production expenses.

While Prudential was not willing to contract for a machine, it signed an agreement with Eckert and Mauchly, in August 1947, where it funded development of the computer system in return for an option to buy one later. If the option was exercised, the money provided for development would be applied to the purchase. The agreement promised to complete the design and several prototypes of several key elements of the computer system by the end of 1947. Once more Eckert and Mauchly were overly optimistic in their time estimate. By the end of 1947, they had no yet completed the prototype, and Prudential could have insisted that half its funds be returned. Instead, it agreed to amend the contract several times to allow Eckert and Mauchly's company more time to fulfill its obligations. Prudential extended the deadlines because it was impressed with the progress being made and the development contract made it dependent on Eckert and Mauchly. In the end, Prudential signed a contract in December 1948 for building a computer system. The contract called for one card-to-tape converter and two tape-to-card converters, devices that would allow Prudential to retain its punch-card data processing systems. This was essential for Eckert and Mauchly extending their market to encompass non-numeric data processing, for example, in insurance companies. The Prudential contract described Eckert and Mauchly's complete computer system, which they had named UNIVAC a year earlier, Universal Automatic Computer. It had a central computer, tape drives, alphanumeric key-to-tape encoders, and line printers. In order to answer demand, Eckert and Mauchly had developed their original ENIAC and EDVAC number cruncher design into an alphanumeric design for data processing to succeed extensive punched card business.

4 Establishing Business of Computers

Eckert and Mauchly left the Moore School of University of Pennsylvania in March 1946, because they saw bright possibilities of computer business and they founded a partnership as the basis for their work. They focused on developing a computer and attaining computer-building contracts through 1946 and 1947, and Mauchly travelled extensively to win over customers. In this period, they established contacts with A. C. Nielsen Company and Prudential Insurance Company, which contracted for computers in 1948. In addition, the records show that Mauchly had contacts to about twenty additional private and public organizations prospects in 1946–1947, which did not produce contracts.

Eckert and Mauchly only incorporated their business in December 1947 and it was named Eckert-Mauchly Computer Corporation. Though the company attained several substantial contracts in 1948, its financial problems became more severe during that year. Since the start of the year, Mauchly worked hard to attack additional customers based upon a strategy to produce the company out of its crisis. The company was desperate to securing adequate capital to assure the government and private companies that they could complete contracts that they would make, and the company failed to raise substantial new capital by issuing additional stocks in April 1948.

However, in the summer of 1948, new capital came from American Totalistor Company of Baltimore. John Straus, its vice president, saw possibilities of computers applied as totalisators. He convinced his company to invest $500,000 in in return for 40 percent of the voting common stock of Eckert–Mauchly Computer Corporation. American Totalisator's support kept Eckert and Mauchly's company floating for fourteen months, during which development on UNIVAC continued. In October 1949, Eckert and Mauchly's company received an additional $100,000 from American Totalisator. Anyway, the company's problems were not yet solved. Nine days later, Henry Straus was killed when his small airplane crashed. Straus had been the prime force behind Totalisator's support and his death terminated the flow of funds from this company.

As a direct result of Straus's death, Eckert and Mauchly spent the remaining months of 1949 seeking financing from loan companies and research foundations. Finally, they sought to sell their corporation to a major manufacturer. They approached producers of calculating equipment, such as Burroughs, IBM, National Cash Register, and Remington Rand. Subsequently, they approached major industrial producers, such as General Motors.

Remington Rand was first to act, and on 1 February 1950, it purchased all the shares of the Eckert-Mauchly Computer Corporation. It became a subsidiary of Remington Rand and functioned as a separate division. It delivered the first UNIVAC computer to the Bureau of the Census in March 1931. By October 1954, Remington Rand had delivered twelve UNIVACs and had orders for four more.

5   Mess of Making Business of a Revolutionary New Technology

I started the paper by citing John W. Mauchly's reminiscence, in 1973, of the shaping of what became the UNIVAC computer. He admitted that the shaping process was protracted, which he explained by observing, "…it always takes a long time to change people's minds, and it takes even longer for us to change an institution."

He was correct that institutions – which he conceptualized as private and public organizations – had to change, but this only occurred once computers were installed. In the late 1940s, the organizational change of customer to demand computers had short duration compared to the at least five years, which Eckert and Mauchly spent in designing and building the first large computer. In contrast, Mauchly persuaded the Census Bureau in five months to order a computer system, A. C. Nielsen Company used between two and three months to reach a decision, and Prudential Insurance Company reached their decision in less than a year. However, it took much more time to establish the trust needed for these organizations to sign contracts. They were uncertain of Eckert and Mauchly's company's financial capability, and they did not want to be dependent on technology which perhaps never would materialize.

The demand for reduction of uncertainty and dependency gave room for the National Bureau of Standards to establish itself as the national computer intermediary facilitating civilian and military contracts.

Further, Mauchly underestimated the extent of developing a revolutionary new technology twenty-five years after it took place, as he and Eckert did while they explored the new technology between 1943 and 1951. Before starting computer production, they had to establish company standards for designing and building completely new technology, based upon many components with reliability problems. Through this process, the scope of their computer's planned applications grew from the original number cruncher (ENIAC and EDVAC), to the numerical statistics calculator for the Census Bureau and A. C. Nielsen Company, and to the alphanumeric data processing machine for Prudential Insurance, which was named UNIVAC. Each extension of applications added a new element of uncertainty to the project. However, Eckert and Mauchly rejected an enquiry in 1946 of developing their computer for totalisator applications, which illustrates that they did not pick all requests. Their choices of customers remained within the scope they envisioned in the spring of 1946 and gradually expanded their business opportunities.

At each expansion, Eckert and Mauchly accepted new uncertainty, because they depend on one more customer to fill their company's extensive need for funds to complete their previous assignment. Their perpetual search for new customers, made Mauchly commit extensive time to locate and persuade new customers. Often, Eckert, who should have committed all his time to complete their technical project, accompanied him. The records of Eckert and Mauchly's company provide a hectic picture of searches for funding that took time and delayed the project. Already in the summer of 1947, they had also to borrow money from Prudential Insurance to be able to keep their computer development project floating. In 1948, they received substantial capital from American Totalisator. However, only access to the large financial resources of the Remington Rand conglomerate, in 1950, facilitated completion and production of UNIVAC computers.

Eckert and Mauchly's first large computer and their business were shaped through dependency on a series of customers for expertise on future use of computers and funds for innovating computers. At first glance, the technical development process and the search for additional customers may seem chaotic, and, certainly, they held many chaotic elements. However, Mauchly was correct in 1973 to claim that he and Eckert all the way went for a general objective, which they accomplished though in Remington Rand, a different business context than they originally anticipated.

IBM Manufacturing in the Nordic Countries

Petri Paju

Cultural History Department, University of Turku, Finland
petpaju@utu.fi

Abstract. Unlike other foreign computing companies, in addition to sales and service IBM early on also established production facilities in the Nordic countries. To provide a better understanding of the role of IBM in these countries, the article surveys IBM manufacturing in the region: what was produced, and where were these functions located? The term "production" is understood in a rather narrow sense, as manufacture. The results show that for several decades, IBM produced punched cards in four Nordic countries, but that after 1960 there has been only one IBM factory for hardware in the region, located in the Stockholm area. The article also discusses the reasons for Sweden's importance in IBM manufacture, and suggests that Nordic companies contributed to IBM manufacture through subcontracting.

Keywords: Computer history, hardware production, IBM World Trade Corporation, Nordic countries, punched card, subcontracting.

1 Introduction

From World War II to the 1980s, one of the most influential actors of the computer industry in the Nordic countries was IBM, the International Business Machines company. Throughout the period, this American multinational corporation was the data-processing market leader in all five countries belonging to the Nordic cultural region. Unlike many other foreign computer companies, in addition to sales and service IBM early on also established production facilities in the Nordic countries. IBM's wide international connections had many implications for national developments, from Iceland to Finland. As in many other parts of the world, IBM was or became a contested player in Scandinavia too, no doubt partly because of its formidable size and dominance. According to some current beliefs, IBM was often perceived as, or argued to be, a counter-force to the national computer industries. To understand better the role of IBM in the Nordic area, this article discusses IBM manufacturing in the Nordic countries.

Some parts of IBM production in the Nordic area may be well known, but not the whole or big picture. In the book *History of Nordic Computing*, Hans Andersin wrote about IBM's role in the early development of computing in the Nordic countries. A recent study has argued that IBM's success in Europe was partly due to its production structure, which was organized in terms of the whole continent [1, 2]. IBM has

J. Impagliazzo, P. Lundin, and B. Wangler (Eds.): HiNC3, IFIP AICT 350, pp. 215–227, 2011.

usually been dealt with on a national basis, although IBM itself was comprised of several levels and perspectives, national as well as multinational. During most of the period covered in this article the Nordic IBM subsidiaries were part of the IBM World Trade Corporation; this organization did business everywhere except in the United States, where IBM sales were managed by the IBM Corporation.

In the article, I ask the following questions: What did IBM produce in the Nordic area? Where were these functions located? The term "production" is understood in a rather narrow sense, as manufacture, i.e. mainly plants that produce things. Other productive activities, such as training and software writing, are thus excluded. A further question is, did the Nordic IBM plants in turn make a special contribution within IBM?

To some extent, this article contributes to the discussion of the effect of these operations, including their possible influence on the national information technology industries in these countries. In addition, it provides information – although indirectly – on IBM's customers and computer users and their concentrations in the region.

The paper is based on a varied array of material and literature. I have used some archival sources from the IBM Corporation in the USA and from IBM Finland, as well as IBM publications, including IBM's internal staff magazines. For the most part, however, my main sources consist of the secondary literature, such as academic studies.[1] The article is part of a larger, ongoing research project, which examines the co-shaping of computer expertise in Europe in the Cold War era, and visions of European capabilities, using IBM technology. To grasp the long evolution of IBM's manufacturing in the Nordic area, I need to start from the state of data processing before the computer [3].

2   IBM Enters the Nordic Countries

The first national IBM subsidiary in the Nordic area was established in Sweden, in 1928. At the time, however, IBM had already had sales agents in most Nordic countries for several years. The first IBM or Hollerith machines had been delivered even earlier. In fact, in 1894 Norway became one of the earliest countries outside the United States to test the punched card machines developed (for purposes of census tabulation) by Herman Hollerith in the 1880s [4]. In 1911, Hollerith's technology became a key product for the company that was renamed IBM in 1924. Soon afterwards, IBM founded its first factories in Europe, located in France and Germany.

The Nordic national IBM companies were founded in the period from 1928 to 1967 (see Table 1). These dates, and their order, may have played a role when IBM management chose locations for IBM facilities, so they merit some attention. The Swedish subsidiary was established first, and evidently became an administrative centre for IBM's expansion in the region. This history probably offers some explanation for the large part that Sweden would play in further IBM development in the Nordic region.

---

[1] See also the article by Eric Malmi, Timo Honkela and myself, in this volume.

Table 1. The Establishing of Nordic IBM Country Organizations

Year	Country	Organization type
1928	Sweden	Subsidiary
1935	Norway	Subsidiary
1936	Finland	Subsidiary
1950	Denmark	Subsidiary
1967	Iceland	Branch Office

The Danish agent was evidently doing so well that IBM waited until the late 1940s to push for a national subsidiary there. From 1950 onward, when the IBM World Trade Corporation (WTC) was established, this new company, with its global reach, included a newly formed IBM subsidiary in Denmark. In Iceland, prior to 1967, IBM had had a national representative from 1948, coordinated from Denmark. In Reykjavik, the Icelandic capital, IBM punched card machines were first introduced in 1949 [5].[2]

3 Punched Card Production

IBM started production in the Nordic countries in 1932, with the manufacture of punched cards. Unsurprisingly, it was Swedish IBM that was involved, since it was the only IBM Company in the region. In 1932 the Swedish IBM company build a Carroll Press, named after its designer, the IBM engineer Fred Carroll. In the first year, eighteen million cards were printed. The punched card plant moved to Vällingby in 1954. Punched card printing peaked in 1969, when the factory in Sweden produced one billion cards. Card manufacture ended in Sweden in 1980 [6]. In other words, IBM Sweden was printing punched cards for almost fifty years.

Although often unappreciated as a key part of data processing in its time, punched cards were of crucial importance to the data processing business and to IBM. The cards themselves were used in most things IBM and its customers did, but especially in large-scale data processing; for a considerable time, nothing could be done without those actual pieces of special paper. For IBM, moreover, the cards had been a highly profitable and steady source of income already in the 1930s, and they continued to give the company financial stability [3, 7]. Thus, a significant part of IBM's business was the production and delivery of punched cards.

IBM punched cards needed in Finland, for instance, were first shipped from Germany and later from Sweden. In Helsinki, the first Hollerith cards had been ordered by the Statistical head office in 1922. After 1932, with the inception of the Swedish plant, punched cards for the Finnish IBM agent and later for the IBM subsidiary (est. 1936), as well as for customers, were probably supplied by IBM Sweden [8].

The period of World War II brought a wave of IBM production to the Nordic countries. This was probably because of difficulties with IBM punched card

---

[2] For a history of the IBM branch office in Iceland, see Sverrir Olafsson's article in this volume. For information on the Danish IBM agent and early IBM business in Denmark, see Søren Duus Østergaard's article in this volume.

deliveries. Between 1940 and 1943, punched card plants were established in Norway (1940), Finland (1942) and Denmark (1943), although the Danish plant was owned by the national IBM agent [8–10]. It seems remarkable that IBM Sweden was able to help both the Danish IBM agent and IBM Finland in establishing card plants, considering that Finland was in a state of war and Denmark was occupied by German troops [8].[3] Nevertheless, along with eventual assistance from IBM Sweden this period reveals some tension and competition among the IBM companies.

For the Finnish subsidiary, securing a punched card factory was not all that straightforward. As mentioned, in the late 1930s IBM Finland received its punched cards from Sweden. In wartime, these deliveries could not be guaranteed, and IBM Finland came up with the idea of producing its own punched cards. The CEO of IBM in Finland, Einar Dickman, visited IBM Sweden's card plant in August 1940, during the interval of peace in Finland between the Winter War of 1939–1940 and the Continuation War, which began in the summer of 1941. (Sweden of course maintained neutrality during World War II.) Dickman calculated that if Finnish IBM made its own cards, one of the printing machines in Sweden would became idle and could be moved to Finland. He suggested this to the European headquarters, but IBM Sweden did not agree; they said they needed all of their machines. In 1942, however, a used printing machine was imported from IBM Sweden to Helsinki, where a Finnish IBM punched card factory operated during 1942–1946 [8, 11].

During the war, IBM Finland also received some help from IBM Sweden and IBM Norway. In addition to spare parts, they occasionally sent engineers for service tasks while Finnish engineers were at the front or otherwise serving the war effort [12].[4] Help was also sought from a Polish expert, but apparently, the Germans wanted to keep him [11].

In using punched cards and in IBM's business with them, the most important thing was card quality: not only in a general sense, but more specifically because bad card quality made the machines jam and IBM service had to fix them. Since the IBM machines were rented to the customers, service meant extra costs for IBM. The need to minimize costs made card quality so essential for business.

The importance of card quality is indicated by the fact that in 1946 IBM Finland again started importing cards from Sweden; the old printing press in Helsinki could no longer produce cards of sufficient quality. Moreover, because of the growing post-war demand the Swedish subsidiary could not deliver cards for Finland in sufficient quantity. The Finns therefore applied to the World Trade Division in New York for a new printing machine to be placed in Finland [8, 11].[5] It is clear that the Swedish and Finnish IBM companies had different interests in card production. The national subsidiaries negotiated over this question with and through IBM headquarters. Within the multinational company, this certainly exemplifies *international* competition over company facilities and functions. Such negotiations among IBM nationals may have also reinforced the parties' national feelings.

---

[3] For the card plant's situation in Denmark, see Søren Duus Østergaard's article in this volume.

[4] Cf. According to Anttila [11] it was often difficult to get that (or any) help. Anttila had access to the original correspondence, which is now missing.

[5] The IBM World Trade Division was the form of organization in 1947, right before the establishment of the World Trade Corporation.

Finally, in 1952, an IBM punched card factory (re)opened in Helsinki. The card plant began production despite difficulties in the first years. The greatest problems were in meeting the high standards that were required for functional paper cards. The paper for the cards was manufactured by and bought from a medium-sized Finnish pulp and paper company, the G. A. Serlachius factory at Kangas, near Jyväskylä [8]. IBM card manufacture continued in Finland until the late 1970s, for twenty-six years. All this was certainly an important argument for the IBM Finland's national significance.

In the 1960s, the same Finnish pulp and paper company started selling and exporting its material to foreign IBM subsidiaries as well. Finnish IBM printed cards for Finland, but it also exported them to other IBM subsidiaries. Interestingly, in the mid-1970s the Finnish subsidiary, as a subcontractor, also exported cards to the Soviet Union [13]. These were most probably delivered to the IBM operation coordinated from Moscow.

One consequence of the punched card press and related technology transfer to Finland was that the manager of the IBM press, Ulf Enbom, resigned from IBM in 1957 and started a card plant of his own in 1958. He co-developed new machinery for card printing and competed with IBM Finland by producing punched cards. In the 1960s, however, the new company could not compete and had to close down [14].

In 1950, when the Danish IBM subsidiary was established, it also took over the punched card press there. In 1970, 70 percent of all Danish computer systems used punched cards as their input medium. At the time, card production was mostly carried out within the country and accounted for some one billion cards [9]. Thus IBM Denmark, the clear market leader, continued to produce cards there at least well into the seventies. In Norway the peak of IBM's punched card production, six hundred million cards a year, was achieved in 1970, a year later than in Sweden, indicating the long-lasting demand for the cards [15].

For all these national plants, quality control and testing were essential. In these respects, IBM's international network of transnational resources played a major role in the manufacture of cards and other "information record" devices. In the Finnish case, tests were performed by the Finnish subcontractor and by an IBM print technology laboratory in Stockholm. Another IBM laboratory, located in Sindelfingen, West-Germany, tested the color ingredients for the color tapes (used in IBM typewriters). There were also several other IBM units involved, although not in dealing with punched cards [16]. In other words, the international IBM network made a big difference for national card production sites as well. Evidently, most of these IBM laboratories served all of the IBM card plants in Europe. This made the plants' available transnational IBM resources hard to compete with by means of national resources alone – particularly with regard to card quality.

4 Hardware Manufacturing

In addition to punched cards, other IBM manufacturing in the Nordic area started properly in the early 1950s in Sweden and Norway. In his compilation of information on national IBM history in Europe in the late 1960s, James Connolly mentions that IBM Sweden produced its first hand key punches already in 1941 [17]. It was in 1951, however, that IBM commenced assembling electric typewriters in Stockholm (at Norra Stationsgatan). Two years later, in 1953, the Stockholm factory produced its thousandth electric typewriter. These typewriters were made in Sweden until 1961 [10, 18], when other production in Sweden was expanded.

In 1952, IBM Norway started producing time recorders. In the late 1950s, IBM Norway also manufactured electric typewriters for a few years [15]. By 1959, the Oslo Plant had produced its five thousandth IBM 780 job cost and attendance time recorder [10].[6] Production in Oslo continued until 1960, when it was moved to other countries as IBM reorganized or cut its manufacturing [15]. In 1964, IBM World Trade ended its time recorder business altogether [10].

In 1954, all IBM manufacturing in Sweden was concentrated at a new factory in Vällingby, in the Stockholm area. At the new premises IBM workers printed punch cards, assembled electronic typewriters and punched-card machines, and made time recorders. [6] The punch card machines produced were the IBM 082 sorter, the IBM 416 tabulator and the IBM 513 reproducer.[7] Initially the factory employed 120 people [10].

Tellingly of Sweden's modernization in city planning, and of IBM's place in this development, Vällingby, the location of the IBM factory complex, was the first "town of the future." It was an "ABC City" — an acronym for "Arbete-Bostad-Centrum," or "work and residential center" – a suburb designed to offer its residents everything they needed, similar to an independent city. It was inaugurated in 1954, the same year IBM moved in [19]. The new city and its architecture attracted public attention in Sweden and even internationally.

In 1961 IBM enlarged the Vällingby factory, although they also stopped producing typewriters the same year [10]. The expansion was needed for the manufacturing of new products. In 1960 the factory had commenced the production of two new punched card machines, the IBM 088 and the IBM 1402. The IBM 088 was a collator, a machine that shuffled separate decks or card piles together into one or more decks [17, 20]. The IBM 1402 was a card reader punch, originally designed as part of the IBM 1401 data processing system. In 1967, the plant began manufacturing another peripheral for the IBM 1401 computer, the IBM 1403 printer [10].

The IBM 1401 was the first transistorized computer system for smaller businesses, which could continue using the punched cards and get a computer relatively cheaply. The 1401 system was announced in 1959 and became IBM's breakthrough model in computers until its withdrawal in 1971 [7, 21], see also [2]. With the peripheral machines, which were integral to the computer system – the IBM 1402 and especially the printer IBM 1403 – production in Sweden contributed to and shared in IBM's worldwide success.

5   The IBM Factory in Sweden Focuses on Printers

Thanks to its fast-growing sales, IBM erected a new factory at Järfälla (or Jarfalla, the form used in English) in 1970. The Järfälla municipality, like Vällingby, is located in

---

[6] Cf. Nerheim & Nordvik [15], who give 1957 as the year of the five thousandth IBM 780.

[7] The factory's products changed from time to time. The products listed in this article were the main items produced, but the list is not comprehensive.

the greater Stockholm area. In fact, the new factory site was located only a few kilometers from the older site at Vällingby [22]. With the exception of the punched card plant, which remained in Vällingby until its closure in 1980 [18], all IBM manufacture in Sweden was relocated to the Järfälla premises.

Already in 1970, the factory was making printers for all of Europe. During the seventies, several new printers went into production in Järfälla. After the introduction of the IBM system 370 in 1970, for instance, came the IBM 3211 line printer. In 1976, the Järfälla plant shipped its first IBM 3800 laser printers [10]. Most of the production at the factory was for export [18].

According to information provided at an international press conference at Järfälla in 1971, 95 percent of products were exported to 108 IBM countries. Out of about 3,300 IBM employees in Sweden, a little over 1,000 worked at the factory. This manufacturing supported a large number of subcontractors from several countries [23].

Printers had become the target area for Swedish IBM production. It may be relevant here that the Swedish company Facit had been highly regarded, by IBM executives among others, for its peripheral devices. In late 1958 the top management of IBM World Trade met with Facit executives at the IBM World Trade Corporation's New York headquarters; IBM expressed ample interest in co-operation with Facit, especially because of the latter's expertise in peripherals, including printers. However, soon afterwards, in 1959, IBM suddenly withdrew from these plans and continued as competitively as ever [24].

In this focus on printers, it is possible that IBM was impacted by Swedish know-how, leading IBM World Trade to choose to focus on printer production at its Swedish factory. In Sweden, IBM might be able to hire printer specialists from or around Facit, or at least to weaken Facit's competitive status in manufacturing, by this production decision and the related hiring and subcontracting.

6 Subcontracting for IBM's European Plants

Most of the Nordic countries contributed some subcontractors to IBM's manufacturing in Europe. In Finland, for instance, subcontracting via IBM Finland started in the early 1960s, when several foreign IBM subsidiaries began ordering the custom-made stiff paper for their punched cards from the same supplier, the Serlachius pulp and paper company, that had been supplying the Finnish IBM card factory since 1952 [25].

Importantly, subcontracting was apparently one thing the IBM subsidiary could increase in response to the criticism that IBM's business consisted too much of just importing hardware and software to Finland. This debate and the subsequent actions (on both sides) were part of a larger European response to the debate over the American challenge in the late 1960s. The debate of the late 1960s and early 1970s included the 1967 book *Le Défi Américain*, by Jean-Jacques Servan-Schreiber. The next year the book was published in English as *The American Challenge*, as well as in Swedish and Finnish translations; the Finnish title was *Dollarin maihinnousu* (Invasion of the Dollar, 1968). A similar debate, and the IBM reaction, especially in the form of increasing subcontracting, was going on in all the Nordic countries; in fact, the only Nordic country with no subcontractors for IBM plants was Iceland. Subcontracting possibilities were in fact seriously investigated in Reykjavik too, but no business justification could be found [26].

IBM Finland appointed a coordinator for subcontracting in 1970. He reported both to the European Purchasing Competence Center (EPCC) which coordinated subcontractors in Europe and IBM's European Plants, and to the CEO of IBM Finland [27]. In the late 1960s, the price level in Finland was low by international standards, making the country more attractive for IBM buyers [25]. Just as IBM production was organized continentally, so evidently was subcontracting as part of IBM production structures.

Already in 1971, the value of Finnish subcontractors' deliveries to foreign IBM companies equaled thirty to 40 percent of IBM Finland's imports, and the figure was expected to grow during the seventies. In 1976, some twenty companies in Finland made products for IBM companies in Europe. These deliveries secured around two hundred jobs annually [25, 28]. Three years later IBM estimated this figure at 250 jobs. In the 1980s, a significant producer for IBM's personal computers was the large Finnish consumer electronics company Salora, later merged with Nokia, which delivered monitors to an IBM factory in Italy [29, 30].[8]

In Norway, there were some twenty subcontractors in 1985 delivering to IBM's European factories [15]. In addition to subcontracts, actual production could also be transnational or trans-border, when for instance in 1983 a Danish subcontractor was chosen to manufacture the new IBM 4250 printer in support of the IBM plant at Järfälla, Sweden [10].

On the demand or IBM side, the Järfälla plant, as the one Nordic IBM factory, was by far the biggest IBM customer for subcontractors in the Nordic countries. In 1971, the new factory utilized approximately five hundred subcontractors [23]. Out of this significant number of businesses, presumably many were from Sweden and the other Nordic countries.

By its choice of subcontractors, the IBM World Trade Corporation benefitted from the strengths of individual companies in the Nordic countries; and perhaps vice versa, the Nordic companies had an impact on IBM products. The supplier and product examples above represented the contributions to and involvement in IBM's European production system of Finnish, Norwegian and Danish subcontractors.

7 IBM and Other Production

What about other computer vendors – did they produce something similar in the Nordic region? One of IBM's rivals, the (French) Bull Company originated in Norway; but the construction of Bull punched card machines was relocated to France already in 1931 [4]. By 1967, Burroughs had a demonstration centre in Sweden, but no actual manufacture in Scandinavia [17]. It was mostly Nordic, more specifically Swedish and later Finnish (Nokia) computer companies that maintained production facilities in several Nordic countries. Compared to other major computer companies, IBM was clearly the one most involved in computing-related production in the Nordic countries.

---

[8] The Salora Company also manufactured monitors for several other computer companies [30].

However, IBM not only produced things in the Nordic countries, but also the reverse: it sought to undo or to discourage competition. According to Hans Andersin, who was at IBM Finland, and on two assignments in Sweden, all during 1956–1965, IBM headquarters (IBM World Trade Corporation HQ in New York, presumably) had specialists whose job it was to prevent the establishment of national computer industries, obviously also in the Nordic countries. They offered cooperation and sub-contracting agreements and/or advised against competing with IBM. IBM, for instance, tried – unsuccessfully – to discourage the Finnish Cable Factory, later Nokia, from embarking on the computer business in the early 1960s [1].

8 Discussing the Bigger Picture

In this article, I have addressed the question of IBM manufacturing in the Nordic countries before the 1990s. Previously, the stories of IBM subsidiaries in Scandinavia have been framed primarily in national terms. I hope to have shown that a wider, international Nordic perspective brings significant benefits for understanding IBM in each of the Nordic countries. Further, the picture of IBM production structures has become considerably clearer.

On the one hand, the printing of punched cards started early on in Sweden and spread, in the war time and soon after, to all four Nordic subsidiaries (see Table 2). In punched card manufacture, all the subsidiaries took part in IBM's transnational coordination and co-operation structures. The only exception in the region was the IBM branch office in Iceland, which was less independent than a national subsidiary and had no IBM manufacture; it merely imported punched cards from the USA [26].

The four IBM card plants in the Nordic countries serve as a reminder of the great importance of punched cards to the data-processing business. For a considerable time, at least half a century, punched cards were essential for most IBM data processing. Millions and millions of those precisely shaped pieces of special paper were used in most of the activities of IBM subsidiaries – activities consisting of sales and services, which have mostly been ignored in this article. In these operations, IBM personnel made most of their contacts with customers and computer users. A major reason for establishing and maintaining IBM punched card plants in the four Nordic countries was no doubt the proximity to customers, giving easy accessibility and minimizing transportation costs. This was one way in which Nordic IBM customers indirectly influenced and benefitted from IBM activities in the region and from their location.

The distribution of other manufacturing was much more uneven. As IBM's production system was European, the Nordic region did not form a coherent unit in the system but was integrated into the larger production network. Clearly, Sweden was the big player in IBM manufacture among the Nordic country organizations and locations (see Table 2). Within the Nordic region, the most significant hub of IBM production developed in the Stockholm area. In the 1950s, other manufacture was temporarily located in Norway. From 1960 onwards, the only IBM manufacturing site for hardware in the Nordic countries was IBM's Swedish factory.

Table 2. New IBM Plants & Location by Country in the Nordic region up to the 1990s

IBM	1930s	1940s	1950s	1960s	1970s	1980s
Sweden	Punched-card (P-C) press		Factory, misc. products; typewriters, punched card machines	New products, printers	New Järfälla site, manufacturing printers for Europe	P-C Press closed (-80)
Norway		P-C Press	Factory, esp. time recorder production (until -60)			
Finland		(P-C Press)	P-C Press		Subcontracting, P-C Press closed	
Denmark		Agent: P-C Press	P-C Press			
Iceland				est. 1967 as an IBM Branch Office		
					All but Iceland: Subcontracts	

There were probably numerous reasons why Sweden, industrially the most advanced and successful of the Nordic countries, became the location of so much IBM manufacture. An excellent explanation is offered by the national computer markets: the first IBM computers in the Nordic region were installed in Sweden in 1956.[9] According to the World computer census in December 1966, the number of computers in the Scandinavian countries was (roughly, at least) as follows [32]:[10]

Sweden   350
Denmark   175
Norway   150
Finland   90
Iceland   3

Clearly, Sweden was the earliest and biggest national market, in digital computers too, in the Nordic countries. However, it also had the toughest competition. Among the Nordic countries, it was Swedish professionals who had the highest hopes for a successful national computer company; this meant that IBM was also heavily criticized, especially when the Swedish companies could not sustain the competition, see [24, 33]. Perhaps this competitive situation contributed to the fact that Sweden was able to attract a lot of IBM functions and operations.

Until the mid-1960s most of both national Swedish IBM facilities and international Nordic IBM operations were located in or around the Swedish capital [34]; later

---

[9] The first IBM computers followed in Norway (1958), Finland (1958; also the first computer in the country), Denmark (1959), and Iceland (1964; the first computer in the country) [1]. See also [31].

[10] Iceland was not included in this census source. Its figure is based on [26].

Copenhagen started gaining IBM functions, see [1, 9]. To a perhaps significant level, IBM companies could also be national and even nationalist in competing for the allocation of IBM operations. This question too requires further study.

Was there some specifically Nordic contribution to IBM? One such area was probably the focus of IBM's Swedish manufacturing plant on peripherals and especially on printers from the mid-1960s onward. Eventually, Sweden provided printers for IBM in all of Europe. In each Nordic nation, subcontracts to IBM's European plants were another instance where the national Nordic companies could use their individual strengths and capacity.

9 Conclusion

Unlike any of its major competitors, IBM early on established manufacturing facilities in the Nordic region. These IBM activities have received limited attention, but they may offer a tool both for a better understanding of IBM in the Nordic region and for exploring Nordic contributions to IBM. For decades, IBM produced punched cards in four Nordic countries, whereas after 1960 there was one IBM hardware factory in the region, located in the Stockholm area. For several reasons, discussed above, IBM concentrated its Nordic hardware manufacturing in Sweden. There (and elsewhere in Europe), companies from four Nordic countries contributed to IBM manufacture through subcontracting. In addition, the IBM factory in Sweden specialized in printer production, which probably included local contributions. Studying those contributions requires further evidence and scrutiny.

Overall, IBM may perhaps have been more Nordic than most of its competitors, including those which were Nordic themselves. By Nordic, I mean here that some manufacturing was performed in most of the Nordic countries (as opposed to being done in one, two or three of them), and that IBM cooperation among the Nordic countries was inclusive, usually including all or most of its Nordic organizations. Moreover, the findings presented in this article suggest that IBM manufacturing in the Nordic countries was linked to its success in the region; the relationship between economic success and manufacturing, however, calls for further research.

Furthermore, IBM involved Nordic IBM staff in building its international and transnational operations models. Meanwhile, IBM itself was influenced by and incorporated the contributions of its Nordic subsidiaries. The precise nature of this influence in each individual national environment remains to be examined: what did it mean for their information technology industries? How and why the international patterns of operations of the Nordic IBM companies evolve as they did? More Nordic cooperation and contributions can be uncovered by studying IBM education and R&D work in the region [14]. Perhaps studying IBM's operation pattern in the Nordic region can help us to understand how IBM operated in other regions as well.

Finally, the ending of the Cold War division of Europe around 1990 brought many changes for IBM manufacturing in the Nordic countries. In 1989, the Järfälla plant became a subcontractor to an independent LexMark Company owned by IBM. Two years later IBM sold this part of its business, including printer production, to another American company. In 1994 IBM sold its majority share of the Järfälla plant [18], see also [11].

Today, a reorganized IBM continues its operation in the Nordic area, but its manufacturing has moved on. What remains are memories of it and probably some influence on the information technology industries in the Nordic countries.

Acknowledgments. This research project started as part of the European Science Foundation EUROCORES Research program, "Inventing Europe: Technology and the Making of Europe, 1850 to the Present," and has benefitted from its collaborative research project, Software for Europe. My part of it has been funded by the Academy of Finland. Thanks are due to the staff at the IBM Archive and to James Cortada.

References

1. Andersin, H.E.: The role of IBM in starting up computing in the Nordic countries. In: Bubenko Jr., J., Impagliazzo, J., Sølvberg, A. (eds.) History of Nordic Computing, pp. 33–43. Springer, New York (2005)
2. Schlombs, C.: Engineering International Expansion: IBM and Remington Rand in European Computer Markets. IEEE Annals of the History of Computing 30(4), 42–58 (2008)
3. Cortada, J.W.: Before the Computer. IBM, NCR, Burroughs, and Remington Rand and the industry they created 1865-1956. Princeton university press, Princeton (1993)
4. Heide, L.: Punched-Card Systems and the Early Information Explosion, 1880-1945. The Johns Hopkins University Press, Baltimore (2009)
5. Kjartansson, Ó.: Data Processing with Unit Record Equipment in Iceland. In: Impagliazzo, J., Järvi, T., Paju, P. (eds.) History of Nordic Computing 2. IFIP AICT, vol. 303, pp. 225–229. Springer, Berlin (2009)
6. Hallberg, T.J.: IT gryning. Svensk datahistoria från 1840- till 1960-talet. Studentlitteratur, Lund (2007)
7. Campbell-Kelly, M., Aspray, W.: Computer. A History of the Information Machine. Basic books, New York (1996)
8. Dickman, E.: Några data beträffande förhållandena på hålkorts-området i Finland före 1937 (and other parts). Av Einar Dickman, antecknade – huvudsakligen – ur minnet under (December 1961 – January 1962) (Some facts about conditions in the punched card field in Finland prior to 1937. In Swedish) Manuscript, located at the IBM Finland Archive (unpublished)
9. Heide, L.: Hulkort og EDB i Danmark 1911-1970. Forlaget Systime A/S, Århus (1996)
10. Sayers, K.W.: A Summary History of IBM's International Operations 1911-2006, IBM 2006., 2nd edn. IBM Archive. Somers, New York (2006)
11. Anttila, P.: Big Blue Suomessa. O. y. International Business Machines A. b. 1936-1996. (Big Blue in Finland. O. y. International Business Machines A. b. 1936-1996, in Finnish). Published by the author, printed in Salo (1997)
12. Dickman, K.: Uudet tuotteet – tuttu ympäristö (New products – familiar environment, in Finnish). In: Tienari, M. (ed.) Tietotekniikan alkuvuodet Suomessa (The first years of information technology in Finland, in Finnish.), Suomen Atk-kustannus Oy, Helsinki, pp. 316–339 (1993)
13. Nuutila, T.: Suomen IBM:n atk-tarvikeosasto tänään (IBM Finland's information records division today, in Finnish.) IBM Katsaus 15(3), 46–47 (1976)

14. Paju, P.: The many levels of IBM operations in Europe. Combining national and transnational in IBM Finland. In: Alberts, G., Durnová, H., Nofre, D., Paju, P., Sumner, J. (eds.) Computing in many languages. European practices and identities in the early Cold War era (2011) (forthcoming)

15. Nerheim, G., Nordvik, H. W.: Ikke bara maskiner. Historien om IBM i Norge 1935-1985. Universitetsforlaget, Oslo (1986)

16. Tietoa kortilla – jos nauhoillakin. Suomen IBM:n ATK-tarvikeosasto, IRD, Information Records Division (Information on card – and also on tapes. IBM Finland's Information Records Division, in Finnish). IBM Katsaus 10(2), 42–45 (1971)

17. Connolly, J.: History of Computing in Europe. IBM World Trade Corporation, New York (1967)

18. IBM Svenska ABs historia, http://www-05.ibm.com/se/ibm/sweden/history/ (accessed May 25, 2010)

19. Johansson, I.: Stor-Stockholms bebyggelsehistoria. Markpolitik, planering och byggande under sju sekler. Gidlunds, Stockholm (1987)

20. It happened in Sweden. IBM World Trade News, 13 (12), 5 (1961)

21. IBM Archives, http://www-03.ibm.com/ibm/history/exhibits/mainframe/mainframe_PP1401.html (accessed June 7, 2010)

22. Agenda, a meeting of the executive committee of IBM World Trade Corporation. New York, February 24, 1969. World Trade Corporation, office of the secretary, board of directors, box 16. IBM Archive, Somers, New York (unpublished)

23. Välitöntä tunnelmaa Järfällassa. (Unreserved feeling in Järfälla, in Finnish.) (No author, presumably Katri Kettunen) Suomen IBM uutiset, 6(3), 10–11 (1971)

24. Petersson, T.: Facit and the BESK Boys: Sweden's Computer Industry (1956-1962). IEEE Annals of the History of Computing 27(4), 23–30 (2005)

25. Winberg, A.: Suomen IBM:n harjoittama alihankintatoiminta (Subcontracting activity coordinated by IBM Finland, in Finnish). IBM Katsaus 15(3), 48–49 (1976)

26. Email letter from Sverrir Olafsson to Petri Paju (November 2, 2010)

27. Suomen IBM 1969. Vuosiraportti. (Yearly report of IBM Finland in 1969, in Finnish.) IBM Finland, Helsinki (1969)

28. Suomalaista uusvientiä. (New Finnish export, in Finnish.) (No author, presumably Katri Kettunen.) IBM uutiset, 7(2), 1 (1972)

29. Lahti, S., Lehtinen, J. (eds.): Suomen ATK-tuotannon vuosikirja 1979. (Yearbook for ADP production in Finland.) Raportti n:o 53. VTT, ATK-palvelutoimisto, Espoo (1979)

30. Lavonen, P.: Radiopajoista matkapuhelinteollisuuteen. Salon elektroniikkateollisuuden historia 1925-2005 (From radio workshops to mobile phone industry. History of the electronics industry in the town of Salo 1925–2005, in Finnish). Town of Salo, Salo (2005)

31. Paju, P.: National Projects and International Users: Finland and Early European computerization. IEEE Annals of the History of Computing 30(4), 77–91 (2008)

32. World Computer Census as of December, 1966 (Digital comp. systems), from Computers and Automation for January 1967. (Translated into Finnish.) ATK:n Tieto-Sanomat 2 (4) 31 (1967)

33. Johansson, M.: Smart, Fast and Beautiful. On Rhetoric of Technology and Computing Discourse in Sweden 1955-1995. Linköping Studies in Arts and Science 164. Linköping University, Linköping (1997)

34. Lindegren, O.: IBM Nordic Education Center – Lidingö. ATK:n Tieto-Sanomat 5(1), 12–13 (1970)

The Presence of the IBM Branch Office in Iceland, 1967–1992

Sverrir Ólafsson

Formerly of IBM Iceland
sverrirolafs@simnet.is

Abstract. During the years 1967–1992, IBM World Trade Corporation established and operated a branch office in Iceland. At the time, IBM WTC was that part of the IBM Corporation that handled IBM operations outside the U.S. This paper addresses operational elements and the impact of a large multinational company on the business life of a small society.

Keywords: IBM Branch Office, IBM Iceland.

1 Introduction

From the beginning of the 1950s, IBM hardware had been installed at some relatively large companies, organizations, and government agencies in Iceland. This hardware was predominantly bought from IBM Denmark. The increasing complexity and technical advancements in the 1960s created a need to extend service and technical skills in order to satisfy customer demands. In Iceland, these increasing requirements put pressure on the local agent whose role had primarily been to install the IBM hardware and keep it operational during its lifespan.

A decisive aspect in this regard was the introduction of the IBM 1620 scientific processor in Iceland in the mid-1960s. It was evident that new skills and advanced knowledge was mandatory in this rapidly increasing industry to serve adequately customers and prospects. Furthermore, it became clear that these new requirements would exceed the agent's financial and technical capacities. At the initiative of the management of IBM Denmark and after considering some alternatives, the establishment of an Icelandic IBM branch office in Reykjavik was deemed feasible. This office would take over the entire IBM operations, related to data processing equipment, from the agent, while office products (mainly sales and maintenance of IBM typewriters) remained with the dealer.

The formal establishment of the IBM branch office took place on 2 May 1967 after necessary legal issues had been resolved. The transfer of personnel and assets took place from that date and the agent became the general manager of the Icelandic IBM branch office.

The IBM agent employed the author of this paper in 1965 as the manager of its Service Bureau. He was involved in the establishment of the IBM branch office in 1967, held various managerial positions during its lifetime and took part in closing

J. Impagliazzo, P. Lundin, and B. Wangler (Eds.): HiNC3, IFIP AICT 350, pp. 228–233, 2011.

branch operations in 1992. Thereafter and until his retirement in 2008, the author served with IBM's successor, Nýherji. This article is based on the author's book titled, "Employed by IBM" [1].

2 Legal Issues – Limited Operation

It was no easy task establishing a company of foreign ownership with residence in Iceland. There was a lingering skepticism towards foreign enterprises operating locally, as the history of relations with foreign powers in this previous Danish colony had not been favorable. In addition, local legislation did not provide for the operation of foreign entities on Icelandic territory and, furthermore, proved to be prohibitive in many ways. These were challenging impediments to overcome.

With the assistance of proficient and local legal counsel as well as support from IBM Denmark and IBM World Trade Corporation in New York, a path was found through the local legislation, which satisfied all the clauses. The Ministry of Social Affairs issued a permit in January 1967 authorizing IBM World Trade Corporation to operate a branch office in Iceland that enabled locally installed data processing equipment to be serviced. It is notable that this authorization was restricted to only two years and foreign employees were subject to job permits. Only technical and application service enterprises or service bureau and rental businesses were supported. Sales of equipment had to take place directly between the purchaser in Iceland and IBM WTC in New York, all of which was of no consequence since it was mostly a rental business at that time. Most companies lacked the capacity, at the time, to purchase data processing equipment. The unnecessary restrictions were subsequently abolished; local people were employed, the fear of foreigners had no substance, and in the course of time, it was easy to get the permit extended.

3 Operational Control and Measurable Results

The Icelandic economy is small and vulnerable. At the end of the 1960s, the prices of the country's main export products fell significantly. Foreign currency costs doubled, as did the service that IBM Iceland provided. The results of the first trading years were disastrous as business fell to a minimum. However, IBM was admirably tolerant and understanding with regard to the branch office's difficulties, which were caused by this external and unexpected recession. The locals are renowned for their patience and tenacity. Thereafter, business recovered and at the beginning of the 1970s, operations were starting to run smoothly.

From then on, the presence of IBM and the Icelandic branch led to many positive changes in the young and growing data processing industry of Iceland, and the financial stability of the branch was a fact. Nevertheless, Icelandic branch should be self sufficient in all aspects and could not rely on any external support. Competent staff members were recruited and sent to IBM's education centers overseas to gain and to bring back the new knowledge of a new technology. In addition, teachers and instructors were hired from abroad to give seminars for employees and customers. Thus, a vast import of knowledge, which was not available in the public education system of the time, took place in the early years of the branch office. While IBM international accounting practices were implemented, plan dissemination and financial budget proposals were put into international channels. Furthermore, business results had to be produced on time and reported effectively. The aspects of control and discipline were implemented into accounting and financial matters; internal audits from IBM Denmark and corporate audits from IBM European headquarters, which scrutinized all the basic elements of the operations, took place at least once a year. Such visits were tough and not always a sought after pleasure for managers.

4 Business Ethics and Personnel Policy

In the late 1950s and early 1960s, the IBM Corporation was sued in the U.S. for violating the antitrust act. This case was resolved by a consent decree in which IBM agreed to adapt to certain business rules and implement them worldwide, which included Iceland where an IBM branch office was now operating.

The introduction and implementation of IBM Business Conduct Guidelines and IBM's Basic Beliefs were the backbone of the business, and all employees were expected to read and live up to their requirements. Focus was on good and reasonable business ethics, which should be based on trust, credibility, loyalty and fairness. The branch should be a "good citizen" in all aspects, customers and colleagues should be shown utmost respect. Furthermore, all relations with customers should be equitable, and orders should be delivered sequentially without deviations. Competition should be handled fairly, which was soon noticeable in the marketplace. In addition, business information would be treated properly, donations would be limited as would the acceptance of presents; any kind of bribery was totally prohibited and subject to dismissal. It was evident that a business unit, which had an experienced and highly sophisticated business culture, was in place and proposed to operate with this culture as its cornerstone.

5 Political Unrest

Successful operations, good business results obtained in a fair and equitable way as well as reasonable taxation paid to central and local governments should normally be considered desirable and beneficial from a local point of view. However, there may also be persons or parties that do not agree. The 1970s, the decade of mainframes, was in many ways a successful period for the young branch office, not least in the public sector. Its success was so extensive that loud protests, questioning the impact of multinational companies like IBM, were heard in the local media. These companies were accused of having a policy that structured the data processing industry so that it served their own needs best, obtained excessive profits, enjoyed substantial benefits from lack of competition, made questionable alliances with local companies, and did not serve the best interest of the country. They were even said to enjoy excessive benefits from local companies by pricing their products and services according to foreign currency. Furthermore, the transfer of profits and funds to the parent company abroad, after taxation, was also found to be questionable and not subject to normal control as regulated. Even the rental of equipment was thought to be questionable compared to outright purchase. With its 95 percent market share, IBM was said to be in a key position to control the entire data processing industry in Iceland. It was likewise indicated that IBM was the only company that had unlimited access to the country's foreign currency reserves and should it decide to terminate its operation it would be a disaster for the country. Such were the accusations in a nutshell.

The matters of the IBM branch were even subject to formal inquiries in the Parliament. The Minister of Commerce, responding to the inquiries from some leftist members of the House, explained the grounds on which IBM operated in Iceland and stated that the company was profitable and a good taxpayer in Iceland. He considered that pricing was normal and rental a more favorable option than purchase, but it was, of course, the customer's right of choice. The branch office operated under equitable and fair local legislation. During this debate, the branch tended to remain silent, an attitude that was strongly recommended by superiors at headquarters. This tactic was probably quite correct, and gradually the fuss died down.

The above stated views were probably instigated by visions or different opinions, but were minority views, which at all times should have the right to be expressed. On the other hand, the positive indirect impact of the IBM branch office, during its operating life for almost a quarter of a century, was abundant and multifarious.

6 To Be a Good Citizen

From the very beginning, the key objective for the establishment of the Icelandic branch was to run a prosperous business in Iceland, pay taxes locally, similar to any local company, and remit the profits after tax to the parent company. But IBM also had the role of being a good citizen, which can be exemplified by the following instances.

In 1973, a volcanic eruption took place on the island of Heimaey, off the south coast of Iceland. All the five thousand inhabitants were evacuated to the mainland, where they were registered in order to keep track of the entire community for which housing, new jobs, new schools, and so on, had to be found. IBM donated technical assistance by creating records of the entire community, a contribution for which the company received a document of thanks from the Red Cross.

During its operation, IBM donated mainframe equipment to the academic community and the University of Iceland. This was well received by a vast majority, but skeptics voiced their disapproval maintaining that IBM was, above all, securing its marketplace with these donations of selected equipment.

In addition, IBM sponsored a translation center operated by the University of Iceland, where IBM publications were translated to the local language. This was a policy of IBM worldwide at that time, apparently regardless of the size of the marketplace and business volumes, a strategy that dwindled later on for obvious reasons. While it lasted, this contribution greatly supported the academic community, bringing new skills and technology to linguistic research.

Furthermore, IBM's policy of selling products to its branches worldwide for basic production costs without any markup was very beneficial to the Icelandic society. However, this policy was never fully understood by government officials and politicians, and of surprisingly minor interest to heads of commerce. As a result, high taxation, in terms of income tax in Iceland, meant that the IBM branch was amongst the biggest taxpayers in the country for several years. On the other hand, at times, this was subject of envy and misunderstanding, as it was often concluded that the markup in Iceland was too high, even though prices were generally quite comparable to IBM worldwide prices, and thus fair and equitable.

The IBM branch in Iceland supported the local community in many other ways. For a time, they were the main sponsors of the Icelandic Symphony Orchestra; they also made donations to cancer research, public education, and supported chess, sports and the arts. Perhaps the most vital contribution was the integration of the special Icelandic alphabetic characters into the international character tables, which meant that the complete Icelandic alphabet became a standard. This was of utmost importance for the Icelandic language, not least when the intensive use of personal computers began in the 1980s. The key person in this matter, together with local technicians, was Wilhelm F. Bohn, a German engineer who was honored with the Order of the Falcon for his outstanding contribution to the Republic of Iceland, one of two IBMers who have had that honor, the other being Viggo Troels-Smith, general manager of IBM Denmark.

7 Selling Boxes

The bread and butter of the IBM branch during the 1970s and 1980s was the sales and service of the mainframe systems of the IBM 1401 series and later of the IBM 360 series, as well as the successors to the IBM 370 and IBM 4300 series. This period included two installations of the large 3090 series; these dinosaurs weighed tons at each installation and were later replaced by much more compact units. A big boom started when the series of IBM Systems 32, 34, 36, and 38 were announced. Their successor, the AS/400, was also extremely successful. The branch had started the application development for these midrange installations, which was very successful; however, a strategic worldwide IBM decision, at one point, declared that they would not provide this kind of service any more, stating that this should be handled by software houses without competition from IBM. While this decision was not favorable for the IBM branch, it resulted in the establishment of a range of local software houses in the early 1980s, which thereafter more or less took over the application service for IBM customers.

The success of the IBM branch office in selling boxes, which began in the early 1980s, would never have materialized if the branch had not obtained full operational licenses to sell and support products directly in its own name. The branch was now entirely comparable to any local enterprise in a fully competitive business environment. IBM now had a considerable market share in all major industries such as banking, insurance, transportation, fish-freezing plants, governmental service, and major enterprises. In addition, the IBM branch supported the establishment of important service institutions such as the Bank Data Center, which assisted all the local banks with a variety of services. Furthermore, the IBM branch hired one of the first dedicated data communication lines to the country, in order to be able to better support their local customers in Iceland. The IBM Data Center was also of immense support to the branch and IBM customers with regard to application service.

However, IBM was not very successful in one specific part of the business, the IBM personal computer or the IBM Personal System. The pricing of this new computer, determined centrally at headquarter units, was at all times out of line, making it therefore easy for competitors to sell more computers than IBM. Quality and endurance were of a lesser priority for units that were outdated, in terms of capacity, in two to three years. IBM lacked the necessary pricing flexibility, and selling this new unit, as a mainframe unit did not work well. Consequently, IBM later relinquished this business and sold the PC segment to a Chinese company.

8 To End in Prosperity

At the beginning of the 1990s, the IBM branch was a flourishing enterprise, financially sound, employing around eighty people, operating from its own property, and an unquestionable presence in the local community. It seemed therefore paradoxical that after a thorough investigation by IBM, they decided to terminate the operation of the IBM branch in Iceland.

It was a matter of common knowledge that the size of the IBM business unit in Iceland had been a matter of concern for some time. The unit had increasing problems adapting to all the control demands on which Big Blue (IBM) insisted. In addition, IBM products alone were considered too limited in number to justify a sound operational unit. It would be better for IBM to support a new company with the amalgamation of another, thus improving service to the local market and its customers. Big Blue was willing to support such an organization with one third of the initial share capital. The new company would take over all the previous sales and services of the IBM branch, as well as most of the former IBM employees. This was the start of the successor to the IBM branch, Nýherji, which was established on 1 April 1992.

In life, everything has its time; life begins and ends. This applies to business life as well. The life of IBM Iceland was fruitful and respected. The branch office was more Icelandic than many Icelandic companies were. IBM left Iceland with dignity. Its integrity and loyalty to the community was significant, its rules of operation were honest and just. IBM's business ethics were unique and unprecedented; the business results were fair and reasonable. It brought wealth and prosperity into a small society.

Nevertheless, IBM left Iceland and, by its leaving, the society lost too much business control, integrity, fairness, equitable handling, good citizenship, reasonability, respect for the individual, and other business merits. This was unfortunate for those who remained, but that saga would probably be the subject of another article.

Reference

1. Ólafsson, S.: Í vist hjá IBM: Svipmyndir úr sögu IBM á Íslandi. Skýrslutæknifélag Íslands, Öldungadeild, Reykjavik (2008)

Personal Computers: A Gateway to Personal Computing

Kari Kotiranta

Tiedetila – ScienceFarm
Alkulantie 265, 42930 Katajamäki, Finland

Abstract. This article is a personal journey, from the early days of batch processing to the modern personal computing era. The journey begins in the early 1970s and starts with the punch cards at the computer centre of the University of Jyväskylä. The use of minicomputers (HP 2100 series) gave a different view – how to collect and process data with a computer. Honeywell timesharing systems made it possible to use the computer near to me, in the classroom. Early personal computers gave a feeling of freedom. In this article, I describe how the hobbyists promoted the development of computing and discuss how I took part in early software production and its use. Lastly, I briefly consider what it means to have a connection to the world using a computer at home.

Keywords: Early university computing, hobby-built computers, personal computers.

1 Introduction

What is personal computing? My definition of personal computing is that it must meet the following criteria: easy access to a computer, suitable applications, ease of use, and connection to the internet. This article is a personal journey from early batch processing to modern personal computing.

2 Early Steps in Computing

In 1970, when I started to study computer science at the University of Jyväskylä, it did not have its own central computer – only keypunch machines in the computing center where students keypunched their FORTRAN programming exercises into the cards. The punched cards were sent to a company called Valmet, which was located on the other side of the town. This company executed the programs punched into the cards and returned them to the students the following day, with a printed listing of the execution results. One of the learning materials was a book titled *Tietojenkäsittely* (Computing) written by Malinen [1]. In the first chapter, he writes that one needs computers to organize data and that they can be used to maintain existing systems, collect data, and design new systems [1]. It was quite an insightful beginning to computing. At that time, a computer was used for three purposes: to learn how to use a computer, to develop programs for scientific applications, and to process scientific data with statistical programs.

J. Impagliazzo, P. Lundin, and B. Wangler (Eds.): HiNC3, IFIP AICT 350, pp. 234–239, 2011.

In 1971, the university acquired its own Honeywell 1642, an interesting computer that had a time sharing operating system. Several terminals were placed around the university campus and computer use gained new dimensions – no longer was it necessary to go to the computer center with your punched cards, the psychology department had a terminal ready for typing. This terminal was an interactive Teletype model 33 KSR, writing on paper. For example, using a statistical software application (SURVO) was easier than the earlier work with the punched cards, because it was only necessary to answer the questions that the computer presented. Mustonen [2] developed an early version of SURVO in 1966, and the timesharing version was introduced for Honeywell at the beginning of 1970.

The presence of the terminal in the department of psychology generated new ideas about how to use the computer to add value to the department's teaching and research. For example, it was possible to create tests in which the students could respond using the computer. The problem was that there was no ready-made software for such purposes, thus researchers had to develop the programs themselves. The easiest way to program was to use the BASIC programming language. One of the first computer programs that were designed for teachers was OPSAM, which Mikkonen & Mikkonen [3] developed to measure and analyze educational achievements. The program was a small statistical library to analyze tests - to evaluate whether the test items were relevant or not.

Five years later, Mikkonen [4] tried to analyze teaching methods using a computer program, "OVV-opetusmenetelmien vertailu ja valinta." The goal was to help teachers choose the most suitable teaching method; when the teacher should use an overhead projector, when printed materials should be distributed, and so on. His premise was that when the teacher answers questions about the content of the lecture, the computer should recognize the parameters of the teaching situation.

At the beginning of the 1970s, I was able to use another computer at the University of Jyväskylä, a HP 2116C which was situated at the Faculty of Sport Sciences. The HP 2116 computer featured an analog to digital converter and was mainly used to analyze measured data that was collected by the instrumentation recorder. The system administrator, who would thereafter input about fifty computer words one by one, using switches on the front panel, started the computer in the morning. The code entered was a BBL (Basic Binary Loader), which had to be loaded first using switches. Then the MTS (Magnetic Tape System) was loaded, and the programs and data were accessed using the magnetic tape.

During 1974 and 1975, I studied at the University of Turku that had an IBM 1130 computer that used punch cards. Some computer exercises were carried out using a HP 2100 mini-computer at the Department of Methodology. The computer had almost the same features as the HP I used in Jyväskylä, but differed in its use; instead of processing collected analog data, it was used to calculate the statistical analysis of research material.

At the University of Oulu in 1976, I again came across a Honeywell computer. Time had passed and the computer was now five years old, but there was a new terminal, a Nokia NOP 30. It was a wheel printer, which meant that it printed quality text. After a few days of experimenting, we developed a simple line editor. Although not great, the editor was better than the normal typewriter since it could at least save and print the text.

Students had found a weakness in the Honeywell computer by creating a disk query that was very complex and then using many terminals to run the query so that the computer had no time to read and return the work within the shared four seconds limit. The result was a one-hour outage. These outages were one of the reasons to acquire a new central computer, which the University of Oulu did; it bought a UNIVAC in 1977. Students responded by writing on the bulletin board: "Bye bye Honey – welcome UNIVAC."

One phase in the history of computing in Finland ended. There had been five Honeywell computers in universities and it had been a good beginning. They were modern mainframe computers – the idea of externalized services and computing was gradually reintroduced to a wider audience with the rise of cloud computing in the early twenty-first century.

3 Personal Computers – From Hobbyists for Hobbyists

Byte Magazine came out in 1975 and I subscribed to it from the beginning until it published the last copy. The magazine presented the possibilities of microprocessors and even the concepts of suitable home computers. Finnish electronic journals, such as the Yleiselektroniikka and Elektroniikka magazines, were also following the trend. The year 1977 was revolutionary in personal computing; in that year, Osmo Kainulainen designed a Telmac computer construction kit for the company Telercas. He also wrote seven articles for a technical magazine, Elektroniikka, about how to build your own microcomputer and how to understand microprocessor technology [5]. At the same time Apple, Commodore, and Tandy Radio Shack presented their first home computer models. A year later, the Swedish ABC80 computer, the "'hemdator," entered the market. All of them influenced the Finnish microcomputer culture and each brand had its own fans.

I ordered a Telmac "microprocessor," as personal computers were then called, and after much soldering and assembling it was completed. The computer had an RCA 1802 processor, an RCA monitor program, a pseudo machine language, and a Tiny-BASIC interpreter.

A computer in your own home gave one the freedom to develop programs, play games, and do research. Until that time, the computer had always been at the end of an outgoing terminal line, with the terminal situated in the university department. Now it was on my table, and I was able to control its operation myself – it was a thrilling experience.

As an assistant in psychology, I had a lot of use for a computer. However, at that time, the tax authorities did not understand why a psychology assistant would need a computer and the related literature. "It is not widely known that a psychology assistant needs to work on a computer" was the curt reply on my application for a tax deduction.

4 Personal Computers at Work

The first work-related development was a piece of cross tabulation software, which was the first component of a statistical software program named PATO [6]. I also obtained a new tool for presenting psychological phenomena. It was possible for me to take my computer to the university so that my students could test themselves using the computer programs, which included a perception test, a reaction time test, and simple personal tests.

I proposed that personal computers should be bought for the faculty of education at the University of Oulu. This was in 1978 when the first commercial personal computers – the ABC80, the Apple II, and the Commodore Pet – were entering the market. The computer chosen was the Luxor ABC80, but purchasing a computer was not simple, because authorization was needed from the Ministry of Education. The request was made and after a few months, a purchase permit that was personally signed by the Minister of Education was on my desk.

In 1979, the first teaching experiments were carried out at the primary school of the Department of Teacher Education. The computer produced simple arithmetic tasks and provided feedback to the responses. There were two computers, which the pupils used in groups of three. While two groups at a time worked on the computers, the other students did the exercises using pen and paper. Was it effective learning? That I do not know, but everyone was eagerly involved. Teacher trainees were also interested in new teaching methods using the computer.

In the summer of 1982, I organized the first computer training courses for teachers at the University of Oulu. Some companies sponsored the courses by providing the computers, which were all BASIC programmable and there was no operating system. Programs were loaded from diskette or cassette and the teaching consisted of general information about the computers and programming exercises. Some of the teachers made simple programs for their pupils while others tried to understand how to use the computer programs.

University researchers needed statistical methods and statistical software, and creating these programs became an important development target for us. In 1982 the school board offered funding for the development of educational materials, and although I applied for resources, my request was not approved. In my disappointment, I contacted the authority to find out why my application had been refused. The answer was roughly as follows: "We are of the opinion that those micro-computers are not suitable for any real work – and therefore no money or time should be invested in them."

The first version of a statistical package for microcomputers was produced in 1982. It was ported to nearly all microcomputer brands, including HP, Tandy, Luxor ABC, Metric, Commodore, and many others. The software was very popular in universities and other pedagogical institutes, and it was also used by some companies. We realized that it was worth the time and money to develop software for microcomputers.

Personal computers also enabled digital text processing and documentation. One of the most used categories of computer software was, and still is, word processing. It was overwhelmingly practical compared to typing with a typewriter. In the early days there were word processing machines and microcomputers with word processing software. Professional text writers used word-processing machines and researchers typed on a microcomputer. The new technology offered easier ways of writing research papers and books.

The potential of text processing and documentation captured our interests as well. We produced the first version of the word processing software EDITO in 1982 [7]. It was one of the first text editors produced in Finland, and it became widely used by journalists and researchers. Another Finnish text editor, TEKO, was produced by Valtion Tietokonekeskus (the State Computer Centre) and used in public administration. A widely used foreign competitor was Wordstar. Many microcomputers, such as Osborne and Kaypro, had Wordstar floppy disks included.

There was no dominant operating system, which was a difficult situation for programmers. The software had to be ported to many different systems. A similar situation now exists with mobile phone operating systems; there are many different systems such as Symbian, Android, Meego, iOS, Windows Phone, and so on. When IBM introduced their Personal Computer (PC), a dominant standard was born. The IBM PC had an open architecture and anyone could create his or her own version of the IBM computer. There was DOS (Disk Operating Software), which was the same for all IBM clones. It was a godsend for programmers – only one platform for which to make software.

5 Personal Computing for Everyone

Old mainframe computers such as the Honeywell and Univac computers provided software for commercial and research use. They were mainly used for calculation purposes and you often needed the help of an operator to organize jobs to be carried out. It was not personal computing.

Four turning points accelerated the development of personal computers. The first was the open construction of the IBM PC in 1982. Its open specification made it possible to generate IBM clones. The second turning point was the graphical user interface, which was developed for the Xerox Alto, an early personal computer developed at Xerox PARC in 1973. Apple adopted it for Lisa in 1979 and Macintosh in 1984. In 1983, Microsoft announced the release of Windows for its own operating system (MS-DOS). The third turning point was the beginning of competition that reduced the price of personal computers; the fourth was the availability of computer programs. There were really only two platforms and it was quite easy to produce software. All of this happened before 1995.

One day in 1975, at the university cafeteria, someone voiced the idea of a global computer network. All computers would be linked and able to retrieve information from all over the world. After a moment's thought, we came to the conclusion that it would not be possible.

The first web browser, Mosaic, was developed in 1992. Local telephone companies began to sell internet connections during 1993–95. Modem connections came first, then ISDN. Now the world was open. Every home computer was able to connect to the world, thus completing the latest step for personal data processing.

Over the years, the personal computer has provided me with improvements for carrying out psychological tests and measurements, producing stimuli, and collecting data. I could use it for statistical analysis and as a teaching aid. Years ago, microcomputers developed into word processing machines. Now in 2010, personal computing is necessary for me in my everyday life at home and at work. Personal computers and personal computing have come to stay.

References

1. Malinen, P.: Tietojenkäsittely. Werner Söderstöm Oy, Porvoo (1971)
2. Mustonen, S.: Tilastollinen tietojenkäsittelyjärjestelmä SURVO 66. Monistesarja, Moniste, no. 2, Tampereen yliopiston tietokonekeskus, Tampere (1967)
3. Mikkonen,V., Mikkonen, J.: OPSAM: Opintosaavutusten mittaus. Tammi, Helsinki (1971)
4. Mikkonen, V.: OVV-opetusmenetelmien vertailu ja valinta. Sitra, Helsinki (1975)
5. Kainulainen, O.: Mikroprosessorista 'mikrotietokoneeksi' Osa I. Elektroniikka, 13–14. Insinöörilehdet Oy (1977)
6. Kotiranta, K., Lindqvist, J.: PATO tilasto-ohjelmisto. Mikrovuo Oy, Oulu (1982)
7. Kotiranta, K., Lindqvist, J.: EDITO käsikirja. Mikrovuo Oy, Oulu (1982)

Norwegian Computer Technology: Founding a New Industry

Yngvar Lundh

Østre vei 26, 3152 Tolvsrød, Norway
`yngvar@ifi.uio.no`

Abstract. Norway had a successful computer industry. A small group of young research engineers who saw a new era and started "from scratch" founded it. They were able to harness and exploit the rapid development by a basic technical research project.

Keywords: Computer, display, hardware, light pen, magnetic core, memory, reliability, transistor.

1 Introduction

In the early 1960s, a small group of enthusiastic young engineers developed some basic computer technologies. They built their own basic knowledge and created digital circuits, devices and systems, based on technical literature and academic visits to the United States. They made no contact with similar projects. In the late 1960s, members of the group initiated and had the quintessential knowledge in *Norsk Data*, *Informasjonskontroll* (ND) and a new division of *Kongsberg Våpenfabrikk*. These were successful industrial enterprises; ND became large indeed. This is my account on the way the fostering of the technology and the enthusiasm occurred.

2 Study

As a student of electrical engineering at the Norwegian Technical University – NTH – I was looking forward to my final thesis term in 1956. I had come across a book about the "Mark1"-effort at Harvard and other "electronic brains." I asked docent Jens Balchen whether he might be interested in giving me a topic in that area. Balchen had made an impression by his open mind and his singlehanded development of the analog computer "Diana." I had invited him to tell us about it in our radio club, where I spent my spare time with fellow students rebuilding the ham radio station that had been nonexistent since the war.

After a while I was told that nobody at NTH had the knowledge to suggest a topic for study of electronic brains. However, Balchen's friend research engineer Karl Holberg of the Norwegian Defense Research Establishment – NDRE – at Kjeller, proposed a topic. They invited me to do my thesis work there and to investigate an idea, proposed in a journal. That method could multiply, add and divide numbers

J. Impagliazzo, P. Lundin, and B. Wangler (Eds.): HiNC3, IFIP AICT 350, pp. 240–248, 2011.

represented by frequencies of pulse trains. I called it "Siffer frekvens systemet" [1]. Programmable computers were very costly indeed, and cheaper means of computing might be useful in automatic control, signal processing etc. I subsequently worked for NDRE until 1984.

3 Solid State Devices?

In that investigation, I built a set of modules to be interconnected and used for experiments. The modules were binary dividing chains and counters, all implemented by vacuum tubes. During that term and for the next couple of years I did much reading about circuits and devices that might be usable for digital systems. I became concerned by reports of the limited lifetime of vacuum tubes and the ensuing unreliability of systems.

One fellow student's diploma work had been to investigate if a small, much heralded, component, called transistor, might be useful for hearing aids. His professor brought him a sample from an American laboratory. The student had sadly concluded: No. However, transistor radios came on the market. Solid-state components became a promising possibility for replacing tubes in the future. Many practical factors made that choice a long-term one. Between various assignments at NDRE after my graduation, I was able to do a fair amount of reading about solid-state devices. I was especially intrigued by magnetic devices also. Could we possibly use them for implementing logic functions?

I tried to obtain answers to some more or less wild questions and ideas by the assistance of graduate students. Both professors Balchen and Westin at NTH and Tangen at the University of Oslo (UiO) accepted some of my ideas for topics of thesis work for their students, some of them quite brilliant. I served as their advisor and they did their studies as members of our research group at Kjeller. All of us gradually became captivated by the possibilities we saw in digital technology.

4 From the United States

I saw reports about "mathematics machines" such as BESK, DASK and NUSSE, but – rightly or wrongly – I decided to seek solutions that were more promising. I was warned by prominent research committee members that such machines, now in development elsewhere, would have adequate capacity for the foreseeable mathematics market, hence precluding need for Norwegian effort in that area. I decided to spend some time in the United States, where computer technology now apparently was actively being developed and exploited. From august 1958 through 1959 I worked at MIT in the famous Servomechanisms Laboratory, first as "guest" living on a fellowship awarded by the Norwegian research council, later employed by MIT as manager of a project to develop a "pulsed analog" computer. Besides auditing classes in signal theory and automata, I spent much of my time in the special lab established around a computer called TX-0.

As a computer, the TX-0 was somewhat odd as it was built for a special purpose. It was, however, a truly programmable computer; it had a good directly driven CRT display, and – most important – its circuits were all transistorized. Moreover, it was available! I could sign up for time and then use it solely for my own purposes. That was rather different from MIT's main computer center. It featured a monstrous IBM-machine occupying its special wing of the building, with users delivering stacks of punched cards through a window and receiving thick printouts.

Part of the time I went around the back of the "little" TX-0, studying circuit details using an oscilloscope. Additionally, I learnt how to program it, meticulously punching machine code on to paper tape. My proud top success was when the Boston Globe published a story about my program that enabled people to play Tic-tac-toe with the computer, using a "light-pen" that could paint on its display screen. Well, machine code – someone developed a program to translate "mnemonic" three-letter codes, a precursor to assembly code, making the bits of the machine code much easier to remember.

All of this made me entertain ideas that we must develop such machines back home, only much better ones. Karl Holberg, who stopped by the lab on one of his visits in the US, supported the idea heartily. I was even more dedicated after visiting a conference in Boston, where Kenneth Olsen displayed a "programmed data processor" – PDP-1 – a computer to become quite important later, the incipient "minicomputer." Olsen, who told me his parents had come from Fredrikstad, Norway, had started Digital Equipment Corporation after finishing his central role at designing the TX-0 and much else at MIT's Lincoln Lab. We had DEC's logic modules at the TX-0 lab.

5 Building a Development Team

Back at Kjeller in 1960, I was first disappointed to learn that finding resources for developing a computer would take time. However, something else came up. Someone had theorized on ideas that digital techniques could possibly enhance signals buried in noise. This idea could develop into an important project; someone would be happy to finance a digital signal processor if one could build it. I was lucky to be able to propose one. Money became available and there was a need to see results soon. An intense development program began. It resulted in a machine consisting of four large cabinets full of transistorized digital circuits. It worked as planned, processing signals. The only thing it could do was that process, but it did perform it in real time, which was beyond what known programmable computers could do at the time.

To deliver that machine quickly, we had to employ some new engineers. We soon became a group of young engineers. Two of them, fresh after completing their thesis work in digital electronics were Lars Monrad Krohn and Per Bjørge. A period of intensive development began. We viewed some issues very seriously and they were probably decisive for our success.

6 Transistors!

Without doubt, transistors would be the active components! Some were now commercially available, but critical characteristics varied greatly. We needed hundreds of transistors. Circuits were carefully designed using classification of each component type to make the circuit perform to specifications even in the most unfavorable combination of values. We called it a worst-case design. We designed and implemented a few building blocks on printed circuit boards. Typical modules were a "flip flop" and an "inverter." We could implement any digital logic using the modules. Great care ensured standardized compatibility; each module carefully documented with practical rules for interconnection.

Fig. 1. "Siffergruppen" and the "Lydia" digital signal processor. From left: Per Bugge-Asperheim, Svein Strøm, Per Klevan, Lars Monrad-Krohn, Per Bjørge, Asbjørn Horn, Olav Landsverk, Yngvar Lundh (Ove Raffelsen not present).

Extensive work went into the mechanical design of racks, "drawers," guides for cards, and interconnection plugs. It is fair to say that Monrad-Krohn was an essential force in that design process. He spared no effort to meet requirements to ensure reliable performance and he inspired the entire group with his overwhelming energy and his uncompromising determination. Bjørge was an eminent designer of circuits meeting worst-case requirements. A pioneering spirit was growing. "Printed circuits" was something we had heard of, but never seen. Numerous considerations aiming for reliability went into combined effort of the little team of engineers fresh out of university (Fig. 1). The complete machine, named "Lydia," was put to work in March 1962.

Our development must have made impression. It now became possible to think of a general purpose, programmable computer, a dream not forgotten since my return from MIT. Holberg, now leader of a large project, foresaw the need for a machine to handle experiment data and assigned Siffergruppen, now an honorable name, to build one.

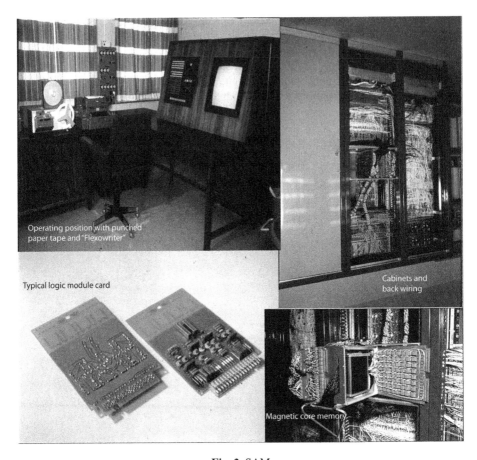

Operating position with punched paper tape and "Flexowriter"

Typical logic module card

Cabinets and back wiring

Magnetic core memory

Fig. 2. SAM

The goal of the new project "build a computer as fast as possible" was unusually vague. However, reflecting on our ambitious attitudes prevailing at that time, "mathematics machines" were exotic news items. The project was named SAM, for simulator of automatic machinery. The same team, augmented by a couple of new candidates who had just completed their theses and became associated members of the group developed it. SAM, a fast programmable computer for that time, was developed and built. It was used for experiments at NDRE until 1973. Since then, it has been an exhibit at the Technical Museum in Oslo.

7 Component Prices

Transistors then on the market were much better than those we had used in Lydia, but way too expensive. We estimated need for more than one thousand. However, I had noted a tendency of extreme price falls happening to new components that became winners in the market. Hence, we carefully studied ambitious market launches of very fast transistors. The advent of the planar process had made possible competing production of equivalent transistors. Semiconductor companies now recognized that "second sourcing" of components was now a necessity in the market rather than something to avoid. These were two factors of unquestionable importance for the use of semiconductors in computer circuits from the early 1960s. Gambling on a dramatic drop in prices, I bought samples of some promising transistors. Prices were exorbitant, so I could only buy three samples for testing and circuit design. We were lucky to pick winners in that race. A few months later when we needed a great number of those transistors, prices had fallen even more than expected. The speed of our new logic circuits had increased several hundred times over those of Lydia. We retained the mechanical standards of cards and interconnection.

In a process over several months, the overall design of the computer was defined in detail. It ended up with features that turned out to point ahead while some were dead ends. I had kept my belief in magnetic components. For the main computer memory, I meant to see a future for thoroidal magnetic cores. Reportedly, they were promising and some companies began to offer them commercially. A study-process made us end up buying from Philips a complete matrix of 64x64x25 bits. Olav Landsverk was responsible for careful design of driving and sensing circuits, including error detection logic. That became the main memory of SAM and it worked fine. I became intrigued by a possible design of an associative memory, using multi-aperture magnetic cores, and soon, we started the circuit design for it. SAM's instruction set contained commands for the associative functions. I found out later in the design work that some clever commands using the ordinary memory would outperform the associative ones. So, we abandoned the idea of associative memory – fortunately. The concept of index memory emerged during those months. We purchased some "very fast" experimental memory modules using thin magnetic film deposited on glass rods for it. Suitable drive circuits were designed, and they worked. I believe the experience of that effort was more valuable than the resulting improvement of computing power. We pursued a number of ideas during some quite creative and busy months.

From my experience with the TX-0, I was convinced of the value of a display screen for which a pen light made interactive. We did not see computer screens for many years to come, of course. I had found a rather special device, called the Charactron Shaped Beam Tube. It projected character symbols on the screen by a form of electron optics. Purpose was to make the display faster and more responsive in interaction. The Charactron was large, it required very special drive circuits indeed, and was expensive. Moreover, it was sensitive of the earth's magnetic field and had to be completely shielded in a "mu-metal" casing. A new member in our group, Knut Korsvold, made the entire design. He met a design challenge of unusual complexity, and succeeded. The display worked reliably. A little device called light pen also comprised some tricky problems. Bugge Asperheim developed a working light pen connected to the display.

The complete machine was developed, built and was working by mid-1964. Later some further additions were made to it. In August 1964, we presented several papers about SAM the NordSAM conference in Stockholm [2].

8 Confirming Experience

During the same period, when SAM was under development, we received another challenge. The telecom administrations of Sweden, Denmark and Norway had decided they wanted to begin experiments with satellite communications. They needed a system to steer a large antenna for experiments. Ground stations for that purpose had been built in some other countries. They were computer controlled, but that made them too expensive for the Scandinavians' budgets. I was asked for a suggestion, and luckily was able to come up with a proposal that the telesatellite committee accepted. Using the well-proven Lydia type modules, we built a special purpose machine that could predict the pointing coordinates of the antenna. Jan Garwick, astronomer and head of NDRE's mathematics section, helped me with the mathematics of approximation of the predicted ephemeris data of satellite orbits, by second-degree polynomials. The machine used the principles of "Siffer frekvens systemet" that I had investigated in my thesis.

The electronics filled four large cabinets of card modules. The machine, "Rasmus," was installed July 1964 at the antenna station at Råö in Bohuslän. Einar Evensen of NDRE developed the powerful servo system that converted the analog output signals from Rasmus into physical pointing angles of the large antenna. The 25-meter disk was a radio telescope built for astronomy. It became available to the telesatellite committee for telecommunication experiments, and now enabled the telecom administrations to demonstrate, for the first time, direct transmission of TV-signals from California to Scandinavia. Again, a special purpose computer had become the solution in real time control.

9 Software

Various bits and their combinations defined the instruction set of SAM. Commands had three letter "mnemonic" names. We recognized the need for an assembly program. Martin Vånar doing his thesis work in our group was inspired by Jan Garwick's ideas of program structures. Vånar wrote a great assembler called Samba. (Garwick's group became a source of some powerful software innovations, but that was later). Monrad-Krohn now came back from a sabbatical year at MIT, full of new ideas and enthusiasm, especially about programming. Thinking that Samba was too complicated, he quickly wrote an assembly program called Asem. It became the dominant software tool for programming SAM. The ideas of operating system programs did not really occur to us until a little later.

10 Industrialization

We learned many lessons during these years. First, we began to understand the workings of computers. We saw that it was possible to make them. We learned how to use them, how to do things, and what not to do. From the end of 1964, Monrad-Krohn headed Siffergruppen, when I had to leave for another assignment. The group went on growing and developed newer and better machines. SAM-2 was developed for some real time applications. Growing knowledge was valuable. Integrated circuits had now become a reality. Features of SAM indicated what was good, and what was less valuable. We built experience.

Some new young engineers and students joined from time to time. Rolf Skår was one of them. As a period of industrialization began, several members of the group left, to join the new organizations. In 1967, time had come to go out and industrialize this know-how. Three members of Siffergruppen, Lars Monrad-Krohn, Per Bjørge, and Rolf Skår, took the initiative to found a new company, later called Norsk Data – ND. Martin Vånar founded a consulting company – Industrikontroll. Kongsberg Våpenfabrikk – KV – employed Olav Landsverk and others. Several books were written about that period [3].

A computer for field artillery was the next great opportunity that came up. It ultimately became a great success for KV. In a short time, commercial ideas and marketing realities had pervaded the group. Technical arguments between the two emerging industrialists ND and KV appeared belligerent. The atmosphere smelled hostile. Probably the competition was a useful stimulus, though, viewed in retrospect.

Both launched their series of "minicomputers" – in competition. As for myself, I wished them success, but after careful consideration, I decided to stay with NDRE and attend to some other opportunities. Each of the companies achieved significant success. ND became large and for a while, it was the largest corporation in Norway, measured by stock value [4].

11 Trust and Success

Our success was partly due to the "state of the art" in that period. We were able to make early use of some unique devices as they became available, hence getting a good start on the international scene. Most important was the rapid development of semiconductor components and circuits. Our results were ready for commercial exploit when minicomputers were making computing affordable for many new applications. There was a large and rapidly growing market.

Even with that, the success had not happened, were it not for the ability of those young engineers. They designed intricate computer electronics with enthusiasm and certain knowledge. It could be done, and it should be! Some of the design details of those early experimental circuits were quite difficult ones. Resources were small, creativity was great, previous experience was nil. We were reading about many types of difficulty leading into trouble elsewhere. That gave us respect for potential dangers. We were thus motivated for careful design, trying to think of everything that could possibly go wrong. Specifications, limits and tolerances became household words. Throughout our little organization, everyone was conscious of the great potential of this wonderful new digital technology. We had promised that we could do it. We all thought that it was always up to us, only to ourselves, to succeed.

A significant reason for the success was *trust*. Karl Holberg gave us the permission to go ahead and develop SAM. It can best be called basic technical research. He shared my vision that digital techniques were to become important. He invented a possible application in a quite different large project, set aside a sum of money and assigned Siffergruppen to the task. In his own joking language, he said he stole the resources. Had we not succeeded in demonstrating unique performance and promising technology, that joke might have turned rather sour. He never told us what to do, but trusted us to do what we had promised. The enthusiasm and responsibility felt by every member were most valuable results of that trust. Young people were stimulated to take responsibility and do what they were good at doing. Self-confidence carried over into the industry it spawned, and continued to grow.

References

1. Lundh, Y.: Digital Techniques for Small Computations. J. of the Brit. I.R.E. 19, 37–44 (1959)
2. Holberg, K., Lundh, Y., Bjørge, P., Landsverk, O., Raffelsen, O., Korsvold, K., Bugge-Asperheim, P.: Regnemaskinen SAM. Elektroteknisk Tidsskrift special issue (August 1965)
3. Wicken, O.: Norsk datahistorie. Prizewinning essay, Ingeniørforlaget/Teknisk Ukeblad (1989)
4. Heradstveit, P.Ø.: Eventyret Norsk Data: En bit av fremtiden. J.M. Stenersens forlag (1985)

The Founding, Fantastic Growth, and Fast Decline of Norsk Data AS

Tor Olav Steine

Formerly of Norsk Data AS
torolav@online.no

Abstract. Norsk Data was a remarkable company that in just twenty years went from a glimmer in the eyes of some computer enthusiasts to become number two in share value at the Oslo Stock Exchange. Within a few years thereafter, it collapsed, for no obvious reason. How was this tremendous success possible and why did the company collapse?

Keywords: Collapse, computer, F16, industry, minicomputer, Norsk Data, Nord, simulator, success, Supermini.

1 The Beginning

1.1 FFI

A combination of circumstances led to the founding of Norsk Data[1] in June 1967. Several brilliant researchers came together at the Norwegian Defense Research Institute (FFI)[2] in Kjeller outside Oslo, Norway. Under institute director Finn Lied, division director of telecommunications Karl Holberg initiated a digital group and appointed Yngvar Lundh as its project leader. Lars Monrad-Krohn was appointed leader of the digital lab.

Yngvar Lundh had experience as a researcher at MIT (Cambridge, MA) during a stay in 1959, Monrad-Krohn followed with a similar appointment in 1962–64, while Per Bjørge, another brilliant computer developer, did his own MIT tour during 1966.

These researchers were impressed with the fast development of computer technology at MIT [1, 2] and soon FFI was itself active in the field, building two military systems, SAM and SAM2. Due to the fact that SAM2 was being built with the new Dual-In-Line (DIP) Integrated Circuit technology, it also had civil potential.

In time, the idea of launching a spin-off company for the civilian market was born. Consequently, Lars Monrad-Krohn and Per Bjørge, together with Rolf Skår and Terje Mikalsen, founded ND in June 1967. Monrad-Krohn, Bjørge, and Skår all worked for the company, with Monrad-Krohn as the unquestioned leader. Although Terje

---

[1] The company name was initially Nordata, Norsk Data Elektronikk A/S, later changed to Norsk Data AS for international simplicity.
[2] Forsvarets forskningsinstitutt (FFI).

J. Impagliazzo, P. Lundin, and B. Wangler (Eds.): HiNC3, IFIP AICT 350, pp. 249–257, 2011.
© IFIP International Federation for Information Processing 2011

Mikalsen was not employed by the company, he convinced his ship-owner father-in-law to invest in it; even Monrad-Krohn's mother and a number of FFI friends and colleagues bought shares in the company.

1.2 The First Bumpy Years

The first few years were bumpy – a balancing act between failure and success, with the latter depending on special contacts, a few key sales, and a highly motivated team of employees. NorControl AS, a company making control systems for ships, employed Terje Mikalsen, who had studied with Rolf Skår at the Norwegian University of Science and Technology. There he helped convince his boss, Ibb Høivold, to use a general purpose computer as an integral part of their system for a new ship, thus providing ND with its first customer. The basis for this vital project, supported by the National Research Fund, had already been established the year before.

Taimyr was an ordinary bulk carrier, commissioned by the Norwegian ship-owner Wilh Wilhelmsen, for which Norcontrol supplied the on-board electronic control systems. The radar was to be extended with a Nord-1 computer (the first ND computer, designed by Per Bjørge) for automatic collision avoidance. This computer was delivered to SINTEF (a large independent research organization carrying out projects for many companies) in Trondheim, remaining there a year before it was moved on board the ship.

The development of the system included a new assembly code generator (Mac), a new operating system (Sintran), and application programs written in Fortran. The operating system was named Sintran (from SINtef and forTRAN) and functioned flawlessly for years!

Other critical early sales were to SINTEF itself, which ordered the first minicomputer with virtual memory in 1968, and to the University in Bergen (UiB). The contact person at UiB developed a positive attitude toward the newly formed computer vendor and later moved to become the central contact for most purchases from the Norwegian government institutions.

In 1970, ND teamed with Siemens and obtained a contract to build a packet-switching network (based on Norsk Data's new Nord 2B machines) for the Norwegian Air Force Supply Service. Dave Walden, who had been part of the BBN (Cambridge, MA) team that developed the ARPANET packet switch (precursor of the Internet router), spent the year 1970–71 working at ND and leading the software implementation for the network [3]. Before returning to BBN in September 1971, Dave Walden recommended Bo Lewendal, a brilliant Swedish-American who was unemployed after two years developing a large time-sharing system for Berkeley Computer Corporation (BCC) [4], to Rolf Skår, then software development manager at Norsk Data.

When Lewendal arrived in 1971 he asked Rolf Skår for permission to develop a time-sharing system for the Nord-1 computer. Since everybody was on holiday during the summer, he spent a few weeks in solitude working on his project, and at the end of the summer, Nord TSS was functioning in its first, rudimentary form.

Other key personnel from FFI, SINTEF, and directly from the universities were attracted to the company. Norsk Data became *the* place to be for ambitious engineers with an interest in computers.

2   The Demanding Customers

In the next few years, a number of specific, often difficult, contracts enabled ND's continued survival and expanding reputation for computer technology and customer service. Only a few of these activities can be mentioned in this paper.

2.1   CERN

In 1973, ND was invited to bid on a contract with CERN, the giant research institution outside Geneva. Among other things, the task was to monitor the new SPS particle collider ring. There was considerable competition for this prestigious contract. Fortunately, Norsk Data shareholder Thor Lingjerde was at CERN at the time and managed to arrange on-site demonstrations of the Nord-1 computer. Norsk Data, with the first time-sharing system in any minicomputer (a further developed Nord TSS), eventually won the contract in 1973, after fierce competition from other European bidders and from Digital Computer Corporation of Maynard, MA. Several of ND's key people used their own cars to deliver various parts of the equipment from Oslo to Geneva, staying there for days and weeks to make things work.

At that point in time, this contract was the key to the very survival of the company. Rolf Skår summed it up as follows: No Bo Lewendal, no time-sharing system. Without the time-sharing system, no CERN contract, and ND would have been bankrupt in 1973!

The extraordinary effort from key personnel during this delivery made Norsk Data's management aware of the fact that sometimes a single programmer or technician is much more important for the future of a company than any executive or chairman. The shaping of the company's personnel policy was made on that basis and it became rather different from other, similar companies in the following years.

The people working at CERN itself represented the best brains in Europe. They influenced the further progress of Norsk Data computers through active involvement with the ND developers.

Two key persons at CERN, Robert Cailliau and Tim Berners-Lee, aimed to solve the problem of organizing the vast amount of documents necessary within CERN, by using "hypertext."

Their first attempt was called Enquire, developed on a Nord 10 computer [5]. Tim subsequently implemented it in a windows fashion on a Next computer. In 1993, the world wide web was launched internationally, and one could safely say it turned the world upside down, helped by Marc Andreassen's Mosaic browser. Cailliau later served as a chairman for the W3 Consortium for many years.

2.2   The Norwegian Meteorological Service (MET)

Per Ofstad, who was the head of the University of Oslo's (UiO) computer center, conceived the idea of a special computer for fast computations as a "slave machine" to an ordinary computer. The concept was mentioned to Lars Monrad-Krohn, who thought the idea was good and achievable, but would be costly to develop. Nevertheless, a year later the institute decided to acquire such a system from ND. Since the project would tie up ND's development resources for a long time, the company offered the system at a substantial price, and the project was launched at high risk. It was delivered on time, and the Nord-5, the world's first 32-bit super-minicomputer was born, which later evolved into the ND 50, 500, and 5000 series of computers.

2.3 Singer Link – The F16 Simulator

In 1977, the NATO countries of the Netherlands, Belgium, Denmark, and Norway joined forces in the "weapons deal of the century" to purchase new fighter planes to replace their mixed and ageing fleets of jet fighters. Such international weapons contracts often involve "offset" contracts, that is, some of the development work is given to companies in the purchasing countries.

Norway had little to offer with respect to offset projects (a few went to Kongsberg Vaapenfabrikk). In the search for viable offset projects, one of the bidders for the pilot training simulators, Singer Link, which needed fast computers for its simulators, approached Norsk Data.

The newly employed head of education, Jan Bjercke, looking for a desk of his own, found the forgotten telex request from Singer Link in a drawer. Jan knew about the newly developed Nord-5 and proposed that four of them be combined into a system for each simulator. Such a proposed system could easily cope with the requirements. The new Nord 10 with virtual memory and new operating system, Sintran III, had just been released; a new Nord 50 and a multiport memory were also developed, allowing several Nord 50s to be connected to each Nord 10.

Thus, the combination of the virtual memory from SINTEF, Sintran from SINTEF and the Taimyr project, Nord-5 from the MET projects, and a new multiport memory comprised the basis of a new and especially demanding project – a powerful online computing system for flight simulation! Jan Bjercke and Rolf Skår (who became ND's Managing Director a few months later) traveled to the USA to finalize the sale.

Although the project was very demanding for a relatively new computer vendor, the systems were delivered and accepted on their scheduled dates (something the customer had not previously experienced). A demanding customer can be very useful to an evolving computer vendor.

2.4 The Norwegian State Railway System (1976)

In 1976, the Norwegian State Railways (NSB) planned a new system to keep track of all its freight cars, which involved arranging trains at the shifting station in Alnabru outside Oslo and optimizing car maintenance. The system, which could save millions through a better utilization of the car pool, was named GTL (Gods Transport Ledelse – "Gods" had no divine link; it simply means "cargo" in Norwegian[3]). The system required a Transaction Processing (TP) monitor capable of handling 150 terminals and

---

[3] Hence, the "Gods Expedition" at the station "Hell" outside Trondheim in mid-Norway is a major tourist attraction…

heavy on-line traffic with a 24/7 operational capability. (ND's competitors were US-based mainframe vendors.)

ND knew that a single minicomputer would be unable to deliver this capacity. Thus, all the terminals in the network were connected through ND's new Nordnet, and all the transactions would appear at a single pair of threads. The TP system divided the work between four Nord 10s, each handling specific tasks. The machines could be backups for each other, and inter-CPU communication was also through Nordnet. The database management component of the freight car system was the SIBAS system (previously developed SINTEF in Oslo) – a traditional CODASYL DBMS first implemented on a Nord 1.

The system was delivered on time, functioned as planned, and served with impressive stability and performance during its entire lifetime.

2.5 Product Strategy

New technologies were quickly applied, demonstrating that the organization had the courage to take on the formidable risks of new applications and still be able to deliver on time. What this implied about the efforts, skills, and motivation of ND's employees in the early days is worthy of a study of its own.

As in subsection 2.1–2.4 above, projects were often built upon each other. It may not have been a conscious plan, but limited resources made it necessary, thus teaching ND how to "rationalize" its products (keep the number of products at a compact level, but make sure they interact well and can be combined in a flexible manner).

This ability was one major key to the profitability of the company during the following years of rapid growth. Competitors, on the other hand, often had competing lines of products that were sometimes mutually incompatible. ND avoided this and could therefore keep a smaller staff for development, technical support, and customer education.

3 The Years of Fast Growth

3.1 Stock Listings

The company became very successful, showing rapid growth and excellent financial results. However, cash was required to finance growth, which the original owners alone could not support; they had to turn to the stock market in Norway. Annual returns showed steady, profitable growth attractive to potential stockholders, resulting in increasing share prices. In addition, there was a periodic share split to maintain the stock price within an attractive "value band."

However, ND eventually grew too big for the Oslo Stock Exchange and Norsk Data was listed on the London Stock Exchange in 1981. This was a major breakthrough regarding access to larger scale financing. In the same year, 1981, Norsk Data was also listed on the "Over the Counter" stock exchange in New York after Terje Mikalsen and CTO Tor Alfheim had presented the company to the investment bankers at Morgan Stanley (CEO Rolf Skår had to stay home due to a back injury). The bankers had "a good feeling" about the company, which had not been felt there since Digital Equipment Corporation some years before. When

Terje Mikalsen presented this news at the annual sales meeting in Lillehammer in 1981, a sense of awe swept the room. Before the sales meeting ended, the stock price doubled, initiating an upward journey that lasted for almost ten years.

3.2 The "ND Spirit"

During ND's first few years the focus was on technology and products, but it soon became clear that it was the attitude of the employees that was the company's most important success factor for the future.

The concept of an "ND-spirit" became a vital element in developing a highly motivated staff capable of obtaining the extraordinary results that were achieved during the following years. CTO Tor Alfheim illustrated the ND spirit by putting a blank sheet on an overhead projector in front of the employees: "You cannot see it" he said "but it is here," holding the blank sheet in the air as evidence.

The employee policy was consciously planned and implemented by the early founders, Lars Monrad-Krohn in particular. These guidelines were given to every new employee:

Work: You spend at least half of your waking time at work – get the most out of it!

Solutions: Do not choose the easiest solution; choose the one you think is right!

Work pressure: The reward is usually proportional to the difficulties.

Things you dislike: Do something about them; improve them if they are important enough.

Work instructions: Until you are certain someone else has taken over the responsibility, it is your own.

Colleagues: Find out which ones are important to you (organizational chart disregarded) and treat them accordingly.

Instincts: Be skeptical of some instincts, do some of the things you dislike the most, talk to some of the persons you dislike the most.

Performance: If you are honest with yourself, you are the best judge.

Improvements: You are allowed to propose improvements, even if you are not perfect yourself.

Obedience: If you are convinced that you are right, stick to it.

Personality: Be yourself. Like yourself. Improve yourself.

Mistakes: Admit them.

Chances: Take them.

The company was geared for rapid growth in a technologically complex and changing world and had no time for formalism or time-consuming procedures. Efficiency was a key success factor and the best way to obtain this was on the basis of a philosophy derived from the late Col. Ole Reistad[4], which ND, in essence, adopted: "Do whatever

---

[4] Mr. Ole Reistad led the Norwegian military Olympic team to its win of a gold medal in St. Moritz in 1928. One exercise was a downhill race to a goal 3000 feet below. His command became legendary: "We'll regroup at the bottom," implying that everyone had to find the best path down the hill, and then join ranks. They won, of course.

you find most efficient to obtain our common goals, and make sure to adjust your activities with the others when needed."

Not everyone thrived in this environment, and some missed education, information, and instructions for what to do next. On the other hand, for those who had a curious, open-minded and independent attitude to life in general, this was heaven on earth.

3.3 "Management by Eating around"

The top managers of ND had a formidable task. They not only had to satisfy a rapidly increasing group of anxious stockholders, but also had to know and react to developments in the highly complex market while managing their own people who were busy doing equally complex work to meet the challenges of the same market.

Thus, ND management eschewed relying on weekly or monthly reports, attending seminars, or hiring consultants in order to understand future technology trends. Instead, they gathered the information directly from the sources themselves – no intermediaries or delays in becoming informed.

An important aspect of staying informed and synthesizing the essence of information into knowledge upon which to base decisions that shaped the company's future took place in the ND canteen. Management always arrived late for lunch and spread out at the various tables. Business discussions during the meals were common, especially when a main executive was present. Information was obtained directly by the people who needed it from the people who knew. And over the long term, management could observe how the staff members developed, who was ready for promotion and who might need some guidance.

Management by eating around was never a specifically stated policy within ND – it was just practiced. (There was no partitioning of the canteen into blue collar, white collar, and executive areas.) This ND approach worked until the computer industry changed toward the end of the 1980s.

4 Crisis and Downfall

4.1 What Happened

In 1981, IBM had launched the Personal Computer era [6] and the machine independent operating system Unix was beginning to win ground in the research world [7]. Their common denominator was an "open architecture," and customers welcomed the possibility of not being bound to computer vendors with their proprietary software systems.

The proprietary mini-computer era was drawing to an end, and the entire computer industry was rocked by a paradigm shift (a disruptive transition in technology) that lasted for a decade or so [8]. All traditional computer vendors struggled to adapt to the classic situation.

- o Existing customers who loved existing products continuously asked for the addition of more features.

o The new open standard products had fewer functions than the established proprietary ones, but were less expensive, both in purchase price and in life cycle operating costs.

o If an established vendor launched open standard products, it also undermined its more profitable, proprietary product line.

Hence, most computer vendors tried to resist the transition while giving 'lip service' to the new trends. In order to maintain profitability, a vendor that put all its efforts into open standard products needed to sell in greater volumes, which thus required a slimmer sales- and support organization.

"Lean and mean" became the winning formula.

4.2 Why Norsk Data Failed

In 1986 and 1987, Norsk Data was ranked among the most successful computer companies in the world, according to the lists established by the Datamation magazine [9]. ND's position as the third most profitable computer company in the world was only outranked by Cray Research and Microsoft [10].

However, close examiners of the 1986 results may have noted a slight reduction in the growth of profits and that some development costs had been added to assets in the books, a change from ND's prior policy of treating all development costs as expenses. Norway had become an oil producing country, but a significant drop in oil prices made the government, ND's largest customer, less willing to invest in more computers. This was a major reason for the pressure on profits.

Norsk Data did not manage the transition! A shift in technology would have required a total change in company culture and customer support; existing customers would not accept any reduction in the support level for their recently purchased products.

The situation was difficult for ND's management, oriented as it was to growth and not to restructuring. Yet ND reacted early and in a reasonably competent manner. A new Unix line was developed, and PCs were added to the product range and integrated with the existing line of minicomputers. The company realized early that the minicomputers would be reduced to "network servers" in the future, and the ND 5000 line of new computers was consistently called a "server" line.

In 1989, after a considerable loss was posted in the accounts of the previous year, a major reorganization and restructuring of the company was necessary. The company was divided into several new business units, three of which were sales organizations, and two were a service division and a "box mover" style telephone sales component for PCs and auxiliary equipment. Computer production and development was separated into a company (Dolphin) selling servers.

Vacant positions for the new companies were posted internally, and all employees had to apply for a job in the new structure. Unfortunately, eight hundred people became redundant in the initial process, and a further five hundred were dismissed two years later. A rationale for the restructuring was to save some of the investors' money by selling off the various companies in the new organization, the companies that were seemingly adapted to the anticipated future structure in the computer business.

Behind the scenes, attempts were made to join forces with, or to sell Norsk Data to companies such as Apollo Computer, Nixdorf, Siemens, ICL, and even Sony. None of these were successful. The Nixdorf deal was the most promising one, and a final meeting was planned during the 1986 CeBIT Fair. However, Heinz Nixdorf died of a heart attack on a dance floor just prior to his planned meeting with Rolf Skår. The German operation, which mostly sold CAD/CAM systems[5], was eventually bought by Intergraph.

In 1986, when the situation still seemed to be relatively good, Norsk Data used a number of its shares as security for a loan from Deutsche Bank in Germany. The loan was to be repaid in full a few years later. When the company could not repay the loan, it was taken over by the Norwegian bank, Den Norske Bank, which sold it to Telenor, the major Norwegian telecom operator, for less than they could write off in taxes (due to the inherent losses in the Norsk Data accounts).

All that remains of Norsk Data are the skills and competence of former ND employees who went on to companies such as Ergo Group, EDB, Telenor, Umoe, to mention a few. The hard-core CPU developers are still alive and active in Numascale [11], a company spin-off from Dolphin. Led by Mr. Kåre Løchsen (a major designer of the legendary ND 500 – used in the F16 flight simulator), they develop revolutionary technology for massive multicomputer clusters, thus carrying the tradition of the ND spirit into the future.

Acknowledgments. My thanks to Per Bugge-Asperheim, Lars Monrad-Krohn, Bo Lewendal, Rolf Skår, Kåre Trøim, and Dave Walden for early days information. In addition, thanks to Dave for proofreading.

References

1. Green, T.: Bright Boys: 1938-1958—Two Decades that Changed Everything. A.K. Peters Ltd, Natick (2010)
2. Norberg, A.L., O'Neill, J.E.: Transforming Computer Technology: Information Processing for the Pentagon, 1962-1986. Johns Hopkins University Press, Baltimore (2000)
3. http://www.walden-family.com/dave/archive/net-history/lfk.pdf
4. http://coe.berkeley.edu/news-center/publications/forefront/archive/forefront-fall-2007/features/berkeley2019s-piece-of-the-computer-revolution
5. http://infomesh.net/2001/enquire/manual/
6. http://www-03.ibm.com/ibm/history/exhibits/pc/pc_1.html
7. http://en.wikipedia.org/wiki/Unix
8. http://en.wikipedia.org/wiki/Disruptive_technology
9. http://en.wikipedia.org/wiki/Datamation
10. http://www.cray.com/Home.aspx
11. http://www.numascale.com/

---

[5] CAD = Computer Aided Design, CAM = Computer Aided Manufacturing.

The Norwegian National IT Plan, 1987–1990: Whence It Came, What It Was, and How It Ended

Arne Sølvberg

IDI – Institute of Computer and Information Science,
NTNU – The Norwegian University of Science Technology,
Trondheim, Norway
asolvber@idi.ntnu.no

Abstract. In the late 1970s and early 1980s most of the technically advanced nations organized national R&D programs for speeding up the intake of information technologies in industry and society as a whole. In addition, Norway organized a National IT plan that ran for four years from 1987–90. The idea of having a national plan was initiated in 1982–83. This paper shortly covers events of around ten years from 1982 until 1991. There is a short description of the relevant processes and of the central actors, and of the technical and political background where the planning processes took place. There is also a short analysis of why things came about as they came, what the consequences of the plan were, and whether we could have done things differently. The main priority of most of the other national IT plans was to support their computer industries through public financing of relevant research. The Norwegian IT plan came with a wider agenda. Not only was it to be a support plan for the Norwegian IT industry, but it was to be a plan for transforming society as a whole, from the industrial to the post-industrial stage. Therefore, the Norwegian IT plan can be seen as a result of negotiations among the "narrow" industrial interests and the wider interests of the emerging information society.

Keywords: Industrial development, information society, IT education, national IT plan, research funding.

1 Introduction

During the 1970s, there was a worldwide "waking up" to the increasing impact of computers in many strands of society. Computers transformed the technical fabric of organizations, and they were finally perceived to transform the workings of the whole society. The term "information society" was coined during this period. Information technology was seen as the central technology for increasing productivity, for providing competitive advantage to industry and for providing military might.

During the late 1970s and early 1980s, this gave rise to national research and development plans in most of the industrially developed world. For a long time the United States had a number of concerted efforts organized under the umbrella of defense. Japan organized a targeted effort to break the U.S. monopoly on

J. Impagliazzo, P. Lundin, and B. Wangler (Eds.): HiNC3, IFIP AICT 350, pp. 258–270, 2011.

supercomputers and to apply artificial intelligence to further their already world leading automation industry – the so-called fifth generation program. The largest European nations (Germany, France and UK) followed suit and embarked on large national R&D programs that included support for their ailing computer industries. They were quickly followed by some of the technically advanced smaller nations in Europe such as The Netherlands, Sweden, and Denmark. On the European Community level, the ESPRIT program was organized during the early 1980s.

Initiatives appeared during the early 1980s to organize a similar national support program in Norway. Of importance was the "me, too" argument: all other comparable nations developed their IT competences on a broad scale; therefore, it had to be important, and unless Norway followed suit and invested in IT like the others, we risked falling behind as a society and could soon find ourselves on the garbage heaps of history. An opposing view was that "we are too small," Norway cannot make any difference in the development of the new technology, "let's wait and see" and apply the new technology when it has proven its value elsewhere, and – computers are just a temporary fad, all the fuss will soon be over.

The Norwegian national IT plan emerged as a compromise between many competing views: urgency versus "it's a fad, we're too small," placing the main emphasis on industrial modernization versus main emphasis on supporting a rapid transformation of Norway into a post-industrial society. Common for all of the competing views and scenarios was a need for increasing the IT-competent workforce. There was wide agreement for increasing the number of IT-graduates, and consequently a wide agreement for increasing the country's education capacity in information technology. Unfortunately, it was early when they decided not to establish a leadership having overall control of the program. The different ministries required the direct control of their own IT-budgets. This decision resulted in weak leadership and lack of coordination and overview.

The economic volume of the IT plan was determined during the post-mortem evaluation. The average total annual budget for the three-year period 1987–89 was 1,190 MNOK. This was an increase of 62 percent over the 1986 budget for comparable activities. Measured in "fresh money" this represents an increase over the 1986 budget of a total amount of 1,330 MNOK over the three years (445 MNOK/year). IT plan activities were budgeted also for 1990, as originally planned. The collapse of the IT plan in early 1990 makes it difficult to estimate the activity level, and I have therefore omitted 1990 from the comparisons.

The process of the making of the Norwegian plan has been well documented in Trond Buland's doctoral thesis [1]. I was personally heavily involved both in the initiation phase and in the post mortem evaluation. In this paper, I explain some of the reasoning behind the choice of strategy in the initial phase, in particular as far as my own participation is concerned. I relied heavily on Buland's thesis for those parts of the political processes where I did not participate personally.

2   The Political Landscape

The Norwegian IT plan emerged in a domestic political climate, which increasingly appreciated the importance of research and technology. The emerging information technology was seen as particularly important. It became the dominant view that change was coming, and as a country we had to prepare. Whether the feeling of change-is-in-the-air warranted special support actions from the government was another issue. By the mid-1980s, the attitude change had been completed. Enough political actors were ready to support technology-based innovation with targeted actions.

The political approach to industrial development was very traditional. They saw industry built on natural resources, capital and labor. The political left favored an interventionist approach of financing new industry, e.g., electronic industry, through public capital, and the political right favored a market-oriented approach. Much of the debate was concentrated on cost of labor and capital.

Neither the political left nor the right had much belief in the possible benefits of investing in research. Both sides were deeply influenced by traditional economic thinking. The political left favored a Keynesian approach to dealing with the economy. The political right trusted the market to stimulate the "right" research in "right" volume. The prevailing view among economists was that one could not find trustworthy correlations between investment in research and economic results for a country. The Norwegian political system was (and still is) heavily influenced by the economists' worldview. Therefore, money for research was viewed more as luxury expenditure than as a factor for increasing the wealth of the country.

The lack of success of the political responses to the economic downturn during the 1970s showed that neither side could come up with a successful formula for turning the tides. Many saw the Norwegian industry increasingly consisting of sunset industries, which would not be able to pay high enough wages as the competition from the third world countries stiffened. This paved the way for other approaches. The lack of success in taming the economic storms of the late 1970s, the stagflation had weakened the influence of the traditionalists and it had strengthened the hand of the "industrial modernizers." During the late 1970s and early 1980s, several government committees analyzed the emerging trends. The recommendations all pointed in the direction of stimulating technological development. This "game changer" was accepted over the complete political spectrum. Therefore, the scene was set for change.

Because of the recent discovery of North Sea petroleum, the Norwegian economy was in such a good shape that the new economic realities were seen later than in many other countries that were less lucky. Most of the other countries were already several years ahead of Norway in their search for remedies. Many of them had already singled out IT as one of the more promising avenues to industrial modernization. Therefore, it was no big surprise that IT became central also in the Norwegian debate. One may say that IT was destined to take a center stage position.

The political and bureaucratic establishments were short on IT-expertise. One important exception was one of the leading conservative politicians, Petter Thomassen. He came from a civilian job as leader of one of the larger regional computer centers of the 1970s. He had published a political debate book in 1980 about data policy, in English translation the title was "Into the DATA-society" [4]. In retrospect, it seems clear that Petter Thomassen had a very constructive role in developing cross-political support for shaping the IT plan.

The cross-political support for the plan is also evidenced by the fact that there were two changes of government during the plan's life. The initial planning was done under a center-right government, which was replaced by a center-left government in 1986, which in again was replaced by a center-right government after the general election in 1989. Petter Thomassen held central political positions during the whole period. He chaired the Parliament's Finance Committee during the plan's initiation phase in 1984–85, and he was Minister of Industry during the winter of 1985–86, and from early the autumn of 1989.

3 Phases

Seen in the clarifying light of hindsight, the formation of the national IT plan had four distinct phases: initiation, institutionalization, implementation, and end game. The initiation phase consisted of several initiatives for establishing public support plans for using and developing the new technology. Several ministries proposed support actions for IT-research and IT-education, as well as for modernization in general within their own areas of responsibility. None of the proposals for increasing the general support to IT made it through the government budgeting process. During 1984–85, two new initiatives emerged; one came from a "group of concerned information technologists," and one from the electronic, telecommunication, and automation industry. These two initiatives managed to form a coalition, which mustered wide enough support to bring them to a next phase of institutionalization of the proposal process, which finally produced a proposal that made it through the government budget process.

The institutionalization phase started with the merging of the two initial initiatives. The merging was organized by the government's organization for public funding of technical and industrial research – NTNF. Additional proposals were brought into the planning process, e.g., the previously unsuccessful plans from the ministries. New actors brought into the debate wider societal concerns in addition to the more narrow industrial concerns of the initiation phase. Decision and budgeting for a national IT plan came as the result of political negotiations and harmonization of all of these additional concerns, amid a fierce opposition from the Ministry of Finance ("the Treasury") who in every country is predetermined to oppose any new spending plan. The harmonization resulted in a relatively unfocused "open" plan. Many had contributed, but few of the contributors were given back much of substance.

The implementation was characterized by a "me, too" run for resources. All of a sudden, everybody was deeply involved in IT, and consequently had a right to compete for the relatively modest additional monetary resources that came with the national plan. The management of the IT plan was not able to resist the "stampede." There was a continuous fight among the various stakeholders for controlling the direction and money flow of the IT plan. The national IT "plan" became a "plan by addition." New items were added into the "plan," the proponents hoping to get on the list of worthy money-receivers. The "plan" ended in a way as a listing of a substantial part of Norwegian activity that included IT.

The end game started already in 1989, one year before the end of the IT plan. Labor lost the elections in 1989 to the center-right. We had a change of government philosophy from a "big government planning" to a "small government market driven" approach. The public and political support for the IT plan evaporated during the autumn of 1989, also deeply influenced by the deep crisis in the IT industry of the late 1980s. The minicomputer producers were out-competed by the emerging new players in the field, the PC producers headed by Microsoft. The support program that started in 1987 witnessed a collapse of major parts of Norwegian IT industry already in 1989. The political response was negative: the Norwegian IT plan had not worked. Conclusion: money down the drain, a total fiasco for Government intervention in affairs that should be left to the market. The Minister of Industry established a post mortem evaluation committee in January 1990, one year before the IT plan officially should come to an end [2].

4   Initiation 1984–85

The IT plan was first budgeted by the Government in 1987, which was made public early autumn of 1986. Prior to this, there had been a long process of establishing coalitions that had enough political power to release public money for a national support program of sufficient size. As is usual in these kinds of processes, there are different interests and different worldviews and these must be consolidated and harmonized through negotiations.

Three "networks" emerged during the initiation phase: one very informal "network" of Ministry bureaucrats, one formal and institutionalized network of electronic industries, and one informal and loose network of IT professionals.

The bureaucratic network was a loose and informal coalition of bureaucrats in several key ministries who agreed on the importance of information technology as a central force in shaping the post-industrial Norway – the information society. Many of the ministries had large IT stimulus programs in their own areas of responsibility, but there was no coordination among the many programs. The bureaucratic "network" was not in any way organized, and consisted of people who knew that they shared opinions about the importance of IT, and who were local drivers for modernization through IT within their own areas of bureaucratic responsibilities.

The industry network was organized by the interest organization of Norwegian electronics industries, EBF – Elektronikkindustriens Bransjeforening (in Norwegian). The leaders of EBF emerged as very active and forceful spokespersons for the modernization of Norwegian industry through increased application of IT.

The IT professionals' network grew out of the Department of Computer Science (IDB – Institutt for Databehandling (in Norwegian) at the Norwegian Institute of Technology (NTH – Norges Tekniske Høgskole in Norwegian). NTH in 1996 became part of NTNU through a reorganization of the academic institutions in Trondheim.

Together with my good colleague Professor Reidar Conradi, I had a central role in the network of "concerned IT-professionals" as was the informal name of the network. Much of the following describes how this network was formed and how it operated. For an extensive and "balanced" description, the reader is referred to Buland's doctoral thesis [1].

4.1 The Ministerial Support Plans

Several of the different ministries had their own IT plans, in many cases plans of considerable size. The central ministries were for Industry, Education, Culture & Science, Administration & Consumer affairs, and for Communication. The latter was responsible for the telecommunication sector as well as for roads and railways.

IT-interested bureaucrats from these ministries produced a number of initiatives starting in the early 1980s, some of them successful, some of them not. The Ministry of Education initiated in 1984 a support program for increasing the use of IT in elementary and secondary schools. The Ministry of Communication worked with plans for modernizing Norwegian telecommunication. The Ministry for Administration was working with a national plan for IT and developed a first proposal in the autumn of 1984, a proposal that was presented for the other ministers early 1985. The proposal was for a program of 750 MNOK over six years with 350 MNOK for education, 300 MNOK for research, and 50 MNOK for public administration [1]. The Ministry for Industry worked through NTNF – The Norwegian Research Foundation for Technical and Natural Science research – to develop a plan for microelectronics research and innovation.

The activities of the various ministries lacked coordination. A first attempt to produce a coordinated proposal came in late 1984, when the Ministries for Industry, Communication, and Culture & Science (responsible for universities and research) produced a common proposal for an IT support plan of 300 MNOK over two years. There were two major items in the plan, one for supporting IT education and one for supporting IT research. In spite of all the good work done by the bureaucrats, concrete result were lacking in the government's budget for 1986. Nevertheless, all of these proposals and programs together provided a fertile ground for developing a proposal for a national support program that could win a final political approval for the 1987 budget.

4.2 Education: A Major Concern

Organized education in IT started at the Norwegian universities during the early 1960s. Teaching was seen as a service for the established subjects. The teaching load was draconic, the research resources were slim, and IT gained in importance. At NTH we started in 1978 an IT specialist education, which became an instant hit with the students. The Computer Science Department (IDB = Institutt for Databehandling) had ten to twenty times as many applicants as we had available places. The industry was crying out for more and more graduates. There were, however, no signs that we would be given more resources by NTH. The situation was also very discouraging at the other universities. IT education was to a large degree seen as a "cash cow", bringing in money, but being used for research by the established academic disciplines, not for IT research.

At IDB, we became increasingly worried by the lack of relevant IT research in Norway. In most other technically developed countries large R&D programs for IT were underway. Unless Norway did similar investments, it stood the chance of being left behind, using yesterday's technology for solving tomorrow's challenges. At IDB, we tried to make the case for increased public investment in IT education and research both internally and externally, but to no effect. The internal budget fights at the universities made it very clear that it was unrealistic for a new discipline to "wrestle" enough money away from the established disciplines. Increasing the availability of external research resources seemed to be the only hope to survive "in style."

At IDB we came to the conclusion that our best chance was in trying to make available more public resources for the IT field as a whole, in the hope that some of the money would trickle down to us. In 1982, we decided to increase our efforts on the national political scene. This was to the dismay of the leadership at NTH, but we decided to go ahead in spite of that. We had lost belief in NTH's willingness to support us in our efforts to find more resources for IT as a discipline. NTH was willing and able to support increased resources for IT as a support for already existing disciplines, but there was much internal opposition to expand the resource frames for the discipline itself.

4.3 "The Group of Interested Information Technologists"

There was no hope that on our own we could make available enough money, neither for our local needs nor for what we thought that the country ought to have for IT R&D. We needed powerful allies. The obvious candidates were the companies who could not find enough IT-graduates. The discrepancy between demand and supply of IT graduates could be observed in the late 1970s, to become severe around 1984–85. Industry complained that the lack of enough graduates inhibited their growth and undermined their competitive positions. For the university, having the IDB department team up with industry was a perfect win-win situation. The objective was clear: to organize a government sponsored IT plan for investment in R&D, comparable to those of other countries.

The first step was to investigate whether there was any chance of broad support for an initiative in this direction. The idea was favorably received when we presented it at a panel debate in Trondheim early 1984. We developed a sketch for an investment plan of around 400 MNOK/year over three to five years. I wrote a letter to Petter Thomassen, who I knew professionally, and who at the time chaired the Parliament's Finance committee, enquiring whether he thought that the idea had a chance of surviving politically. He encouraged me to continue with the initiative, indicated that 400 MNOK/year was a lot of money, and gave me the good advice of thinking about those who we would have to recruit in order to get political support for finding the money. The sketch was developed during the next months, and this first plan was (somewhat humoristic) called DATAKUP – skisse til nasjonalt Kunnskaps UtviklingsProgram i DATAteknikk (English: sketch of a national knowledge development program in data technique).

The next step was to form a group of likeminded people who were in positions to influence the wider technological and industrial environment. Based on the DATAKUP sketch, we (at IDB) took an initiative to form an informal "Gruppe av interesserte informasjonsteknologer" (English: Group of interested information technologists). The group was established in June of 1984 and it consisted of ten persons, including myself as its informal chair, and my good colleague at IDB, Assoc. Prof. Reidar Conradi who served as the group's secretary. The members of the group were leaders of central IT-companies and of the IT operations of some of our largest companies.

The group further developed the original sketch into a DATAKUP plan of 800–1,200 MNOK over three to five years, strongly profiled towards knowledge development, for education and industry, in a "technology-push" fashion.

4.4 STRAPIT – The Electronic Industry's Plan

The Norwegian electronic industry faced a similar situation as we did at the universities. Their foreign competitors enjoyed large infusions of public money for IT research and development. The lack of similar funds from Norway was a threat to their survival. Norway had at the time several domestic IT equipment producers who enjoyed commercial success, e.g., Tandberg Data produced computer terminals and Norsk Data had been very successful with their mini-computers.

The electronic industry was small, counting only 13,000 working places, and was vulnerable, and might not able to follow up on the rapid technological changes of the times. The CEO of Tandberg Data, Ralph Høibakk, was chair of EBF (the interest organization for the electronic industry), and launched a planning process for the future of the industry. The initiative was called STRAPIT – Strategic Plan for Norwegian IT industry towards year 2000 [2]. The final proposal had a volume of 2,800 MNOK over five years. It was primarily an innovation plan for the electronic industry and was based on a market-pull philosophy.

The EBF chair Ralph Høibakk agreed to be a member of "the group of interested information technologists," together with the then chair of EBF's research committee, Helge Christensen. They were also members of the STRAPIT board. The personal overlap between the two groups secured that the DATAKUP and STRAPIT initiatives were kept on track, and supported each other rather than competed. The two initiatives found a natural separation of tasks. DATAKUP concentrated on basic research and education, and STRAPIT concentrated on industrial issues, both for the IT industry and for the wider Norwegian industry as users of IT.

One item of the STRAPIT report was concerned with forecasting the future size of the electronic industry segment in Norway. Three different scenarios were painted, one of low growth, one of medium growth and one of high growth. These numbers were to play a decisive role in the following political struggle, which was leading up to the decision on whether to form a national IT plan.

The two groups presented their reports during the summer of 1985. The scene was set for the next part of the initiation phase, the institutionalization, which was leading up to the political decision.

5 Institutionalization 1985–86

It was clear to everybody involved with DATAKUP and STRAPIT that NTNF had to play the major role in transforming the two initiatives into one plan, which had sufficient industrial and political backing. Late spring/early summer 1985, prior to the publishing of the DATAKUP report, I contacted the new Director of NTNF. He was the retiring rector of NTH, professor of Electrical Engineering at NTH and familiar with the electronic industry and telecommunication. In the preceding years, I had much to do with him on the reorganization of the IT education at NTH. I proposed that he should take the DATAKUP and STRAPIT initiatives, merge them into one NTNF initiative, and present a proposal to the political establishment. He immediately saw both the needs of the country, and the possibilities for giving NTNF a leading role in the implementation of a national IT plan.

The traditional role of NTNF was to handle industrial research and innovation on behalf of the Minister of Industry. The ministry and NTNF worked closely together. NTNF established a group of six representative persons to merge the existing proposals into a common plan for NTNF to propose to the Minister of Industry. The group was chaired by Reidar Kuvås, who was a central person in Norwegian electronic research and industry, and was an "NTNF-insider." Three others (including the secretary Helge Kildal) had been deeply involved with STRAPIT. Then there was the CTO of the Norwegian Tele-monopoly (Televerket), and I, who represented the "Group of interested IT-technologists." The technical-industrial bias was undisputable.

The NTNF group was established in February 1985 and delivered its proposal in May 1985 after only three months of work. It was easy to agree within the group on the main elements of the proposal, which consisted of five sub-programs for Education, Equipment procurement, Knowledge development, Product development, Applications & Dissemination. It was a plan for industrial modernization.

It soon became very clear that a single Ministry was not strong enough to win a budgetary fight with the Ministry of Finance on a proposal, which required "fresh money". The economists in the Ministry of Finance did not believe that investment in technological research was worth the money. A broader alliance of Ministries was necessary in order to overcome the resistance from the ministry of Finance, and find "fresh" money. The industry political perspective was too narrow for finding sufficient support. A wider perspective of bringing the whole society into the information age was necessary in order to forge a strong enough alliance. The vision of "the information society" subsumed the vision of "industrial modernization."

In the course of the next five to six weeks after the NTNF plan was proposed, the "bureaucratic network" managed to work out a sketch for a four-year plan, which was supported by five ministries, and which was presented to the government's budget conference at the end of June 1985. The proposal contained the five subprograms of the NTNF proposal; but it had widened its rationale enough to get the support of all five ministries in a plan, which still was focused on industrial modernization.

The vision of "the information society" brought new actors into the negotiations, and increased the budget dimensions of the proposals to levels beyond what was possible. The Ministry of Finance was very clear in demanding that no "fresh money" should be given, and that an IT plan would have to be constructed within the ordinary budget frames of the participating ministries. During the spring of 1986 the fight among the different ministries for the directions of the programs, and for the "fresh money" for the furthering of the different causes, brought little progress in the planning. Nothing much happened over the winter, to the increasing frustration of the people behind the two main initiatives, DATAKUP and STRAPIT.

At NTH we were disappointed with the lack of tempo. We tried in vain to re-awake our network of "Interested information technologists." I had been contacted by NTNF after the NTNF report and requested whether I wanted a role in the next phase. I had declined. The indications were that an IT plan would become reality. I saw an important role for NTH in IT education and research, and wanted to be on the receiving side of the money flow. I now regretted that I had not chosen to have a more active role. Whether this would have had any positive effect is, however, more than doubtful when judging the powerful political forces that were in play.

The center-right government was replaced by a center-left government in May of 1986. The new government was positive to motivated politically support programs for selected industrial sectors, while the center-right was generally skeptical to such exercises. The new Minister of Industry took immediately initiative to continue and speed up the planning process. The deadline for having a proposal for the 1987 budget was approaching. Three issues were of particular importance for shaping a winning coalition during the next months: job creation in the electronic industry, regional policy, and the organization of the IT plan activities. The Ministry of Finance had not given up on their defense of the nation's treasure chest, and strengthening of the pro-plan coalition was necessary.

STRAPIT had done three calculations of the size of the electronic industry measured in new jobs, for low growth, medium and strong growth. It was estimated that the strong growth scenario would create 60,000 new jobs within the next fifteen years. These 60,000 new jobs became a concrete goal in the political debate, and "against 60,000 new jobs even a Ministry of Finance will fight in vain" [1, p. 249].

During the summer of 1986, the various Ministries were asked to report which IT-activities they would propose as part of a national IT plan. The Ministry for Districts and Labour (in Norwegian: Kommunal- og Arbeidsdepartementet) worked out an overview of activities where IT could play a role. Those were many. From that point in time, also regional policy started to play a role in the formation of the national IT plan.

The organization question was a tricky one. There were two opposing views. The industrialists' view was to organize the activities as a project with a strong leadership, which should report to the Minister of Industry. The opposing view was that the different ministries should take responsibility for their own budget items, and that a coordination group with limited power should be established. There was wide agreement that it was not desirable to establish a new government agency, and that the existing organizational apparatus should be used. The compromise was to establish a secretariat in NTNF, which reported directly to the Minister of Industry. None of the other ministries was willing to hand over money and control of their own IT activities to the Minister of Industry. The compromise was necessary in order to secure the support of all involved ministries.

After the political negotiations during the autumn the NTNF proposal's original five subprograms had been extended with three new subprograms, one for telecommunication research within the existing publicly owned telecommunication monopoly (Televerket), one for establishing regional competence centers, and one for increasing in-house industrial research financed by the industry. The four-year plan had become reality. The proposal for "fresh money" in the 1987 budget was 300 MNOK.

6 Implementation 1987–90

The IT plan was in for a bumpy ride. It was not a "plan" in the conventional meaning of the word. It consisted of a number of individual plans. Each individual plan was budgeted and controlled by different ministries. The IT plan was the addition of all of the "sub-plans". There was no overriding idea that went beyond visionary statements about the future "information society". There was no overriding strategy, no concrete goals and for the plan as a whole, and no organizational instruments for forging decisions on the sub-plans on how the money should be used. The various ministries did not lightly give up their budgetary control over the activities for which they were responsible.

The first coordination group (Norwegian: Nasjonal Styringsgruppe for Informasjonsteknologi) had a dual responsibility. It advised the Minister of Industry on the whole IT plan, and had the operational responsibility for the IT-research budget of NTNF. The group lasted only a little over one year; it was replaced in March 1988 by a new coordination group called NUIT (Norwegian: Nasjonalt Utvalg for Informasjonsteknologi). NUIT was organized directly under the Minister of Industry. NTNF's money remained in NTNF. The various Ministries' money remained in the Ministries. NUIT emerged as a lightweight coordination committee without own resources. NUIT lasted only for approximately one year and a half. Starting January 1, 1990, the coordination responsibility was given back to NTNF where it remained until the official end of the plan in December 1990.

Each of the sub-plans functioned, and planned work was performed according to plans. The major deficiency was that there was little or no synergy. The overall results of the efforts did not become larger than the sum of the components. The fresh money was not put to use in a planned way following an overall strategy. The first coordination group started to develop a strategy half a year out in the IT plan, by early autumn 1987. The Minister of Industry became increasing impatient, replaced the group by NUIT who restarted the strategy work. By mid-1988, there was still no strategy.

The IT plan had a high political profile. The media interest was also high. As the general election of 1989 came closer, the political pressure intensified for showing concrete results. The "promised" 60,000 new jobs still existed in the political landscape, and they did not materialized during the second year after the plan was initiated! The center-left lost the 1989-election and the IT plan was doomed.

7 End Game 1989–90

The end game started shortly after the new center-right government took over after the general election of the autumn of 1989. The pressure for an evaluation of the IT plan was strong. Petter Thomassen was back as Minister of Industry. I contacted him and asked that I became member of the evaluation committee. This was granted. The evaluation committee was established by government decision on January 12, 1990, and delivered its report on June 1, 1990.

The post-mortem reconstruction of the IT plan classified the activities into five major activity areas: for education (18 percent), equipment (11.5 percent), research

(8.5 percent), product development (15 percent), and applications (47 percent); the numbers indicating the part of the total budget allotted to the activity area (NÆR90). The financing that followed the IT plan was to provide a continuation and strengthening of ongoing efforts within all of these broad activity areas.

The strengthening of activities was unevenly distributed over the five activity areas. The average annual budget increases compared to the 1986-level were allotted to education (57 percent), equipment (107 percent), research (2 percent), product development (52 percent), and applications (80 percent). From these numbers it is evident that the application area had more than 50 percent of the "fresh money," trailed by education (18 percent), equipment (16 percent), and product development (13.5 percent). Research was the big loser, and got nothing (0.5 percent). Compared to the annual inflation rate the research area lost ground and came out worse after the national IT plan than before this substantial national investment in information technology.

One should be careful when evaluating these numbers. Some of the activity areas were headed for substantial budget increases already before the IT plan was initiated. Much of the increased activity in the application area would have happened anyway, independently of having an IT plan or not, although not as fast without the IT plan as with the plan. However, for the most part, the increased activity in education and product development would not have happened without the IT plan.

The Norwegian IT plan was comparable to other countries' IT plans, measured in budget per capita for comparable activities.

8 Concluding Remarks

In the aftermath of the IT plan, the field of IT was dead as a political subject for the next six to eight years, until the start of the dot.com wave. There were many bloody bureaucratic noses in the various Ministries. As seen from the outside, the government bureaucrats seemed to do their best to forget the whole "episode." IT became invisible. The effect of this is felt to this day. The political interest in IT evaporated after the national IT plan, never to have been revived other than in political rhetoric.

One area that received substantial new resources was IT university education. Fortunately, the positive effects of financing an expansion of the university education for IT-specialists may have made the IT plan "exercise" worthwhile. This led to Norway having many competent persons for the next big wave in IT, the internet revolution that set in during the 1990s.

The IT plan had a wider political fall-out. The evaluation report contributed to an ongoing debate about the "segmented" state. A widely supported view was that the segmentation brought about by the internal organization of the government bureaucracy prevented "holistic" planning. The IT plan provided a relevant case study. The basis for the plan was a general technology which had potential for changing every segment of society, and indeed has done so from 1970 and onwards. The IT plan was an obvious case for cooperation among the different "segments" of society. Even so, that did not happen. The conservation forces were too strong. Buland (BUL96) proposes that the fate of the IT plan was an important argument for the restructuring in 1994 of the Norwegian publicly funded research organizations. Norway had a large number of research financing agencies for, e.g., industry (NTNF), basic research (NAVF), food, fisheries, and so on. They were all merged into one organization, NFR – Norges Forskningsråd.

However, nothing had been done with the ministerial "fiefdoms." To this day (2010), the various ministries control their own research budgets for IT and they provide NFR with money that has many strings attached. These "many strings" prevent synergy in the sense that several ministries can easily agree on financing IT research of common interest.

References

1. Buland T.: Den store planen. Norges satsing på informasjonsteknologi 1987-1990, dr.polit. avhandling, Det samfunnsvitenskapelige Fakultet, NTNU (1996)
2. Elektronikkindustriens Bransjeforening (EBF): STRAPIT: Strategisk plan for norsk informasjonsteknologi industri fram mot år 2000, Oslo (1985)
3. Næringsdepartementet: Evaluering av Nasjonal Handlingsplan for informasjonsteknologi 1987-1990. Rapport fra evalueringsutvalget oppnevnt ved kongelig resolusjon (January 12,1990), Oslo (June 1,1990)
4. Thomassen P.: Inn i DATA-samfunnet, Oslo (1980)

Before the Internet: Early Experiences of Computer Mediated Communication

Jacob Palme

Department of Computer and Systems Sciences,
Stockholm University, Stockholm, Sweden
jpalme@dsv.su.se

Abstract. In the 1970s, some people believed in using computers for making almost any information available to anyone and for supporting information exchange and discussions regardless of geographical distances. These ideas were, at that time, novel and revolutionary. Some people regarded these ideas as dangerous; for example, the Swedish Data Inspection Board (Datainspektionen) forbade people from storing email messages for longer than one month as well as from discussing political and religious issues using computerized forum systems. Although people tried hard to implement systems and had some limited success, the ideas became successful with the public usage of the internet in the 1990s. Many had hoped to realize this much earlier.

Keywords: Bulletin board systems (BBS), computer conferencing, computer mediated communication (CMC), forum software, personal protection legislation, privacy legislation.

1 Introduction

Some people feel threatened by computers; others feel computers enhance their opportunities. I have been using these machines since 1963 and have been working in the area of Computer Mediated Communication (CMC) since 1975. This paper attempts to summarize my own early experiences and attempts to use computers as an aid for human communication.

2 Public View of Computers in the 1970s

The public attitude to the effects of computers on society in Sweden in the 1970s was that computers would:

1. Impoverish work tasks, causing more repetitive work and diminishing the capability of employees to influence their work situation and improve their skills. In addition, computers or unskilled labor would replace skilled professionals such as typesetters.
2. Become tools of the government as well as large companies and organizations to control people to an unprecedented degree.

J. Impagliazzo, P. Lundin, and B. Wangler (Eds.): HiNC3, IFIP AICT 350, pp. 271–277, 2011.

3. Become unavoidable entity to maintain industrial competitiveness, despite the two aforementioned serious drawbacks, because if we do not use computers we will be outcompeted by other countries [1].

It is not surprising that people had this view of computers in the 1970s. At the time, computers were so expensive that only the government and large organizations, not ordinary people, could afford to use them as tools.

3 A Few People Had a Different View

However, a few people worked with computers and recognized the potential for something vastly different. For example, Torgny Tholerus [2] wrote a paper titled "Computers for Everyone" (Swedish title "Allmänhetens informationssystem"), which proposed that computers could be used as tools for a new kind of free speech – where anyone was able to have their say in ways which enabled everyone to listen.

I myself, Jacob Palme [3], wrote a paper titled "The General Public Information System" proposing people should use computers to handle textual messages, where anyone could write what they wanted and everyone could access the information and comment on it. I also wrote an article for the newspaper, Dagens Nyheter, in 1975 [4] proposing that the new Swedish National Encyclopedia should be published on computer networks, available to everyone, instead of as a set of printed volumes.

Murray Turoff said that computers were like books of white paper, where anyone could write on the pages and everyone could read what other people had written. In 1978, Murray Turoff and Roxanne Hiltz wrote a book [5] titled "The Network Nation," which describes much of what the internet has become today. On two occasions in the late 1970s, Tomas Ohlin invited Murray Turoff and Roxanne Hiltz to Stockholm, to present their ideas to a group of people including myself, Ohlin, and Tholerus. Turoff's talk was pivotal in stimulating our work in this area.

In 1971, Tomas Ohlin wrote an article for the Svenska Dagbladet newspaper [6] proposing home terminals so that people would have better access to government documents and be able to take part in computerized citizens' panels to enhance democracy. Between 1978 and 1981, Tomas Ohlin was the secretary of several government committees (e.g., the information technology committee, Informations teknologiutredningen, and the commission on new media) which, among other things, proposed that simple, low-cost home terminals could provide access to databases of linked pages, and that consumer information should be available through the same terminals [7].

What we all had in common was that we regarded computers as tools for making all information available to everyone. We thought that people could use computers to give more information to more people and allow more people to make their ideas available to others. This was contrary to the then public view of computers as tools used by the government and large companies to watch over and control ordinary people. None of us expected that it would take more than ten years before our expectations would become reality.

Today, many ideas of Ohlin, Palme, and Tholerus came to realization everywhere, with the internet providing the basis of the free exchange of ideas and knowledge, where anyone can put forth whatever they want, and where everyone can read what others have written. Nevertheless, in the 1970s, we were a kind of underground movement trying to advance our ideas in the rather unwilling public opinion of the time.

In the mid-1970s, Ohlin was working at a government agency for research funding. Together with a small group of partners, Ohlin started the Telecommunications and Regional Development (Terese) project in Sweden that included studies of pioneering communication software. This project, carried out through social trials of computer conferencing in the north of Sweden 1976–77, used the then unknown Planet narrowband communication system, with fifty writing terminals equipped with acoustic modems. They applied the system to applications concerning transport, education, and health services, among others.

4 Development of the KOM System

A small number of people, mainly researchers at DSV, KTH-NADA, and FOA (the Defense Research Establishment of Sweden), also used Planet. All were fascinated by its potential. At that time, the Swedish government decided that FOA should divide into parts at different locations around Sweden. This decision made it possible for me to get FOA to finance the development of a new, more powerful forum system [8].

Our system became rather popular; at its peak in 1987, it had thousands of users. Although small compared to the internet of today, it was the largest of its kind in Sweden at that time. We also connected to the internet in 1982, the cost partially funded by Skandinaviska Enskilda Banken. This internet connection was restricted to email and mailing lists, and did not constitute full internet connectivity.

We conducted a number of studies on the effects of this kind of software [9]. From the results, we were able to conclude, among other things, that people agree more often than they disagree in online discussions, that online discussions increase the communication between people organizationally or geographically, and that this increase is especially noticeable with regard to younger people, non-management, and those without higher education. Older people, management, and those with higher education already seemed to have access to cross-organizational and cross-location communication through travel, before using computerized communication. We also found that computerized communication increased the equality between different people with regard to them expressing their opinion, compared to previous communication methods.

In 1982, we distributed the system, installing it on three computers at QZ (the Stockholm University computing center, at that time, including FOA), at DSV, and at KTH-NADA with the exchange of messages between the systems. For many years, the system was a major tool for internal communication within DSV. Today, DSV uses First Class for this purpose.

Our first attempt at starting this system met with disaster; the Swedish Data Inspection Board [10], a government agency for the control of computer usage, had forbidden the use of our system. According to the Data Inspection Board, our system allowed people to store "free text" in which they could write "anything they wanted," while the Data Act, according to their interpretation, forbids storing information in computers except for certain specified fields with explicit limitations on what could be stored in them! The principals at FOA did not dare appeal this decision to the Swedish government, although such an appeal would have been an interesting test of whether freedom of speech through computers was legal or illegal. Instead, the principals at FOA and the Data Inspection Board negotiated an agreement that prohibited us from writing any messages on subjects designated as sensitive information, according to the Swedish Data Act, such as political and religious opinions, among others! We were also obliged to delete all personal emails after thirty days and all discussion messages after three years!

We finally received permission, started the system again, and promptly disobeyed the rules, discussing such sensitive political issues as whether or not one should allow nuclear power. I also archived all public discussions for more than three years, contrary to the instructions from the Swedish Data Inspection Board, posting a selection of them on the internet [11] for anyone to view even today. I am still waiting for the Data Inspection Board to prosecute me for this breach of the agreement.

5 A Threat to Personal Privacy

Case 1: "The credit card company notes that Mr. X and his wife are registered for a double room at a hotel in London. At the same time, his wife uses her credit card to pay her hairdresser in Sweden." This is a typical example of the arguments given by people about the threat of computers to personal privacy.

Case 2: An American computer company decided to add to their internal email system a facility that lets the sender check if and when someone reads an email. This caused an uproar among employees who felt that such a facility was an invasion of their personal privacy.

Case 3: In 1979, we introduced the KOM forum system, which gave users many opportunities to check on each other. A KOM user could see to which forums another user subscribed, when that user last visited a particular forum, when a user read a personal message, and so forth. In spite of such opportunities, very few complained that this was an invasion of privacy. Why? We did add a facility that enabled KOM users to say that other users should not see their personal information. However, almost no user employed this facility to protect their personal privacy. Why not, if there is such a large risk with regard to intrusion of personal privacy using computers?

Case 4: Nevertheless, there was a conflict in one case. The director of studies at a university department started a mandatory forum for information to teachers. After some weeks, he made a printout of the KOM page showing the teachers that had not participated regularly in this forum and he put a copy into all their actual mailboxes. His admonition on this copy "You are all obliged to participate in this Forum!" caused uproar among the teachers.

In trying to analyze these cases, my conclusion is as follows: When people complain about "a threat to personal privacy," their real objection is actually against the use of computers to try to control them. The reason so few KOM users (Case 3 above) complained was that they designed KOM mainly to be under the control of each user. According to KOM users, KOM enabled them to control their usage. They could choose to which forums to subscribe, when to go to a forum, in which order to read news, as well as what to read and what to disregard. Due to this design, they did not feel that KOM was trying to control them.

People thought their personal privacy was threatened when they felt that large companies and organizations "spied on them" and used this information to gain power over them. Since KOM was not (usually, Case 4 as an exception) used in this way, people did not feel that KOM threatened their personal privacy, although KOM did allow users to see much personal information about other KOM users.

This is very important, because if we believe that the problem regards a threat to personal privacy, we may try to resolve it with methods that make the problem worse and not better. By understanding that the real issue is about control and power, we can solve the real problem through the design of software that does not impoverish the user and by making it difficult for large organizations to use the computer to control people.

6 What were People Really Afraid of?

This fear had made me think about how computer systems should be designed so humans make decisions, not computers [12].

In other cases, the Swedish Data Inspection Board has tried to forbid an author from writing a book with personal information in it. The author appealed this decision to the government, which wisely said that freedom of speech is more important than the Data Act. The board then prosecuted a person who used the internet to criticize practices of Swedish banks. The lower court found the person guilty, but not guilty in the highest court of appeal.

The Data Inspection Board will probably not prosecute me for violating their rules, because they could be somewhat ashamed of their history of trying to prevent freedom of speech on the internet. They have attempted to do this a number of times, but the courts most often declared their decisions illegal on appeal. Apparently, those appeal decisions were based on a better understanding of the democratic principles protected by the Swedish constitution than the Data Inspection Board's understanding of the same principles.

In 1982, I asked a friend of mine, Olle Wästberg, who was a member of the Swedish Parliament at the time, to submit a private member's bill specifying that freedom of speech should override the Swedish Data Act. The parliament rejected the bill without any specific reason!

Our computer system for information exchange attracted a great many users, but it received mixed reactions from the media. Some journalists wrote positive articles about the opportunities, others wrote scandal articles, selecting the most ridiculous texts written by any of our thousands of users and presenting them to discredit our system. At that time, my belief was that the media were afraid of losing their monopoly in providing information to a large number of people.

Other organizations made several attempts during the 1980s to develop similar systems, some met with partial success, others not. Notable failures were the Teleguide system in Sweden and the Prestel system in the U.K. However, a notable success was the Minitel system in France. Minitel was the only system that existed before 1990 that is comparable to the internet today. Why did Minitel succeed, when others did not? The main reason is that Minitel allowed any information provider to put whatever they wanted on the Minitel network. Just like the internet of today, the competition between information providers generated many services where some failed while others were very successful, was the reason for the success of Minitel and the internet.

7 Conclusions

- The success of human society is based on the flexibility of humans and their willingness to adapt their activities to different circumstances.
- Humans are most happy and productive when they can influence their living environment and contribute to solving problems together.
- Laws and regulation are a form of communication between humans. They are in reality only guidelines, people have to adapt to varying circumstances and interpret and apply the rules with understanding and human compassion. If everyone had to adhere 100 percent to all laws and regulations, human societies would no longer function.
- Laws and regulations written on paper usually present no problem. However, if the laws and regulations are programmed onto computers so computers control what is allowed and not allowed, serious problems will often occur. In the best case, people will only be unhappy and unproductive; in the worst case, a major catastrophe could occur.
- The design of computer software must allow flexibility and human choice. Humans should interpret laws and regulations, not machines.
- Making software more complex so that it includes more specific handling of special circumstances will often only make it worse. Instead of complex software, it should be flexible and open-ended.
- There is a human tendency when designing software to include "proper procedure" and "experience how things should be done." This tendency can easily produce unusable or unsuitable software.
- A possible exception to the above occurs when we need to enforce security rules to overcome human weaknesses.

References

1. Palme, J.: A Personal History of CMC, Honorary Publication Dedicated to Yvonne Waern (2000),   http://www.tema.liu.se/people/chrga/yw65/start.html, http://people.dsv.su.se/jpalme/s1/a-personal-history-of-CMC.pdf
2. Tholerus, T.: The General Public Democratic Information System, Datalogilaboratoriet, Uppsala (1974)

3. Palme, J.: The General Public Information System. Data, no. 3 (1974)
4. Palme, J.: Lägg nationalencyklopedin på data [Put the National Encyclopedia on a Computer Medium]. Dagens Nyheter (February 28, 1975)
5. Turoff, M., Hiltz, S.R.: The Network Nation, Addison Wesley, Reading (1978); Revised edn. MIT Press (1993)
6. Ohlin, T.: Local Democracy in Telecommunications Age, Svenska Dagbladet (August 8, 1971)
7. Ohlin, T.: In "New media," the Commission on New Information Technology, Dept. of Education, Sweden (1981)
8. Palme, J.: History of the KOM Computer Conferencing System,
   http://dsv.su.se/jpalme/s1/history-of-KOM.html
9. Palme, J.: Experience with the Use of the COM Computerized Conferencing System. FOA Report C-10166E (1981). Revised (1984),
   http://dsv.su.se/jpalme/reports/c10166.pdf
10. The Swedish Data Inspection Board,
    http://www.datainspektionen.se/in-english/
11. Palme, J.: Det var en gång för länge sedan: Diskussioner ur KOM-systemet vid QZ, Sveriges första BBS: Dokument ur den svenska datorhistorien,
    http://dsv.su.se/jpalme/qzkom/
12. Palme, J.: Can Computers Decide What Is Right and Wrong? (1999),
    http://dsv.su.se/jpalme/reports/right-wrong.html
13. Palme, J.: Protected Program Modules in Simula 67. Modern Datateknik,(12), p. 8

The Baby Networks:
Nordic Positions Before the Internet

Tomas Ohlin

Formerly of Linköping University and Stockholm University
tomas@telo.se

Abstract. This paper discusses the computer network situation immediately before the arrival of the internet. In various countries, there were a number of isolated network "islands," following different standards of technical characteristics called videotex. The paper discusses the different regional standards that were used and what types of services were made available, and asks what role the Nordic countries played in this development and in the transition to the internet.

Keywords: CEPT-3, internet, Minitel, Prestel, standards, TCP/IP, TeleGuide, videotex, Viewdata.

1 The International Background

One does not have to be religious to be challenged about how it all started. All of a sudden, there were islands, and all of a sudden, island organizations started ferry lines of connection. The internet was born and, after a few years, there were so many users. Then, who defined the islands? Were there islands everywhere, even in the Nordic countries? Moreover, what language did they speak for connection?

There are several priests in this church. How did it start? Was it a big network bang—a concentrated point of supreme intelligence that simply blew up?

Some of us who were there refer to the story of a growth of small islands that enlarged intermittently. Surely, the course was not quite smooth. Many analysts stressed early ARPA computer connections and their technically formatted messages. Some refer to university computer connections that developed between academic computer science departments, while others point directly to early versions of TCP/IP and preach that only with this standard did it all become possible. Many of us applaud Tim Berners Lee, who received all his medals for defining the web grammar.

The technological pioneers were active in the 1960s. The DARPA collection of large – primarily military – computers became technologically connected at that time, becoming the ARPANET. The same period also already saw the development of the TCP/IP protocol. Pioneering connection experiments took place in several countries in the 1970s, and time-sharing also appeared on the market, building up local star networks around centralized computer stations.

Tim Berners-Lee and his scientific group published their ideas about the world wide web much later, in 1989. The HTML and HTTP languages and the URL grammar were born soon afterwards, around 1990–91.

J. Impagliazzo, P. Lundin, and B. Wangler (Eds.): HiNC3, IFIP AICT 350, pp. 278–286, 2011.
© IFIP International Federation for Information Processing 2011

2   The Importance of the 1980s

So what happened between the 1970s, the times of the ARPANET and its followers, and the 1990s when the internet arrived? The answer is that the period of the 1980s was the time of videotex, internet's forerunner.

What role did that type of system and technology play? How can we describe this development, technology, structure, and/or user influence?

Applications had an important role here. Several mail-oriented systems, as well as computer conferencing, emerged at different points of time in the 1970s. Thereafter, interactive services based on those systems spread in the 1980s. Nevertheless, when did user oriented networking really "start"? In addition, were Nordic developers and enthusiasts around, at the time of the "birth"?

There are different types of answers to this. Certain experts tend to stress the importance of the basic technology and network structure, while others refer to the situation of the information providers, and yet a third group take the perspective of the user and analyze types of services.

How did so many technologically inexperienced users suddenly become aware of these new possibilities of contact? How did it eventuate that hundreds of thousands of users started to connect through early mail forms, and that certain large groups began to use numerical addresses like 3615 (in France), to connect to communications, advertising, and telephone type services through new terminal devices, or home or office equipment? This all happened long before the PC.

3   Characteristics of Videotex Systems

We cannot completely exclude the comments about technology here, since it influenced network structure. Videotex was a type of communication characterized by a type of transmission, speed, interactivity, and user-screen presentation form. Transmitted on packet switching networks and with coordinated gateway protocols, the message transmission speed of videotex was 1,200 bps in and 75 bps out. The presentation screens contained 24 rows and 40 columns for characters and picture elements.

At the approach of the 1980s, the challenge regarding the character representation language for videotex in Europe stood between the UK – with its Viewdata system, renamed Prestel, and France – with Teletel and the Minitel terminal (whose production cost was 100 Euro!). France had a clear formal lead; in user numbers, which had increased enormously (in 1984, there were already 1.8 million Minitel users and, in 1993, 6.3 million users). Nevertheless, the cultural differences played a role, and a number of European countries chose Prestel instead of Teletel for their networks.

An attempt to unify the standards based on compatibility problems was tried by the central European telecom organization CEPT, which defined a common videotex standard in the late 1970s. Implementations were introduced at the beginning of the 1980s. An increasing number of countries successively chose the CEPT-3 as standard, since it was flexible and technically efficient. However, several countries had already invested in Prestel and Teletel.

The Nordic countries that found themselves, individually, with the initial choice of the Prestel standard, later changed to CEPT-3. However, these decisions were mainly unilateral.

Important parts of the struggles concerning the standards were fought based on applications. A number of large companies invested in services that depended on standards and, as it transpired, during the 1980s, the network operators were not strong enough to force the unification of standards. In addition, the global plurality of videotex made cooperation difficult. For example, in the U.S., the NAPLPS standard (North American Presentation Level Protocol Syntax) grew in the 1980s, while in Canada, which was an early videotex enthusiast, the more graphically able Telidon standard was used quite extensively. On the other hand, in Japan, the flexible CAPTAIN could present the Japanese language visually, which Japanese applications naturally needed. This confusion about global standards did not help national cooperation.

The terminals used for videotex came from a line of major equipment producers, including some from Nordic countries. During the latter part of the 1980s, software that made communication in videotex format via PC possible became available for PCs.

In the Scandinavian countries, this network concept for the information market was first called "teledata." The Swedish PTT, Televerket, used the term "Datavision" for a time, but the U.S.-rooted term "videotex" [1] was finally chosen by many in the middle of the 1980s.

4 Pioneering Work

From the 1970s and onwards, an important influence emerged in the U.S. regarding services that early emphasized message communications. Public mail and computer conferencing appeared before 1970 [2]. Jaques Valle and Bob Johansen at the Institute for the Future, in Menlo Park, were also among the early creators of new social contact systems.

With regard to the Nordic development, mentioning these pioneers is relevant. Turoff and Hiltz were visitors and discussion partners not only in Sweden (on several occasions from the middle of the 1970s), but also in Vallee. In particular, Johansen visited Sweden on numerous occasions until the end of the 1980s, discussing and implementing project ideas. These pioneers were influential and in 1977, Bertil Thorngren and Tomas Ohlin implemented public mail applications in the north of Sweden [3]. In addition, Jacob Palme developed his important KOM system in 1978, after inspiration from Turoff and Hiltz [4].

However, for Europe in general, France defined a user market, although, in all honesty, France received its inspiration from the United Kingdom. Around 1970, Sam Fedida at the British Post Office experimented with a connection between the telephone and the television. The issue was expanding and finding new applications for the telephone network. His invention, called "viewdata," allowed the user to "see the text." Fedida aimed at the home user, whose telephone usage at the time was low.

Ceefax complemented viewdata in the UK, which was a TV bound one-way teletext service that used a few upper lines of the TV picture for centrally produced text and comments. This was followed in numerous countries, as centralized TV bound short text services were evident and understandable.

At the same time, French experiments were being carried out [5]. In 1970, services for numerical calculations via the telephone were presented in Issy-les-Moulineaux. Issy continued to be early with its creative appetite. Later in 1972, the French telecom research institute CCETT was established, in order to bring together telephony and TV research. At the SICOB fair the same year, flexible message output was shown, both in synthetically vocal form and visually. In Vélizy, a practical demonstration of a screen presentation was attempted. Telecommunications analysis expanded and, in 1975, the French X.25 bound Transpac data network was presented.

In 1975, much to the surprise of the French developers, they discovered that the UK intended to start a Viewdata service very soon. The French were hurt. In 1976, President Valéry Giscard d'Estaing asked Simon Nora to produce a visionary report about the information society. This work, by Simon Nora and Alain Minc [6], would become important for the expansion of applications and for user understanding of public network services. With support from the French government, it helped pave the way for Minitel and for its successors also internationally. There were other visionary reports at that time (such as the "Instant world" report, produced by the Canadian government, work led by Douglas Parkhill, Canadian Ministry of Communications), but they were not many.

These descriptions of the information society made it apparent that both the private and the public sector would be interested in new types of communications. Contributions indicated that the citizen as well as the consumer was interested. Applications and services of a democratic nature started to appear; questions were raised about the possibilities of electronic voting.

Pioneers such as Yoneiji Masuda in Tokyo, defined a space where thoughts about cooperation could be expressed on public platforms. Masuda visited Sweden on several occasions at the end of the 1970s, and even discussed Nordic public applications, in his monumental book "Information Society" [7]. He proposed a democratic arena that provided citizen access on the new online platforms.

5 Early Videotex Networks

At the beginning of the 1980s, a number of different national videotex networks were created, several of them conceptually inspired by the French system. Packet switching technology was used for the supporting structures.

The influence of the French videotex system had certain characteristics:

- o a decentralized system structure allowed local hosts to be connected everywhere in the network,
- o flexible payment was centralized, combined with telephone bills,
- o public e-mail was introduced,
- o Annuaire Electronique, a centralized telephone book, was provided online in France.

These characteristics of the pioneering French systems were not introduced in the videotex systems of all other countries, but they played important roles in these countries' national expansion. Table 1 lists which standard was utilized and the year of the official launch of videotex services (trials were conducted earlier) in European countries.

Table 1. Launch of videotext

Country	Launch	Standard
Austria	1984	Prestel
Belgium	1986	Prestel
Denmark	1985	Prestel / CEPT-3
Finland	1986	Prestel
France	1984	Teletel
Germany	1984	CEPT-3
Italy	1985	CEPT-3 / Prestel
Netherlands	1984	Prestel
Norway	1986	Prestel / CEPT-3
Sweden	1982	Prestel (CEPT-3 in 1987)
Switzerland	1986	CEPT-3
UK	1980	Prestel

6   The Nordic Connection

In several countries, there were groups of enthusiasts who recognized what was happening. Widespread interactivity attracted attention, creating interest and tension. Established technological market forces took a stand, usually restrictive at the beginning. Furthermore, several representatives of the existing telecom networks and industries considered the initially small islands of videotex users as competitors.

Finland was an early videotex country. Inspired by the French development and through early personal contacts, they began to conduct experiments in Helsinki at the beginning of the 1980s. The leading newspaper, Helsingin Sanomat, was active, together with the inspired developer Jaako Hanukselä. An analysis was made concerning online news and experiments were carried out locally and shown at Nordic conferences. Other early producers of Finnish information included the business chain SOK.

In Denmark, the Danish PTT was conducting videotex trials, called Teledata, from 1980 onwards; the official market introduction occurred in 1985. Norway conducted Teledata field trials already from 1979 onwards, with the commercial launch in 1986.

In the middle of the 1980s, a number of types of service applications, including grocery sales, travel reservation, and insurance and banking services were tried in almost all Nordic countries.

In some, a politically based public analysis was initiated. One of the forces behind this was the mass media, but after the first shock, newspapers and TV became nervous. Was this a serious threat to the ordinary paper bound press?

In Sweden, a parliamentary commission, Informationsteknologiutredningen [8], including leading politicians, was formed in 1978. Its secretary was Tomas Ohlin. The newspapers had been actively supporting the creation of this commission; they were concerned about the possible competition from electronic information forms. The results of the commission's analysis were rather broad, it was noted that this media change would take time. Actually, the regulation of commercial online information (advertisements) was politically proposed, but never implemented. Similar commissions or public analysis groups were created in other countries.

The late 1970s and the beginning of the 1980s were times of analysis. Existing market forces had to become involved.

7 User Influence

In several countries in the 1980s, information providers formed branch-oriented organizations. For example, in Sweden, Videotexföreningen was formed in 1983, and later expanded into InformationsProducentFöreningen, IPF (with active chairman Tomas Persson). Internationally, the Association for Videotex Information Providers already existed. The driving market forces behind the development of Swedish videotex were Aktievisionen (financial services, developed by Paul Östling), LantbruksData (services for farmers), ATG (administrative services for gambling), TINA (Teledata I Norr, with regional services), and Riksdagen (public information services), as well as banks and insurance companies.

Videotexföreningen developed ethical guidelines for videotex already in 1985 [9]. These were among the first such guidelines published globally.

A group of Swedish industrialists created the company TeleGuide in 1988. The organizations behind this company were IBM, Esselte, and Swedish PTT – Televerket. The aim of Teleguide was to repeat the French success with Minitel, for home applications.

Plans were to develop further the Swedish PTT videotex network. A dedicated terminal equipped with a smart card reader, aimed at the electronics market, was bought from Loewe in Germany. In 1990, they advertised the following TeleGuide services:

o Telephone address book
o Banking
o E-mail
o Postal services
o Public debates
o Online market
o Postal services

o Financial services
o Public information
o Mass media information
o Travel
o Insurance
o Information retrieval
o Games

Several of these services were in early forms of development, but the marketing was offensive.

Due to a lack of collective financial support, plans for joint Nordic activity were drawn up but not implemented. The TeleGuide company did not receive any public support and was only able to attract 22,000 customers. The PTT interest decreased over time and, after three years, the project was discontinued. It had been too early; there was no market for its services.

8 The PTT Positions

The activities of the PTTs [10] were offensive at the beginning; telephone based profits were still substantial. However, conceptually, the plans were conservative, from user perspectives. The old single market thinking ruled. PTTs employed many engineers, who at times had a limited understanding of small-scale online market services for the office and home.

There were, however, certain markets that were offensive at an early stage, often based on powerful organizations such as farmers' services, medical drug markets, banks, and insurance companies. In order to service these markets, the PTTs kept the X.25 network and its videotex counterpart network, in good shape technically. Nevertheless, not everyone was quite willing to accept new market thinking, small-scale usage as well as strong competition.

After a thorough analysis, the Swedish PTT videotex network was discontinued in 1992–93. Although the internet was not fully available at the time, there was an expectant feeling among experts that the different videotex networks would have difficulty cooperating well. Compatibility problems among network dialogues were substantial.

In addition, information providers were dissatisfied with the, in essence, monopolistic PTT. Opposition was evident with regard to the making of certain policies. Reasons for closing the Swedish PTT videotex network were:

o Videotex was a cultural problem for PTT
o Telecom markets were beginning to be liberalized, no monopolies
o Resources were scarce, with no state support
o The videotex network (CEPT type) was expensive
o The number of users was too small
o TeleGuide was closed
o The compatibility problems between networks were too costly
o New types of equipment appeared, teletex, ISDN, smart phones

9 Problems for the Small Network Islands

At the beginning of the 1990s, national videotex networks were becoming aware of problems. The market was not expanding to expectations; new technology (new terminal types, and the PC) and new system structures were appearing. It transpired that the problems that had become relevant for the Swedish PTT had also become relevant for others. In this respect, there were Nordic contacts.

However, French Minitel had shown what later was to become an internet market. The Teletel network that formed the base for the Minitel success (reaching over seven million terminals) was created according to certain principles of decentralized system structure, centralized payment, a "killer app" (phonebook), plus e-mail.

In many countries, there were attempts to duplicate this, for example, the Swedish TeleGuide. This system failed because the application development policy was too narrow, financial support was lacking, as was, subsequently, customer interest.

10 Transition from Videotex into the Internet

No doubt, there were a number of advantages with the videotex format such as low cost, ease of use, flexibility, and interactivity. There were also disadvantages such as slow speed and a lack of graphical sophistication

For a medium of its time, these characteristics were important and no doubt showed the way for the internet. Videotex was a fantastic medium because it was so early with direct user interactivity and influence. Several of internet's later successful services stem from videotex developments in the 1980s.

Historically, it is certainly not the first time that small decentralized services, after initial development problems, pave the way for a broader, centrally combined and successful system. In the early 1990s, many observers had noted Minitel and the different videotex islands, and they had been increasingly convinced that this was a development on which to expand.

In this author's opinion, there is no doubt that the internet would have taken much longer to arrive were it not for the experiences gained from the regional videotex systems. The concepts of the electronic market and the open platforms were already established when the internet arrived.

Videotex had an obvious educational effect on the coming online market. It was the first widely distributed system, which enabled users to become acquainted with controlled interactivity, with early public access, thus becoming a pioneer system for democratic dialogue.

It is often important to be at the right place at the right time. Successful inventions have historically arrived at a time when there is sufficient user understanding. The invention of a technical standard and a network grammar is a beautiful achievement. However, large groups of users form the basis for the real gold medals.

Strangely enough, in 2010 there are still a number of Minitel terminals in France. Phonebook services and personal mail are, to some extent, still used with this equipment, although such use must surely be declining. It is amazing, however, that a network invention from the 1970s can survive for over thirty years in these times of explosively rapid technological development. Videotex paved the way for the internet, and platforms for the many, although there is a lesson in that social platforms need time to mature.

11 Conclusion

If not for videotext, the internet would have arrived on the international (including the Nordic) user market several years later than its actual introduction. Some reasons for this relate to user maturity. Videotex enabled millions of new network users to gain an understanding of the new system. Although not an earthquake in the technical sense, its speed and standardization was only low. It was, however, a system that introduced user interactivity, which was a substantial contribution to network expansion. Suddenly, users found themselves with influence.

What can we say about Nordic contributions? Although the Scandinavian countries were early, they were not at the forefront. However, they did provide important test markets for the coming videotex systems. Actually, during discussions with Frank Burgess, general manager of Prestel in the middle of the 1980s, he confirmed quite clearly that expansion into the Nordic markets had been a necessity for Prestel, and this had provided training for other market developments. Burgess visited the Nordic countries frequently and was keen to maintain close contact with Scandinavian representatives.

This is also relevant for the introduction of CEPT-3. There was close contact between the Nordic countries and CEPT representatives in the middle of the 1980s. The Scandinavian countries were important start-up markets that were used to test several aspects, both technically and with regard to new applications. The Nordic countries were important partners for the expansion of videotex and they helped pave the way for the internet, about ten years later.

References

1. Ohlin, T.: Videotex. Riksdataförbundet, Stockholm (1986) (available via Tomas Ohlin)
2. Hiltz, S.R., Turoff, M.: The Network Nation. New Jersey (1978)
3. Ohlin, T., Thorngren, B.: Projekt TERESE. Styrelsen för Teknisk Utveckling, Stockholm (1976-1977)
4. Palme, J.: History of the KOM Computer Conferencing System (1978), http://people.dsv.su.se/~jpalme/s1/history-of-KOM.html
5. Abadie M.: Minitel Story. P. M: Favre Publi S.A., Paris (1988)
6. Nora, S., Minc A.: Linformatisation de la societé. Paris (1977-1978)
7. Masuda, Y.: Information Society, Tokyo (1976)
8. SOU 1981:45. Informationsteknologiutredningen. Stockholm (1981)
9. Ohlin, T., Synnerstad, K.: Etiska riktlinjer för videotex. Videotexföreningen (1985)
10. Lernevall, S., Åkesson, B.: 11.8 Videotex. In: Svenska Televerket, Del VII, Från myndighet till bolag 1966-1993. Televerket: Telia, Norstedts förlag, Stockholm (1997)

Development of Internet Technology and Norwegian Participation

Yngvar Lundh

Østre vei 26, 3152 Tolvsrød, Norway
yngvar@ifi.uio.no

Abstract. Ideas emerged over several years. From 1968, some fundamental techniques developed in an admirable cooperation between academic groups. The technical development was at its most active during a decade from the early 1970s in a close collaboration between ten groups, eight in the USA, one in England, and one in Norway.

Keywords: Networking, packet switching, resource sharing, TCP/IP.

1 Introduction

Computer networking was not new. From the early 1960s airline ticket reservations could be made in minutes from almost anywhere. What made that possible was SABRE, a large computer network resulting from collaboration between American Airlines and IBM. That operation began about 1960. IBM, the largest computer manufacturer and leader of the industry in many ways, had their own system network architecture – SNA. Most major computer companies had their networks in the 1960s, useful for large companies and organizations. Each network was populated by hardware and software native to the respective computer company. Internet technology was the result of basic technical research and development by a collection of research groups in which none of those companies took part.

2 Ideas

Resource sharing was the mantra of many early contributors to the internet's development. We may trace some ideas back as far as the late 1940s. In a famous article "As we may think" in *The Atlantic* magazine in 1945, Vannevar Bush, leading science and technology advisor in the USA, outlined some visions of how machines could be made to extend the power of the brain for logic, memory, and communication. He compared it to machines that increased the power and productivity of hands. Many important contributions later referred to his work.

The Soviet Sputnik event in 1957 stimulated an upswing in American public investment in basic research. One effort was the establishment of the Advanced Research Projects Agency – ARPA. A leader of ARPA, J.C.R. Licklider, discussed

J. Impagliazzo, P. Lundin, and B. Wangler (Eds.): HiNC3, IFIP AICT 350, pp. 287–296, 2011.

some possibilities. He wrote some notes in 1962, apparently inspired by Vannevar Bush, inviting proposals. Lawrence (Larry) Roberts, then working at MIT, responded and produced some basic ideas of generalized computer networking.

One of Roberts' classmates from MIT was Leonard Kleinrock [1]. In his PhD thesis, he discussed the possibilities of packet switching, a method of "chopping up" long messages into small packets that were encapsulated with administrative information and sent separately through the net. A network of transmission channels interconnected by computers in the nodes would be able to route and transmit the packets through the net to their destinations. Hence, high-speed lines, necessary for quick response, could be shared for improved economy. At about the same time Paul Baran at the Rand Corporation issued a note discussing similar ideas. Later, they re-issued Kleinrock's thesis as a book that attracted great demand.

3 The Arpanet: A Great Laboratory

In 1966, ARPA employed Larry Roberts to lead a project, building a computer network. It was named "Arpanet." The company Bolt Beranek and Newman – BBN – in Cambridge, Massachusetts received a contract to implement it. Robert (Bob) Kahn was a leading engineer in the project.

Ideas pertinent to resource sharing among computers abounded in academic places in the US during the 1960s. A comprehensive demonstration, later to become celebrated, was held at Stanford University in 1968 by Douglas Engelbart. He showed a number of new ideas such as a display screen, mouse, hypertext, and workstations interconnected in nets.

Delivery of components of the Arpanet began in September 1969, first to UCLA. By the end of that year a network between four places was working: UCLA, SRI, UCSB, and the University of Utah. Kleinrock was professor at UCLA. Vinton (Vint) Cerf was one of his students.

The net continued to grow. By 1972, it comprised some thirty universities and research organizations. The main component was an interface message processor (IMP) in every network node to route and transmit packets. One or more computers, called host machines, could interface with the IMP. At that time, a computer was a large investment that few could afford. Therefore, just the possibility of sharing computing power was an enticement. A "terminal IMP" (TIP) had the additional feature to allow direct connection of interactive terminals, teletype or more fancy typing machines, enabling people without a computer to make use of host machines in the Arpanet via inexpensive terminals. A number of academic groups began collaborative projects exploiting resource sharing in a wide sense. Leased lines, mostly at the (American) standard transfer capacity of 56 kb/s, interconnected the IMPs. Each IMP was connected to two or more other IMPs, hence always providing alternative routes for traffic in a mask network. That was a significant difference from commercial computer networks.

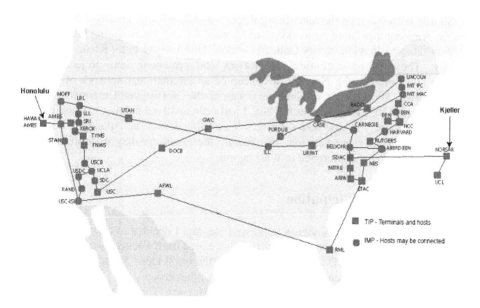

Fig. 1. Arpanet, September 1974

The Arpanet used layered protocols allowing dissimilar machines of various origin and purpose to interact. It offered basic forms of the services such as e-mail, telnet, file transfer, and remote job entry. Packets handled all information transfer.

An important part of Arpanet was the network control center (NCC) at BBN. It could observe various traffic statistics at IMPs. Transfer times of each packet could be measured. Packets could be time stamped and observed at selected points along its path to measure where time was spent. Each IMP could be reprogrammed from the NCC. The Arpanet became a large laboratory for networking techniques. The centralized control facility allowed experiments, covering rather extensive geographical distances, managed efficiently with a minimum of travel.

Another important facility was the network information center (NIC) at SRI. It was a repository of a series of notes called request for comment (RFC). Many of them are still available [2]. It was a library of information pertaining to Arpanet and activities around it. A comprehensive network directory was issued and updated at intervals.

4 Resource Sharing

Bob Kahn arranged a public conference and a broad demonstration of a number of collaboration projects in Washington, DC in 1972. It was an impressive display of resource sharing. Isolated fields of study such as mathematical analysis, natural language translation, weather forecast, and many others were producing extraordinary results and they opened challenging novel roads of progress. A networking culture developed from the start of Arpanet. The services and functions were less powerful and flexible, but the stimulating environment of open networking was fertile.

Shortly before that conference, Larry Roberts and Bob Kahn, greatly stimulated by the far-reaching aspects of networking, saw a need for also investigating international aspects. They visited University College London (UCL) where Peter Kirstein grew an interest. They visited institutions in Norway and presented their project. ARPA already collaborated with Norway. It concerned an international network of seismic observatories. Working as research engineer at the Norwegian Defense Research Establishment (NDRE) at Kjeller in 1965, I had been involved helping to establish the Norsar observatory. It now had a 2.4 kb/s leased line across the Atlantic. I attended Roberts' and Kahn's presentation. Inspired by the prospects they gave of resource sharing, I went to the conference in Washington.

5 Norwegian Participation

The demonstrations in Washington impressed me, and I decided to collaborate. I was invited to participate in meetings of a group that called itself Packet Switching Project Working Group – PSPWG – and learnt some of the basic ideas. I made new contacts at ARPA, SRI and UCL and with other members of that group.

It turned out to be difficult to create interest in Norway. That precluded financing a separate project. So I permitted myself to spend some time studying networking, as part of another project on digital communications. I proposed a topic for graduate student Asle Hesla who began unraveling the mysteries of layered protocols. From 1975, I "borrowed" two research engineers from another project, Pål Spilling and Åge Stensby. Later I received two more engineers, Finn Arve Aagesen and Øyvind Hvinden; they were allowed to serve their military duty at NDRE, an arrangement for fresh university graduates on some rare occasions when their unit could renounce them. NDRE is part of the Norwegian Department of Defense. However, the ARPA project was civilian. At NDRE we had great interest and need for basic technology. Projects with civilian goals were acceptable. Ultimately, in the late 1970s my "Arpanet group" was five people. I had it formalized as project "Paradis" to study packet switched radio channels and distributed information systems. Its own budget was zero. NDRE management was positive to my general ideas, and I let Spilling spend two months in Peter Kirstein's group at UCL for a good start.

ARPA sponsored a TIP at Kjeller, installed in the summer of 1973. Improved modems transmitting 9.6 kb/s were connected in the existing cross-Atlantic line. Multiplexers rendered 7.2 kb/s for the TIP while the seismic traffic kept its 2.4 kb/s. Shortly thereafter, a second European node was assembled at UCL connected by a line from Kjeller. The next node outside the US was installed in Germany in 1980.

Hoping to stimulate interest in Norway, I arranged a seminar at Kjeller in May 1976 and invited some twenty persons from academia and industry. I obtained an international grant allowing me to invite Douglas Engelbart to present his ideas on "Computer Augmentation of the Human Intellect." The experienced and charming inventor lectured his ideas to us for three whole days. He brought and demonstrated his invention, the workstation with CRT and mouse. That was years before people even had seen such screens. My disappointment was sad when the only comment I heard from the audience was "baroque"! Moreover, I could not find interest outside Kjeller.

Fig. 2. Workstation demonstrated 1968

6 Developing the Goals

An important encounter took place in the INWG-group of IEEE in August of 1974. That international group spent two whole days on board the Stockholm-Åbo ferry. Sacrificing the view while cruising through the beautiful Åland archipelago, we discussed computer networking. Desirable goals and potential problems unraveled thoroughly in working groups sharing two conference rooms aboard. Many members of the PSPWG were there. In the next several years, some of the same persons began meeting every three months. Venues rotated between the ten groups of researchers from ARPA, SRI, BBN, Linkabit Company, ISI, UCLA, Comsat, MIT, UCL, and NDRE. These meetings were essential during the most active period of internet's technological development until the early 1980s.

In the following years, goals for technical development had matured; they were successively set and reexamined during PSPWG meetings based on theoretical and experimental work at the various sites and they presented, discussed and documented intermediate suggestions, questions, and results. Bob Kahn, employed by ARPA from 1973, was the quiet and efficient leader of those meetings. Jon Postel of ISI was the gifted author of many clear and precise documents – RFCs. Vint Cerf was a most active participant in the discussions. Typically, he pursued all questions persistently until the group considered every conceivable situation. Individuals communicated intermediate discussions and practical arrangements by email between meetings.

Table 1. PSPWG meetings

Date	Venue	Host
10-11 Aug 74	Åland Ferry	INWG of IEEE
4-5 Sep 75	Linkabit Co, San Diego, California	Irwin Jacobs
12-13 Nov 75	UCL London, England	Peter Kirstein
12-14 Feb 76	DCA and ARPA, Washington, DC	Bob Kahn
29-30 Apr 76	BBN, Cambridge, Massachusetts	David Walden
29-30 Jun 76	NDRE, Kjeller, Norway	Yngvar Lundh
23-24 Sep 76	UCLA, Los Angeles, California	Leonard Kleinrock
9-10 Dec 76	UCL, London, England	Peter Kirstein
10-11 March 77	Comsat, Washington, DC	Estil Hoversten
8-10 Jun 77	NDRE, Kjeller, Norway	Yngvar Lundh
17-19 Aug 77	Linkabit Co, San Diego, California	Irwin Jacobs
31 Oct- 2 Nov 77	BBN, Cambridge, Massachusetts	Bob Bressler
1-3 Feb 78	UCLA, Los Angeles, California	Wesley Chu
3-5 May 78	UCL, London, England	Peter Kirstein
31 Jul-2 Aug 78	MIT Lincoln Lab, Lexington, Massachusetts	James Forgie
1-3 Nov 78	Linkabit Co, San Diego, California	Estil Hoversten
8-11 May 79	BBN, Cambridge, Massachusetts	James Forgie
4-7 Feb 80	SRI, Menlo Park, California	
14-15 May 80	MIT, Cambridge, Massachusetts	David Clark
7-9 Oct 80	UCL/RRE, Malvern, England	Peter Kirstein

In summary, the most important goals were as follows. A) Any type of information transport medium should be made useful for optimal packet transport. B) Any type of traffic should be managed in accordance with its specific need. C) The network should be robust and working without any central control. All the work during the development had those goals in distinct view. It took several years of development to identify what that meant in all detail and to generate the practical solutions.

7 Emerging Solutions

7.1 Network of Nets

It soon became clear that A) could not be met with the simple packet handling algorithms of the Arpanet. They assumed lines of given fixed characteristics between IMPs. Other media, notably wireless ones were different. Bob Kahn and Vint Cerf launched the ideas of a network of **inter**-connected **net**s. An article in the IEEE Transactions on Communication in 1974 [3] documented their ideas. Cerf was then professor at Stanford University. He led a group of graduate students actively working on the respective issues. One of them was Dag Belsnes, on leave from the University of Oslo. The main idea was to consider each type of transmission medium as a separate net, and to optimize the transmission algorithm for that medium. Pertinent details of packets and their handling could be shaped for optimum transmission in that medium. The individual nets would be interconnected by gateways that would repackage each packet, fragment it if need be, and deliver to the next net in size and shape optimized for that medium.

7.2 Traffic Types

They recognized that various traffic types required different accommodations in the net. Two types of traffic were illustrated as examples. Some media are more prone to noise than others are. A noisy channel may cause transmission errors. They can be corrected by retransmission(s), repeatedly if necessary, until it achieves exactness. It is not always best to insist that all traffic should be error free, though. If packets carry the symbolic value of funds, no one would disagree that absolute correctness is paramount. A few seconds delay is less important. As another example, if the packets contain coded speech, such delays are detrimental, while a lost or damaged packet may hardly be observable in the received sound picture, and it is better to leave it alone.

Requirement C), of robustness without central supervision and control, means that the functions that transmit packets through the net, as well as the gateway functions, should be self-sufficient, including routing of packets on their way to destination, always capable of working without supervision. Today's routers perform all those functions. The intricate logic took many years of idea generation, trials, errors and testing to perfect. During some tests, queues of packets could pile up in the IMPS, causing deadlocks that people had to unlock. The internet ultimately became self-healing. Packets route through the many interconnected nets according to the internet protocol (IP). The end-to-end transfer of a message between two entities – typically two programs, one in each host computer – is handled by the transfer control protocol (TCP) according to required reliability and urgency. Today's computers come furnished with operating systems equipped to perform, among so many other tasks, the logic of "TCP/IP."

7.3 Different Channels

To optimize transfer of packets in a transmission medium requires understanding of that medium's nature. A local net of radio stations sharing a frequency is set up to transfer packets one by one between any two stations. Many concepts are possible for handling such a situation. The routers need to transfer packets and verify that they actually went through. The performance criterion – optimum exploitation of the channel's capacity in terms of transferred bits per second of the actual message – was characterized by means of "throughput and delay" diagrams. The aim is to transfer maximum bit rate at minimum delay. If many stations compete by offering much traffic, there will be queues, losses, retransmissions, and ensuing delays. It takes clever algorithms to optimize the exploitation of different channels for varying traffic demands.

That became critical for packet transmission through satellites. The travel time for a packet via a synchronous satellite some 36,000 km away is a limiting factor for achieving stability in packet transfer. It was a challenge to develop algorithms for optimum use of a shared satellite channel. Theory and experiments using three independent ground stations resulted in the CPODA algorithm for packet switching in shared satellite channels. Mario Gerla documented it in Kleinrock's group at UCLA.

Another transmission medium is cable, especially useful in local areas. Robert (Bob) Metcalfe, then at MIT, developed the Ethernet. It used an ingenious scheme of running a coaxial cable around the area. Each host used a device disrespectfully penetrating the shield of the cable at any point. The Ethernet name alludes to using an algorithm similar to that of a radio net. Cables have later been more courteously used one for each host, while active electronic circuits in a "hub" mimic the ether.

7.4 Theory and Experiments

All the work on development of optimized algorithms and protocols included comprehensive theoretical analysis. Kleinrock's group at UCLA, famous for its achievements in traffic and queuing theory, was productive in that area. Experimentation was made by generating and observing traffic. A large number of situations were thoroughly investigated. That is probably the single most important reason for the internet technology to have become so useful. The development of network technology took place in a laboratory – the Arpanet – used at the same time by resource sharing projects having actual "real life" needs. It generated practical traffic that one could observe. Moreover, it was a living reminder of practical needs and possibilities. In addition to the "natural" traffic, they used generators for artificial traffic. They could vary the offered traffic in controlled ways, including increases to saturation. For observation, the NCC could also insert instrumentation functions in IMPs that sent traffic measurements to the various researchers, automatically by e-mail. I could control and observe transatlantic packet experiments while sitting at my desk.

Satellite experiments were made using three ground stations and a free channel of the "Spade" system in the Intelsat IV satellite. Comsat and British Telecom were helpful in providing support at stations in Maryland and England. After some persuasion, the Norwegian Telecom Administration (NTA) provided free use of their shared Nordic ground station at Tanum, Bohuslän including housing of a "satellite IMP" and a line to Kjeller. Ole Petter Håkonsen of NTA was helpful in allowing that. Hence, we could investigate packet satellite transmission from late 1975.

8 Close Collaboration

The development was carried out in close collaboration between the groups. People discussed ideas, propositions, theoretical analysis, and experimental verifications at the three monthly meetings and by email in between. Everybody felt ownership of the problems and resulting solutions. Accordingly, experiments were carried out working together as practical needs suggested. Sometimes experiments required direct "hands on" simultaneous attention. As an example NDRE, UCL and BBN carried out experiments using speech codecs developed by MIT's Lincoln Lab. Several groups were active, leading up to a successful demo of three-site transatlantic internet speech conferencing. It comprised several carrier channels including packet satellite.

The group at BBN had major roles. They were responsible for everyday reliable operation of the net as well as extensions and modifications. They were helpful in setting up experiments and implementing revisions of network functions.

9 Over to Internet

In 1983, the internet technology had reached a stable state that allowed its use on the net. Parts of the Arpanet lingered on, but from about 1986, it was all "Internet." Commercial traffic was forbidden, but was later permitted from 1991. In 1993, the web was launched as a new service on the network and a really rapid growth began.

After the main network development was completed in the early 1980s, various other people in Norway (as elsewhere, of course) had heard of the Arpanet. Interest began to emerge at some other academic places. Spilling spent a "sabbatical year" at SRI from 1979 to 1980. He was helpful in making the network become available beyond NDRE in Norway in the 1980s. He began teaching classes in computers and communications. He joined NTA's research department and had actively taught in the area of computers and communications at UNIK, Kjeller. Aagesen and Hvinden have also worked in the area of computers and communications since then.

Some of us believed that the new communication forms such as email had potential as general public services. I suggested that the Norwegian Telecom Administration should develop public email. Technical director Ole Petter Håkonsen accepted my proposal and I joined the NTA in 1985. During the rest of the 1980s, that effort led to a limited success when company called "Telepost" began to provide electronic mail service. Telepost grew quite fast and issued email address books. Two difficulties are of historical interest. The international standardization processes by CCITT and others had now produced some new "recommendations," notably X.25 and X.400. We based our Telepost development on those. However, in reality they were less practical and could not compete with the internet standards. Secondly, the new "value added services" were not politically acceptable as monopolies. Hence, a radical new political environment for telecom began to emerge during the 1980s.

Significant networking efforts took place at universities in Oslo, Bergen, Trondheim, and Tromsø in the 1970s and 1980s, independently of the efforts at NDRE and the internet technical development. Considerable general knowledge accumulated, especially in connection with the Uninett project. The good knowledge base and enthusiastic people supporting the Uninett became interested in the internet from the mid-1980s and took a substantial role from then on, making use of the net and expanding it in Norway from the late 1980s. In the mid-1990s the phenomenon "internet" began to be mentioned in the media and becoming generally known.

10 Success

I have mentioned these examples of the development as representative of the environment in which it took place. Admirable teamwork in collaboration with enthusiastic persons allowed a Norwegian group the privilege to participate actively. I can best characterize it as "basic technical research." Research may be fertile if driven by a vision well defined as a goal and bravely pursued. That was prevailing feeling of the two or three dozen engineering researchers most central in the development of the internet's technology and the foundation of its success.

References

1. Kleinrock, L.: An Early History of the Internet. IEEE Communications Magazine, 26–36 (August 2010)
2. RFC Homepage, http://www.rfc-editor.org/
3. Cerf, V., Kahn, R.: A Protocol for Packet Network Intercommunication. IEEE Transactions on Communications (May 1974)

The Internet Development Process:
Observations and Reflections

Pål Spilling

University Graduate Center (UNIK), Kjeller, Norway
paal@unik.no

Abstract. Based on the experience of being part of the team that developed the internet, the author will look back and provide a history of the Norwegian participation. The author will attempt to answer a number of questions such as why was The Norwegian Defense Research Establishment (FFI) invited to participate in the development process, what did Norway contribute to in the project, and what did Norway benefit from its participation?

Keywords: ARPANET, DARPA, Ethernet, Internet, PRNET.

1 A Short Historical Résumé

The development of the internet went through two main phases. The first one laid the foundation for packet switching in a single network called ARPANET. The main idea behind the development of ARPANET was resource sharing [1]. At that time computers, software, and communication lines were very expensive, meaning that these resources had to be shared among as many users as possible. The development started at the end of 1968. The U.S. Defense Advanced Research Project Agency (DARPA) funded and directed it in a national project. It became operational in 1970; in a few years, it spanned the U.S. from west to east with one arm westward to Hawaii and one arm eastward to Kjeller, Norway, and then onwards to London.

The next phase, the "internet project," started in the latter half of 1974 [2]. The purpose of the project was to develop technologies to interconnect networks based on different communication principles, enabling end-to-end communications between computers connected to different networks. It was organized as an international project financed and directed by DARPA with Bob Kahn and later professor Vint Cerf as project leader. The internet project had twenty to thirty participants from academia and research institutions in the U.S., four from University College London (UCL), and two from FFI in Norway. Professor Vint Cerf at Stanford University, with his team of PhD students, developed the initial specifications of the TCP. In addition, Dag Belsnes from the University of Oslo had leave of absence and stayed nine months in Cerf's group from April 1974. His task was to analyze the internet protocol (TCP/IP) to find possible weaknesses in it. Three sites – Stanford University, BBN (Bolt, Beranek and Newman) in Boston, and University College in London (UCL) – were responsible for independent implementation of these specifications. Then, these independent implementations were thoroughly tested against one another. At the end

J. Impagliazzo, P. Lundin, and B. Wangler (Eds.): HiNC3, IFIP AICT 350, pp. 297–304, 2011.
© IFIP International Federation for Information Processing 2011

of 1979, the technology was mature enough to be proposed and subsequently accepted as a standard for the U.S. defense in the middle of 1980.

At the end of 1972, DARPA initiated a mobile network development, called the Packet Radio Network (PRNET) [3]. It was inspired by the Aloha project in Hawaii, based on the use of radio-based links, for terminal access to a set of central computer facilities in Honolulu, from various islands in the Hawaiian archipelago. In addition, DARPA had a desire to develop a packet-based satellite network [4].

These activities may in part be considered as incentives for DARPA to interconnect networks based on different technologies. In addition, Bob Metcalf at XEROX-PARC developed the local area network, called Ethernet, in 1973. SRI International conducted the first true internet demonstration in November 1977, involving ARPANET, SATNET, and PRNET.

2 Why was Norway Invited to Participate in the Internet Project?

The Nuclear-Test-Ban-Treaty and the close vicinity to Russia made Norway an attractive location for a seismic detection facility, to detect underground atomic test explosions. The Research Council of Norway, with funding support from DARPA, established NORSAR (Norwegian Seismic Array) in 1970 at Kjeller. A 2.4 kb/s line was installed from NORSAR to the Seismic Data Analysis Center (SDAC) in Washington DC. The line went via cable to the British satellite ground station at Goonhilly, and then by satellite to the U.S. When the Nordic satellite ground station at Tanum Sweden became operational in 1971, the NORSAR-SDAC line was relocated to go via Tanum.

DARPA had initially wanted to cooperate with Donald Davies, a research scientist at the National Physics Laboratory (NPL) in the UK. Davies had developed a packet-based network, enabling distributed terminals to connect to a set of host computers [5]. Because England just had applied for membership in EU, this forced NPL to focus on European research issues. This made it impossible for DARPA to link its ARPANET to the network at NPL and cooperate with Davies.

DARPA then turned to Norway, inviting the research department of the Norwegian Telecommunications Administration (Telenor-R&D) and FFI to participate in the development of satellite-based packet communications, believed to be of importance to the Norwegian shipping industry. In addition, the collaboration between DARPA, UCL, and FFI would make it more efficient and cheaper to link up both UCL and FFI to ARPANET, via the NORSAR – Tanum – SDAC line. Telenor showed little interest in participating, while the invitation was accepted by FFI. As a result, an ARPANET packet-switching node was installed at NORSAR in June of 1973. The ARPANET nodes, called Interface Message Processors (IMPs) were developed in two versions, one version provided attachment for four host computers, the other provided attachments for three hosts and sixty-three terminals, called IMP and TIP respectively. In September 1973, another node was installed at UCL and it was connected with a leased line to the node at NORSAR. FFI's participation in the internet project started in the beginning of 1975. Somewhat later, after several meetings between FFI and Telenor, Telenor was willing to provide, free of charge for the duration of the project, the uplink to the satellite and a 48 kb/s line from Kjeller to the satellite ground station at Tanum, Sweden.

3 The Main Norwegian Contributions

The internet project was actually the integration of several interconnected projects, and included the internet development project, the SATNET project, the packet radio project, and the packet speech project. In the period 1976 through 1979, FFI was heavily involved in the development of SATNET [6]. The purpose of the SATNET project was to explore the feasibility of operating a 64 kb/s channel in the INTELSAT system, multiplexed between a set of ground stations in a packet switched modus. Three ground stations were involved in the project, one at Etam in West Virginia on the U.S. East Coast, one at Goonhilly at the English West Coast, and the third one at the Nordic satellite ground station in Tanum, Sweden. To enable the packet-switched operation of the satellite channel, packet-switching nodes called Satellite-IMPs (SIMPs) were installed in the ground stations – interfacing with the satellite channel equipment. Each SIMP was then interconnected, via a leased line, with a gateway computer connected to the ARPANET. The gateway, a PDP-11/45, connected to the Tanum-SIMP was located at FFI.

The SATNET research program, directed by Bob Kahn, was performed as a joint effort between Linkabit Corporation in San Diego, University of California in Los Angeles (UCLA), Bolt Beranek and Newman (BBN) in Boston, Communications Satellite Corporation (COMSAT) in Gaithersburg, Maryland, University College London (UCL), and FFI in Norway. Linkabit had the project's technical leadership. BBN was responsible for the development of the SIMPs, including the various channel-access algorithms the participants wanted to test. The project participants met about four times a year, with the meeting location circulating among the participating institutions.

Yngvar Lundh, with Pål Spilling as the main work force, headed the Norwegian contingent. Finn-Arve Aagesen, later a professor at NTNU in Trondheim, stayed with the project for twelve months. He was responsible for performing simulation studies of the most promising channel access algorithm, the "Contention-based, Priority-Oriented Demand Access" algorithm (C-PODA). Pål Spilling developed management software on a FFI-based computer, to control artificial traffic generation in the SIMPs, and to fetch data collected in the SIMPs during measurements. Several access algorithms were studied experimentally, among others TDMA, Reservation-TDMA, and C-PODA [7]. Kleinrock's Network Measurements Group at UCLA also performed measurements and simulations.

FFI participated in Packet-Speech experiments performed in 1978–1979 in collaboration with among others MIT Lincoln Laboratories just outside Boston. The packet speech activity was part of the SATNET project. Lincoln Lab had developed a speech vocoder (voice coder and decoder), under contract with DARPA, providing a stream of 2.4 kb/s digitized speech. The vocoder was interfaced with the PDP-11/45 at FFI, with a similar arrangement at MIT Lincoln Lab, and later at UCL. During the speech experiments, the PDP-11/45 acted then not as gateways, but as speech host. In addition, the PDP-11/45 contained a conference management program, also developed by Lincoln Lab, which handed over the "floor" in a FI-FO queue manner, to the parties indicating their wishes to talk.

Pål Spilling performed a set of measurements to determine the profile of packet-speech traffic. The programming of the PDP-11/45, performed in connection with the experiments, is a good example of resource sharing. The computer was located next-door to Spilling's office. The programming tools were located in a machine at Information Sciences Institute (ISI) in Los Angeles. Using a terminal in his office, connected to NORSAR-TIP, Spilling could log on to the computer in Los Angeles, write the necessary modifications to the control program, and have it compiled and uploaded across the network into the PDP-11/45 next door to Spilling's office. A so-called cross-network debugger (X-NET), also in the TOPS-20 machine, facilitated the downloading. This enabled Spilling to debug the modified control program loaded into the PDP-11/45 [8], before it was used for the experiments.

FFI participated in several packet-speech demonstrations. At one of the regular project meetings, held at UCL, Yngvar Lundh could not attend in person. He therefore made use of the conference facility and thereby could participate in the meeting from Norway. The quality of the speech when compressed to 2.4 kb/s was noticeably impaired, but packet transmission through this early internet connection worked fine in real time.

In 1979–80, Pål Spilling stayed sixteen months with SRI International in Menlo Park California, working on the ARPA-funded Packet Radio Network (PRNET). There he made a proposal to improve the software architecture in the PR-nodes to have a better logical layering of the program structure [9]. He also performed extensive experiments on packet-speech performance with QoS-control [10], and suggested a "Busy Tone" method to overcome the "hidden terminal" problem in wireless communications [11].

4 Competition between Alternatives

Simultaneously with the growth of the ARPANET in the early 1970s, we saw the emergence of other competing communication concepts, like CYCLADE in France presented by Pouzin in 1973, the European Informatics Network (EIN) [12] presented in 1976, and the CCITT's Orange Books containing the X.25 standards published in 1977 [13]. In 1983, the International Standards activities presented the "Reference Model for Open Systems" and then in succession a set of layered communication protocols [14]. The dominating feature of X.25, and the ISO standards in general, was the virtual circuit principle, in contrast to the flexible connection-less datagram mode of operation in the ARPANET and later the internet. A virtual circuit in the packet switched arena is the equivalent of the end-to-end circuit establishment in the telephone network. The dominant part of the Norwegian research community, including NTA-R&D was for a long time convinced that packet communications had to be based on virtual circuits.

The management at FFI and NTA-R&D, and the Norwegian communication research community at large did not believe in the internet technology before the end of the 1980s and the beginning of the 1990s. In general, most communication experts believed that the TCP/IP suite of protocols eventually would be replaced by internationally agreed standards. Therefore, when we attempted to create interests for participation in the further development of this technology, the responses were negative.

5   International Communication Standards Activities

The national authorities and the academic communities believed strongly in international standards. It was relatively easy to obtain funding for participation in standards activities. As seen from the outside, the standards work was less committing than the intense work that went on in the DARPA community. Standards were worked out on paper within a study period of four years, and when ready accepted more or less without practical experience. Later, when standards were to be implemented and tested out, deficiencies were surely detected and the standards had to be revised, and then re-proposed as standard in the next study period. In contrast the DARPA research went via specifications, implementations, testing, modifications, more testing and refinements, and when mature and stable enough, finally adopted as standard. This included also a set of support functions like "name to address mapping," "service type to service-access-point mapping," and "IP address to MAC address mapping," to make the combined protocol layers work efficiently and user friendly.

When the ISO communication standards came out in the middle and latter half of the 1980s, after a substantial work effort, a set of standards had been defined for each layer in the reference model. These standards included many options. Before the standards could be implemented, one had to make use of workshops to agree on the options to use in practice. This took quite a while. It is worth mentioning that the options agreed upon, made the ISO standards, for all practical purposes, functionally equivalent to the internet protocols.

Agreed international standards were not openly available. They had to be purchased for a certain fee. In contrast, all internet protocol specifications and related documentations were freely available.

6   What Did Norway Benefit from Participating in the Development Project?

In the middle of 1982, Spilling was invited to move over to Telenor-R&D. He got the impression before he moved that they had interests in the internet technology. This turned out to be wrong. Only one of the research scientists there was interested in participating in the internet project. However, an advantage of being a member of the research staff at Telenor-R&D gave Spilling the opportunity to establish a small Norwegian internet. It was operational from 1983–84 through 1986–87, interconnecting informatics departments at the universities in Oslo, Bergen and Trondheim, and NTA-R&D. The network at NTA-R&D was interconnected, via the Nordic satellite ground station at Tanum and SATNET, with ARPANET in the U.S. Due to his participation in the internet project, Spilling was able to obtain the Berkeley version of UNIX. This UNIX version had the whole internet protocol suite integrated in the system. This implied that influential Norwegian academic research people obtained experience with UNIX and could make use of internet services and communicate with colleagues in the U.S. This demonstrated that the internet communications worked well and provided a set of reliable, effective, and attractive services.

UNINETT, the Norwegian academic communications network, was established in the first half of the 1980s. The goal was to interconnect the computer centers and the main research groups of the Norwegian universities. Due to political pressures, the network should be based on European supported connection-oriented standards.

In 1984–85, a major grant was given to the academic networks in the Nordic countries, with the goal to interconnect the national networks. Due to the very slow progress in the ISO standardization process, a multiprotocol transport service was developed and established, providing X.25, DECNET, IP, and possibly other alternatives. These interconnected networks, called NORDUNET, had its interconnection hub located in Stockholm. From there were leased lines to the Center for Mathematics and Computer Science (CWI) in Amsterdam, to CERN in Switzerland, and to the internet in USA (Princeton). This meant that all the academic networks in the Nordic countries got access to the internet. Gradually IP got a solid foothold, with the result that the other alternatives faded away. This was very fortunate when the SATNET project was terminated in 1989, because now all Norwegian IP-based traffic went via the hub in Stockholm.

The knowledge and experiences gained in participating in the DARPA projects led to the establishment of a computer communications research group and an early curriculum in computer communications at the Department of informatics at the Oslo University. Yngvar Lundh and Pål Spilling initiated this effort and gradually led to the establishment of similar activities at all universities in Norway.

7 Discussions and Conclusions

For a long time, there was a low interest in Europe, including Norway, regarding the internet technology. The opinion among communications research people in Norway was that the internet technology in a few years would be replaced by agreed international standards, like X.25 or ISO. For the Norwegian participation in the internet project, this resulted more or less in a one-man-show performed by Spilling. This of course greatly reduced the opportunity for a broader and more powerful contribution.

In December of 1973, half a year after NORSAR-TIP was installed, a Norwegian ARPANET committee was established to promote and coordinate possible Norwegian participations in DARPA activities. It consisted of members from the Research Council of Norway, and various research organizations. A condition for connecting to NORSAR-TIP, or making use of its terminal service, was that this should contribute to the furthering of the technology and be beneficial to both FFI and NDRE. The committee did not come up with any constructive proposals and dissolved itself in 1975.

When the internet technology, including its basic user services inherited from the ARPANET, was accepted as a standard for the American defense in 1981–82, it was about ten to fifteen years ahead of the marked. The network was mainly used by research people, and was not open to everyone. The first commercial web browser (Mosaic) was available in 1993. Approximately, at the same time the network was opened up for commercial use, resulting in an explosion in the desire to use the internet and its services.

When the internet protocol (IP) was developed and standardized, it contained in its header two 32-bit addresses, one for the destination address and one for the source address. This was thought to be more than sufficient. However, it turned out to be far too small in order to cope with the globalization of the internet. Nobody at that time had the faintest idea about the immense use of the internet today, in the public domain, in the business domain, and in the private sector.

The internet technology gradually convinced the whole world that this technology was efficient, reliable, and easy to administer, in contrast to the CCITT's X.25 concept and the ISO standards. American companies dominated the production of computers and their software, and they were delivered with the internet protocols integrated in their operating systems. They were unwilling to implement, say the ISO standards, unless customers (European companies) paid the costs. Moreover, nobody did that. This meant that very few people, globally speaking, were exposed to other alternatives.

There was a general antipathy in Europe, including Norway, regarding defense matters, and especially everything that was connected with the U.S. defense. This contributed to the low interest, in Norway and in Europe as a whole, for the internet technology.

The Nordic countries have the highest percentage of internet users in the world. This is in part due to the early exposure to this technology, first in the academic world and later in the public sector. NTA (Telenor) was among the first telecom operators in Europe, around 1994–95, to be convinced to offer internet access to customers. This is certainly due to the close exposure to this technology over a long period at NTA-R&D.

References

1. Roberts, L., Wessler, B.D.: Computer Network Development to Achieve Resource Sharing. In: Spring AFIPS Conf. (1970)
2. Cerf, V., Kahn, R.E.: A Protocol for Packet Network Interconnection. IEEE Trans. Comm. Tech. (1974)
3. Kahn, R.E., Gronemeyer, S., Burchfiel, J., Kunzelman, R.: Advances in Packet Radio Technology. Proc. IEEE (November 1978)
4. Jacobs, I., Hoversten, E.: General Purpose Packet Satellite Network. In: Proc. IEEE Spec. Issue on Packet Communications Network (November 1978)
5. Davies, D.W.: Communication Networks to Serve Rapid Response Computers. In: IFIP Congress (August 1968)
6. Spilling, P., Lundh, Y.: Features of the Internet History, The Norwegian Contribution to the Development. Telektronikk 3, 113 (2004)
7. Spilling, P., Lundh, Y., Aagesen, F.A.: Final Report on the Packet Satellite Program. Internal Report E-290, FFI-E (1978)
8. Spilling, P., McElwain, Forgie J.W.: Packet Speech and Network Performance. Internal Report E-295, FFI-E (1979)
9. Spilling, P.: Low-Cost Packet Radio Protocol Architecture and Functions – Preliminary Requirements. Technical Note 1080-150-1, SRI International (October 1980)
10. Spilling, P., Craighill, E.: Digital Voice Communications in the Packet Radio Network. In: ICC 1980, Seattle (1980)

11. Spilling, P., Tobagi, F.: Activity Signaling and Improved Acknowledgements in Packet Radio Systems. Packet Radio Technical Note 283, SRI International (1980)
12. Porcet, F., Repton, C.S.: The EIN Communication Subnet Principles and Practice. In: Proc. of ICCC, Toronto (1976)
13. Series X Recommendations. The Orange Book, ITU, Geneva (1977)
14. Basic Reference Model. ISO 7498-1 (1983)

From the ceremony at Stanford University in 2005, celebrating thirty years since the start of the internet development. We see from left to right: Pål Spilling, President John Hennessy of Stanford University, and Vinton Cerf. There are thirty-two names on the bronze plaque, among which Dag Belsnes, Yngvar Lundh, and Pål Spilling are from Norway.

The Use of Interpretation for Data Acquisition and Control: Its Impact on Software Development and Project Management

Otto Vinter

Otto Vinter, Software Engineering Mentor, Sthensvej 2F
2630 Taastrup, Denmark
vinter@ottovinter.dk

Abstract. For over a decade, I and a number of other software engineers introduced, developed, improved, and expanded the principle of interpretation for data acquisition and control task descriptions; initially a simple description and execution tool to assist plant engineers, but in the end a software development framework for modeling, managing, and executing large, complex projects in this domain.

Keywords: Data acquisition, interpretation, modeling, project management, process control, software engineering.

1 Introduction

For the first data acquisition and control system in 1969 for the Danish power plant Vestkraft Blok2 (Fig. 1, Appendix 1, [1, 2]), we simply wanted to create a tool (simple process language) that would make it easier and more flexible for plant engineers to define their measurements and calculations, and thus dispense with the limited and predetermined ("hard coded") operations on process data based on flags in data tables.

In 1978, at the completion of the process control system for the Copenhagen Mail Sorting Center, the principle of using interpretation on a data-model of the system (Fig. 3, Appendix 2, [3, 4]) had evolved into a software engineering framework that not only influenced the system architecture, but all phases of software development from detailed requirements, design, coding, testing, and release staging, to project management, estimation, planning, scheduling, configuration management, quality procedures, and documentation.

2 The Early Data Acquisition Systems

At the beginning of the 1960s, the use of computers started to spread from pure mathematical applications to the process control industry. However, both buyers and suppliers were very cautious about letting the computer take full control of the

J. Impagliazzo, P. Lundin, and B. Wangler (Eds.): HiNC3, IFIP AICT 350, pp. 305–314, 2011.

Fig. 1. The power plants at Vestkraft. Blok2 is the tower on the left. See Appendix 1 for details.

industrial processes. The acquisition of analog signals and their conversion to binary numbers was not very well known, and disturbances from the electrically noisy environment of high-power machinery could severely affect the low-level signals at maximum values of 24 mA and 10 V. Consequently, the first computer systems were only used for logging measurement data; performing simple conversions and calculations, and presenting the operators of the plant with alarms and reports.

These data loggers were programmed like the hard-wired electronic instruments they intended to supplement. The early programs were sequential monolithic structures that scanned the data acquisition channels and stored them in memory resident tables after conversion and simple alarm checks. Other programs would later read these tables, perform calculations, and generate reports. Around the mid-1960s, the first multiprogramming monitors appeared which allowed programs to execute in parallel, for example, data acquisition programs could execute in parallel with report printing programs. However, the structure of the programs did not change very much; they still retained their basic monolithic form. Now there were just more of them, executing in parallel.

3 The Original Idea of a Dedicated Process Control Language

In these early systems, in order to describe the processing that would take place on the data, a number of flags (bits) were kept for the variables of each measurement, along with its status and value. They defined what conversion routine to use, whether alarm limits should be checked, or what other calculations should be performed. When a data processing program scanned the data tables, it examined the flags individually (in a specific sequence) and called the relevant routine (basically a huge case structure).

Therefore, the plant engineer who designed the actual processing had the difficult task of defining the data tables and processing flags; and he had to do it in the computer's native machine code. Due to the limited number of predefined flags and the fixed sequence in which they were scanned, it was often difficult to describe the processing that was desired.

We wanted to improve this situation by developing a data acquisition and control language closer to the concepts of a plant engineer, to gain flexibility by replacing the flags and fixed processing sequence and allowing the engineer to select the processing from a range of language commands. The introduction of such a process language was not new. Other dedicated data acquisition and control languages were being developed for similar systems at that time. However, the trend was to compile such languages into (monolithic) executable programs.

4   The Introduction of the Interpretation Principle

We could not allow ourselves the luxury of compiler for the language, because our development system was the same as the executing system, and therefore had severe limitations regarding memory, backing store, and peripherals. Furthermore, at that time, compiled code was known to lack the necessary performance for real-time applications. We therefore decided to define the language in a macro-like format which could be easily translated into command data-structures.

The command data-structures were made self-contained, for example, the references to the software routines to execute the macro-command and the parameters were stored together. Since each routine was designed for the specific purpose of handling its parameters, the length of each command data-structure could also be calculated and stored in the structure.

As we did not have a file handling system either, we had to organize the layout of command data-structures and data variables on the backing store ourselves. At specific places, the translator would insert special commands to load the next segment of command data-structures from backing store to memory, and commands to swap segments of variables that had been updated with others which would be needed next.

At predefined intervals, a simple program (interpreter) executing in one of the multiprogramming processes scanned the model containing the command data-structures. It would sub-routine jump to the routine referenced in the first command data-structure. When that routine returned, the interpreter added the stored length of the command data-structure (parameters) to point to the beginning of the next command data-structure, call that routine, and so on, until an end-of-data-structure command was encountered. In this way, data processing was no longer contained in a monolithic program; it had turned into an extremely flexible set of small dedicated routines in a data-model that was interpreted rather than executed.

Several routines (macro-language commands) would normally have to be called to accomplish one complete processing of a plant variable (Fig. 2), but the type of checks, conversions, calculations, and the order in which they were performed, was no longer limited or predefined by the real-time processing program.

```
; Create new value for TFd and add to sum in TFdS10
/802                        ; TFd, steam temperature for HT
  :IWR,    K=802            ; Initialize working registers (variable 802)
  :LSV,    V802             ; Load state and value for TFd (variable 802)
  :ECAV,   R1T25            ; Evaluation control of analog value (range, terminal)
    L1                      ; skip conversion and checks if compensated by operator
    L2                      ; Skip conversion in case of a measurement failure
  :CRE,    K=150            ; Convert resistance element (parameter value)
  :ILCMM, K=-200,Pih=6000   ; Instrument limit control (min, max)
2:TPC,    V802              ; Test for failures and update status (TFd)
  :TCCV,   V219             ; If compensation use value for TOH (variable 219)
1:PCM,    K=-50, Pah=5650   ; Plant status control (hysteresis, maximum)
  :SSV,    V802             ; Store new state and value (TFd)
  :SUM,    V3301            ; add to TFdS10 (variable 3301)
```

Fig. 2. Processing commands for a temperature variable at Vestkraft Blok2

5   New Opportunities Because of the Interpretation Principle

Having one central data-model, which is interpreted rather than executed, opened up for a number of advantages in the development and customization of data acquisition and control systems. New language commands could be easily defined; a small dedicated component (routine and parameter description) designed, coded and added to the macro-translator. Nothing had to be changed in the on-line system's processes (programs); the data-model was simply replaced.

In addition, defects were easier to locate because they were confined to the new component (or the macro-translator), as there was no direct communication (e.g. calls) between routines, only through the data values and their status.

6   Testing in a Simulated Environment

The principle of interpretation allowed us to test new components in a simulated environment (e.g. off-line) using only those parts of the data-model that were needed for testing the component. Dedicated test drivers and stubs (simple test commands included in the macro-language) were inserted in the test data-model to check whether the new routine produced the correct (expected) results under different conditions of input data. For each call, the drivers and stubs stepped through a list of test inputs (test cases).

A logging facility was inserted (another test component in the data-model) that could print the data values and status used by the component (routine), along with the result data and new status it generated (stored). From this, it was only a small step to include expected results in the test lists and let the logging facility mark any incorrect results in the print. Automated regression testing in a simulated environment had now been introduced as a natural thing.

Even late in the 1970s, software programmers were scarce and we usually had to teach them everything: assembler language, linkers, loaders, bootstrapping, running the system, and, of course, good practices of basic software engineering (it was not called that at the time). Using the principle of interpretation and simulated test environments made introducing rather primitively trained developers on a project much easier and safer. They were able to find and correct their errors early during unit tests in the coding phase, and quickly became seasoned developers on-the-job.

Testing in a simulated environment also meant that we were able to implement a defined process for promoting partially completed systems through several levels of environments (unit testing, system testing, and production) complete with automatic regression test data and test procedures.

7 Effects on the Software Architecture

The principle of interpretation of a data-model influenced all aspects of our software development. The most immediate effect was, of course, on the software architecture; based as it was on a comprehensive model of the industrial plant, and an easily adaptable and flexible set of software components.

All data values and their status were fetched, updated, and stored in the model. Furthermore, all connections and communication between the modeled physical components of the plant took place through their representations in the model. In addition, all other types of handling and control were also designed into the model and represented as "abstract" components, for example, conversions, averages, accumulations, calculations, progress timing, storage management, plant sub-systems (groups), as well as "physical" output devices and set-point controls.

Alarms, reports, logs, and other output data about the operation of the plant were generated from data in the model and communicated via a number of message buffer queues to dedicated reporting processes running in parallel to the acquisition and control process, so that processing and output tasks could perform independently of each other [5].

Input to and output from the message buffer queues were protected by semaphores, and buffer overruns were handled so they did not influence the operation of the acquisition and control process. The principle of interpretation was also used to describe the layout, contents, and generation of reports.

8 Effects on Project Management

Project planning, scheduling, and management were impacted by the data-model architecture. Due to the limited complexity of each component, it was easy to estimate how long it would take to implement it, and actual data from previously developed components quickly created a solid basis for new estimates. Each component could be developed and tested almost independently of other components, so it was relatively easy to assign components to the available developers in the project plan and perform follow-up on development progress.

However, this did not eliminate the need for the overall design of the components system, which always involved senior developers. Sometimes it turned out to be a bottle-neck and generate overruns on its estimates.

We finally managed to deliver our projects almost on time and budget, and with very few defects in operation.

9   The Applications of the Interpretation Principle

The interpretation principle and data acquisition and control language commands from Vestkraft Blok2 were reused and improved for another power plant (Nordkraft Sektion4) and adapted for a sugar production plant (Saxkjøbing Sukkerfabrik).

However, the comprehensive software engineering framework, described above, was not realized until the Copenhagen Mail Sorting Center (Fig. 3). In this system, all physical components of the plant were modeled as components in the data-model.

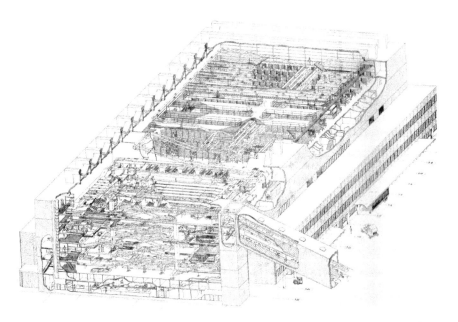

Fig. 3. The Copenhagen Mail Sorting Center. See Appendix 2 for details of the modeling.

10   Why the Principle Did Not Catch On

Firstly, the advent of new computer and software technology in the late 1970s and early 1980s meant a complete change in data acquisition and control systems from comprehensive centralized systems to a network of small dedicated minicomputers, microprocessors (PLCs), which required less complex software systems.

Secondly, the response time of a system interpreting a data-model is never faster than the time it takes to scan the data-model. This works for most industrial processes which only change slowly. However, direct control loops (PID) and other fast reactions to input must be handled by separate processes executing in parallel. As prices for computers went down, and hard-wired instrumentation went up, the trend was to use computers to engage faster and more directly with the control of the industrial plant.

11   A Final Twist in the Tale

In the late 1980s, I was product manager for a new line of automatic test equipment at Brüel & Kjær. Our goal was to develop a set of virtual (e.g. software-based) measuring instruments. In addition to those, we wanted to develop a comprehensive test and measurement environment, where engineers could develop their own test and measurement projects, combining the instruments of their choice with calculations, sequencing, loops, and controls. Numerical results and graphs were to be combined into reports that showed whether the product being tested has passed or failed.

We had many heated discussions on how to design this test and measurement environment. There was a clear divide between the experienced test and measurement engineers and the brilliant software engineers, some just out of the university. For my part, I was impressed with the advances in computer speed and compiler capabilities; it seemed that object-oriented development was becoming an important principle for the future. Therefore, we decided to base the test and measurement environment on the compilation of our measurement components rather than the interpretation.

We struggled for several years to make this design work, but did not succeed. In the end, the project was cancelled. A couple of years later, a U.S. company (National Instruments) launched a, since then, rather successful test and measurement environment based on the interpretation of simple measurement, calculation and control components, which could be combined graphically (2D) in an easy drag, drop, and connect fashion. These simple test and measurement components resemble the language commands we had used in the early days for the industrial plants, albeit in a more modern, colorful, and graphic way.

The lack of speed in interpretation, which we had feared so much, was not a problem for test and measurement engineers, partly due to the increased speed of computers and partly because many test and measurement processes change at a slow rate.

In hindsight, this example shows that the interpretation principle can still be the right way to solve a complex problem, given the right conditions. And, by the way, Microsoft Excel is actually another example of the successful use of the interpretation principle.

Acknowledgments. I wish to thank Peter Kraft, who was project manager on the Vestkraft project, where the initial idea of using the interpretation principle for data acquisition and control systems was born. Furthermore, I wish to thank Bent Bagger and Ebbe Sommerlund, who were my primary supports on the Copenhagen Mail Sorting Center project, where the full impact of the principle was realized. Also, my gratitude goes to many people for their assistance in recovering our common past from our combined rusty memories and dusty archives.

References

1. Kraft, P., Vinter, O.: Rapport over proceskontrolsystemets opbygning hos I/S Vestkraft Esbjerg. Regnecentralen (1970)
2. Nedergaard, N.: Procesregnemaskinen på Vestkraft. Elektroteknikeren, 66. årgang nr. 4 (1970) (see also nr. 23 for a description of the whole plant)
3. Prag, P.: Datamatstyring af transport- og sorteringsanlæg i Centralpostbygningen i København, Rådgivning og projektering. In: NordDATA 1977 Proceedings (1977)
4. Vinter, O.: Datamatstyring af transport- og sorteringsanlæg i Centralpostbygningen i København, Transportdatamatstyringen. In: NordDATA 1977 Proceedings (1977)
5. Kraft, P., Mossin, E.: Datastrømme, elementer til kommunikation i et proceskontrolsystem. In: NordDATA 1972 Proceedings (1972)

Appendix 1: The Vestkraft Blok2 Power Plant

The power plant was built in 1969 (Fig. 1, Fig. 4). It had an electric capacity of 250 MW, plus a heating capacity of 160 Gcal/h that covered the needs of Esbjerg city. The turbo-group was from BBC and the boiler unit from Babcock & Wilcox. All of the plant controls were handled by conventional electronic equipment. For the complete supervision of the plant, a digital computer system from A/S Regnecentralen was installed [1, 2].

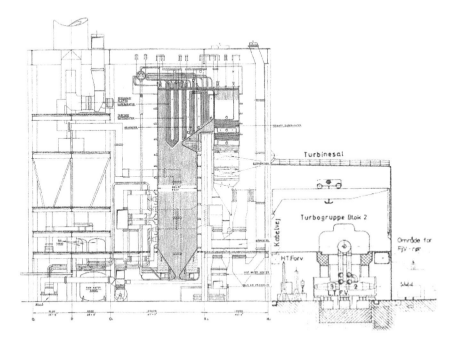

Fig. 4. A view into Vestkraft Blok2. A combination of two original drawings, matched to fit the correct proportions of the plant. The boiler section with its heating supply units to the left and the turbine section to the right.

Every ten seconds, all bearing and coil temperatures from major motors, pumps, and generators were measured and analyzed by the computer. A special supervision of boiler drum, oil burners and air pre-heaters was also carried out; approximately 250 analog measurements.

Every minute, another 250 analog values were measured and analyzed; among others, 170 super-heater pipe temperatures. The latter were particularly important because close supervision of these could increase maintenance intervals and prevent breakdowns. All relevant measurements were accumulated over time. Performance and load calculations were carried out and used to improve the management and performance of the plant.

The RC4000 computer configuration was: 32kB memory, 512kB drum storage, 512 analog inputs, 216 digital sense inputs, 48 digital interrupt inputs (for counting), and 48 digital outputs.

Appendix 2: Modeling of the Copenhagen Mail Sorting Center

The software system for the Copenhagen Mail Sorting Center (Fig. 3, [3, 4]) was developed from 1974–1978. The center was designed to handle the 130,000 parcels and 3 million letters that arrived and departed each day on trucks or trains following a strict schedule. The main contractor was Boy Transportmateriel A/S.

The center comprised approximately one thousand conveyor belts which, if started or stopped at the same time (especially when loaded with mail bags or parcels), would have a severe impact on the power lines supplying the building. Therefore, each conveyor belt was modeled as a component in the data-model of the software system, with two flags indicating its ability to receive and deliver mail respectively.

When mail is delivered at the receiving end of a belt, its predecessor component turns its able-to-deliver true, and the belt component then issues a start command (bit) to its belt's motor. While the motor is running, the component calculates when mail will reach the other end of the belt, at which point it raises its able-to-deliver flag. This is detected by the succeeding component, which then starts. If the succeeding component is not able to receive mail (its able-to-receive flag is false), the belt motor will be commanded to stop.

This also happens when mail is no longer delivered from the belt's predecessor (its able-to-deliver flag turns false). The component will allow the belt to continue to run until a calculation determines that the belt is empty. Then the belt motor is commanded to stop and the component's ability-to-deliver flag is set to false. The effect propagates down the line of conveyor belt components (Fig. 5).

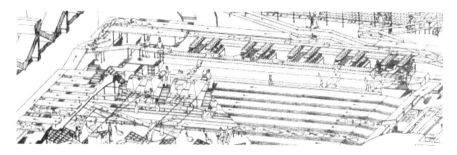

Fig. 5. Details of conveyor belt connections

When a belt is intended for storage, the predecessor component is a photo cell component at the start of the belt, rather than another belt component. The photo cell, however, is modeled with similar flags, and the storage belt only moves as long as the photo cell component has its able-to-deliver flag true, for example, while mail is blocking the view of the photo cell. In this way, mail is compacted on the belt. When mail reaches the other end of the storage belt (usually controlled by a photo cell component at the end of the belt now signaling able-to-receive false), the storage belt will indicate able-to-receive false to its predecessor (the photo cell component at the start of the belt). This not-able-to-receive flag is reflected to its predecessor (the component delivering mail to the storage belt). A storage management component will then choose another parallel storage belt to receive further mail. When emptying a storage belt, the belt component will act as a normal transporting belt, but it will still keep the able-to-receive flag false, so that no new mail will be received until the belt is completely empty.

Thus, the use of these "able-to" flags can control the progress of mail throughout the mail center, irrespective of the type of equipment modeled, and only keep those conveyor belts running that are in use. The "able-to" flags are the only way in which the modeled components communicate, and the flags are examined at each cycle through the data-model.

The center was controlled by five duplex hot stand-by computer systems for each section of the mail sorting process, a number of microprocessors, and a supervisory computer for the operators connected via asynchronous communication lines. The control computers were Control Data (CDC) Cyber 18-17 with 32–88kB memory, a memory-to-memory high-speed bus, and no backing stores.

Computer Systems Performance Engineering in Trondheim: Origins and Development, 1970–1995

Peter H. Hughes

Department of Computer and Information Science,
NTNU, Trondheim, Norway
peterh@idi.ntnu.no

Abstract. Developments covered by this review include early experimental work on Univac mainframes, a contribution to early debate regarding the application of queue-network analysis, the development of bespoke benchmarking techniques, one of the first interactive load generators, and modelling tools for system sizing and for simulation. We show how addressing problems that arose from practical needs has benefited both university teaching, and industrial practice. The period covers the transition of performance *evaluation* as a set of ad hoc modelling and measurement techniques to performance *engineering*, which aspires to be an integral part of systems design and development. Cross-fertilization and collaboration with developments internationally form an important part of the activities reported.

Keywords: Benchmarking, model-support environments, performance engineering, queue-network analysis, simulation, system sizing.

1 Introduction

The computer center at SINTEF in Trondheim, later known as RUNIT, was a pioneer in the practice and teaching of computer systems performance evaluation. Today, NTNU is one of a very few teaching establishments in the world with computer systems performance engineering as an established part of the undergraduate curriculum [1]. In this paper, we trace some of the activities and developments, which contributed to this long journey.

In scope, the paper deals with those applications of performance evaluation related to computer systems capacity management and information systems development. Other application domains, such as computational software optimization, hardware design, and the design of telecommunications systems are not considered.

Over the period of twenty-five years, some eight researchers were involved, augmented by a number of master-level students. At any one time, the core research group numbered between two and five. The treatment is broadly chronological, with some parallel threads for clarity of exposition. In the final section, we consider the larger context in which these activities took place and make some general observations.

J. Impagliazzo, P. Lundin, and B. Wangler (Eds.): HiNC3, IFIP AICT 350, pp. 315–322, 2011.

2   The Mainframe Era: Measurement, Modelling and Experimentation

The work began with a practical need, mainly to understand capacity aspects of the expensive UNIVAC 1100 series mainframes introduced to Scandinavia in the late 1960s and early 1970s. The performance of mainframe computers and their operating systems was at the time something of a mystery. They were extremely complex engines with opaque scheduling policies and a range of adjustable parameters, the tuning of which was a dark art. Even senior technical personnel at Univac had difficulty with the more esoteric areas of the EXEC8 operating system.

A performance evaluation group came in existence at Trondheim in 1971. The purpose was to guide decisions on tuning, upgrade and future investment. The approach was apparently simple: select a representative set of programs and data and use this "benchmark" to measure the capacity of alternative system configurations. The predictive accuracy of this approach depended on the benchmark being sufficiently representative of the user workload and on the measurements obtained being sufficiently comparable. Neither requirement was easy to fulfill. This early experimental work turned out to have a wider impact in the following three directions.

(i) The Art of Benchmarking
Firstly, we developed techniques whereby benchmark tests became the basis of reproducible experiments, in which both workload and system state were carefully controlled. This was a complex challenge, involving an understanding of a large, disparate set of user programs and data, analysis of system log-files, and special instrumentation of the operating system [2]. We developed the idea of a benchmark beyond its origin as an arbitrary reference point, to become a model of an actual user workload. The reward for this rather laborious investment was that we were able to offer a customized benchmarking service to other computer centers with procurement projects. Internationally, we were invited to contribute to a state-of-the-art report for the industry on computer measurement [3].

(ii) Models of Multiprogramming
The second contribution was less direct, but at least as significant. Certain results due to Geir Moe [4] gained international recognition as a rare experimental validation of the new theory of queue-network analysis.

A purely measurement-based approach to performance prediction is limited by the range of configurations, which are available for testing and by the cost of such an exercise. It was natural to consider a modelling approach to reduce the number of measurements required. Modelling of computer systems was however in its infancy.

Moe had developed a simulation model for multiprogramming based on simple probabilistic assumptions. This model displayed some intriguing asymptotic behaviour. About this time, at a conference of the British Computer Society, Conway Berners-Lee, from the UK computer firm ICL, provided a queuing network interpretation of multiprogramming systems [5]. Armed with Berners-Lee's analysis, Moe was able to explain the behaviour of his simulation model and show that it was consistent with a queuing network model. Moreover, results from the model were consistent with results obtained in the benchmark experiments [6].

It was both difficult and expensive to do controlled experiments with large mainframes. It turned out that our painstaking benchmark tests constituted one of the very few measurement experiments worldwide that provided evidence for the queue-theoretic interpretation. At the time there was much controversy regarding the validity of queue-network models. Real systems do not have exponential service times and other mathematically convenient Markov properties, and it was not clear until years later, how far queue-theoretic predictions could be relied upon.

(iii) Synthetic Programs
It quickly became apparent that modelling and measurement together could provide powerful insights. Performance measurement, in combination with queuing theory, simulation and statistics, was helping to demystify mainframe computers and to untangle the complexity of computer system behaviour. We investigated some key issues surrounding the role of so-called synthetic programs in benchmarks. Was it legitimate to model computer workloads with artificial programs and data? Which properties should we preserve? [7, 8] How might a set of programs be statistically representative of a workload? [9]

3 The Birth of an Academic Subject

At RUNIT in 1972 a teaching unit was formed which became the new *Institutt for Databehandling* (IDB) at *Norges Tekniske Høgskole* (NTH), led by professor Arne Sølvberg. After various reorganizations, these two entities were subsumed in larger ones, leading eventually to the present structure: the *Institutt for Datateknikk og Informasjonsvitenskap* (IDI) at NTNU.

Following an initiative by Sølvberg, we packaged and distilled some of our practical experience for teaching purposes [10]. The new subject came to be entitled *Systemering III*, a sequel to the systems design courses *Systemering I* and *II*. This association anticipated by more than a decade the link between performance evaluation and design now implicit in terms such as *software performance engineering* [20]. The course content was gradually extended to both practice and theory by contact with industry and the wider academic community.

Globally, research in the mathematical analysis of queuing networks proceeded in parallel with the practical side of performance engineering, as is still the case today. Although mathematical textbooks appeared, there was little to support the more holistic engineering approach we wished to develop. In 1978, the situation was transformed by the appearance of Domenico Ferrari's comprehensive and scholarly work, *Computer Systems Performance Evaluation* [12]. This text became the foundation of the subject for years to come.

In the same year, the author received an invitation to present our work on benchmarking techniques as part of a summer school in Urbino, Italy, led by Ferrari. The gathering attracted many leading researchers in the field. The widening of horizons provided by this experience was of long-term benefit to the course in Trondheim.

In the late 1970s, the theory of operational analysis was developed [13]. Based on directly measurable quantities, this provided a simpler approach for analyzing multi-programming systems. Our earlier simulation results also supported an operational interpretation. Indeed, some of the invariance rules derived in [6] are equivalent to operational laws. Alternative theories were passionately debated for some years, until the protagonists of the several mathematical camps learned to accommodate one another [14].

In 1984, a second landmark textbook appeared in which the new queue-network solution technique known as "Mean Value Analysis," was expressed in operational form [15]. This relieved our syllabus of an overload of queuing theory.

4 Interactive Computing: Mini-Computers, Hardware Monitors and the RUNIT Interactor

By the late 1970s, the importance of interactive computing was increasing and the minicomputer revolution was undermining the position of mainframe computing centers. In a changing economic climate, the performance group at RUNIT became a cost center, which had to finance itself from industrial consultancy and research grants. The group made a successful research proposal in collaboration with the Norwegian computer manufacturer Norsk Data A/S to develop one of the world's earliest interactive load-generators: the RUNIT Interactor [16]. This device could monitor and learn the keystrokes of a human operator, scale up and emulate a controlled load, and measure the resultant response times.

The Interactor was used in numerous benchmarking studies in the state sector under Norway's *Statens rationaliseringsdirektorat*. It subsequently became one of Norsk Data's principal tools for remote stress testing over telephone links (e.g., from Oslo to Stockholm). The Interactor attracted commercial interest from Denmark and the UK. In today's climate, it would undoubtedly have been a prime candidate for commercial exploitation.

The Interactor stimulated the development of other experimental techniques. It was frequently used together with a performance monitor, which could be software- or hardware-based depending on the target system. This required intimate acquaintance with either the workings of the target operating system, or the circuitry of the hardware "back-plane" to which measurement probes were to be attached.

A second important technique was the development of executable workload models. These consisted of two parts: scripts, which emulated user-to-computer interactions, and target programs whose execution was invoked by the scripts. The target programs could consist of real programs and data. However, this approach limited our range of investigation. We therefore developed a prototyping system known as PILOT to study the performance of CODASYL database systems before they became operational. PILOT generated synthetic workloads with appropriately randomized keys and artificial data for the target database schema [17].

5 Simulation Modelling and Model-Driven Design

At IDI a course in discrete-event simulation had been introduced, based on the Simula language. This course was transformed by the introduction of an elegant Simula class known as DEMOS (Discrete Event Modelling on Simula) [18]. DEMOS was developed at the University of Bradford in the UK by Graham Birtwistle, who had worked on the Simula project in Oslo. It was the outcome of practical experience with applying simulation to industrial problems. The original SIMULATION context of the Simula compiler was low-level and complicated to use. DEMOS exploited the powerful extendibility features of Simula by providing a small set of high-level synchronization constructs. These constructs lend themselves readily to a graphical representation known as "activity diagrams." In Trondheim, we enhanced the DEMOS activity diagrams to develop an accessible undergraduate teaching method. This enabled us to focus more on the core techniques of discrete-event simulation, and less on the details of the simulation language.

The Process Interaction Tool (PIT) developed in the UK later adopted the enhanced activity diagrams [19]. PIT was a unique tool, which supported the construction of simulation models via a graphical interface [20]. It has been used in industry for models ranging from hardware design, to telecommunications, to real-time financial settlement. The appeal of the DEMOS constructs is demonstrated in their adoption by simulation tools in other object-oriented languages such as C++ and Java. A modern example is DESMO-J from the University of Hamburg.

6 Sizing, Configuration and Deployment

Computer systems have a coarse-grained modularity arising from separately developed software and hardware units configured together for particular applications. The choices made regarding dimensioning and deployment of such modules directly affect performance. The industrial experience with this problem in the 1970s in the UK and Norway caused us to develop a semi-formal quantitative framework known as "Structure and performance Specification" (Sp). The first description of Sp appeared in 1983 [21]. Collaborative projects established with Norsk Data and subsequently with ICL in the UK [22] led to a succession of prototype Sp tools.

Sp has exhibited a long staying power. It proved capable of modelling successive generations of computer and software architecture such as enterprise systems and mobile platforms; these conceptions did not exist at its inception. Recent work [23] suggests that Sp offers a more powerful alternative to the "deployment diagram" currently offered by the Unified Modelling Language (UML). Moreover, we have found that Sp provides a vital part of the conceptual foundation needed for the teaching of Performance Engineering [1].

7 Graphical Workstations and the Integrated Modelling Support Environment

The 1980s saw the emergence of powerful graphical workstations with potential to construct and solve detailed models. This gave an enormous stimulus to the development of new performance tools based on various modelling paradigms. In parallel with this development, the new generation of object-oriented databases was emerging.

At IDI, a separate line of research was investigating model-driven design in the context of information systems. Most work in this area was conceptual and functional rather than quantitative. It proved feasible in combination with Sp to address some of the quantitative issues [24]. Several doctoral dissertations investigated related topics [25–27].

In 1989–1992, the various strands of research and development described above came together in a European Research project under the Esprit 2 program. This was IMSE, an Integrated Modelling Support Environment, which involved nine industrial and academic partners from five European countries [28]. Trondheim was an active partner [29]. The conceptual basis of IMSE was developed via a UK predecessor project known as SIMMER [22]. Sp and PIT tools were integrated with queue-network, petri-net, simulation, and workload analysis tools in an object-based system having a common meta-model and a common graphic support system. An experimenter tool was built that exploited the common framework provided by the meta-model. IMSE was a pioneering environment that had a strong influence on the development of performance engineering across Europe, still traceable today.

8 Conclusions

This condensed case history provides a basis for the following observations.

A. It contains concrete demonstrations of some familiar principles such as

    i. practical needs leading theoretical advance,
    ii. application of the classical scientific method,
    iii. synergy of research and teaching,
    iv. vital role of the international community.

B. It demonstrates the importance of taking a long-term view. No one could have predicted in 1970 how the field of performance engineering would develop or the challenges it faces today. Many thought that the subject would not survive in the face of Moore's Law. Yet Moore's Law is now becoming obsolete and the field is well established.

C. Mobility of individuals between industry and academia was extremely valuable, perhaps even essential, to the development of this field in Norway. Cross-fertilization with the United Kingdom, with its larger industrial base, had mutual benefits. The SINTEF model of industry-related research seems to this observer to have been particularly advantageous.

D. With a great deal of effort and some delay, the evolution of the teaching material reflected step-changes in the state of the art. Course content improved markedly with the arrival of landmark texts in 1978, 1979, and 1984. Our thoughts could make bigger strides and we created more room for applications. The need to keep up with constantly changing technology balanced these gains. The syllabi we developed were not contained in any one text. Although methodology and mathematics changed infrequently, the applications that gave meaning for successive generations of students changed much faster.

E. The context in which the early work took place was quite different from today. At the beginning of the period, computing itself received scarce recognition in

Norway as an academic subject. Although we had benefited from RUNIT's good economy, obtaining funds from research committees was extremely difficult and uncertain. We were indebted to the good offices of a few far-sighted individuals and to the personal enthusiasm and commitment of many team members and students.

F. We could have done better at exploiting our research and development results. This would have required more mentoring early on and more financial investment at crucial times. We can now better appreciate such needs. Nonetheless, we had the privilege to work in a very supportive environment.

This review over a quarter-century ends in 1995. We conclude that performance engineering has not only been a valuable practical subject but also a strong stimulus to research. The dynamic interplay of measurement and modelling continues to throw up challenging questions about the systems we create as computer systems engineers.

Feedback from alumni and industrial contacts indicates that inclusion of performance engineering in the education of computing engineers in Trondheim is greatly valued. Nonetheless, projects and systems everywhere often fall short in performance, sometimes with disastrous consequences. As system complexity rises, high-level software engineering becomes increasingly remote from its physical effects. Clearly, there is more education and more research to be done.

References

1. Hughes, P.H.: Lecture Notes in Performance Engineering IDI, NTNU (1995, 2010)
2. Hughes, P.H.: Developing a reliable benchmark for performance evaluation. In: Proceedings, NordDATA 1972 Conference, Helsinki, Finska Dataförbundet rf, vol. 2, pp. 1259–1284 (1972)
3. Hughes, P.H.: Towards Precise Benchmarks. Infotech International Limited State of the Art Report 18 Computer Systems Measurement (1974); ISBN 8553-9170-7
4. Moe, G.: Computer Performance Analysis using Simple Queuing Models. Lic.techn. thesis, NTH (1973)
5. Berners-Lee, C.M.: Three analytical models of batch processing systems. In: Proceedings British Computer Society Conference 1972, pp. 43–52 (1972)
6. Hughes, P.H., Moe, G.: A structural approach to computer performance analysis. In: AFIPS Joint Computer Conferences, Proceedings of the National Computer Conference, New York, pp. 109–120 (1973)
7. Barber, E.O., Asphjell, A., Dispen, A.: Benchmark construction. ACM SIGMETRICS Performance Evaluation Review 4(4) (1975); ISSN:0163-5999
8. Hughes, P.H.: Benchmarks, Workloads and System Dynamics. In: Invited paper, Infotech International Limited, Conference on Performance Modelling and Prediction, London (1977); ISBN 8553-9410-2
9. Barber, E.O.: A question of balance. D.Ing dissertation, Division of Computer Science, University of Trondheim (1981)
10. Asphjell, A.: Ytelsesvurdering av datamaskinsystemer. Teaching Notes, RUNIT/ NTH (1976)
11. Smith, C.U.: Performance Engineering of Software Systems. SEI Series in Software Engineering. Addison-Wesley, Reading (1990); ISBN 0-201-53769-9

12. Ferrari, D.: Computer Systems Performance Evaluation. Prentice-Hall, Englewood Cliffs (1978); ISBN 0-13-165126-9
13. Denning, P.J., Buzen, J.P.: The operational analysis of queuing network models. ACM Computing Surveys 10(3) (1978)
14. Denning, P.J.: A tale of two islands (a fable about operational analysis). ACM SIGMETRICS Performance Evaluation Review 9(4) (1980)
15. Lazowska, E.D., Zahorjan, J., Scott Graham, G., Sevcik, K.C.: Quantitative System Performance. Prentice Hall, Englewood Cliffs (1984); ISBN 0-13-746975-6
16. Hughes, P.H., Dispen, A., et al.: Applications of the RUNIT Interactor. In: Proceedings, NordDATA 1981 Conference, Copenhagen, Dansk Databehandlingsforening, vol. 3, pp. 286–291 (1981)
17. Hughes, P.H.: PILOT – A Synthetic Prototype Generator for Database Applications. In: Potier, D. (ed.) Proc. International Conference on Modelling Techniques and Tools for Performance Analysis, North Holland, Paris (1984)
18. Birtwistle, G.M.: Discrete Event Modelling on Simula. MacMillan, NYC (1979); ISBN 0-333-23881-8
19. Pooley, R.J., Hughes, P.H.: Towards a standard for hierarchical process oriented discrete event simulation diagrams part II: the suggested approach to flat models. Transactions, Society for Computer Simulation 8(1), 21–31 (1991)
20. Barber, E.O., Hughes, P.H.: Evolution of the Process Interaction Tool. In: Proceedings, Association of SIMULA Users Conference, Pilsner, Czechoslovakia (1990)
21. Hughes, P.H.: A structural analysis of information processing systems (with application to the sizing problem). Inst. for Databehandling NTH. (1983)
22. Hughes, P.H.: Design of a Performance Modelling Environment. In Proceedings, Association of SIMULA Users Conference, Stockholm (1986)
23. Hughes, P.H., Løvstad, J.S.: A generic model for quantifiable software deployment. In: Proceedings International Conference on Software Engineering Advances ICSEA 2007. IEEE, Los Alamitos (2007), doi:10.1109/ICSEA.2007.4; ISBN 0-7695-2937-2
24. Opdahl, A.L.: Sensitivity Analysis of Combined Software and Hardware Performance Models: Open Queuing Networks. Performance Evaluation Journal 22(1) (1995)
25. Opdahl, A.L.: Performance Engineering during Information System Development. Dr.Ing dissertation, IDT, NTH Trondheim (1992)
26. Vetland, V.: Measurement-based Composite Computational Work Modelling of Software. Dr.Ing dissertation. IDT, NTH Trondheim (1993)
27. Brataas, G.: Performance engineering method for workflow systems: an integrated view of human and computerised work processes. Dr.Ing. dissertation, IDI, NTNU (1996)
28. Pooley, R.J.: The Integrated Modelling Support Environment. In: Balbo, Serazzi (eds.) Proc. 5th Int. Conf. On Modelling Techniques and Tools for Computer Performance Evaluation, Turin, pp. 1–16. North Holland, Amsterdam (1991); ISBN 0 444 88989 2
29. Brataas, G., Opdahl, A.L., Vetland, V., Sølvberg, A.: Final Evaluation of the IMSE. Technical Report, IMSE project deliverable D6.6-2 SINTEF/University of Trondheim (1991)

Provisioning of Highly Reliable Real-Time Systems

Harold (Bud) Lawson[1] and Kurt-Lennart Lundbäck[2]

[1] Lawson Konsult AB, Albavägen 25, 181 33 Lidingö, Sweden
bud@lawson.se
[2] Arcticus Systems, Box 530, 175 26 Järfälla, Sweden
kurt.lundback@arcticus-systems.com

Abstract. The development and deployment of highly reliable real-time systems is an important technical as well as societal concern. Many systems are dependent upon timely and correction function; for example in key automotive components, aircraft components, military equipment, and so on. Based upon some early architectural developments in Automatic Train Control, collaboration has led to further development of the concepts and products for highly reliable real time systems. Arcticus Systems has provided products based upon the concepts for several Swedish system suppliers in various branches. In this paper, the history of these developments is described, the consequences of a missed opportunity to take a leading role in the automotive branch are discussed and potential future directions are presented.

Keywords: Automatic train control, real time systems, safety-critical, vehicle components and systems.

1 Introduction

In this paper, experiences with the provisioning of highly reliable real-time systems are described from the perspective of two small actors; namely Arcticus Systems AB and Lawson Konsult AB. During the 1970s, Harold Lawson was an architect for the software system of the world's first microprocessor based Automatic Train Control (ATC) system delivered to the Swedish Railways (Statens Järnvägar, SJ). The concepts and principles upon which this design was based proved to be a highly reliable and extremely small robust real-time solution. In 1990, a project was started by Mecel AB to explore how to develop a distributed real-time architecture for vehicles. Nutek supported this project and it brought together several companies and university researchers. It was at this point that co-operation between Lawson Konsult AB and Arcticus Systems AB began. Since then Arcticus Systems have continued to refine the concepts and have delivered their real time operating system Rubus OS to amongst others, Haldex, Volvo Construction Equipment and Hägglunds. Further, Arcitcus Systems has had a continual relationship to research work in this area with Mälardalen University.

J. Impagliazzo, P. Lundin, and B. Wangler (Eds.): HiNC3, IFIP AICT 350, pp. 323–330, 2011.

2 Automatic Train Control

The experiences with the Automatic Train Control (ATC) system have been described in two publications [1] and [2] the latter of which was presented as a keynote address at HINC2. Only a brief summary is provided here. In 1975, the consultant services of Harold Lawson were contracted by Standard Radio to assist Sivert Wallin, chief designer, in the conceptualization of the ATC architecture. Following a review of the work done to date on the software, Harold Lawson and Sivert Wallin re-examined the fundamental requirements of the ATC function and developed the problem oriented architectural concepts that has successfully provided product stability as well as a sound basis for further development under the entire life cycle of the ATC on-board system product. The following three core concepts were developed and have been driving factors during the product life cycle.

Time Driven: The major conceptual aspect of the design is the treatment of the system as being continuous in time as opposed to being discrete event driven. This was motivated given the fact that a 250 ms resolution (dT) of the state of the train in respect to its environment was determined to be sufficient to maintain stability. It became clear that the simplest approach was to execute all relevant processes (procedures) simply during this period.

Software Circuits: As the result of the time driven concept, a cyclic approach became the basis for the solution where short well-defined software procedures performing required transformations behave like timed circuits. The naming of this concept was developed later when the concepts of the architecture were applied in the research project described later in this paper.

Black-Board Memory: In order for Software Circuits to have access to key status information, variables are retained in a black-board where both reading and writing are permitted.

This simplification of concepts led to the fact that the processors only needed to be interrupted by two events. One interrupt to keep track of time (1 ms) and one interrupt when information from transponders (located on the track) is available. The 250 ms dT is more than adequate to perform all processing. Adding more structure to the problem, for example, via the use of an event driven operating system approach would have had negative consequences in terms of complexity, cost as well as reliability, testability and risk thus affecting safety.

The "circuit like" structure of software led to highly simplified coding of processes (procedures). While it would have been useful to deploy a higher-level language in the solution, it was deemed unnecessary due to the low volume of code that was expected. Experience has indicated that this was a reasonable decision at that time. On the other hand, it was decided to comment the code in a higher-level language. In earlier versions of the product, the Motorola MPL (a PL/I derivative) was employed. In later versions, a more Pascal like annotation has been consistently employed. In system tests, MPL, respectively Pascal versions have been executed in parallel with the execution of the assembly language version in order to achieve system verification.

The Standard Radio developed ATC system has been functioning in most all locomotives in Sweden since the early 1980s. Ansaldo of Italy now owns this on-board system. It has been implemented in a few new versions reflecting special needs that developed including the introduction of the X2000 high speed trains as well as the need to run trains over the Öresund Bridge to Copenhagen. The modifications continued to apply the concepts that were earlier developed. We can conclude that there has never been a train accident that could be attributed to faults in this control system. Ansaldo utilized the concepts from this original solution in a product based upon the Ada programming language that was provisioned to and is still operating on New Jersey Transit in the USA.

3 Early Arcticus Products

Arcticus Systems originated in 1985 and its first product called O'Tool was influenced of the rendezvous concept of the Ada programming language. At that time, it was a state of the art solution for Real Time Operating System (RTOS). Several languages had evolved during the 1970s including Pascal and C, followed by Ada that provided for real time task management. Another language that was modified in order to provide RTOS capabilities was EriPascal (developed by Ericsson).

O'Tool became a viable RTOS solution for microcontrollers implemented in the C programming language. This development transpired in close cooperation with IAR Systems in Uppsala that was a pioneer in applying C in microcontrollers and where worlds leading at that time. An increasing number of microcontroller applications (embedded systems) where developed and the market grow quickly in the late 1980s and early 1990s.

Many system developers where not accustomed to utilizing an RTOS and experienced problems in respect to excessive overhead and especially with fault diagnosis. RTOS technology in general and even O'Tool provided event driven functionality. An external event provided the trigger to initiate a task/function that after processing decided about reaction.

Event driven systems have the difficulty of not being able to guarantee response time and behavior, especially in the case where multiple events happen in close proximity or in a sequence that was not planned for in the system solution. We where often involved in customer contact to resolve faults in their applications. Thus, our experience from customers convinced us that reliable event driven systems are not achievable via event driven solutions.

The need for university education in respect to RTOS systems grew during the late 1980s and O'Tool, due to its small size became popular in courses at the KTH Mechatronic institution as well as at Mälardalens University.

IAR Systems marketed O'Tool world wide as a complement to their C compiler. Thus, we had several customers from various countries.

4 Collaboration Leading to New Concepts

Via an agreement that Arcticus had with Mecel in 1990–91, we participated in an EU research project Prometheus that was a supported by amongst others, Renault. This resulted in a preliminary implementation of an RTOS concept called VDX (Vehicle Dynamic Executive) based upon communication on a CAN/VAN-bus. VDX was a traditional event driven RTOS that had the problems that were discussed earlier.

Based upon Mecel's and our own experience and analysis and even based upon the VDX project it was concluded that embedded real time systems should not be based upon an event driven approach. Such systems tend to be complex and difficult to guarantee their behavior. They concluded that the RTOS contributed significantly to the systems complexity.

Mecel together with a number of small companies including Lawson Konsult and Arcticus Systems as well as researchers from Chalmers, SICS and Uppsala University initiated a research project for constructing of distributed safety-critical vehicle system as a part of the Nutek Swedish Road Traffic Informatics program. The project was called the Vehicle Internal Architecture (VIA) and it transpired between 1992 and 1995. The project budget was about twenty million SEK.

4.1 Vehicle Internal Architecture Project

Based upon experiences from the Automatic Train Control system as well as research performed at the Vienna Technical University under the direction of Professor Herman Kopetz, the project group defined an architecture based upon time synchronized communication and execution (Time Triggered execution model) in a distributed environment. The project incorporated the fundamental program architecture for the construction of safety-critical systems and related methodology. Even hardware construction for safety-critical systems was considered in the scope of the project.

Now, fifteen years later we can see that the VIA architecture is very actual and that the vehicle industry has begun to implement according to the concepts that were developed earlier. Within a few years, distributed safety-critical functions will be put into mass production.

In addition to Time Triggered execution, Event Driven execution was incorporated in the VIA architecture for parts of the application that only had a soft real time demand.

4.2 Red and Blue

Our colleague Professor Jan Torin from Chalmers was drawing a picture to illustrate the difference between the Time Triggered and Event Driven functions. He happened to use Red and Blue markers and so these two categories became differentiated via color. This differentiation has continued and been extended with a green color in the Rubus OS. Rubus OS provide three categories of run-time services:

Green Run-Time Services. External event triggered execution (interrupts).

Red Run-Time Services. Time triggered execution, mainly to be used for functions that have hard real-time requirements, i.e. meeting their deadlines is critical to the operation.

Blue Run-Time Services. Internal event triggered execution, to be used mainly for functions that have soft real-time requirements, i.e. meeting their deadlines is not critical to the operation.

4.3 Software Circuits

The implementation of small short procedures performing transformations that was integral in the ATC application carried over into the implementation of the Time Triggered functions defined in the VIA project and in the Rubus OS.

Due to their timed nature and the transformation properties, they behave much like timed hardware functions and thus in the VIA project where given the name Software Circuits.

4.4 Distributed Control

An important aspect of the VIA architecture was the introduction of distributed control; that is, no coordinating centralized function synchronized activities. Synchronization occurs due to the time functions provided by the communication bus. There are now several standards and products based upon this concept such as FlexRay, TTCAN, and TTP. The results of the VIA project where reported in two international publications [3] and [4].

5 New Arcticus Products

The positive experiences with ATC as well as the VIA project has led to the development of new products. Thus, our history has influenced further developments.

5.1 Haldex Four Wheel Drive Coupling Device

Haldex made an agreement in 1996 with Volkswagen to provide a new type of product called the Limited Slip Coupling Device for four-wheel drive vehicles. Since Haldex AB did not have the required resources and competence to construct the hardware and software of this control system, and at the suggestion of project leader Anders Cedeberg, Arcticus AB was contracted to provide the software platform based upon Rubus OS. The role for Arcticus was to construct a platform for the selected 16-bit microprocessor from Infineon with drive routines for the I/O units that where incorporated. Arcticus also developed a simulator for the functional testing in a PC environment.

Arcticus and Lawson Konsult participated in the discussions with Volkswagen (the acquirer of the product) concerning architecture and implementation that contributed to the fact that Haldex was selected to supply the base platform. Originally, Volkswagen's position was that Haldex would only deliver the mechanical parts and hardware electronics.

Because Arcticus and Lawson Konsult had a central role, we convinced Haldex to develop a set of processes based upon the ISO/IEC 12207 standard on software life cycle processes as well as a Safety Case indicating that the product and its development were verifiable.

Haldex having a long history of developing mechanical products and was not accustomed to this new type of product development. This resulted in the fact that budgeted development costs and product planning were not realistic and caused problems for the project and Haldex corporate leaders due to delays. After a few years though Haldex could demonstrate the functioning coupling device and eventually received confidence from their customer (Volkswagen) to also take responsibility for the control functions that were implemented in software.

Haldex have now gone through five generations of the coupling device for Volkswagen and have many other automotive manufacturers as customers. Rubus OS with associated development environment are still utilized and continue to function in an excellent manner.

5.2 Model Based Development for Volvo Construction Equipment

Volvo Construction Equipment, like Haldex, had limited resources in the mid 1990s for the construction of software based control systems. Volvo CE selected to base their software development upon Rubus OS and to build a software platform based upon the Rubus concept. Arcticus responsibility was to assist in the construction of a platform for the selected 16-bit microprocessor from Infineon as well as the associated I/O units.

Approximately 1997 Volvo CE decided to promote a component based development model that was developed by researchers at Mälardalans University and successively has been further improved by Arcticus as the Rubus Component Model. To support this development a language and compiler was developed that automatically generates an execution schema for the Red Kernel. Both the component model and the related tools were further developed into a second and third generation release around 2000 and 2008, respectively.

The generation of products containing ECU (Electronic Control Units) developed by Volvo CE since 1997 have been based upon the Rubus component model and its development environment. The environment provides a graphical representation with data flow between software circuit input and output ports.

The unique property of the Rubus component model and related development tools is that non-functional requirements like deadline controller and automatic schema generation including the program execution disturbance caused by interrupts are considered in the analysis.

Volvo CE has via the Rubus Component Model and tools been able to exploit nearly 100 percent of the theoretic capacity of the processor that is utilized.

Arcticus has participated in a research project at Mälardalens University and Volvo Construction Equipment aimed at refining the component model that was developed for Volvo to even include Event Driven programs in the model. The project was called MultEx and was performed between 2005 and 2008. Arcticus has now after fifteen years of model based development in industrial environments a combined structural modeling with integration of function modeling, for example, SIMLINK and MathLab, plus a unique execution model.

5.3 Further Development of the Component Model for Hägglunds

The military system provider Hägglunds decided in 1996 to base its real time software architecture upon the Rubus OS. In 2007, Hägglunds decided to work towards model-based development based upon our MultEx project and this resulted in the use of Rubus Component Model, version 3. Thus, the tool was restructured for supporting Rubus CM3 as well as to handle many of the problems from our ten years of experience with Volvo CE. The first version of the tool and model was delivered to Hägglunds in 2008 and has been further refined in cooperation with Hägglunds. This forms the basis for their new platform for military equipment based upon Rubus products.

Together with Hägglunds we now participate in a project that is aimed at supporting the analysis of communication between network nodes called EEMDEF (2009–2012) sponsored by KK-Stiftelsen (the Knowledge Foundation). This work will lead to the next generation of component model; namely Rubus Component Model 4.

This vision of EEMDEF is to develop a framework that allows modeling and analysis of execution requirements (e.g. response times, deadlines, jitter, memory consumption and other metrics relevant for control systems) on an abstraction level that is close to the functional specification (i.e. abstracting away implementation details such as physical and logical allocation of functionality).

5.4 Industry-Academic Research

Arcticus continuously has cooperated with state of the art research programs at Mälardalen University. This has provided a strong input for the development of Arcticus products and also provided the research project with practical relevant industrial requirements. For further information about this collaboration, consult; http://www.mrtc.mdh.se/projects/multex/ and
http://www.mrtc.mdh.se/projects/eemdef/.

6 A Missed Opportunity

Interestingly that more than fifteen years after the VIA architecture project the architectural features developed then are currently in focus. Some reflections concerning this development are as follows.

- Development proceeds slowly with a time lag of perhaps more than 10 years from research to practice for embedded system development companies. It is a question of developer competence and corporate leadership, all the way from initial education to the time that they progress to decision-making positions in a development project.

- It takes time to develop commercial products that achieve customer acceptance (10+ years). This concept is especially for a small company that provides a new type of product that is unproven and does not follow existing standards.

- Combating the "Not Invented Here" (NIH) phenomenon.

- Sweden is a leading nation in the area of real-time research and we can retain this competence lead and amplify it. If we do not this, many Swedish inventions will die out or move to other countries. We seem to be poor at commercializing and supporting the excellent research and development efforts.

- Large companies like standards. In many cases, standards are sought that do not provide technical advantages. If we follow the standard, we cannot go wrong and take no chances even if there is a better technical alternative.

7 Conclusion

Think if the VIA project had been pushed forward in Sweden. The opportunity existed in the mid 1990s. We see that European standards today are largely based upon the German auto industry such as OSEK and Autosar for real-time systems that are built upon the traditional event-driven solution. Sweden could have had this leading role.

References

1. Lawson, H., Wallin, S., Bryntse, B., Friman, B.: Twenty Years of Safe Train Control in Sweden. In: Proceedings of the International Symposium and Workshop on Systems Engineering of Computer Based Systems, Washington, DC (April 2001)
2. Lawson, H.: Provisioning of safe train control in nordic countries. In: Impagliazzo, J., Järvi, T., Paju, P. (eds.) HiNC2. IFIP AICT, vol. 303, pp. 13–28. Springer, Heidelberg (2009)
3. Hansson, H., Lawson, H., Strömberg, M., Larsson, S.: BASEMENT: A Distributed Real-Time Architecture for Vehicle Applications. In: Proceedings of the IEEE Real-Time Applications Symposium, Chicago, IL (May 1995); Also appearing in Real Time Systems. The International Journal of Time-Critical Computing Systems 11(3) (1996)
4. Hansson, H., Lawson, H., Bridal, O., Ericsson, C., Larsson, S., Lön, H., Strömberg, M.: BASEMENT: An Architecture and Methodology for Distributed Automotive Real-Time Systems. IEEE Transactions on Computers 46(9) (1996)

Information Modeling: Forty Years of Friendship

Stig Berild[1] and Eva Lindencrona[2]

[1] Santa Anna IT Research Institute AB, 581 83 Linköping, Sweden
stig.berild@gmail.com
[2] Vinnova, 101 58 Stockholm, Sweden
eva.lindencrona@vinnova.se

Abstract. Information systems design was the theme for a research group at Stockholm University under the leadership of Professor Janis Bubenko, Jr. The research group was called Computer Aided Design of Information Systems (CADIS). The CADIS group developed modeling methods and, at the same time, computer support for the modeling of information systems. The methods were stepwise defined based on early practical applications. Formal modeling languages were defined. The computer support tools turned out to be powerful and grew into a full Database Management System (DBMS), which was further developed into a commercial product (CS5). The CS5 DBMS was based on binary relations. The CADIS approach to modeling and to the DBMS was too early to be commercially successful; however, the basic ideas behind the modeling and the DBMS have survived several generations of "new" approaches to modeling as well as to the DBMS.

Keywords: Binary relations, CASE tools, conceptual modeling, CS5, DBMS, information modeling.

1 Introduction

Forty years ago a group of enthusiasts started a research project at the Royal Institute of Technology, Stockholm, under the leadership of Professor Janis Bubenko, Jr. The aim of the research was to develop a new, computer-aided methodology for information systems design. The research project was named Computer Aided Design of Information Systems (CADIS). The methodology aimed to be more flexible, user oriented, and more efficient than the earlier "water-fall" kind of methodologies. Furthermore, what was new by then, the methodology should be computer supported. The computer support – the tool – should be capable of storing the specifications of an information system during its different stages of refinement. These types of tools were later called Computer-Aided Software Engineering (CASE) tools. For the methodology, it was recognized at a very early stage that there was a need for specifications expressed as information and data structures. In addition, it was discovered early on that such specifications needed a CASE tool capable of storing complex structures. A database solution was necessary. Well-defined information and data structuring languages were also needed. This required a powerful but at the same time easily managed DBMS. No such DBMS was available at that time. It was time to step on the information modeling bandwagon.

J. Impagliazzo, P. Lundin, and B. Wangler (Eds.): HiNC3, IFIP AICT 350, pp. 331–338, 2011.

2   The 1970s

2.1   General Overview

Binary modeling languages had their main period in the 1970s. Langefors [1] was a pioneer with the "elementary message" concept; Bubenko, Jr. [2], Abrial [3], Senko [4] and many others were involved. With Chen [5] came an interest shift towards different types of Entity-Relationship (ER) Modeling Languages. A number of different types of ER modeling languages were defined, mainly as part of some academic research projects. Each language obviously had to include some unique construct – useful or not.

Starting another thread, Codd 1970 wrote [6]. The Relational Model (RM) was born as well as the third normal form. Soon a number of normal forms were defined in research environments. They had their short time "in fame" and then faded away. Usefulness did not seem to be an interesting aspect.

ER-model advocates and RM advocates had their disputes. ER models were mainly aimed at designing conceptual models based on user requirements during the design phase of a database application. Relational schemas were supposed to express the logical structure within the database. Furthermore, the graphical language could hardly be trusted, as it lacked formal definition, or at least an operational language to manage the models.

In 1975, the ANSI/X3/SPARC Study group on database management systems [7] presented its report that introduced a context and a three-layer architecture for database systems. The context was called the "universe of discourse" and the three layers were the external, the conceptual and the internal models. The ANSI/SPARC architectures clarified the need of different models for different purposes, and its terminology and definitions became "de facto" standards among researchers and database developers.

2.2   For Us

Work on methodology for information systems design continued within the CADIS group [8]. A number of different modeling approaches were presented during these years. We used the ANSI/SPARC architecture to compare and identify the usability of different modeling approaches. An analysis of different modeling approaches was presented early in a PhD dissertation [9].

Inspired by the work of Langefors and Bubenko, Jr. as well as by binary languages in general, a CASE tool was developed and implemented. The CASE tool was in itself a DBMS where data elements were expressed and stored as triplets or basic statements (<subject>, <predicate>, <object>). The use of triplets is certainly not unique today – but it was at the time. It was soon discovered that this DBMS could not only easily be used for storing design specifications, but also as a general DBMS. Such a DBMS based on triplets turned out to be extremely flexible and efficient.

During the following years, information systems design became primarily database design and the research on methodology came to focus on formal specification languages. At the same time, the research and development of a CASE tool turned out to be focused on a general DBMS system including features such as query language, integrated programming language, multi-user environment, transaction management, and so forth rather than emphasizing computer aided solutions. Results were presented at international conferences such as [10] and [11], as well as in a published book [12].

The different versions of the DBMS were called Cadis System 1-5 or the shorter CS1-CS5. The design was a binary model, the schema and implementation was the same binary model. In addition, the integrated programming language was using triplets for storage and retrieval. It represented ease and flexibility in a nutshell. This nutshell also made way for a new approach in systems design; prototype development or experimental programming, as it also came to be known. They could design and implement information systems with full functionality in fractions of the time usually needed using conventional methods. This in turn made it possible to test things, try different functionalities, get a feeling for different user interfaces, which gave the real users a possibility to be directly involved in the system development.

3 The 1980s

3.1 General Overview

The interest for CASE tools and information modeling did not take off as anticipated. Some were using these models merely for conceptual modeling, focusing on the concepts used in an organization, rather than as an input to schema design and implementation. Others really used, for example, ER modeling as part of the design of a database application. However, the bridge from an information model to an RM model was not that easy when it came to real and complex models. The automatic generation of RM schemas was tried, but implementations often needed adjustments from third normal forms down to second normal forms and the like, for performance and other reasons. Keeping the information model and the bridge accurate and updated during the life of the application was not in sight. Modifications were made directly in the RM schema, no wonder CASE tools and information modeling did not take off. Well, to be fair, they did in the Nordic countries. Notwithstanding, this pushed formal specifications, relational DBMS and schemas to the forefront. The relational approach ruled the 1980s.

3.2 For Us

For the CADIS group, research took two directions. On the methodology and modeling side, focus was now on practical tests and the development of formal modeling languages, while on the DBMS side the prototype was developed into a commercial product.

In 1984, Janis Bubenko, Jr. established the Swedish Institute for Systems Development (SISU). Much of the CADIS research on methodology, modeling, and formal specification languages was now carried out at SISU. The SISU was open to cooperation between research and industry, which led to the practical testing of modeling as a design method for systems- and database applications. Actually, some of the very first practical modeling tests were carried out by SISU. The first SISU publication – SISU Analysis Nr 1 [13] – was completely devoted to modeling and to reports on its practical use. At the same time, formal specification languages were developed. Languages named C-mol and D-mol were developed and presented in reports and papers [11]. Such languages were improved stepwise based on requirements experienced during the practical tests [14]. In addition, the first Swedish textbook on conceptual modeling was published and used in university courses [15].

On the DBMS side, we stood by our binary models. The DBMS was commercialized under the name of DREAM. A number of applications were implemented using DREAM as the supporting database management system. The binary model approach proved to be useful for simple as well as very complex database applications. Complexity in data structures was not a problem, neither were large volumes of data. We were all excited and proud of having developed such a powerful, yet easy to use, database management system. However, according to the commonly held view at the time, databases should be relational. The fact that we were a small company that represented a product not in line with the commonly held truth of the time did not make things easier for us. Consequently, the development efforts had to be reduced after a while. Market pressure towards mainstream DBMS based on the relational model put the creative part of our DREAM to an end.

4   The 1990s

4.1   General Overview

Object-oriented (OO) programming languages became increasingly popular in the 1990s. They represented an approach where data and behavior were integrated into objects. In fact, OO languages were not new at all, although most of the "OO-evangelists" had probably never heard of Simula. Nevertheless, Java soon became popular. Consequently, everything should be an object, even things stored in databases. The objects were just using the database as a place of rest during their dynamic lives. Database and program logic was naturally integrated. Suddenly, all entities in databases should include behavior, even if the information in the database represented a snapshot view of some reality of interest.

For lack of better ideas, the behavior often took the form of "store," "delete," "check value" of the entities in the database, which did not really relate to the behavior of some entity but to the DBMS working with these entities. So what ...? Every well-renowned market research company predicted that object-oriented DBMS would replace Relational DataBase Management System (RDBMS) in a few years. Well, things did not turn out that way – for obvious reasons. Information about some reality and work on that information is different things. This, however, does not mean that object databases are useless. They are excellent for certain types of applications, for instance, those where the application is a reality in its own right, instead of representing some external Universe of Discourse (UoD).

Object-oriented applications needed support from CASE tools, which consequently had to support some object modeling language. Now things started to become interesting, or rather, funny. A fight between proponents of several different design methods and their modeling languages began. Each method had its front figure or so-called "guru." It seemed as if they had not noticed the ER modeling language discussions a decade earlier. Consequently, they represented nothing new except for the inclusion of a simple description of "behavior" in each object type. Each one of these languages was argued to be somewhat better than all the others. Seen from a distance, this fight was nothing more than a strange and somewhat ridiculous episode in the era of information modeling.

Eventually, Object Management Group (OMG) understood that continuing these fights was counterproductive to the future of modeling. OMG took the initiative to melt the different languages down to just one, a language that was later (1996) standardized as the Unified Modeling Language (UML). With UML came a renewed interest in CASE tools. Furthermore, Extendable Mark-up Language (XML) and the increasing demand for information exchange between systems brought in a slight interest in semantics. A tag was attached to each information element, which had to reflect some meaning and understanding of the information element. While a tag did not replace the need for information modeling, it helped to sow an interest in modeling.

4.2 For Us

From 1990 and onwards, a smaller group continued to support DREAM. Applications continued to be supported and new ones were developed. They still exist and work well even today. About 1990, STANLI, a Swedish Standards Institute organization, drew up an interesting approach for information exchange of geographic oriented information, which should be communicated through a central hub. This hub was meant to be responsible for the delivery of information from one party to another. In this role, the hub was also supposed to have the mandate to manage and specify what types of information should be allowed to be communicated. The specification was meant to be in the form of one or several information models. Not only did this model restrict the allowed information, it also represented a uniform semantic view of this information. The hub was supposed to play the role of a "market place" for geographically oriented information. This approach represented new thinking with its focus on interoperability and – even more interesting – interoperability in combination with conceptual models as "rule setters." In fact, the importance of conceptual models for this purpose is still today not fully understood. The semantics is merely being specified using Document Type Definitions (DOD) – and later XML Schema Definition (XSD). Nevertheless, a DOD or XSD schema is not the same as a conceptual model – they complement each other. The conceptual model gives a neutral view of some UoD of interest for exchanging information, while an XML schema defines the content of a specific type of exchange (message type). Regardless, SISU was asked to specify a modeling language for information models. In 1991, the first version of the STANLI modeling language was introduced. It was based on all the experience collected over a number of years within SISU. The STANLI language was based on a binary view of information and included a number of facilities for expressing semantics. At the time, it had more expressiveness, by far, than most existing languages. This language came to be used extensively, both in connection with geographic information and for modeling in general. To a large extent, the language came to be used for purely conceptual modeling, focusing on the meaning of concepts rather than on designing structures for relational schemas. The STANLI language is still frequently used in Sweden. Conceptual modeling was at the forefront!

5 The 2000 Decennium

5.1 General Overview

The message type definition capability in XML was initially at a very basic level. This changed with the XSD standard from Worldwide Web Consortium (W3C) in 2001. In many ways, XSD had the same expressive power as ordinary modeling languages, although it was intended to express structure and some message type semantics. Nevertheless, the interest for semantics was on the rise.

With the web came the need to specify information about resources on the web (photos, videos, documents, sound). For some strange reason, this type of information came to be called metadata. Some used "metadata" to refer to information models, while others thought of metadata as data describing data elements in databases. Furthermore, no one seemed to have heard of the ISO standard 10027 "Information Resource Dictionary System framework" where different layers of information are clearly defined.

Anyway, the XSD metadata was believed to be so special that it needed its own modeling language. The first version of Resource Description Framework (RDF) became a recommendation of W3C in 1999. Surprisingly enough, RDF was nothing more than triples, i.e., based on a simple binary model. There is nothing wrong with that; however, why reinvent an existing thirty-year-old language just because the UoD is new? Furthermore, why not give at least some references to old sources? The good thing with RDF was that it helped open up a new phase in modeling and in information management, not just for metadata, but for data in general. Data no longer had to be managed in relational databases. With RDF and later recommendations, W3C helped open the door to binary modeling and revitalizing the interest in binary databases. Binary modeling was "on the table" again.

The RDF proponents soon found that RDF could also be used for other types of information than metadata, in fact, for any types of data. What a surprise! The academic world found all this interesting and started to build new features into RDF. Web Ontology Language (OWL) was born, which was mainly reinventing the wheel again. It had features similar to those in ER-modeling languages and UML (not to forget the STANLI language) but with one major different feature; allowing instance and type specifications to coexist. With RDF and OWL, a model could not be called an information model or conceptual model; it had to be called ontology.

RDF and OWL have their proponents in academic environments. However, in industry and elsewhere, UML became the dominant modeling language, mainly thanks to the support from OMG. Interestingly enough, it came to be used more and more for ordinary information modeling, i.e., without behavior as an ingredient.

Internet interoperability was on the rise. Then along came Service Oriented Architectures (SOA) with Web Services Architecture as the most well-known alternative. XML and XSD were part of this movement into information exchange.

No longer was information just stored in databases, it was moving around on the web. No longer were applications something internal to an organization. They were redesigned as services and open to the global community to use as long as it was benefitting the business.

5.2 For Us

Information of different kinds – be it data, metadata, model data, or anything else – constitutes the base ingredient that gives the web its purpose, meaning and soul. It is about knowledge sharing, cooperation, and information exchange in its most general sense, and it is about information and service interoperability (exposure, discovery, interpretation, exchange, and use).

Lacking in SOA was and is a layer expressing an independent view exchange of some UoD of interest. It was and is believed that XML and XSD are doing the job. However, as it has already been pointed out, message structures using XSD and UoD based information models are not the same, they complement each other.

Furthermore, is XML really the optimal way of delivering information? Not necessarily. Information could just as well be delivered as chunks of triples or elementary messages. Together, these triples express exactly the same thing as a message expressed in XML. Moreover, these chunks may be sent as a file with the same internal format as "our" binary database. The chunk is, in this way, a database in itself and, as such, operable through the usual database interface. Suddenly, not only messages, but also whole databases could exist moving around in cyber space or in a permanent place. Why not mark this change of view by replacing "database" with "information cluster."

Our interest in information modeling has continued and a number of projects have been carried out. One example of such a project was Eurocontrol/OATA (Overall ATM/CNS Target Architecture), a major air traffic control project aiming at improving the overall performance, safety, and sustainability of European air transport. A very large and complex UML model played a major role in the OATA specification. Other examples are projects in the health care sector.

6 Final Thoughts

We started with binary models in the CADIS project, went through all the turbulence during the years, and have just reached the end of the National Information Structure project [16] where STANLI has been used as the modeling language.

DREAM applications are still in use. STANLI is still a valid choice as a modeling language, and will so be in future projects.

Binary modeling combining simplicity and enough expressiveness is an attractive combination. The fact is that we still draw bubbles and arrows on napkins during lunch discussions, prefer to use simple general-purpose graphical tools when they are available, and sometimes work with more advanced tools in formal projects. So much has happened during the years, but most things are still the same.

The described forty years constitute a full loop of information modeling and modeling languages.

References

1. Langefors, B.: Theoretical Analysis of Information Systems. Studentlitteratur, Lund, Sweden (1966,1973)
2. Bubenko, Jr., J.A.: The Temporal Dimension in Information Modelling. In: Proceedings of IFIP WG 2.6 Working Conference on Architecture and Models in Data Base Management Systems (1977)
3. Abrial, J.R.: Data Semantics. In: Klimbie, Koffeman (eds.) Data Management Systems, North-Holland, Amsterdam (1974)
4. Senko, M.E.: Conceptual Schema, Abstract Data Structures, Enterprise Descriptions. In: Morlet, Ribbens (eds.) International Computing Symposium. North-Holland, Amsterdam (1977)
5. Chen, P.P.: The Entity-Relationship Model – Toward a Unified View of Data. ACM Transactions on Database Systems (1976)
6. Codd, E.F.: A Relational Model of Data for Large Shared Data Banks. Communications of the ACM (1970)
7. ANSI/X3/SPARC Study Group on Database Management Systems, Interim Report (1975)
8. Bubenko, Jr., J.A., Berild, S., Lindencrona-Ohlin, E., Nachmens, S.: Information Analysis and Design of Data Base Schemata. TRITA-IBADB- 3091, Department of Information Processing and Computer Science, Royal Institute of Technology and Stockholm University (1975)
9. Lindencrona-Ohlin, E.: Determination of Information Structures. TRITA-IBADB-0098; Department of Information Processing and Computer Science, Royal Institute of Technology and Stockholm University (1976)
10. Berild, S., Nachmens, S.: CS4: A Tool for Database Design by Infological Simulation. In: Proceedings of Very Large Data Base Conference (VLDB 1977), Tokyo (1977)
11. Lindencrona-Ohlin, E.: A Study of Conceptual Data Modelling. PhD dissertation. Chalmers Technical University and University of Gothenburg (1979)
12. Janning, M., Nachmens, S., Berild, S.: CS4 – An Introduction to Associative Data Bases and the CS4 System. Studentlitteratur, Lund (1979)
13. SISU Analys, Nr 85/1: Konceptuell modellering, SISU – Svenska institutet för Systemutveckling (1985)
14. Lindencrona-Ohlin, E., Bubenko, Jr., J.A.: Towards a Formal Syntax for a Data Modelling language –DMOL, SYSLAB Working Paper Nr 63 (1983)
15. Bubenko, Jr., J., Lindencrona, E.: Konceptuell modellering – Informationsanalys, Studentlitteratur, Lund (1984)
16. The National Board for Health and Welfare: Nationell informationsstruktur, http://www.socialstyrelsen.se/NI

Scandinavian Contributions to Object-Oriented Modeling Languages

Birger Møller-Pedersen

Department of Informatics, University of Oslo, Norway
birger@ifi.uio.no

Abstract. The history of Scandinavian contributions to modeling languages is interesting in many respects. The most interesting part of the history is that some of mechanisms were conceived very early, years before modeling became mainstream. It is well-known that object-orientation started with SIMULA in 1967, but it is less known that SIMULA formed the basis for a modeling language already in 1973, and that the Ericsson AXE software structure (1976) was one of the foundations (via SDL) for composite structures in UML2. It is also interesting that there has been a development towards making mechanisms less particular: while early modeling languages had special structuring mechanisms, UML2 now cover this by composite classes. In addition, early modeling languages were executable, in fact they were combined modeling – and programming languages. After a period where modeling was just for the purpose of analysis and design, the trend is now towards executable models, i.e. almost going back to the original Scandinavian approach.

Keywords: Languages, modeling, programming.

1 Introduction

This paper tells part of the story of the Scandinavian contribution to modeling languages. We restrict ourselves to the contribution to the de facto standard language for modeling, UML in its current version UML2 [1]. Instead of just making a chronological account of what happened when and who were involved, the story is told with emphasis on language mechanisms, and the paper is organized correspondingly.

For the account of when things happened, we have decided to do it based upon published material, although we are aware that activity often started earlier, see Fig 1.

2 Object-Orientation

Object-orientation as part of UML has a straightforward history. The main sources are the Booch [2] and OMT [3] methods, and these are in turn based upon the concepts of object-oriented programming originating with SIMULA. Booch and OMT were not the first methods for object-oriented modeling, but they directly influenced UML. The OOSE method [4] contributed with Use Cases.

J. Impagliazzo, P. Lundin, and B. Wangler (Eds.): HiNC3, IFIP AICT 350, pp. 339–349, 2011.

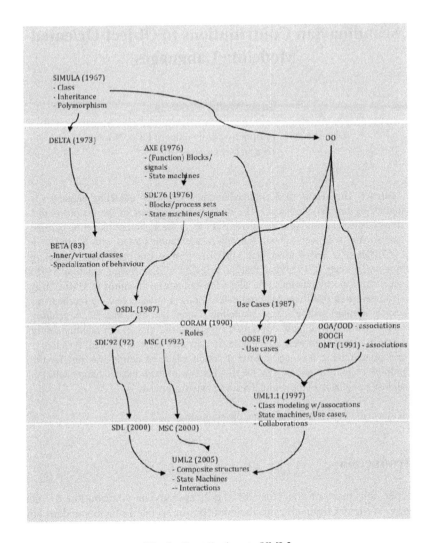

Fig. 1. Contributions to UML2

SIMULA was developed by Ole-Johan Dahl and Kristen Nygaard at the Norwegian Computing Centre, Oslo, in the 1960s [5, 6]. A comprehensive history may be found in [7] and in [8].

SIMULA I was a simulation language. It was realized that the concepts in could be applied to programming in general, and the result was the general-purpose language SIMULA 67 – later on just called SIMULA. The SIMULA I language report of 1965 opens with these sentences:

The two main objectives of the SIMULA language are:

o To provide a language for a precise and standardized description of a wide class of phenomena, belonging to what we may call "discrete event systems".
o To provide a programming language for an easy generation of simulation programs for "discrete event systems".

Thus, SIMULA was considered as a language both for system description and for programming.

It turned out that many users of SIMULA seemed to get more understanding of their problem domain by developing a description than from the actual simulation results. The modeling approach of SIMULA was therefore refined in **DELTA** [9], a pure description language ('description language' was the term for 'modeling language' at that time).

DELTA supported the description of true concurrent objects and used predicates to express state changes and continuous changes over time. DELTA had a goal similar to that of the object-oriented analysis and design (OOA/OOD) methodologies (e.g. Coad and Yourdon [10]) that appeared subsequently in the mid-80s, followed by OMT and Booch.

After the initial ideas of SIMULA, there were two different developments of object-oriented programming: the 'modeling approach' and the 'programming approach'. The main difference between these is on the understanding of objects, classes and subclasses. The modeling approach regards objects as models of phenomena from the application domain, classes as models of domain concepts and subclasses as models of special concepts. SIMULA defined the modeling approach. The programming approach puts emphasis on subclassing as a language mechanism for reuse of code. A subclass does not have to define a subtype of the type of the superclass, and the subclass is free to redefine properties of the superclass. Object-oriented methods in the 1980s followed the modeling approach.

The approach to language design used for **BETA**[1] [11] was highly influenced by the SIMULA tradition. BETA should be a combined modeling and programming language. The first account of BETA is [11]. The history is described in [12].

It was realized already with SIMULA that the class/subclass mechanism was useful for representing concepts including specialization, but there was no formulation of a conceptual framework for object-oriented programming. For BETA it was therefore necessary do develop such a conceptual framework. [13] provides a definition of object-oriented programming with a modeling approach.

It was from the beginning decided that BETA should support for full concurrency. As will be seen below, this early Scandinavian work on object-orientation had similarities with the AXE software structure in that it supported concurrent, active and communicating objects.

The primary goal of the OMT++ [14], OMT+ [15], and Octopus [16] efforts by Nokia Research Center was improved methods for embedded systems, and not new language mechanisms.

---

[1] The BETA-project started as a research project (Bent Bruun Kristensen, Ole Lehrmann Madsen, Birger Møller-Pedersen, and Kristen Nygaard). The main implementation effort was done as part of the Nordic Mjølner project.

3 Structuring Mechanisms

3.1 Blocks and Block Structure

In the telecom industry, specifying systems as a set of interconnected blocks was common practice already in the seventies as reported in [17]. SDL was one of the first standardized notations for specification with support for such structuring mechanisms [18].

AXE Blocks. In 1976 the paper [19][2] in Ericsson Review presented for the first time the software structure of the AXE system. This was a result of some years of applying software technology to the area of switching, and in line with most similar efforts, it was based upon non-synchronized communication (by means of signals) between processes. The new thing was the organization of the software in terms of blocks with well-defined interfaces.

The experience with the AXE system brought into development the SDL'76 and SDL'80 by Ivar Jacobson, Nils Lennmarker, and Anders Rockström[3]. SDL used blocks with possible substructures of blocks and concurrent, non-synchronized processes with behavior defined in terms of state machines and with well-defined interfaces in terms of signals.

SDL'84 and SDL'88 saw the formalization of both the communication part and the data modeling part [20][21]. The reason was that different tools then would have the same interpretation, and that SDL could be used not only for documentation, but also for making executable specifications.

While **block structure** in AXE and SDL was a direct specification of what an execution consists of in terms of instances (composition), block structure in programming languages means pure *nesting* of definitions. Early programming languages had procedures/functions nested within procedures/functions. SIMULA introduced nesting of classes. From being a purely technical mechanism, nesting ended up being conceived as a means (in [22] coined *localization*) for describing concepts that depend on an enclosing object.

Nesting in terms of inner classes has made it into main object-oriented programming languages and into UML2.

Object-oriented SDL (OSDL/ SDL'92) was proposed in 1987 [23][4]; in 1992 these concepts became part of the language [24][5]. Object-oriented SDL introduced block

---

[2] The reason for one author on this paper is probably that Hemdahl was the key person behind this, although many persons were involved in this undertaking.

[3] Work on SDL started already in 1968, when CCITT decided to find out what to do about telecom and software technology. Telecom operators were the driving forces (e.g. the Swedish Televerket, Gösta Lindberg (CTO)). Anders Rockström joined this effort in 1974.

[4] Started as part of the Mjølner project (Dag Belsnes, Hans Petter Dahle, Birger Møller-Pedersen), where the idea was to develop a new language. After discussions, especially between EB Technology and the Swedish partners (where Anders Rockström and Ferenc Belina were involved), it was decided to go for an extension of SDL.

[5] The standardization work of OSDL was done as part of the Norwegian SISU-project, where Øystein Haugen and Rolf Bræk joined, and as part of the EU-projects SPECS and FORTE, where Ove Færgemand and Anders Olsen from TeleDanmark joined. Anders Ek was a key person involved from Telelogic.

types and process types, and gates as connection points for communication links between blocks and processes. In addition, specialization (subtyping) was defined for block and process types. For block structuring, the implication was that block subtypes would inherit the internal block structure of the super block type.

OOSE 1992. From the AXE software structure OOSE had blocks with internal structure, and each block had an own behavior in terms of a state machine.

ADL/ROOM. Work on Architecture Description Languages (ADLs) began in the early nineties. This area has produced a number of modeling languages. In 1994, ROOM [25] combined statecharts and structuring mechanisms like those of SDL (by capsules, ports and connectors).

Subsystems. When UML1[6] was adopted in 1997, none of these structuring mechanisms had become part of the language. It had no notion of block (AXE/SDL/OOSE) or capsule (ROOM); an object could only have behavior in terms of methods and not a main behavior as an active object (process).

UML1 had, however, the notion of Subsystem, being a mixture of a Classifier and a Package. As a package, it could contain (among other things) a State Machine, but this was nothing like the behavior of a block. In addition, there are no communication links between subsystems. The paper [26] gives a description of subsystems.

ADLs had Components as the parts of a structure. For some reason Components in UML1 was not a mechanism for structuring systems, but more a mechanism for deployment. This has, however, been changed in UML2.

3.2   Composite Classes

When OMG in 1999 embarked upon making the second version of UML (UML2), a group of telecom users (Alcatel, Ericsson, and Motorola) of SDL handed in joint requirements [27]. Structuring of large, complex systems was one of the main requirements.[7]

SDL had block diagrams with the only purpose of specifying the architecture of systems ([28] and [29]). In contrast to this, UML1 had class diagrams with classes and relations between classes. Although composition was one of these relations, this could not be used for the structuring of systems, with the implication that UML users had to use packages and subsystems for this purpose, see [30].

The 1992 version of SDL supported object orientation by block types and process types, and corresponding subtypes. These types would correspond to classes in UML (when it arrived in 1997), so the obvious requirement for UML2 was that classes should be able to have an internal structures.

ROOM capsules had much of the same properties as SDL'92 blocks. In 1999 the ROOM concepts became parts of a UML profile UML-RT [31]. Fortunately the

---

[6] UML1.1, the first version of UML with Scandinavian contribution. The Swedish company Objectory, founded on the OOSE method in 1987, was acquired by Rational in 1995 and contributed with Use Cases and predefined method stereotypes. UML versions up to 1.5 – Karin Palmkvist and Gunnar Övergård contributed to Use Cases, Interactions, Collaborations, and Subsystems.

[7] Scandinavian contributors to UML2: Øystein Haugen and Birger Møller-Pedersen (at that time with Ericsson).

UML2 saw the SDL2'92 and ROOM concepts as structuring concepts within UML proper and not in a profile. As pointed out in [32], the way in which UML-RT combined UML with ROOM was not the way to do it; they advocated what more or less became the reality: that structuring mechanisms became integrated with class models.

The discussions described above lead to the notion of composite structures and in turn, these were used to define composite classes and collaborations. A composite structure consists of parts (sets of objects of a given type) connected by connectors. Connectors either connect parts directly or connect ports on parts. The composite structures of collaborations also form the contexts for Interactions, so these parts are well integrated in UML2. This is illustrated in [33].

The following citation from [34] is summing up structuring mechanisms of UML2:

> The basis for this set of features comes from long-term experience with various architectural description languages, such as UML-RT, ACME, and SDL. These languages are characterized by a relatively simple set of graph-like concepts: basic structural nodes called parts that may have one or more interaction points called ports and that are interconnected by communication channels called connectors.

A detailed correspondence between SDL and UML2 is described in [35].

Languages with support for modeling of architectures typically have language mechanisms designed especially for this purpose. One may easily imagine that the same thing could have happened when introducing this in UML2, i.e. making up a new language mechanism just for this purpose. Fortunately, both SDL and ROOM had been there before. In UML2, therefore, it was recognized that the composite structures, which were needed in order to model architectures, could be seen as a special case of composition of classes. This implied that composite structure became an inherent property of objects, and by being defined for classes, inheritance also applied to structure: inheritance implied inheritance of parts, ports and connectors.

4 Object Behavior

Mainstream object-oriented languages have most of the original concepts from SIMULA: classes and objects, subclasses, virtual methods, polymorphism, etc. An exception is the SIMULA notion of an active object with its own action sequence (in addition to behavior in terms of methods). Strangely enough, many other programming languages had not adopted this.

In SIMULA, it was regarded as obvious that objects had their own behavior, in addition to behavior associated with methods. Objects were not just intended for the modeling of data entities, but also for processes with their own behaviors.

The AXE design had similarly function blocks with their own behavior (in terms of a state machine), the same with processes in SDL'76. OOSE did not carry this over from AXE and SDL.

UML1 did not have a separate object behavior, although it had the notion of active objects. Booch and OMT followed the trend in programming languages to do this by means of a special method.

UML2 introduced a so-called ClassifierBehavior, so that classes may have a behavior. This extension comes from SDL, ROOM, and UML-RT, and it links back to the original AXE and SDL idea of processes as the main kind of objects.

Although **state machines** were part of AXE, this was not the only source of inspiration for state machines in SDL'76. The use of state machines was common in telecom and process control systems. UML1 had state machines, but they were for some reason intended for the specification of the behavior of collaborations, and not for the objects taking part in the collaborations, at least according to the semantics specification of UML1. The state machines of UML1 comes from [36], where objects and state machines were combined. In 1987, Harel introduced structuring mechanisms for state machines, hierarchical statecharts, with composite states containing states and transitions.

SDL-2000 adopted the hierarchical state machines of statecharts, extending them with entry/exit points [37], a kind of interface for composite states, so that states could be entered/exited without having to know to the details of the composite states. Entry/exit points for states are supported by UML2.

5 Use Cases

The story behind Use Cases is easy to track down. The first paper on Use Cases is from OOPSLA'87 [38], and this paper in turn points to two sources of inspiration: the way functions (we would call it services today) were described as part of the AXE development within Ericsson, and the IFIP'86 paper [39], where the notions of task and roles in system development were introduced. Use Cases also rest on the shoulders of both the Norwegian and Swedish approaches to participatory design.

Use Cases are sometimes criticized for leading to functional decomposition of systems instead of the object-oriented decomposition based upon objects. However, use cases were conceived in a setting where the system design was made by means of blocks, so use cases were the means by which it was possible to describe properties of the system independently of how it should be structured in terms of blocks.

Use Cases have been a success independent of UML and they are not really dependent on being tightly integrated with the rest of the UML.

6 Collaborations

Collaborations have two Scandinavian contributions: role modeling and realizations of use cases.

The role modeling method, OORAM[8] [40] is a method that emphasizes objects and the collaborations of objects playing different roles. It is covered in the survey [41], and it has been demonstrated at OOPSLA conferences since 1986. Collaborations in UML1 were based upon presentations of the method to the OMG.

Realization of use cases by means of collaboration was presented at the UML conference in 1999 [42]. Collaborations were not part of OOSE, however, one of the

---

[8] Based upon a former role modeling method [48]. Trygve Reenskaug was member of the UML Core Team, and part of small group that made the first proposal for UML1.1.

co-authors on the book on OOSE contributed to the realization of use case by means of collaborations.

Collaborations were revised (in light of composite structures) as part of UML2, in a way that supports OORAM better than the Collaborations of UML1.

7 Interactions (Sequence Diagrams)

When SDL was standardized for the first time in 1976, the telecom field (including AXE) also used proprietary variations of sequence diagrams (called Message Sequence Charts – MSC). The 1988 SDL User Guidelines had a short section on message sequence charts as an auxiliary diagram that could be used in combination with SDL.

A paper [43] triggered the first standardization of Message Sequence Charts (MSC) in 1992[9]. MSC-2000 [44] refined earlier structuring mechanisms such as MSC references and inline expressions.

UML1 selected a somewhat different dialect similar to, but not identical to MSC-92, as the foundation of sequence diagrams, and did not support reuse and hierarchy.

The approach in [45] formed the basis for Interactions in UML2[10], and the two dialects have reached more or less the same expressiveness, see [46].

8 Conclusion: Executable Models or Unified Modeling and Programming

It all started out with a combined modeling and programming language (SIMULA), with software structuring (AXE) tightly integrated with a programming language, and a modeling language with an execution semantics (SDL). Although one of the main strengths of object-orientation is that it provides a unified approach to modeling and programming, modeling languages developed independently of object-oriented programming languages, and drifted away from execution and became languages in support for analysis and design. Recently we have witnessed the need for executable models, not just for special domain specific languages, but for modeling in general, and this has called for initiatives like Executable UML [47]. One may say that this is just a return to how it was in the beginning, but the difference is that executable models may still just translate to implementations in existing programming languages, yielding both a model and a program artifact. If development environments for modeling languages for executable models will not be able to match development environments for programming languages, then users still have to cope with both a modeling language and a programming language, and based upon experience the code artifact will be the dominant. Really returning to the original approach would imply going for a combined modeling -and programming language, see [48] for an account of that. Class models and state machine models will obviously be part of such a combined language, with e.g. interaction models for the specification of execution

---

[9] A key contributor at the time and subsequently (until his untimely death in 2002) was Ekkart Rudolph of Siemens, Munich.

[10] Øystein Haugen (at that time with Ericsson) was leading this work for UML2.

semantics, while other parts of modeling languages are obviously just intended as support for analysis methods, as with Use Cases.

Acknowledgments. Thanks to Anders Rockström, Rick Reed, Pär Emanuelsson, and Anders Olsen for providing valuable input, and to Stein Krogdahl for careful reading and commenting.

References

1. OMG: UML: Unified Modeling Language 2.0. OMG. ptc/2004-10-02 (2004)
2. Booch, G.: Object-Oriented Analysis and Design with Applications. Benjamin/Cummings, Redwood City (1991)
3. Rumbaugh, J., et al.: Object-Oriented Modeling and Design. Prentice Hall, Englewood Cliffs (1991)
4. Jacobson, I., et al.: Object-oriented software engineering: a use case driven approach. Addison-Wesley Professional, Reading (1992)
5. Dahl, O.-J., Myhrhaug, B., Nygaard, K.: SIMULA 67 Common Base Language (Editions 1968, 1970, 1972, 1984). Norwegian Computing Center, Oslo (1968)
6. Dahl, O.-J., Nygaard, K.: SIMULA—a Language for Programming and Description of Discrete Event Systems. Norwegian Computing Center, Oslo (1965)
7. Dahl, O.-J., Nygaard, K.: The Development of the SIMULA Languages. In: ACM SIGPLAN History of Programming Languages Conference (1978)
8. Krogdahl, S.: The Birth of Simula. In: Bubenko Jr., J., Impagliazzo, J., Sølvberg, A. (eds.) History of Nordic Computing. IFIP WG9.7 First Working Conference on the History of Nordic Computing (HiNC1), Trondheim, Norway, June 16-18. Springer, New York (2003)
9. Holbæk-Hanssen, E., Håndlykken, P., Nygaard, K.: System Description and the DELTA Language. Norwegian Computing Center, Oslo (1973)
10. Coad, P., Yourdon, E.: Object-Oriented Analysis. Prentice-Hall, Englewood Cliffs (1991)
11. Kristensen, B.B., et al.: Abstraction Mechanisms in the BETA Programming Language. In: Tenth ACM Symposium on Principles of Programming Languages, Austin, Texas (1983)
12. Kristensen, B.B., Madsen, O.L., Møller-Pedersen, B.: The When, Why and Why Not of the BETA Programming Language. In: HOPL III: The third ACM SIGPLAN Conference on History of Programming Languages, San Diego (2007)
13. Madsen, O.L., Møller-Pedersen, B.: What Object-Oriented Programming May Be—and What It Does Not Have to Be. In: Gjessing, S., Chepoi, V. (eds.) ECOOP 1988. LNCS, vol. 322, Springer, Heidelberg (1988)
14. Aalto, J.-M., Jaaksi, A.: Object-Oriented Development of Interactive Systems with OMT++. In: TOOLS 14 – Technology of Object-Oriented Languages and Systems. Prentice Hall, Englewood Cliffs (1994)
15. Kruusela, J.: Object oriented development of embedded systems with the octopus method. In: Lectures on Embedded Systems – European Educational Forum School on Embedded Systems Veldhoven, The Netherlands, November 25-29, Springer, Heidelberg (1996)
16. Awad, M., Kuusela, J., Ziegler, J.: Object-Oriented Technology for Real-Time Systems: A Practical Approach Using OMT and Fusion. Prentice Hall, Englewood Cliffs (1996)
17. Jacobson, I.: Language Support for Changeable Large Real Time Systems. In: OOPSLA 1986 – Object-Oriented Programming, Systems Languages and Applications, Portland, Oregon (1986); ACM Special Issue of Sigplan Notices

18. Rockström, A., Saracco, R.: SDL–CCITT Specification and Description Language. IEEE Transactions on Communications 30(6) (1982)
19. Hemdal, G.: AXE 10 – Software Structure and Features. Ericsson Review 2 (1976)
20. Haff, P., Olsen, A.: Use of VDM within CCITT. In: VDM 1987 VDM – A Formal Method at Work, pp. 324–330. Springer, Heidelberg (1987)
21. Belina, F., Hogrefe, D.: The CCITT Specification and Description Language SDL. Computer Networks and ISDN Systems 16 (1989)
22. Madsen, O.L., Møller-Pedersen, B., Nygaard, K.: Object-Oriented Programming in the BETA Programming Language. Addison Wesley, Reading (1993)
23. Møller-Pedersen, B., Belsnes, D., Dahle, H.P.: Rationale and Tutorial on OSDL: An Object-Oriented Extension of SDL. Computer Networks 13(2) (1987)
24. Olsen, A., et al.: Systems Engineering Using SDL-92. North-Holland, Amsterdam (1994)
25. Selic, B., Gullekson, G., Ward, P.T.: Real-Time Object-Oriented Modeling. John Wiley & Sons Inc., Chichester (1994)
26. Övergaard, G., Palmkvist, K.: Interacting Subsystems in UML. In: Evans, A., Caskurlu, B., Selic, B. (eds.) UML 2000. LNCS, vol. 1939, pp. 359–368. Springer, Heidelberg (2000)
27. OMG: UML 2.0 RESPONSE ON REQUEST FOR INFORMATION from Ericsson, Motorola, and Alcatel, Version 1.0. (1999)
28. Fischer, J., Holz, E., Møller-Pedersen, B.: Structural and Behavioral Decomposition in Object Oriented Models. In: ISORC International Symposium on Object-oriented Real-time Systems, New Beach, CA (2000)
29. Bræk, R., Møller-Pedersen, B.: Frameworks by Means of Virtual Types—Exemplified by SDL. In: IFIP TC6 WG6.1. Joint International Conference on Formal Description Techniques for Distributed Systems and Communication Protocols (FORTE XI) and Protocol Specification, Testing and Verification, PSTV XVIII (1998)
30. Garlan, D., et al.: Modeling of Architectures with UML. In: The Third International Conference on The Unified Modeling Language, York, October 2-6 (2000)
31. Selic, B.: Using UML for Modeling Complex Real-Time Systems. In: Mueller, F., Bestavros, A. (eds.) Languages, Compilers, and Tools for Embedded Systems. Springer, Heidelberg (1998)
32. Rumpe, B., et al.: UML+ROOM as a Standard ADL? In: 5th International Conference on Engineering of Complex Computer Systems (1999)
33. Haugen, Ø., Møller-Pedersen, B., Weigert, T.: Structural Modeling with UML 2.0. In: Lavagno, L., Martin, G., Selic, B. (eds.) UML for Real. Kluwer Academic Publishers, Dordrecht (2003)
34. Selic, B.: UML 2: A Model-driven Development Tool. IBM Systems Journal (2006)
35. Møller-Pedersen, B.: From SDL to UML2 – from an ITU Specification Language to an OMG Modeling Language. Telektronikk, 1 (2009)
36. Harel, D., Gery, E.: Executable Object Modeling with Statecharts. IEEE Computer (1997)
37. Møller-Pedersen, B., Nogva, D.: Scalable and Object Oriented SDL State(chart)s. In: IFIP TC6/WG6.1 Joint International Conference on Formal Description Techniques (FORTE XII) FORTE 1999. Beijing (1999)
38. Jacobson, I.: Object Oriented Development within an Industrial Environment. In: OOPSLA 1987 – Object-Oriented Programming, Systems Languages and Applications. ACM, Orlando (1987)
39. Nygaard, K.: Program Development as a Social Activity. In: Information Processing 1986 – IFIP 10th World Computer Congress, Elsevier Science Publishers B.V., Dublin (1986)

40. Reenskaug, T., Wold, P., Lehne, O.A.: Working with Objects: The OOram Software Engineering Method. Manning/Prentice Hall, Englewood Cliffs (1996)
41. Wirfs-Brock, R.J., Johnson, R.E.: Surveying Current Research in Object-Oriented Design. Communications of the ACM 33(9), 113–116 (1990)
42. Övergaard, G.: A Formal Approach to Collaborations in the Unified Modeling Language. In: UML 1999: The Unified Modeling Language – Beyond the Standard, Second International Conference. Springer, Fort Collins (1999)
43. Grabowski, J., Rudolph, E.: Putting Extended Sequence Charts to Practice. In: 4th SDL Forum. North-Holland, Lisbon (1989)
44. ITU: Message Sequence Charts (MSC), Recommendation Z.120. Geneva (1999)
45. Haugen, Ø.: From MSC-2000 to UML 2.0 – The Future of Sequence Diagrams. In: 10th International SDL Forum. Copenhagen (2001)
46. Haugen, Ø.: Comparing UML 2.0 Interactions and MSC-2000. In: SAM 2004: SDL and MSC Fourth International Workshop, Ottawa (2004)
47. OMG: Semantics of a Foundational Subset for Executable UML Models (2009)
48. Madsen, O.L., Møller-Pedersen, B.: A unified approach to modeling and programming. In: Petriu, D.C., Rouquette, N., Haugen, Ø. (eds.) MODELS 2010. LNCS, vol. 6394, pp. 1–15. Springer, Heidelberg (2010)

Dansk Datamatik Center

Dines Bjørner[1], Christian Gram[2], Ole N. Oest[3], and Leif Rystrøm[4]

[1] DTU, Denmark
bjorner@gmail.com
[2] DTU, Denmark
chr.gram@ddf.dk
[3] DDC-I Inc., Phoenix, Arizona 85020, USA
ooest@attglobal.net
[4] Danish Road Directorate, Copenhagen, Denmark
rystroem@mail.dk

Abstract. In 1979, a software research and development center was created to demonstrate the power of systematic and formal methods in software development. One of the first and biggest projects at Dansk Datamatik Center (DDC) was to develop an Ada compiler and run-time system. DDC made the first department of Defense (DoD) validated Ada compiler in Europe, and the Ada project was carried on in a subsidiary called DDC–I, Inc. This paper describes the background and start of DDC and some aspects of the formal development method called "Rigorous Approach to Industrial Software Engineering" (RAISE) as well as other DDC activities.

Keywords: Formal methods, software development, technology transfer.

1 A History of DDC

The idea of Dansk Datamatik Center (DDC) 🏢[1] was first aired by Christian Gram of the Department of Computer Science at the Technical University of Denmark (DTU) and discussed with his colleague Dines Bjørner during the spring of 1979. Software development in business, administration, and industry was then still very unsatisfactory. Already in 1968, the NATO Science Committee arranged a conference on software engineering [1] on "a problem crucial to the use of computers, viz. the so-called software, or program, developed to control their action." Many projects were late, more expensive than estimated, and full of errors. "The phrase 'software engineering' was deliberately chosen as being provocative, in implying the need for software manufacture to be based on the types of theoretical foundations and practical disciplines, that are traditional in the established branches of engineering." Even after a second conference on the same problem area, problems with software development in practice continued. We felt in 1979 that computer scientists had

---

[1] The DDC 'cube' was designed by Danish Design award winning Ole Friis.

J. Impagliazzo, P. Lundin, and B. Wangler (Eds.): HiNC3, IFIP AICT 350, pp. 350–359, 2011.
© IFIP International Federation for Information Processing 2011

developed foundations and theories that – if properly implemented – could make programming a more professional, engineer-like profession and allow developing large, reliable programs on schedule.

We contacted ATV, the Danish Academy for Technical Sciences, an umbrella organization for a significant number of 'Science-Engineering-Technology' institutes working to help industry applying the newest technologies in their field. ATV responded positively, and ten of the largest users and/or producers of IT in Denmark agreed to become members of the institute, each paying 100,000 DKK per year. DDC was created in September 1979 as an ATV society for advanced software development. The members of DDC were Christian Rovsing A/S, Crone & Koch edb, Danish Defense Research Establishment, Datacentralen af 1959, Jydsk Telefon A/S, Kommunedata, Regnecentralen af 1979 (RC), Sparekassernes Datacenter (SDC), Teleteknisk Forskningslaboratorium (TFL) and ØK Data. An attempt to make Danish financial institutes interested in DDC failed.

Most projects used formal specification methods – VDM, the Vienna Development Method [3, 4] developed at IBM, and later RAISE, Rigorous Approach to Industrial Software Engineering [5], a method co-developed at DDC.

A main goal was to act as a link between Danish IT companies and Danish/European IT research; in order to make DDC capable of using the most advanced software design and development tools.

DDC had very little cooperation with the IT research in Nordic countries. We felt that there was not the same interest for and emphasis on the use of formal methods for software development. Because Denmark was a member of EU (and the only Nordic member at that time), it was natural for us to seek partners and financial support among EU members. However, from 1984 we cooperated with the Swedish Försvarets Materielverk on the Ada project, and later with Ericsson and Bofors.

The Ada compiler project was so successful that a separate company, DDC International A/S, was created in 1985 to market, sell, and further develop the Ada system. DDC International later created the limited company, DDC-I Inc., which is still in the market, and the Ada system and other systems developed at DDC-I were sold in USA, China, and other countries. Some years ago, the headquarters moved to Arizona, USA.

Over the years, some of the original member companies lost interest in DDC and its services and it became difficult to find funding for the kind of projects, DDC wanted to further. After almost ten years, it was decided to close down DDC, but some larger projects were carried on under new hats. The development of Ada systems continued in DDC-I. The RAISE project and the people working on it were transferred to the Danish software house CRI Inc. (CRI) that completed the project and used it as a base for the Large-scale Correct Systems (LaCoS) project using formal methods.

2   The Use of Formal Techniques at DDC

Both the CHILL and the Ada compilers were developed roughly as follows. The static and dynamic semantics of the languages were described in denotational form. Then, in several stages of refinement, they systematically developed more and more concrete prescriptions, covering both static and dynamic semantics for sequential and parallel language features [6]. These prescriptions (in the VDM language) included the expression of a number of "standard" compiler requirements for microprocessor-based compilation as well as execution platforms. From the concrete requirements prescriptions multi-pass compilation administrators were developed and subsequently, the N passes of the compiler were coded (for Ada N was 9) [4, 7].

In both projects, the VDM approach was one of systematic development: Formal specifications of all phases, stages and steps; however, it used no formal proof of correctness. See Section 3.2 for more details.

3   DDC Activities 1979–89

The thirty to thirty-five member professional staff worked with *advanced software development projects* (the CHILL and Ada compilers), *research* (the CHILL and Ada formal definitions), *explorative studies* (formal methods appraisal, office automation), and *other activities* (seminars, courses, and other dissemination).

3.1   The CHILL Projects

The Formal Definition of CHILL

In 1978, Prof. A. Kjerbye Nielsen, director of TFL, asked Dines Bjørner to follow the development of the CHILL programming language by an international group of the C.C.I.T.T.[2] (today ITU[3]). It was the intention to attempt a formal description of CHILL. Through the work of Dines Bjørner, his colleague, Hans Bruun, and some master students formal descriptions were researched and experimentally developed at DTU. Once DDC was established, that work was completed at DDC [8, 9].

The benefit of making formal descriptions may be illustrated by the following. Hans Bruun found – during his painstaking analysis and in discussions with members of the C.C.I.T.T. group – a tiny identifier scope issue that, if simply removed, would shorten the definition by some 20 percent. The group ended up nullifying that scope issue – significantly simplifying any CHILL compiler.

The CHILL Compiler Development

In 1979, before the formation of DDC, work started on the development of a compiler for the full CHILL language (CCITT High Level Language). Peter Haff and Søren Prehn did the work, funded partially by TFL. The CHILL compiler was for the full CHILL programming language – including, for example, its three "independent" sets of parallel programming constructs. When completed, the compiler became public property by TFL and DDC and it played a significant role in the teaching of CHILL worldwide [9].

---

[2] Comité Consultatif International Téléphonique et Télégraphique.
[3] International Telecommunication Union.

3.2   The Ada Projects

The Ada Compiler Project

The Danish/Italian Collaboration and the Initial Contract

The Ada programming language had been designed on behalf of the U.S. Department of Defense as a new cure-it-all standard programming language targeting development of embedded software. At the time more than two hundred languages were in use within the U.S. DoD and significant savings would be possible if this number could be reduced to just one, Ada.

The Commission of the European Communities (CEC) had set aside significant funding for the development of a European Ada compiler system because the CEC thought that similar savings might be possible within European software development. A French/German consortium was slated to receive the funding for this European Ada Compiler System.

Shortly before the call for proposal ended, DDC formed a consortium with Olivetti (Italy) and Christian Rovsing (CR) (Denmark) and in record time de- veloped a bid for the funding.

Several months of hectic technical evaluations of the DDC/Olivetti/CR proposal followed. It was very inconvenient for certain people in the CEC, that this Danish/Italian consortium competed for money intended for the French/German consortium. Each time we went to Brussels for another technical evaluation, the experts found some 'show-stoppers' not discussed at the previous meeting. Nevertheless, in early 1981, it ended up with a contract where 50 percent funding came from the CEC and 50 percent from Danish sources. DDC's part of the project was to develop a portable Ada compiler for small computers.

Some years later, after the Ada standard finalized, DDC won a contract for developing a formal specification of the language. We considered that a significant acknowledgment of VDM and of DDC's high technical level.

Technical Approach

The driving method behind the development of the DDC Ada Compiler System was the Vienna Development Method (VDM) [3, 4] and the demonstration of the viability of using VDM was initially perhaps considered more important to DDC and its members than the end-product itself.

In 1980, a team of master's students from DTU had developed a formal definition of Ada and of the underlying execution model [10]. This specification became the foundation for the actual compiler development. The compiler was developed as a number of refinements of this specification.

It was a requirement on the Danish/Italian consortium that the Ada compiler should be suitable for mini computers with limited memory resources. It was therefore designed as a multi-pass compiler, and the systematic development of the Ada compiler was basically refined into buckets, where each bucket would correspond to a compiler pass.

Even though the Ada language and the host computer platform underwent changes in this period, the project became a success and resulted in a commercial viable product. The DDC team even managed to achieve formal U.S. DoD approval (validation) of the compiler ahead of the French/German project [11, 12].

The project – part of which was research-oriented – exceeded the original budget by less than 20 percent, but it was on time, which was significantly better than most software projects.

The First Commercial Sales

DDC presented the DDC Ada compiler project and the use of VDM at several conferences [11, 12]. These presentations showed not only the high level of correctness of the compiler but also provided productivity numbers which showed that VDM was a cost-effective development method even when used without the support of computerized tools which only became available much later [5, 13].

Those technical presentations persuaded Nokia to license the DDC compiler technology for developing an Ada compiler for a proprietary minicomputer. Without any sales and marketing organization, DDC made its first commercial sale of what became known as the DDC OEM Compiler Kit.

Honeywell heard through Nokia of the DDC technology. Honeywell had two projects needing an Ada compiler, a mini computer and a mainframe system. They talked with the French/German consortium but ended up placing both orders with DDC. Significant sales were also made to the COSTIND, China and NEC, Japan.

The Formation of DDC International (DDC-I)

Several other OEM contracts followed. In 1985, DDC created a subsidiary, DDC-I, to commercialize the DDC Ada Compiler System. The system became an important part of many projects (aircrafts like Boeing 777, MD-80 and MD-90, satellites, and various military programs) and in 2010, it is still generating revenue for DDC-I.

Commercializing the other outcome of the project, the successful use of VDM, turned out to be much more troublesome. The industry was not ready to adopt formal methods until some twenty years later, where formal methods had become mandatory in validation of, for example, the Multiple Independent Levels of Security (MILS) operating systems.

The Formal Definition of Ada

During the early 1980s, a lively discussion forum supported by CEC resulted in the CEC supporting the R&D of a formal definition of Ada. A group was formed, again anchored in Denmark (DDC) and again with Italian partners at the universities in Pisa and in Genoa, Istituto di Elaborazione della Informazione (IEI) and CRAI, respectively. The Ada formal definition project (1984–87) was truly a research project. It was not known from the outset how the result would look [14–18] such as which specific abstraction and modeling techniques to deploy or which abstractions to use. During the project a number of exciting research problems were solved and many scientific papers were published.

3.3 The RAISE Project

The RAISE project had two parts: a precursor project, FMA, and a main project called the RAISE development project.

The Formal Methods Appraisal Project

During the developments of the CHILL and Ada compilers the need for a revision of VDM was identified. Other formal techniques to software development and especially additional formal specification constructs were introduced in the late 1970s and the early 1980s. In 1983, DDC obtained funds for a formal methods appraisal (FMA) study [19, 20]. It ended with a number of requirements that formal specification languages should satisfy when applied to problems involving distributed, real-time and concurrent systems.

The RAISE Development

We make a distinction between the RAISE pro-ject and the RAISE product.

The RAISE Project

After the FMA project, a Danish/British consortium was formed and eventually DDC, ABB (Asea Brown Bovery, DK), ICL (UK) and STL (UK), obtained a contract with the CEC for researching and developing a successor to VDM.

Thus, RAISE was initially developed under that contract, from 1985 to 1990, with the aim of providing a unifying improvement over formal methods such as VDM, Z, CSP, Larch, and OBJ. From 1990 to 1995, RAISE further developed (after DDC) in the Large-scale Correct Systems (LaCoS) project using formal methods.

RAISE stands for Rigorous Approach to Industrial Software Engineering and it introduces the use of formal (mathematical) techniques in the development of software; that is, in requirements analysis and formulation, specification, design, and development.

The RAISE Product

There are three facets to the RAISE product. (i) The RAISE Specification Language (RSL) which provides a rich, mathematically based notation in which requirements, specifications and steps of design of software may be formulated and reasoned about. RSL is a wide-spectrum language since it facilitates abstract, axiomatic styles of description as well as concrete, operational styles. It may be used from initial domain and requirements analysis through design to a level at which the specification may be translated into code. (ii) The RAISE method provides a set of techniques and recommendations for ways to use RSL in the various life-cycle phases of software development as well as techniques for verifying properties of specifications, implementations, and their relationships, formally, rigorously or informally. (iii) The RAISE Tool Set, which supports the use of RSL and the RAISE method.

RAISE comes with comprehensive documentation. Books on the language RSL [13] and the method [5] are provided, and further information is available on internet [21–24].

3.4 Office Automation Projects

DDC concluded several office automation projects during its existence. In 1981, a study was performed describing office automation systems. An office automation system was understood as a computer-based system assisting the office staff in their daily tasks. At the time, there was a growing amount of literature and commercial products concerning office automation. The two main purposes of the project were:

o   to contribute to the understanding of the office automation area by establishing a taxonomy and a terminology for the area;
o   to contribute to the further development of the area by specifying a generic office automation system (a system with special features for adaption to the tasks and working methods of a specific office).

The project also helped technology transfer, as persons from DDC together with persons from DDC members carried out the project.

In the taxonomy part of the project [25], the concepts of the office automation area were identified, analyzed, and classified. In the terminology part general terms, concepts and abbreviations used within office automation were explained and listed alphabetically. More than seventy items were explained.

To overcome the problems with a general office automation system: not fulfilling the requirements of a specific office, tailored system; being expensive to update as the needs of an office changes – a generic office automation system was specified and characterized. The generic office automation system was modeled using the VDM formal specification language. The model was also described informally and could thus be used by persons without knowledge of the VDM language.

Another office automation project was FAOR, Functional Analysis of Office Requirements. The project was supported by the CEC. Organizations from UK, Germany and Denmark participated in the project from 1983 to 1987. The Danish participant was a DDC member, ØK Data with DDC as subcontractor.

The purpose of the project was to develop a method that could help systems analysts to analyze and specify the office automation requirements to IT- systems. The work processes in an office for which IT-support was needed in the 1980s became more and more complex and were often unstructured. The FAOR project addressed this challenge of analyzing the complex office work and specifying functional requirements to IT-solutions. The method gives the analyst detailed instructions for the analysis and refers to a set of techniques and tools to use. The method was tried in field studies within the FAOR project with good results. The project is described in [26].

3.5   Technology Transfer

Cubus

In 1987, DDC expanded its technology transfer activities, bringing its knowhow out to Danish IT companies, by introducing a quarterly magazine Cubus.[4]

The main content in Cubus was technical and scientific articles. They covered subjects in which DDC had deep insight from actual project work. The articles were mainly addressed to an IT-knowledgeable audience, but they did not require special knowledge in the subject covered. Cubus also had articles for a wider audience and overviews/summaries of conferences, and it listed new DDC project reports.

---

[4] Please note the DDC 'cube' adorning the beginning of this paper.

Seminars and Courses

DDC also arranged seminars and courses covering sub- jects from DDC projects and topics of general interest, but within the area of software design and development. Examples of seminar subjects included topics such as object-oriented programming, why and how to change Ada, local area data net, and selling Danish software worldwide.

Reports

The results of DDC projects were largely publicly available through reports prepared during the projects. The reports appeared in the magazine Cubus and they sold for the reproduction costs.

4 Appraisal of DDC

In the mid 1980s, some forty people worked at DDC. Half of them had a master's degree in computing. The two large compiler projects Ada and CHILL lead to usable and useful products. However, in the longrun it was difficult to derive advantage and profit from these products. Ada did not gain the expected widespread use despite its U.S. DoD and CEC support. The knowledge and the rights for the Ada system were transferred to the subsidiary DDC–I Inc., which earned money but not sufficient to give a surplus to DDC. CHILL was developed for Danish teleauthorities as a new standard language for the international telecommunity CCITT, but after completion, CHILL did not generate income for DDC. At the same time, these products had very little interest for several of the DDC members.

A third large project was the RAISE software engineering method. Its scope was too ambitious to be of immediate interest to DDC's members. The project was transferred to the software company CRI Inc., where it was completed, used, and marketed with some success.

Besides the above compiler-oriented projects, DDC had a number of smaller software development projects, including user-friendly software and administrative database projects.

To assess what benefit DDC achieved for the Danish software milieu is difficult. However, in our opinion the major effects of DDC were as follows.

o   Some of the larger Danish IT users and producers became aware of modern software development techniques.

o   A reliable, DoD-verified Ada system was produced and became the basis for the incorporated company DDC-I Inc. still existing.

o   RAISE and LaCoS – methods and tools for large-scale reliable software development – were developed and brought to market by CRI Inc., which took over leading staff and all project rights from DDC.

o   Between fifty and a hundred young master's students in computer science obtained experience using advanced software technology and they carried it with them into other companies in Denmark and abroad.

o   DDC completed a number of large projects with better performance and higher product quality than was common in the 1980s.

Where DDC failed was to major Danish companies of the benefits of using reliable software development based on formal methods. (But, DDC did not try very much.) However, some of DDC's software engineers went to work for CRI Inc. (later sold to Terma), where they proceeded using formal methods "lite" in major European Space Agency and U.S. defense industry projects.

Acknowledgments. This is not the time and place for thanking those many people and institutions that made DDC possible. Nevertheless, we do wish to acknowledge the help of Assoc. Prof., Dr. Hans Bruun (emeritus). Without his diligent and painstaking investigations of how to formalize the static semantics of CHILL and Ada, DDC could not have gotten off the ground. In writing this paper, we received help from Messrs Peter L. Haff, Klaus Havelund and Jan Storbank Pedersen, and we acknowledge their help with gratitude.

References

1. Naur, P., Randall, B. (eds.): Software Engineering: The Garmisch Conference. NATO Science Committee, Brussels (1969)
2. Løvengreen, H.H.: Metodikker og værktøjer til konstruktion af programmel (KOMET). Report DDC-05, p. 229 (February 1981)
3. Bekič, H., Bjørner, D., Henhapl, W., Jones, C.B., Lucas, P.: A Formal Definition of a PL/I Subset. Technical Report 25.139, IBM Laboratory, Vienna (December 1974)
4. Bjørner, D., Jones, C.B. (eds.): The Vienna Development Method: The Meta-Language. LNCS, vol. 61. Springer, Heidelberg (1978)
5. George, C.W., Haxthausen, A.E., Hughes, S., Milne, R., Prehn, S., Storbank Pedersen, J.: The RAISE Development Method. The BCS Practitioner Series. Prentice-Hall, Hemel Hampstead (1995)
6. Bjørner, D.: Programming Languages: Linguistics and Semantics. In: International Computing Symposium 1977, pp. 511–536. European ACM, North-Holland Publ. Co., Amsterdam (1977)
7. Bjørner, D., Jones, C.B. (eds.): Formal Specification and Software Development. Prentice-Hall, Englewood Cliffs (1982)
8. Haff, P.L. (ed.): The Formal Definition of CHILL. ITU (Intl. Telecomm. Union), Geneva (1981)
9. Haff, P., Olsen, A.V.: Use of VDM within CCITT. In: Mac An Airchinnigh, M., Jones, C.B., Bjørner, D., Neuhold, E.J. (eds.) VDM-Europe 1987. LNCS, vol. 252, pp. 324–330. Springer, Heidelberg (1987)
10. Oest, O.N., Bjorner, D. (eds.): Towards a Formal Description of Ada. LNCS, vol. 98. Springer, Heidelberg (1980)
11. Clemmensen, C.B., Oest, O.N.: Formal specification and development of an Ada compiler – a VDM case study. In: Proc. 7th International Conf. on Software Engineering, Orlando, Florida, pp. 430–440. IEEE, Los Alamitos (1984)
12. Oest, O.N.: VDM From Research to Practice. In: Kugler, H.-J. (ed.) Information Processing 1986. IFIP World Congress Proceedings, pp. 527–533. North-Holland Publ. Co., Amsterdam (1986)
13. George, C.W., Haff, P., Havelund, K., Haxthausen, A.E., Milne, R., Bendix Nielsen, C., Prehn, S., Ritter Wagner, K.: The RAISE Specification Language. The BCS Practitioner Series. Prentice-Hall, Hemel Hampstead (1992)

14. Reggio, G., Invarardi, P., Astesiano, E., Fantechi, A., Giovani, A., Mazzanti, F., Zucca, E.: The Draft Formal Definition of Ada, The User Manual of the Meta-Language. Technical report, CRAI/IEI/University of Genoa (January 1986)

15. Astesiano, E., Bendix Nielsen, C., Fantechi, A., Giovani, A., Karlsen, E.W., Mazzanti, F., Reggio, G., Zucca, E.: The Draft Formal Definition of Ada, The Dynamic Semantics Definition. Technical report, Dansk Datamatik Center/CRAI/IEI/University of Genoa (January 1987)

16. Botta, N., Storbank Pedersen, J.: The Draft Formal Definition of Ada, The Static Semantics Definition. Technical report, Dansk Datamatik Center (January 1987)

17. Storbank Pedersen, J.: VDM in Three Generations of Ada Formal Descriptions. In: Mac An Airchinnigh, M., Jones, C.B., Bjorner, D., Neuhold, E.J. (eds.) VDM 1987. LNCS, vol. 252, Springer, Heidelberg (1987)

18. DDC, Univ. of Pisa, CRAI, CNRS IEI Pisa, Univ. of Genoa (ed.): The Draft Formal Definition of Ada. 3 parts. Dansk Datamatik Center (1987)

19. Prehn, S., Hansen, I.Ø., Palm, S.U., Gøbel, P.: Formal methods appraisal, first report. Technical Report DDC 86/1983-06-24, Dansk Datamatik Center, Lyngby (1983)

20. Prehn, S., Hansen, I.Ø.: Formal Methods Appraisal. Technical report, Dansk Datamatik Center (1983)

21. George, C.W.: Download for the RAISE Tool Set United Nations University's International Institute for Software Technology, P.O. Box 3058, Macao SAR, China, `ftp://ftp.iist.unu.edu/pub/RAISE/methodbook/`

22. George, C.W.: UNU-IIST's RAISE Web Pages United Nations University's International Institute for Software Technology, P.O. Box 3058, Macao SAR, China, `http://www.iist.unu.edu/raise/`

23. Storbank Pedersen, J.: Information about industrial use of RAISE Terma Inc., Herlev, Denmark, `http://spd-web.terma.com/Projects/RAISE/project.html`

24. Storbank Pedersen, J.: Terma Information about the RAISE Tool Set Terma Inc., Herlev, Denmark, `http://spd-web.terma.com/Projects/RAISE`

25. Bundgaard, J., Schmeltz Pedersen, J., Storbank Pedersen, J., Hansen, K., Kvorning, P., Nilsson, B.: Kontor-Automations-Systemer (KAS) – Et studieprojekt. DDC document: DDC 04/1981-04-30

26. Schmidt, K.: Kontorarbejde og kontoranalyse. In: Cubus (July 1987)

SISU: The Swedish Institute for Systems Development

Janis A. Bubenko, Jr.

Department of Computer and Systems Science
Royal Institute of Technology and Stockholm University
Forum 100, SE-16440, Kista, Sweden
janis@dsv.su.se

Abstract. The research institute SISU aimed at supporting the public sector as well as Sweden's business and industry in introducing modern methods and tools when developing information systems within their organizations. SISU was founded in 1984 by support from twenty-four companies and organizations and the Swedish Board for Technical Development (STU). In its peak period around 1993, SISU had forty employees and a turnover of 35 million Swedish crowns. The institute carried out a large number of national as well collaborative, EU-supported projects. One result of the projects was the forming of innovative Swedish companies and development of IT-products. SISU was discontinued in the year 2000 primarily due to lack of financial support.

Keywords: ESPRIT, information systems, methodology, research, software tools, technology transfer.

1 Background

The Swedish Institute for Systems Development (SISU) was a research institute aimed at supporting the public sector as well as business and industry in introducing modern methods and tools when designing and developing information systems within their organizations. This narrative presents reflections on why SISU was established, how it was financed, what its main achievements were, and why it was discontinued. In order to have a better understanding of the story, we will first present a brief survey of the computer hardware situation as well as of the systems development method and tool situation in Sweden in the early 1980s.

To know the number of people aged 16–74 who used the internet[1] at home was a question of no relevance in the early 1980s. The internet simply did not exist. Instead Sweden was populated with a fairly large number of mainframe computers, at least when it comes to their physical size. Companies or public organizations owned the computers. My guess is there were between two thousand and three thousand of them installed in Sweden in the early 1980s. From a performance point of view, these computers could not even compete with a laptop of 2010. They had a processor speed of about 0.5 MIPS, a memory of 64–128 kilobytes and a secondary magnetic disk

---

[1] For some, not accounted for, reason SCB's (The Swedish Bureau of Census) statistics about computer use in Sweden ends with persons aged 74. The author of this paper is 75.

J. Impagliazzo, P. Lundin, and B. Wangler (Eds.): HiNC3, IFIP AICT 350, pp. 360–367, 2011.
© IFIP International Federation for Information Processing 2011

memory of 25–50 Megabytes. Magnetic Tape units were frequently used. Many online, terminal based applications started to appear. The terminals used had simple, text-oriented displays. Graphics oriented terminals were extremely rare. Personal computers started to appear but except for a few Apple Macintosh personal computers, the operating systems were not windows-oriented.

IBM dominated having a 70 to 75 percent share of the market. In many cases the 360 computer (IBM 360/30, 360/40, 360/50) had replaced the IBM 7090, 7070 and 1401-type of computers. Other vendors such as Digital Equipment Corporation (DEC), Datasaab, ICL, Univac, CDC, and others competed on the remaining 25 to 30 percent share of the Swedish market. Minicomputers such as DEC's PDP-11 and VAX computers were not unusual in technical applications. They also introduced the UNIX operating system and made possible local mail use between users in a company. Later this developed into a more global email system where computers were calling each other in order to transfer mail. In the early 1980s, an email address consisted of a chain of computer names the mail had to pass in order to be delivered to its final destination. The data transfer speed was very modest: about 1,200 bits per second. As said above, the world wide web did not exist at this time, but IBM had its own worldwide network connecting IBM installations. Another well-known net was the ARPA-net connecting many US universities. Compatibility between computers did not exist, except for within a particular vendors' product line. For this reason, transferring of software from one vendor's hardware to another vendor's hardware was a non-trivial task, even when the software was written in a high-level language.

Computers, or rather computer centers, were normally run by the "data processing (DP) department" or "division" of the company. Practically all company information systems were produced "in house" by a company's own system analysts and programmers or by consultants. Standard software packages were rare. This situation gave the DP departments a strong position in companies and organizations. The manager of the DP department was often also member of the top managing group of the company. Information was considered valuable and expensive.

The market of "methods for computer use" or "methods for information systems development" during the 1970s in Sweden was dominated by data processing system departments of large companies (e.g. Ericsson, Telia, ABB, SCA, Volvo, etc.) and by a few large consulting companies such as Programator, ENEA, Data Logic, and Statskonsult. Most of them had their own, semi-structured, "home-made" method handbook. Vendor companies, most notably by IBM, demonstrated considerable method influence also. The user organization "Riksdataförbundet" and its service organization Servi-Data also carried out a number of projects aimed at description and comparative analysis of practical methods for systems development. Practically all these methods were practical and informal, some even having their roots in punched card oriented approaches.

In summary, method use in organizations was primitive. No generally accepted method for system development existed. System development tools started to appear but were hardly used. Lack of interactivity and graphical workstations made the use hard. Graphical representation of system flow and data diagrams was still quite primitive.

2 What Could Academics Offer?

Academic education and research in systems development had just begun. The ISAC and the CADIS[2] research groups at the Royal Institute of Technology and Stockholm University (KTH & SU), influenced by the works of Börje Langefors[3], were among the first in Sweden to work on theoretical aspects of methods for systems development. The ISAC group had already established a research institute called "Institute V" supported by a number of organizations in practice. ISAC was concerned manly with the early system development stages. Otherwise, contacts between the academic world and the field of practice were relatively sparse. We in the CADIS group and later in SYSLAB[4] were primarily concerned with implementation aspects of information systems design, including design of databases. We felt it also necessary to expose our ideas and results to the field of practice, in order to improve the quality of systems design and development work in Sweden.

What did we have to offer besides our enthusiasm and optimism? We had a fairly good grasp of the method situation concerning models of systems and information (data). We were also working on prototypes for implementation of CASE tools as well as for tools to develop object oriented office information systems.

By doing research on system development, we were of the opinion that much could be improved in practice. Standardization and improvement of methods, use of computer-based tools for system design and development were needed as well as a strict and less "local, home-made flavor" inspired evaluation and use of methods. In addition, in method education, much could be improved and new and modern methods could be taught. We also felt that the methods and prototypes we were working on had the potential to be "inherited" by companies and then developed further into marketable products, methods as well as software.

Therefore, in 1983 we started our work to establish a research institute forming a bridge between the academic world and practice.

3 Founding of SISU

The SISU institute was founded in 1984 as a natural consequence of two research efforts – the research groups CADIS and SYSLAB as well as of our collaboration with some companies in business and industry. Instrumental in the process of forming SISU was SYSLAB's industrial advisory group[5] headed by Rune Brandinger, then the CEO of Valand Insurance Company. In 1983–84, researchers from the department, including

---

[2] CADIS (Computer Aided Design of Information Systems) a research group at KTH & SU between1969 and1979, mainly sponsored by STU (Swedish Board for Technical Development).

[3] Börje Langefors became Sweden's first professor in "Administrative Data Processing" at KTH and SU in 1966.

[4] SYSLAB is the SYStems development LABoratory at the department, established in 1980.

[5] Members of the group were Krister Gustavsson, Statskontoret, Gunnar Holmdahl, ASEA Information Systems, Göran Kling, Volvo-Data, Sten Martin, Swedish Defence, Per Olof Persson, Riksdataförbundet, Sven-Erik Wallin, Esselte Datacenter, and Kurt Wedin, Vattenfall.

the author, together with the advisory group, contacted a large number of Swedish organizations in order to obtain financial support for forming a research foundation. Considerable support was obtained. A "supporting user and partner organization" called "Intressentföreningen för SVensk Informationssystemutveckling" (ISVI)[6] was established. SISU's research plans for the first three years, 1985–87, were worked out and documented in a "Framework Program" (ramprogram). All members of ISVI guaranteed to support SISU's research according to the Framework Program.

STU[7] and twenty-one supporting organizations and companies initially financed SISU. The Swedish government decided, in the autumn of 1984, to establish the operation of the industry research institute SISU starting January 1, 1985. The 1985 budget of SISU was about 8 million SEK. A number of researchers[8] moved from SYSLAB to SISU during 1985.

4 Initial Activities

The main goal of SISU was to act as a bridge between the worlds of practice and academia. Initially, SISU's main areas of activity were: 1) The Information Center (information dissemination, education), 2) Management of Information and Data Resources, 3) Methods and Tools for Problem-oriented Systems Development, and 4) Interactive Systems – Office Information Systems. The idea was to take some results of CADIS and SYSLAB and develop them into "prototype products" which could be demonstrated in practice. Two of these were OPAL (later renamed to AVANCE) and RAMATIC.

OPAL was a prototype system for distributed object management. This system would be used to build advanced and interactive office information systems. The architecture of OPAL was strongly object-oriented. The language PAL was developed for defining office applications [1]. The basic idea of OPAL was to decrease drastically the effort needed to implement advanced office applications.

RAMATIC was a meta-CASE tool, i.e. a tool to build CASE-tools for different methods and description techniques. In this way, we would be able to generate CASE tools for our supporting organizations, which all were using more or less different models and techniques for describing systems. RAMATIC was later used for building system-modeling tools in a number of Swedish organizations as well as in several international projects financed by the European Union's Framework programs.

Another legacy from SYSLAB that further developed at SISU was the conceptual information modeling knowledge and tradition. It later contributed to developing strong participatory business and enterprise modeling approaches as well as computer supported modeling tools within SISU.

---

[6] ISVI members in 1984 were: ASEA, Datalogic, DBK, ENEA, Ericsson, Försvarsstaben, Götabanken, IBM, Infologics, Kommundata, Programator, SAAB-SCANIA, SE-banken, Skandia, Statskonsult, Statskontoret, Televerket, Valand, Vattenfall, Volvo-Data and Volvo-PV.

[7] The Swedish Board for Technical Development.

[8] Matts Ahlsén, Lars Bergman, Peder Brandt, Stefan Britts, Janis Bubenko, Jr., Roland Dahl, Tord Dahl, Mats-Roger Gustavsson, Christer Hultén, Lars-Åke Johansson, Eva Lindencrona, Stefan Paulsson, Lars Söderlund, Håkan Torbjär, and Benkt Wangler. SISU's first secretary was Marianne Sindler.

All SISU's initial software prototype building was made on SUN-1 Workstations under SUN Unix and programmed in C. Ericsson had donated five SUN-1 workstations to SISU. These computers were considered quite powerful at this time.

5 National Projects

In its "peak period" (1990–93) SISU had an annual turnover of about 35 million Swedish crowns and about forty employees. The institute generated and carried out a large number of national collaborative projects, where the supporting organizations from ISVI took an active part. Hence, many persons from the supporting organizations received advanced training. One such project was TRIAD that generated and documented a vast amount of knowledge in business modeling in organizations. TRIAD also produced a by-product: a very easy to use, simple Macintosh based graphical modeling tool called Business Modeler. Regretfully, Business Modeler was not exploited outside the TRIAD project. Other examples of national projects are HYBRIS and Effective IT.

HYBRIS developed a hypertext-based tool that allows inexperienced computer users to navigate in and retrieve information from large corporate databases at a conceptual level. The information contained in the databases is represented in a graphical conceptual model – the information map. Queries are formulated by pointing and clicking directly in the information map.

Effective IT was a fairly large, two-year, umbrella project that ran from 1993 to 1995. It was initiated by a preliminary study project ordered by Sweden's ministry of industry and business and by NUTEK (a successor of STU). The aim of Effective IT was to investigate the possibility to define a national research program for improved and more effective use of IT in Swedish business and industry.

6 Collaborative European Projects

SISU understood early the scientific, technological, and the economic importance of joining European Union's ESPRIT program. Work on forming of consortia and on preparing project proposals started in 1987. SISU managed to be accepted as partner in a number of EU-projects such as KIWIS (2424), TEMPORA (2469), Nature (6353), F^3 (6353), INTUITIVE (6593), LYNX (6816), and several more. In the mid-1990s, about half of SISU's staff was engaged in EU-supported projects. During the period from late 1980s until the year 2000, SISU participated in more than twelve EU-supported projects, These projects pursued a number of advanced topics such as federated knowledge bases, temporal-deductive information system modeling, multimedia object management, accessing information in heterogeneous corporate databases, advanced techniques in requirements engineering, computer supported collaborative work, and several more topic areas. This collaborative work gave later openings for forming spin-off companies such as CNet, Projectplace, and ALKIT.

7 Main Contributions

Which were the main contributions of SISU to Sweden's professional society? The most concrete effects are formation of new pioneering IT-companies and through them, the transfer of innovative method and software tool knowledge and technology to usable products. IT-companies formed include NeoTech, CNet, Projectplace, and ALKIT. The next concrete contribution is more than 15 academic degrees (Licentiate or PhD degrees) awarded to SISU employees. SISU played an active role in supporting such studies, financially as well as scientifically. Other contributions include spreading of the "Culture of Conceptual Modeling for Business and Information Systems Development" to many Swedish organizations[9]. One of the names for this activity is "Enterprise Modeling" which now has grown into an international academic as well as a practical discipline. This discipline is now being exposed in conferences related to requirements engineering, information systems engineering, enterprise resource planning, and to practice of enterprise modeling (see for instance PoEM [2]). Another important contribution of SISU is bringing Swedish enterprises to participate in EU's research projects in particular in the ESPRIT program (European Strategic Program for Research and development in Information Technologies). Overall, SISU's activities on the European research arena gave Sweden improved recognition in international research in IT. Above all, it gave many young Swedish researchers and IT-engineers a taste and feeling for working on the European market. SISU was also instrumental in starting up the well reputed international CAiSE (Conference on Advanced Information Systems Engineering) conference series now celebrating its twenty-second annual conference [3].

SISU continued its operations until 2000, during the last two years as part of a research company Framkom. The foundation had a concluding passive period 2000–04. SISU's managing directors were Janis Bubenko, Jr. (1985–92), Thomas Falk (1992–94), and Eva Lindencrona (1995–98) and Mikael von Otter (1998–2000).

8 Why Was SISU Discontinued?

The reason for the discontinuance of SISU is a crucial question and difficult to answer. As expected, there were several contributing causes. One of them is economic disturbances and recession in Sweden. In the beginning of the 1990s, the interest rate climbed to 500 percent. The so-called "IT-bubblan" started in latter part of that decade. Companies found it more and more difficult to justify expenses on supporting IT research, in particular in companies classified as IT users rather than IT developers such as the Ericsson company. However, Ericsson had problems as well, as we remember. Telia (Swedish Telecom) also had difficulties as had most IT-consulting companies. Ericsson and Telia both were supporting SISU to more than 50 percent of SISU's total budget. Both these companies discontinued their support in the late 1990s. This discontinuation contributed strongly to the demise of SISU. Participation in EU-projects in mid-1990s was considerable. It generated some money, but all EU-support was spent on producing project deliverables. The above reasons obviously made it very hard for SISU's management to obtain sufficient financing to run SISU as an independent research organization and not as a consulting company.

---

[9] As an example, the modelling approach has been used by the National Board of Health and Welfare in order to describe and display Sweden's "national information structure" (http://ni.socialstyrelsen.se).

Nevertheless, my feeling now, more than fifteen years after the peak period of SISU, still focuses on another reason that is perhaps quite essential for the decline of the institute. This reason is that to apply research results in practice necessitates an undertaking requiring high-competence user organizations, considerable time, and human resources. SISU's supporting organizations were in the 1980s and 1990s perhaps not ready to make such long-term commitments. In this sense, our initial expectations about our supporting organizations and their capability for technology transfer and take-up were far too optimistic. What could be the reason for this situation? In my opinion, it is the relatively low degree of research and development orientation of the education underlying employees of most of our supporting organizations. The academic education in Sweden in computer and systems science and in the neighboring topic "Informatik" has, since its start in the end of 1970s, had a very low fraction of education in the mathematical and engineering sciences. This has fostered, I believe, an attitude among our supporters that excellence in systems development is something that can be bought, by acquiring advanced products, instead of developing skills and competence of the organization itself.

On the other hand, we have to be a bit critical about ourselves as well. We began in 1985 by building two extremely complex prototypes. Resources required to implement them were perhaps five to ten times larger than we had available, but we did not know it then. Consequently, OPAL/AVANCE was never completed and we could not find any Swedish company willing to invest the resources needed for its completion. RAMATIC was practically used in a few projects. In addition, here we failed to find a Swedish company willing to carry the complex work further towards a product. We had better luck with some prototypes in the 1990s, but this was because the prototypes were constructed as products by the staff who originally designed them at SISU.

We had better luck with the exploitation of methods and knowledge for business and enterprise modeling. Knowledge from this field was disseminated to many organizations and hundreds of professionals.

9   Concluding Remarks

SISU existed during a fifteen-year period. The technical conditions in the beginning of the period and at its end were vastly different. In 1985, computing was mainly done on incompatible mainframe computers. Few workstations or PCs existed. In the year 2000, the internet was in full swing and computing in Sweden was largely done by compatible personal computers. The market had grown to more than a million of PCs, but they did not require the kind of complex software SISU had been developing. The most characteristic thing was the speed with which everything evolved. Such a quickly evolving world of telecommunications and computing calls for different research priorities and research transfer initiatives compared to what existed in 1985. An intriguing question might be, is there a market for a research institute with a similar direction as SISU? That is, does a market exist for the dissemination of information system development methods and tools that existing today? Personally, I think there is a true need for that, but the task to convince business and industry to understand that need and to put any money in such a venture is most likely quite discouraging.

One may find more information about SISU at http://www.sisuportal.se/ (developed by CNeT) which contains more than 250 documents produced during the 1985–2000 period. A description of SISU's knowledge and technology transfer activities can be found in [4]. The forty-year history of the Department for Computer and Systems Science [5] includes reports about CADIS and SYSLAB and in that way forms the background to the establishment of SISU.

References

1. Björnerstedt, A., Britts, S.: AVANCE: An Object Management System. In: Object-Oriented Programming Systems, Languages and Applications, San Diego, CA (1988)
2. Stirna, J., Persson, A. (eds.): The Practice of Enterprise Modelling. LNBIP, vol. 15. Springer, Berlin (2008)
3. Steinholtz, B., Sølvberg, A., Bergman, L. (eds.):Second Nordic Conference on Advanced Information Systems Engineering, CAiSE 1990. Springer, New York (1990)
4. Bubenko Jr., J.A., Lindencrona, E.: Experiences from Technology Transfer Initiatives at SISU. In: Johannesson, P., Söderström, E. (eds.) Information Systems Engineering: From Data Analysis to Process Networks. IGI Publishing, Hershey (2007)
5. Bubenko Jr., J.A., Jansson, C.-G., Kollerbaur, A., Ohlin, T., Yngström, L. (eds.): ICT for People: 40 Years of Academic Development in Stockholm. Department of Computer and Systems Sciences at Stockholm University and Royal Institute of Technology, Kista (2006)

Cloud Computing in the 1970s:
The Discovery of Hash Based Relational Algebra

Kjell Bratbergsengen

Department of Computer and Information Science (IDI)
The Norwegian University of Science and Technology (NUST/NTNU)
kjellb@idi.ntnu.no

Abstract. Cloud computing was not a known term in the 1970s. However, this is about work done from 1975 to 1990, which with today's terminology partly could have been termed, cloud computing. This article is about how we discovered hash-based methods for doing relational algebra, searching for efficient algorithms to run on a future parallel computer. We found the algorithms; however, Norsk Data never built the parallel computer. We built four parallel computers ourselves, but first we implemented the hash based relational algebra algorithms in TechRa, a system for mono computers, and obtained excellent results. Being able to establish a lab, developing machines, software and algorithms led to a very rich research period from 1985 to 1990, involving many PhD and master students. We had the world record in both sorting and relational algebra on our parallel computers for a while. We commercialized our research in 1989 with many positive effects, but with negative effects to the university activities in the field.

Keywords: Database research, history of research projects, parallel computing.

1 The Database Group

A small database group was formed at NTH and SINTEF in 1972 lead by Kjell Bratbergsengen, then assistant professor at NTH. The group built several file and database systems right from its beginning: AKUFIL [1], INDSEQ [2], Ra1 [3], Ra2 [4], and a backend database machine Ra3 [5]. AKUFIL was a specialized file system for storing matrices. INDSEQ was an indexed sequential file system used in an internal project CASCADE led by Arne Sølvberg. Inspired by a similar system on our UNIVAC 1107 computer, we used block splitting on overflow (at both data and index levels); our architecture was really close to what is known as B*-trees today. RA1 was used to store the first BIBSYS database and it served BIBSYS for more than fifteen years until it was followed by ADABAS on a new IBM computer. RA2 was developed for Kongsberg Vaapenfabrik (KV); the first application was their bill of material database. Later, KV in Scandinavia also marketed RA2. RA2 featured sequential, indexed sequential and hashed access to records at the first level. Below each first level record, there could be a general tree of records of different types.

The database group was very familiar with the CODASYL work. It existed a Norwegian system SIBAS, based on the CODASYL proposed standard. SI developed

J. Impagliazzo, P. Lundin, and B. Wangler (Eds.): HiNC3, IFIP AICT 350, pp. 368–374, 2011.
© IFIP International Federation for Information Processing 2011

SIBAS and Norsk Data marketed it; there was no room in Norway for more systems of this type. Our market was lighter and faster systems.

The database group started as a common group for NTH and SINTEF. Bratbergsengen was employed by the university, the first two members; Knut Hofstad and Kjell Wibe were both employed by SINTEF. They operated very integrated the first ten years, however, as the SINTEF group grew and financing needs alike, they became more independent of each other.

2 The ASTRA Project

In 1970, Edgar F. Codd published his seminal paper "A Relational Model of Data for Large Shared Data Banks." This was a totally new way of organizing data, but it was regarded as useless caused by very long execution times. The model favored programmer productivity. Finding methods to get reasonable execution times seemed impossible, and became a great challenge. Relational algebra is the "instruction set" of relational database systems.   Instructions included selection, projection, join, intersection, union, difference, division and aggregation. Operands were tables or files if you like, so are also results. Algorithms for doing relational algebra were normally nested loop algorithms or sort based. These methods were terrible for large operands. A number of research projects tried to find effective ways to implement the relational model the next fifteen years [6–12]. Because of the time-consuming algorithms, all the listed projects involved building some type of new hardware, either parallel disks or machines with smart or especially associative memory. The list of projects is not complete.

Norsk Data saw a market for selling more hardware, and together we worked out a research proposal to the Norwegian Science Foundation – the ASTRA project in 1977. We should develop a relational database system for parallel computers. The database data was to be stored in main memory. Norsk Data engineers had figured out that main memory would reach the same price as disk in quite a few years. Main memory storage and parallel machines should solve the problems with long execution times. However, Norsk Data engineers were not equally acquainted with disk technology and disks became cheaper too. Eventually this led to the end of the project. However, the main result of the project was the discovery of efficient methods for doing relational algebra. It is easy to parallelize selection.   All the other relational algebra operations are all based on finding records with matching values of their operation keys – a set of attributes specified for the operation. In the seventies, nested loop or sorting for larger operands was used to find records with equal key values. Both methods are hard to parallelize.

2.1 Hash Based Relational Algebra Algorithms

The basic idea behind hash based relational algebra methods is quite simple. If two records have the same key value, their hash values would also be the same. If two hash values are different, their keys must be different. If two hash values are equal, their keys *might* be equal, but not necessarily. To avoid testing too many unequal keys for equality, the hash value space is adapted so the probability of synonyms is small. Synonyms: two different key values giving the same hash value. We also use a hash formula on the primary key to compute the home node (the node where it is stored) of a record. Only one node is activated for storing, deleting, or modifying a record given that the primary key is known.

The first phase of all relational algebra operations (except selection and non-equijoin) is a redistribution of all the operand records to the target node determined by the hash value of the operation key. Then the operation is completed on the target node; the global task is split into N local tasks. N is the number of nodes on the parallel computer. The method requires a minimum of internal synchronization and features a built in load distribution mechanism, i.e. the hash based redistribution of operands.

Redistribution of operands required an internode network with high capacity and good scalability. The analysis of different networks was documented in [13]. We looked at different ring structures, records might move one or both ways, and the rings were intersected to reduce the average number of hops during redistribution. We ended up with an extreme variant, a ring of only two nodes, able to handle many nodes; the number of intersecting dimensions became larger. This is how we discovered the hypercube. The hypercube was chosen because it scaled perfectly and it had simple routing rules. The number of nodes in a hypercube is $N=2^D$ where D is the number of dimensions. We could also call D the diameter of the hypercube, which is the maximum number of hops to relocate a record. The average number of hops is D/2. In [13], we also described hash based relational algebra in very vague ways; we protected pour methods! We discussed patenting, but had no experience, no one to ask for advice, and no resources for financing.

The ASTRA project was quite ambitious; it also had a language development goal. The relational model was integrated into a modified SIMULA, the new programming language was named ASTRAL, see [14] and [15]. The database – or permanent data was declared in the outer block of the program. This block was never left conceptually. New programs were inserted as procedures into the persistent outer block. We managed to write a compiler for ASTRAL before the project was called off. Major contributors were Tore Amble and Tor Stålhane.

3 After ASTRA Came TechRa

As it became evident that Norsk Data would terminate the project because the assumptions about main memory price versus disk price did not hold, we realized that we had to build the parallel hardware ourselves.

However, this author got a request from a KV subsidiary – SYSSCAN Mapping, they needed at database system for storing geographic data. SYSSCAN Mapping pioneered digital maps. Kvatro AS (KV avdeling Trondheim) got a contract for building a brand new relational database system, with some added features for storing free text and especially sequences of x, y, z coordinates. The relational algebra was of course realized using hash-based methods. Roy Lyseng, fresh from NTH, was employed by Kvatro to lead the project, which was mainly staffed by RUNIT people. Kvatro marketed TechRa successfully for more than twenty years. It was a lightweight and very efficient database system. The usefulness of hash based relational algebra methods on a mono computer system had been evidenced.

4 The Period of the Hypercube Laboratory (HCL)

How the methods worked on a real parallel computer had still to be tested. Realizing hash based relational algebra on a parallel computer moved the possible bottleneck from disk I/O or bus/memory system to the network connecting the nodes of the parallel machine. For some years, the author worked on a VLSI chip for setting up lines through the hypercube. However, no serious attempt to produce it was made, it simply was too expensive.

In 1983, we came across dual ported memory chips. Could we use them for communication between computers or nodes in a parallel computer? A test set up with three PCs was built during the Christmas holidays in 1983, and it worked. Dual port RAM was less efficient than using line switching between nodes; however, it was considered efficient enough for a demonstration system. After getting NFR support, a project was set up to build a parallel computer with eight nodes to demonstrate parallel algebra. David DeWitt and his group at University of Wisconsin had worked out a benchmark for relational database systems in 1983 [16]. The most popular test was the DeWitt join test, joining two tables; Table A containing 1,000 records each 182 bytes long and table B containing 10,000 records also 182 bytes long. We "promised" NFR to do the test in less than 3.0 seconds. We did it in 1.8 seconds. The same test was run on several computers: TechRa on ND540 used 17 seconds, 32 seconds on a VAX 11/750. Ingres – one of the leading systems at the time – used 156 seconds on a VAX 11/750 [17]. CROSS8 was the name of this first operational parallel computer. It was finished in 1985. It had a direct connection – one common dual port RAM of 1,024 bytes – between each pair of nodes, which explains its name. Each node was a single board computer with a SCSI disk. Each node had also a DPRAM in common with a supervising PC, which controlled the whole system. We experienced DPRAM to a very flexible and useful tool for developing new hard- and software. A curiosity: During start up, DPRAM was mapped in as boot memory, after start up the same area was used for transferring messages.

We built three more parallel computers: HC16-186, HC16-386 and HC64-486 all with hypercube topology DPRAM message passing network. The first number (16, 64) is the number of nodes, and the last number denotes the Intel processor used. Each node was a single board computer designed and built by us. HC64-486 was never completed. It was up and running with four nodes; however, the HCL then closed down.

Shifting from direct communication in CROSS8 to indirect communication in the HCxx-systems was an issue. The CPU had to use some time to move records in transit between nodes. However, it turned out not to be a problem. HC16-186 and HC16-386 were fairly stable systems and they were used to improve the database algorithms, and a large number of parallel algorithms were developed and tested by our PhD and master students. We had the world record in sorting for a period; in 1989, 100 MB was sorted in 180 seconds on HC16-186 [18].

In 1989, we were ready to commercialize our research, and we established the company HypRa AS with seven shareholders from the research group. The new company should develop a database for Telenor. It soon became clear that Telenor wanted a transaction-oriented system with extremely high reliability. Parallel algebra systems – which was really ready to go commercially at that time; it was not in Telenor's interest. The commercialization became a catastrophe to database research at the department. The lab disappeared, so did the people and there was no money to reestablish the loss. Despite being the founder and board chair of the company, I could not go along with it and I left HypRa in 1991. The high throughput, extremely reliable, transactional database for telecom operations required another ten years of research, but that is another (success) story. HypRa AS went through several transformations, Teleserve, Clustra, Sun Microsystems Trondheim, and was recently bought by Oracle. The database activities produced a large number of master candidates, very competent in database technology and parallel computing which strengthened Trondheim as the database city.

5 What We Achieved and Learnt

We discovered and demonstrated the usefulness of hash-based algorithms for doing relational algebra. These methods are part of all major data base systems today, both for mono machines and parallel machines. Our early experiences with parallel machines were taken further within HypRa and the companies that followed from HypRa; developing high capacity and highly reliable database systems.

The work on hypercube networks or more generally, high capacity highly scalable networks had not been continued after the three last prototypes. The reason: We had not pursued this track and other off the shelf hardware had been good enough. Work on hypercube networks or scalable networks could be reconsidered as we now have computers with thousands of nodes.

We established a permanent commercial activity on core database technology in Trondheim and Norway. We should have done more on publishing our work, especially the first years. That would have improved our worldwide standing, although we do not complain.

To protect our results we badly needed assistance. Today the universities in Norway have systems for this. However, it is surprising how long it takes to develop ideas before they are put to work. We discovered hash-based algebra in 1978, a vague publication was done in 1980, and a full publication of the methods and their results demonstrating their superiority came in 1984 [19]. Ten years later, at SIGMOD 1994, all the major database vendors of that time (IBM DB2, Sybase, and Oracle) indicated that they are now working on implementing hash-based methods in their systems.

Commercialization is very risky. It took away people, the lab, and financing. The database group was never reestablished to the same level. Partners from industry and research institutes had only an eye for protection of their commercial interests and they took no responsibility for continued research and production of more candidates at the university. Continued activity at the department was considered as a threatening competition to the commercial offspring.

During the five intensive years at the Hypercube laboratory, we produced a large number of master candidates with hands on experience from data management and parallel computers. We covered a broad field from VLSI design to parallel programming and algorithms and advanced database technology: parallel core database algorithms, transaction handling and fault tolerance techniques on a parallel system. Access to bright candidates with relevant education was cited as a major reason for international companies to establish branch offices in Trondheim (Yahoo, Google).

Instead of moving projects away from the university, it would have been much better for continuity in research to keep the commercial activities within the department, or at least central parts of it. The same experience repeated itself when the FAST group moved away from our department.

Having a common goal, a laboratory and being able to build prototypes is of highest value. It requires financing to keep laboratory personnel and develop new hardware. The lab is bringing people together, a common working and *social* arena for graduate and undergraduate students, researchers and professors. Problems, hard to find from theory alone, popped up such as deadlock in the record redistribution algorithm. Crossing hypercube dimensions in arbitrary order caused deadlock. Crossing hypercube dimensions in any fixed order (all records obey this order) avoids deadlock. Of course, this is what we learnt in operating systems and transaction scheduling theory! In parallel systems, we must handle failures, the more nodes, the higher probability that one of them will fail. Working with cloud technology in the 1970s and 1980s was a very successful educational project. Many of the PhDs and masters from the project have key positions in advanced IT projects today.

Acknowledgments. Torgrim Gjelsvik was the first researcher at HCL. He did most of the practical work building new machines and writing the low-level software. Ole John Aske was the second researcher at HCL and he worked mainly with developing software. They made everything work and helped. PhD students Øystein Torbjørnsen, Eirik Knutsen, Petter Moe, and Olav Sandstå were also part of the HCL kernel. A large number of students did their project works and master thesis within the lab. Some developed the system further and many used the hypercube computers to get their first experience with writing and implementing parallel algorithms. I am very grateful to all of you, the ASTRA and TechRa projects participants and members of the database group. Thanks also to the Norwegian Science Foundation who financed both the ASTRA and the Hypercube projects.

References

1. Bratbergsengen K., Hofstad K., Nødtvedt E.: AKUFIL – et filsystem for lagring og gjenfinning av matriser. Brukerveiledning, Oppdrag nr. 140404.0 SINTEF (November 15, 1972)
2. Bratbergsengen K., Johansen T.: INDSEQ Et indeks-sekvensielt filsystem for Univac EXEC-8 og IBM System 360/370 OS, CASCADE arbeidsnotat nr. 23 (April 24,1972)
3. Bratbergsengen K., Hofstad K.: RA1 – et vertsspråkbasert databasesystem. Metode og systemdokumentasjon, SINTEF prosjekt nr 140413 (December 1, 1973)
4. Bratbergsengen, K., Kongshaug, P., Kvitsand, S.: RA2 – Brukerveiledning, SINTEF prosjekt nr. 142515 (January 13,1977)
5. Bratbergsengen, K., Hofstad, K., Wibe, K., Midtlyng, J.O.: Databasemaskiner – en riktigere måte for å omsette databaseprogramvare, Data no. 3 1977 og NordDATA 77 (June 1977)
6. Ozkarahan, E.A., Schuster, S.A., Smith, K.C.: RAP An Associative Processor for Data Base Management. In: NCC 1975 (1975)
7. Su, S.Y.V., Lipovski, G.J.: CASSM –A Cellular System for Very Large Databases. In: VLDB 1975 (1978)

8. Leilich, H.O., Stiege, G., Zeidler, H.C.: A Search Processor for Data Base Management Systems. In: VLDB 1978 (1978)
9. Langdon, G.G.: A Note on Associative Processors for Data Management. ACM TODS 3(2) (1978)
10. DeWitt, D.J.: DIRECT – A Multiprocessor Organization for Supporting Relational Database Management Systems. IEEE Transaction on Computers C-28(6) (1979)
11. Maller, V.A.J.: The Content Addressable File Store – CAFS. ICL Technical Journal 1(3) (1979)
12. Oliver, E.J.: RELACS An Associative Computer Architecture to Support a Relational Data Model, PhD Dissertation, Syracuse University (1979)
13. Bratbergsengen, K., Larsen, R., Risnes, O., Aandalen, T.: A Neighbor Connected Processor Network for Performing Relational Algebra Operations. Paper presented at 5th Workshop on Computer Architecture for Non-Numeric Processing, March 11-14. Pacific Grove, California (1980)
14. Amble, T., Bratbergsengen, K., Risnes, O.: ASTRAL: A Structured and Unified Approach to Database Design and Manipulation. In: Proc. Database Architecture Conference, Venice (1978)
15. Bratbergsengen, K., Stålhane, T.: A feature analysis of ASTRAL. In: Brodie, M., Smidt, J. (eds.) The Relational Task Group - Feature Analysis of Relational Database Systems. Springer, Heidelberg (1981)
16. Bitton, D., DeWitt, D.J., Turbyfill, C.: Benchmarking Database Systems. A Systematic Approach. In: VLDB 1983 (1983)
17. Bratbergsengen, K.: Algebra Operations on a Parallel Computer - Performance Evaluation. In: The 5th International Workshop on Database Machines, Karuizawa Japan, October 5-8 (1987)
18. Baugstø, B.A.W., Greipsland, J.F.: Parallel Sorting Methods for Large Data Volumes on a Hypercube Database Computer. In: Boral, H., Faudemay, P. (eds.) IWDM 1989. LNCS, vol. 368, Springer, Heidelberg (1989)
19. Bratbergsengen, K.: Hashing Methods and Relational Algebra Operations. In: VLDB 1984 (1984)

The TEMPORA Approach:
Information Systems Development Based on Explicit Business Rules with Time

Benkt Wangler

Department of Computer and Systems Sciences
Stockholm University, Forum 100, SE-16440 Kista, Sweden
benkt.wangler@dsv.su.se

Abstract. This paper provides an account of the project TEMPORA, run from 1989 to 1994 and sponsored by the European Union, in which the Swedish Institute for Systems Development (SISU) and the research institute SINTEF from Norway were two of the partners. The project aimed at developing a prototypical systems development environment that involved the time dimension and it was based on the explicit representation of business rules. The Nordic partners played important roles in the project, in designing, building, and evaluating modeling formalisms and tools, as well as in designing methodological support.

Keywords: Business rules, information systems development environment, time dimension.

1 Background

During the 1980s, IT professionals started to become increasingly aware that the most fundamental part of information systems was the business rules embedded in the software. Such rules are, more or less, all the conscious rules that govern the business. They derive from business objectives (customers have to pay their invoices within ten days), laws and regulations (each car must have a registration number), and laws of nature (a child can only have one genetic mother). These rules are implemented into the various programs of an information system, without much help in keeping track of them. What rules are there? When a rule changes, which code do I have to change? Those questions required answering when a change occurred in a system.

Another trend starting somewhat earlier was the interest in the temporal dimension. That is, how does one take requirements involving time (e.g. a rule such as: "in order in one state to be divorced, you have to have been married in some previous state") into consideration during requirements capture and how should databases and information systems be designed with regard to representing and coping with time. The research that was carried out concerned understanding and implementing time in an information system context that resulted in various kinds of temporal logic and in temporal databases usually realized in the relational database model.

J. Impagliazzo, P. Lundin, and B. Wangler (Eds.): HiNC3, IFIP AICT 350, pp. 375–382, 2011.

TEMPORA [1] was a project within the European ESPRIT program aimed at developing practical methods and tools for systems development that integrated rule-based methods and temporal reasoning. Involving time meant that one could express the requirements for historical information and that rules may refer to time. As indicated in Fig. 1, the TEMPORA development discipline ranged from business analysis all the way through to design and implementation.

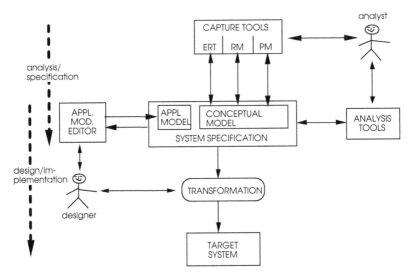

Fig. 1. The TEMPORA systems development environment

Central to the environment was a conceptual model comprising three parts: a structural entity-relationship-time (ERT) specification, a rule model, and a process model. Around this specification, we developed methods and tools both for capturing requirements and creating/analyzing the model and for taking it further to implementation.

The remainder of the paper briefly presents the project, and then concentrates on the conceptual model and the evaluation of its feasibility. The paper concludes by accounting for some experiences of the project as a whole.

2 The Project

As mentioned, TEMPORA was a European research project running under the ESPRIT 2nd framework program in which the Swedish Institute for Systems Development (SISU) and SINTEF, a Norwegian research institute, were two of the partners. Since Sweden and Norway were not members of EU, national authorities funded the work. The other partners were:

- the Belgian company BIM (cf. BIM-Prolog), which was formally responsible vis-à-vis the European Union (EU),
- the University of Liege in Belgium,

- the University of Manchester Institute of Science and Technology (UMIST, now part of the University of Manchester), which acted as project leader,
- Imperial College, London,
- Logic Programming Associates (LPA), a London based company, and
- Hitec, a company from Greece.

The author of this paper led the SISU effort. The project had a considerable budget and lasted for just over five years, from January 1989 to the beginning of 1994.

The responsibility of SISU was to design and specify the semantics of the ERT notation, to develop the drawing tools for ERT and the process model, and to contribute to the parts of the methodology that concerned early phases of requirements modeling. The Swedes were also responsible for evaluating the usability of all three notations.

The Norwegian partner shared many of these responsibilities, also bringing and adapting the PID formalism into the project. Both Nordic partners made substantial contributions to the project. In general, universities and research institutes conducted the more research-oriented tasks, while industrial partners were providers of technology.

There were regular plenary meetings about four times a year at locations offered by the various partners, as well as, at times, extra meetings between some of the partners to solve specific issues. Once a year, one of the plenary meetings was used a whole day for review and discussion with a representative from the European Commission and an independent reviewer.

3 What We Did

The idea of TEMPORA was to build a systems development environment based on the explicit representation of business rules in notations that were easy to use and understand, and which should also make it possible to represent requirements that involved time. The environment should provide support in devising system requirements expressed in these notations and from which an executable prototypical system could be derived. Hence, we proposed the following:

- A conceptual schema representation comprising a triplet of interrelated notations:
  - Process interaction diagrams (PID), a graphical process modeling language similar to dataflow diagrams but enhanced with triggers,
  - ERT, an entity-relationship (ER) type of language where one could mark for which entity and relationship types one wanted their temporal behavior to be preserved,
  - External rule language (ERL), an elaborate, though still reasonably easy to understand and use, textual version of a temporal logic
- Tools for use in formulating statements in these languages and in analyzing the resulting conceptual model. The tools were implemented using RAMATIC, a meta-case platform developed at SISU.

- A generator that could take a model built in these languages as input and transform it into an executable system. The generator and resulting system were implemented using BIM-Prolog and a relational database system (SYBASE).
- Methodware, rather elaborate procedures, guidelines, and advice regarding how the analyst/designer should think, reason, and use the above languages and tools during the process of capturing and formulating a model in those languages and, through such use, finally devise executable software that fulfill the requirements represented in the model.

In the following two sections, I briefly present and provide examples of the representation of time, and the business rule notation.

3.1 The Temporal Dimension

Semantic data models of the past focused on data representation without any in-depth consideration of the temporal and behavioral aspects of information modeling. In [2] we explored the enhancements to a binary entity-relationship model necessary to express requirements for temporally related information. We employed a time model in which time proceeds in ticks. Hence, central to this model were time points represented by ticks and periods starting at a certain tick and ending at a later one. Periods corresponding to those of our own calendar down to a sufficiently narrow granularity were also included.

When adding the temporal dimension to models belonging to the ER family, we must consider

- Enhancing the relational database to incorporate temporal information, and
- Augmenting the graphical and textual modeling formalisms with time concepts, so that temporal requirements, integrity constraints, and other rules involving time can be specified.

The topic of adding the temporal dimension to the relational model had received considerable attention in the database literature. It was made clear that two types of temporal information can be recorded in addition to attributes/tuples, to fully capture the evolution of an attribute/tuple over time, these being the

- Event time which records, as a series of time points, the time period over which we know (or think) a piece of information holds in the Universe of Discourse (UoD), and
- Transaction time which records, as a series of time points, the time period during which the information is stored in the database.

In practice, the event time is of most interest, since the modeling of the UoD is usually the objective of an IS. The transaction time is only of use in meta-rules which review the activities of the IS and that would need to know what information the system used at any point in its execution. Since the latter was not the purpose of TEMPORA, the temporally extended ER type of model developed within TEMPORA incorporated the event time and not transaction time. It did this in the form of time-stamps (start- and end-time) attached to the database representations of entities and relationships for which one wanted to keep track of history.

Hence, the ERT language was augmented with the possibility to T-mark the entity types and relationships for which one wished to keep track of the period of validity, that is, the period for which they hold. Fig. 2 shows an example of an ERT model. The T-mark on certain entity classes and relationships expresses that instances of these are valid (hold) only for a limited period, as represented in the database. Instances of classes that have no T-mark hold for all time, as in a standard database system. A "car" has a certain life span from production to destruction. During this time, it may have several registration numbers and several owners, each with a certain life span. In addition, a person may have a certain life span. As we delete instances of classes that are not T-marked, they are erased from the database. Instances of classes and relationships that are T-marked will stay in the database after they are "killed," but they will not hold as true any more. The dashed lines indicate relationships derivable from other relationships.

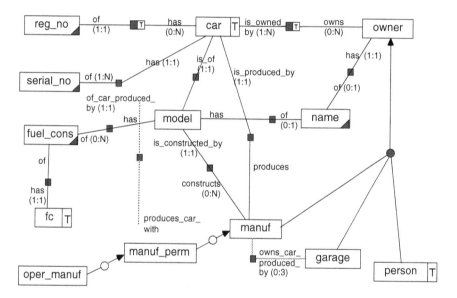

Fig. 2. The ISO-case ERT schema

With reference to this model, rules referring to time may be expressed by means of temporal logic, which is a modal logic able to express that some condition should hold "some time in the past," "in the next state," "always in the future," and so on. In addition to such temporal relations, the ERL language was augmented with various logical and temporal operators and connectors. Examples appear in the next section.

3.2 Business Rules

Business rules are essentially of three kinds [3]:

- Constraints expressing restrictions on permissible states of the information base,

- Event-condition-action rules expressing that if a certain event occurs, and provided a pre-condition holds, a certain action should be conducted, i.e., the database management system should somehow ensure that a certain post-condition is made to become true,
- Derivation rules expressing how certain information, which is not explicitly stored in the database, may be derived from information stored in the database.

In addition, a rule may be *static*, referring to a single state of the database, or *dynamic*, referring to several states. Cardinality constraints of relationships such as the ones expressed in Fig. 2 are examples of static constraints.

To be expressed as precisely referring to explicit states of the database, the rules must be presented in great detail. A few examples of static and dynamic rules expressed in ERL and referring to Fig. 2 follow below.

a) Sample static constraint: "The serial number is unique for all cars of one manufacturer." In ERL, this rule may be stated as: "if at some point there are observations that there are cars produced by the same manufacturer and these observations do not concern the same car, then their serial numbers cannot be the same."

```
If Manufacturer.M produces car.C1 and manufacturer.M
produces car.C2 and not C1 = C2 then not car.C1 has
serial.no = car C2 has serial.no
```

b) Sample dynamic constraint: "Each car has one serial no for its entire lifetime." `always_in_future` is a temporal operator referring to all future states in the lifetime of the car.

```
If car.C has serial.no = X then always_in_future (car.C
has serial.no = X)
```

c) Sample dynamic ECA-rule: "Only in January may a car be registered as being produced in the previous year." The rule may be formulated as below, where registration time is the start time of the "car has reg_no" relationship. Some_time_in_past is a temporal operator referring to all states preceding the current one. This_year, this_month and last_year are temporal literals referring to the corresponding periods.

```
When car.C has reg_no if some_time_in_past(car.C and
just_before not car.C and Prod_year = this_year) then
Prod_year = this_year or this_month = 'January' and
Prod_year = last_year
```

In the communication with the customer/user, rules are often expressed ambiguously. By stating the rules in ERL, formulations are demanded that in a precise way refer to the temporal database, although they sometimes have to be explained to those not used to thinking in temporal database and ERL terms.

3.3 Evaluation

The TEMPORA approach was tested in parts and in total, using a number of smaller and larger cases. One of the first cases we used was the so-called ISO case, involving forty-seven more or less complex statements and rules governing car registration in a fictitious country (cf. Fig. 2 and rule examples of Section 3.2 and [3]). It transpired that it was indeed possible to model all the rules, but that some of them became complex and actually required a great deal of "Prolog programmer thinking."

The largest case used for testing the modeling environment concerned building a complete model of the order system at Sweden Post. This case generated several hundred business rules at different levels of abstraction, some of which were quite complex. Although the case again showed that it was possible to model all the rules, it also demonstrated that keeping track of such a huge mass would require a much more elaborate and efficient way of structuring and handling them in the model repository.

The case that was used to test the complete environment was much smaller, but demonstrated that it was indeed possible to derive a working system with functioning transactions, albeit the system was very small and the user interface primitive.

4 Concluding Remarks

Ultimately, we did not use many results directly, but the thinking and the understanding of business rules affected other work on business modeling at SISU. Above all, the project was a great learning exercise generating much useful knowledge and experience per se. The TEMPORA approach itself might have resulted in a realistically useful environment, if we had another fifty person-years to build it. The project was also a tremendous exercise in working together as an international team. The Nordic partners worked quite closely together on the modeling formalisms and the methodology, sometimes meeting in Trondheim or Stockholm. In addition, email proved to be a really useful tool for communicating. It is indeed a challenge to write down your thoughts in such a way that makes them possible for others to grasp.

Additionally, we further advanced the knowledge on information modeling, business rules, and representation of time in new ESPRIT projects such as F3, Nature, and Ores, in which SISU took part. F3, which means From Fuzzy to Formal, was a project that focused on the early stages of requirements capture, representation, and management. Nature (Novel Approaches to Theories Underlying Requirements Engineering) intended, as the name indicates, to strengthen the foundations of requirements engineering. Finally, Ores was a project that built a temporal database manager and tested it on electronic medical record applications for a Spanish hospital.

The OMG Business Motivation Model [4] is largely formulated along the same line of ideas that were put forward in TEMPORA. Business rules are the rules governing the business and, as such, they are important assets of the business. They are derived from a means-end breakdown of business objectives, from man-made laws and regulations, or even from laws of nature. However, in order to be incorporated into computerized information systems, they need to be broken down into detail and stated very precisely, with regard to the database

The representation of time in requirements and in databases was subject to quite a lot of research in the 1980s and early 1990s. It seems, however, that the interest for general solutions to problems of the temporal dimension has decreased lately. One can wonder why. Perhaps it is too hard conceptually and technically, or it may be that the time for generic and usable solutions has not yet arrived. Nevertheless, a temporal extension to SQL, TSQL2 [5], has been developed and there are at least a couple of relational DBMS implementations that accept statements in this language.

In general, the project partners got along very well, although a few did not contribute too much to the project, probably because they were not allocated clear enough tasks. Having participated in several international projects of this size, it is the author's experience that it is very important for each of the partners to be assigned work that matches their competence and interest. A controversial issue in the project concerned the rule language and its implementation. This was resolved in a way that perhaps made one of the partners less pleased. However, as a whole, the project was a very valuable experience that provided much useful knowledge that transferred into education programs at the related universities. It also resulted in many lasting relationships and continued collaborative research between researchers in Norway and Sweden.

Acknowledgments. The author wishes to thank all the members of the TEMPORA team, in particular Rolf Wohed (SISU), Anne Helga Seltveit (SINTEF) and Peter McBrien (Imperial College).

References

1. TEMPORAConsortium: TEMPORA: Integrating Database Technology, Rule-Based Systems and Temporal Reasoning for Effective Software. ESPRIT Proj. E2469 (1988)
2. McBrien, P., Seltveit, A.-H., Wangler, B.: An Entity-Relationship Model Extended to Describe Historical Information. In: Proceedings of International Conference on Information Systems and Management of Data, CISMOD 1992, pp. 244–260. Indian National Scientific Documentation Centre, Bangalore (1992)
3. Wangler, B.: A Conceptual Schema with Time: Modelling the ISO-Case with TEMPORA. In: Jaakkola, H., Kangassalo, H., Kitahashi, T., Markus, A. (eds.) Information Modelling and Databases, pp. 313–333. IOS Press, Amsterdam (1994)
4. Business Rules Group: The Business Motivation Model: Business Governance in a Volatile world (1.3) (2010),
   http://www.businessrulesgroup.org/bmm.shtml
5. Wikipedia: Temporal Database,
   http://en.wikipedia.org/wiki/Temporal_database (last visited June 11, 2010)

RAMATIC: A Case Shell Platform

Lars-Åke Johansson and Mats Gustafsson

Alkit Communications AB
Sallarängsbacken 2, 431 37 Mölndal, Sweden
{johansson,gustafsson}@alkit.se

Abstract. Computer-aided software engineering (CASE) tools are important aids in supporting the building, changing, and maintenance of different types of large models in the area of business and information systems development, in order to maintain quality and consistency at a satisfactory level. The aim of the Swedish Institute for Systems Development (SISU) was to help the public sector as well as Swedish business and industry introduce modern methods and tools when they develop information systems for their processes. Founded in 1984, SISU has worked vigorously to develop and maintain information systems and tools. Various modeling techniques often support system development methods to achieve different types of results addressed by the method. Computer-based tools to help users reach a certain level of quality can effectively aid the use of modeling techniques. The tools must be flexible in order to enable in-use learning, change of methods, and the modeling techniques themselves. RAMATIC was one of the world's first meta-CASE tools. The meta level of the tool allows adapting to change in representation and functionality without programming.

Keywords: Case, case shell, information systems development, methodology, methods, modeling, models, research, specifications for information systems, systems development, software tools, technology transfer.

1 Introduction

Expressive, powerful, and goal-oriented methods as well as the adaptive use of these methods are important for developing businesses, identifying information needs, and designing and developing adequate information systems in an effective way. These are important experiences stemming from several decades of work in the area. Some of the causes for these requirements are complex interrelated business and customer problems, as well as the possibilities and structures of existing and new tasks.

Several types of methods, which have different aims and focus on separate aspects, must support the business and systems development process. Every component of the process has an aim and the methods should focus on these targets. For example, one goal of a specific part of the development process is to create a model of all information needs (based on a defined value-based process), which in turn is based on relationships to concepts in a semantic-oriented concepts model. In later steps, the information requirements must relate to different kinds of symbols for expressing the information.

J. Impagliazzo, P. Lundin, and B. Wangler (Eds.): HiNC3, IFIP AICT 350, pp. 383–389, 2011.
© IFIP International Federation for Information Processing 2011

Successful methods comprise support for effective communication between dissimilar groups of people involved in the development of various aspects of the business, information support requirements, and of the information systems themselves. For example, there may be different groups of people involved in business development, e.g. people working with management and control, process and cross-organizational development, concepts and semantics orientation, terminology, information analysis, component design, and database design. All of these groups need descriptions and models that can support communication both between and within each group. The experiences of the last decades indicate that the created concepts described in different models of various efforts must be consistent within different aspects to create successful change in businesses.

Such communication and consistency work can be supported by numerous types of expressive and powerful modeling techniques: models that are value-process oriented, as well as models for concepts, information, work flow, data, event analysis, organizational unit and responsibility, data bases, components, user interface and interaction, and so on. In all these models, there may be relationships and dependencies that need to be maintained.

In order to manage these model structures, which change continuously, powerful computer-supported modeling tools for the work are needed. In a business and information development effort, models like these can become excessively large, and must be kept consistent. As personal computers and workstations became dominant at the beginning of the 1980s, the CASE group from SISU recognized the possibilities of introducing new types of tools, the computer-assisted software engineering (CASE) tools. Early on, such tools were basically drawing tools that helped to create models such as information models and dataflow diagrams. The conceptual content of these models was, at best, stored in a repository from which, in some cases, one could generate part of the database design and some rudimentary software. However, one important experience was that the conceptual content of the models and the way to connect the models are of the utmost importance, and that graphical presentation is one of several projections of the models.

Modeling techniques changed, based on experiences of use and new needs. For example, there may be a need to describe new aspects related to the analysis and development work. It may therefore be necessary to extend the modeling techniques with new modeling concepts and constructs. There could, for example, be a need to describe both value-based, and flow-oriented processes. Ideally, CASE tools should also be able to adapt to these types of changes.

2   The Development of RAMATIC

RAMATIC is a CASE shell initially developed in 1980 at SYSLAB in Gothenburg; SISU further developed it at the beginning of 1984. RAMATIC is adaptive concerning the modeling techniques one wants to use; it allows changes to these techniques (new modeling techniques can be supported, and changes to existing techniques can be allowed), because the CASE tool is controlled by a definition layer (the meta model layer).

The modeling techniques, including modeling concepts and their relations and attributes, are described in the meta model layer. Modeling concepts are clustered into model types and modeling concepts in different model types can have relations. Rules for how modeling concepts can be related are defined. Modeling concepts may or may not have spatial representation. Symbol outlines are defined in relation to model concepts. Accordingly, the meta model language is used to define the modeling techniques, and the tool can be regarded a meta controlled case tool.

3 Spatial and Conceptual Representation of Models within RAMATIC

The CASE tool builds a graph-independent representation of the model the user wants to create. However, graphs are only one way of building the model, as they are one of many projections of model parts. The user can choose what parts of the model should appear in different types of graphs. This means that the model can be divided in different ways using various kinds of criteria, depending on the structure goals for the model [1].

The conceptual representation of the model is stored in the conceptual database (CDB), while the spatial representations of the model are stored in the spatial database (SDB) [2]. Spatial aspects of the models consist of symbol outlines and placements of symbols in graphs, and so on. However, the CDB and the SDB representations are related. For example, a particular business concept can appear in several graphs, which show different relationships, depending on the division of the model.

The CDB is used to describe other aspects of a model's "node" than graphical representation aspects. For example, a "term" in an information flow model can have attributes, such as a term name, short-term name, relations to the flow, relations to attributes in a concept model, creation date, change date, and so on. The CDB is primarily important because it expresses the content of the model. Furthermore, it creates a variety of consistency and completeness analyses of the models.

The RAMATIC tool has a set of powerful functions that oversee large model clusters. It can also generate graphs to project the content of models based on certain criteria that interest the user. One of them is the "projection" function that allows the user to generate a "neighborhood view" of a model, starting with a focus on a particular model node independent of the model's division into graphs. A special graph is instantly generated that focuses on the particular "center" model concept and the projection of all the desired relationships of a certain type in the concept, independent of graphs stored in the SDB. The neighborhood can be narrower or wider depending on user choice. The structure of the CDB is important for supporting this user facility.

Another important function is "merge to large model" which creates a large flat graphical projection of several hierarchically organized data flow diagrams (users appreciated these functions). The tool platform can also offer a set of powerful checks for model consistency and completeness.

Several types of database systems have been used to store models within RAMATIC, which had a design that allowed the change of database systems. At the outset, a Swedish binary-oriented database system CS5 [3] was used and shown to perform well for the actual application.

4 Technical Prerequisites

Graphical presentations of models help a wide range of people involved in the efforts of system development to read, understand, and comment on models. When RAMATIC was first developed, the ability to project graphical drawings on computer screens was limited. Initially, the CASE group at SISU used large CAD-oriented CRT screens, but the graphical facilities in computers and their screens improved systematically.

When RAMATIC was developed, tasks that are today regarded as simple, such as placing a circle and an arrow on the screen, created significant enthusiasm. Soon thereafter, however, multi-color graphical terminals were available for the projection of drawings. Affordable high resolution terminals were, however, limited, which forced those involved with modeling to divide the models into parts.

Several years later, RAMATIC was further developed on UNIX-based SUN 1 work stations. The graphics were good but only available in one color. Later, RAMATIC migrated to other operating systems, such as Windows, which allowed other industry groups to use the meta-CASE tool.

Rapid changes in computer performance, an emerging variety of operating systems, and graphics management in computers led to the architectural goals of making RAMATIC independent of operating systems, vendor-specific graphics, and database-specific storage. This ensured that different industry users could run the application independent of computer platform and vendor lower level specific systems.

5 Different Types of Models Supported by RAMATIC

During this period, the industry and organizations around SISU became more interested in structured methods. Costs for the development of systems increased. Methods and modeling techniques became significant for the design and specification of business and information needs to support the business processes. Tools that can support the refinement and consistency of large models are important, because they can manage analysis and design work, leaving more time for creative ventures.

RAMATIC supported new method concepts, both at the national and international level. For example, companies such as Volvo Car Corporation, and Ericsson used it in industry. Volvo began using data modeling according to SASMO (Scandinavian Airline Systems Modeling, IRM Consult). This was a part of the IRMA (Information Resource Management Architecture) method. Volvo created a company version of SASMO called PV-SASMO. RAMATIC supported this version of the modeling language, and the company wanted it used within the organization. Here, people gained much experience in modeling and in the use of CASE tools.

RAMATIC was also used for research and development purposes. One important international project that it supported was the TEMPORA project (an EU project within the ESPRIT Program), which created new innovative method parts focusing on, for example, the temporal aspects of business realities. Particular model types were developed for this, including TEMPORA-ERT (Entity Relationship Time). RAMATIC supported this modeling technique as an adaptive tool. One of the challenges was to handle time-varying entity and relationship classes through time stamping, so that one could associate a time period class. The TEMPORA models could also generate executable system parts from the models' constituent specifications.

The EU project F-cube (1992–94) also used RAMATIC by developing a rich modeling language that included concept models, process/function models, actor models, and non-functional requirements models. The F-cube meta model was composed in RAMATIC using the TEMPORA-ERT modeling language.

SISU developed a powerful modeling technique called conceptual modeling language (CMOL). It included several important modeling concepts and expressions that were useful in many demanding industrial modeling efforts associated with SISU. RAMATIC also supported this modeling technique. CMOL included modeling concepts such as entity, relation, data, event types, and attribute relations.

The Swedish method SVEA (Strukturerad Verksamhetsinriktad Arbetsmodell) was used by several Swedish businesses and governmental organizations, including the Swedish telecom operator Telia. RAMATIC also supported this method and its modeling techniques. The method contained a business routine description model, a data modeling technique, and a business flow model. Many Swedish actors pointed out the usefulness of RAMATIC support of the method, since few international CASE-tool vendors saw it as an opportunity [4]. RAMATIC also supported more internationally well-known flow-oriented modeling techniques like Yourdon [5].

6   Changes in Methods, Models and Tools

In the 1980s and 1990s, several industry organizations around SISU became interested in systematic methods, modeling techniques, and repository-oriented tools like CASE tools. Ultimately, industry became very interested in these types of aids. One lesson learned was that overly simplistic methods and modeling techniques are not sufficient for complex industry problems, as simple models cannot express many aspects of the business and its environment sufficiently well. RAMATIC played an important part in organization learning in which it attempted to manage large models. The experience was that models that were too simple could not express some aspects of the business and its environment to a sufficient depth, and that more expressive modeling techniques demanded more powerful modeling support tools.

As RAMATIC had quite powerful representation facilities, user focus turned to a flexible and usable interaction interface. The interaction facilities led to many ideas on how to attain an easier-to-use interface for many of the powerful check and analysis functions.

Both researchers and industry actors showed considerable interest in the tool. In particular, researchers took much interest in the meta level – several articles were published on the subject at the time, not least by researchers at Finnish universities [6–9].

RAMATIC allowed users to achieve several types of quality in large models, focusing on aspects of completeness and consistency. RAMATIC also had a good conceptual representation of the models' content, which made it possible to create a set of checking facilities that could run instantly to perform specific checking and analysis sessions. These sessions would run when the models had reached a certain level of readiness.

Aspects of completeness quality could interact with different groups of users. One example of this concerns domain descriptions for all attributes of an information model, describing whether all terms in the flow of a flow model regarding relationships to an information model.

One important observation related to CASE tools regards the level of the methods. Methods can involve more of an iterative way of working when a CASE tool is used, since one can make outlines of a set of models at the initial stage, and the models can be more detailed in an iterative way, when the scope and the goals for the business change are decided at a strategic level. A CASE tool allows a user to return and change the models in a controlled manner, enabling the quality management of the results.

7   The Market for Meta-CASE Tools

The market for modeling tools is not significant. However, there are defined markets for systems and business development that relate to the methods, tools, and knowledge about how to use these aids. Many of the customers are interested in the adaptability of modeling tools. The lessons learned from RAMATIC are that users in the different types of customer organizations are beginning to think about and propose requirements with regard to extend the modeling techniques. In this matter, they want the tool to be extended in terms of supporting the use of the modeling technique.

Therefore, the interest in the adaptability of modeling tools is relevant. However, not all users are interested in using the meta languages to change their modeling tools. In large organizations, allowing every user to change important description techniques that many individuals use may not be beneficial. In some organizations, it may be convenient to have pre-adaptable tools, in order to change the tools within certain limits.

In other cases, customers are interested in further developing and changing the modeling techniques they use in a more direct and continuous way. For example, one could extend an existing modeling technique, define a new modeling technique, and establish new relationships between modeling concepts in order to express important semantic relationships. In regard to the latter case, one illustration is the relationships between concepts and value-based process models in which motivated ("expert") users are willing to learn a fairly difficult meta modeling language, to be able to define new and changed modeling concepts.

Examples of two meta-oriented CASE tools already established on the market are MetaEdit [10] and Qualiware [11]. These tools were established after the initial development of RAMATIC, which was mostly used for research and development, but also by the industrial partners associated with SISU.

References

1. Johansson, L.-Å.: Graphics in Requirements Specifications of Information Systems. In: Proc. CAMP 1983, Berlin (1983)
2. Bubenko, Jr, J.: On Model Types and their Conceptual and Spatial Representation in RAMATIC. SYSLAB (1982)
3. Janning, M., Berild, S., Nachmens, S.: CS5, Preedition. Databaskonsult DBK AB (1984)
4. Johansson, L.-Å.: RAMATIC: A Computer-Aid for Modeling Activities (Use Situations). In: Proc. SPOT-3, SYSLAB, Chalmers Tekniska Högskola och Stockholms Universitet, Göteborg (1984)
5. Yourdon, E.: Modern Structured Analysis. Prentice-Hall, Englewood Cliffs (1989)
6. Lyytinen K., Smolander, K., Tahvainen, V.P.: Modelling CASE Environments in Systems Development. In: Proc. of CASE 1989 the First Nordic Conference on Advanced Systems Engineering. Stockholm (1989)
7. Orlikowski, W.J.: CASE Tools and the IS Workplace: Some Findings from Empirical Research. In: Proc. of the 1988 ACM SIGCPR Conference on the Management of Information Systems Personnel, April 7-8 (1988)
8. Rossi, M., Gustafsson, M., Smolander, K., Johansson, L.-Å., Lyytinen, K.: Metamodeling Editor as a Front End Tool for a CASE Shell. In: Loucopoulos, P. (ed.) CAiSE 1992. LNCS, vol. 593, Springer, Heidelberg (1992)
9. Smolander, K., Tahvanainen, V.P., Lyytinen, K.: How to Combine Tools and Methods in Practice – a Field Study. In: Steinholtz, B., Bergman, L.D., Solvberg, A. (eds.) CAiSE 1990. LNCS, vol. 436, pp. 195–214. Springer, Heidelberg (1990)
10. MetaEdit+, www.metacase.com, MetaCase, Texas, USA, and Jyväskylää, Finland (2010)
11. Qualiware Denmark (2010), http://www.qualiware.com

Computer Science Education at Helsinki University of Technology: The First Ten Years (1968–1978)

Hans Andersin, Reijo Sulonen, and Markku Syrjänen

Aalto University School of Science and Technology
Department of Computer Science and Engineering
P.O. Box 15400, FI-00076 Aalto, Finland
{hans.andersin,reijo.sulonen,markku.syrjanen}@tkk.fi

Abstract. When Helsinki University of Technology (HUT), after a period of basic programming courses, set out to offer their students a full curriculum of computer science courses, they did it in their own way. Instead of the usual mathematically oriented university curriculum, most of the courses were slanted towards the practical needs of the surrounding industry. In addition to this, they kept an eye on what was new and coming throughout the world in the field of computer science. The paper focuses on the development during the first ten years, 1968–1978. Course headings and people involved in teaching are mentioned. The research activity is described briefly.

Keywords: Computer science curriculum, industry relations, research activities, student activities.

1 The Very Beginning

In meeting the growing demand for university-level education in computer science, Helsinki University of Technology (HUT) offered some courses in programming (within applied mathematics) and systems analysis (within industrial engineering) from as early as the mid-1960s. Computer technology and the technical applications of computers had already been present in practical research and development projects at various institutions of HUT since the 1950s. The market wanted more and in response to this HUT founded the chair of computer science or, as we called it, "information processing science."[1] Hans Andersin, having recently presented his PhD dissertation (computer simulation of organizations), was nominated to become the first holder of the chair. He was given the "abundant" resources of two assistants, a secretary, and some office space.

The ACM Computer Science Curriculum [1] that was first published in the late 1960s was heavily slanted towards the theoretical fundamentals of computing and so were the first computer science professors worldwide. HUT was a notable exception. Andersin's background was partly technological, having been involved in building a

---

[1] From the early 1970s, Prof. Leo Ojala, at the Department of Electrical Engineering, started a line of activities in the area of digital systems. This gradually grew to a substantial effort in what can be called theoretical computer science. The history of this branch is not considered in this paper.

J. Impagliazzo, P. Lundin, and B. Wangler (Eds.): HiNC3, IFIP AICT 350, pp. 390–398, 2011.
© IFIP International Federation for Information Processing 2011

computer in the 1950s, and partly in computer applications and operations from his previous employers, IBM and the State Computer Centre. Critics from industry blamed HUT for teaching students programming languages such as Algol, while industry used Cobol and Fortran. The close ties with industry guided the new team at HUT more than the ACM Computer Science Curriculum did.

2 Setting the Goals

The first steps taken by the new team were to formulate its version of the computer science curriculum and a strategy to implement it. In retrospect, we were guided by the following principles:

1. Every student at HUT should at least know programming (the "computer literacy principle");
2. HUT should be able to offer a wide variety of computer-related courses from the newest trends in computing to the practical needs of Finnish industry (the "smorgasbord principle");
3. Close contacts should be maintained with Finnish industry (the "serving principle");
4. From the beginning there should be an international flavor to every aspect of our computer science activity (the "internationality principle");
5. One or a few niches have to be found and defined for the research focus for the new institution of computer science at HUT (the "niche principle");
6. Being young and creative, students should become involved in sharing responsibilities. This was more a necessity than a cognitive action dictated by the limited resources (the "participation principle").

These principles guided us through the first ten years, 1968–1978. In this paper, we will deal mainly with questions relating to points 1, 2, 4, and 6. The other points will be covered more thoroughly in future papers. Contacts with industry were maintained by arranging a yearly conference, OtaDATA, during which the students and invited speakers presented an update on the latest developments in the field, inside and outside HUT, to a paying audience. The OtaDATA association of teachers and students arranged the OtaDATA conference. OtaDATA contributed to covering a part of the expenses of running the computer science activity. Most of the master's theses were directly done for and paid for by industry and were thus industrially oriented. Even though the creation of the information processing curriculum and the huge number of students it attracted dominated all the activities during the first years, serious efforts were dedicated towards starting research in areas reflecting the capabilities and orientation of the initial team. The initial research focus was on computer graphics and interactive systems and especially on the use of computer technology in the graphical industry [3]. Another mainstream in early research was simulation, which led to a textbook used at several Scandinavian universities [4]. Teaching programming techniques led naturally to the research areas now known as software engineering. Our close connections with Finnish industry created the tradition of searching for research problems in unexplored and innovative computer applications outside academia. All these initial steps have remained as underlying themes and principles characterising the research activities. Our first PhD thesis, presented in 1975, dealt with high-level concepts for a computer graphics programming language [5]. The first PhD thesis on programming methodology was presented in 1975 [6]. What was started during those early years has a strong following at Aalto University today. The early research activity of the laboratory of information processing science at HUT will be presented in more detail at a later stage.

3 The First Curriculum

From the academic years 1969–1970, a well-defined curriculum was open to all students [2]. One could say that the "smorgasbord principle" was applied to its full extent. The curriculum contained four course groups:

- *Computer Science I (Programming).* In 1969, this group of courses was still provided by the Applied Mathematics department and it was based on the Algol language and the Elliot 803 computer of the computing centre of the university. From 1970 onwards, our institution (the Computer Science Laboratory) took over these basic courses. The new courses included computer architecture, computer and programming language modules (Basic, GPSS, Simula, Fortran, LISP, APL, Snobol, Analitic, and Cobol), data and file structures, time-sharing systems, the structure and use of the PDP-15, computing systems from the point of view of the user, computing systems (hardware), theory of formal grammars and automatically constructed recognisers, the FAS programming language and its compiler for administrative systems, the Macro 15 language, the PDP-15 foreground/background monitor, data transmission and communication, the UNIVAC assembler, compilers, and operating systems.

- *Computer Science II (Information Systems Design).* This course consisted of several modules such as theoretical analysis of information systems, systems design methods, project work, and special features of the design of real-time systems, GPSS, Simula, and other programming tools in systems design.

- *Computer Science III (Computer Applications).* The topics of this course varied from year to year. Examples include administrative data processing systems, management information systems, Cobol programming, technical-scientific and mathematical-statistical applications, applications in construction engineering and in the construction industry, applications in community planning, applications in production planning and management and in industrial production in general, management applications, marketing applications, and real-time applications.

- *Computer Science IV (Seminars).* The topics of the seminars varied widely during the years. Topic examples include integer programming, processing of symbols, graphs (theory, algorithms, applications), information retrieval, computer graphics, real-time systems, computer technology, linear programming, artificial intelligence, MIS, logical-linguistic foundations of computing, production planning, modeling and computer simulation, management of information systems design, Nordic projects, operations analysis and models, minicomputers, community planning and registers, computer applications in hospitals, how to choose a computer, text processing, the computer as a tool for a product designer, compilers, information systems from an economic point of view, special problems in using large-scale computing systems, translation of natural languages, socio-economic models, measuring the performance of computing systems, project management, software engineering, sorting and search, proving the correctness of programs, distributed data processing systems, and computers and society.

4 The Role of Seminars

The seminars were very popular among both students and outsiders. They were often conducted by visiting professors, researchers from other Finnish and foreign institutions, senior students, laboratory engineers, and representatives of industry. Each seminar was obliged to produce a publication covering the topic selected. Many of these publications were sold to industry by the student association OtaDATA. The list of names of the seminar coordinator-lecturers reveals that many persons who have had an outstanding influence in industry or academia started their career here, e.g. at least eight future university professors started from here. The leftist political movements of the 1970s motivated the almost-yearly seminar on Computers and Society. This seminar was criticized by some people (students and staff) who did not like the idea of separating "good Soviet data processing from bad Western data processing."

5 Computer Science for the Masses versus Specialization

An important change happened in 1971: the basic programming course was separated from the rest of the curriculum and a new course on computing technology was created. It tried to answer the question "what every engineer should know about computers and computing." The topics covered included principles of computing, computer hardware (on a very general level), introduction to information systems design, and an overview of applications. In this way, we adhered to the "computer literacy principle." Both these introductory courses were open to, or even compulsory for, all students of HUT. The curriculum, consisting of Computer Science I-IV, was now devoted to students specializing in computer science after having already passed the first two introductory courses. The more advanced courses contained in computer science had turned out to be very crowded, partly with less devoted students. So, the purpose of the new basic courses was to satisfy the crowds and give us time to concentrate on our own students.

6 The New Credit Unit System

From the academic year 1972–1973 on, all the studies at HUT were reorganised in the form of a credit unit system. A credit unit was defined as one week (i.e. 40 hours) of work. One academic year added up to 40 such credit units and the requirement for the M.Sc. degree was 160 credit units of studies plus writing a M.Sc. thesis, "worth" 20 credit units. The studies of the first two academic years were the same for all students from the same department; for the last two academic years a student was supposed to select a major subject (40 credit units) from a list specified by the department where he/she was studying, and a minor subject (15 credit units, in principle, any subject taught at HUT). The remaining 25 credit units were freely selectable.

The contents of the computer science major and minor varied during the ten years covered by this paper. Table 1 provides a snapshot from the end of the era.

Table 1. Content of CS major and minor towards the end of the 1968–1978 period

Prerequisites:	*Major subject:*
Introduction to Programming	*Core courses*
Computing Technology	Programming Techniques
Minor subject:	Individual Computer Science Project
Compulsory courses:	Information Systems
Programming Techniques	Programming Project
Computer Science Project	Data Structures and File Systems
Optional courses:	Computer Systems
Two courses from the following list below	*Other courses of the major*
must be taken	12 different courses (including seminars)
Computer Systems	Programming languages (Fortran, Algol, Cobol, Assembler, Simula)
Information Systems	
Data Structures and File Systems	

The computer science major was open to students from the departments of technical physics, electrical engineering, and mechanical engineering. In practice, this meant that students graduating with a major in computer science were quite evenly distributed among these three departments. Students taking the minor subject came from all over the university.

7   The Importance of Individual and Team Projects

An early requirement for computer science students was to carry out an individual (sometimes team) project involving the solution of a real-life problem. This praxis taught the student many practical and theoretical facets of computing better than any lecture could do. The project is still one of the most important parts of the educational process of computer science at HUT today. In addition to this, the M.Sc. thesis was built around a thorough problem-solving exercise carried out (and paid for) by an enterprise.

8   Curriculum and Course Planning

From its tiny beginnings in 1968, the curriculum and the number of persons involved in implementing it grew tremendously towards the end of the period 1968-1978. The number of students and M.Sc. theses also increased steadily. The number of PhD's was still relatively small compared to the situation today. The funds that were available were still very limited. To alleviate the problem young people became inspired and motivated by new and trendy things, with lots of voluntary work contributions. Some extra money was earned from industry with the sales of OtaDATA seminar publications and OtaDATA conference proceedings. These resources were used for arranging planning meetings at various course centers in Finland and abroad (including the Canary Isles!). Combining pleasure with work was, and still is, a good way of rewarding personnel; it formed a tightly knit working team.

9   International Connections

The "internationality principle" mentioned above implied the necessity of international contacts for the newly founded CS laboratory. Fulbright scholarships and other systems for financing visiting scholars from the U.S. to Finland and vice versa were utilized fully. Four professors from U.S. universities visited us for shorter or longer periods and made great contributions, both in teaching and in research activities. These professors were James Moore, Harold Highland, Robert Hacker, and Thomas H. Brown. All the computer science professors of HUT spent sabbatical years at leading U.S. universities (Andersin at Brown, Sulonen at Brown and Stanford, and Syrjänen at Stanford). The bilateral cooperation between Finland and the Soviet Union in the field of cybernetics also led to exchanges of researchers, both with Moscow (Igor Pedanov) and Tallinn (Ants Work, Leo Vyhandu). Besides the international relations, we profited from having visitors from neighboring universities in Finland (e.g. Reino Kurki-Suonio, Pentti Kerola, and Martti Tienari) and Sweden (Janis Bubenko, Jr.).

10   Computer Resources

In 1968, when the new CS laboratory was established, there were exactly two computers at the whole university. The computing centre had an Elliot 803 to run mainly Algol programs; the first programming course (Introduction to Programming) was based on the Algol language. This computer was operated on the principle of a "closed computer room": a program was given in on a coding sheet and the results were delivered later, usually the next day.

In addition, there was an IBM 1620, which curiously enough, had been bought as "additional equipment" for the Elliot computer. While the Computing Centre was located in the main building of the university, this "additional equipment" resided in the Department of Electrical Engineering. It could be programmed in the Fortran III language and used freely. The computer itself was strictly hidden, but it could be used through a "terminal" consisting of a combination of a card reader and a line printer located in an open lobby. For one of the authors of this paper this was the first computer he could use independently, which was a fascinating experience.

In 1970, two important steps forward were taken. A time-sharing computer of the HP 2000 type was installed in the computing centre, with several teletype terminals situated all over the campus, with one also in our laboratory. This computer interpreted programs written in the Basic language, and thereafter the Introduction to Programming course was based on Basic instead of Algol.

In addition, the Bank of Finland bought a "great computer" of the Univac 1108 II type, to be shared by all Finnish universities. Physically this computer was located in the State Computing Centre, which was only one kilometre from our university. All the universities were connected to this computer by "fast" telecommunication lines. A "terminal" to that computer, once again consisting of a combination of a card reader and a line printer, was located in our laboratory.

The Univac, in addition to its "huge" computing power, supported several "new" programming languages, including Fortran IV, Cobol, and Simula 67, with implications for our curriculum. Earlier, teaching programming languages beyond Algol or Fortran III had required special arrangements with partners outside the university.

Also in 1970, a PDP-15 computer including a graphic processor was installed in our laboratory for the computer graphics project. This computer was devoted to research purposes, but during the years, some courses about its operating system and its macro-assembler language were given, mainly in order to educate potential new members of the research staff.

The situation remained essentially the same for several years, until in 1977, we received a PDP-11/34 computer and in 1978, the computing centre gained a "medium-sized" DEC-20 computer. In 1978, the PDP-11 became the first computer in Finland to run the UNIX operating system (enabling exotic features like email to be used) and DEC-20 was the first computer at our university to run Prolog programs, but these developments are outside the scope of this paper.

11   Conclusion

The authors of this paper were surprised and overwhelmed by the great interest that the students at HUT showed in computer science courses and other activities right from the start. The largest lecture halls of HUT were filled to the last seat and some of our colleagues were complaining that the CS laboratory absorbed too many of their students and resources. The first ten years of computer science at HUT were characterized by a new social phenomenon: students from all different departments convened around a common interest – computer science. The most important features characterizing the first ten years of computer science at HUT were the wide variety of courses offered, the high level of activity of the students, and the research niches selected.

The current situation in computer science at HUT is, of course, very different from what it was during its first ten years. Nevertheless, labels currently associated with a good part of the current computer science department such as active, popular, good international relations, successful research projects, and good relations with the surrounding industry lie deeply rooted in the principles, strategies, and objectives formulated more than forty years ago and which guided the developments during the first ten-year period.

References

1. ACM Curriculum Committee on Computer Science. Curriculum 1968: Recommendations for the Undergraduate Program in Computer Science. Communications of the ACM, 11(3), 151–197 (1968)
2. The OtaDATA biyearly information newsletters 1969-1978
3. Enlund, N., Andersin, H.E.: The Early Days of Computer-Aided Newspaper Production Systems. In: History of Nordic Computing 2. IFIP AICT, vol. 303, pp. 238–249 (2009)
4. Andersin, H., Sulonen, R.: Simuleringsteknik. Studentlitteratur (1972)
5. Sulonen, R.: High-Level Concepts for a Graphical Programming Language, PhD Thesis, Espoo (1975)
6. Syrjänen, M.: On Construction of Correct Programs as a Two-level Process, PhD Thesis, Espoo (1975)

Appendix

Names of People Involved in Computer Science Teaching at HUT during the First Ten Years [2]

Aho Pekka
Alander Jarmo
Andersin Hans
Andersson Patrick
Arppe Heikki
Björk Bo-Christer
Blomqvist Berndt
Brantberg Robert
Brown Thomas H.
Bubenko Janis
Bäckström Bertel
Eloranta Eero
Enlund Nils
Granskog Christer
Hacker Robert
Hakonen Erkki
Hallavo Erkki
Hallivuori Matti
Hannus Seppo
Heino Juhani
Helme Jukka
Highland Harold
Hoikkala Pekka
Husberg Nisse
Hytönen Veikko
Jauhiainen Osmo
Kallioja Tapio
Kamppari Olli
Kanerva Antti
Kangas Kauko
Keijola Matti
Kerola Pentti
Kervinen Esko
Keränen Heikki
Kiiras Juhani
Kilpi Matti
Klimscheffskij Roni
Knuuttila Raili
Koivisto Kari
Korhonen Martti

Koskela Lauri
Koski Timo H.A.
Kotovirta Tuomas
Kukkasjärvi Aimo
Kukko Arvo
Kuronen Aune
Kurki-Suonio Reino
Kuronen Timo
Laaksonen Kimmo
Laukkio Tuuli
Leino Tapio
Lifländer Veli-Pekka
Linnakko Ilkka
Lokki Olli
Loponen Hannu
Louhenkilpi Timo
Lukumaa Juhani
Lundström Lars
Makkonen-Eloranta Kirsi
Martonen Esa
Moore James
Mykkänen Jussi
Mäkelin Matti
Mäkinen Alpo
Nevalainen Risto
Nyholm Bo
Nyström Gunnar
Oberly Mark
Oesch Klaus
Oksala Tarkko
Olkkonen Tauno
Orelma Arto
Parkkinen Matti
Pedanov Igor
Pekkanen Kauko
Pennanen Juha
Perttula Matti
Perttula Pekka
Peussa Markku
Pietarinen Ilmari

Pihlajatie Jorma
Puhakka Matti
Pulkkis Göran
Rehnström Peter
Reimavuo Jyrki
Ristimäki Heikki
Roman Ilkka
Roos Kurt-Erik
Ruikka Seppo
Runeberg Bernhard
Ruohoniemi Aimo
Saikkonen Heikki
Seppänen Edvin
Seppänen Jouko
Sihto Matti
Silvennoinen Juha
Siro Kristel
Sulonen Reijo
Suvanto Hannu
Syrjänen Markku
Sääksjärvi Markku
Takala Tapio
Talpila Antti
Tamminen Hannu
Tienari Martti
Tiihonen Timo
Tuukkanen Annikka
Törnudd Elin
Uusitalo Matti
Uusitupa Seppo
Valli Tapio
Varvikko Kari
West Håkan
Vepsäläinen Ari
Vesterinen Kaarina
Work Ants
Vyhandu Leo
Vähäkylä Pekka
Yrjölä

Provincial Designer Design:
A Creative Mix of Hard Restrictions and Soft Visions
of an Information Systems Educational Program

Darek Haftor[1], Stig C Holmberg[2], Ulrica Löfstedt[2],
Christina Amcoff Nyström[2], and Lena-Maria Öberg[2]

[1] School of Business, Stockholm University, 106 91 Stockholm, Sweden
dh@fek.su.se
[2] ITM / Informatics, Mid Sweden University, 831 25 Östersund, Sweden
{stig.holmberg,ulrica.lofstedt,christina.amcoff,
lena-maria.oberg}@miun.se

Abstract. This paper presents a brief historical account of the unorthodox design of an educational program for information systems development. The design and development of this program was initiated in 1977 at the University College of Östersund, today the Mid Sweden University. The presented account provides a description of the somewhat unusual context of this initiative, which was regarded as a weakness by conventional standards, but became an opportunity in this particular situation. The intellectual inspirations and sources for the design of this program are characterized and followed by a presentation of the very content and operating mode of the educational program. The final part presents the various outcomes that the program gave rise to, in terms of students' professional careers observed.

Keywords: Historical reflections, informatics, systems design, systems sciences.

1 Introduction

Due to a misplaced "X" in the governmental distribution matrix for higher education, a study program in Information Systems Development (ISD)[1] was started in Östersund, Sweden, at its University College, in 1977 (hereafter the *Östersund-program*). Despite such an accidental start in a rural milieu far from the epicenter of Nordic computing, it fostered a systems culture and nearly one thousand students have successfully completed their ISD studies. The purpose of this paper is to provide a short historical account of this unorthodox educational program. Its challenging context is first briefly characterized and then followed by an account of the key sources of intellectual inspiration. The mode of operation and the design of the very content are described thereafter. This account concludes with some highlights of the outcomes generated by this unusual educational program for information system development.

---

[1] "Systemvetenskapliga linjen" in Swedish.

J. Impagliazzo, P. Lundin, and B. Wangler (Eds.): HiNC3, IFIP AICT 350, pp. 399–408, 2011.

2 The Context

The Östersund-program was established and developed under very specific conditions. Consequently, there was no history and no tradition in computing or computer-related education at hand; neither the host university nor the local industry showed any particular interest or engagement in the activity. Furthermore, resources were very limited and the research activity was simply low. While these factors at first glance were regarded as negative for the development of a successful educational program, they actually turned out to constitute a positive foundation for the development of the Östersund-program.

The developmental milieu became very energetic and open to inputs from all over the world. As there were few external restrictions imposed, the faculty teaching this program had almost unlimited freedom regarding experimentation and creative design approaches. Not being bound to expensive hard- and software also made it easy to follow the rapid development within the various Information and Communication Technologies (ICT). Due to the limited initial research opportunities, the educational program itself became the main research and development laboratory and target [1].

3 The Inspiration

Although the igniting spark came from Uppsala University, the design of the Östersund program was initially mainly inspired by the research and teaching activities conducted at the Royal Institute of Technology (KTH), Stockholm. The new Department for Information Processing (called 'Administrative Data Processing', or 'ADB' in Swedish), led by Professor B. Langefors [2], constituted a significant part of that initial input; however, major influences also came from several other departments at KTH.

Over the years, Professor K. Ivanov [3] at Umeå University and Professor K. Samuelson at KTH [4] in Stockholm have had a distant yet important influence on the developmental activities in Östersund. Quite soon, however, Östersund became part of an international network of researchers with links to academic nodes such as St Gallen [5], Fribourg [6], Washington [7], Hull [8], and San Fransisco [9, 10] among others. We only realized later that the extensive international networking and cooperation had become somewhat of a hindrance to greater national and Scandinavian cooperation. With regard to technological development, the key inspiration came from Sommerville [11] and Wirth [12] and, to some extent, from professional organizations such as the IEEE Computer Society [13] and the ACM [14].

4 The Operation

The operation of the program can be characterized by both conservation and change. The vision to support human activity systems [9] with the best information systems possible remained unchanged for the whole period. The ways and tools for reaching that goal, on the other hand, were under constant change. That change was driven by a program improvement system (IPS) which, in fact, was an expanded and completed course evaluation system. Nearly all the stakeholders, that is, the lecturers, students, external experts, and industry representatives were engaged in IPS. In that respect, we came close to Banathy's [17] vision of a third generation of design methods. All possible information was gathered here during the year and people used it as input to annual design seminars. In those, the program was designed with the help of Ackoff's [16] idealized design.

This cycle of operation-design ran very well for several years, but was eventually overwhelmed by changes in the host organization. Hence, the freedom and energy gradually disappeared and the responsibility was removed from the lecturing faculty.

5 The Design

The Östersund program successively evolved over the years. Its idealized design [16] was finally grounded on the following cornerstones.

5.1 The Program Focus

Contrary to conventional ISD educational programs [18], the Östersund program had the problem-*domain* as its main area of attention (Fig. 1). In that respect, the program followed the user-orientation already advocated by Langefors [2]. This also made the program more process-oriented and thus less content-oriented, compared to the more conventional arrangements [18]. In that respect, the program honored Popper's searchlight knowledge paradigm [20].

Furthermore, on the basis of Beer's [19] dictum that techniques and tools should not be regarded as a challenge as long as one knows what one wants to do, very little explicit time was assigned to the study of different technologies, techniques, and tools along the solution arsenal, in Fig. 1 (as represented by the vertical axis). Far from all the students agreed on this point, but we still hold to the assumption that a relevant amount of technical meta-knowledge is the best approach for the optimal application of a rapidly moving technology front.

The design focus in Fig.1 represents the core program goal of forming skills to solve human information and communication problems, by applying the best available techniques in an ingenious way. Very soon, however, we discovered that information systems design was just a special case of a more generic design science. Hence, Simon [15], Warfield [7], Ackoff [16], and Banathy [17] became the main sources of inspiration for our design courses.

Thanks to Samuelson [4], the program was, from the beginning, embedded in a systemic framework. Hence, the term "system informatics" (systeminformatik) was coined as a label. Ulrich [6] helped us here not to overdo the systems approach.

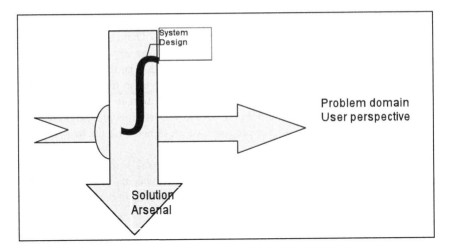

Fig. 1. The figure illustrates two dimensions of the conception of the Östersund-program; the *Problem-domain axis* constituted the main focus of attention for the students, i.e., how to define relevant problems and opportunities; while the *Solution-arsenal axis* constituted the tool-box and meta-learning capabilities offered the students to handle problem solutions in a successful manner

5.2 The Expanding System Complexity

One core principle that guided the design and execution of the Östersund program was to increase successively the complexity of the systems studied by the students [21]; from deterministic and foreseeable systems, through teleological and living systems [24], to the social and very complex systems. From the very start, a process for the effectiveness of individual study was provided to the students, which proceeded from the computer and program systems, the information and workflow systems, and concluded with organizational and inter-organizational systems. In subsequent semesters, very complex real-world systems were studied and re-designed according to viable system design principles [19].

5.3 Creativity and Problem Solving

One should characterize systems development and problem solving by a high degree of creativity. On this point, different innovative activities such as "six-thinking-hats" and "the devil's advocate" were applied, in order to minimize the limitations of undesired thinking [23]. Brainstorming, brain-drawing, and brain-writing techniques were also used to support the students' lateral thinking and idea generation.

The studies were further characterized by a high degree of problem solving, due to the assumption that students can solve any problem if they are given the chance [25]. Hence, the practical assignments were normally not "tested in advance" and the teaching team did not have the "right" solution.

5.4 The Learning Approach

"Learning by doing" is a stimulating way of learning in line with Schön's [22] *"learning by experience and reflections."* In the program assignments termed "close to reality," the students appreciated the assignments, which were often executed together with different stakeholders. The ability to communicate with "real" stakeholders, presenting different ideas and negotiating proposed solutions, was identified as an essential skill for the future developers of information systems. Hence, in this respect, the program conformed with Ackoff's [25] position that case studies and fictive descriptions can never work as well as authentic cases.

According to Warfield [7], the working environment is an important component in the design result. Therefore, the program abandoned the computer-lab concept and instead created environments that resembled normal working places as much as possible. In this, the students were free, within certain limits, to equip and use their theme labs according to their own liking.

5.5 The Theme Semesters and the Course Teams

In order to avoid fractionating in allowing the study of complex real-world problems, courses of a certain length were found necessary. Hence, the idea of educational "theme semesters" was born. The program mainly comprised the following semesters: (a) personal effectiveness in academic studies, (b) computer systems, (c) information systems, (d) organizational systems, and (e) knowledge creating systems.

Furthermore, in order to cover all the aspects of long and wide ranging courses and to give students the best possible study conditions, the concept of "course teams" was initiated. A course team was a group of faculty members, responsible for a theme semester; it had to collaborate closely in order to run the given semester. A guiding principle for the constitution of a course team was to provide it with comprehensive coverage and to expose students to a variety of complementary knowledge and facilitation. A model building on Warfield's [7] Sigma Five was developed as a guide for the teams' working mode.

5.6 The Inter-course Interaction

"You always work for some client." This expression can characterize a key quality of the Östersund program, namely, that the various semesters had to interact with each other. The idea of utilizing results generated by student groups in one theme semester as inputs to other student groups in another theme semester included three theme semesters. In this case, "the Realization of Information Systems" was guided by the systems requirements from "the Design of Information Systems" which, in turn, was guided by the systems requirements obtained from the "Strategy and Management Organizations," as shown in Fig. 2. Hence, designs from semester five were given to semester three for realization, while organizational strategies and more local management plans, formulated within semester six, were given to semester five students for the design of an appropriate information system. All this gave rise to valuable communication and negotiation exercises, including conflict resolution and management!

5.7 The Meta Learning Capability

Within a fast moving area such as ICT, the ability to learn during the whole professional period is judged more important than what you have learned during your

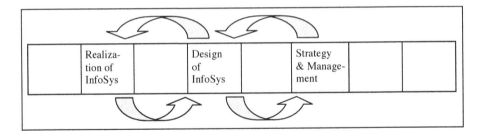

Fig. 2. The figure illustrates a key feature of the Östersund program: outcomes generated by students from one theme-semester constituted the inputs (i.e. systems requirements) for students in another theme-semester

undergraduate studies. Hence, in accordance with Popper [20] and in an effort to foster desirable meta-learning skills, the program was filled with the following meta-learning moments:

- bachelor students had to make an independent compilation and assessment of current relevant research results;
- bachelor students had to make an independent implementation of a new research result into an actual professional activity (bachelor thesis);
- master students had to plan and implement their own work for a full semester, in accordance with given outcome targets, which was to develop a new idea or research result into a viable business or organization;
- master students had to independently plan and realize a minor research project, the result of which had to be reported in the form of a scientific paper.

Beside the fact that most students found these tasks particularly challenging and stimulating, the results were often surprisingly good. For example, several students had their paper presented at international academic conferences and some succeeded in publishing their paper in international scientific journals, while still others received best paper awards. This brings us to the last part of this historical account, some of the outcomes produced by the Östersund program.

6 The Outcome

Plans and design may be one thing, while results and outcomes often turn out to be something quite different. In order to provide a snapshot of some of the results generated by the Östersund program, four former students were asked to submit testimonials with regard to what they judged to be the most significant aspect in the Östersund program. A summary of their testimonials follows.

6.1 The IS Professional Perspective

The Östersund program aimed to prepare the future "systems professionals" for a successful intervention of human, industrial, and social affairs, by means of embedding ICT-artifacts into such contexts. Three key capabilities that the program provided students with, which aim to fulfill this ambitious target, are discussed here.

The first capability is decomposing the social and technological complexity by providing skills that conceptualize any intervention situation in terms of three layers of the intervened systems. The first of these three layers is the *ICT-artifact layer*, with all its techno-aspects such as programming, configurations, and testing, among others. This capability was provided to the students by means of education and training that centered on the construction of software and database systems and enabled the future systems professionals to understand the workings of the various ICT. The second layer, the *workflow layer*, addressed the understanding of the work processes, in and between organizations, which are enabled by ICT-artifacts. This conceptualization was provided to the students by means of education and training that centered on the analysis and design of various workflows and the identification of the requirements of the supporting ICT-artifacts. With this capability, the future professional was able to understand the logic of human activity systems, its challenges, and the potential value that modern ICT-systems may or may not contribute to the workflows. The third layer, the *organizational layer*, addressed a whole organization, or a set of such, and was comprised of various interacting workflows, including the different resources (technological, human, and financial), as well as their regulatory and intentional properties.

This triplex, *artifact-workflow-organization*, provided the future professionals with "intellectual spectacles" that enabled successful conceptualizations, interpretations, and designs, as well as the management of the various professional challenges at hand.

The second capability of the systems professional focused on the articulation and handling of the *gap between theoretical-knowledge and professional-practice*. All professions have their hidden, tacit, and professional knowledge that cannot be reduced and communicated via standard textbooks. Hence, by exposing the future systems professional to a well-designed mix of theoretical bodies – e.g., software engineering theory or organizational behavior – and then a stepwise real-life application of these, followed by critical evaluation, the capability of bridging the gap between the abstract and the concrete was established!

The third capability addressed the distinction and opposition between *analysis and design*. The ability to analyze, understood as comprehending what exists by taking it apart (at least conceptually), is important and well provided to most of us by our western cultural tradition. However, even the best analysis capability cannot help us with the creation of a new and wanted reality. The latter requires the design capability, often allocated to "the strange artists"! By providing an exposition for the theoretical foundations – such as the systems sciences – and the practical hands-on doings of analysis and design, the ability to master these two mental and operational approaches, in a conscious and purposeful manner, was provided to the future systems professional!

The three capabilities of the systems professional include the artifact-workflow-organization hierarchy, the theory-practice abyss, and the analysis-design dialectics. They were not enough for the successful intervention of human, industrial and social affairs by means of modern ICT-artifacts. However, they did contribute significantly to a mastery of the real-life complexity in a manner that the systems professional would like to possess!

6.2 Lecturing Perspective

Working together in the course teams, with academic teachers at different levels, was a positive experience for all involved – students and teachers alike. The students became less dependent on one or a few teachers, which provided better student access to the right competence for student-teacher dialogue and discussion.

After some initial difficulties, the teachers also found working in a group more stimulating than working in isolation. A course team together with the students also became more like a normal working group in industry and less like an artificial educational composition.

We also found that the introduction of new teachers became much easier to handle than before. Changes in faculty staff were also easier since the senior member of a course team tutored assistant teachers and newly engaged teachers. Course material such as assignments, laboratory lessons, instructions, and different kind of practices, were also handed over to the new staff member of a team; in that sense, no one "owned" their teaching material; it was the property of a course team. In summary, the most positive outcome from the teamwork included:

o limiting students' and other faculty members' *dependencies* on a particular staff member;
o high *student access* to teachers with the relevant competence;
o increased *quality* and continuous improvements as part of the course team work;
o a well-functioning *teacher-tutor* system;
o an increase of *student and teacher democracy* in planning and decision-making.

6.3 The Researcher Perspective

The Östersund program created good potential for an academic career and provided a solid foundation for work as a researcher. Indeed, several former students are now either full or associate professors at various universities and in various disciplines.

The strong focus on methodology provided by the Östersund program prepared students for a professional research career. There were also several opportunities for the students to practice research already during their studies, for example, when writing the thesis. The objectives required of the students were high: to present the thesis work at international conferences and then to submit it for publication in academic journals – challenging goals which several students did indeed accomplish. This also exposed the students to what it means to be a researcher.

A second key feature of the Östersund program that was beneficial for a future career in research was its multi-disciplinary focus. This included a variety of subjects starting with mathematics, statistics, and computer sciences, proceeding with economics, business and management sciences, then to psychology, sociology, political sciences and the law, and to various philosophical domains, which together with the coordination of the Systems Sciences aimed at a holistic comprehension of the Information Systems thinking and practice.

A third key feature of a more practical nature was the opportunity offered to the students to participate in ongoing research projects conducted by senior staff members at the department, all of which prepared students for research work.

6.4 The Doctoral Candidate Perspective

To what degree did the program prepare students for the exciting work as doctoral candidates? According to an old Swedish proverb, *practice gives skills*. From that point of view, the Östersund program prepared a doctoral candidate for an eventual academic career in the following ways.

The formulation of relevant *research questions* and research problems is an important part of the doctoral research process. In the pedagogical model of the Östersund program, the undergraduate students became responsible for their own learning process. At the end of the program, students also had to formulate questions for their bachelor and master thesis work. Those core elements of the program have provided a good foundation for the ability to formulate questions and research problems.

Communicating with different stakeholders is another ability that is typically needed for a doctoral candidate. The Östersund program included several training opportunities in communication, both with companies and with the academic world. There was the obligatory writing of the bachelor thesis and then the master's thesis; the latter in a research paper format, for example.

The Östersund program had a *methodology focus* that prepared the undergraduate students for solving problems in a methodical and reflective manner. This provided an important capability for a doctoral research process, partly due to the experience of using different types of methods, but also due to the contribution of new insights that emerged from using different methodological perspectives. All those educational qualities shaped independent and self-motivating students.

7 A Final Question

The vision of the Östersund program for information systems development was specified as, "Helping students to master methods and techniques that are not yet invented. In this way, to make students fit to handle future problems that have yet to present themselves..

Retrospectively, and observing the ongoing trends within the information systems development profession, a challenging question had emerged in the minds of the designers of this unique educational program, namely: to what degree is such a vision too idealistic to fit into the *modern factory* metaphor that currently prevails in our universities? [3]

References

1. Holmberg, S.C.: A Study Program Design in Retrospect. In: Gasparski, W., Mlicki, M., Banathy, B.H. (eds.) Social Agency, Dilemmas and Educational Praxiology, pp. 291–307. Transaction Publishers, New Brunswick (1996)
2. Langefors, B.: Theoretical Analysis of Information Systems. Studentlitteratur, Lund (1966)

3. Ivanov, K.: Whither Computers and Systems? In: Bubenko, J., Jansson, C.G., Kollerbaur, A., Ohlin, T., Yngström, L. (eds.) ICT for people, pp. 125–134. DSV, Stockholm University, Stockholm (2006)

4. Samuelson, K.: Informatics and Systems Science. In: Bubenko, J., Jansson, C.G., Kollerbaur, A., Ohlin, T., Yngström, L. (eds.) ICT for people, pp. 195–200. DSV, Stockholm University, Stockholm (2006)

5. Espejo, R., Schwaninger, M.: Organisational Fitness. Campus Verlag, Frankfurt (1993)

6. Ulrich, W.: Critical Heuristics of Social Planning. Wiley, Chichester (1994)

7. Warfield, J.N.: A Science of Generic Design. Intersystems Publications, Salinas (1990)

8. Jackson, M. C.: Systems Approaches to Management. Kluwer, Plenum, New York (2000)

9. Checkland, P.B.: Systems Thinking, Systems Practice. Wiley, Chichester (1981)

10. van Gigch, J.P.: System Design Modeling and Metamodeling. Plenum, New York (1991)

11. Sommerville, I.: Software Engineering. Addison-Wesley, New York (1989)

12. Wirth, N., Gutknecht, J.: Project Oberon. Addison-Wesley, New York (1992)

13. IEEE Computer Society, http://www.computer.org (accessed June 10, 2010)

14. Association for Computing Machinery, http://www.acm.org (accessed June 10, 2010)

15. Simon, H.A.: The Science of the Artificial. MIT Press, Cambridge (1969)

16. Ackoff, L.R., Magidson, J., Addison, H.J.: Idealized Design. Wharton, Upper Saddle River (2006)

17. Banathy, B.H.: Designing Social Systems in a Changing World. Plenum, New York (1996)

18. ACM: IS 2010 Curriculum Guidelines for Undergraduate Degree Programs in Information Systems, http://www.acm.org/education/curricula/IS%202010%20ACM%20final.pdf (accessed June 10, 2010)

19. Beer, S.: Brain of the Firm. Wiley, Chichester (1981)

20. Popper, K.R.: Objective Knowledge, An Evolutionary Approach, revised edn. Oxford University Press, Oxford (1979)

21. Boulding, K.E.: General Systems Theory-The Skeleton of Science. Management Science 2, 197–206 (1956)

22. Schön, D.A.: Educating the Reflective Practitioner. Toward a New Design for Teaching and Learning in the Professions. Jossey-Bass, San Fransisco (1987)

23. deBono, E.: http://www.edwdebono.com/index.html (accessed March 1, 2010)

24. Miller, J.G.: Living systems. McGraw-Hill, New York (1978)

25. Ackoff, R.L.: Education. In: ibid (ed.) Ackoff's Best, pp. 147–167. Wiley, NY (1999)

Teaching Image Analysis at DIKU

Peter Johansen

Datalogisk Institut, University of Copenhagen (DIKU)
Universitetsparken 1, 2100 Copenhagen, Denmark
peterjo@diku.dk

Abstract. The early development of computer vision at Department of Computer Science at University of Copenhagen (DIKU) is briefly described. The different disciplines in computer vision are introduced, and the principles for teaching two courses, an image analysis course, and a robot lab class are outlined.

Keywords: Computer vision, image analysis, pattern recognition, robot vision, University of Copenhagen.

1 Introduction

Teaching image analysis at DIKU began in 1979 when the author returned from a one-year sabbatical at the University of Hawaii at Manoa. The university had astronomy as an area of excellence. Hawaii has the best "seeing" on earth, meaning that the image of a point source like a star in a telescope is subject to the least atmospheric disturbance anywhere on earth. The reason of course is that the shortest distance from the Islands of Hawaii to the nearest continent is about 3,000 miles, resulting in minimal air pollution. At that time, a telescope was built with a very sensitive digital sensor, perhaps the first digital sensor on an astronomical telescope. A project was underway as a joint project between USA, Switzerland, and the USSR. The purpose was to classify the surface of the moon from multispectral images and if possible, to detect mineral deposits.

2 Signal Analysis

At that time, the author had no experience in digital analysis of images, but found the concept so intriguing that he decided to embark upon analysis of images by programming a computer. As a first step he signed up for a course in optics - as it turned out not a very useful beginning, then starting to familiarize himself with digital signal analysis. As it later dawned on him, signal analysis was mainly concerned with linear processing of 1D time series, and in particular, applications of the Fourier transform. The fast Fourier transform is a beautiful algorithm, and it was tempting to start a voyage of discovery into signal analysis of 2D signals. Filtering an image of a star in order to undo the damage of atmospheric distortion seemed a good starting point. This way imaging defects by an optical sensor could be minimized. It was a

J. Impagliazzo, P. Lundin, and B. Wangler (Eds.): HiNC3, IFIP AICT 350, pp. 409–415, 2011.

laudable endeavor, but not central to image analysis. Of course, information in an image should be as credible as possible, but the real problem was what to do with an image once it had been massaged to provide optimal information. Furthermore, linear methods in signal processing originated in analysis of electrical circuits, and concepts and terminology was characterized by electrical engineering. No doubt, signal processing was important but, as the author was to discover, statistical analysis was also central. An important initial application of image analysis was processing of microscope images in medical research. Immense gains could be made by automating manual visual classification of slides. In this application, so-called mathematical morphology was used very early. This approach is complementary to signal processing with origin in electrical engineering. Mathematical morphology is non-linear, and this extension of classical concepts in signal processing was very much needed in image analysis. Images could be cleaned in a much better way, and non-linear filters opened up for new applications.

3 Pattern Recognition

Astronomers used spectral images. An area was imaged in different bands of the electromagnetical spectrum. This way each location (picture element or pixel for short) was associated numbers expressing the reflected light at the different bands. Mathematically, a digital image was an array of multiples of numbers, not just of single numbers. The basic systematic way to classify an area was to group number multiples into groups of similar multiples. This is the basic problem in multispectral pattern recognition. At the Technical University of Copenhagen (DTU) in Denmark, satellite images were being analyzed this way. Images of Mestersvig in Greenland were investigated for possible mineral deposits. For a mathematician turned computer scientist this application opened up a bewildering set of problems. A pixel did not contain precise information but was the filtered response of a sensor by its point spread function. A pixel pertained to a point location on the ground, and was influenced by neighboring points. In an application, geologists would know the minerals at selected spots. Thus, in the image one could designate areas with known deposits as *training areas*. Thus, all multiples at the training areas were known to reflect a certain mineral. This meant that educated guesses could be made for minerals at unvisited locations by computing the training area with most similar multiples. "Most similar" had to be defined, and here mathematical statistics was the necessary tool. One describes the distribution of multiples as a multidimensional probability density distribution, and one estimates its parameters from information obtained from relevant training areas. Even, if no training areas were known, it was often possible to group similar multiples into classes, and, this way segment the image into different classes. The discipline is called unsupervised pattern recognition and supervised, when training areas are known.

4 Image Scale

If images were taken from a different height, what was the relation between the pictures? This problem was important, when information from different sensors

should be combined. In 1985, Ruzena Bajczy visited Copenhagen University, and in an invited lecture, she mentioned the work of Andrew Witkin on Scale space. This meant a mathematically fruitful way of defining the effect of varying spatial aperture of a sensor. When an image is analyzed, a description must combine an overall description with small significant details: different scales are necessary for interpretation. As an example, shadow boundaries are sometimes more and sometimes less sharp. In order to locate a less sharp boundary one has to analyze a larger environment of the image, than when the boundary is well defined. The Perona-Malik filter uses a small aperture at image points with large gradient and a larger aperture when the image gradient is smaller. In this manner, different points in an image are processed at different scales.

5 Human Visual Perception

A human makes the interpretation of an image, be it a medical doctor screening an X-ray image or a biologist studying a histological microscope slide. Thus, even more complexity is introduced into automatic analysis, since one has to understand and preferably model human visual perception. Not only that, but the interpretation is conditioned on previous experience. A study of human visual perception and memory was called for. Fortunately, the neurology of visual perception was much studied. The Hubel and Wiesel discovery of brain areas with specialized and specific visual functions initiated an avalanche of new discoveries of how the brain decodes images. The book *Vision* by David Marr from 1982 had international impact, and hid DIKU as a bomb. He treated biological vision from a computational point of view. As an example, the function of a ganglion cell in the retina can be described as a linear filter, and ganglion cells come with different apertures. This permits the retina to analyze an image at different scales.

6 Information Theory

A fundamental question presents itself: Interpretation of image data depends on the application. In general, one wants to model the phenomenon that one wants to understand. Then one determines the parameters of the model. A computer scientist would ask, which program (model) would generate the data that one observes. Without constraints, this question has many answers, including the trivial one: The model is a listing of the data. The question has to be rephrased: Find the program given reasonable restrictions. A possible restriction is to find a simple model. This way the model would describe one's understanding of the data. For example, Kepler's equations for motion of the planets express our understanding of planet motion. Likewise, one would like to obtain a description of a 3D scene from a 2D image, and one wants a simple description. The vocabulary of the description is elements of the language for building the model. One would like to obtain a description of the pathology of a medical image in concepts relevant for the illness investigated. The precise formulation of how to find the simplest model for a set of data was first made by Kolmogorov, when he stated that the complexity of a set of data is the number of bits needed to represent it. Thus, one is forced into information theory in order to understand how data can be represented using the fewest number of bits. This approach provides a mathematical definition of parsimony, also called Occam's razor: One describes a phenomenon by the simplest explanation. Obviously, the shortest program to generate a set of data is the optimal way to compress a data set. We need to understand data compression as well. Jorma Rissanen made statistical models explicit, stating in his *Minimum Description Length Principle (MDL)* that the best model is the one that possesses the least joint complexity of the model and the data that it generates. Here the complexity of a model is the information needed to describe its parameters.

7 Active Vision

In 1983, Ruzena Bajczy gave a lecture at the Scandinavian conference on image analysis. She did research on robotics that is programming motion of a machine based on visual input. Until then, at DIKU we had concentrated on signal analysis including the fast Fourier transform as the basic theory of image understanding. Ruzena Bajczy introduced the concept of active vision. How does a device – a robot – decide where to direct its sensor? Analysis of its sensors, in particular its images, should tell it where to direct its camera next in order to obtain maximum information about the object to describe or to avoid. This introduces the perception-action cycle into the pêle-mêle of knowledge needed for image analysis! One wants that information from an image that is sufficient to compute the next position of the sensor – and for a movable robot, the robot's actuators. This threw us into description of the 3D world from image inputs. We started by two fundamental investigations: Generating depth from two images of a stationary object taken from different angles, and computing the motion of a moving object from a stationary camera. For this purpose, we built equipment that made it possible to program the motion of an object and to locate a camera at different position. We settled on a turntable that we could move along a rail. On the table, we could position either the object, or the camera. The equipment permitted us to quantify the precision of our computation of depth and motion, since we could set up an experiment with known parameters for position and motion. Four PhD theses resulted from this early development [1–4].

Later we changed to small movable robots, that is platforms on which were mounted a camera and a computer that controlled actuators for the platform's wheels. The prototype project would be to program the robots as a swarm according to the rules used by Reynolds' "boids": Agents should move at the same speed, close to each other, but not too close. Furthermore, we mounted communication equipment on the platforms, thus permitting the robots to communicate.

A robot interacting with its environment is a dynamical system. The theory of dynamical systems predicts that for certain values of system parameters, infinitesimal changes of parameter values could make the system change behavior from well behaved to chaotic. A challenge, which we never came to realize in the lab, would be to implement the transition from period doubling to unpredictability.

8 Teaching Computer Vision

How is one to teach this enormous complexity inside a computer science curriculum? One approach is to teach the basic disciplines first, followed by their application to image analysis. We discovered by experience that, since the involved disciplines are so many, it is difficult to decide if one should select a few or teach a little of each. Furthermore, we found that focus is easily lost over too long a time span, that is, when too many (≥ 2) courses are needed. At DIKU a successful lecture series has resulted, which is built on a set of weekly exercises. Each exercise introduces necessary theory in connection with an application. An exercise is a program that should be modified or extended. This way theory is seen as necessary for results, theory and application were seen as depending on each other, the students' attention were caught and their creativity unleashed. The same concept was used for image analysis and for active robot vision.

This setup functions well in a computer science education, since the students would be proficient in programming in advance of classes, permitting focus on the subject matter, and permitting more advanced applications.

Two classes have crystallized from our efforts: An image analysis class, and a robot lab class. Both classes were built on the same concept: In advance a set of weekly exercises were programmed as small applications. The students were to apply the programs and to do application motivated modifications. The lectures presented the theory in advance of the exercise. This way theoretical concepts and applications were always together. Advanced theory would always be demonstrated with practical applications. It is surprising how advanced theory a simple application needs, if it has to be well understood, and how advanced applications can be build from little well understood theory. The experience was that if a firm ground could be made for a simple and convincing application, the students themselves would extend the theory and the application.

Exercises were carefully designed, and constituted the backbone of the classes. The exercises were non-trivial. For instance, the first exercise in image analysis was to segment a grey level image. This is possible with threshold logic for a simple image; the application was to compute the total value of coins on an image. For an image analysis expert trivial, but for a novice without experience in image analysis, a surprisingly large set of concepts are introduced by a single exercise. Then segmentation of a color image followed, then image segmentation, and motion analysis.

The robot lab class would start by implementing avoidance behaviour by fuzzy control. Then students would program self localization using particle filtering. The final exercise would be on robot cooperation, but so far we have not yet succeeded to program the robots to behave like one of Reynolds' swarms.

9 Literature

Below are mentioned a selection of textbooks and papers that have influenced the development of computer vision at DIKU in the period 1980–2008. Edda Sveinsdottir's research in computer tomography can be found in [5, 6]. Image analysis and pattern recognition was typically taught using a background textbook [7] supplemented by lecture notes. The book by Bishop [8] on pattern recognition was very welcome, when is appeared in 2006. Its flavour is mathematical statistics, and computer science students would need some mathematical background to fully profit from the book. Andrew Witkin's paper on scale space [9] introduced us to the idea of analysing a signal at different scales. Koenderink [10] extended scale from 1D signals to 2D signals, that is to images. Its application to image analysis is well explained by Lindeberg in his paper [11], in which he gives instructive examples. Information theory was introduced by Claude Shannon [12], and his initial text is still very readable. The minimum description length (MDL) principle is well described by Hansen and Yu [13]. Kolmogorov complexity and its applications are explained in the textbook by Li and Vitanýi [14]. Active vision introduced by Bajczy is well presented in a paper by K. Pahlavan and T. Uhlin and J.-O. Eklundh [15]. The elegant emerging flocking behaviour of locally acting agents is presented in a paper by Reynolds [16]. Devaney [17] is an introductory textbook on dynamical systems from a mathematical point of view. The elegant and powerful technique of particle filtering can be found in the paper by Isard and Blake [18].

Acknowledgments. Ruzena Bajczy from University of Pennsylvania, and Jan-Olof Eklund from the Royal Institute of Technology in Stockholm have been instrumental in providing advice and inspiration for the development of computer vision at DIKU. Edda Sveinsdottir and the author initiated the development of image analysis at DIKU as a follow up on Edda's research in computer tomography. Enthusiastic cooperation of members from the image group at DIKU is acknowledged. I wish to thank Søren Olsen and Jon Sporring for editorial comments to this presentation.

References

1. Arnspang, J.: Local Differential Kinematics in Surface Vision. PhD thesis, DIKU, University of Copenhagen (1987)
2. Olsen, I.: The Design and Analysis of a Feature Based Stereo Algorithm. PhD thesis, DIKU, University of Copenhagen (1988)
3. Henriksen, K.: Projective Geometry and Straight Lines in Computational Vision. PhD thesis, DIKU, University of Copenhagen (1990)
4. Nielsen, M.: From Paradigm to Algorithms in Computer vision. PhD thesis, DIKU, University of Copenhagen (1995)
5. Høedt-Rasmussen, K., Sveinsdottir, E., Lassen, N.A.: Regional Cerebral flow in Man Determined ny Intra-arterial Injection of Radioactive Inert Gas. Circulation Research XVIII (3), 237–247 (1966)
6. Sveinsdottir, E., Larsen, B., Rommer, P., Lassen, N.A.: A Multidetector Scintillation Camera with 254 Channels. The Journal of Nuclear Medicine 18(2), 168–174 (1977)
7. Sonka, M., Hlavac, V., Boyle, R.: Image Processing, Analysis, and Machine Vision. Brooks/Cole, Thompson (1999)
8. Bishop, C.M.: Pattern Recognition and Machine Learning. Springer, Heidelberg (2006)
9. Witkin, A.: Scale Space Filtering. In: Proceedings of the International Joint Conference on Artificial Intelligence, Karlsruhe, pp. 1019–1021 (1993)
10. Koenderink, J.J.: The Structure of Images. Biological Cybernetics 50(5), 363–370 (1984)

11. Lindeberg, T.: Feature Detection with Automatic Scale Selection. International Journal of Computer Vision 30(2), 79–116 (1998)

12. Shannon, C.E., Weaver, W.: The Mathematical Theory of Communication. Illini Books edn. (1963)

13. Hansen, M.H., Yu, B.: Model Selection and the Principle of Minimum Description Length. Journal of the American Statistical Association 96(454), 746–774 (2001)

14. Li, M., Vitanýi, P.: An Introduction to Kolmogorov Complexity and its Applications. North-Holland, Amsterdam (1993)

15. Pahlavan, K., Uhlin, T., Eklundh, J.-O.: Active Vision as a Methodology. In: Aloimonos, Y. (ed.) Purposive Vision, ch. 1. Lawrence Erlbaum, Mahwah (1994)

16. Reynolds, C.: Flocks, Herds and Schools: A Distributed Behavioral Model. In: SIGGRAPH 1987: Proceedings of the 14th Annual Computer Graphics and Interactive Techniques (Association for Computing Machinery), pp. 25–34 (1987)

17. Devaney, R.L.: An Introduction to Chaotic Dynamical Systems. Addison-Wesley, Reading (1989)

18. Isard, M., Blake, A.: Condensation – Conditional Density Propagation for Visual Tracking. International Journal of Computer Vision 29(2), 5–28 (1998)

Simula: Mother Tongue for a
Generation of Nordic Programmers

Yngve Sundblad

Human-Computer Interaction, Computer Science and Communication
KTH, 10044, Stockholm, Sweden
y@kth.se

Abstract. With Simula 67 Ole-Johan Dahl and Kristen Nygaard invented object-oriented programming. This has had an enormous impact on program development tools and methods in the world, well accounted in conferences and books, on programming languages and object-oriented programming, and on software pioneers. Early influenced were computer scientists in the Nordic countries who from about 1970 had Simula as the main programming tool, "mother tongue." This paper gives a first-hand account of experience of a unique early introduction of object-oriented programming for higher education in computer science and in computer programming, which provided powerful program development tools long before other educational institutions, especially as it coincided with the introduction of powerful interactive systems. The paper also challenges the misconception that Simula is primarily a tool for simulation by illustrating how it was used to teach general computer science and programming concepts with more general-purpose constructs than most contemporary languages, except perhaps Lisp.

Keywords: Computer science education, Nordic programmers, object-oriented programming, Simula.

1 Introduction

"*From the cold waters of Norway comes Object-Oriented Programming*"; this is the first line in Bertrand Meyer's widely used textbook titled, "Object Oriented Software Construction" [1].

Based on the previous development of Simula I in 1961–65, Ole-Johan Dahl and Kristen Nygaard in 1967 introduced Simula 67, an extension of Algol 60 with the basic concepts of object-oriented programming [2, 3].

The development of those concepts and the language Simula, the contributions of Ole-Johan Dahl and Kristen Nygaard, and their impact are well described in history of computing publications. We find accounts in books resulting from the ACM conference on History of Programming Languages, 1979 [4], the IEEE conference on History of Object-oriented Programming, 1994 [5], and the SD&M conference on Software Pioneers, 2001 [6, 7].

The development of computing education in the Nordic countries has been thoroughly described in several sessions at the History of Nordic Computing conferences in 2003 and 2007, as in [8].

J. Impagliazzo, P. Lundin, and B. Wangler (Eds.): HiNC3, IFIP AICT 350, pp. 416–424, 2011.
© IFIP International Federation for Information Processing 2011

Fig. 1. O.-J. Dahl & K. Nygaard

Here, I will concentrate on the impact of Simula on computing education in universities in the Nordic countries. More specifically, as it affected computing education in Sweden and even more specifically at KTH and at Stockholm University.

Ole-Johan Dahl and Kristen Nygaard first presented Simula to us in 1968 at a seminar. As teachers of programming to engineering and science students mainly in the procedural paradigm of ALGOL-60 and to some extent Fortran, we saw Simula as a revelation. We immediately grasped and saw the power of the object-oriented concepts extending the syntax of Algol, which until then was our main programming tool (with some use also of Fortran and Basic).

We have kept contacts with the Scandinavian academic object-oriented programming environments, especially in Aarhus, Lund and Oslo, but the experience accounted for here could certainly be complemented by experience from other Nordic computer science educational institutions.

2 Simula Concepts

There is a misconception, especially in the US, that Simula was just a tool for simulation applications. Simula's main importance was the introduction of impressively powerful new concepts that are useful for and facilitate development of interactive and other computer applications as the predominance of the object-oriented concepts today shows. Someone coined that it is an acronym for "SIMple Universal Language." The main new concepts were the following.

- *Class* of similar Objects (in Simula declaration of CLASS with data and actions)
- *Objects* created as *Instances* of a Class (in Simula NEW object of class)
- *Data attributes* of a class (in Simula type declared as parameters or internal)
- *Method attributes* of, patterns of action (in Simula declared as PROCEDURE)
- *Message passing*, calls of methods (in Simula dot-notation)
- *Subclasses* that inherit from superclasses
- *Polymorphism* with several subclasses to a superclass
- *Co-routines* (in Simula Detach – Resume)
- *Encapsulation* of data supporting abstractions

3 Teaching Computer Science Concepts with Simula

Simula soon assumed a role as a second course language (after Algol or Fortran or Basic) in many academic programming environments. As an example, at KTH in Stockholm, all students from 1975 to about 1990 used the "Algol part" (the procedural subset) of Simula in their first programming course [9] while many students took a second course in object-oriented programming with the entirety of Simula [10]. At Stockholm University, Simula used teaching objects, program structures, and data structures until 1997, illustrated by a comprehensive textbook from 1993 [11]. Also at Lund University, Simula was used in education until 1997 as illustrated by a textbook from 1992 [12].

From 1972 onwards, this was a uniquely early introduction of object-oriented programming for education, applications and research, with continued development and spread to national industry and international academics environments.

Simula was also our tool for teaching program and data structures, with no real competitor except Lisp, which took over in the computer science specialist education in the late 1980s through the brilliant textbook and lectures on "Structure and Interpretation of Computer Programs" by Abelson and Sussman at MIT, using the Lisp dialect Scheme [13].

At the Stockholm Computer Centre, we taught an ongoing education one-week course in Simula twice a year from 1972 to about 1980, with about twenty participants from industry, academia, and defense research, mainly with backgrounds in Fortran. Thus, several hundred developers received an early introduction in object-oriented programming.

In computer science departments in the Nordic countries, there has been a variety of languages and systems used in teaching object-oriented programming since 1980, but the basic concepts go back to Simula and they were taught to our current generation of teachers by the older generation using Simula. We illustrate this by a list of Simula descendants used at KTH: Smalltalk, LOOPS, C++, Modula-2, now Java and Python.

We now take up some basic concepts that constitute a major computer science and programming education, introduced via Simula already in the early 1970s.

3.1 Data Structures

In the 1970s data structures were put on a firm theoretical footing by many researchers, e.g. Ole-Johan Dahl [14] and [15], Tony Hoare [14] and Nicolas Wirth [16], with the "formula" *Algorithms + Datastructures = Programs*.

In [6, p. 85], Dahl states, "The most important new concept was data structures with associated operators." That concept is very important and elegant in Simula but equally important are other new concepts in Simula such as class and inheritance.

The Simula reference variables that safely (strongly typed) can reference objects, with other references as attributes, give easy tools for building up stacks, queues, lists, trees, lattices, etc., that are proper data structures for different applications.

Together with the built-in framework SIMSET for building circular double-linked circular lists with head the references in Simula made systematic teaching of data structures powerful as illustrated in the textbooks [10–12, 14–18].

An elegant example is the following class for binary tree nodes with a method for scanning, which applied to the root makes a scan in post order. The "trick" is that it terminates because INSPECT-ing NONE has no effect.

```
CLASS node(left, right); REF(node) left, right;
BEGIN
    PROCEDURE scan(x); REF(node) x;
    INSPECT x DO BEGIN
        scan(left);
        scan(right);
        visit(THIS node);
    END of scan;
END of node;
```

3.2   Class and Subclass – Encapsulation and Inheritance

The encapsulation of data and algorithms (methods) into classes made it possible to structure programs in new ways, in many cases more appropriate and giving better overview than in the strictly procedural ways of the then predominant Algol and Fortran.

Subclass mechanisms allowed hierarchical structures and abstractions that also help students to structure and make less error-prone programs. The polymorphism, several subclasses of an abstract superclass, with rules for handling and using/overriding name collisions, gave the more advanced students powerful tools.

3.3   Co-Routines and Discrete Event Simulation

An advanced feature of Simula, that allows defining the class of parallel processes and the SIMULATION framework, is the Detach-Resume-Call mechanisms.

The Detach and Resume() procedures in processes allow stopping and handing over control between them as does Detach and Call() between a class instance and the main program. These allow simulated parallelism for applications that are naturally described as co-routines and they were used as basis for true parallelism [19].

In the advanced Simula courses, SIMULATION was usually introduced, at KTH with a special textbook [20], while co-routines were treated for the most interested students.

3.4   Computer Graphics and Interaction, Model-View-Controller

We soon realized that computer graphics and interaction are very well suited for object-oriented structures and programming. It is natural to see the entities on the screen as objects, their actions and our interactions with them as invoking their methods.

In his brilliant work on Sketchpad, as early as 1963 [21] Ivan Sutherland invented several object-oriented concepts for handling the graphics on the screen such as objects, methods, and sub-objects although he does not develop it into a language but rather a hands-on system.

When introducing graphics into our courses in the 1970s, for plotters and vector and character terminals, Simula was natural to use for describing the objects and of keeping track of them is through display lists, which also is easy to implement with SIMSET in Simula [22].

Then, in the early 1980s, came the graphic workstations to us in academic Scandinavia, although developed in the US already in the mid-1970s, with Simula inspired tools such as Smalltalk.

The structuring of interactive graphic applications into MVC – Model-View-Controller, also has Nordic Simula origin, through Trygve Reenskaug, then visiting scientist at Xerox PARC [23].

MVC was introduced into our courses with Smalltalk around 1985 and is now commonly used in most programming tools for building interactive graphic applications.

4 Teaching Programming Practices with Simula

Here we look at some programming practices that emerged in the 1970s and were supported by Simula and its implementations.

4.1 Structured Programming and Programming Style

A buzz concept in the 1970s was structured programming with the "religions" hope of solving the "software crisis," i.e. the galloping costs for development of large programs. Structured Programming also had a sound scientific basis formed in the early 1970s by theorists as Ole-Johan Dahl, Edsger Dijkstra and Tony Hoare with their ground-breaking book [14], Don Knuth and Niklaus Wirth, and practitioners as Kristen Nygaard, and Kernighan & Plaugher [24] at Bell labs.

These practices were taught extensively in our basic and advanced programming courses in Simula and survive today with other tools.

4.2 Dialog Programming Environment

A key factor in the success of using Simula in our education was its implementation on current computers. The first implementation we met in 1971 was on the IBM 360, but the real breakthrough came with the implementation for our first large dialog system, DEC-10. A Swedish team developed in the early 1970s a system for the DEC-system 10 [25], which was also basis for a dissertation at our department [26]. Ole-Johan Dahl states that "the DEC-system 10 implementation contributed considerably to the spread of Simula" [6, p. 85].

The experience of using Simula on text terminals led to abandonment of punched cards completely in 1976 and letting all our students take turns in using 30 terminals versus the DEC-10 at Stockholm Computer Centre (QZ). That led to slow response and complaints from other users. Hence, when they ported Simula to the DEC-20 and we were allowed to break the centralization dogma in Swedish academic computing, we acquired the department's own DEC-2020, "Nadja" in 1979, mainly for running Simula. The Algol part was taught to all KTH students and the entirety of Simula in second courses for students such as in engineering physics, electrical engineering, and mathematics. We soon had to expand with a DEC-2060 ("Vera") and one more DEC-2020 ("Venus"). The names represent Hope-Faith-Love in different languages.

The programming environment on the DEC computers had nice features such as the:

o SIMDDT debugger, [27], for inspection of variables at breakpoints and on forced interruptions when infinite loop is suspected, etc.
o SIMED program text editor, capitalising reserved words, making standard procedure names having first letter as capital and making proper indentations
o FQC collecting run time statistics
o SAFEIO, for safe input, not accepting input of "wrong" type

When the personal workstation revolution came in 1984, we moved some courses with Simula in computer science, programming, graphics, and interaction over to the Macintosh that survived until 1997, thereby abandoning the DEC computers in 1988. Developments and experiences in this area appear in [28–30].

Fig. 2. DEC-2020 computer "Nadja," used extensively for up to thirty parallel students' interactive development and running of Simula programs 1979–88. It was revived 2010, started at first effort, here with the proud author. Historically important as the first mainframe academic computer owned (and run) by a department (NADA, KTH) and not by the six centralized computer centers, one in each university region in Sweden.

4.3   Simula as an Inspiration for Smalltalk

Alan Kay at Xerox PARC was one of the first American researchers that, by coincidence, learned about the Simula concepts and saw the power of object-orientation. Together with Adele Goldberg, he used it in the definition and development of the epoch-making Smalltalk language from 1972 onwards [31] and [32]:

Fig. 3. Alan Kay & Adele Goldberg

Then there was Simula, which the designers thought of as an extension of Algol. It was basically a preprocessor to Algol the way C++ was a preprocessor for C. It was a great concept and I was lucky enough to see it as almost a new thing. ... If you combine Simula and Lisp – Lisp didn't have data structures, it had instances of objects – you would have a dynamic type system that would give you the range of expression you need. ... It is not too much of an exaggeration to say that most of my ideas from then on took their roots from Simula – but not as an attempt to improve it. It was the promise of an entirely new way to structure computations that took my fancy. As it turned out, it would take quite a few years to understand how to use the insights and to devise efficient mechanisms to execute them.

In our courses on graphics and interaction, Smalltalk took over the role as a more powerful tool than Simula from about 1985, when we got the first decently efficient implementation on Sun and Tektronix stations, until about 2000. Now packages in Java play that role.

5   The Simula Heritage in Computer Science Education Today

Algol is "the Latin" of procedural programming, i.e. the dead language that most modern such languages build on. Similarly, Simula is "the Latin" of object-oriented programming.

Simula and its object orientation as inspiration in developing programming tools received recognition by the creators mentioned below:

- o 1970s: Smalltalk (Alan Kay), Modula-2 (Niklaus Wirth), LOOPS (Dan Bobrow)
- o 1980s: Eiffel (Bertrand Meyer), C++ (Bjarne Stroustrup), Objective C (Brad Cox), Object Pascal (Niklaus Wirth, Anders Hejlsberg)
- o 1990s: Python (Guido van Rossum), Java (Jim Gosling), Objective Ada (Jean Ichbiah), C# (Anders Hejlsberg)

Some of these are extensions of existing programming languages such as general as LOOPS (of LISP), or procedural as C++, Objective C and C#, Objective Ada, Object Pascal, Java, leading to compromises and sometimes less "clean" constructions.

The extensions of procedural languages with stronger industrial backing than Simula such as C and Pascal gave object-oriented variants a much wider use. A notable example is C++, developed from C by Bjarne Stroustrup with a Scandinavian Simula background; it is still widely used in spite of its sometimes "dirty" constructions. Another is Java, where the strong backing by the Sun Corporation and the sensitivity for needs of portable devices such as mobile phones, has made it widely used. A third is C#, with its strong backing by Microsoft Corporation.

The other languages are new developments, often with elegant clean ways of expression in the Simula tradition: Smalltalk (with the "clean" paradigm that everything is objects), as well as Modula-2, Eiffel, and Python (with their strong influences of the later abstract data type and assertion theories). Some of these are quite broadly used in academic teaching but not dominant in industry.

In most academic computer science and programming educational environments as well as in the programming industry, these offsprings of Simula are the main tools used. Thus, Simula must be seen as a great success, although it is quite natural that new developments make old programming languages obsolete.

Acknowledgments. The experiences and lessons on teaching computer science and programming with Simula have been shared with many colleagues, especially those at the KTH department, NA (Numerical Analysis) from 1970 renamed into NADA (Numerical Analysis and Computer Science) in 1979; the trend also affected other Swedish and Nordic computer science departments. Stefan Arnborg, Serafim Dahl, Örjan Leringe, Kjell Lindqvist, and Staffan Romberger, all at NADA, Kalle Mäkilä, Mats Ohlin and Jacob Palme, all at FOA (now FOI), and Sten Henriksson and Boris Magnusson (Lund University) deserve special mention.

References

1. Meyer, B.: Object Oriented Software Construction. Prentice-Hall, Englewood Cliffs (1988)
2. Dahl, O.-J., Myhrhaug, B., Nygaard, K.: SIMULA Common Base Language. Norwegian Computing Centre (1968, 1970)
3. Birtwistle, G. M., Dahl, O.-J., Myhrhaug, B., Nygaard, K.: SIMULA BEGIN. Studentlitteratur/Auerbach, Philadelphia (1973)
4. Nygaard, K., Dahl, O.-J.: The Development of the SIMULA Language. In: Proceedings of the ACM SIGPLAN History of Programming Languages Conference, pp. 243–272. ACM, New York (1979)
5. Holmevik, J.R.: Compiling SIMULA: A historical study of technological genesis. IEEE Annals of the History of Computing 16(4), 25–37 (1994)
6. Dahl, O.-.J.: The Roots of Object Orientation: The Simula Language. In: Broy, M., Denert, E. (eds.) Software Pioneers, pp. 78–90. Springer, Heidelberg (2001)
7. Dahl, O.-.J., Nygaard, K.: Class and Subclass Declarations. In: Buxton, J.N. (ed.) Simulation Programming Languages, pp. 158–174. North Holland, Amsterdam (1967); reprinted in Broy, M., Denert, E. (eds.) Software Pioneers, pp. 91–107, Springer, Heidelberg (2001)
8. Krogdahl, S.:The birth of Simula. In: History of Nordic Computing Conference 1, Oslo (2003), http://heim.ifi.uio.no/~steinkr/papers/HiNC1-webve

9. Romberger, S., Sundblad, Y.: Grundläggande Programmering i Simula. Teknisk Högskolelitteratur, Stockholm (1978)
10. Sundblad, Y., Romberger, S., Leringe, Ö.: Fortsatt Programmering i Simula. Teknisk Högskolelitteratur, Stockholm (1980)
11. Dahl S., Lindqvist, K.: Objektorienterad programmering och algoritmer i Simula. Studentlitteratur, Lund (1993)
12. Holm, P.: Objektorienterad programmering och Simula. KFS, Lunds Studentkår (1992)
13. Abelson, H., Sussman, G.J.: Structure and Interpretation of Computer Programs. MIT Press, Cambridge (1985), http://mitpress.mit.edu/sicp/full-text/book/book.html
14. Dahl, O.-J., Dijkstra, E.W., Hoare, C.A.R.: Structured Programming, pp. 175–220. Academic Press, London (1972)
15. Dahl, O.-J., Belsnes, D.: Algoritmer og Datastrukturer. Studentlitteratur, Lund (1973)
16. Wirth, N.: Algorithms + Datastructures = Programs. Prentice-Hall, New Jersey (1975)
17. Pooley, R. J.: An introduction to programming in Simula. Blackwell Scientific Publications, Great Britain (1987)
18. Kirkerud, B.: Object-Oriented Programming with SIMULA. International Computer Science Series. Addison-Wesley Publishing Co., Reading (1989)
19. Palme, J.: Making Simula into a programming language for real time. Management Informatics 4(4), 129–137 (1975)
20. Siklósi, K.: Simula-Simulation. Teknisk Högskolelitteratur, Stockholm (1980)
21. Sutherland, I.: Sketchpad, a Man-Machine Graphical Communication System. Ph.D. thesis from MIT republished as Technical report no. 574 by Cambridge University (1963, 2003)
22. Haugen, Ø., Skifjeld, K.: Class graphics – A powerful tool in Interactive Computer Graphics. In: Proc. 10th Simula Users' Conference Norsk regnesentral (1982)
23. Reenskaug, T.: Models –Views – Controllers. Xerox PARC Learning Research Group internal memo (1979)
24. Kernighan, B.W., Plauger, P.J.: The Elements of Programming Style. McGraw-Hill, New York (1978)
25. Arnborg, S., Jones, R.W., Noble, K.H.M., Weston, P.J.: Simula 67 for the DEC System 10 Computer. FOA P Rapport C-8304-M3 (E4), Försvarets Forskningsanstalt, Planeringsbyrån, Stockholm (1971)
26. Arnborg, S.: Programming language implementation. Doctoral Thesis, Numerical Analysis, KTH, Stockholm (1972)
27. Palme, J., Wennersten, I.: SIMDDT – for conversational debugging of SIMULA programs. Simula Newsletter 5(2) (1977)
28. Dahl, S., Sundblad, Y.: Mac Simula Application Framework. In: Proc. 18th Simula Conference, Plzen (1990)
29. Sundblad, Y.: Teaching Object-Oriented User Interface Design. In: Proc. Apple European Univ. Consortium, Heidelberg (1988)
30. Kjelldahl, L., Sundblad, Y.: Experience from ten years of student projects oriented towards graphic interaction. Computers and Graphics 20 (1996)
31. Feldman, S.: A conversation with Alan Kay. Queue 2, 20–30 (2004)
32. Kay, A.: The Early History of Smalltalk. In: Bergin Jr., T.J., Gibson, R.G. (eds.) History of Programming Languages – II, pp. 511–578. ACM Press, Addison-Wesley Publ. Co., New York, Reading (1996)

Precursors of the IT Nation: Computer Use and Control in Swedish Society, 1955–1985

Isabelle Dussauge[1], Johan Gribbe[2], Arne Kaijser[2], Per Lundin[2], Julia Peralta[2], Gustav Sjöblom[3], and Björn Thodenius[4]

[1] Dept. of Thematic Studies – Technology and Social Change, Linköping University
581 83 Linköping, Sweden
isabelle.dussauge@liu.se
[2] Div. of History of Science and Technology, KTH
100 44 Stockholm, Sweden
{johan.gribbe,arne.kaijser,per.lundin,julia.peralta}@abe.kth.se
[3] Div. of Technology and Society, Chalmers University of Technology
412 96 Göteborg, Sweden
gustav.sjoblom@chalmers.se
[4] Dept. of Management and Organization, Stockholm School of Economics
113 83 Stockholm, Sweden
bjorn.thodenius@hhs.se

Abstract. This paper is a presentation of a research project that aims at writing the history of computing in Sweden in the mainframe age from a user perspective. Rather than beginning with the history of hardware, this project takes as its point of departure the way in which actors in different sectors of society used computer technology in order to achieve a higher degree of control over crucial processes, whether through electronic data processing systems, process control or technical/scientific computation.

Keywords: Control, historiography, history of computing, IT-history, Sweden, users.

1 Introduction

This paper is a presentation of the research project "Precursors of the IT Nation: Computer Use and Control in Swedish Society, 1955–1985."[1] The aim is to draw upon the experience and sources accumulated in the project "From Computing Machines to IT" and to write the history of computing in Sweden in the mainframe age from a user perspective [1, 2]. The focus of this paper is on the wider context and central concepts, rather than the details of the work process.

In the last twenty-five years, Sweden has consistently received the designation as an IT nation. When the Economist Intelligence Unit made a ranking of IT competitiveness in 2009 with Sweden ranked third [3]. Through the 1990s and 2000s, similar rankings by IDC and Forbes consistently landed Sweden in one of the top

---

[1] The program is funded by Handelsbanken Research Foundations.

J. Impagliazzo, P. Lundin, and B. Wangler (Eds.): HiNC3, IFIP AICT 350, pp. 425–432, 2011.

spots.[2] The high level of computer diffusion, internet penetration, and computer literacy has been a constant feature of the adoption of computer-based information technology in Sweden since the advent of the personal computer in the late 1970s.

When the PC became widely available in the early 1980s, digital computing already had a thirty-year long history. The purpose of this project is to provide the first comprehensive research on the way people and organizations used computers during this period. We will not deal explicitly with the continuities to the eras of personal computing and the internet or with any outright comparison with other countries. Rather, the project aims at providing an understanding of the first thirty years of computing in Sweden in its own right.

The history of digital computing in Sweden begins with the efforts of the state towards transferring computer hardware and skills from abroad after World War II. In November 1948, the Swedish Board for Computing Machinery was appointed and in November 1953, the first digital computer, the Binary Electronic Sequence Calculator (BESK), went into use. A group of young Swedish engineers, some of whom sent by the board to the United States on fellowships to study the new technology of digital computing constructed the BESK. At that time, BESK was an advanced computer, and leading computer scientists including John von Neumann, Howard Aiken, and Konrad Zuse, visited it [4]. Due to BESK, Sweden became one of the leading nations in the development of this new technological field.

The BESK project often becomes the point of departure for the history of computing in Sweden. The main topic of discussion centers around the reason the national computer project failed in the early 1960s after such a successful start. Although BESK was ahead of its time and despite its high expectations, the project did not result in the development of an internationally competitive computer industry. In 1957, the chief engineer Erik Stemme and most of the technical staff left the project for the electronics firm Åtvidabergs Industrier (later Facit) to develop scientific and administrative mainframe computer systems for the commercial market [5]. They abandoned the project after only a few years as its proponents realized that Swedish firms would not be able to compete with IBM and other American firms. Instead, Erik Stemme and the progenitors of BESK later devoted themselves to a rather successful development of peripheral equipment to computers. Annerstedt has argued that the lack of government support was a key factor in this negative development [6]. Other researchers have challenged his analysis but the overall emphasis remains on the issue of why a national computer industry did not materialize [7, 5].

The international historiography of computing is marked by a similar focus on the early development of large mainframe computers such as the ENIAC and the rise of the leading hardware manufacturers like IBM, Univac, DEC, and ICL. We now have an impressive collection of literature on the development of computer hardware [8–11]. Recently, the research has extended to software development [12, 13]. However, there is a tendency in the existing studies to deal with the development of computers more or less in isolation, without relating them to the wide range of users of computers and their appropriation of computer technology [14].

---

[2] For example, Sweden topped the IDC/World Times Information Society Index (ISI) between 2000 and 2003.

The focus on the manufacturing of computers rather than their use is especially misleading for small nations like Sweden, where it imported from abroad the vast majority of computers in use and computerization relied more on the appropriation of imported technologies than on domestic hardware development. Our ambition is to take computer users as the point of departure for a new and different historiography, which does not point in the direction of a failed computer industry, but to a Swedish tradition of rapid adaptation to computer technology. The most important long-term consequence of the activities was not the accumulation of expertise about the construction of computers, but the fostering of a considerable number of very competent users. In total, more than 1,300 people attended the board's training courses between 1952 and 1961 [15]. Civilian and military scientists, engineers, and administrative personnel, who disseminated knowledge of the new technology to different sectors of society, used BESK and its various modified copies (SMIL at the University of Lund, SARA at Saab in Linköping, DASK in Copenhagen, and the Facit EDB machines sold by Åtvidaberg) extensively. For example, meteorologists from Stockholm University used BESK to carry out the first numerical weather forecasts. Moreover, in 1961 when the Swedish Defense Research Agency (FOA) purchased an IBM 7090 mainframe computer for advanced scientific calculations, they could benefit from many years of practical experience of programming and use of advanced digital computers. From the late 1950s, the competence created by the training courses and technical-scientific computations was increasingly integrated with experience of other forms of information technology. Punch-card machinery for administrative purposes had been in use in Sweden since the 1910s and the installed value of IBM punch card machinery in Sweden doubled between 1956 and 1960. Numerically controlled machine tools and process control technologies increasingly integrated with digital computers. In parallel with the activities at the board, other processes prepared users for the computer age.

In the project, we follow this thread from the Swedish Board for Computing Machinery, from punch-card equipment and from early process control and industrial automation technology, and we analyze the subsequent development of computer systems in Sweden from the perspective of the users. Computer technology did not spread by itself; actors in different sectors of society appropriated it to achieve a higher degree of control over crucial processes. This appropriation often entailed the development of new applications that brought users in touch with computer suppliers, consultants, and the new professional groups of programmers and systems developers.

If we are to understand the early appropriation of computer technology and thus the historical roots of the IT-nation, we must look in detail at the specific traits that characterized computing before the personal computer revolution of the 1980s. Mainframe computing associated with the centralized and hierarchical structures of Fordism rather than the dynamic networks of the information age had characterized the first thirty years of computing in Sweden [16]. Many economic historians and sociologists have identified the computer, together with microelectronics and telecommunications, as the core of a third industrial revolution or the coming of an information age [17–20]. Regardless of the particular perspectives, these scholars are mainly concerned with computers as we know them from the 1980s and onwards: distributed, networked, and flexible. We argue that while there certainly was a revolutionary turning point in the 1980s, there were also continuities from the age of mainframe computing which deserve further study.

Between the macro-level descriptions of information ages and industrial revolutions on the one hand, and the detailed orientation towards technology and manufacturing on the other, there is a huge gap, which this project intends to fill. We believe that historians have an urgent task in writing the history of how users of computers appropriated the globally available computer technology, adapted it to their own purposes, and constructed computer systems to extend their control of people and activities.

2 Computers and Control in the Fordist Age

The period covered in this project is the years 1955 to 1985, which corresponds to the *era of the large, centralized, mainframe computers*. The first computers of the 1950s were gigantic in size; they required very large investments and had limited storage capacity and compatibility with other systems. As a result, they were associated with large organizations, a centralization of information processing, and often with large projects for specific purposes. Over time, these characteristics became less marked, as prices fell, smaller computers appeared, and networked computing became more widespread. Nevertheless, we argue that the period from 1955 to the early 1980s characterizes an era of mainframe computing. While there certainly were currents pointing to the future paradigm of personal computers and distributed computing, the mainframe maintained its dominance of the concept of computing.

Because of the scale economies, mainframe computing was strongly associated with *large organizations* and *large projects*. Only large organizations were capable of the high investment and high volume of information processing necessary for owning and running a computer system. Small- and medium-sized organizations could gain access to computing only through service bureaus; therefore, they had a limited ability to develop tailor-made computer systems. Instead, they used computers for the mechanization of previously manual routines. In larger organizations, computer systems development often took shape in the form of projects to develop completely new capabilities. In a project, experts with different kinds of competence and different kinds of experience came together for a limited time in order to develop a certain endeavor. Tasks could evolve informally beside the ordinary hierarchies [21]. These projects were complex and people usually carried them out as collaborative efforts between a number of organizations, mostly involving both suppliers of computer technology and the future users.

We will study a number of large computer projects in different sectors of society. In many cases, the aim of such projects was rationalization for cost-cutting purposes, a mechanization of manual routines that did not fundamentally change the way of doing things. In other cases, the purpose of computer systems development acquired a meaning of developing new capabilities that allowed organizations to do new things in new ways. It is important to observe that the initial objectives were not always achieved – several of the projects studied failed or did not lead to the intended consequences, as systems development was influenced by external actors or by the forces unleashed by the new availability of information.

As described above, the central idea of the project is that *actors appropriated* computer technology to achieve *control*.

Appropriation refers to the way in which technologies are constructed in a negotiation between the original technology and the users [22]. The computer hardware used in the Swedish systems differed little from the one used abroad. Computer technology was available from a global pool and circulated globally. As noted above, previous research has tended to follow an American paradigm where a strong relation exists between domestic computer manufacturing and computer use. While Sweden had a domestic computer industry at the time, its total output amounted to only a tiny share of the Swedish market. IBM alone had a market share of two-thirds through most of the period of study and other foreign suppliers such as DEC, ICL, Bull, Univac, and Wang followed it. Therefore, computer diffusion is far more relevant than computer manufacturing from the point of view of computerization in a small nation as Sweden. The computer systems developed in the encounter between the mostly multinational suppliers and the domestic users, often in long negotiations and with the participation of other actors such as consultants and academic experts. This perspective also raises the question of the extent to which the computer projects that we study reflect a generic, international model of computerization and to what extent they reflect Swedish particularities [23]. While this issue can only be fully explored in a comparative study, it nevertheless raises important questions about the relevance of Swedish particularities within each of the subprojects (e.g. policy of military non-alignment, one of the world's most extensive welfare states, an unusual predominance of big business, a Swedish tradition of infrastructure governance) [22].

Control is the pivotal concept of this study. Following Cortada's perspective, computer systems constituted a *digital hand* by which certain actors acquired a new tool for the processing of information and controlling a wide range of activities [24–26]. At the same time, it must be stressed that the control efforts were ambiguous, often fostering counter reactions from those who subjected greater efficient control, sometimes leading to other outcomes than expected, and nearly always resulting in some degree of internal struggle for mastery of information control. Thus, control is not monolithic, and important questions are what forms of control resulted from these changes: Control by whom, of what, and over whom? Moreover, what were the consequences for those subjected to control? This question will be a connecting thought for all four subprojects.

To understand fully the relation between computer systems and control, we must define how the development of computer technology interacted with different actors and social groups. Since systems development took place within large projects, identifying the structures and boundaries of these projects will be a primary task of the project. Which actors entered and left the project? What were their relative roles? The new forms of control affected the relative power of managers, IT departments, finance departments, salesmen and workers within organization as well as the relations to a large number of external actors. The key issue here is to identify the articulation of ideologies of control and resistance based on computer technology. How did computer systems development mesh with different professional cultures? Different categories of users integrated computers in their professional identities in different ways, with huge ramifications for the development of organizations as well as computer systems. In other words, the era of mainframe computer projects was a social construction, as different actors appropriated the computer technology to achieve new forms of control. Through their efforts, they constituted and created the precursors of the IT nation Sweden.

3 Subprojects

3.1 Controlling the Citizens

Controlling the Citizens sheds light on the construction and implementation of computerized systems for the production, accumulation and processing of individual data within public authorities in the Swedish welfare state during the period 1955–1985. We have taken case studies from the Swedish Public Employment Services (AMS) and from preventive health care screenings.

Computers were an important tool in the rationalization of administrative tasks: for instance, for the British public administration, they became instruments for the control of welfare procedures and thereby for some aspects of the citizens' behavior [27]. In Sweden, politicians and civil servants saw computerization as a way to eliminate loopholes in the tax systems and to enhance welfare services. One major aspect of these developments was the establishment of computed files: records and information systems for the classification and retrieval of data over the citizens.

The hypothesis is that with the introduction of computerized systems, the institutions of the welfare state reshaped their practices of control of social problems (e.g. unemployment) and individual or public responsibilities (e.g. employability).

3.2 Controlling the Firm

In the world of big business, electronic data processing initially represented a continuation of that mechanization of clerical routines already under way, using punch card and other electromechanical equipment. However, computer-based information systems soon became the basis for new and extended control systems and they were integrated in the management of the firm, and thus in its power relations. The subproject deals with how different individuals and social groups – owners (especially Marcus Wallenberg), CEOs, vice presidents, line organization middle management, external consultants (notably Stanford Research Institute), rationalization experts, computing professionals, and labor unions – appropriated computer technology to extend their control of the firm and its environment. The focus is on the electrical engineering giant ASEA, a major user of computers for data processing, technical computation and process control, as well as an increasingly important supplier of systems for process control and industrial automation. The ASEA case complements the research by Atlas Copco and Volvo. The subproject, moreover, includes research on the service bureau industry as the main provider of computing services for small and medium-sized firms in the age of mainframe computing.

3.3 Controlling the Battlefield

Another area in which computerized systems were introduced during this period was the armed forces, where digital technology opened up new ways of controlling the battlefield. The main purpose of the subproject *Controlling the Battlefield* is to study the development and implementation of computerized command and control systems in the Swedish Armed Forces during the Cold War. More specifically, the project is articulated around two separate case studies: the introduction of digital real-time computers in the air defense system in the 1950s and 1960s, and the failed attempt by the Swedish Defense Staff to implement computerized systems in support of military decision making in the 1970s and 1980s. The case studies are the radar-based air defense network STRIL-60 and the computerized command system LEO.

3.4 Controlling the Flow

Castells' notion that the control of flows is the main source of power in the modern network society inspires this subproject [20]. We focus on flows of different types and analyze how the introduction of computers enabled new forms of control of these flows from the mid-1950s onwards. The flows that are included in the study are *flows of current* (the electricity infrastructure at Vattenfall and Sydkraft), *flows of money* (interbank clearing, SIBOL, giro systems, and ATMs in the banking industry), and *flows of goods* (the distribution networks for goods).

Acknowledgments. We are grateful to Handelsbankens forskningsstiftelser for supporting the research for this paper.

References

1. Lundin, P.: From Computing Machines to IT: Collecting, Documenting, and Preserving Source Material on Swedish IT-History. In: Impagliazzo, I., Järvi, T., Paju, P. (eds.) History of Nordic Computing 2: Second IFIP WG9.7 Conference, HiNC2, Turku, Finland, August 21-23 (2007); Revised Selected Papers, pp. 65–73. Springer, Berlin (2009)
2. Lundin, P.: Documenting the Use of Computers in Swedish Society between 1950 and 1980: Final Report on the Project From Computing Machines to IT. KTH, Stockholm (2010)
3. Economist Intelligence Unit: Resilience Amid Turmoil. Benchmarking IT Industry Competitiveness 2009 (2009)
4. Swedish National Archives, Arninge, Swedish Board for Computing Machinery Archives, D IV:1 Besöksbok (1949-1959)
5. Petersson, T.: Facit and the BESK Boys. IEEE Annals of the History of Computing 27, 23–30 (2005)
6. Annerstedt, J.: Datorer och politik. Cavefors, Staffanstorp (1970)
7. De Geer, H.: På väg till datasamhället. Kungliga tekniska högskolan, Stockholm (1992)
8. Campbell-Kelly, M., Aspray, W.: Computer: A History of the Information Machine. Basic Books, New York (1996)
9. Ceruzzi, P.: A History of Modern Computing. MIT Press, Cambridge (1998)
10. Hallberg, T.: IT-gryning: Svensk datahistoria från 1840- till 1960-talet. Studentlitteratur, Lund (2007)
11. Yost, J.R.: The Computer Industry. Greenwood Press, Westport (2005)
12. Mowery, D.: The International Computer Software Industry. Oxford University Press, Oxford (1996)

13. Campbell-Kelly, M.: From Airline Reservations to Sonic the Hedgehog: A History of the Software Industry. MIT Press, Cambridge (2003)
14. Misa, T.J.: Understanding How Computing Changed the World. IEEE Annals of the History of Computing 29(4), 52–63 (2007)
15. Sjöblom, G.: The Programming Priesthood Comes to Sweden – Computer Training in the 1950s. Unpublished manuscript, presented at the Division of History of Technology and Science, Royal Institute of Technology (November 2, 2009)
16. Appelquist, J.: Informationsteknik och organisatorisk förändring: Teknik, organisation och produktivitet i svensk banksektor, 1975-2003. Lund Studies in Economic History 36. University of Lund, Lund (2005)
17. Freeman, C., Louca, F.: As Time Goes By: From the Industrial Revolutions to the Information Revolution. Oxford University Press, Oxford (2001)
18. Magnusson, L.: An Economic History of Sweden. Routledge, New York (2005)
19. Schön, L.: En modern svensk ekonomisk historia. SNS förlag, Stockholm (2007)
20. Castells, M.: The Rise of the Network Society. Blackwell, Malden (1996)
21. Hughes, T.P.: Rescuing Prometheus. Pantheon Books, New York (1998)
22. Hård, M., Jamison, A.: The Intellectual Appropriation of Technology. MIT Press, Cambridge (1998)
23. Aspray, W.: International Diffusion of Computer Technology, 1945-1955. Annals of the History of Computing 8, 351–360 (1986)
24. Cortada, J.W.: The Digital Hand. Volume 1: How Computers Changed the Work of American Manufacturing, Transportation and Retail Industries. Oxford University Press, Oxford (2004)
25. Cortada, J.W.: The Digital Hand. Volume 2: How Computers Changed the Work of American Financial, Telecommunications, Media and Entertainment Industries. Oxford University Press, Oxford (2005)
26. Cortada, J.W.: The Digital Hand. Volume 3: How Computers Changed the Work of American Public Sector Industries. Oxford University Press, Oxford (2007)
27. Agar, J.: The Government Machine: A Revolutionary History of Computing. MIT Press, Cambridge (2003)

Text Mining and Qualitative Analysis of an IT History Interview Collection

Petri Paju[1], Eric Malmi[2], and Timo Honkela[2]

[1] Cultural History Department, University of Turku, Finland
petpaju@utu.fi
[2] Department of Information and Computer Science
Aalto University School of Science and Technology, Finland
eric.malmi@gmail.com, timo.honkela@tkk.fi

Abstract. In this paper, we explore the possibility of applying a text mining method on a large qualitative source material concerning the history of information technology in one nation. This data was collected in the Swedish documentation project "From Computing Machines to IT." We apply text mining on the interview transcripts of this Swedish documentation project. Specifically, we seek to group the interviews according to their central themes and affinities and pinpoint the most relevant interviews for specific research questions. In addition, we search for interpersonal links between the interviews. We apply a method called the "self-organizing map" that can be used to create a similarity diagram of the interviews. We then discuss the results in several contexts including the possible future uses of text mining in researching history.

Keywords: Documentation project, IBM, IT-history, methods development, self-organizing map (SOM), Sweden, text mining.

1 Introduction

Research on the history of computing has, for a considerable time, involved developing methods, especially the application of oral history methods for conducting interviews, as Thomas Misa wrote in the book *History of Nordic computing 2* [1]. However, until recently, the field has shown limited interest in developing methods of its own or in using computational methods. Notwithstanding, new experiences from a couple of projects has brought attention to using the internet and other electronic means in *creating* sources for research. This contrasts with the tradition of collecting source material from the archives or publications but is closer to the established practices of interviewing for research purposes. One of these recent projects is the Swedish documentation project "Från matematikmaskin till IT" (http://ithistoria.se/), in English "From Computing Machines to IT," which during 2007–2008 had produced a large database concerning the Swedish history of information technology. This collection of information includes among other things (more than) 160 interviews and 50 organized group discussions, or witness seminars, almost all available as transcripts in the Internet [2]. They are in Swedish language, and therefore understandable in most of the Nordic area. Nevertheless, because of its

J. Impagliazzo, P. Lundin, and B. Wangler (Eds.): HiNC3, IFIP AICT 350, pp. 433–443, 2011.
© IFIP International Federation for Information Processing 2011

formidable size, the "data" is difficult to handle as a whole and especially so to a non-Swede or non-expert who is unfamiliar with the many details of the subjects, people and (national) topics.

In this paper, we explore the possibility of applying text mining on the interview transcripts of the Swedish documentation project. Specifically, we seek to group the interviews according to their central themes and affinities and pinpoint the most relevant interviews for specific research questions. In addition, we have searched for links between the interviews and we use those links to outline interpersonal connections of the group of interviewees.

However, our study includes seventy-four interviews so it does not cover all of the interviews conducted in the project. The choice of the interviews was based on the selection of transcribed texts at the beginning of this study.

We apply a method called the "self-organizing map" [3] that can be used to create a similarity diagram of the interviews [4]. In the following, we shortly introduce the method, present the analysis results and discuss them in the contexts of the history of computing, the Nordic countries and as a methodological tool for future challenges with the masses of historical electronic sources.

2 Methods

The self-organizing map (SOM) algorithm [3] has been developed for the analysis and visualization of large masses of complex data. It projects data non-linearly on to a two-dimensional plane in such a way that the original structure of the data is retained as well as possible. The outcome of the SOM analysis is a map in which entities, such as people, words, sentences, or documents, are positioned on the map according to similarity with respect to some property. The SOM serves several analytical functions. First, it provides a mapping from a high dimensional space into a low-dimensional space, thus providing a suitable means for analysis and visualization of complex data. Second, the SOM reveals topological structure of the data. The topological distance between two points in the map is proportional to the distance between the points in the original input space.

The SOM algorithm originally grew out of early neural network models, especially models of associative memory and adaptive learning [5]. The underlying motivation was to explain the spatial organization of the brain's functions, as observed especially in the cerebral cortex. Nonetheless, the SOM was not the first step in that direction. The spatially ordered line detectors of von der Malsburg [6] and the neural field model of Amari [7] preceded the development of the self-organizing map. However, the self-organizing power of these early models was rather weak. The crucial invention of Kohonen was to introduce a system model that is composed of at least two interacting subsystems of different nature. One of these subsystems is a competitive neural network that implements the winner-take-all function, but there is also another subsystem that is controlled by the neural network and which modifies the local synaptic plasticity of the neurons in learning [8]. The learning is restricted spatially to the local neighborhood of the most active neurons. Only by means of the separation of the neural signal transfer and the plasticity control has it become possible to implement an effective and robust self-organizing system [9].

From a present-day point of view, the SOM, as an unsupervised statistical machine learning method, compares to classical unsupervised quantitative research methods such as multidimensional scaling or clustering. The SOM has been extensively used to analyze numerical data in many areas, including various branches of industry, medicine, and economics and the number of references to SOM-based research articles is currently over eight thousand [10–12]. This popularity of the SOM in a large area of scientific disciplines has raised Kohonen to be (one of) the most cited Finnish scientists in any field. The use of the SOM has also been extended into the analysis of text data (see, e.g., [4, 13]). It can be used for the study of large amounts of material such as e-mails, web sites, interview transcripts, etc.

Janasik et al. have shown that the SOM-based text mining process improves the quality of the inferences drawn by researchers doing qualitative research [14]. The SOM specifies a holistic conceptual space. The meaning of some item in an analysis is not based on a predefined definition but is the emergent result of a number of encounters in which the item is used in some context. Moreover, the emergent prototypes on the map are not isolated instances (as in many forms of cluster analysis), but they influence each other in the adaptive formation process [14]. In its emphasis on the grounded nature of knowledge, the SOM approach aligns well with the central epistemological presuppositions of traditional and revised grounded theory (see e.g. [15]). In grounded theory, the concepts and conclusions are drawn from the research material rather than determined beforehand as hypotheses to be tested. This is also the approach taken commonly in modern historical research.

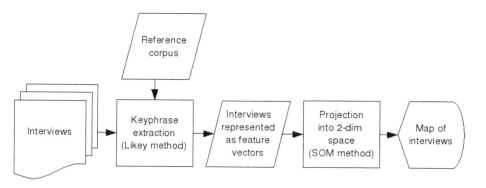

Fig. 1. The basic processes in creating map of interviews.

In our analysis, the interviewees are automatically positioned on the SOM according to the central themes discussed in their interviews (see Fig. 1 as an illustration of the overall process).

The themes are automatically extracted from the texts using language-independent keyphrase extraction (Likey) method [16]. Likey utilizes a reference corpus to highlight keyphrases that occur frequently in an interview compared with the reference corpus. Likey approach to extracting keyphrases is based on observations about the statistical properties of natural language. We use the distribution of phrase frequencies in texts to determine the significance of a phrase in a document by comparing it to the corresponding frequency in a baseline reference. In a related method introduced by Damerau, terms are ranked according to the likelihood ratio and the top m terms are used as index terms [17]. Likey produces keyphrases using relative ranks of n-gram frequencies. It is a simple language-independent method: the only language-specific component is a reference corpus in the corresponding language. Likey does not utilize any commonly used language-dependent (pre)processing such as stemming, stop word lists, part-of-speech tagging or syntactic parsing [16]. The availability of the software implementing the method may be requested from one of the authors (TH).

In the present analysis, we use a concatenation of all the interviews as the reference corpus for the Likey method. The effect of using Likey is that we are reasonably independent of researchers' biases. On the other hand, the choice of the reference corpus is a subjective matter. Choosing the whole corpus of interviews could be a rather neutral alternative but it has some specific effects. For instance, it does not select the acronym "IBM" as a keyword by the method as it is common in this corpus in general. If some other corpus, such as Europarl (the extracted proceedings of the EU Parliament), were used a word like "IBM" would end up in the list of keyphrases.

When the keyphrases have been selected (this can also be conducted manually instead of using the Likey method), a term-document matrix can be formed. In the matrix, each row corresponds to a document (interview), and each term (keyphrase) is represented by a column. The cells in the matrix then contain the number of occurrences of each term in each document. We may normalize the matrix by dividing the number in each cell by the row sum. This operation makes sure that documents of different length are considered in the analysis in a balanced manner. This matrix can then be given as input to some statistical software package that contains the SOM algorithm. In our case, we have used Matlab software, specifically the SOM Toolbox developed for Matlab (available for free at http://www.cis.hut.fi/projects/somtoolbox/). One can find more detailed information on using SOM-based text mining for qualitative research in [14].

In addition to the central themes, we also extract the references between the interviewees. Specifically, a directed link from interviewee A to interviewee B is drawn if A mentions B's surname in the interview. Thus, we get a social network of the interviewees drawn from top of the SOM.

3 Results

The resulting SOM is presented in Fig. 2. The interviewees that have had common themes discussed in their interviews are located close to each other. In a color picture, the lighter the area between two people, the more in common their interviews have.

To visualize different perspectives of this SOM, a terminology distribution diagram for each central theme is created (in short: theme map). The terminology distribution diagrams of the most popular themes are presented in Fig. 3 and Fig. 4. A dark area on a terminology distribution diagram implicates that on the SOM the interviewees within the same area have discussed the theme indicated in the title of the sub-diagram. For example, from the diagram on "numerisk analysis" (numerical analysis) one can see that the interviewees on the bottom-left corner of the SOM have mentioned numerical analysis in their interviews. Furthermore, some of these interviewees have also been discussing human-computer interaction (Fig. 4: "människa-datorinteraktion").

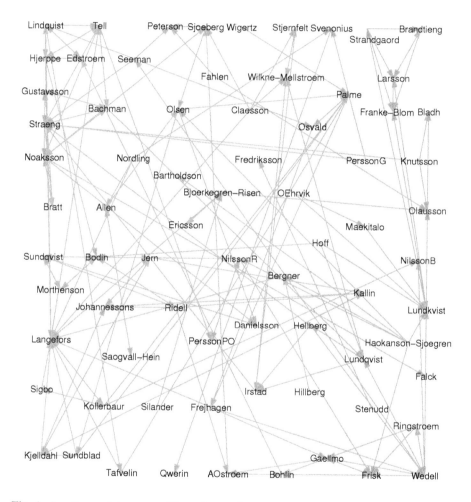

Fig. 2. A self-organizing map of interviewees based on interviews produced in the Swedish documentation project "Från matematikmaskin till IT." The interviewees that have had common themes discussed in their interviews are located close to each other. Also references between the interviewees are indicated: a directed link from a person to another is drawn if the first mentions the surname of the other in his or her interview.

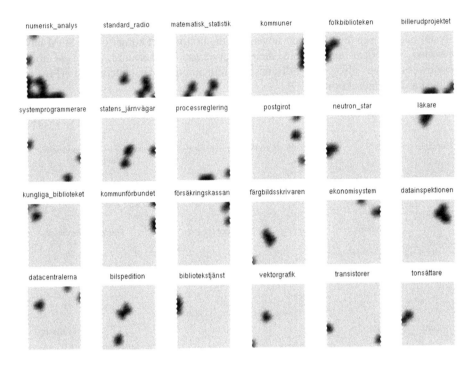

Fig. 3. A terminology distribution diagram of twenty-four themes commonly discussed in the interviews. Areas with dark color in each sub-diagram indicate that the theme has been handled in the interviews that have been mapped in the corresponding area on the SOM. For instance, the lower right corner of the sub-diagram "billerudprojektet" is dark which coincides with the corner where the surnames Wedell and Frisk are located (see Fig. 2). To learn how to interpret the theme maps imagining them on top of the SOM map (Fig. 2), see Fig. 5 (on the Billerud project).

Comparing the theme area of the human-computer interaction with the SOM map (Fig. 2), we can see that the interviewees (Lars) Kjelldahl and (Anita) Kollerbaur and perhaps their neighboring interviewees discussed this topic. After looking at other theme area maps, we notice these two have also talked about "Simula" (the programming language), "vektorgrafik" (vector graphics), and to a lesser extent "färgbildsskrivaren" (color printer) as well as the already mentioned numerical analysis.

The terminology distribution diagrams thus allow us to find the interviewees who have mentioned certain themes. It has to be emphasized that each diagram illuminates a particular aspect of the same map. Thus, a particular area on each diagram, for instance the upper right corner, always refers to the same items, in this case particular persons and their interviews. The theme maps can also be used for finding correlations between the themes. There is, e.g., an intuitive connection between the planes "patienterna" (patients) and "medicinsk information" (medical information). In addition, some less obvious connections can also be found, such as:

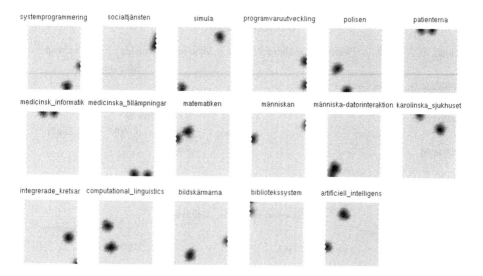

Fig. 4. A terminology distribution diagram of another seventeen themes commonly discussed in the interviews (see the caption of Fig. 3 for more details)

"försäkringskassan" (social insurance office) –
"kommunförbundet" (association of local governments)
and
"ekonomisystem" (accounting system) –
"datacentralerna" (computer centers).

A total of 188 interpersonal references were found from the interviews. These connections are visualized with arrows (ties) and they include 35 mutual ties. Majority of the ties are short suggesting that two interviewees, one of whom has mentioned the other, are likely to have discussed similar topics as well. In other words, the structure of the map based on the contents of the interviews coincides well with the structure of the social network. From yet another point of view, one can say that people who have similar interests also tend to know each other. If the same number, i.e. 188, interpersonal references were created randomly between the interviewees, the average length of the ties would be considerably longer than in this real case, and the network diagram would appear much more complex.

The social network also brings out the interviewees with many references. Three interviewees with the most references are Börje Langefors (13 references), Björn Tell (7), and Gunnar Wedell (7).

4 Discussion and Conclusions

In this section, the above results will be discussed in the contexts of the history of computing, especially in the Nordic countries and as a methodological tool for future challenges with the masses of historical electronic sources.

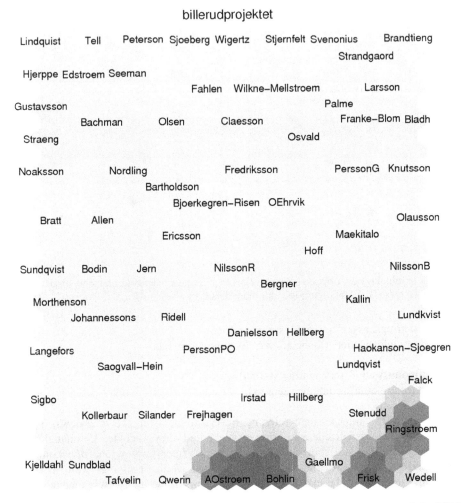

Fig. 5. An enlarged terminology distribution diagram or theme map shown on top of the SOM map indicates which interviewees talked about the Billerud project. They were, from right to left, (Karl Johan) Åström, (Torsten) Bohlin, (Tage) Frisk, and (Ingemar) Ringström.

As a test case towards qualitative analysis, we have utilized the SOM maps especially in studying IBM in Sweden. With the help of, for instance, keywords provided by the editors of the interviews, we identified the bottom right hand corner as having a high concentration of IBM related people and topics. From the theme area maps we see that "billerudprojektet" (Billerud project), "systemprogrammerare" (systems programming), "processreglering" (process control), and some other themes come up in that section of the SOM. A closer look at the interviews indicated that this corner has gathered interviews about the IBM Nordic Laboratory, established in 1960 near Stockholm and clearly one focus point of the documentation project. Further, reading the close-by interviews we can quickly find other related interviews, such as the ones dealing with the ALGOL compiler project of the IBM laboratory. Especially Bengt Gällmo and Birgitta Frejhagen talked about the ALGOL project. Another job of the IBM laboratory was a process control project in Billerud Company, depicted in one of the theme maps (see also Fig. 5). We thus get a good chance of finding most of the relevant information on such details promptly. However, the big picture of, for instance IBM's influence in Sweden or effects on the interviewees' careers, is much more complex and requires close reading of several of the interviews in the SOM's 'IBM corner'.

Since IBM was originally not chosen as a possible SOM theme because of its very high frequency in the data, we wanted to see how common it really is in this material. We decided to compare the words IBM and Ericsson to see their spread in the SOM data.

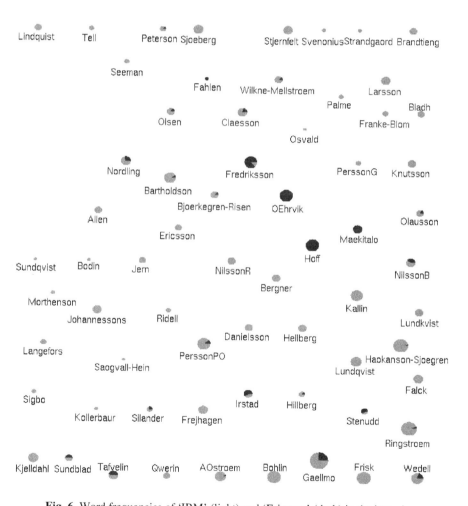

Fig. 6. Word frequencies of 'IBM' (light) and 'Ericsson' (dark) in the interviews

This map (see Fig. 6) reveals that IBM, unsurprisingly perhaps, is very commonly referred to in the interviews of the documentation project. The mapping also indicates an Ericsson concentration (Oehvik, Hoff) that could be interesting.

We hope to have shown that the SOM method can contribute to analyzing data also in history research and furthermore, can be useful for a special field such as history of computing in the Nordic countries. Especially when the Swedish language is applied, as in this documentation project under analysis, the data is understandable in most of the Nordic area. The SOM makes the data of even such a formidable size, and rich with countless details of subjects, people and (nationally specific) topics, accessible for a non-Swede and/or for a non-expert user.

In the future, we suggest using the SOM method for historical data (also in English) and as a new way of producing user guidelines for large information archives such as in the field of history of computing and those in the Charles Babbage Institute at the University of Minnesota. Moreover, with ever-increasing amount of electronic source materials becoming objects of historical scrutiny in the future, we foresee many uses for text mining with the SOM method in organizing the analysis of such electronic source collections.

Many historians oriented towards qualitative research may find it challenging to use a method such as terminology extraction or the SOM, with which they potentially do not have any prior experience. For the moment, before easy-to-use implementations of the necessary software are available, we recommend that these kinds of studies be conducted in collaborative and interdisciplinary contexts because this would ensure that various aspects of the necessary methodological expertise are available. This is particularly true for automatic terminology extraction and some advanced uses of the SOM [14].

Acknowledgments. We warmly thank Prof. Reijo (Shosta) Sulonen who with his vision brought the authors of this paper together. His discussions with Prof. Yrjö Neuvo originally generated the basic ideas behind this study. We are also grateful to Academician Teuvo Kohonen whose work, including the development of the self-organizing map algorithm, has been foundational to a whole research area.

References

1. Misa, T.J.: Organizing the History of Computing: 'Lessons Learned' at the Charles Babbage Institute. In: Impagliazzo, J., Järvi, T., Paju, P. (eds.) HiNC2. IFIP AICT, vol. 303, pp. 1–12. Springer, Heidelberg (2009)
2. Lundin, P.: Documenting the Use of Computers in Swedish Society between 1950 and 1980: Final Report on the Project "From Computing Machines to IT." Working Papers from the Division of History of Science and Technology, TRITA/HST 2009/1, Stockholm (2009)
3. Kohonen, T.: Self-Organizing Maps, 3rd edn. Springer, Berlin (2001)
4. Honkela, T., Kaski, S., Lagus, K., Kohonen, T.: WEBSOM – Self-organizing maps of document collections. In: Proceedings of WSOM 1997, Workshop on self-organizing Maps, pp. 310–315. Helsinki University of Technology, Espoo (1997)
5. Kohonen, T.: Self-Organization and Associative Memory. Springer, Berlin (1984)

6. von der Malsburg, C.: Self-organization of orientation sensitive cells in the striate cortex. Kybernetik 14, 85–100 (1973)
7. Amari, S.: Topographic organization of nerve fields. Bulletin of Mathematical Biology 42, 339–364 (1980)
8. Kohonen, T.: Self-organized formation of topologically correct feature maps. Biological Cybernetics 43, 59–69 (1982)
9. Kohonen, T., Honkela, T.: Kohonen network. Scholarpedia 2(1), 1568 (2007)
10. Kaski, S., Kangas, J., Kohonen, T.: Bibliography of self-organizing map (SOM) papers: 1981-1997. Neural Computing Surveys 1, 102–350 (1998)
11. Oja, M., Kaski, S., Kohonen, T.: Bibliography of Self-Organizing Map (SOM) Papers: 1998-2001 Addendum. Neural Computing Surveys 3, 1–156 (2003)
12. Pöllä, M., Honkela, T., Kohonen, T.: Bibliography of Self-Organizing Map (SOM) Papers: 2002-2005 Addendum. Technical Report TKK-ICS-R23, Helsinki University of Technology (2009)
13. Lagus, K., Kaski, S., Kohonen, T.: Mining massive document collections by the WEBSOM method. Information Sciences 163(1-3), 135–156 (2004)
14. Janasik, N., Honkela, T., Bruun, H.: Text mining in qualitative research: Application of an unsupervised learning method. Organizational Research Methods 12(3), 436–460 (2009)
15. Castellani, B., Castellani, J., Spray, S.L.: Grounded neural networking: Modeling complex quantitative data. Symbolic Interaction 26(4), 577–589 (2003)
16. Paukkeri, M.S., Nieminen, I.T., Pöllä, M., Honkela, T.: A Language-Independent Approach to Keyphrase Extraction and Evaluation. In: Scott, D., Uszkoreit, H. (eds.) COLING 2008, 22nd International Conference on Computational Linguistics, Posters Proceedings, Manchester, UK, August 18-22, pp. 83–86 (2008)
17. Damerau, F.: Generating and evaluating domain-oriented multi-word terms from text. Information Processing and Management 29(4), 433–447 (1993)

A Classification of Methods and Contributions in the Historiography of Nordic Computing

Henry Oinas-Kukkonen[1], Harri Oinas-Kukkonen[2], and Veronika Sušová[3]

[1] Faculty of Humanities, History, Centre of Excellence in Research, P.O. Box 1000
FIN-90014 University of Oulu, Finland
Henry.Oinas-Kukkonen@oulu.fi
[2] Department of Information Processing Science, P.O. Box 3000
FIN-90014 University of Oulu, Finland
Harri.Oinas-Kukkonen@oulu.fi
[3] Veronika Sušová, Independent Researcher
(formerly of Charles University, Prague, the Czech Republic)
susova76@hotmail.com

Abstract. The relevance and need of proper scientific methods in the research of computer science history was debated in the closing session of HiNC2 (Turku, August 2007). This text extracts a classification of research approaches and methods from HiNC1 and HiNC2 papers and offers a classification of computer science history to help understand the various research contributions in the field. It recognizes two basic divisions and five dominant approaches in the current research on the History of Nordic computing. The need for a clearer definition of the research methods and approaches in the contributions is evident, and there seems to be a need to broaden the conceptual apparatus.

Keywords: Approaches, classification, historiography, history of Nordic computing, methodology.

1 Introduction

The interest and effort devoted to studying the history of computing (HC) have grown remarkably in the past few years. There are many reasons for this, such as information systems and technologies becoming much more mature to manage by organizations and end-users, and many key people behind past IT innovations having perhaps retired but are still available for research purposes. However, the selection and use of proper scientific methods for carrying out computer science history research seem quite immature. This paper proposes a classification of research approaches and methods, using the first two History of Nordic Computing conferences (HiNC1 and HiNC2) as examples. The paper helps to clarify the various research contributions in the HC field, by describing the current methods and focus areas in them. It also supports future HC studies by combining theoretical and philosophical approaches with practical research methods and analysis.

1.1 Aim and Scope in HiNC1 and HiNC2

HiNC1, organized in Trondheim, Norway, in 2003 was rather hardware-oriented. The first sentence about the aims and scope of this conference in the call for contributions stated, "Nordic computing started with hardware such as BARK, BESK, and DASK." The historical time period proposed covered a period from the time of early computers until around 1985. Nevertheless, among other issues, attention was also given to information systems theories and methodologies, and the development of education and curricula in computer science by computing pioneers [1].

HiNC2, organized in Turku, Finland in 2007 paid more attention to the commercial products, conferences organized, and applications produced, with special focus on the software. The timeframe of interest clearly emphasized even more recent contemporary history. The call for contributions stated, "The conference concentrates on the period from the 1960s to the 1980s, but does not want to omit any part of history. Papers from the 1990s with relation to the past years are also most welcome." Attention also included politics, its role in advancing computing in the Nordic countries, and its relations and exchanges with the Former Soviet Union. In a similar manner, the Baltic countries, in particular the roles of Estonian computer pioneers and their experiences, achieved increased interest. Thus, the history of international relations became intertwined with the history of Nordic computing [2].

1.2 Historical Methods and Historical Sources

An ideal article is one that clearly defines historical questions and chronological scope, relying on the historical primary sources and indirect secondary ones that are explicitly presented and characterized in the introduction of the work. The combination of different sources, for example, oral history and archival or written texts, makes a research result more credible. In brief, an ideal article is coherent in defining its research questions and concepts, as well as in its selection of sources used for answering these questions [37].

The research questions and selected historical sources direct the researcher to seek additional research methods from other disciplines (e.g., network theory) to complement the "standard" methods of history such as source criticism, the cornerstone of utilizing historical sources. In brief, source criticism involves an interrelated set of steps: a focus on the origins of a source, its brief description, questions of source originality, and the authority of its author/s, or competence and trustworthiness of the observer. Finally, a very important step is the interpretation of the source, which occurs in direct relation to research questions. A goal of objectivity also applies to the scientific research, even though it may not be achieved by a strict epistemological definition. We submit for criticism and debate the history of the research into past events, which has emerged.

1.3 Historical Methods and Historical Sources in HiNC

We focus next on two mutually interrelated issues. Firstly, we discuss the question of using historical methods and historical sources through the analysis of the research contributions of the first two HiNC conferences, from the introduced perspective of historical science and its core methods. If a contribution extensively follows aspects introduced in section 1.2, we regard it as an advanced use of historical methods; however, if it does not do so, we regard it as a limited use of historical methods. Existing debates related to the historical sources, their use and epistemological problems in the recent historiography, fall outside the scope of this article's purpose and space allowed.

Secondly, we pay attention to the topical approaches of the papers and briefly to their conceptual apparatus to grasp the present scale of interest and scope in the HiNC field. Most of the papers deal with the period 1970–1995 and they are categorized according to the research contributions' current historiographical understanding of the history of Nordic computing until 2007. Our aim is to demonstrate the current state of art in this field and to illustrate some of the key problems in the HC field.

2 Two Lineages and Five Major Approaches of HiNC1 and HiNC2

2.1 Two Basic Divisions in Current Nordic HC Research

The HiNC1 conference generated forty-one historical papers for publication [3], whereas HiNC2 included thirty-two such articles [4]. These papers seem to fall into two main lines of research.

In Fig. 1, we show two basic divisions of research into the history of computing that also well reflect the current research into Nordic HC. We can characterize the first as research through historical methods and patterns involving text-based studies of written documents of any kind, as well as research based on material sources or artifacts, and oral history methods. The second division involves a broader recording of historically valuable texts/sources in the form of memoirs and autobiographies.

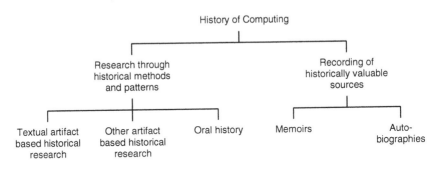

Fig. 1. Two basic divisions in the history of computing (HC) research

2.2 Historical Methods and Historical Sources in HiNC1 and HiNC2

There have been seventy-three papers in the previous HiNC conferences, including many examples [38] of good, professionally applied research practices in using historical methods and sources. Due to limited space, we can only exemplify two of them here. The articles written by Petri Paju [5] and Anders Carlsson [6] are examples of well-designed historical research. In accordance with his research question, Paju uses a variety of historical sources, including oral history, archival and published material, related to the topic, and offers a brief introduction on the sources utilized.

Carlsson also explicitly uses historical sources. In particular, he emphasizes publically investigated material, but also takes into account some technical journals and archival sources that he applies to his research question.

There are also articles dealing with historical developments, in which the proper use of historical methods is limited. This limitation occurs when any historical sources used are not mentioned, whether primary or secondary, or references are omitted, thus causing confusion for their readers, since the origin or source of the authors' conclusions and findings are not traceable.

The following constitutes a list of typical mistakes found in the current HC research papers utilizing historical research methods:

- Confusion between history and memoirs (e.g., objectivity problem)
- Lack of references of any kind and/or omitting some of the key sources or references
- Reliance on only one type of source in the context of a broad research question
- Lack of criticism of the sources used
- Lack of proper links between sources and research questions

Not understanding what is history and what are memoirs seems to be quite problematic. From the orthodox historiographical viewpoint, we cannot regard memoirs and autobiographies as a genre of historical research (due to, e.g., the reliance on one's own publications or memory as a main or only source). Thus, in the purest sense of historical research, these memoirs or autobiographically-based articles should perhaps be categorized as the recording of historical sources rather than the historical research *per se*. Nevertheless, the HiNC1 and HiNC2 papers are not uniform in this aspect. There are a number of instances in which memoirs merge with the use of secondary historical sources, which makes classifying these papers especially difficult, at least from the perspective of historical science [7].

In spite of the difficulty in classifying these kinds of works, they provide a special case for historians, since HC as a research topic involves a period extending only some sixty years. This short time span makes it possible for individual actors who have participated in the given developments to bring their personal memories to the public's attention. Thus, it offers a unique opportunity to conduct historical research. Nevertheless, research into HC should clearly differentiate between a participant perspective and purely historical research into the published works. The latter normally deals with the past by using a historical source as its main method of approaching the topic from the *non-participant perspective*. This perspective is generally believed to be more objective and, for this reason, it gains much wider acceptability among historians.

2.3 Topical Approaches in HiNC1 and HiNC2

An analysis of the topical approaches and concepts utilized in the HiNC conferences helps to grasp the current situation in the field, identify main areas of interest, and perhaps recognize its blind spots. We can identify five main approaches in these papers as shown in Fig. 2.

Table 1. Contributions in the HiNC1 and HiNC2 conferences [3, 4]

	HiNC1 [3]	HiNC2 [4]
Research through historical methods		
- Advanced use of historical methods	Carlsson, Oinas-Kukkonen et al., Paju, Suominen et al.	Oinas-Kukkonen et al. (b), Paju, Pohjolainen
- Limited use of historical methods	Benediktsson et al., Benediktsson, Berntsen, Elgsaas & Hegna, Espelid et al., Klüver, Kollerbaur, Krogdahl, Lawson, Reenskaug, Saarikoski, Skog, Yndestad	Elgsaas & Hegna, Jørgensen (b), Kimppa et al., Kjártaksson, Nordal, Oinas-Kukkonen et al. (a), Nykänen & Andersin, Reunanen & Silvast
Recording of historically valuable sources	Andersin, Asker, Bruhn, Dahlstrand, Fontell, Henrikson, Iivari, Kurki-Suonio, Lindencrona, Lindgreen, Magnússon, Nordhagen, Ofstad, Olle, Ruge, Sanders, Thorvaldsen & Wibe, Tuori, Vahl	Benediktsson, Bubenko (a), Bubenko (b), Dahlstrand, Engh, Enlund & Andersin, Hugoson, Järvi, Järvinen, Lawson, Thorbergsson, Tyugu, Väänänen & Mertanen
Historiographies, contributions to cultural studies, preservation of history, theory of history		Ferro & Swendin, Heinonen & Reunanen, Jørgensen (a), Lundin, Misa, Tittonen

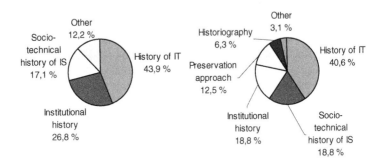

Fig. 2. Topical approaches in (a) HiNC1 and (b) HiNC2

History of information technology: This approach focuses on the chronologically conceived development of a particular computing-related technology or the computer (machine) itself such as computers and computer networks. Its main aim is to offer a descriptive rather than an interpretative analysis that often represents a highly expert view on the topic. Due to such a narrow scope, this approach often lacks socio-political contexts or a broader social dimension, and limits itself to the particular case study in its account [8, 9].

Socio-technical history of information systems: In this approach, which addresses IS/IT use, social aspects of computing, and computerization, the social impacts or socio-political contexts of IS/IT use and development remain as the focus of research interest. Computer development is conceived as a social process in which different social actors and forces, like politicians, political parties, trade unions, states, cities, regions, and multinational firms, may be involved, and where its social or cultural consequences are addressed as well [10–12]. The scope in this approach tends to be more interpretative than descriptive and it analyzes different aspects of the relations between information technology and society from the historical perspective.

History of computing institutions: Institutional history is quite prominent in HiNC papers. Such an approach involves recounting the history of a particular firm [13], research or computer center [14], or university, including a history of the institutionalization of computing science and curricula development [15–17].

Historiographical approach to computing: This approach addresses rather theoretical questions of computing history studies and discusses, among others, the aspects of relevant historical sources, their critiques and use, possible research designs, and organizational issues. The articles by Thomas Misa (2009) on both the research theory and organizational experience of the Babbage Institute in the USA [18] and the one by Anker H. Jørgensen (2009), which questions the historical knowledge or awareness among IT specialists and students, provide examples of the historiographical approach [19]. This low number illustrates that the theoretical questions and historiographical discussions about HC were rather underrepresented so far among the analyzed conference papers.

Preservation approach to computing: While the fifth approach overlaps the historiographical approach to some extent, it nevertheless emphasizes the preservation of written sources and material artifacts related to the computing history and organizational questions of preservation institutions (museums) [20].

Other topical approaches: We could not categorize some papers with our classification framework. This group is composed of various papers that mainly have different research topics such as the role of women in computing history [21], or the relationship between science fiction and technological innovations [22].

3   Conceptual Apparatus in HiNC1 and HiNC2

HC is a new area of study; in this sense, it seems to be in search of an identity. Our focus on the HC conceptual apparatus illustrates to what extent HC is open to various interdisciplinary approaches and to what extent it seems to develop its own theoretical agenda in relation to the broader social scientific analysis.

In sum, various concepts such as computerization [23], technology transfer [24], internationalization [25], transfer of knowledge [25], computer fiction and techno-scientific democracy [21], digital heritage [26], techno-biography [19], and data policy [27], among others, have been addressed in the HC field. All these concepts obviously relate HC with the broader social scientific discussions and, as a result, help to make the field increasingly important for the further understanding of social change in contemporary societies.

Transition, continuity or discontinuity, or other historical concepts associated with the time and space of the historical events were not positioned as central research subjects in the first two HiNC conferences cf. [28, 29], which was probably due to the defined aim and scope of these events.

In general, a number of HiNC papers emphasize the confined contextual frameworks restricting their scope to questioning the particular IT or institutional developments without taking into account broader social, political, economical, and cultural contextual aspects. Furthermore, some inspirational grand concepts of other social sciences have been considerably underrepresented so far. Contemporary social thinking dedicates a great deal of work to the conceptualization of social and technological changes of the last century. As examples, we could just mention a few possible concepts of recent sociology, like Manuel Castell's network society and informational capitalism [30–32], cultural critic Steven Shaviro's controversial and provoking notion of soft fascism [33], or various studies oriented towards the virtual society [34]. Finally, the productive use of concepts can be noticed in the historical writing itself. For example, Paul E. Ceruzzi's notion of the digitalization of the world picture links HC to the more established field of the history of science and ideas [35] or Thomas P. Hughes' works about the history of technologies [36]. We can see the current underrepresentation of social research because of the predominance of a minimalist conception of HC, discussed next.

4   Conclusion

There seem to be two general conceptual methods in Nordic HC. The expert-oriented concept approaches HC as a confined research field in which chronological developments of computing play the role of inside-community *chronicle*. It is significantly relevant for the future understanding of early computing histories as well as for the identity of a community. A broader-scoped concept, which is more, oriented towards social, political, economic, and cultural contexts, as well as the interrelations, impacts, and influences of computing links HC to the agenda of recent social research and its conceptualizations.

The main problem related to the historical methodology and objectivity is a mismatch of history and human memory. One could take a more precise sectional division of future HiNC papers along with two lineages in Nordic HC. We should pay more attention to combine two practices into a welded cooperation between participating actors and non-participating historians, where personal memoirs would become the background of other historical sources.

The analysis in this paper indicates that despite the epistemological and methodological problems related to source criticism and the increasing inter-disciplinarity of historical science, this practice still represents a crucial historical method.

The main points mentioned above are embedded in historical/social research and computing. An intensified dialog about relevant methods, concepts, and theories is very productive.

In sum, all the published works in the history of Nordic computing have so far added important aspects to the body of knowledge in this relatively new field of HC. Nevertheless, future contributions of HC research should more clearly characterize how the research in each case was conducted by addressing the research methods and sources more explicitly. Our classification of the approaches may help in doing so.

Acknowledgments. We wish to thank Gustav Sjöblom and the reviewers of this paper for their constructive comments.

References

1. First Conference on History of Nordic Computing, HiNC 1: Call for contributions, NTNU, Trondheim (June 16-18, 2003), http://hinc.dnd.no/CFP-v4.pdf
2. Second Conference on History of Nordic Computing, HiNC 2: Call for contributions, Turku (August 21-23, 2007),
   http://hinc2.utu.fi/call_for_contributions2.pdf
3. Bubenko Jr., J., Impagliazzo, J., Sølvberg, A. (eds.): History of Nordic Computing: IFIP WG 9.7 First Working Conference on the History of Nordic Computing (HiNC1), Trondheim, Norway, June 16-18, 2003. IFIP International Federation for Information Processing, vol. 174. Springer, New York (2005)
4. Impagliazzo, J., Järvi, T., Paju, P. (eds.): HiNC2. IFIP AICT, vol. 303. Springer, Heidelberg (2009)
5. Paju, P.: Computer Industry as National Task. The Finnish Computer Project and the Question of State Involvement in the 1970s. In: Impagliazzo, J., Järvi, T., Paju, P. (eds.) HiNC2. IFIP AICT, vol. 303, pp. 171–184. Springer, Heidelberg (2009)
6. Carlsson, A.: On the Politics of Failure. Perspectives on the "Mathematics Machine" in Sweden, 1945-1948. In: HiNC1, pp. 95–110 (2005)
7. Bubenko Jr., J.: Information Processing – Administrative Processing. The First Courses at KTH and SU, 1966-1967. In: Impagliazzo, J., Järvi, T., Paju, P. (eds.) HiNC2. IFIP AICT, vol. 303, pp. 138–148. Springer, Heidelberg (2009)
8. Yndestad, H.: Micproc. A Fast 16-bit Microprocessor. In: HiNC1, pp. 289–296 (2005)
9. Lawson, H.B.: Provisioning of Safe Train Control in Nordic Countries. In: Impagliazzo, J., Järvi, T., Paju, P. (eds.) HiNC2. IFIP AICT, vol. 303, pp. 13–28. Springer, Heidelberg (2009)
10. Henriksson, S.: When Computers Become of Interest of Politics. In: HiNC1, pp. 413–423 (2005)
11. Oinas-Kukkonen, H., et al.: Development in the Growth Base of the 'Oulu Phenomenon'. In: HiNC1, pp. 425–448 (2005)
12. Reunanen, M., Silvast, A.: Demoscene Platforms: A Case Study on the Adoption of Home Computer. In: Impagliazzo, J., Järvi, T., Paju, P. (eds.) HiNC2. IFIP AICT, vol. 303, pp. 289–301. Springer, Heidelberg (2009)
13. Andersin, H.: The Role of IBM in Starting Up Computing in the Nordic Countries. In: HiNC1, pp. 33–44 (2005)
14. Suominen, J., Paju, P., Törn A.: The Wegematic 1000 Computer Centre, 1959-1964. In: HiNC1, pp. 463–485 (2005)
15. Espeldid O.T., et al.: Research and Curricula Development at Norwegian Universities. In: HiNC1, pp. 137–154 (2005)
16. Dahlstrand, I.: The Development of University Computing in Sweden 1965-1985. In: Impagliazzo, J., Järvi, T., Paju, P. (eds.) HiNC2. IFIP AICT, vol. 303, pp. 130–137. Springer, Heidelberg (2009)
17. Benediktsson, O.: Early Curricula in Computer Science at the University of Iceland. In: HiNC1, pp. 123–130 (2005)
18. Misa, T.J.: Organizing the History of Computing: 'Lessons Learned' in the Charles Babbage Institute. In: Impagliazzo, J., Järvi, T., Paju, P. (eds.) HiNC2. IFIP AICT, vol. 303, pp. 1–12. Springer, Heidelberg (2009)
19. Jørgensen, A.H.: What do IT-people know about the nordic history of computers and user interfaces? In: Impagliazzo, J., Järvi, T., Paju, P. (eds.) HiNC2. IFIP AICT, vol. 303, pp. 38–44. Springer, Heidelberg (2009)

20. Lundin, P.: From Computing Machines to IT: Collecting, Documenting and Preserving Source Material on Swedish IT History. In: Impagliazzo, J., Järvi, T., Paju, P. (eds.) HiNC2. IFIP AICT, vol. 303, pp. 65–73. Springer, Heidelberg (2009)
21. Lindencrona, E.: Where Were the Women? In: HiNC1, pp. 405–412 (2005)
22. Ferro, D., Swedin, E.: Computer Fiction: "A Logic Named Joe": Towards Investigating the Importance of Science Fiction in the Historical Development of Computing. In: Impagliazzo, J., Järvi, T., Paju, P. (eds.) HiNC2. IFIP AICT, vol. 303, pp. 84–94. Springer, Heidelberg (2009)
23. Klüver, P. V.: Technology Transfer, Modernisation, and the Welfare State. In: HiNC1, pp. 61–78 (2005)
24. Bedeniktsson, O., et al.: Computerisation of Icelandic State and Municipalities. In: HiNC1, pp. 45–60 (2005)
25. Oinas-Kukkonen, H., Kerola, P., Oinas-Kukkonen, H., Similä, J., Pulli, P.: Information Systems and Software Engineering Research and Education in Oulu until the 1990s. In: Impagliazzo, J., Järvi, T., Paju, P. (eds.) HiNC2. IFIP AICT, vol. 303, pp. 185–194. Springer, Heidelberg (2009)
26. Heinonen, M., Reunanen, M.: Preserving our Digital Heritage: Experiences from the Pelikonepeijoonit Project. In: Impagliazzo, J., Järvi, T., Paju, P. (eds.) HiNC2. IFIP AICT, vol. 303, pp. 65–83. Springer, Heidelberg (2009)
27. Elgsaas, K., Hegna, H.: The Development of Computer Policies in Government, Political Parties and Trade Unions in Norway 1961-1983. In: Impagliazzo, J., Järvi, T., Paju, P. (eds.) HiNC2. IFIP AICT, vol. 303, pp. 156–170. Springer, Heidelberg (2009)
28. Oinas-Kukkonen, H., Pulkkinen, J., Anttila, T.: Continuity and Discontinuity in the History of Discoveries and Innovations. In: Faravid 32/2008. pp. 185–201 (2008)
29. Oinas-Kukkonen, H.: From Bush to Engelbart: 'Slowly, Some Little Bells Were Ringing'. IEEE Annals of the History of Computing 29(2), 31–39 (2007)
30. Castells, M.: The Rise of the Network Society. The Information Age: Economy, Society, Culture, 1st edn. (1996) vol. 1. Blackwell Publ., Oxford (2010)
31. Castells, M.: The Power of Identity. The Information Age: Economy, Society, Culture., 1st edn.(1997) vol. 2. Blackwell Publ., Oxford (2010)
32. Castells, M.: End of Millennium. The Information Age: Economy, Society, Culture, 1st edn.(1998) vol. 3. Blackwell Publ., Oxford (2000)
33. Shaviro, S.: Connected-Or What it Means to Live in the Network Society. University of Minnesota Press, Minneapolis (2003)
34. Woolgar, S. (ed.): Virtual Society? Technology, Cyberole, Reality. Oxford University Press, Oxford (2002)
35. Ceruzzi, P.E.: A History of Modern Computing, 1st edn.(1998) MIT Press, Cambridge (2003)
36. Hughes, T.P.: Networks of Power: Electrification in Western Society, 1880-1930. Johns Hopkins University Press, Baltimore (1983)
37. Howell, M.C., Prevenier, W.: From the Reliable Sources: an Introduction to Historical Methods. Cornell University Press, New York (2001)
38. Staudenmeier, J.M.: Technology's Storytellers: Reweaving the Human Fabric. MIT Press Cambridge, Massachusetts (1985)

Research Directions Profile in the Computing Museum of the Institute of Mathematics and Computer Science, University of Latvia (IMCS)

Rihards Balodis, Juris Borzovs, Inara Opmane,
Andrejs Skuja, and Evija Ziemele

Institute of Mathematics and Computer Science, University of Latvia
Raina bulv.29, LV-1459, Riga, Latvia
{Rihards Balodis,Juris Borzovs,Inara Opmane,Andrejs Skuja,
Evija Ziemele}imcs@lumii.lv

Abstract. The article describes the development of information technology in Latvia, in IMCS, to the middle of the 1990s. The history of IMCS represents the usage of computers in typical computing centers in the former Soviet Union and the transformation from computing center to research institution. It also represents Latvian collaboration with the Nordic countries that provided political, scientific, and technological support. Historical documents, computer parts, and photos are collected in the Computer Museum of IMCS.

Keywords: Computing museum, history of computing technology, Latvia, research institute.

1 Institute of Mathematics and Computer Science

The Institute of Mathematics and Computer Science at the University of Latvia (IMCS) was established in 1959 as a computing research center. Although it was part of the University of Latvia, the government set it up and from the beginning, it always had its own budget. The funding of the Institute of Mathematics and Computer Science was through government research grants and contracts. It was the fourth computing research center in the Soviet Union, established with the goal of developing Latvian industry. Since the founding of the institute, the best computing machines available in the USSR were installed and used there. Over the years the use of computing technology and the relevant scientific technological field itself, had changed significantly.

The number of people employed at the institute varied over the years, ranging from 120 to 450. Currently, 230 employees work at IMCS and it is the largest and most relevant research institution in Latvia in the fields of information technology, mathematics, computer science, and computer linguistics. In recent years, new scientific groups were established for the development of interdisciplinary research and e-infrastructures (e.g., GEANT, GRID, and cloud computing).

J. Impagliazzo, P. Lundin, and B. Wangler (Eds.): HiNC3, IFIP AICT 350, pp. 453–461, 2011.
© IFIP International Federation for Information Processing 2011

2 History of Computer Use in IMCS

Over the years, computing machines in IMCS were replaced with more advanced and progressive units, along with the development of technology. Engineers wanted to keep up with rapidly changing technologies and collected more interesting computer parts. The Computing Museum, established in 1984, was founded by IMCS and actually also constitutes the history of IMCS. Since IMCS is currently the largest information technology research center in Latvia, to some extent it also constitutes the history of Latvian information technology. The documents and equipment in the museum reflect the computing machines of a passing age, their description, and the tasks solved with them.

Currently, the Computing Museum occupies 230 m^2, holds 13,116 exhibits, of which 504 are equipment units, 287 mainframe and workstation parts, 98 computers, and 44 printers. The museum exhibits were complemented with photographs and documents that seemed to have historical value.

The museum has an exhibit for each computing machine used in IMCS. It is either in the form of a photograph, a separate computing unit or component, or as in several cases the complete machine. The history shows how in the transition from Soviet model computers (BESM and MINSK) to Western computers (e.g., IBM and PDP) cloning had taken place and how the regaining of Latvian independence changed the assessment values of technology. For example, efficiency started to play an important role and thus the operation of the service demanding ES EVM was prematurely suspended. The former engineer of IMCS with more than forty years of work experience, who describes the exhibits with illustrations from his own background, heads the museum.

2.1 First Computers in IMCS

The original computers became operational during the initial stages of the development of the information technology field in the USSR. The first, a BESM-2, went into commercial production in 1958. IMCS acquired the machine; it had production number "5" – a fact that serves as substantial evidence for the role and competence of the computing center. BESM-2 was a demanding machine that required a great amount of engineering work, but IMCS's engineers were innovative and could introduce several important upgrades that enabled the respective machine to be more efficient. In this regard, IMCS had one of the best results in the entire Soviet Union.

At the end of the 1960s, IMCS started using the Minsk series computers. The machine had a decimal (decimal-binary) notation with the point fixed after the lower bit; numbers and instructions were coded with a variable-length sequence of characters. In addition, the instruction set had a variable number of addresses for operands, and the instruction addresses were normalized and indexed.

The circuitry and instruction set of Minsk-23 completely differed from those computers that had existed before it. The machine was the first domestic computer with alphanumeric logic as well as a variable word and instruction length. A multitasking mode was also realized in Minsk-23. The Minsk-32 closed the Minsk computer series.

Table 1. First computers used in IMCS

Usage years	Computer
11.04.1961–21.08.1970	BESM-2 (first generation, vacuum tubes, 5,000 op/s)
29.06.1964–03.04.1972	BESM-2M
11.04.1967–06.04.1978	BESM-4 (second generation, transistors, 20,000 op/s)
	Computer modernization with FACIT ECM 64
1968–1975	Minsk-22, Minsk-23, Minsk-32 (7,000 op/s)

In very special cases, IMCS bought Western computers, for example, IMCS had been granted funds to buy the GE415. This allowed IMCS scientists to compare the level of computer technology progress in the USSR and the West and to comprehend the tasks that were necessary for software development. GE415 was a second-generation computer with transistors that executed 40,000–90,000 op/s. GE400(s) computers were time-sharing information systems produced by General Electric, introduced in 1964 and exported until 1968. IMCS used the GE415 from 03.09.1969 until 03.04.1983.

2.2 Mainframes in IMCS

Soviet economic planners decided to use the IBM design, although some prominent Soviet computer scientists had criticized the idea and suggested that one of the Soviet indigenous designs such as BESM or Minsk should be chosen instead. The first work on the cloning began in 1968; production started in 1972. Thereafter, the first subseries of the ES EVM, released in 1969–1978, included models 1010, 1020, 1030, 1040, and 1050, which were analogous to System/360, and the more rare and advanced models 1022, 1032, 1033 and 1052, which were incompatible with the IBM versions. The electronics of the first models were based on TTL circuits; the later machines used the ECL (emitter-coupled logic) design. ES 1050 had a maximum of 1 MB RAM and 64-bit floating point registers. The fastest machine of the series, the ES 1052, was developed in 1978. (Note that data regarding computer models and their relevance to cloned models come from Wikipedia.)

The second subseries, released in 1977–1978, included the models 1015, 1025, 1035, 1045, 1055 and 1060, all analogous to the System/370.

Table 2. Mainframe types used in IMCS

Usage years	Computer types
16.05.1974–31.12.1978	ES EVM-1020 (3. generation, integrated circuits, 11,800 op/s)
1976–31.12.1987	ES EVM-1022 (80,000 op/s)
02.1980–31.12.1987	ES EVM-1022-02 (80,000 op/s)
12.1982–1990	ES EVM-1060-02 (100,000 op/s)
02.03.1983–06.1989	ES EVM-1055M (450,000 op/s)
25.10.1989–10.1992	ES EVM -1037" (4,000,000 op/s)

After Latvia regained independence, the operation of ES EVM was suspended in 1992 due to the costs of service, electricity, and the numerous maintenance staff.

2.3 Workstations in IMCS

The SM-4 was a Soviet PDP-11/40 computer clone. SM EVM was a general name for several types of Soviet minicomputers. Production started in 1975. Most types of SM EVM are clones of the DEC PDP-11 and the VAX. The common operating system was MOS, a clone of UNIX. The IZOT was a Bulgarian produced model.

Table 3. Workstation types used in IMCS

Usage years	Computer types
23.03.1981–06.1989	SM-4 (180,000 op/s)
24.03.1985–05.1989	IZOT-1016S
30.04.1987–1990	IZOT-1055S
07.06.1989–1990	IZOT-1080 (4,500,000 op/s)

2.4 Microcomputers and Personal Computers in IMCS

Acorn's BBC Micro computer dominated the UK educational computer market during the 1980s and early 1990s, drawing many comparisons with Apple in the US. The Wang 2200 was cloned by the Soviet Union and produced as "Iskra 226." DVK was a computer series of DEC PDC-11 and PDP-11, while the Elektronika BK was a series of 16-bit PDP-11-compatible Soviet home computers, almost perfectly compatible with the DEC LSI-11 line. These computers were used in schools for informatics classes: one KUVT and many BK or Yamaha, later AGAT (Apple-II). The KUVT was based on a Z80 CPU (in fact, an Eastern clone of Intel 880), and used SCP, a CP/M compatible operating system. It was widely used in Russia and other East European countries for office and educational purposes. Iskra 1030 was a Soviet 8086 compatible personal computer.

At the end of the 1980s and the beginning of the 1990s, the rapid transition to Western personal computers started.

Table 4. Microcomputers and personal computer types used in IMCS

Usage years	Computer types
1985–1993	Acorn UK education class
1986–1993	Previous generation of personal computers:
	ISKRA-226
	DVK
	KUVT-86
	BK-0010
	Robotron – 1715 (East Germany)
	Yamaha (JAPAN)
1989–1993	ISKRA-1030, IBM XT, AT, Mazovia, PS2

3   Profile Components – Signs of Age

What were the original tasks solved and how did the technology help? The following is a brief overview.

a. IMCS had a scientific spirit - there were many technological deficiencies in the first industrial Soviet computers that demanded refinements, which were carried out in IMCS by an innovative laboratory of engineers and electricians;
b. The installation of the first computers substantially contributed to the growth of research, particularly in the development of methods for the mathematical modeling of various physical processes, in the development of software, and research in theoretical computer science (Tables 5 and 6);
c. Along with the research, practical information systems for the Latvian economy were developed (Table 7);
d. From the 1970s onwards, cloning was a trend, but IMCS retained its initiative in carrying out original research. IMCS cloned only one system – CRJE (DUVZ), the adoption of Conversational Remote Job Entry (Clone of CRJE) for OS ES EVM (Clone of OS/360).

Mathematical scientists and highly qualified engineers worked in the institute. Owing to practical tasks – mainly solving specifically commissioned assignments with methods of mathematical modeling – the initiative emerged to develop such software that solved specific assignments and large groups of them. Thus the first IT research directions appeared. Original software was developed – compilers and software development tools (Table 6), for example, computer usage counting system, software development, and complex systems modeling languages and tools (later GRADE, MOLA), now – semantic WEB (term coined by W3C director Tim Berners-Lee).

Three activity directions of the institute were the result of specific assignments – the development of information systems, mathematical models in natural sciences, and research in computer science. The history of IMCS illustrates how very limited computing resources contributed to the evolution of theoretical research fields.

Table 5. Research directions developed in IMCS

Research direction	Description
Software debugging and testing	From the development of automation tools for practical needs to theoretical research and experimental systems
Inductive synthesis of algorithms from examples	Theoretical research and experimentation
Specification languages	For telephone exchange, real time systems and business models
Software development tools	Research and development of tools
Modeling and simulation of discrete processes	Theory, practical simulation of telephone exchange call load balancing
Computational linguistics	Latvian language research with computers
Graph theory	From theory to printed circuit board design
Mathematical methods and modeling of physical processes	Theory and computer modeling

Table 6. Notable original software developed in IMCS from 1970 to 1980

Programming language or software tool	Description	Computer (operating system)
Fortran	Compiler implementation; compiler had restrictions	BESM-4
SMOD	Macro command system for information system development	Minsk-32
TRANS	Automation of translation, debugging and execution of programs	Minsk-32
PL/I	Original PL/I Compiler. Interpreter of PL/I commands for software debugging in visual PL/I machine. PL/I Handbook, printed twice in Statistika (Moscov), Polish translation of book (Warsaw)	OS ES EVM (Clone of OS/360)
RIGAL	Language and tools for Compiler implementation	OS ES EVM (Clone of OS/360), SM-4, IZOT
SDL (System description Language)	Real System specification language: tools used for system prototyping and debugging.	SM-4, IZOT
MAUS (Computer usage account system)	System that counts usage of all computer resources (processor, peripherals, I/O operations) and calculates expenses.	OS ES EVM (Clone of OS/360), MAUS included in the base of the operating system and maintained in all Soviet produced computers

Table 7. Information systems developed in IMCS from 1970 to 1980

Description	Computer (operating system)
Wholesale store for agriculture, including accounting system	Minsk-22, Minsk-32
City traffic simulation system	BESM-4
Operative planning system for production in enterprise	GE-415
Information system for electronics production at Factory Komutators	Ge-415
Construction and building management system	Ge-415
Higher education student registration system	OS ES EVM
Agricultural resources optimization for land usage	OS ES EVM
Pension calculation and payment system	OS ES EVM
Informatics in schools	PC

4 Collaboration with Nordic Countries

Hereafter we illustrate the extensive cooperation with the Nordic countries that commenced in the 1990s.

Over the ages, the Baltic Sea has separated and united Latvia and the Scandinavian states. Only 500 kilometers separates Riga from Stockholm and there is only a distance of 200 kilometers between Ventspils and Visby. During the Soviet years, cooperation with the Nordic countries was uncommon; an exception was the modernization of BESM-4 with FACIT ECM 64 (ECM 64 is the magnetic tape storage unit or the Carousel Memory, developed by Facit Electronics AB, Stockholm).

After Latvia gained its independence, cooperation with the Nordic countries started and it brought political, scientific, and technological support. Three directions of cooperation follow.

4.1 Collaboration with Oy International Business Machines AB, Tietokuja 2, Helsinki

The first initiatives in IBM commencing its operation in Latvia began in the spring of 1991; however, a contract between IMCS and the IBM branch in Helsinki was signed in May of 1992. Within the framework of the contract, IBM and IMCS provided each other with mutual consultations. The IBM operation in Latvia was equally important to the development of IMCS and the development of the information technology field in Latvia in general, encouraging its dynamic growth with technology exhibitions, annual industry conferences, and other cooperative ventures.

4.2 Collaboration with the Swedish Institute

The Swedish Institute (SI) is a public agency that promotes interest and confidence in Sweden, around the world. After the Baltic States (Estonia, Latvia, Lithuania) regained their independence at the beginning of 1990, the Scandinavian countries helped considerably to establish relations between them and the Western academic community. The SI provided the possibility for Latvian information technology scientists to visit and work for a short period at KTH in Stockholm, Chalmers University of Technology in Gothenburg, as well as at Uppsala, Linköping, and other research centers. Two co-authors of this paper also enjoyed the hospitality of Professor Janis Bubenko, Jr. during their sabbatical leave at the Royal Institute of Technology in 1991. Through increased contacts and new networks, knowledge and innovative ideas could be shared and applied to many future research areas. Professor Janis Bubenko, Jr. (Royal Institute of Technology) and Professor Arne Sølvberg (Trondheim Technical University) jointly established the biannual international conference "Baltic Databases and Information Technology." The ninth DB&IS has taken place in 2010. Both professors are still working on the Advisory Committee of DB&IS.

Professor Janis Bubenko, Jr. has received the Honoris Causa Doctor award from Riga Technical University (2004) and the University of Latvia (2010).

4.3 Collaboration with NORDUnet

After the restoration of Latvian independence, IMCS began to work on building an IP network. In 1992, IMCS leased the Lattelekom and ESTI telekom analog communication channel to Tallinn. As of 1993, NORDUnet provided help in developing an IP network for research and educational purposes. Their help was useful both technologically and financially. Controversies over which network solution (X.25 or IP) was the most appropriate had lasted until 1995; Lattelekom with its technology supported X.25 and NORDUnet's actively defended introduction of the internet platform.

In 1995, LATNET (a network maintained by the Laboratory of IMCS) had a 64k link via Tallinn to Helsinki (FUNET) and a 128k link to Stockholm KTH (NORDUnet). Two links had implemented load sharing, so the aggregated capacity was 192k (which was at 100 percent capacity during the day). The five largest universities, about ten research institutions, three libraries, and many other non-profit organizations were connected to LATNET. Inside LATNET, new service providers were emerging such as LANET (another Latvian Academic Network) and Bank Communications Center.   LATNET received almost no local assistance for the support of academic users; some sponsorship came from commercial users and a great deal from the Nordic Council of Ministers and PHARE (The Program of Community aid to the countries of Central and Eastern Europe), who were paying for international lines and donating equipment. Unfortunately, no one wanted to pay all the people who operated it; commercial users sponsored the small daily expenses, local lines, and dial-up pools.

The wireless internet access network in Latvia was started in 1993 when the IMCS (LATNET) installed the first citywide wireless LAN link to connect a remote university campus to the central building, a distance of five kilometers between them. At that time, spread spectrum wireless LAN technology was little known.   The inspiration to start these tests came from a Cylink demonstration of spread spectrum link of wireless data at the INET'93 workshop in San Francisco, and from the staff at KTH network operations center in Stockholm who brought the first wireless LAN cards to Riga in the autumn of 1993.

The work [1] summarizes the Nordic countries' point of view on the cooperation with LATNET (at present Sigmanet), the laboratory of IMCS.

The first contacts with Baltic computer scientists were created when the NORDUNET program was still operational. Members of the NORDUnet community were active in this new collaboration. In Finland, Estonian scientists interested in building data networks contacted FUNET. In Sweden, the Latvians first approached the Swedish Institute for Computer Science (SICS). In Norway, Rolf Nordhagen, from the University of Oslo, cooperated with the Lithuanians. Rolf Nordhagen recalls that in fact the first outside network connection from a Baltic country was established from Vilnus, Lithuania, to the Norwegian Uninett via satellite already by 1991.

Mats Brunell, the project manager of the NORDUnet program, was working at SICS when the Latvian Institute of Electronics and Computer Science contacted the Swedish to establish research collaboration. The Baltic researchers expressed their interest in getting a connection to NORDUnet and via NORDUnet also to the internet.

Brunell began to organize a project for Nordic–Baltic networking collaboration. After a visit to Riga, Latvia, in May of 1991, Brunell initiated the BALTnet project with the objective of establishing communication services with the Baltic States, primarily for the research and education community. The funding for the project was sought and received from the Nordic Council of Ministers; it granted 7.5 million Danish crowns for the BALTnet project.

The BALTnet project came into being in 1993 and Mats Brunell became its project leader. He continued in this task until 1995. Then the BALTnet project was moved from SICS to the University of Oslo and Rolf Nordhagen took over the management.

The goal of BALTnet was to support the development of Baltic education and research networks. The work was accomplished by organizing seminars for Baltic networkers, buying equipment for research institutes and financially supporting international connectivity. In addition, the Nordic networking specialists helped Baltic scientists to establish contacts with other European networkers and with networkers in the United States.

Peter Villemoes considers that the NORDUnet community played a very important role in the Baltic countries when the three countries were building their first research networks. According to Villemoes, the early collaboration and connection to NORDUnet and to the Internet had a beneficial effect on Baltic networking – collaboration with the Nordic countries ensured that "of the former Soviet states, the Baltic countries became the most advanced in networking."

The success of networking in Latvia and in all the Baltic States was based on international cooperation and help, including the support of the Nordic Council of Ministers. For example, LATNET (at present Sigmanet) was the Latvian partner in the BALTnet project established by the Nordic Council of Ministers in 1993.

Reference

1. Lehtisalo, K.: The History of NORDUnet: Twenty-Five Years of Networking Cooperation in the Nordic Countries,
   http://www.nordu.net/history/TheHistoryOfNordunet_simple.pdf

What Can We Learn from the History of Nordic Computing?

Summary of Panel Discussion

Discussants: Harold (Bud) Lawson (Sweden), Søren Duus Østergaard (Denmark), Ingeborg Torvik Sølvberg (Norway), and Nina Wormbs (Sweden)

Moderator: Tomas Ohlin (Sweden)

The panel discussion took place during the second day of the conference. Professor Hans Andersin (Finland) had planned to participate but was unable to do so. Historian Dr. Lars Ilshammar (Sweden) was invited to participate with prepared questions for the panel.

The panel members had prepared introductory statements that expressed specific comments about the historical development. In regard to this, before the conference, Hans Andersin had distributed comments addressing the role of cooperation with government in forming an information society that would otherwise, to a great extent, have turned out to be guided by university research and industrial achievements.

At the start of the session, the panel members were given time to make introductory comments. The panel addressed the limited role of women's activities in the development of computing as well as the role of the type of education given during that time. With a different type of education, could the development have been different?

The panel noted the challenge of the increasing complexity of systems developed from early times and onwards. Did this lead to a complexity that was too great and unstable, and if so, what can be done? It also pointed out that there can be different types of historical lessons learnt depending on who is being taught. Some lessons address the needs and practices of applied research; others are structural and address cooperation, or relate to specific achievements in industry and, to some extent, the broader society.

A discussion followed between the members of the panel. Comments were made about the role of education for early development, and about the varying rates of progress during different historical phases. What types of external conditions had been instrumental for the different phases?

Lars Ilshammar added comments regarding who questioned how possible lessons learnt could be of value for further historical research after pointing out the experiences gained from three HINC conferences. Is there need for increased methodological refinement? He added that as computing has become increasingly transnational over time cooperation over borders may become more relevant, inviting more comparative approaches. Ilshammar also added that it may be of interest to question how Nordic activities had contributed to the view on information systems in which systems structures have changed from standby computers to ever-enhancing networks.

J. Impagliazzo, P. Lundin, and B. Wangler (Eds.): HiNC3, IFIP AICT 350, pp. 462–463, 2011.
© IFIP International Federation for Information Processing 2011

With this as background, panelists commented about the role of computing history as an emerging new field of research and the possibility of finding value from more established scientific fields with historical contact.

It was then noted that early Nordic computing development had, to some extent, reaped some benefits from certain types of governmental support, and surely also from cooperation between industry, education, and research. However, central parts of the development of Nordic computer systems can hardly be said to have been the sole fruit of explicit governmental planning.

After a number of remarks from the panel, the discussion was opened up for comments and questions from the public. Numerous aspects were added, among them observing the importance of lessons learnt from insufficient concern about systems security and supporting compatibility between system dialects.

In a review of the points made during the panel discussion, certain aspects were emphasized. These often took the form of questions rather than answers:

- How can we address the concept of Nordic influence in a situation where the Nordic countries acted separately, to some extent?
- Was there a geographically related type of influence, concerning shared responsibility?
- Did the Nordic computing mentality (e.g., cooperation in systems work and user influence) transcend internationally?
- What role can historians play in the further analysis of computing development in an information society?
- Could the Nordic influence have taken a different path if computing scientists and engineers allocated greater concern to computing security in its early stages of development?

In summarizing the panel discussion, we note that the discussion raised more questions than answers provided. For future endeavors, statements were made about the importance of specific types of education that already start at elementary school. The need for increased security concern was also noted. Comments were added about the importance of a more evident gender balance in different phases of the historical development. These comments are important for future types of analyses, where lessons from the past may be a historical ladder upward and forward. A concluding remark of the panel discussion was as follows:

The Nordic countries are now part of the world, a situation where cooperation may be of increased value. It is worth remembering that we are only at the beginning of a movement into the online society, a development that contains much change.

Author Index

Amcoff Nyström, Christina   399
Andersin, Hans   390

Balodis, Rihards   453
Barth Jacobsen, Bjørn   108
Bátiz-Lazo, Bernardo   92
Berild, Stig   331
Bjørner, Dines   350
Borzovs, Juris   453
Bratbergsengen, Kjell   368
Bubenko, Jr., Janis A.   360

Cortada, James W.   1

Dussauge, Isabelle   56, 425

Engh, Jan   137

Gram, Christian   350
Gribbe, Johan   22, 425
Gustafsson, Mats   383

Haftor, Darek   399
Hagenson, Norodd   35
Heide, Lars   207
Hellstrøm, Jan   101
Holmberg, Stig C.   399
Honkela, Timo   433
Hughes, Peter H.   315

Jørgensen, Anker Helms   168
Johansen, Peter   409
Johansson, Lars-Åke   383

Kaijser, Arne   28, 425
Kajbjer, Karin   74
Karlsson, Tobias   92
Klein, Gunnar O.   65, 74
Kotiranta, Kari   234

Lawson, Harold (Bud)   323, 462
Lindencrona, Eva   331
Löfstedt, Ulrica   399
Lundbäck, Kurt-Lennart   323
Lundh, Yngvar   240, 287
Lundin, Per   187, 425

Malmi, Eric   433
Møller-Pedersen, Birger   339

Nagell, Bjørn   13
Nordberg, Ragnar   74

Öberg, Lena-Maria   399
Oest, Ole N.   350
Østergaard, Søren Duus   196, 462
Ohlin, Tomas   278, 462
Oinas-Kukkonen, Harri   444
Oinas-Kukkonen, Henry   444
Ólafsson, Sverrir   228
Opmane, Inara   453
Orrghen, Anna   127

Paju, Petri   215, 433
Palme, Jacob   271
Peralta, Julia   56, 425

Rolandsson, Lennart   159
Rystrøm, Leif   350

Saarikoski, Petri   150
Sjöblom, Gustav   83, 425
Skuja, Andrejs   453
Sølvberg, Arne   258
Sølvberg, Ingeborg Torvik   43, 462
Spilling, Pål   297
Steine, Tor Olav   249
Sulonen, Reijo   390
Sundblad, Yngve   176, 416
Suominen, Jaakko   117
Sušová, Veronika   444
Syrjänen, Markku   390

Thodenius, Björn   92, 425

Vinter, Otto   305

Wangler, Benkt   375
Wormbs, Nina   462

Ziemele, Evija   453